fifth edition

CONSUMER BEHAVIOR

AN APPLIED APPROACH

NESSIM HANNA // RICHARD WOZNIAK // MARGARET HANNA

PROFESSOR EMERITUS, NORTHERN ILLINOIS UNIVERSITY • NORTHERN ILLINOIS UNIVERSITY • SAN QUENTIN CORRECTIONAL FACILITY, SAN QUENTIN, CA

Kendall Hunt
publishing company

Book Team

Chairman and Chief Executive Officer   Mark C. Falb
President and Chief Operating Officer   Chad M. Chandlee
Vice President, Higher Education   David L. Tart
Director of Publishing Partnerships   Paul B. Carty
Senior Developmental Editor   Lynnette M. Rogers
Vice President, Operations   Timothy J. Beitzel
Production Editor   Elizabeth Cray
Cover Designer   Faith Walker
Web Project Editor   Erica Nelson

Cover images © Shutterstock, Inc.

Kendall Hunt
publishing company

www.kendallhunt.com
Send all inquiries to:
4050 Westmark Drive
Dubuque, IA 52004-1840

BRIEF CONTENTS

CONSUMER BEHAVIOR *AN APPLIED APPROACH*

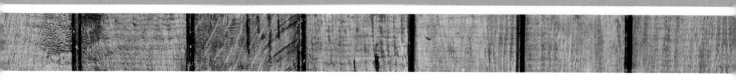

CONTENTS

PART 2 INDIVIDUAL INFLUENCES ON BEHAVIOR   77

PART 3 SOCIAL AND CULTURAL INFLUENCES ON BEHAVIOR 345

CONSUMER BEHAVIOR *AN APPLIED APPROACH*

FOREWORD

The conceptual foundation of consumer behavior relies heavily on theories, concepts, and models developed in the behavioral sciences with proper orientation toward business, particularly marketing, situations. The analysis and understanding of human behavior are usually based on the S-O-R (Stimulus-Organism-Response) model generally followed by the authors of *Consumer Behavior: An Applied Approach*, Fifth Edition, as suggested by the framework outlined in the preface of the book. Accordingly, behavior is said to be determined by forces within the individual as well as in the situation.

The authors cover the five psychological processes of perception, learning, attitudes, motivation, and personality. The manifestations of these processes obviously differ from one person to another. This is why people vary in their responses even to the same business events and marketing situations. Yet a marketer usually looks for common forces among people toward which he or she directs the marketing policies and promotional programs. Some of these forces can be found in the social environment and cultural spheres that bond people together. Since these forces differ from one society to another, it is expected that consumer behavior would vary across nations. A careful consideration should be given, therefore, to the unique forces that characterize the social and cultural milieu of each country.

The past thirty-five years or so have witnessed the prevalence of the *system's approach* in the management and organizational literature. The approach emphasizes, among other things, the *interdependencies* among various parts of the organizational system. This approach has found its way to the general orientation of the book through the cross-functional approach, so cleverly articulated by the authors, and as highlighted by the chapter-opening vignettes, end-of-chapter cross-functional debates, and points of view. This orientation has been further strengthened in the current fifth edition and is an important distinguishing feature of the book.

The authors have also adopted active individual, group, and self-learning approaches, with extensive use of the most up-to-date tools of information technology. Real-life applications are emphasized through the real-world opening vignettes; global, ethical, and in-practice application boxes; and cases about known companies in the United States and overseas, thus enriching and broadening the scope of students' knowledge about American business experiences and what is happening worldwide. This will enhance both the marketability of the book in other countries and the globalized trend of educational programs everywhere.

"This is a wonderful book that I have very much enjoyed reading. I strongly recommend it to colleagues in universities here in the United States and overseas."

— Ahmed A. Abdel-Halim, Ph.D., Professor Emeritus, Alexandria University, Egypt, Former Dean, College of Business & Economics, United Arab Emirates University, UAE Former Management & Marketing Dept. Chair, Illinois State University at Normal-Bloomington, Illinois

PREFACE

During the recent "Great Recession" that took place from mid-2007 through mid-2009, the economy greatly contracted, and over 8 million jobs were lost. At that time, these conditions had a dramatic effect on consumers and on their spending patterns. To cope with these negative realities, many consumers learned to abandon more expensive alternatives and trade down to store brands, purchase smaller and more energy-efficient cars, and shop at discount stores or wholesale online venues.

The last few years since these events took place, however, major changes to this gloomy picture emerged. Americans started to observe gradual but positive changes in the economy. With the start of 2016, only the memories of these hard times appear to remain. The overall unemployment rate had fallen below 5 percent, inflation was in check at 1.7 percent, interest rates remained low, the stock market indices were close to their all-time high, and energy prices remained within reach of almost everyone.

As the economy continues to recover, the Bureau of Labor Statistics projects that consumer spending will grow by 2.6 percent annually through 2022, and that employment will increase by 1 percent annually to reach almost 95 million jobs by that same year. However, against this rosy portrait of our economy today, there are still many challenges that continue to cloud the future economic climate of our nation. Primary among those is the issue of national security, where both the reality and the perception of security threats have negatively influenced our progress. Examples of such threats include the rise of the Islamic State (ISIS); wars in Syria, Iraq, and Afghanistan; rebellion against racial inequities; widespread gun violence; distrust of public officials; the prevalence of cyber crimes; the dire consequences of climate change; as well as tensions and conflicts with other nations in our political sphere.

The problems that America is facing today are not simply domestic. They are worldwide phenomena encompassing both developed and developing nations. This global inclusion is an expression of the interdependency—for better or for worse—that has developed between nations today. The recent trend toward increased global cooperation among blocks of countries was envisioned with the objective of obtaining high standards of living for all participants. Thus, the traditional perspective of isolation as the principle of choice among countries is no longer useful or practical in organizing and enhancing economic activities. This same principle of interdependency that works well in the global arena also holds great merit when applied to conventional marketing practices on the micro level.

Within the confines of the interdependency concept and its proven positive effect on business operations, firms today should no longer be viewed as collections of separate and independent units or departments, where each specializes in a singular activity such as engineering, purchasing, finance, accounting, selling, or human resources. Rather, today's successful business operations are based on sophisticated organizational arrangements that apply the team approach to managing operations—where representatives from various disciplines within the organization interact and equally cooperate in bringing new products and services into the marketplace. This cross-functional view of contemporary business operations had been the core of success for countless foreign firms, especially in Europe and Japan.

We feel so strongly about the cross-functional approach that we have brought it into *Consumer Behavior* in two major ways. First, every chapter's accompanying website materials include a cross-functional debate exercise tied to the chapter's opening vignette. These are intended to help students apply the chapter's principles to other business-related disciplines such as accountancy, management, finance, production, and law. For example, the opening vignette in Chapter 5 on the topic of "Consumer Attitudes" addresses the rise of ISIS as a threat to the civilized world. The presentation is extended to cover the various tactics the group employs to motive radical and troubled individuals to join the movement.

This is not all. The cross-functional approach is brought in a second way. Each chapter contains three cross-functional points of view in the website material. These segments expose students to related disciplines and show them the interrelationship of marketing and consumer behavior to the other functional areas of business. For example, in Chapter 5, the three cross-functional points of view focus on:

- *Finance and Economics*—how consumers' attitudes toward the health of the economy affect its actual performance,

- *Politics*—smear campaigns that political candidates often use to win votes, and
- *Strategy and Ethics*—the fashion industry's tendency to create different seasonal fashions every year in an effort to generate sales.

The cross-functional approach is only one of many things we have done in *Consumer Behavior*. All of these things have a common goal: to get students involved. Thomas Jefferson once wrote, "Tell me and I'll forget, teach me and I may remember, involve me and I'll learn." We wanted to bring this principle to life in the consumer behavior field.

ORGANIZATION AND FEATURES OF THE TEXT

The text is broken down into three major parts. After a brief introduction, coverage starts with the individual influences on our consumption behavior, then broadens the perspective to include relevant social/cultural forces. The three parts of the subject treatment are:

- **Part One:** The first part sets the groundwork of the text, and includes Chapters 1 and 2.
- **Part Two:** The second part deals with individual influences on our consumption behavior, and includes Chapters 3 through 8.
- **Part Three:** The third part addresses social and cultural influences on our consumption behavior, and includes Chapters 9 through 14.

Numerous features of the text will keep students interested in the subject and will help them visualize applications of consumer behavior principles. Specifically:

- An **opening vignette** and corresponding **Internet exercise** at the beginning of each chapter ease readers into the topic. The Internet exercise directs students to visit one or more websites to help answer relevant questions. For example, at the start of Chapter 5, students are invited to visit a website in order to learn more about the radical ISIS movement and our strategy to defeat it in its propaganda war.
- Each chapter contains three entertaining and informative **applications boxes** that tie in with the chapter material. Each box is linked to the Internet and contains thought-provoking questions. For instance, in Chapter 5, these boxes are:

- ○ **"Consumer Behavior in Practice":** This vignette presents a glimpse of the youth-focused American society and the continued interest of people to enhance their physical appearance—thereby significantly raising market revenues from cosmetic surgery procedures to $17.5 billion.

- ○ **"Global Opportunity":** A vignette regarding the massive $5.5 billion Shanghai Disney Resort that the company designed to capitalize on the popularity its famous characters, such as Mickey, Minney, and Fairy Tale Princesses; yet in the meantime, woo the Chinese by a new cast of culturally relevant symbols and characters.

- ○ **"Ethical Dilemma":** A vignette on the legalization of marijuana in Colorado, and the ability of consumers to walk into a dispensary and make a marijuana purchase. These dispensaries, however, also stock a wide variety of marijuana edibles that look like cookies and candies, with an obvious appeal to children. Many children accidentally ingest such novelties by mistake, potentially causing them great harm.

- • A **running glossary** of terms is provided in the page margins to highlight key terms and help students review chapters at a glance. In ad-

dition, a **comprehensive alphabetical glossary** covering all chapters appears at the back of the book.
- Each chapter ends with a **summary**.

FEATURES OF THE WEBSITE DIRECTED TO STUDENTS

New to the fifth edition is a website that engages students with interactive components. The contents of the students' website include the following:

- Five review questions cover key points in the chapter.
- Three discussion questions specifically designed to test students' ability to apply the concepts learned in the chapter to other issues in the business world.
- A Cross-Functional Point of View.
- A Cross Functional Debate.
- An original one-page chapter case covering an issue or business problem in the contemporary marketplace. These cases include: "Drones: The Pros and the Cons," "Teen Peer Pressure," "Beauty for Billions or Billions for Beauty?", and "Enabling the Disabled." Each case is followed by questions designed to get students to seek additional information about the company and its business environment—from the Internet and social media.
- Video links that relate to chapter content.
- Two article summaries that relate to chapter content.
- PowerPoint slides for each chapter.
- An interactive self-test gives students feedback on their level of comprehension for the key content of each chapter.

FEATURES OF THE WEBSITE DIRECTED TO THE FACULTY

A password-protected website includes:
- **Answers to questions** that include responses to review questions and solutions to case studies.
- **A test bank** that includes approximately 1,000 questions—a combination of multiple-choice and true-false items—prepared by the authors.
- **A PowerPoint presentation** that includes lecture outlines as well as schematic diagrams found in the textbook.

- **Data-driven exercises** that include three "Be the Consultant" cases, each placed at the end of the text's three parts.

ORGANIZATIONAL FRAMEWORK OF THIS TEXT

The diagram in Exhibit P.1 is a simplified representation of the treatment given to the subject of consumer behavior throughout this text.

The framework commences with a depiction of the consumer research process, whose objective is partially to provide information about consumers' needs, characteristics, and preferences for various brand alternatives. This first step is followed by the segmentation process, which involves dissecting the potential market for a product or service into a number of subgroups, each with its own unique but identifiable needs and preferences. Marketing managers can then decide which segment or segments to pursue.

EXHIBIT P.1

An Organizational Framework for the Study of Consumer Behavior

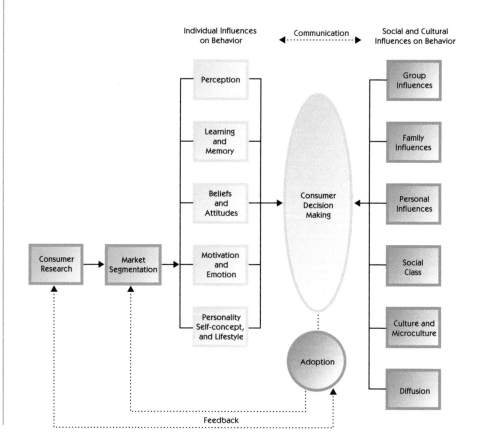

The framework then proceeds to consider the two broad sets of factors that largely influence consumer choice making; namely, individual influences and social and cultural influences. The first group, labeled *individual influences*, includes personal factors such as perception, learning, attitudes, motivation, and personality. Marketers attempt to influence consumers' perception, learning, and attitudes through product offerings, advertising, or salespeople, and other individual factors such as personality are taken as givens.

The second major group of influencing factors on decision making is brought about by the environment of which the consumer is part. This group of factors is labeled *social and cultural influences*. Components of this set include group, family, and personal influences. In addition, this set encompasses the ramifications of social class and culture on consumption patterns, as well as the effect of diffusion efforts brought about by change agents. The reason for including diffusion as part of the social and cultural influences on behavior is that other people's acceptance and use of products and services have a bearing on our own decision to accept and use these same products and services. For instance, person-to-person communication through the electronic media is not a one-sided phenomenon.

The framework addresses the communication flows between the environment and the consumer. Such communication, either interpersonal or mass, determines the probability and direction of consumer choices. This process is shown as a two-sided flow between the individual and the social and cultural forces. Each set of factors mutually influences the other.

In light of the interaction of these two broad sets of forces, consumer decisions are made. In response to influence from an ad, a recommendation from a friend, or a temporary price reduction, consumers may decide to purchase or adopt a product. The framework thus shows adoption as an outcome of decision making.

Although adoption seemingly represents the last link in the decision-making process, most marketers consider it the start of a relationship with the consumer. Postpurchase evaluations occur as consumers begin to use a product. Product performance is evaluated against consumer expectations and sacrifice of resources. The result of this evaluation directly influences whether or not the consumer repurchases the same brand. This relationship in the framework is shown as a dotted-line feedback loop that connects adoption with the consumer.

The role of consumer research reappears at this juncture. Through research, marketers can determine consumer reactions and attitudes toward the brand as well as explain and predict future purchase intentions. A dotted line between feedback and consumer research reflects this interaction.

ACKNOWLEDGMENTS

We are fortunate to have worked with some wonderful people who generously gave their time and effort to make this textbook and its ancillary package a reality. We are particularly indebted to Ms. Sara McGovern and Ms. Elizabeth Cray, Project Coordinators; Senior Developmental Editor; Mr. Paul B. Carty, Director of Publishing Partnerships; and all the kind folks at Kendall/Hunt who made the publication of this fifth edition a reality.

We sincerely hope that every professor or student who uses this textbook finds it to be as interesting and enjoyable an experience as we have encountered in the process of writing it.

Nessim Hanna
Richard Wozniak
Margaret Hanna

ABOUT THE AUTHORS

The lead author **Dr. Nessim Hanna** received his Ph.D. in Marketing from the University of Illinois at Urbana. He is Professor Emeritus of Marketing, Northern Illinois University, DeKalb, and former Vice President and Chief Marketing Officer of Efficient BioSystems, Inc., located in Darien, Illinois. His areas of expertise in the fields of consumer behavior, pricing, international marketing, and cross-functional business disciplines prompted many domestic and international universities to invite him as Visiting Professor to teach and to help in establishing their curricula. Included in this group are schools such as The American Graduate School of International Management (Thunderbird, AZ); Norwegian School of Management (Oslo, Norway); Hong Kong Baptist University (Hong Kong, China); the University of Petroleum and Minerals (Saudi Arabia); and the University of Cairo (Egypt).

Dr. Hanna has published intensively in the fields of consumer behavior, marketing management, pricing, and international marketing. He has over thirty-five articles published in refereed journals, such as *Journal of Marketing, Psychology and Marketing, and Journal of Academy of Marketing Science*. In addition, he has published over forty refereed conference papers. He is also the author of several textbooks on pricing and principles of marketing, as well as global business operations and institutions. His *Pricing Policies and Procedures textbook* has been translated into the Czech, Polish, and Russian languages.

Dr. Hanna is on the editorial board of numerous domestic and international professional business journals. He has done consulting for and has conducted executive seminars on behalf of many companies and organizations, such as General Motors, Motorola, Honeywell, ServiceMaster, ARAMCO, Petromin, and Saudi Airline Top Management Group, as well as most recently for the Middle East Securities Executive Training Center. He has served as a keynote speaker for many organizations, including SAMMY, The National Association of Purchasing Managers, The American Management Association, and The American Marketing Association.

Dr. Hanna was appointed by The American Marketing Association Global Division as Coordinator of the International Activity Group (IAG) for the entire Middle East. He also established a number of faculty-student exchange programs between U.S. universities and other overseas institutions, such as the Norwegian School of Management and the Hong Kong Baptist University, among others. Presently, research, writing, and consulting occupy the majority of his time.

Supporting author **Mr. Richard Wozniak** received his B.S. in Marketing, B.A. in Spanish, and M.S. in Marketing from Northern Illinois University. He was a faculty member in the Department of Marketing, College of Business, at Northern Illinois University, in DeKalb, from which he has now retired. He has taught undergraduate and graduate marketing and business related courses for the past thirty-five years. In addition to his teaching, Mr. Wozniak has extensive business experience in the fields of retailing and wholesaling, working with companies such as Masterpiece Studios, Marshall Fields (now Macy's), A. Marcus, and Rockford Tool. Mr. Wozniak also does consulting for various not-for-profit organizations, including the Roman Catholic Archdiocese of Chicago. Mr. Wozniak has presented a number of papers on the topics of teaching statistics and research methods at regional conferences and has coauthored journal articles on retail pricing. Mr. Wozniak's invaluable contributions to this book involved word processing of the entire manuscript and its online supplements, preliminary editing of the chapters, as well as selecting the YouTube videos which are found in the text's website.

Supporting author **Ms. Margaret Hanna, APN, WHNP-BC, CCHP,** is presently a healthcare provider at San Quentin Correctional Facility in San Quentin, California, a position she has held since 2006 after leaving her previous post as President of DermaCare Clinic, Inc., in west-suburban Chicago. Ms. Hanna brings a fresh perspective to this project as she synthesizes her expertise in medicine with her skills in the business field. In addition to her demanding career, she has authored and published many articles on various business issues related to the field of healthcare marketing. She has also presented papers on healthcare issues at business and medical conferences, both domestically and abroad. Ms. Hanna has conducted seminars for healthcare administrators, has served as a consultant for a number of medical groups and U.S. hospitals, as well as contributed her time and effort as a faculty advisor and mentor to medical interns from the University of California–San Francisco and Samuel Merritt University in Oakland. Her business practice provided tremendous insights for the applied approach followed in this textbook, and her editorial capabilities added depth and clarity to its coverage.

PART 1

GROUNDWORK OF THE TEXT

© Joshua Resnick/Shutterstock.com

CHAPTER 1
Introduction to Consumer Behavior   3

CHAPTER 2
Segmentation, Targeting, and Positioning   37

CHAPTER 1
INTRODUCTION TO CONSUMER BEHAVIOR

LEARNING OBJECTIVES

- To comprehend the dynamics of the Consumer Behavior discipline.
- To recognize the multidisciplinary nature of this subset of human behavior.
- To gain insight into factors that influence purchasing decisions.
- To develop a basic understanding of the marketing concept.
- To explore the dynamic trends that shape our society.
- To grasp implications of the macro and micro trends on behavior.

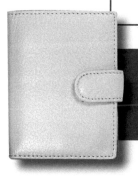

KEY TERMS

consumer behavior	agents of change	m-commerce
marketing concept	e-commerce	

People in the United States are probably the most diet-conscious consumers in the world. In 2015, The Boston Medical Center reported that 45 million Americans go on a diet each year. Typical dieters spend $33 billion on weight-loss products in their pursuit of a more trim and fit body. They routinely consume foods with labels such as *diet, light, reduced calorie, low cholesterol,* and *low fat.* Store shelves are loaded with low-calorie food products ranging from Diet Coke to Slim-Fast. According to a recent DataMonitor report, the diet business in the United States mushroomed to over $59.8 billion at the end of 2014, and grew by 1.4 percent in 2015. Significant demand for weight-loss and diet products has helped to diversify this market and partition it into a number of distinct market segments that include diet foods and beverages, artificial sweeteners, diet pills and plans, medically supervised programs (e.g., weight-loss surgery), as well as health clubs, just to name a few.

Yet during the past twenty years, there has been a dramatic increase in obesity in the United States. According to the most recent data from the Centers for Disease Control and Prevention (CDC), the rate of obesity in 2015 exceeded 35 percent in three states—Arkansas, West Virginia, and Mississippi. Twenty-two states, at that time, had rates over 30 percent; forty-five states were above 25 percent; and every state was above 20 percent. Arkansas had the highest adult obesity rate of 35.9 percent, while Colorado had the lowest at 21.3 percent—a major concern, since studies reveal the fact that the annual medical cost of obesity in 2015 was around $147 billion measured in terms of 2008 dollars.[1]

Whatever the reason, marketers are quick to capitalize on this and other consumer behaviors in the marketplace. Producers and marketers alike have adjusted their product offerings and strategies to accommodate consumers' desires to feel good about themselves. For example, clothing manufacturers who used to produce most garments in slender cuts have faced dwindling sales as consumers can no longer fit themselves into their usual clothing sizes. In response to consumer weight gain coupled with the corresponding phenomenon of weight-gain denial, clothing manufacturers embarked on a tactic known as vanity sizing. *Vanity sizing* is the practice of enlarging the actual size of garments but keeping the same smaller-size designation on the label. For example, a garment currently labeled size 8 may actually be a formerly size 10 item. Consumers psychologically feel better about a brand that allows them to fit into small sizes, suggesting they still have the figure and physique of yesteryear.

Airlines and theaters are working to eliminate complaints from dissatisfied customers who feel that seat dimensions are unsuitable to their body frames. Automakers are designing larger and wider models that are capable of accommodating the obese. Similarly, furniture makers are producing larger, sturdier chairs, couches, and bed frames that can withstand excessive body weight. One industry in particular now faces an intriguing question. In the field of promotion, advertisers are wondering whether the slim, trim, or even waiflike look of yesteryear's models remains relevant, or whether the era of full-bodied models is here to stay.[2]

Issues related to diet and weight have created abundant opportunities for marketers in the areas of food and beverages, clothing, and exercise. Think of some such products that you purchase. Are they priced, promoted, or distributed differently from regular products? Why or why not? Check out a company involved in the diet-weight business by visiting Weight Watchers at www.weight-watchers.com. *Also visit a plus-size and super-size ladies' fashion company at* www.modeloth.com *and* www.navabi.us. *What motives do these companies stress to get consumers to buy their products or services?*

WHAT IS CONSUMER BEHAVIOR?

Welcome to the field of consumer behavior. As an interdisciplinary field of inquiry, consumer behavior focuses on the consumption-related activities of individuals. It investigates the reasons behind and the forces influencing the selection, purchase, use, and disposal of goods and services in order to satisfy personal needs and wants.

The field of study known as consumer behavior is a fairly young discipline. In fact, the first textbooks that specifically addressed the topic were written only as recently as the 1960s. Among the pioneers in the discipline of consumer behavior were James F. Engel, David T. Kollat, and Roger D. Blackwell, as well as John A. Howard and Harold F. Kassarjian, whom many have come to regard as the pioneers of consumer behavior.

Consumer behavior is a subset of a larger set of activities consisting of all human behavior. It includes everything that occurs as prospective customers for products and services become actual customers. Interestingly enough, much of consumer behavior does not necessarily involve purchasing per se. It also encompasses such activities as browsing, influencing others, being influenced by others, and complaining about and returning products, as well as exposure to the media.

More specifically, the study of consumer behavior investigates the way individuals choose, purchase, use, and dispose of goods and services in order to satisfy personal or household needs. Savvy marketers today think of consumers in terms of their product and service needs throughout their lives. This view, which is known as the *customer lifecycle*, focuses upon the creation and delivery of lifetime value to the consumer during every interaction in a consumer's relationship with a firm. This relationship extends throughout the various stages of the purchase process, starting from one's interest and search for a product, to purchasing it, to using it, to replenishing or replacing it, to finally retiring or recycling it. In each one of these customer lifecycle stages, marketers attempt to improve their customer

consumer behavior
the study of how consumers select, purchase, use, and dispose of goods and services to satisfy personal needs and wants

centricity through a better understanding of customer interactions or consumers' *touchpoints* with the firm. The goal of Customer Touchpoint Management (CTM) is to enrich customers' experiences with the firm during all interactions, both personal and mechanical, that they would normally experience during their relationship lifecycle with the firm.

Some of the influences that shape consumer choices and tendencies are internal processes, such as our own thinking, feeling, and desiring. Other influences spring from environmental factors, such as social forces (whether group or interpersonal) and economic, situational, retail, and promotional considerations. Somehow, all these forces combine and dynamically interact to produce shopping behavior, the objective of which is to satisfy human needs and wants.

Many forces combine to produce shopping behaviors; the objective of which is to satisfy human needs and wants.

The term *consumer behavior* differs from a similar term, *buyer behavior*, in that buyer behavior is an umbrella term often understood to encompass business-to-business purchasing as well as personal consumption. Business-to-business buying entails the procurement processes and activities of producers and intermediaries in the marketing channels, as well as the acquisition procedures of other organizations and institutions. Business-to-business buying is beyond the scope of this text, which primarily focuses on consumer behavior.

Human behavior is an extremely complicated subject, and consumer behavior is no less complex. Analysis of consumer behavior in the field entails surveying numerous theories and published research studies that offer insight into purchasing tendencies. The ultimate goal is to help marketers better understand the processes and activities of consumer behavior, and thus to anticipate how marketing strategies and tactics will influence consumers and affect the products and services various types of consumers will buy. In other words, as marketers come to understand consumer behavior, they are better able to predict how consumers will respond to various environmental and informational cues. For example, the September 11, 2001 attacks on the United States, as well as the more recent assaults on Paris, France and San Bernardino, California in 2015, and the heightened level of apprehension and anxiety that followed, caused many Americans to reexamine what really matters in their lives. Many are focusing more on keeping their homes and families secure, purchasing products that promise safety, and seeking better understanding of foreign cultures. Marketers can then configure and fine-tune their strategies and tactics accordingly. Additionally, in today's highly competitive marketplace, a sound understanding of consumer behavior helps marketers gain a competitive advantage and establish positive and lasting customer relationships.

APPROACHES TO THE DISCIPLINE OF CONSUMER BEHAVIOR

In today's world, goods are produced and services are planned in anticipation of future demand. Meanwhile, consumer preferences and tastes constantly change. Styles quickly become fashionable and then go out of vogue. It becomes increasingly important that marketers know what consumers need and want, how they spend their resources, and how they decide where to shop, when to buy, and what to purchase. In short, timely knowledge of consumer behavior is a prerequisite for marketing success. For instance, companies that were able to anticipate the surge in consumers' need to feel secure developed numerous successful products and services ranging from home security systems to "smart" credit cards with chips that deter fraudulent use.

The discipline of consumer behavior can be approached in a number of ways. At the individual level, we can examine intrapersonal influences on consumption such as perceptions, learning, attitudes, motivations, and personality. We can then broaden our view to examine group, interpersonal, cultural, and cross-cultural influences. Conversely, we can also begin by examining cultural and social forces that influence consumption and then narrow down the focus to personal factors. In this text, we begin our investigation of consumer behavior at the level of individual influences and then broaden our focus to consider social and cultural influences.

Throughout the stages of its development, the study of consumer behavior borrowed heavily from other fields of knowledge to enhance our understanding of human consumptive activities. In this sense, the investigation of consumer behavior can be viewed as interdisciplinary, spanning the spectrum of the behavioral sciences. Among the disciplines that contribute most to the understanding of consumer behavior are psychology, sociology, social psychology, cultural anthropology, and economics.

Psychology investigates the mental processes and behavior of individuals as they react to stimuli in their environment. Researchers of consumer behavior and marketing practitioners make extensive use of psychological concepts, including perception, learning, memory, motivation, emotion, personality, and self-image.

Unlike psychologists, sociologists generally focus on groups and social institutions as primary units of analysis. *Sociology* canvasses the collective behavior of individuals as groups, organizations, institutions, and entire societies. Researchers of consumer behavior and marketing practitioners alike are interested in status and role structures within various groups, as well as group norms and values.

Social psychology probes the way individuals relate to other individuals and function together within groups. The purchase of many products is socially motivated, and many products and services are used in group settings. In this regard, researchers of consumer behavior and marketers are interested in reference groups and opinion leaders that consumers look to when they make purchasing decisions.

Anthropology delves into people in relation to their culture. In addition to examining the influence of society on individuals, anthropologists explore artifacts and behavior patterns from the past. They also conduct comparative studies that cross cultural boundaries. Studies of cross-cultural consumer behavior are particularly valuable for marketers involved in global business.

Economics examines people's production and the exchange of resources for goods and services. In economic terms, the study of consumer behavior emphasizes *demand* more than *supply*, assuming that offering a supply of goods and services that truly matches market demand is preferable to undertaking the task of creating demand for what sellers happen to supply.

No single discipline adequately explains all aspects of consumption. For example, pure economic theory could lead one to assume that consumers always behave rationally, act on complete market information, and maximize the satisfaction they obtain from every dollar they spend. Traditional economics cannot account for the influence of internal forces, such as human needs and wants, attitudes, emotions, personality, and risk perception. Nor does it take into consideration the impact of external factors, such as culture, social class, the situational context, reference groups, opinion leaders, word of mouth, and marketing communications.

Psychology, sociology, social psychology, anthropology, and economics as well as other fields offer diverse perspectives from which marketers hope to gain meaningful insights about the factors that influence consumption patterns.

WHAT DO BUYING DECISIONS INVOLVE?

To see what consumer behavior entails, consider the hypothetical case of Mr. and Mrs. Donato and their two young children, John and Kathy, as together they contemplated the acquisition of a family pet. After weeks of deliberating, the Donatos had decided to get a puppy. Nearly all the households in the neighborhood had dogs, and John and Kathy had repeatedly asked their parents for one. The parents believed it would teach their children a great deal about responsibility and caring for others. The tasks of feeding the dog, walking it, grooming it, training it, and cleaning up after it were therefore delegated to the children.

The family borrowed several books about dogs from the local library, searched the Internet, and visited social media sites to learn exactly what they were getting themselves into. Professional breeders were one source; others included pet shops, animal shelters, and individuals who ran classified ads in the local newspaper offering puppies for sale. After considering these sources, Mr. and Mrs. Donato decided to take John and Kathy to visit the local pet shop.

The parents had no strong preference for any particular breed or gender, and several large and small breeds, as well as mixed breeds, were available. The prices varied markedly, ranging from $800 for a purebred, show-quality malamute to $150 for a six-month-old mixed breed. Although Mr. and Mrs. Donato had originally agreed to spend no more than $400 on the purchase, John and Kathy instantly fell in love with a frisky gray-and-white husky that carried a price tag of $500.

Mr. and Mrs. Donato had a number of questions to ask the salesclerk. In just a few moments, they needed to learn as much as possible about caring for the new addition to their household. The clerk informed the Donatos that the city required dog owners to buy a license and that periodic shots were needed. The family bought a brush, a collar and leash, a feeding bowl, some toys, and a large basket where the dog could sleep.

© ANURAK PONGPATIMET/Shutterstock.com

A professional breeder happened to be waiting in the store's checkout line. She advised the Donatos that huskies need plenty of exercise and a large, fenced-in yard. She reminded them that responsible owners have their animal spayed or neutered in order to help control the pet population. She also recommended obedience school in order to train the pet properly.

The Donatos asked the breeder about the type and amount of food that would be best for the dog. Choices emerged again regarding which brand to purchase and the quantity to buy, as well as where to buy it. Better-quality foods were often available for cheaper prices at pet superstores. This fact, however, did not preclude the possibility of buying dog food from the pet store where the family bought the puppy. The only problems with buying the food there were limited choices and higher prices.

Selecting a veterinarian was not an easy task either; a dozen were listed in the Yellow Pages. The parents sought the advice of other pet-owning friends. Fortunately, a colleague at work recommended a competent veterinarian who charged reasonable prices for the required services. After checking out the vet's references on social media, the Donatos called her for an appointment.

CONSUMER BEHAVIOR: THE FORCES BEHIND HUMAN ACTIONS

This brief scenario illustrates a number of important concepts drawn from the field of consumer behavior. The decision occurred within a *family* setting where the parents *rationally* sorted out and weighed the pros and cons. Afterward, different family members played different *roles* in the *decision process*. The children were the *initiators* of the process. The parents were *motivated* to make the purchase by a desire to teach their children a sense of responsibility, which they deemed an important *cultural value*. Mr. and Mrs. Donato must have *perceived* that buying a pet was a worthwhile investment. A particularly favorable *attitude* toward dogs, as compared to cats or other animals, was instrumental in the decision to acquire the puppy.

The decision to purchase the puppy was a *high-involvement* process, because adopting a dog is significant and relevant to the way a household functions. Consequently, a considerable amount of *pre-purchase deliberation* might be expected. Interestingly, the final selection may have been somewhat *impulsive*, because the narrative offers no evidence that the members of the family had read up on the traits of the chosen breed. Experience alone will tell whether the characteristics of the husky will match and complement the *personalities* and *lifestyle* of the owners.

The influence of *reference groups* came into play when the parents considered the fact that most families in their *middle-class* neighborhood owned dogs. In addition, Mr. and Mrs. Donato relied on the professional breeder as an *opinion leader* when they sought advice about food for the pet. *Word-of-mouth communications* helped them select a qualified veterinarian.

Purchase of the puppy brought about the *need* for additional expenditures on various products and services. Pet food and various accessories need to be purchased when the puppy is brought home. A trip to the vet is required for shots, and the puppy may be sent to obedience school for training. After the dog has become fully integrated into the household, many *low-involvement* purchases may also be made, such as toys, biscuits, and doggie treats.

CONSUMER BEHAVIOR IN PRACTICE

A Computer with Good Taste

Before the start of the weekend, you may have had a chance to sit at your computer intending to select a number of movies from a site such as Netflix. As you access the site and begin to choose your movies, suddenly in front of you on the screen appears a number of suggested films Netflix sent to you because the company felt confident that you were going to like them. In fact, many of us go ahead and pick a number of movies based upon Netflix's recommendations. There are two reasons why we do this: the first is an attempt to reduce our effort in choosing from an overwhelming selection of movies; and the second is the fact that those suggested by the site seem to suit the type of movies we enjoy watching.

As a consumer, if you have ever had such an experience, you have witnessed the functioning of what is known in the industry as a "recommendation engine." It is software that gives you advice about what you might enjoy buying, listening to, watching, or even reading the next time you consider ordering.

Recommendation engines are an outgrowth of a technique called collaborative filtering, which presumes that the behavior of a large group of people can be used to make educated guesses about the behavior of a single individual. For example, if researchers determine statistically that most people who liked the *Star Wars: The Force Awakens* movies also tended to like the movie *Star Trek Beyond*, the system makes an educated guess that a particular individual who happened to like a *Star Wars* movie will also like *Star Trek*. However, the system is not as simple as it sounds. It is actually doing something scientifically more elaborate and complex within its algorithmic guts. The system is processing an astounding quantity of data about the audience using sophisticated mathematical formulas and models. It is attempting to second-guess complicated human emotions and attitudes, as well as both conscious and subconscious motivations.

The collaborative-filtering concept is based on the fact that the system has no knowledge of the product, movie, piece of music, or piece of art in question. It is basically concerned with and is simply measuring the audience's reaction to it. The logic here is that if a large number of people state that they have enjoyed say two movies, two pieces of music, or two other products, the software digs in to infer the attributes or aesthetic properties that those two items share or possess in common. As members of the audience, we may not even be aware of the aesthetic properties of the items in question. Better yet, these properties may not even have a recognizable name or be verbally describable. However, in a statistical sense, the characteristics are said to coexist in these two items.

While marketers seem to have great hopes for recommendation engines' ability to boost sales and simplify our choice processes, one drawback of that mechanism may be its limiting nature. It tends to lock customers in basically the same circle or vicinity as where they began—reducing their opportunity for exposure to new and different spheres.[3]

Over the past decade, collaborative filtering has become a popular technique used by merchants of many retail products, movies, music, books, and art objects. Amazon.com was the pioneer of these automated recommendations. Others who followed suit include Netflix, Apple, YouTube, and Google, as well as eBay. Visit Netflix.com. In your opinion, do such suggestions facilitate or restrict consumers' choice behavior? Cite the pros and cons you think support or discredit this technology. Comment on the statement, "Today, marketers have succeeded in revealing consumers' conscious and subconscious motives and have been able to delegate elements of our choice behavior to mere software."

THE ROLE OF THE MARKETING CONCEPT IN EXCHANGE PROCESSES

The activities of buying, selling, and marketing are certainly not new to the world. On the contrary, these tasks in some form or another are as old as the existence of humans on the planet. Cultural anthropologists have discovered murals on the walls of Egypt's more than 5,000-year-old Pharaonic temples that depict ships bringing ostrich feathers, ivory, rare woods, and monkeys into the country. These items were traded by merchants from Lebanon, Assyria, and Ethiopia in exchange for Egyptian chariots, wheat, and horses. It is only in recent times, however, that business practitioners have come to appreciate the vital role of the consumer as the core of all marketing activities. Firms today increasingly subscribe to an operating philosophy known as the marketing concept, in which the consumer is the focal point of company activities—production, new-product research and development, pricing, distribution, and promotion. The marketing concept embodies "the view that an industry is a customer-satisfying process, not a goods-producing process. An industry begins with the customer and his/her needs, not with a patent, a raw material, or a selling skill."[4] In this regard, the task of marketing is frequently described in terms of generating, expediting, and consummating exchanges between buyers and sellers in order to satisfy consumer needs and wants.

> **marketing concept**
> an operating philosophy in which the consumer is the focus of all company activities

Inherent in any discussion of consumer behavior is the notion of exchange. Exchange occurs when resources of any variety are transferred between the parties to a transaction. In other words, exchange means relinquishing something of perceived value (cash, credit, labor, goods) in return for acquiring something else of perceived value (products, services, ideas). For successful exchanges to occur there must be at least two parties—each of which possesses something desired by the other. Each party must be able to communicate with the other and to deliver on any commitments that are made. In addition, each party must believe that it is desirable—or at least acceptable—to deal with the other, and both parties must be free to accept or reject any offer from the other party.[5] Exchanges occur between individuals and other individuals, between individuals and organizations, and between organizations and other organizations.

The material possessions we own, the services we use, and the activities we engage in are largely by-products of marketing actions that somehow have influenced our purchasing behavior. We all witnessed the *Frozen*-themed merchandise craze in 2015, which prompted many consumers to purchase

agents of change
entities that actively strive
to reshape consumers'
beliefs and behaviors

and collect such items. In a similar way, the make, model, and year of the car you drive, the services of the bank you frequent, and the sports outing you may have planned are some of the components of daily life that are influenced by marketers and their role as agents of change.

Some writers even go to the extent of stating that marketing is "the creation and delivery of a standard of living."[6] That is to say, in our society, marketers as agents of change have brought about the high standard of living to which we have grown accustomed. The claim is that our lives have become happier, more varied, and interesting due to their efforts.

In this view, what we purchase is based on what we see and learn. Much of what we see and learn results from marketing tactics, such as glamorous advertising, clever promotions, creative store displays, and the availability of a multitude of convenient and helpful customer services. For example, many of us would have been unable to purchase our homes or most of the durable goods we own if it were not for the creative financing and credit policies that marketers provide.

Although many of these marketing efforts help us to experience a more enjoyable lifestyle, at the same time we are victims of some such efforts. Consider, for example, the automakers' policy of introducing new auto models annually. This action makes the previous year's model, at least psychologically, seem old. This strategy prompts many car owners to upgrade to the new model. Similarly, think of the fashion industry's seasonal changes in clothing styles. When the new styles appear, most fashion-conscious consumers feel obligated to replace their suddenly outdated wardrobe.

In such cases, do marketers have *the right* to act as agents of change for the public? Many societies attempt to find ways to cushion the effect of some of these changes through social action groups and governmental regulatory agencies. In addressing these changes, however, the challenge often lies in the difficulty of determining whether the change in the long run is beneficial to the entire society.

THE INFLUENCE OF MACRO FORCES ON CONSUMER BEHAVIOR

Children born in recent years take for granted a world their grandparents could not have envisioned. During the twentieth century, humans have witnessed unprecedented technological progress. Never before has the pace of change been so brisk. The first half of the twentieth century brought about the invention of automobiles, airplanes, radio, television, and telephones as well as many household appliances such as refrigerators, washing machines, and clothes driers. During the second half of that century, computers, satellites, and interactive media have altered the way we communicate. Supersonic jets and feature-loaded automobiles have changed the way we travel. Ingenious financial networks and investment programs have reshaped the way we plan for retirement. High-tech medical equipment and miracle drugs extend our lives. In the twenty-first century, eclectic forms of marketing made possible by handheld devices and the social media have reconfigured the way we exchange information and the way we shop.

As a result of a virtual information explosion, consumers now constitute the most knowledgeable generation in history. Computers, tablets, and smartphones have made it easier than ever for consumers to get whatever they need—products, services, or information—wherever and whenever they want it. For example, mobile commerce services now include banking, brokerage, couponing, purchase and delivery, location-based recommendations and directions, browsing, auctions, ticketing, and advertising, just to name a few. In the marketplace, innovative and facilitating methods such as electronic devices, planners, computers, and robotics offer a more efficient and labor-saving alternative to the traditional ways of doing business. Communication easily occurs via e-mail, Facebook, forums, USENETS newsgroups, electronic bulletins, Twitter, blogs, vlogs, instant messaging, text messaging, Skype, and other electronic media. In the field of entertainment alone, thousands of cable and satellite stations from all over the world have come into being. A telecommunications network supported by orbiting satellites makes it possible for consumers to reach anyone in the world and to witness global events as they occur.

As advances in technology have changed consumer lifestyles, marketing practices, in turn, have had to respond. Strategies ranging from precision targeting to customization of products have emerged. Creative selling tactics, advanced networks of distribution channels, and novel ways to motivate consumers to buy, as well as means to finance purchases, have also come about.

Such progress, however, does not come without costs. As consumers become increasingly overwhelmed by the deluge of new product offerings and glut of information, decision processes become more complicated. Today, with Twitter and Facebook, as well as countless apps fed into our smartphones, the flow of messages never ceases. That can be a positive fac-

A woman uses her tablet computer to compare prices at a supermarket.

tor when information serves to empower consumers. Yet, research shows that this glut of information is changing the way we make decisions—and not always for the better.[7] For example, based on an extensive search, a student was close to choosing a particular college. Suddenly, friends swamp his or her media with texts and tweets with reasons for going elsewhere. All this new data may cause confusion or cause the student to alter his or her original choice of school.

In the wake of this profusion of information, some unscrupulous marketers have seized the opportunity to employ puffery, deception, and manipulation to sell their products and services or even to defraud consumers. Concern over unethical practices has motivated many private as well as public bodies to take steps to protect the public from misrepresentation and fraud. Many companies have adopted a philosophy of relationship marketing, in which firms develop a loyal clientele by forming and solidifying long-term customer alliances that are based on trust. Many industries have adopted codes of ethics to which member firms are expected to adhere. When self-regulation has proven to be inadequate, government bodies have had to step in to protect consumer rights.

Today's marketplace is a very different place from what it used to be. Consumers have come to demand convenience and immediate satisfaction of their needs and wants. They expect product-related facts to be instantaneously accessible but seldom use all the available information. These and a host of other trends create opportunities for innovative marketers who are open to change and willing to adapt to a dynamic marketplace.

EMERGING TRENDS IN CONTEMPORARY SOCIETY

In this late second decade of the twenty-first century, certain trends seem to be emerging. The following sections detail four trends that will undoubtedly influence consumer behavior and consequently the way marketers conduct business. The trends are (1) the Dawn of Marketing-Related Innovations; (2) Safety, Security, and Heightened Anxiety; (3) Global Interdependency and Connectivity; and (4) Concern over Affordability of College Education.

THE DAWN OF MARKETING-RELATED INNOVATIONS

With the acceleration of cyberspace technology since 1990, when Tim Berners-Lee created the first World Wide Web browser, a new economic ecosystem was born. Through this innovation, it became possible for anyone to connect to anybody else, anywhere, and at any moment in time.

© Subbotina Anna/Shutterstock.com

From a macro point of view, this early invention not only changed our lifestyle, but also the manner in which we communicate with one another. From a micro perspective, it was a key driver in the growth of e-commerce, which commenced in 1991.[8] From that time on, e-commerce provided a quick and convenient way of exchanging goods, services, and ideas both regionally and globally.

M-commerce, on the other hand, which was born just a few years later in 1997, started in Finland when the first two mobile phones enabled Coca-Cola vending machines to accept payment via SMS text messages. M-commerce uses a number of sophisticated communication devices, including smartphones, PDAs, labtops, iPads, and tablets, among others. In fact, the reinvention of the mobile phone as a touch-sensitive, handheld computer was the major reason for the success of m-commerce.

Beyond the prior advances in cyber technology, today due to our creative spirit, a host of truly innovative products has been and is being introduced into the marketplace. Advances in hardware, software, and automation have netted a number of devices and apps which significantly simplify our tasks, allow us to make better use of our resources, and transform our lives for the better.

Presently, practically everything in our home can be automated or connected to our tablets or smartphones. Available in the market are *wearables* that track and analyze our movements and reactions; *home technologies* including home security, monitoring air quality, and permitting remote child and pet care; *bluetooth* including health meters that track patients' vital signs remotely; and *robotics* that perform functions which formerly required human physical and mental capabilities. Other innovations currently under development or already on the market include

Advances in technology have changed consumer lifestyles, so marketing practitioners, in turn, have had to respond.

e-commerce
buying and selling of products or services over electronic systems, such as the Internet

m-commerce
business transactions conducted via a portable or handheld electronic device

smart refrigerators and dishes that can track expiration dates of packaged foods and measure your food consumption and caloric intake. These innovations allow us to control our environment and manipulate it to adapt to our needs—so that in the end, we can have a more productive, safer, and pleasing lifestyle.[9]

Two of the truly creative products that are expected to revolutionize business and the marketplace in the coming years are drones and self-driving automobiles. A few years ago concerning the first of these, the mention of the word *drones* brought to mind images of military aircraft engaged in espionage and other controversial operation overseas. It was not until Jeff Bezos from Amazon came up with the idea of making prompt deliveries of consumer purchases via drones that this presently popular phenomenon of a new, drone-powered economy became a reality.

While current military applications dominate the global UAV (Unmanned Aerial Vehicles) market, commercial applications are quickly catching up. Drones will soon begin taking on extended roles for businesses that range from transporting e-commerce orders to monitoring security, news gathering and reporting, mail delivery, overseeing traffic patterns, conducting searches for missing people, and changing the way farmers manage their crops. In the United States, until recently, it was extremely difficult to fly a drone for commercial purposes, at least legally. However, at the beginning of 2015, American regulators began to phase in commercial drone flights, starting with operation of small drones weighing fifty-five pounds or less.

This trend accelerated for the remainder of 2015, a year that witnessed an explosion of new businesses that were granted permissions to fly drones. Over nine hundred FAA (Federal Aviation Administration) exemptions to fly drones were issued to farmers, railroads, security services, and medical facilities. Retail and e-commerce, along with a number of related logistics and shipping industries, have the most at stake with regard to the broadened deployment of UAVs. Drones, over the next few years, may well prove to be the missing link in the shipping aspect of the supply chain, which will allow for nearly immediate e-commerce deliveries.[10]

© Maria Dryfhout/Shutterstock.com

Drones today serve a number of business applications, including surveying, security, and delivery.

The second futuristic product innovation is the self-driving car—a self-maneuvering automobile with features that allow it to accelerate, brake, and steer a vehicle's course with limited or no driver interaction. Self-driving cars can be classified into two different varieties: semi-autonomous and fully autonomous. The first type requires the presence of a user/operator while navigating on the road—and because of regulatory and insurance questions regarding their presence in traffic—the release of such vehicles to the market will not likely occur until around the year 2020. The second type (i.e., the fully autonomous cars) can drive from point A to point B and encounter the full range of on-road scenarios without requiring any intervention from a human driver. Companies such as Mercedes Benz, BMW, and Tesla have already released self-driving features that give a vehicle the ability to drive itself.

In the year 2016, a couple of big players—namely, Tesla and Ford—began to publicize their plans for introduction of such vehicles. Tesla, for instance, announced the *Summon,* a car that allows operators to use their smartphones to fetch the Tesla. A driver can stand at the end of his or her driveway and call the car, which in turn automatically opens the garage, starts up the car, and meets the driver wherever he or she is. In fact, Tesla claims that the vehicle can be summoned from just about anywhere.

Ford, on the other hand, has its own concept called *Ford Credit Link*, which will allow a consumer, together with as many as five individuals, to lease a single car. The consumer would use the companion app to determine who is driving when and where in order to be able to coordinate the car's use among its renters. By 2020, observers predict that 10 percent of vehicle owners in mature urban markets will replace their car with access to an on-demand car fleet. It is also estimated that by that time, there will be nearly 10 million self-driving vehicles roaming the roads within the United States alone, considering that Google—as of the time of this writing—is testing its self-driving car, and that Apple is working on its version.[11]

SAFETY, SECURITY, AND HEIGHTENED ANXIETY

Today, we are living in troubled times, compared with the relatively peaceful era that prevailed at the end of the last century. Every day brings gloomy news about terrorism, wars, racism, cyber risk, privacy issues, global warming, and economic uncertainty, as well as other natural disasters, such as earthquakes, wildfires, and floods.

Today, Internet security is a major concern for the government, as well as for commercial operations.

© Den Rise/Shutterstock.com

In these troubling times, emotions tend to follow the same downturn as the path of global events, which causes individuals to feel less secure, more fearful, and increasingly vulnerable. For many people, security implies stability and continuity. Vulnerability, on the other hand, implies the inability to cope with and control prevailing conditions. A heightened sense of insecurity and vulnerability can result in pervasive stress and fear. Such anxiety, as far as marketing is concerned, has a psychological dimension that is likely to affect the behavior of consumers in the marketplace. For example, dire news about terrorism dominates the media today. Images of bombing aftermaths and other atrocities are covered daily in our newscasts and periodicals. We see on TV broadcasts long lines at airport security checks, as we hear about some seemingly innocuous items such as beverages, shoes, and backpacks that have become weapons for deadly attacks. Fear perpetuated by terrorists has a distorting impact on subjective beliefs and individual choices. Terrorism has enduring effects that extend well beyond the immediate loss of human life. Perceived dangers of violence tend to have long-term repercussions, such as posttraumatic stress disorder, a heightened sense of fear, with negative effects on our physical and emotional well-being. These imagined dangers also affect other aspects of society, such as the costs of increased measures to maintain national security; or changes in the choices that individuals make, such as abstaining from buying or traveling. For example, the tourism and hospitality industries in both the United States and abroad have suffered a decline since the beginning of the twenty-first century because of the reduced demand for travel.[12]

Furthermore, new technologies today have created a rich field where cybercrime has significantly flourished, allowing hactivists to unleash illegal acts such as fraud, trafficking, identity theft, and privacy intrusions. Most cybercrime today takes the form of an attack on individuals, corporations, or the government.

Cybercrime spans a wide spectrum of activities. At one end are crimes that involve fundamental breaches of personal or corporate activity, such as identity theft; and at the other end lie transaction-based crimes, such as fraud, trafficking in child pornography, digital piracy, money laundering, and counterfeiting. Cybercrime affects both virtual and reality-based entities. Consider the case of identity theft in contemporary society. Each one of us has a social security number, serving as a de facto identification system. Access to that number affords the opportunity to gather all the data and documents related to each individual and reconstruct that person's identity. An unethical individual may use this information to run up huge bills for unsuspecting victims, forcing the affected individuals, as well as credit card companies, to suffer huge losses. The thief may sell this personal information to other similarly unethical parties, who can use it in the same manner. Alternatively, a criminal might use an individual's name and credit card number to illicitly create a new identity for some other partner in crime. For instance, a thief may contact the issuing bank of a stolen credit card and change the mailing address on the account. This criminal may then be able to accomplish the same for getting a passport or driver's license with his or her own picture, but with the victim's name on it.[13] The depiction in Figure 1.1 raises awareness of cyberthreats.

Other forms of illegal schemes include Internet fraud, an example of which is the Nigerian 419 scam, where an individual receives an email claiming that the sender requires assistance in transferring a large sum of money out of Nigeria, and asks the recipient to cover some of the cost of moving the funds out of the country. For doing so, the cooperating party is promised—but never receives—millions of dollars for his or her services. Other forms of fraud include forgery and counterfeiting currency and other documents—acts that became possible and simple due to the advent of inexpensive, high-quality color copiers and printers.

Worse yet are crimes that attempt to wreak havoc on the hardware that makes up the network, where unscrupulous individuals hack fortunes from the world's financial and communications networks, introduce viruses, penetrate computer bulletin boards, or access government and corporate computer systems. What makes such criminal activities difficult to

FIGURE 1.1

Today, cyberthreat has become one of the most worrisome problems globally.

police by law enforcement authorities is the fact that they occur in cyberspace at global jurisdictions separated by vast distances. This adds another factor in consumers' sense of vulnerability.

Another related scenario is the emerging fear of nuclear power. In 2015, the world's attention has been intensely focused on negotiations between the United States and its coalition of China, the U.K., France, and Germany with Iran—the goal of which was to halt Iran's nuclear program and prevent it from becoming a major player in the nuclear age. Today, there are over 60,000 nuclear weapons on the planet, the majority of which are owned by the United States and Russia, and the remainder by the U.K., France, China, India, Pakistan, North Korea, and Israel. Observers maintain that even in extreme circumstances, most rational governments would avoid launching a nuclear weapon. However, human error, mechanical failure, political struggle, or schemes of terrorist organizations such as ISIS can make this remote possibility a reality. For example, ISIS militants in 2015 announced that they would obtain a nuclear weapon within the following year, potentially from Pakistan. This type of news—even though it centers around terrorist's access to less-sophisticated and crude nuclear materials and weaponry known as "dirty bombs"—can still stir major fear across the board in this country and elsewhere.[14]

When addressing sources of fear, let us not underestimate the significant role played by mass media and social networks in raising and bolstering feelings of doom and gloom. The barrage of downbeat news stories in all media regarding terrorism, crime, police brutality, world conditions, political bickering, business greed, and other negative issues has taken a toll on our psyche and left us with a seemingly hopeless and cynical mindset. Yet, these same feelings of fear and anxiety can bring about community solidarity and harmony, as was evident in the 2015 terrorist attack in San Bernardino, California. In this incident, fourteen people were killed and twenty-two were seriously injured. The perpetrators were a foreign-national Muslim married couple, who targeted a county Department of Public Health. What was horrifying in this attack was the fact that the violence was carried out during a Christmas party at the center where the husband was employed. The perpetrators killed their own colleagues at a facility that had been dedicated to serve persons with developmental disabilities. The community, as well as the whole country, was shocked and saddened by this act, and it remains difficult to ascertain the motives that underlie this type of crime. The citizens of San Bernardino all united in supporting the victims, their families, and the efforts that were taken against this violent act. The community, both domestic and foreign, including police, media, the government, and even Muslim groups living in the United States, joined hands in an effort to lift and support those who suffered loss, fear, and shock.

Another scenario in this coverage is climate change and the phenomenon of global warming. Atmospheric levels of carbon dioxide (CO_2), one of the most prevalent greenhouse gases, have risen above a symbolic threshold of 400 parts per million around much of the globe. This trend has a major impact on global weather systems, causing everything from unexpected volumes of rainfall to extreme heat waves. The rise in greenhouse gas present in the atmosphere is mostly blamed on burned fossil fuels, which moved the gears of the Industrial Revolution and beyond. The demands of a growing population have led to deforestation and intensive use of land, causing greenhouse gas levels to rise. These gases trap heat from the sun instead of radiating it back to space, a process that causes the earth's atmosphere to heat up in what is known as the "greenhouse effect." This climate change has already caused some regions to become significantly colder and others warmer. Sea levels have risen, and glaciers are melting. Entire regions of the country are at risk of heat waves, drought, forest fires, flooding, and natural disasters. Climate change, as such, could ruin food chains and ecosystems, placing our world at risk of starvation, health consequences, and driving humans back into poverty.[15]

This depiction of downloading containers of imported goods is a familiar site at any major seaport today.

© Sheila Fitzgerald/Shutterstock.com

GLOBAL INTERDEPENDENCY AND CONNECTIVITY

Business activities are no longer confined to the domestic market. U.S. and foreign businesses compete in an increasingly interdependent global economic environment. A growing number of U.S. firms export, import, or manufacture products abroad. Similarly, many foreign-based companies now operate in the United States. Whether or not any given business organization is directly involved in exports and imports, nothing can be done to avoid the impact of competition from abroad.

Today, nations are more vulnerable to outside economic disruptions than they were at any time in history. Inflation can spread quickly across national borders. Previously safe domestic industries have been known to disappear due to competition from other world markets. For example, American companies in sectors exposed to global competition have lost ground against a flood of low-cost Chinese products. Distortions in currency exchange rates can also shut out nations' traditional export markets.

Other major global events that are quickly changing world economies include the rise of terrorism, the wars in Iraq and Syria, the unsettled political situation in the Middle East and Iran, the migration of millions of immigrants to Europe and Western nations, the economic rise of China and India, and natural disasters such as tsunamis and hurricanes perpetrated in large part by global warming.

The Internet, as no other communication medium, has given a globalized dimension to the world since it serves as the primary source of information for billions around the globe. Through the use of computers, laptops, smartphones, and iPads, people connected to the Internet now have access to information at their fingertips about global events as they occur. Distance and time factors have become things of the past. News travels as if we were all living in a single village. Just think of the world events that have occurred in the last few years or that are now occurring to be able to grasp the meaning of interdependency and connectivity.

Consider how U.S. financial markets tumbled in 2011 due to the debt crisis in Europe. Ireland and Greece needed bailouts, and Portugal, Spain, Italy, France, and Belgium were drowning in an ocean of unsustainable debt.[16] At that time, the financial concerns of the European Union, the twenty-seven-member nation organization with seventeen countries using the euro as common currency, caused the U.S. stock market, U.S. banks, and value of the U.S. dollar to plunge. The reasons for that negative effect were obvious—European financial instability had touched the United States on four fronts, including the value of our dollar, volume of our exports, stability of our stock market, and liquidity of our banks. For one, the value of the dollar is tied to that of the euro; if one rises, the other falls. A weaker dollar raises the cost of goods we import from overseas. Financial markets are affected by global pessimism, causing reluctance of global investors and multinational corporations to invest in our country. U.S. banks were also negatively impacted, as European banks traded billions of dollars daily with counterparts on Wall Street which were invested in U.S. money markets.[17] The economic and financial impact of the uncertainty caused by the withdrawal of the United Kingdom from the European Union, an event known as "Brexit," remains to be seen.

Further consider the power of social media to incite groups to act on behalf of a cause.[18] Contemplate what ISIS does to communicate. Use of digital media is one of the group's significant strengths helping it to remain a powerful force. Contemplate further the level of sophisticated messaging and social media efforts that ISIS employs to great effect in order to attract members and solicit funds. The group has a multilingual propaganda arm known as *Al-Hayat*. It uses GoPros and cameras mounted on drones to make videos that appeal to its followers. ISIS is skilled in using multiple tools in the platform box, ranging from Twitter to YouTube and Instagram.

Similarly, consider the role of social media during crises, natural or otherwise. For example, during the devastating hurricane Sandra on the East Coast of the United States in the year 2012, social media sites like Twitter, Facebook, and YouTube permitted widespread awareness of the scale and magnitude of the natural disaster, aided the search for missing people, and enabled charities

© Fotokon/Shutterstock.com

to call out for support, donations, and volunteers. For example, social media sites posted guides on how impacted citizens can use the network to communicate and receive vital facts such as safety of individuals or places, evacuation details, medical information for victims, and various forms of support. In addition, the user-generated video site YouTube provided a source for people around the world to view raw footage of the disaster.

Furthermore, consider how politicians today have figured out what social media technologies, such as text messages, blogs, Facebook, and Twitter can do for them. More than ever before, it allows them direct access to various publics, both national and global. It is a means by which they can bypass the professional press and deliver their message unfiltered and unchecked. While in the past, politicians relied on news agencies to write press releases and print them in their newspapers and magazines, social media now allow them to send uncensored messages directly to their publics. Moreover, new media technologies leave an online record that is accessible and searchable by interested citizens, journalists, and historians.

However, the fact remains that access to computers and other similar types of technologies is far from being uniform globally. Every country has its "haves" and "have nots." For example, compared to North America, where the rate of Internet penetration in 2014 was 86.75 percent, the rate in Africa that same year was only 19 percent, in India 19.19 percent, and in Nigeria 37.59 percent.[19] For many people in less-developed countries around the world, acquiring these new electronic devices remains a challenge.

From a consumer behavior point of view, one distinguishing trait of today's global scene is the commonality of needs among consumers in different countries. Whether in Tokyo, Moscow, Berlin, London, Cairo, Hong Kong, or Bangkok, consumers—particularly those in the middle class—have begun to seek the new products and services they have learned about in the conventional media, social media, and online. Walking through the streets of any of these cities, we are likely to observe people wearing Levi's jeans or Nike shoes and using iPods and iPhones.

The ad presented in Figure 1.1 from Microsoft Cloud informs consumers about the company system's ability to connect millions of people throughout the world.

CONCERN OVER AFFORDABILITY OF COLLEGE EDUCATION

In a recent survey of college pricing, the College Board reports that a "moderate" college budget for an in-state public college for the 2015-2016 academic year averaged $24, 061; and a "moderate" budget for a private college averaged $47,831.[24]

ETHICAL DILEMMA

When Big Pharma Digs for Gold

Today, the Center for Drug Control (CDC) estimates that there are 3.2 million Americans infected with hepatitis C (HCV), where approximately half of them are unaware of the fact they carry the virus. This simply points to the fact that HCV has become a major public health threat in the United States.

In past years, there has been a relatively low-cost HCV treatment that achieved moderate success as a cure for a range of HCV cases. This regimen, however, required a lengthy forty-eight-week period of treatment with Peginterferon and Ribaviron, which the majority of patients found intolerable, causing them to discontinue the treatment after a few months from the starting date.[20]

Over the years 2013 and 2014, however, pharmaceutical companies, through partnership with the government and industry, reached a breakthrough in the treatment of HCV in the form of direct-acting antiviral agents against the disease. A number of brands appeared on the market, including Harvoni and Sovaldi (produced by Gilead Sciences), Viekira Pack (produced by Abbvie), and Olysio (produced by Janssen). These breakthrough medications achieved cure rates of 95 percent, with a twelve-week treatment—in addition to causing minimal side effects. As a result, these new treatments established themselves as unprecedented milestones in the management of HCV.

This positive news about the new treatment was initially greeted with great excitement and relief that finally the war against hepatitis C had been won. However, a few weeks later, the medical community and general public were shocked when the wholesale acquisition price tags for these twelve-week treatments were revealed. The supplying pharmaceutical companies announced prices of $83,319 for Viekira Pack, $84,000 for Sovaldi, $94,000 for Harvoni, and $66,000 for Olysio—price levels that would translate into approximately a $1,000-a-day pill per patient. The medical community concluded that if all 3.2 million Americans infected with HCV were to receive this type of treatment, it would net $300 billion in sales to these pharmaceutical companies. Public opinion and the media were quick to condemn these astronomic prices, bashing Big Pharma and calling these prices unconscionable and simply unethical.[21]

In the face of these accusations, spokespersons from Big Pharma defended the pricing practice as mere reflection of the "value" to the patients of these medications. Unlike long-term treatments for hepatitis C via traditional medications, they reason these new ones offer high certainty of cure—thereby reducing long-term health care costs, morbidity, and mortality; as well as enhancing infected individuals' quality of life.

Obviously, these excuses fall apart in view of facts about actual costs of making these drug treatments. Pharmaceutical industry analysts estimate that the actual cost of producing this new treatment is at most $1,000, and probably less.[22] In fact, in selling these same drugs overseas in countries such as Canada, several nations in the European Union, Egypt, and India, the price charged is significantly lower. For example, Sovaldi, for which patients in the United States pay between $84,000 and $160,000 for a twelve- to twenty-four-week course of treatment, is sold in Egypt and India for a mere $900 for the complete course.[23] Gilead Sciences, the company making it, remains profitable even at this reduced price.

The prevailing opinion of medical practitioners is that if Sovaldi's and Harvoni's prices, as well as those of other similar medications that treat HCV, were reduced by 90 percent to, say, $8,000, the drug companies would still end up with at least a $7,000 profit margin per course of treatment, and ethical issues raised with their pricing policies would disappear.

For everyday clinicians treating patients with HCV, the landscape has changed drastically because of these high-cost treatments. The promise of a twelve-week, highly tolerable cure has swelled the ranks of those seeking a cure. However, if all who are eligible for Medicaid coverage were treated with these new drugs, the average cost to any state would rise to over $50 billion per year. These are costs that are impossible for any state to bear ethically and economically for treating just one type of condition. Consequently, most states have put in place strict protocols for the patient to be considered for treatment—thereby denying treatment to thousands of those who are truly in need of help. Visit http://www.medscape.com/viewarticle/844054_print, http://msubiotics.com/2014/10/23/hepatitis-c/, and http:// www.medscape.com/viewarticle/835182_print. The ethical challenge faced by our society today in such a situation is whether the free hand of the market in setting price should be left untouched so as to encourage and maximize innovation; or as a society, we have to deem various areas such as healthcare too important to operate freely without firm ethical parameters. Which of these two viewpoints do you support? Explain why.

This trend of the rising college education costs is making it harder for ordinary Americans to get the education they need. Today, it would take a minimum wage worker an entire year to earn enough money to cover the annual in-state tuition at a public university—a fact that hinders many young and bright people in our society from being able to attend college. With the added news about an overwhelming student loan crisis amounting to over $1.3 trillion, many families and their young children have started to wonder whether the struggle the college graduate faces in getting a four-year degree is worth the cost.[25]

A new set of income statistics from the Economic Policy Institute in Washington, D.C., however, answered the question clearly and confirmed the fact that an important pathway to the middle class to attain high earnings is achieved through higher education. The statistics reveal that the pay gap between college graduates and everyone else in our society has continued to widen over the years. Americans with four-year college degrees earn twice as much per hour compared to people without a degree. This pay gap is predicted to continue to widen in the coming years, even though over the last decade, the average hourly wage for college graduates has not risen much (only 1 percent) to about $32.60, the pay gap has expanded mostly because the average wage for everybody else has fallen to about $16.50.[26]

In this view, college education is essential for both personal and national well-being. The United States, as a highly competitive global economy, needs the best-educated workforce in the world. This goal cannot be accomplished if every year, thousands of bright people cannot afford to attend college, and millions more leave school deeply in debt.

There is, therefore, an urgent need to ensure that every young American who wishes to go to college can get the education that he or she desires, without going into debt and regardless of his or her family income. In fact, there was a time when higher education in the United States was nearly free. The GI Bill, which was implemented after World War II, gave and still provides a free education to millions of veterans, who otherwise would never have been able to afford college—a major reason for the high productivity and economic growth the country enjoyed during postwar years and even into the present. In addition, in most Western nations such as Germany, Denmark, Finland, Norway, Sweden, and Ireland, public colleges and universities are tuition-free.

Many experts, journalists, and politicians today have a vision of a free college education for young American men and women. In addition they call for addressing the challenge of existing student loans through legislation, allowing student-loan borrowers to refinance outstanding loans at lower interest rates, and capping payments at a low percentage of their income. The emphasis, in this view, would be to establish free-tuition college education for all. Just as other countries that offer such opportunities to their citizens, the U.S. government can do the same through taxation. In this view, free-tuition college education would become a citizen's "right" (rather than just a privilege for those who can afford it)—synonymous with security, safety, and protection provided by the state to its citizens.[27]

The ad presented in Figure 1.2 from the Kelley School of Business at the University of Indiana paints a portrait of a successful individual who earned an advanced college degree.

FIGURE 1.2

This ad from the Kelley School of Business at the University of Indiana emphasizes how a university degree can be valuable for the business career of an individual by conveying the success story of a recipient of a master's degree from Kelley.

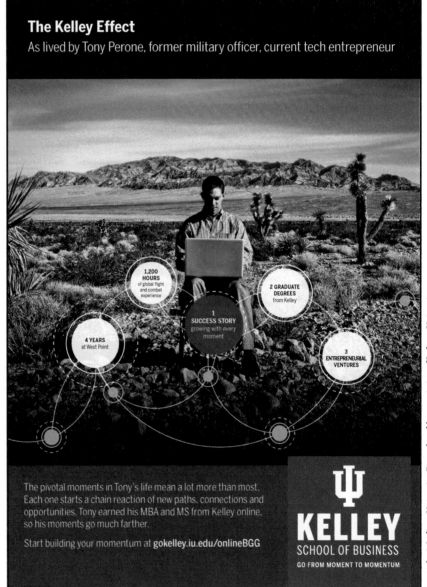

GLOBAL OPPORTUNITY

When Hollywood Actors Speak Chinese

As Hollywood explored opportunities for global expansion of its movie business, China emerged as a fertile ground for possible expansion. This initiative on Hollywood's part arose after the Chinese mainland undertook serious steps to develop its own movie business. Recently, China approached Hollywood seeking partnerships to produce a wave of Sino-U.S. movies for the Chinese market.

What makes China an attractive market is not just the mere size of the country nor its huge population of over 1.3 billion persons, but its emerging middle class, which appears to be interested in just about anything that is Western. Today, China's middle class snaps up everything from Quarter Pounders and Coca-Cola to iPhones and American-made automobiles. However, until recently, this vast potential coexisted amid a lumbering bureaucracy and strict controls that the Chinese government had imposed on foreign businesses. In the movie industry, just as is the case with any other product or service, the challenge is finding an efficient way to get the film to the consumer—in this case, the massive Chinese audience. The China Film Ministry, which decides how many foreign films may be shown in the country, has favored homemade movies. It stocks China's theaters with hundreds of domestic films a year and allowed, until that time, only twenty imported films annually. In 2012, however, a new contract was signed between the United States and China for revenue-share distribution and for raising the film import quota to thirty-four films per year.

As American studios grew more dependent on ticket sales from the Chinese box office, film makers have become more willing to adjust the content of their movies in order to appeal the stringent mandates of the Chinese censors. This trend has had its influence over Hollywood's biggest blockbusters, causing more studios to modify lines of dialogue, alter scripts, or revamp entire scenes in order to make the movies more palatable to the Chinese tastes.

China is now on tract to overtake the United States as the world's largest film market by the year 2017. China's film industry is growing faster than anyone had expected, with ticket sales of $6.5 billion in the year 2016, compared to combined ticket sales in the United States and Canada of around $11 billion. Much of the growth has been driven by popularity of Hollywood blockbusters such as *Jurassic World* and *Avengers: Age of Ultron*, the rising middle-class hunger for movies, as well as rapid growth of multiplex cinemas. In an acquisition deal signed in January 2016, the Chinese conglomerate Dalian Wanda Group bought U.S. film studio Legendary Entertainment for about $3.5 billion. This move makes Wanda the first Chinese firm to own a major Hollywood studio—a clear sign that China has become a growing power in the global movie world.[28]

RAMIFICATIONS OF CURRENT TRENDS FOR CONSUMERS AND MARKETERS

Trends such as those cited in this chapter constitute significant forces that have enhanced our knowledge, broadened our connections with others, guided our carbon footprints, soothed our feelings of insecurity, enhanced our understanding of problems related to financing our higher education, and sharpened our global understanding. Today's consumers have found new ways to become more informed, are savvier, and have become more powerful in the process. Moreover, they have developed a sense of entitlement. That is to say, whether the issue involves health, recreation, ethical matters, or environmental concerns, consumers have high expectations from the businesses that serve them. Adept marketers realize that they must adjust to the opportunities and challenges presented by these and other trends in the marketplace. It remains to be seen which companies will successfully adapt to these trends, precisely how firms will respond, and how consumers and government bodies will react to the actions of business. A thorough understanding of the market environment, consumers in it, and prevailing competitive forces, as well as current product and service offerings, is vital for marketing management, which must draw up a mission statement and set workable strategies for the firm. Marketing and consumer research, thus, become essential tools for providing the necessary data that can yield this market insight. For example, through consumer research, companies gain valuable knowledge about consumers such as their purchasing habits, their product use, and their demographics. Through this process, marketers come to recognize that people possess different needs and wants and that they often satisfy their desires dissimilarly. The varied needs and wants of consumers must be taken into account when companies design their product and service offerings. This realization is the foundation for what is known as market segmentation. Market segmentation allows marketers to see clearly the diversity within their markets and uncover possible opportunities that may exist or to identify niches whose needs have been poorly met by other product and service offerings. Market segmentation together with the closely related concepts of targeting and positioning are the topics that constitute the next chapter.

SUMMARY

For purposes of this text, *consumer behavior* refers to the field of study that addresses how people buy and why they act as they do. More specifically, the study of consumer behavior investigates how individuals plan, purchase, use, and dispose of goods and services that satisfy personal or household needs. Some of the influences that shape consumer choices and tendencies entail internal processes, such as thinking, feeling, and wanting; other influences involve environmental factors, such as social, economic, situational, and promotional considerations. Somehow, all these forces combine and dynamically interact to produce shopping behavior, the objective of which is to satisfy personal needs and wants. The analysis of consumer behavior entails surveying various theories and research studies that offer insight about purchasing tendencies. Marketers need to understand what consumers need and want, how they spend their resources, and how they decide where to shop, when to buy, and what to purchase. In short, knowledge of consumer behavior is an essential prerequisite for marketing success. The ultimate goal of this field of endeavor is to help marketers *predict* consumer behavior.

As we enter the second decade of the twenty-first century, a number of trends will undoubtedly affect consumer behavior and, consequently, how marketers conduct business. This chapter briefly examines a number of these trends. The specific trends covered include (1) the dawn of marketing-related innovations; (2) safety, security, and heightened anxiety; (3) global interdependency and connectivity; and (4) concern over affordability of college education.

In our society, marketers—as agents of change—are largely responsible for bringing about the high standard of living to which we have grown accustomed. Although many of these marketing efforts help us to experience a more enjoyable lifestyle, we are at the same time victims of some such efforts.

CASE SYNOPSIS

What's in Your Burger?

Disclosure of information about the caloric content of restaurant menu items is seen by many as a desirable step toward helping consumers make healthy menu choices. While the FDA in the past has recommended listing such vital nutritional information on all processed foods, only a fraction of major chain restaurants voluntarily place this caloric and fat-content information on their menus. A consumer movement to force restaurants to provide nutritional information has resulted in the passage of an FDA food labeling law which became effective in 2013. Visit the book's website for the case and related exercises.

Notes

1   Centers for Disease Control and Prevention, http://www.cdc.gov/obesity/data/trends.html and Division of Nutrition, Physical Activity, and Obesity.
2   "Land of the Fat," *Scanorama* (December 1994–January 1995), p. 69; Jerry Knight, "America Getting Thinner? Fat Chance," *Chicago Sun-Times* (September 4, 1994), p. 4; Bill Ingram, "Fed Up with False Hope," *Chicago Sun-Times* (September 4, 1994), p. 4.
3   Lev Grossman, "If You Liked This…," *Time* (June 7, 2010), pp. 44–48.
4   Theodore Levitt, "Marketing Myopia," *Harvard Business Review* 53, no. 5 (September-October 1975), pp. 26–44 and 173–181.
5   Franklin S. Houston and Jule B. Gassenheimer, "Marketing and Exchange," *Journal of Marketing* (October 1987), pp. 3–18.
6   E. Jerome McCarthy and William D. Perreault Jr., *Basic Marketing*, 10th ed. (Homewood, IL: Irwin, 1990), p. 8; Malcolm P. McNair, "Marketing and the Social Challenge of Our Times," in Keith Cox and Ben M. Enis (Eds.), *A New Measure of Responsibility for Marketing* (Chicago: American Marketing Associations, 1968).
7   Sharon Begley, "I Can't Think," *Newsweek* (March 7, 2011), pp. 28–33.
8   "Developing an E-Commerce Strategy: What Is E-Commerce?" (Retrieved from a website entitled *Sell Online*.)

9   Tom Demers, "The Best Smart Home Products for DIYers: 50 Smart Home Technology Systems and Devices to Automate Your Home the DIY Way." *Safe Sound Family* (November 19, 2015), http://safesoundfamily.com/blog/the-50-best-smart-home-products-for-diyers/; Andrew Gazdecki, "Smart Technology and the Internet of Things," Bizness Apps blog, http://www.biznessapps.com/blog/2015/06/18/smart-technology-and-the-internet-of-things/.

10   Marcelo Ballıve, "Commercial Drones: Assessing the Potential for a New Drone-Powered Economy," *Business Insider* (October 3, 2014), http://www.businessinsider.com/the-market-for-commercial-drones-2014-2; Ben Popper, "These Are the Companies Allowed to Fly Drones Over the US," *The Verge* (July 7, 2015), http://www.theverge.com/2015/7/7/8883821/drone-search-engine-faa-approved-commercial-333-exemptions.

11   David Pierce, "Tesla Summons Hints at How the World of Self-Driving Cars Will Work," *Transportation* (January 18, 2016); John Greenough, "10 Million Self-Driving Cars Will Be on the Road by 2020," *BI Intelligence* (July 29, 2015), http://www.businessinsider.com/report-10-million-self-driving-cars-will-be-on-the-road-by-2020-2015-5-6.

12   Emily Vuong, "Terrorism, Fear and the Impacts on Economic Rationality," *essa* (October 13, 2013); Karl Vick, "The Migrant Crisis Is a Major Test for European Identity—and Unity," *Time* (September 28, 2015); Dimitra Kessenides, "The Path Beyond the Waves," *Bloomberg* (September 10, 2015), pp. 12–13.

13   FBI Cybercrimes, https://www.fbi.gov/news/.../cyber-crimes2015.

14   Editor's Pick, "Nuclear Weapons, Primal Fears," *HarvardGazette* (December 2, 2010), http://news.harvard.edu/gazette/story/2010/12/nuclear-weapons-primal-fears/; Editorial Board, "Nuclear Fears in South Asia," *The New York Times* (April 6, 2015), http://www.nytimes.com/2015/04/06/opinion/nuclear-fears-in-south asia.html?_r–0); Steven Viney and Stephanie Julett, "TalkAboutIt: Top Five Nuclear Threats the World Faces," *News* (July 24, 2015).

15   Morgan Winsor, "Climate Change Could Force 100M into Poverty by 2030, World Bank Group Report Says," *ibtimes* (November 8, 2015), http://www.ibtimes.com/climate-change-could-force-100M-poverty-2030-world-bank-group-report-says-2173747?rel=rel#1); Clark Mindock, "Climate Change 2015: Green House Gas Emissions Break Records in Atmosphere as Global Warming Fears Rise, 100 Million Could Become Poor," *ibtimes* (November 9, 2015), http://www.ibtimes.com/climate-change-2015-greenhouse-gas-emissions-break-records-atmosphere-global-warming-2175476); Unilever U.S. Stories, "What Is Climate Change? How Can We Take Action?" https://BrightFuture.unilever.us/stories/423885/What-is-climate-change-How-can-we-take-action/.aspx?gclid=Cj0KEQiA5oy1BRDQh6Wd572hsfkBEiQ...

16   Julia Kollewe, "World Stock Market Plunge as Fears of Recession Intensify," *Guardian.co.uk* (August 18, 2011), http://www.guardian.co.uk/business/2011/aug/18/world-stock-markets-plunge-as-fears-of-recession-intensify...

17   Heather Stewart, "Markets in Meltdown Amid New Global Recession Fears," *Guardian.co.uk* (August 18, 2011), http://www.guardian.co.uk/business/2011/aug/18/markets-plummet-global-recession-fear ...

18   Joseph Marks, "Social Media's Role in Arab Spring Still Unclear," *nextgov*, http://www.nextgov.com/site_services/print_article.php?StoryID=ng_20110916_4696.

19   Internet Live Stats, "Number of Internet Users 2015," World Internet Users Statistics and 2015 World Population, www.internetworldstats.com/stats.htm.

20   John Watson, "Hepatitis C: Weighing the Price of Cure," *Medscape* (May 21, 2015), http://www.medscape.com/viewarticle/844054_print.

21   Julie Appleby, "New Hepatitis C Drugs' Price Prompts an Ethical Debate: Who Deserves to Get Them?" *Washington Post* (May 2, 2014).

22   Leonard Fleck, "The Ethical Challenges Raised by Hepatitis C Drugs," *Biotics in the News* (October 23, 2014), http://msubiotics.com/2014/10/23/hepatitis-c/.

23   Roxanne Nelson, "Why Are Drugs Cost So High in the United States?" *Medscape* (November 19, 2014), http://www.medscape.com/viewarticle/835182_print.

24   Caroline Howard, "America's Top Colleges Ranking 2015," *Forbes* (July 29, 2015), http://www.forbes.com/sites/carolinehoward/2015/07/29/americas-top-colleges-2015/#11505aaa#4eed.

25   Bernie Sanders, "Make College Free for All," *The Washington Post* (October 22, 2015).

26   Dustin Swanger, "Student Debt and Higher Education," *Huff Post Education* (July 22, 2014, updated September 21, 2014), http://www.huffingtonpost.com/dr-dustin-swanger/student-debt-and-higher-e_b_5609436.html.

27   Bernie Sanders, "It's Time to Make College Tuition Free and Debt Free," https://berniesanders.com/issues/its-time-to-make-college-tuition-free-and-debt-free/

28   Christopher Zara, "Hollywood Studios Are Self-Censoring Movies to Appease Communist Censors in China, Says U.S. Report," *ibtimes* (October 30, 2015), http://www.ibtimes.com/hollywood-studios-are-self-censoring-movies-appease-communist-censors-china-says-us-2163232; Patrick Frater, "Hollywood Studios Finalize Distribution Contract with China," *Variety* (November 5, 2015).

CHAPTER 2

SEGMENTATION, TARGETING, AND POSITIONING

LEARNING OBJECTIVES

- To grasp the limitations of adopting a mass-marketing strategy.
- To comprehend the concepts of segmentation, targeting, and positioning.
- To identify the major segmentation variables for dissecting markets.
- To explore the various market-targeting strategies.
- To determine criteria for an effective positioning strategy.
- To examine the tactic of repositioning.

KEY TERMS

mass-market strategy
market segmentation
market targeting
positioning
geographic segmentation
demographic
   segmentation

geodemographic
   segmentation
psychographic
   segmentation
AIO inventories
behavioral segmentation
market profile
undifferentiated strategy

multisegment strategy
concentration strategy
customization strategy
mass customization
personalization
perceptual map
repositioning

arketers realize that in order to succeed in today's increasingly fragmented marketplace, they have to isolate key market segments and reach these segments with the maximum possible impact. Innovative programs such as the following can help to attract target-ed customers, enhance customer satisfaction, and increase business:

- GolfNow.com covers news about golfing and allows golfers to book their tee times online 24/7 at more than 6,000 courses in the United States, Canada, Ireland, Scotland, and Mexico. A mere click by a user to schedule a tee time directs the golfer to multiple courses within a twenty-five-mile radius from his or her current geographic location.
- ChristianMingle.com allows single individuals of the Christian faith who are looking to date and marry to find like-minded partners. Ini-tially launched in 2001, the site now boasts more than 15 million reg-istered members.
- DestinationXL.com is an online all-inclusive site that offers an ex-tensive assortment of extra-large-size men's clothing, as well as other accessories. This site serves individuals with large body frames along with other similar online services, such as kingsizedirect.com.
- Hasbro.com is an online toy site that allows parents and others to learn about different toys and games. In addition, the site provides product instructions, details about safety, and information about product re-calls. A part of the site provides answers to frequently asked questions (FAQs).
- Findyourstampsvalue.com is a helpful site for individuals who collect stamps, are looking to purchase stamps, or who are seeking to evaluate their stamp collections. The site provides the values of all U.S. and U.K. stamps, a directory of companies that buy and sell postage stamps, and full personal support in stamp-value searches by collectors.

This chapter addresses the strategies of market segmentation, targeting, and positioning. It also delineates tactics that marketers employ to achieve their sales, market share, and profit goals. The reality is that people possess different needs and wants and often perceive and act on their desires dif-ferently. Rarely do firms today claim that everyone is a prospect for their products or services.

Today, more than ever, marketers recognize the importance of precision targeting. Many have established innovative programs designed to initiate relationships with prospective customers and lure them to the company's brand. Cite one such program you have participated in. How does this program work? Learn more about Kimberly-Clark's initiative by visiting the firm's website at www.parentstages.com. What types of information does the company provide to help parenting, even though many visitors to the site may not be customers of the company? Do you think this strategy is effective? Why or why not?

MASS MARKETING

In 1908, Henry Ford introduced the new Model-T automobile to the market. His concept was simple: use economies of scale to produce a standardized, low-priced automobile that could be purchased in any color the customer desired—as long as it was black. Demand for the Model-T was so great that consumers flocked to purchase the car.

As time passed, the Model-T suffered the consequences of inflexibility because Ford overemphasized standardization and uniformity. Ford's basic premise that customers have homogeneous preferences proved to be incorrect. Consumers' needs for automobiles began to shift toward heavier, closed-body cars that were more comfortable and more colorful. Ford's highly standardized operations, as well as its specialized workforce and facilities, made it difficult to respond to changing customer needs. However, its chief rival, General Motors, had the flexibility to respond quickly to evolving consumer needs by introducing new automobile designs, such as the 1923 Chevrolet, which embodied the innovative features consumers had come to desire. These designs helped General Motors enhance its market position against Ford's Model-T. As a consequence, in 1927 Ford closed down operations for an entire year, at enormous cost, in order to retool and introduce the revised Model-A.

It is clear that Ford, in his Model-T introduction, employed a mass-market strategy, a philosophy based on the assumption of a single, large, homogeneous marketplace with common needs. Focusing on these common needs, Ford introduced only one product to appeal to everyone in the market. Other companies that followed this same strategy have ranged from the early Coca-Cola Company, which originally sold Coke in its familiar eight-ounce green-glass bottle and in only one flavor, to the Bell System, which introduced the early rotary-dial black telephones.

> **mass-market strategy**
> a philosophy that presumes consumers are uniform and that broad-appeal products and marketing programs suffice

Today, however, traditional mass-market approaches aimed at building huge customer or client bases are frequently ineffective. Large groups of consumers are, in reality, heterogeneous, consisting of smaller, more homogenous subgroups with common demographic or lifestyle characteristics. Consequently, mass-marketing approaches have largely been replaced by strategies to match the product to the market.

EXHIBIT 2.1

Components of a Market
Matching Strategy

Segmenting Consumer Markets

Three major steps are necessary and inseparable components of any successful product–market matching strategy. The first step is market segmentation. Market segmentation is the act of dissecting the overall marketplace into a number of submarkets that may require different products or services and thus can be approached with different marketing mixes. The second step is market targeting, which is the process of reviewing the segments that result from implementing the first step and deciding which one or ones the company can feasibly pursue. The selection of which market(s) to pursue is usually determined on the basis of a feasibility study, considering such things as a company's strengths and weakness, the opportunities and threats it faces, as well as a parallel analysis of the competition and overall industry trends. The third step is positioning. Positioning establishes an intended and differentiating image for a company's brand, product, or service. This image should communicate to the target segment(s) the uniqueness of the brand. These three steps are depicted in Exhibit 2.1.

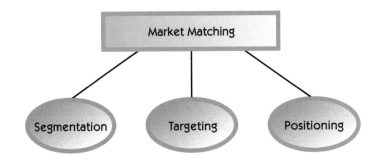

MARKET SEGMENTATION

By segmenting the market into a number of submarkets or *niches*, in which customers have distinct and somewhat similar needs, a marketer can determine which one or ones to target and accordingly design an appropriate marketing mix for serving and reaching each. For example, commercial airlines divide travelers into two major segments: business and leisure travelers. The first segment is characterized by interest in on-time departure and arrival, frequent daily flights, good service, and comfortable seats. Business travelers are less concerned about ticket prices and seldom purchase tickets in advance or remain at their destination over a weekend. Leisure travelers, on the other hand, are more interested in low-priced tickets than in precise departure or arrival times. This group usually purchases tickets in advance and remains at a destination over a weekend. Based on these differences, airlines have designed separate pricing structures for the two segments—a high price for the business traveler and a low price for the leisure traveler. Airlines promote these services differently to each segment, emphasizing those aspects that are important to each.

In order for separate market segments to exist, there should be differences in the responses of the subgroups to product design, price, distribution, or promotion. If each subgroup were to respond in the same manner (for example, by purchasing products in the same amount or with the same frequency), then they would *not* be real market segments. Consumer research can determine likely sources of variation in consumer responses, and it is identifying the *response* that matters: Simply finding differences in consumers' characteristics is not enough.[1]

Marketers may opt to use one segmentation variable or several, whether geographic (location, climate), demographic (age, family lifecycle, gender, race and ethnicity, occupation), geodemographic (consumer clusters and zip codes), psychographic (lifestyle, personality), or behavioral (usage rate, end benefits sought, brand and store loyalty). For example, a fashion firm may use differing climatic conditions between *geographic regions* as the sole segmentation variable. This clothing firm may offer a heavier and warmer garment line for consumers located in colder climate regions of the country and a lighter line for consumers in warmer regions. Alternatively, the firm may elect to employ additional segmentation variables such as *demographics* (offer separate fashion lines for men and for women), geodemographics (offer an expensive line of clothing directed to clusters of consumers residing in certain zip codes based on a scale of affluence), *psychographics* (offer sports lines for joggers, tennis players, and golfers), or *product-relevant behavior* (offer lines of formal and casual wear). Exhibit 2.2 depicts these five classes of segmentation variables, and the next sections cover each one in detail.

Geographic Segmentation

When products are bought, used, or sold differently in various areas of the marketplace, it makes sense to use geography as a basis for market seg-

EXHIBIT 2.2

Segmenting Consumer Markets

mentation. Markets then are divided into subcategories such as regions, counties, cities, and towns that typically reflect varied consumer wants and product usage patterns. This partitioning of the market is called geographic segmentation.

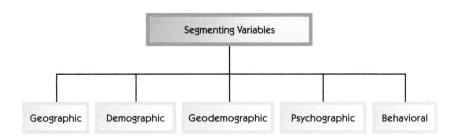

Geographic dissimilarities between regions include climate, location, surroundings, distance, and terrain. These geographic differences precipitate the formation of different tastes, preferences, and activities among consumers residing in various parts of the marketplace. Marketers, in response, may need to develop separate marketing mixes to target consumers in diverse geographic sites. Many companies now *regionalize* their marketing programs and *localize* their products, as well as their advertising and selling efforts, in order to better suit the needs and preferences of individual regions, cities, and even neighborhoods. For example, S. C. Johnson & Son, maker of the Raid line of bug killers, has recently started using a geographic segmentation approach to market its line. The company promotes cockroach zappers in areas of heavy roach infestation such as Houston and New York, and flea sprays in flea-bitten cities such as Tampa and Birmingham.[2] This new segmentation strategy has led to an increase in Raid's market share in sixteen of its eighteen regions. It has also led to an increase of more than 5 percent in the company's market share in the $1 billion-per-year U.S. insecticide market.

When it comes to driving and preferences for vehicles, a greater percentage of consumers in the Southwest drive pickup trucks. More Northeasterners prefer vans, whereas Californians love high-priced imported cars such as BMWs and Mercedes-Benzes. Geography also appears to affect size preferences among car consumers. Whereas Texans like big cars, New Yorkers prefer more compact vehicles.

With Parade, you can cover the entire United States

or just some of it.

As a marketer, Parade offers you the ability to custom make your market. Whether it's metro areas, rural areas, the Corn Belt, Snow Belt or growth areas, Parade gives you a choice of any, or all, of over 300 markets. So no matter who you're trying to reach, you can draw your media plan accordingly.

PARADE

81 million readers in just 48 hours.

Created by Warwick Baker O'Neill for PARADE Magazine. Reprinted with permission of Parade Publications.

FIGURE 2.1

Today many newspapers, magazine publishers, and TV networks realize the importance of covering news and events relevant to local publics. In this ad, Parade magazine emphasizes its custom design, enabling it to serve the needs of both national and local advertisers.

Advertisers on network television often run regional ad campaigns directed to consumers in different areas with their own unique tastes and preferences. Likewise, magazine and newspaper publishers often print different editions to accommodate the needs and interests of readers in diverse geographic areas. Many newspapers, for example, come in urban and suburban editions in order to carry news stories, editorials, and ads relevant to those readers who reside within a specific trading area. The ad in Figure 2.1 illustrates how *Parade*, a magazine inserted into hundreds of newspapers, enables advertisers to cover the national market or selected areas of the country.

Demographic Segmentation

Demographics are the most common basis for segmenting consumer markets. Marketers' preference for using demographic data to segment markets rests on the relative ease of measuring them, as well as their close link to demand for many products and services. Demographic variables such as age, stage in the family lifecycle, gender, income, occupation, education, religion, nationality, and race are commonly used by marketers because they usually correlate with consumer preferences, needs, and usage rates. For example, gender is an important segmentation variable in the case of clothing, cosmetics, skin-care products, and hair-coloring products. Similarly, stage in the family lifecycle is important in determining the need for housing, furniture, appliances, children's products and services, and electronic gadgets. This partitioning of the market is called demographic segmentation.

Another reason for the value of demographic variables as a basis for market segmentation is the wealth of demographic data available from numerous sources, including the U.S. Census Bureau and various commercial and noncommercial entities such as Simmons Market Research and Donnelley Demographics. Demographic data are easily acquired and quite simple to use.

Age

Because consumer capabilities and wants change with age, age can be a significant segmentation tool for many firms. Crayola Company, which typically caters crayons toward four- to eight-year-old children, has recently discovered a significant potential market consisting of girls between the ages of eight and twelve.[3] The company introduced a line of six do-it-yourself boutique-style jewelry kits called *Jazzy Jewelry*. Crayola executives believed that this product line extension was needed because jewelry has become a booming field, with girls becoming sophisticated at a younger age. Kellogg is another company that targets children. Cereals such as Fruit Loops, Apple Jacks, Honey Smacks, Fruity Marshmallow Krispies, Coco Krispies, and Cinnamon Mini-Buns are targeted for children. However, the company also produces other cereals for adults, such as All-Bran, Special K, and Fiberwise.

Harley-Davidson also recognizes that age plays an important role in identifying its market. Harley's core customers (i.e., white males age thirty-five and older) continue to be the focus of the business, even as the company aggressively pursues "outreach" customers—those ages eighteen through thirty-four, women, African-Americans, and Hispanics. Today nationwide, 39 percent of motorcycle owners are fifty-one to sixty-nine years old, according to the Motorcycle Industry Council (MIC). Through the introduction of less-expensive bike models, the company has increased its market share with young audiences. Increasingly, accountants, physicians, and engineers are now entering the ranks of the Harley Owner Group (HOG) in larger numbers.[5]

Similarly, when General Nutrition Company discovered that 30 percent of U.S. consumers age thirty-five and over take vitamins regularly, it opened a chain of natural food and vitamin stores to capitalize on this market segment. Likewise, Coca-Cola in 2015 brought back its "Share a Coke"

The Magic of Hollywood

Walt Disney's *Frozen*, the computer-animated comedy/drama film, was released in November 2013. This musical fantasy became the highest-grossing animated film ever, not only in the United States, but also continued its wildly successful run in global markets. It has become the biggest animated picture ever, bringing Disney total earnings in excess of $1.3 billion.

Outside North America, *Frozen* became the highest-grossing animated Walt Disney film in more than forty-five foreign territories, including the Latin American region—particularly Mexico and Brazil, the United Kingdom, Ireland, Russia, Norway, Australia, China, and Japan, among others. In total earnings, the film's top market after North America was Japan. *Frozen* helped Japan's ailing film industry get back to levels it had not seen since the year 2010. *Frozen*, known in Japan as *Anna and the Snow Queen*, brought $247.6 million in total earnings. The biggest reason for this success was Disney's targeting of the film's storyline to its primary audience (i.e., thirteen- to seventeen-year-old girls). In Japan, this age group plays a vital role in shaping Japanese pop culture. *Frozen* had so many elements that appealed to these teenagers—a tale of a young girl with power and mystique, who finds her own sort of good in herself. Another reason contributing to the film's success in Japan was Disney's great care in choosing high-quality voice actors for the Japanese-dubbed version.

The revenue generated by this film came from both domestic and overseas box office sales, digital downloads, disks, television rights, and a sound track that generated more than 1 million album sales and 7 million Spotify streams. In addition, the film earned money from licensed *Frozen*-themed merchandise, and a DVD that became Amazon's best-selling children's film of all time. The film also received two Academy Awards, a BAFTA (British Academy Film Awards), and a Golden Globe. It prompted official YouTube video views in the hundreds of millions.[4]

Even though many U.S. goods and services have been successful overseas, Hollywood has been in the forefront of industries that has maintained a powerful lead over the worldwide market. Hollywood, nevertheless, has become more dependent on the foreign box office for its profitability on films. Check a site on such dependency by visiting http://www.businessinsider.com/over-seas-audiences-helping-us-box-office-2013-3. *Because of the high cost of movie production at home, as well as declining domestic movie-attendance figures, there is a call in Hollywood to "forget the Oscar," and focus instead on foreign viewers. It appears that this is where the potential for growth in revenues really exists, rather than in seeking honorary American awards. Do you agree? Why or why not?*

directed to teens and millennials, in which young consumers scoop up bottles of Coke in search of their own or a friend's name on the label. The marketing group used 250 most-popular first names among teens and millennials, as well as colloquial phrases placed on the cans, such as "Superstar" and "BFF."

In recent years, more and more companies have been targeting the baby boomers (born between the years 1946 and 1965). On January 1, 2011, the oldest baby boomers turned sixty-five. Every day, for the next twenty-four years, 10,000 more individuals will reach that threshold. In fact, according to the U.S. Census Bureau, their number will total 61.3 million by the year 2029, when all baby boomers will have reached or surpassed the age of sixty-five. This means that the elderly (age sixty-five and older) will make up about 20 percent of the U.S. population by that year, up from about 16 percent in 2016. Companies that offer financial services, leisure goods, pharmaceuticals, and preventative healthcare products and services are finding lucrative opportunities in the boomers segment.[6] The ad in Figure 2.2 informs consumers about VitaFusion, a vitamin formulated specifically for men, women, and boomers.

Family Lifecycle

Stages of the family lifecycle (a series of life phases that families traditionally go through starting with young single individuals and ending with sole surviving spouses) present another demographic segmentation variable. Each stage of the cycle brings changes that, in turn, affect the family's needs, resources, and expenditure patterns. Many hotel chains, such as Hilton, Hyatt, Marriott, and Westin, have had to rethink their pitch to customers based on this segmentation variable. Many two-career couples, with or without children, are unable to take long trips because of their jobs or their children's schooling. To capitalize on their needs, business hotels in downtown areas designed brief weekend escapes for families where Internet access, pay-per-view movies, fitness centers, and diverse dining options are available. These hotels have started offering discounted weekend rates and allow children to stay in their parents' room free of charge. Packages are supplemented with amenities and services including special children's menus, cribs, bed rails, video games, and even flame-proof bathrobes for kids.[7]

The singles market is another significant lifecycle segment. Defined as over twenty-five years of age and divorced, widowed, or never married, this group represents a major market for many products and services. Match.

Courtesy of Northwest Natural Products.

FIGURE 2.2

The catchphrase "just for me" reveals the specific nature of this new VitaFusion vitamin, with its reformulation designed to suit the needs of men, women, and boomers.

com, the largest video dating service, successfully tapped this market and built a multimillion-dollar business, with millions of members located all over the world. This segment is also of prime importance for such diverse products and services as fast foods, apartments and condominiums, entertainment, bars, and liquor.

Changes in the composition of families in the United States and the emergence of nontraditional families such as single-parent households have created new market segments. These segments have become an important targeting focus for support groups such as Parents Without Partners and childcare firms such as Kinder-Care Learning Centers.

A more complete discussion of the family lifecycle, as well as various age groupings that are meaningful to marketers, is presented in Chapter 11. The ad in Figure 2.3 illustrates how G + J offers magazines for women of all ages—teens, expectant and new moms, home enthusiasts, and household decision makers.

Gender

Gender is also used as a basis for segmentation for a variety of products and services ranging from cigarettes to cosmetics. For example, a number of cigarette companies target women through brands such as Virginia Slims. In the diet field, companies such as Weight Watchers' Healthy Choice, Stouffer's Lean Cuisine, and Kraft emerged with a broad line of low-calorie foods that to a large degree are targeted to women. Diet centers, such as Jenny Craig and NutriSystem, also benefit by appealing directly to women.[8] Cosmetic companies have also been in the forefront of gender-based segmentation, offering preparations specifically formulated for men and for women.

FIGURE 2.3

Because needs, resources, and consumption patterns change as people pass through successive stages of the family lifecycle, marketers can successfully use this concept to market products and services designed specifically for consumers at particular stages. In this ad, G + J offers a magazine for every stage of a woman's life.

Likewise, some pharmaceutical companies have found gender segmentation valuable in creating new market opportunities. A number of years ago, Pfizer Pharmaceuticals introduced Viagra to treat impotence, a sexual dysfunction that affects millions of men; and in 2015, Sprout Pharmaceuticals introduced Addyi, the first drug to boost women's sexual drive.

Race and Ethnicity

The sheer size and purchasing power of the growing base of Hispanic-American, African-American, and Asian-American minorities make these groups rich frontiers for U.S. marketers who use race and ethnicity to segment markets. Minorities tend to favor products and media vehicles that are geared toward them. Merely translating the English copy of an advertising campaign into another language or replacing the image of a white model with an ethnic stand-in has insufficient appeal.

Products and services targeted on ethnic bases range from clothing and cosmetics to foods. Urban Fashion store, Zumiez, and DrJays, for example, cater directly to African-Americans by carrying hip-hop themed merchandise. Today, most telephone companies, banks, and large retailers, as well as many government offices, cater to various ethnic groups by employing operators who speak the same languages as callers. Magazine and newspaper publishers cater directly to ethnic groups through publications that reflect their experience and speak to them in a relevant way. Cosmetic companies produce beauty aids and hair-care products that fit the skin tones and hair features of each market segment. Supermarket chains adjust the product mix that each of their stores carry, based on the ethnic makeup of the trading area in which the store operates.

Occupation

Education, occupation, and income tend to be closely related, so much so that they are frequently used together as a composite index of an individual's or household's social class. Despite the high correlation of these three, some companies segment their market based on occupation alone in the belief that it is a more important determinant of consumer behavior than income. Occupational breakdowns include a large number of categories, ranging from professional and technical workers to homemakers.

Pharmaceutical companies, for example, have traditionally been interested in targeting doctors. These companies strive to change physicians' behavior and often attempt to persuade them to prescribe their branded drugs over generics and other competitors' brands. To accomplish this objective, pharmaceutical companies employ a number of strategies that include retaining a doctor as a spokesperson, positioning friendly medical "thought-leaders" in the media, or organizing conferences and free events at posh resorts or expensive hotels in order to "educate" doctors about a particular disease and the company's latest drug to help manage or cure it.[9]

Geodemographic Segmentation

Blending geography and demographics has led to the formation of a new technique known as geodemographic segmentation.[10] This technique is designed to explain and predict behavior by using typologies; that is, by placing consumers into categories whose members are assumed to behave similarly. Geodemographic cluster systems sort U.S. neighborhoods on the basis of their income, educational attainment, occupation, homeownership rate, family type, age grouping, and other characteristics. These systems have proven successful in store-location analyses, directing advertising media buys, locating pockets of prospects for a product or service, and providing direct marketers with a highly effective tool for precision targeting.

The 1980s and early 1990s saw the proliferation of large, data-rich household databases developed by the direct-marketing industry. The U.S. census also provides data on census tracts or block groups. Research firms such as Nielsen, among others, blend the two to create a cluster system in which consumer categories could be assigned to small units of geography, such as zip code, ZIP + 4, or census tract and block group. The assumption is that "birds of a feather flock together." In other words, people who live within the same neighborhood tend to be much alike and buy the same types of products and services. Based on this assumption, a zip code can classify individuals according to their tastes. Exhibit 2.3 shows a map that uses geodemographics for segmentation purposes.

PRIZM

One of the earliest efforts in geodemographics is PRIZM (Potential Rating Index by ZIP Market), which originally was developed by Claritas, Inc., now Nielsen. This geodemographic taxonomy covers aspects of lifestyle segmentation of U.S. consumers, and provides rich consumer behavior information on shopping, financial and technology preferences, as well as media habits both on- and offline. For example, the present Nielsen "MyBestSegments" is based on the original lifestyle segmentation PRIZM, which classified U.S. households into one of sixty-six categories based on census data, supported with leading consumer surveys, and compiled household files, as well as other public and private sources of demographic and consumer information.

To help firms identify demographic trends in their field, and learn about their customers' spending patterns and their lifestyle behaviors, PRIZM offers four industry-specific household segmentation systems: PRIZM, which provides insight about consumers' behavior, their shopping patterns, and media ownership and use; PRIZM Premier, which is the latest evolution of the original PRIZM; P$YCLE, which focuses on consumers' financial and investment behavior, as well as their wealth; and ConneXions, focusing on households' likelihood of adopting and using technology.

PRIZM Premier operates on the principle that there is a universal tendency for people with similar cultural backgrounds, needs, and perspectives to gravitate toward one another. They usually congregate in neighborhoods offering affordable advantages and compatible lifestyles. For instance, the sixty-six market segments of PRIZM Premier include household types that are assigned colorful and distinctive labels, such as "Young Digerati," another called "Up-and-Comers," as well as "Country Comfort" and "Shotguns and Pickups." For example, zip codes classified as "Young Digerati" are the dual-income couples who live in chic condos in the most-fashionable urban areas, whereas "Up-and-Comers" are the recent college graduates hoping to jump-start their careers while still enjoying their free time.

These segments include not only basic demographics as age and household income, but also capture everything from where people buy their clothes to which magazines they read. Through this system, both marketers and consumers can learn just about everything they need to know about a city or a neighborhood. Home buyers, for example, can find helpful information ranging from house values to school ratings. Marketers, on the other hand, can construct a precise profile of consumers in a category. The category "Country Casuals," for instance, is characterized by consumers who prefer trucks, SUVs, and minivans to cars, and are active in home-based activities such as gardening, woodworking, and crafts. Members of the "Shotguns and Pickups" cluster, meanwhile, drive pickup trucks and often own hunting rifles. Nearly one-third of these individuals live in mobile homes.

To view any neighborhood's prime segments, "MyBestSegment" zip code lookup allows interested companies or individuals to view a specific locale's composition by simply entering the five-digit zip code to access the neighborhood's top five segments. The zip code lookup tool, as well as profiles for each of the sixty-six segments can found at https://segmentationsolutions.nielsen.com/mybestsegments/ and https://segmentationsolutions.nielsen.com/mybestsegments/Default.jsp?ID=30&pageName=Segment%2BDetails, respectively.[11]

Used with permission of Nielsen.

EXHIBIT 2.3

ZIP PRIZM Cluster Assignments—Louisville, KY.

Louisville, KY: S. Hancock St. & E Market St.
5 and 10 Mile Radii Showing Dominant PRIZM Cluster by ZIP Code

The PRIZM system assigns colorful labels to describe household types. "Up-and-Comers" are recent college graduates hoping to jumpstart their careers while still enjoying their free time.

A number of other companies in addition to Nielsen provide similar segmentation and targeting tools. Among them is Esri, which has two such systems: Tapestry and a geographic mapping service known as ArcGIS (geographic mapping system). The first system, Tapestry, was designed to help marketers understand a company's customers' lifestyle choices, what they buy, and how they spend their free time. It classifies U.S. residential neighborhoods into sixty-seven unique segments based on demographics and socioeconomic characteristics, and depicts U.S. neighborhoods in easy-to-visualize terms, such as Soccer Moms, Heartland Communities, Trend Setters, and High Rise Renters. An easy-to-use zip lookup tool is available at Esri's website (http://esri.com/data/tapestry/zip-lookup). Tapestry further categorizes the segments into LifeMode and Urbanization groups. Grouping the segments simplifies the differences by summarizing markets that share similar traits. For example, there are fourteen LifeMode groups, representing markets that share a common experience (such as born in the same generation or immigration from another country) or a significant demographic trait (such as affluence). Tapestry groups are also classified into six Urbanization summary groups, in which markets share similar locales (ranging from principle urban centers to rural areas).[12]

This system provides the tools for markets to identify best and worst geographic markets for their specific lines. Through this knowledge, a company can focus its marketing and promotional efforts to the most meaningful segments. Tapestry empowers its users to (1) access Tapestry web maps that provide hundreds of lifestyle measures down to the local neighborhood level, (2) add to these maps dynamic popup infographics, (3) attach Tapestry data to spreadsheets and enrich their customer data with lifestyle information, and (4) prepare presentation-ready, custom reports that include maps, charts, and graphics.

Esri's second system is known as ArcGIS. This system connects people with maps, data, and apps through GIS (short for "geographic information systems") software. Unlike Google Maps which aims its maps to consumers, GIS is a location platform that houses millions of maps available to any company that wants to overlay them with its own proprietary information. GIS is an essential tool for many firms, including municipal business, be it in planning, transportation, public safety, public works, or economic development. For example, customers of Esri include FEMA, U.S. Geological Survey, UPS, oil and gas firms, retailers, utilities, and environmental groups. Recently, Walgreens used Esri technology to choose locations for its new stores. Other effective uses of the system were realized for developers in identifying estate hot zones and viewing population growth trends in real time. Still other applications include managing and sharing data concerning natural resources and public utilities.[13]

Another tool in the segmentation and targeting arena is the PersonicX Lifestage household-level segmentation system, developed by Acxiom, the data analytics firm. This real-time, web-based tool gives marketers a picture of their customers to better understand who they are, where they are, what types of goods and services they use, their buying behavior, and their channel and media preferences. PersonicX, powered by Acxiom's InfoBase data, clusters U.S. households into one of seventy segments, within twenty-one lifestage groups based on specific consumer behavior and demographic characteristics. PersonicX Lifestage can be paired with industry-specific segments for better understanding and predicting behaviors within markets.[14]

EXAMPLES OF HOW ONE SYSTEM (PRIZM) HAS BEEN USED By matching up its PRIZM clusters with information from other databases, Nielsen can tell its clients where their customers reside. For example, for a dog food company, Nielsen was able to determine that dog ownership was highest among *Kids and Cul-de-Sacs* and *God's Country* clusters, and to show the client which zip codes, census tracts, or blocks in the entire nation were characterized by these lifestyles.

In addition to the clustering system, PRIZM also provides consumption indices for a variety of product categories. The higher an area's consumption index number, the greater is its market potential for a specific type of product. For example, PRIZM publishes a market potential index for luxury cars.[15] Compared to the national average (for which the index equals 100), different areas of the country are categorized into five classes according to their sales potential. Areas with *high* sales potential are those with an index of 201 or more. Areas with *above-average* potential have a minimum index of 169. Areas with an index of at least 103 are designated as offering *average* potential. Areas with an index of 94 or less are considered *below average* and those with an index of 45 or less are regarded as offering *poor* potential.

A broad range of companies use PRIZM. Some merge it with their own internal databases or research to understand their markets better. BMW of North America has used Nielsen's marketing data for the purposes of site locations, market analysis, and sales performance analysis of the dealerships in its retail network. Similarly, AOL utilized PRIZM demographic segmentation as a core baseline for analyzing broad-based audience behaviors. By segmenting the audience in this manner, AOL was able to identify which segments used newer emerging technologies with greater frequency. As a result, the company was able to apply the "emerging behaviors" as a filter to further identify its most valuable market segments.[16]

The number of companies keeping databases of individual consumers has exploded. Today, sophisticated computer programs used by marketers can combine information from several databases and put together a detailed picture of specific households or individuals. Similarly, supermarket checkout scanners enable many marketers to track the success of their products in the marketplace. Some experts believe that the future lies with technologies that count real people and actual purchases.[17]

CONSUMER BEHAVIOR IN PRACTICE

"Go On, Cut. You'll Be Brilliant"

Armstrong World Industries is a leader in the floor covering market and has successfully positioned its sheet-vinyl floor covering in the do-it-yourself (DIY) market. Originally, the company had observed that shoppers, after examining Armstrong's in-store displays, walked away without purchasing the product. Research revealed that although women generally drive the purchase decision in the DIY market, men are usually the ones left with the actual chore of installation. Armstrong also learned that fear of making the first cut is the major stumbling block against a purchase. Nearly 60 percent of the do-it-yourselfers cited fear of botching the job when they attempted to install the sheet-vinyl floor the first time.

A few years ago, Armstrong set out to combat this problem with a campaign that made a fail-safe promise to beginners: Make a mistake, and the company replaces the floor covering at no cost. Thus, the "Go on, cut. You'll be brilliant" campaign was born. Along with it, the company provided a *Trim and Fit* kit to help beginners do the job right the first time. The campaign was supplemented with point-of-purchase materials,

permanent and temporary displays, and a toll-free number to provide beginners with installation tips.

The campaign was overwhelmingly successful. The biggest barrier to the purchase of the product had been substantially removed. Beginners were assured that even if they were to make a mistake, they would not have to pay for it. There was simply nothing to lose, so why not go ahead and do it?

Armstrong achieved a strong position in the DIY market because the company understood and empathized with the segment it targeted and spoke the language its prospects understood.[18]

The do-it-yourself market has grown substantially in the United States during the past two decades. To what underlying causes do you attribute this growth? Visit the website of Armstrong World Industries, Inc. at www.armstrong.com. What tactics does this company use to attract do-it-yourselfers? Also visit www.doityourself.com. Determine what types of projects are most likely to be popular among do-it-yourselfers. In your opinion, do any specific demographic or lifestyle traits characterize do-it-yourselfers or differentiate them from those who prefer to purchase already-complete, ready-to-use items?

Psychographic Segmentation

Although age, family lifecycle, gender, occupation, and other demographic variables are usually helpful in developing segmentation strategies, they often fail to paint a precise picture of different market segments. For example, there is little correlation between demographics and such things as consumer desire to travel, propensity for moviegoing, preferences for music, enthusiasm for sports, choice of investment opportunities, and affinity for smoking and drinking. These tendencies can, however, be explained through psychographic segmentation, which is the partitioning of the market based on consumers' lifestyle and personality characteristics.[19]

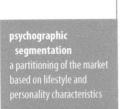

psychographic segmentation
a partitioning of the market based on lifestyle and personality characteristics

AIO inventories
questionnaires that reveal consumers' activities, interests, and opinions in order to create psychographic profiles

Psychographic profiles, descriptive sketches of individuals' lifestyles, are commonly obtained by having people respond to a battery of statements designed to reveal their Activities, Interests, and Opinions, hence the name AIO inventories. For example, an AIO inventory may include statements such as, "I'd rather spend a quiet evening at home than go out to a party" and "I'd feel lost if I were alone in a foreign country." Respondents indicate how strongly they agree or disagree with each statement, usually on a six-point scale. Responses are then cluster analyzed, and results are cross-tabulated with a particular purchasing behavior of interest to the researcher. For example, a psychographic study may correlate ownership of foreign automobiles or interest in certain magazines to specific personality traits.

Today, a number of companies are using a new technique in this field known as *attitudinal data framing*. For example, CUNA Mutual Group, a financial services firm, uses this technique by mining its computer database to search for the motivations that triggered the purchase of financial products made by the company's investors. In other words, the company attempts to discover how and why its customers arrived at their purchase decisions.[20]

Several years ago, Gaines, formerly a pet foods division of General Foods, conducted a psychographic study of dog owners to classify households according to how they felt about their pets and to tie these feelings to the type of food a household's pets were fed most often.[21] In this investigation, five psychographic types of dog owners were identified. *Functionalist* owners, who kept a dog as a means of self or property protection, accounted for approximately 40 percent of the dog owners. These individuals showed little attachment to their dogs. *Family Mutt* owners, whose dogs served as pets for their children, represented about 25 percent and showed just somewhat more interest in their dogs. *Baby Substitute* owners, for whom a dog took the place of a child or a spouse, accounted for about 10 percent.

They showed above-average attachment to their dog. *Nutritionalist* owners, such as breeders and consumers who were themselves diet conscious, accounted for about 13 percent and were very personally attached to their dogs. Finally, *Middle of the Road* owners, about 12 percent of dog owners, showed no distinctive characteristics.

Gaines found strong correlations between these psychographic categories and use of commercial dog food products. Members of the Baby Substitute and Nutritionalist categories bought the least amount of commercial dog food, whereas members of the Functionalist group bought the most. Because of their high degree of attachment to their dogs, Baby Substitutes and Nutritionalists were heavily involved in the choice of dog food, were least concerned about its cost, and displayed high interest in the quality and taste of the dog food. Gaines was able to introduce a line of premium priced and high-quality dog foods to suit the idiosyncrasies and preferences of the Baby Substitute and Nutritionalist segments.

One of the best-known and most widely used psychographic segmentation systems is VALS™, a service of Strategic Business Insights, formerly SRI Consulting Business Intelligence. The VALS™ program is based on the assumption that people buy products and services and seek experience that can fulfill their preferences and give shape, substance, and satisfaction to their lives.[22] The current VALS™ program devises a system for placing consumers into one of eight clusters based on primary motivation and resources/innovation. It is presented in detail in Chapter 7, which deals with personality, lifestyle, and self-concept.

Behavioral Segmentation

A final method used to segment the marketplace for products and services is behavioral segmentation. According to this method, buyers are divided into subgroups based on their attitude toward, usage of, commitment to, or reaction to a product. Identifying market segments based on actual product-related buyer behaviors, such as usage rate, benefits sought, brand and store loyalty, and marketing tactic sensitivity, is a suitable starting point for delineating market segments.

behavioral segmentation
a partitioning of the market based on attitudes toward or reaction to a product

Usage Rate

Usage rate refers to the frequency or quantity in which consumers buy or use a particular product or service. For many products and services, a mere 20 percent of users account for approximately 80 percent of total product or service sales. This phenomenon is so common that it has become known as the *80–20 principle.*

Every product or service category has its users and nonusers. For marketers, it is critical to identify those within the total marketplace who belong to each group. Verizon segments its service customers in order to pinpoint those who contribute most to the firm's profitability. By profiling heavy and light users, Verizon is able to focus primarily on the first group through various price promotions and special service deals. Similarly, airlines, car rental companies, and hotels attempt to lure frequent business travelers, who constitute the heavy users of their services, via upgrades, discounts, and frequent-flier programs.

To attract nonusers, firms often rely on sales promotion in various forms such as product samples, coupons, rebates, bonus-size packages, premiums, outright price reductions, and special offers made available via social media. For example, Wells Fargo Bank's rewards program gives its customers the choice of using their earned points to purchase merchandise, get gift cards, have cash added to their savings account, repay their Wells Fargo loans, or redeem for cash at an ATM.

Benefits Sought

Because different people seek different benefits from the same product or service, it is possible for marketers to use the benefits sought variable as a basis for segmenting the marketplace.[23]

Pharmaceutical companies often segment consumers on the basis of the benefits sought from medicine. Aspirin users take this medication to treat a wide range of ailments including headaches, muscular aches and pains, colds, flu, fevers, and heart conditions. Other persons whose digestive systems are sensitive to aspirin turn to Tylenol (which contains acetaminophen) in order to achieve pain relief without stomach irritation.

The success of online shopping versus shopping at traditional brick-and-mortar stores is largely based on the benefit of convenience to consumers. Toothpaste users seek to fight cavities, to whiten and brighten teeth, to freshen their breath, or even to prevent gum disease. Thus, the benefits that people seek when consuming a given product become the primary basis for segmenting the market.

Brand and Store Loyalty

Brand and store loyalty can also be means to segment the market. Brand loyalty is the tendency of some consumers to repeatedly select the same brand within a given product category. Store loyalty is a parallel tendency of some consumers to repeatedly patronize a particular retail establishment. To promote this tendency, many stores either offer preferred-customer cards or store credit cards to encourage customers to frequent the store. Brand loyalty may also lead to store loyalty, because consumers may prefer to patronize retail outlets that carry a particular brand of product. For example, consumers who like *Craftsman* tools can buy them at Sears or other hardware stores.

Consumers can be classified as loyal or nonloyal, and even among loyal customers, the degree of loyalty varies. Consumers who are brand or store loyal in one product or service category might not be in another category, and their usual loyalties may lessen when competitors offer attractive incentives and inducements to switch brands via sales promotion. For marketers, recognizing such variations is helpful in adopting strategies to enhance loyalty. For example, to build loyalty, marketers have initiated frequent-shopper programs that entice and reward customers with such attractions as tours, cruises, and lavish resorts vacations.[24] For example, in 2015, Starbucks initiated its "Starbucks for life" sweepstakes, which offered one free food or beverage item every day for thirty years if consumers participated in this competition and won.

Marketing Tactic Sensitivity

Just as some consumers are more or less loyal to particular product brands, others are more responsive to certain marketing tactics. Some consumers, for example, are very price conscious, whereas others react primarily to perceived product quality. Still others respond to clipped and viral coupons, customer service, salespersons, advertising appeals, or word of mouth from their peers and from social media.

Many major retailers, such as Sears, sponsor store brands (like Kenmore or Craftsman) that offer value comparable to manufacturers' brands but sell for less in order to attract price-sensitive customers. Marketers of many food, beverage, and personal products offer sales promotion inducements such as coupons, rebates, bonus-size containers, "price-off promotions," and similar methods to lure value-conscious shoppers. For example, Whole Foods built its reputation on carrying organic and fresh foods that many consumers today crave. Full-service department stores, such as Nordstrom and Macy's, employ salespersons on the selling floor who personally wait on customers. Such retailers also offer a wide spectrum of customer services such as personal shoppers, special orders, liberal exchange policies, delivery, free shipping, gift wrapping, and nicely decorated waiting areas in order to attract and keep those customers who are sensitive to in-store experiences.

Advertisers attempt to appeal to relevant buying motives in ads and commercials. Promoters of items such as baby products and life insurance, for example, frequently appeal to consumers' emotional buying motives through themes that emphasize the need to care for loved ones. Auto manufacturers such as Toyota and Honda target customers with appeals that express concern for the environment. Other car companies such as Mercedes-Benz, Jaguar, and Cadillac use status-related motives as the main focus for status seekers. Still others such as Volvo have employed feature-quality themes to appeal to drivers' safety concerns. Some automobile companies rely on imagery to emphasize exceptional style, along with interior and exterior elegance, such as the Mercedes-Benz automobile shown in Figure 2.4.

MARKET TARGETING

So far, we have focused on the market segmentation process. Once this first analytical stage is complete, a portrait of the marketplace emerges. Called a market profile, this portrait includes the number of segments that exist within the larger market and outlines the characteristics and motivations of people or organizations within it, as well as competitors' positions relative to the specific product of interest.

Once the firm has profiled its market-segment opportunities, marketing managers have to evaluate the various segments and decide how many and which ones to target. Because companies vary in their size, financial resources, technical know-how, and marketing capability, they seek the best possible match between their characteristics and the desires and preferences of particular market segments. Whereas some firms with vast production facilities and capital strength, such as auto companies, can pursue a number of market segments at the same time, others that lack financing or other resources prefer to focus on a single segment.

There are four basic types of market-targeting strategies: (1) the undifferentiated strategy, (2) the multisegment strategy, (3) the concentration strategy, and (4) the customization strategy.

Courtesy of Maserati

Undifferentiated Strategy

A firm following an **undifferentiated strategy** essentially views the market as a single large domain with no individual segments. An undifferentiated approach is a *postage stamp* strategy, meaning that the product is identical for everyone far and near. Companies that follow this strategy assume that individual consumers have similar needs that can be met with a single marketing mix. An undifferentiated approach is feasible in the case of homogeneous product commodities, such as sugar, salt, rice, wheat, corn, and some categories of farm produce. Argo cornstarch, for example, uses an undifferentiated strategy and directs its product to the total market.

As we saw earlier in this chapter, companies employ this strategy when the product is relatively new to the marketplace and competition is minimal. The Hershey Company's first chocolate bar or the pioneering companies that produced the original white facial and bathroom tissues are but some examples of firms that have employed undifferentiated targeting. Advantages of this strategy mainly relate to savings in production and marketing costs due to standardization. An undifferentiated approach often makes good economic sense. The combined impact of economies of scale and the

undifferentiated strategy
a view that the market is a single large domain and that one marketing mix suffices

benefits of workers' accumulated experience can produce significant reductions in unit costs.

In many instances, however, undifferentiated targeting emerges by default rather than by design. Companies continue to follow this strategy even after the market expands and competition intensifies. The result is often a stagnant and impotent product offering that commands little appeal. The firm then becomes vulnerable to competitive inroads and can easily lose its dominant market position. For example, Pepsi-Cola was able to capture a large market share from Coca-Cola when it offered different sizes of containers to the market in the late 1950s. Coca-Cola, realizing its failure to recognize the need for a multisegment strategy, followed Pepsi's lead and introduced different sizes and flavors. In so doing, Coca-Cola not only matched but surpassed Pepsi in introducing new flavors and sizes—a strategy that allowed Coca-Cola to regain its leadership position in the industry. The Coca-Cola ad in Figure 2.5 uses the brand's universal reputation to appeal to all types of soft drink consumers.

FIGURE 2.5

The Coca-Cola Company used an undifferentiated strategy when the product first appeared on the market. To some extent, the symbols employed in this current ad reiterate the original undifferentiated strategy.

ETHICAL DILEMMA

The Hoax of Organics

To many people today, the word "organic" conjures up notions of wholesomeness, healthiness, freshness, and a responsible consumer purchase pattern. The prevailing perspective has led organic food sales to more than triple over the past decade, and to increase by 11 percent in the year 2015 to reach $35.9 billion, according to the Organic Trade Association.[25]

Consumers who pay premium prices for organic foods do so because of their fear of pesticides. This concern is due in part to the fact that they lack understanding of the nuances of organic agriculture. The idea that organic farming does not use pesticides is a myth. Organic farmers use the so-called "natural" pesticides to achieve the same effect of their synthetic counterparts.[26] And just like conventional produce, organic produce shows pesticide residue in laboratory tests to be no safer than that used in traditional agriculture.

In a classic study, University of California–Berkley biochemist Bruce Ames and colleagues found that 99.99 percent of the pesticides in the American diet are chemicals that plants produce to defend themselves—not unlike the antibodies our biological systems produce in order to protect us from diseases.[27] Thus, consumers who buy organic foods to avoid pesticide exposure are focusing their attention on just 0.01 percent of the pesticides they consume. Furthermore, many consumers think that the USDA's National Organic Program (NOP) requires certified organic products to be free of ingredients from GMOs—organisms crafted with techniques from genetic engineering. This is also a false assumption—the USDA does not require organic products to be GMO-free.

Add to the situation the many cases of certification fraud, which has become prevalent in recent years. This is due to the fact that certification of organic farming is handled by third-party companies' certifiers who carry out the USDA organic rules on the agency's behalf. These certifiers charge the farmers a royalty fee ranging between 1.5 and 3 percent of the farm's receipts, in addition to $2,000 for inspecting. Presently, inspections from certifiers consist merely of an interview with the farmer and a glance at the copious paperwork documenting the farm's activities—mostly without actually performing laboratory sample testing of the farm's output. This is an honor-based system, where the actual inspection of samples is left to the discretion of the certifier. These conditions clearly leave the door wide open to many cases of fraud.[28]

In our contemporary society, unfortunately the image of "organic" is often connected to faddish words like "natural" and "healthier," as well as banners like "Values Matter"—rhetoric that creates a deceptively discordant image of people who purchase organics as those who care about their own or their children's health versus the thrifty masses who buy conventional food.

In our society today, pressure has been building to switch to an organic diet in order to remain healthy. More and more shoppers are opting for expensive organic foods—a movement that revolutionized the food retailing industry and created a lucrative opportunity for organic food companies. Check out an article covering this recent trend at http://fortune.com/2015/05/21/the-war-on-big-food/. How has growth of the organic trend affected major conventional packaged food companies? In addition, visit the website of Whole Foods at wholefoodsmarket.com and, in particular, view the section on "Values Matter." Do you think that Whole Foods upholds and sets the standards for food consumption in our society? Discuss and defend your position.

Multisegment Strategy

A multisegment strategy entails serving two or more segments and developing marketing mixes to suit the needs of each. For instance, each of General Motors' four core divisions—Chevrolet, Buick, Cadillac, and GMC—offers cars and trucks designed for and targeted specifically to a particular market segment. In this case, all marketing mix elements—including the product (e.g., fuel type, power, size), distribution, price, and promotion—are adjusted to match the characteristics of each targeted segment. Whereas the Chevrolet is designed to appeal to the budget-minded automobile buyer, GM's Cadillac line is targeted to upscale customers. Apple also employs a multisegment strategy for many of its new technologies such as iPhones and iPads. The company analyzes ownership and market potential for all its electronic products among adults and teens. The survey measures household penetration of these technologies among these two groups, and goes further to quantify the purchasing intentions of each.[29]

Firms that follow a multisegment strategy serve a number of different market segments and offer a diversified product line. Market risk is low, because sales decline or losses in some segments are usually cushioned by profits realized in others. However, although a multisegment strategy can generate high sales and reduce market risk, it is accompanied by significant increases in the cost of doing business. To meet the requirements of dissimilar market segments, products have to be modified, which results in higher research and development, engineering, and tooling costs. Smaller production runs of each separate model mean higher costs per unit of output. Administrative costs of managing a diversified line escalate, and promotional expenses incurred to reach diverse market segments mount up.

On the other hand, the unique product features designed specifically to appeal to the peculiarities of each market segment allow the firm to charge higher selling prices. For example, when Apple introduced the *i*Phone, the company decided to charge a premium price.[30] Similarly, Gilead Sciences Pharmaceutical Company charges a price of $100,000 for treatment with the firm's Harvoni hepatitis C medication.

Concentration Strategy

A concentration strategy focuses marketing effort on one segment of a larger market and develops products and marketing programs tailored specifically to the needs and preferences of that segment. For example, the

King Size Direct company, a leading online retailer of big and tall fashions for men, caters specifically to the larger male.[31] The company realizes that millions of men in the United States weigh significantly more than their ideal body weight, enough potential customers to warrant a concentration strategy. To reach them, the firm mails out millions of clothing catalogs each year and an online newsletter to its customers and others who visit the company's website. This newsletter addresses matters concerning King Size weight issues and other topics of interest to this group. Other firms that use a concentration strategy range from distinctive automakers like Ferrari to food companies like Gerber (baby foods).

Advantages of the concentration strategy are many. The firm can achieve a prominent position in the market due to its precise knowledge of the specific preferences of its target market segment. It can enjoy operating economies in design, manufacturing, distribution, advertising, and promotion due to its focused view of the market. Firms using the concentration strategy often build a reputation for leadership in their field by serving the very specific needs of their clients.

Against these advantages, the concentration strategy may prove to be risky. A decrease in the size of the selected market segment, a decline in the segment's purchasing power, a change in customers' tastes, or the entry of a strong rival can spell disaster for a firm that fails to diversify.

Customization Strategy

Many years ago, it was a normal practice for sellers to follow a customization strategy and individualize their goods to meet each customer's requirements. Tailors, shoemakers, clock makers, furniture artisans, and home builders, among others, customized their goods. However, as the marketplace grew in size and diversity, customization lessened, and products had to be produced in advance in anticipation of demand and stored until needed.

Customization, however, has not vanished. In small neighborhood stores, many proprietors know every customer by name and continue to offer personalized service. On a larger scale, some marketers—ranging from magazine publishers and greeting card companies all the way to sellers of personal computer systems—employ this strategy as a viable targeting option. For example, with the aid of computerized databases that contain geodemographic, lifestyle, and purchasing information about individual

customization strategy a personalized marketing effort to suit individual customer's needs

consumers, customized magazine issues now are published that contain ads matching specific subscriber profiles.[32]

The term mass customization has been coined to refer to efforts undertaken by manufacturers and marketers to combine the use of technology along with customer information to tailor products and services to the specific needs of each customer. Examples abound in the marketplace of companies that provide such customized products. In the watch industry, for example, companies such as Timissimo allows customers to create their own customized watches. Buyers can choose from an assortment of cases, dials, bands, and colors—with the option of having a specific design on the dial.

Similarly, mass customization has been accomplished in many industries through the use of 3D printing and other technologies that opened the door for many small companies to compete with the multinationals. Now, for example, laser scanners can create a 3D computer model of a customer's foot, providing the exact measurements for a shoemaker to work from. This opens the potential for these measurements to be taken anywhere in the world. Similarly, 3D technology is being used in the dental industry. Laser scanners can take dental impressions using a 3D computer tomography system, which subsequently produces the orthodontic device needed for straightening a specific adult's teeth. The process and materials used in manufacturing these devices are based on mass-manufacturing technologies, yet each patient's specifications are individually accommodated.[33] Other firms following a mass-customization strategy include Dell's "Build-to-order" computers and the tourism industry by offering package-holiday alternatives.

Mass customization, as a viable targeting strategy, is dependent on the likelihood that management can balance out the extra cost of giving each customer an individualized product or service against the profit potential that would be derived from increased sales and from willingness of customers to pay a premium for those customized products.

Personalization, a concept related to customization, has also been widely used as a targeting strategy. Personalizing standard items such as apparel, business supplies, calendars, baseball caps, mugs, pens, golf items, and greeting cards has become a major selling strategy. Today, even mobile phones—in addition to choice of case color and ringtones—offer interactive wallpaper and MP3 TruTones. In the United Kingdom and Asia, WeeMees, which are used as wallpaper and respond to the tendencies of the user, are becoming popular. By means of videographics array (VGA)

mass customization
a marketing effort that focuses on a single market segment

personalization
making a product personal to the consumer. This concept is related to customization

© Whitevector/Shutterstock.com

The dental industry combines use of technology with customer information to tailor products and services to each customer.

picture quality, phone users can change the screen background with ease. These services, among others, are available to be downloaded through most service providers.[34]

In the gift-giving industries, a number of large companies offer the services of personalization of products. One such company is the well-known Shutterfly that has been the forefront of personalizing an expensive array of products ranging from household items to photos and jewelry.

Personalization is also prevalent in the service industry. In fact, personalization has always characterized the marketing efforts of such service providers as physicians, lawyers, tax consultants, hairstylists, tattoo artists, wedding planners, and interior decorators. The cost and commitment of resources necessary to implement a personalization strategy far exceed those required for producing standardized products or rendering standardized services. However, the higher level of customer satisfaction that results when consumers acquire precisely what they had in mind empowers companies employing this strategy to charge higher selling prices.

Targeting Considerations

In selecting which market segment(s) to serve, a firm examines a number of criteria or features such as size, current sales potential, projected rate of sales growth, ease of reach, and expected profit margin. Not every segment presents a viable target market. Marketing managers evaluate each segment against a number of criteria to determine whether or not it should be pursued. According to Philip Kotler, these criteria include such factors as size, measurability, accessibility, and stability, among others.

Although some companies target the largest market segment or the segment with the greatest growth potential, the biggest or fastest-growing segment is not always the *right* segment for every firm. Small-size firms frequently lack the financial resources or competence to serve the largest market segments adequately. Often, the competition in the biggest and fastest-growing segments is too intense for smaller, weaker firms to break through and survive. Such firms may find it more advantageous to target a smaller segment and gain a large share, rather than target a huge segment and attract only a small share. In the ice cream industry, Ben & Jerry's was originally established as a small operation to produce ice cream for a select market segment within a field controlled by giants, such as Haagen-Das, Breyer's, and Baskin-Robbins—companies that serve the mass market. Ben & Jerry's was so successful in capturing a sizable market segment that it became attractive for acquisition by Breyer's.

POSITIONING

Once marketers have segmented the market and selected the target, their product or service offering needs to be properly positioned. Positioning strategy follows logically from targeting and has no significance apart from it. A product's *position* refers to the manner in which it is perceived by consumers, as compared to competitors' products and other products marketed by the same firm. This mental image that consumers hold of a particular product, service, brand, or store constitutes a significant factor in determining how it will fare in the marketplace. Ponder, for a moment, the images that are conjured up at the mention of brands such as Rolls-Royce and Kia, or stores such as Saks Fifth Avenue and Walmart.

The decisions of marketing managers about what products to offer, prices to charge, promotional activities to undertake, and distribution channels to employ all affect the positioning of a brand in the marketplace. Fortunately, to a large extent, marketers can influence the formation of desirable mental images by planning and implementing a suitable positioning strategy. This process requires careful consideration of all product features as well as determination of the ways in which product characteristics, distribution, price, and promotion differentiate the brand from its competition.

In an effort to create this differentiating image, marketing managers attempt to ascertain how consumers perceive competing brands in the marketplace. One useful technique often employed to accomplish this objective is known as perceptual mapping.[35] Perceptual maps are *n*-dimensional comparisons that allow researchers to construct visual profiles for a number of related brands. For example, in comparing a number of competing brands of pain relievers along the *two* dimensions of *effectiveness in alleviating pain* (the horizontal axis) and *gentleness to the stomach* (the vertical axis), respondents would be requested to evaluate each brand on each of the two dimensions. The means of all respondents' evaluations for each attribute of every brand being compared are then calculated and plotted on a cross-like coordinate axis. A two-dimensional perceptual map appears in Exhibit 2.4. As can be observed in this depiction, some pain relievers seem to have distinct images as indicated by the fact that they appear far apart from one another. Other pain relievers are perceived very similarly, as they appear to cluster together in a quadrant. The distance between any two brands in the map can be viewed as an operational measure of the disparity between their images.

perceptual map
n-dimensional depiction that provides a visual profile of a number of brands for comparison purposes

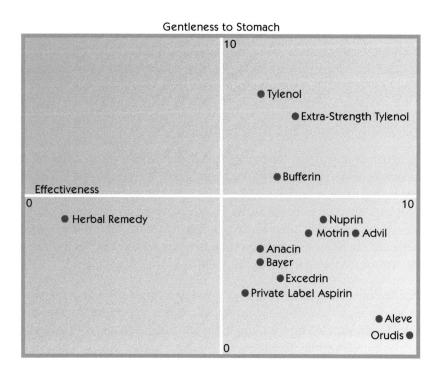

EXHIBIT 2.4

Images of Pain Relievers: A Two-Dimensional Perceptual Map

Product positioning, therefore, is a strategic effort aimed at creating and maintaining in consumers' minds an image that will both distinguish a product from competitive offerings and give it an advantage in selected target markets. However, because not all brand differences are meaningful to consumers, a company should select a differentiating feature that is worthy of being established as a basis for positioning. Any selected feature should satisfy one or more of the criteria for positioning, such as:

- *Desirability*, which implies a benefit highly valued by a large number of consumers
- *Uniqueness*, which denotes originality and exclusivity of the feature
- *Visibility*, which suggests a noticeable departure from features of competing brands
- *Affordability*, which suggests that the price is reasonable and fair

Examples abound in business literature of companies that were less successful in their positioning effort due to selecting marginal or irrelevant features. For example, when a Nexxus shampoo ad positioned the shampoo as capable of "bringing out the best in silver, gray, and white hair," few consumers were likely to admit that they were old and that their advanced age warranted using a shampoo specially formulated for the elderly. As a result, the expected sales did not materialize. Age denial worked as a deterrent to brand acceptance. Similarly, the American Association of Retired Persons (AARP) automatically mails to anyone who reaches fifty-five years of age invitations to join the association. Many of those are still active in the workforce; as such, they perceive retirement as a dormant, "not for me" lifestyle—a fact that causes most of these invitations to be ignored.

Irrelevant Attributes and Positioning

A number of researchers have suggested that it is possible to differentiate products by selecting attributes that *appear* to create a meaningful difference, when in fact, these features are irrelevant or not beneficial to consumers.[36] For example, many outdoor insect killers are differentiated on the basis of adding a pleasant scent to the spray, a characteristic that often reduces their effectiveness as bug killers. Similarly, mouthwashes are differentiated according to taste and color—features that have nothing to do with their potency.

It has been shown that these irrelevant features may work well in the short run. However, in the long run, competitors often recognize the vulnerability of irrelevant features leading to the introduction of new brands that grant consumers authentic benefits.

Repositioning

Sometimes marketers decide to alter the way a product or service is perceived by consumers. The need for such a change may come about in response to a dynamic marketing environment, such as intensified competition, changing consumer tastes or lifestyles, and/or technological advances. Repositioning entails modifying an existing brand, targeting it to a new market segment, emphasizing new product uses and benefits, or altering a brand's image. Modifications in a brand's design, formulation, benefits, or name are likely accompanied by adjustments in its promotion, distribution, and pricing strategies. For instance, a reformulated soft drink in which NutraSweet replaces sugar as an ingredient offers a new benefit—calorie control. Marketers of this beverage may redirect product advertising in order to target consumers who are weight conscious or must restrict their sugar intake. Advertising appeals would likely tout the benefits of the sugar-free product.

Examples of companies that have attempted to reposition their brands abound. For example, many high-tech businesses today have been repositioning themselves as e- and m-commerce operations.

Nokia has been able to reposition itself by changing its core products and by adopting new forms of technology as they became available. Progressive changes in the company's history from its origin as a paper mill in 1865 to a cable manufacturer for a telegraph and telephone business during World War II, to a television manufacturer in the 1980s, and finally to the world's leading maker of cellular phones are a testimony to the transforming power of a repositioning strategy.

Similarly, the history of Apple Computer attests to the role of repositioning in boosting the profitability of a corporation. In 1996, Apple experienced losses in both revenue and market share. It then purchased former-owner Steve Job's software company known as NeXT. In 1997, with late Steve Jobs as CEO, Apple began to restructure its product line using proprietary operating systems and focusing on creativity and style. The result was the emergence of one of the most profitable corporations in the world.

McDonald's presents still another case of how a repositioning strategy can enhance both a firm's competitive position and bottom line. In the early 2000s, McDonald's was under fire from anti-obesity and anti-junk-food critics—a movement that affected its profitability and led to the firm's first-ever losses in the year 2006. However, under the direction of CEO

repositioning
modifying a brand, redirecting it, or stressing different features to boost sales

John Skinner, the company began to change its culture and succeeded in repositioning itself as a food chain committed to offering healthy menu choices for both children and adults within a relaxing and pleasant dining atmosphere. This represented a move that restored profitability to McDonald's.[37]

It should be noted, however, that marketing communications play a key role in the process of repositioning, as this is the main ingredient where images and perceptions are formed in the consumer's mind.

Repositioning usually entails a considerable investment of time and expense on the part of the company, because changing consumer attitudes is a difficult and slow process. Detailed coverage of attitude change appears in Chapter 5.

The first two chapters of this text attempt to sensitize you to the dynamics of the marketplace. Awareness of the emerging trends in the domestic and global market, coupled with recognition of the diversity of consumers' needs and wants, will help you appreciate the complexity of factors that shape consumer behavior. More effort is thus needed to fathom the myriad personal and sociocultural factors that impact buying behavior. The remaining chapters of this book are devoted to exploring individual influences on consumer behavior such as perception, attitudes, and motivations as well as sociocultural influences such as reference groups, opinion leaders, and social class.

SUMMARY

This chapter addresses the topics of segmentation, targeting, and positioning. These are necessary and inseparable components of any marketing strategy. Segmentation entails dissecting the heterogeneous overall market for a product or service into a number of more homogeneous submarkets or niches. Targeting means reviewing and selecting one or more market segments to pursue. Positioning establishes an intended and differentiating image for a product or service.

A mass-marketing approach, in which a standardized product is marketed to the entire marketplace, sometimes makes good economic sense for homogeneous commodity products. In a mass-marketing approach, economies of scale and accumulated experience work together to lower unit costs. Mass-marketing approaches have largely been replaced by market segmentation, which divides a body of consumers into smaller groups with common demographic or lifestyle characteristics. Marketers target specific segments, offer differentiated products, and design programs specifically suited to the needs and preferences of each segment selected.

Segmentation of consumer markets can be accomplished by using a number of variables. Segmentation can be based on geographic, demographic, geo-demographic, psychographic, and behavioral variables. Marketers can opt for single-variable or multivariate segmentation.

A market profile or portrait of the segmented marketplace emerges. Based on this profile, marketers decide which submarket(s) they should pursue or target. Four basic targeting strategies are (1) undifferentiated strategy, (2) multisegment strategy, (3) concentration strategy, and (4) customization strategy. The attractiveness of various market segments is typically evaluated with regard to seven factors: (1) size, (2) potential, (3) measurability, (4) accessibility, (5) compatibility, (6) stability, and (7) defendability. When a company has decided on the segment(s) it elects to target, it develops a product mix and marketing mix appropriate for each segment.

Once marketers have segmented the market and selected their target market(s), their product or service offering(s) need to be properly positioned. Positioning strategy flows logically from the targeting strategy and has no significance apart from it. A product's position is the manner in which it is perceived by consumers in relation to competitors' products and other products marketed by the same firm. Because not all brand differences are meaningful to consumers, a company should select a differentiating feature that is worthy of being established as a basis for positioning. Any selected feature should satisfy one or more of the criteria for positioning that include (1) desirability, (2) uniqueness, (3) visibility, and (4) affordability.

Changes in the marketing environment sometimes cause marketers to reposition their products, changing the way a product or service is perceived by consumers by modifying an existing brand, targeting it to a new market segment, emphasizing new product uses and benefits, or altering a brand's image. Modifications in a brand's design, formulation, benefits, or name are likely accompanied by adjustments in its pricing, distribution, and promotion strategy.

CASE SYNOPSIS

A Starbucks Lifestyle Experience

Starbucks has grown from a single coffee shop in Seattle City in 1971 into a multibillion-dollar corporation today. This success was mainly due to the firm's clear understanding of the market segment it sought to pursue. The company was able to create a "lifestyle experience" that appealed to the business community and socialites alike. The coffeehouse was no longer viewed as just a place to get a cup of good coffee, but rather as a center for socializing and meeting friends. Starbucks implemented a number of successful strategies including those of selecting coffeehouse locations, establishing strategic partnerships with other firms, and following a tested formula for social behavior across the Web. The company's plans to expand internationally focus on China and the Asia-Pacific region due to their huge untapped potential, with expectations of opening 3,000 stores in China by 2019.

Notes

1 David W. Cravens, *Strategic Marketing*, 5th ed. (Chicago: lrwin, 1997), p. 133.
2 Thomas Moore, "Different Folks, Different Strokes," *Fortune* (September 16, 1985), pp. 65, 68.
3 Judith D. Schwartz, "Back to School with Binney & Smith's Crayola," *Brandweek* (September 13, 1993), pp. 26–28.
4 Maria Konnikova, "How Frozen Took Over the World," *The New Yorker* (June 25, 2014); Dorian Lynskey, "Frozen-mania: How Elsa, Anna, and Olaf

Conquered the World," *The Guardian* (May 14, 2014), www.theguardian.com/film/2014/may/13/frozen-mania-elsa-anna-olaf-disney-emo-princess-let-it-go; Alex Stedman, "'Frozen' Becomes the Highest-Grossing Animated Film Ever, *Variety* (March 30, 2014).

5   Joseph V. Tirella, "Is Harley Davidson Over the Hill?" *MSN Money* (March 30, 2009), articles.moneycentral.msn.com/ . . . /is-harley-davidson-over-the-hill.as . . . ; John D. Stoll, Kyle Peterson, and Nick Zieminski, "Legend Rolls on with Newer Looks to Lure Younger Riders—Focus Harley Davidson," *Chicago Tribune* (December 8, 2011), Business Section, p. 2.

6   D'Vera Cohn and Paul Taylor, "Baby Boomers Approach Age 65—Glumly," *Pew Research Center Publications* (December 20, 2010), http://pewresearch.org/pubs/1834/baby-boomers-old-age-downbeat-pessimism.

7   James S, Hirsch, "Vacationing Families Head Downtown to Welcoming Arms of Business Hotels," *Wall Street Journal (June* 13, 1994), p. BI.

8   Mollie Neal, "Weight Watchers' Winning Marketing Strategy," *Direct Marketing* (August 1993), pp. 24–26, 46.

9   Mary Ebeling, "Beyond Advertising: The Pharmaceutical Industry's Hidden Marketing Tactics," *PRWatch* (February 21, 2008), http://www.thwatch.org/node/7026.

10 Donald Cooke, "Understanding Geodemographics," *Business Geography* (January 1997), pp. 32–35.

11 Nielsen SOLUTIONS: Segmentation, http://www.nielsen.com/us/en/solutions/segmentation.html; https://segmentationsolutions.nielsen.com/mybestsegments/; https://segmentationsolutions.nielsen.com/mybestsegments/Default.jsp?ID=30&pageName=Segment%2BDetails; https://segmentationsolutions.nielsen.com/mybestsegments/Default.jsp?ID=20&pageName=ZIP%2BCode%2BLookup&menuOption=ziplookup; https://segmentationsolutions.nielsen.com/mybestsegments/Default.jsp?ID=51&&pageName=Frequently%2BAsked%2BQuestions&menuOption=learnmore; https://segmentationsolutions.nielsen.com/mybestsegments/Default.jsp?ID=51&&pageName=Frequently%2BAsked%2BQuestions&menuOption=learnmore

12 "Tapestry Segmentation: Get More Insights into America's Changing Population," http://www.esri.com/data/tapestry; "Esri Demographics: Tapestry Segmentation," http://doc.arcgis.com/en/esri-demographics/data/tapestry-segmentation.htm; "Esri Explore Your Neighborhood: ZIP Lookup," http://www.esri.com/data/tapestry/zip-lookup.

13 Miguel Helft, "The Godfather of Digital Cartography," *Forbes* (February 29, 2016), pp. 38–39; Heather Clancy, "This Software Entrepreneur Wants Executives to Think Like Cartographers," Fortune.com (November 21, 2014), http://fortune.com/2014/11/21/connected-jack-dangermond-esri/; "What Is GIS? The Power of Mapping," http://www.esri.com/what-is-gis.

14 "Consumer Audience Segmentation and Visualization-Personicx-Acxiom: Sifting and Analyzing Mountains of Consumer Data Is a Daunting Task for Any Enterprise. That's Why Acxiom Offers Personicx. It's Audience Definition Made Easy," http://www.acxiom.com/personicx/; "About Acxiom: The Acxiom Story," http://www.acxiom.com/about-acxiom/.

15 "Internet Solution Gives BMW Competitive Edge," "AOL: PRIZM NE Makes a Difference in Determining Online Behaviors," www.claritas.com/claritas/Default.jsp?ci=2&pn=cs_bmwusa.

16 "Claritas' Case Studies," www.Claritas.com/claritas/Default.jsp?ci=2&pn=cs.

17 "They Know Where You Live—and How You Buy," *BusinessWeek* (February 7, 1994), p. 89.

18 Edward DiMingo, "The Fine Art of Positioning," *Journal of Business Strategy* (March–April 1988), pp. 33–38.

19 Joanna L. Krotz, "Divide and Conquer Your Customers with Psychographics," *Marketing Intelligence* (March 2004), p. 1.

20 Ethan Boldt, "CUNA Mutual Group's Dave Griffith on Attitudinal Data Framing," *Target Marketing* (November 27, 2007), www.targetmarketing-mag.com/story/print.bsp?sid-71956&var=story.

21 Scott Ward, "General Foods: Opportunities in the Dog Food Market," *Harvard Business School Case 578162* (Cambridge, MA: Harvard Business School Publishing, 1978), pp. 1–37.

22 SRI Consulting Business Intelligence, "The VALS Types," 2003.

23 Russell Haley, "Benefit Segmentation: A Decision-Oriented Research Tool," *Marketing Management* 4, no. 1 (Summer 1995), pp. 59–63.

24 Shari Caudron, "Brand Loyalty: Can It Be Revived?" *Industry Week* (April 5, 1993), pp. 11–12, 14.

25 Beth Kowitt, "The War on Big Food," *Fortune* (May 1, 2015), pp. 61–70.

26 https://www.geneticliteracyproject.org/2015/01/04/scientist-mothers-view-organic-and-whole-foods-are-scam-of-the-decade/.

27 Henry I. Miller, "The Colossal Hoax of Organic Agriculture," *Forbes* (July 29, 2015), http://www.forbes.com/sites/henrymiller/2015/07/29/why-organic-agriculture-is-a-colossal-hoax/#2715e4857a0b2e49a07d38e4.

28 https://www.geneticliteracyproject.org/2015/07/22/fraud-or-drifts-usda-finds-43-percent-of-organic-foods-contain-prohibited-substances/.

29 "8th Annual Household and Teen CE Ownership Study," *Market Research.com*, www.marketresearch.com/product/display.asp?productid=1327723&xs=r.

30 Katie Hafner, "/Phone Owners Crying Foul over Price Cut," *New York Times* (December 7, 2007).

31 Vincent Alonzo, "The Bigger They Are . . . The Harder Some Marketers Try to Reach the Larger-Sized, Big-Spending Customers," *Incentive* (June 1995), pp. 57–60.

32 Stan Rapp and Tom Collins, *The Great Marketing Turnaround* (Upper Saddle River, NJ: Prentice Hall, 1990), pp. 97–98.

33 *Ibid.*

34 Harvey May and Greg Heam, "The Mobile Phone as Media," *International Journal of Cultural Studies* 8, no 2 (2005), pp. 195–211.

35 Jack Trout, Steve Rivkin, and Al Ries, *The New Positioning* (Boston, MA: McGraw-Hill, 1995).

36 Gregory S. Carpenter, Rashi Glazer, and Kent Nakamoto, "Meaningful Brands from Meaningless Differentiation: The Dependence on Irrelevant Attributes," *Journal of Marketing Research* (August 1994), pp. 339–350.

37 Lisa Magloff, "Examples of Transformational Change," 2011, smallbusiness.chron.com . . . business&technology.

PART 2

INDIVIDUAL INFLUENCES ON BEHAVIOR

© Charles Amundson/Shutterstock.com

CHAPTER 3
CONSUMER PERCEPTION

LEARNING OBJECTIVES

- To define and comprehend elements of the perception process.
- To explore components of the human sensory system.
- To gain insight into the process of perceptual selectivity.
- To recognize the impact of stimulus, individual, and situational variables on perception.
- To become familiar with the Gestalt view of perception.
- To understand the process of perceptual categorization and inference.
- To grasp the relationship between imagery and consumer perception.

KEY TERMS

perception	individual factors	proximity
exposure	chunk	context
attention	bottom-up processing	figure and ground
sensation	top-down processing	perceptual categorization
synesthesia	absolute (lower) threshold	surrogate indicators
perceptual overloading	terminal (upper) threshold	prototype matching
perceptual vigilance	differential threshold	perceptual inferences
selective exposure	or just noticeable	schema
selective attention	difference (JND)	script
perceptual defense	situational self-image	image
selective sensitization	situational variables	imagery
selective interpretation	Gestalt	brand equity
adaptation	closure	
stimulus factors	grouping	

One of the biggest issues companies have to face head-on is the quality of the image their products project to the public. Perhaps this concern is nowhere more evident than in the automobile industry, where image perception is the major factor determining what make of car consumers select.

To dispel the poor perception about quality of American automobiles compared with cars made overseas, U.S. automakers, starting in 2007, took serious steps toward adopting technologies and innovations whose objectives were to enhance the quality image of domestic vehicles. For example, in recent years, features such as automatic navigation and parking systems, lane-departure warning, collision avoiding mechanisms, side blind-zone alert, and hands-free communication systems (such as calling, radio tuning, climate control, and concierge) have become standard equipment in many recently produced car models. In the case of General Motors, for instance, autonomous driving has claimed a significant share of the more than $7 billion the company has spent annually on research and development over the past three years. GM aims to be the first automaker to bring vehicle-to-vehicle communication to market—that is, cars "talking" to one another in order to avoid collision—in its 2017 Cadillac CTS.

Today, Chrysler, General Motors, Ford, and Tesla have been working diligently to offer cars to match and beat the imports in this arena. In 2016, General Motors, Ford, and Tesla offered a number of outstanding vehicles that were rated among the top ten cars by Clean Fleet Report charts. However, it seems that with these high-quality vehicles, domestic automakers are still struggling to overcome what seems to be a national bias against American-made cars, resulting in many consumers shying away from buying domestic automobiles.

In order to dispel this unfavorable image, domestic auto companies have attempted to alter consumers' quality perception of domestic cars by emphasizing facts regarding the location where these cars are actually being built. Toyota, for instance, assembles its best-selling Camry in the United States, using parts that are 90 percent American made. Conversely, the Ford Fusion is built in Mexico, with 80 percent of its parts manufactured outside the United States. Furthermore, Buick's latest sport utility concept car, the Envision, is built completely in China. Automakers also stress the fact that several foreign cars, including Honda, Toyota, Subaru, Nissan, BMW, and Volkswagen, are actually built in the United States. Thus, the assumption that a foreign-made car is a better quality car is perhaps a widespread misnomer.[1]

As the debate concerning the quality of import versus domestic cars continues, do you agree with the assertion that quality perception is not a "generalized" concept, but rather depends on which specific brand or model is better suited to what an individual happens to be looking for in a car? Cite an example that supports your point of view. Learn more about ratings of car quality by visiting the J. D. Powers and Associates website at http://www.jdpower.com/autos/articles/2016 *and about hybrid and electric cars at* http://www.cleanfleetreport.com/. *In terms of the fore-mentioned automotive innovations, the issue becomes how well consumers will interface with and experience all this technology. Will it really help them, or will it become a secondary burden for people who just love to drive their cars? Explain.*

This chapter begins by examining the stages of the perception process—exposure, attention, sensation, and interpretation—as well as its subjective and selective nature. We also continue to address stimulus, individual, and situational influences on perception. After discussing the Gestalt view of perception, perceptual categorization, and perceptual inferences, the chapter covers the topic of brand imagery, brand equity, and risk perception.

WHAT IS PERCEPTION?

Perception is the process of selecting, organizing, and interpreting sensations into a meaningful whole. In the past, methods of studying stimuli and measuring responses to them were restricted to examining the five senses. Today, however, the view that perception uses merely sight, hearing, smell, taste, and touch to comprehend the environment is inadequate. Although the senses do play a major role in our comprehension of an event, our interpretation of a sensation may lead to a false perception. Perception is highly subjective and therefore easily distorted.

An individual's frame of reference affects the way he or she interprets sensations. For example, two friends may go to see the same movie but leave with different interpretations of the film. Their frames of reference, experience, and expectations are among the factors that influence their evaluations. Not only may different people perceive the same stimulus differently, but the same person may also perceive a given object or situation differently at various times or under different circumstances.

Consumer perceptions are vital to marketers and often underlie the success or failure of products in the marketplace. For example, a glance at the success story of the iPhone 6S is a case in point. Apple witnessed overwhelming success with the 6S model during the first weekend of its launch in September 2015. The iPhone 6S scored very high on the customer

perception
the process of selecting, organizing, and interpreting sensations into a meaningful whole

© baranq/Shutterstock.com

© goodluz/Shutterstock.com

In the year 2016, 207.2 million individuals in the United States owned a smartphone.

exposure
the act of deliberately or accidentally coming into contact with environmental stimuli

attention
the allocation of an individual's mental capacity to a stimulus or task

satisfaction front, with the majority of owners describing it as "simply the best phone ever." The phone also received rave reviews from Gadgets 360, as well as from various publications that praised its extraordinary high-tech features. This has been a familiar theme for Apple's iPhones since the induction of the original model back in November 2007, during which sales amounted to 1.4 million units in just the first ninety days.

Three concepts are intimately related to perception: exposure, attention, and sensation. Acquisition of sensory information is possible only when consumers attend to stimuli they are exposed to. For example, commercials that escape viewers' attention produce no sensation and, thus, have no effect on behavior.

EXPOSURE, ATTENTION, AND SENSATION

The process of perception begins with exposure to a stimulus. Exposure occurs when individuals come into contact with environmental stimuli either accidentally or through their own deliberate, goal-directed behavior. Not all stimuli to which we are exposed, however, get noticed.

Attention refers to the allocation of mental capacity to a stimulus or task.[2] After choosing whether or not to expose themselves to a message, consumers may momentarily pay attention to a specific aspect of the stimulus that is within their range of exposure. Attention can be planned, involuntary, or spontaneous. Planned attention is goal directed; individuals use their attention—such as watching a TV commercial or reading an ad in a magazine—to help them perform a specific activity such as shopping. When external stimuli force their way into our awareness, attention is involuntary. Imagine, for instance, that a fire alarm were to sound as you read this. Your automatic reaction would be immediate involuntary attention to the alarm. Spontaneous attention, on the other hand, may be exemplified by shoppers looking for birthday gifts. They do not concentrate too narrowly on any particular product class; thus they may remain open to other stimuli. A perfume bottle noticed by accident while shopping at a department store is an example of a product that receives spontaneous attention.

Sensation refers to the responses of our sensory receptors (eyes, ears, mouth, nose, touch) to environmental stimuli, and the transmission of this data to the brain via the nervous system. This process represents the acquisition of raw sensory information received through the sense organs—a preliminary step in the processing of information.

SENSORY SYSTEMS

Environmental stimuli or sensory inputs are received through our five senses. Visualize for a moment a young woman shopping in an open fruit market on a sunny summer day. She *sees* the splendid colors of the different varieties of fruit, *smells* the sweet aromas of mangoes and strawberries, *tastes* a sample of a ripe pineapple, *hears* the calls of vendors promoting

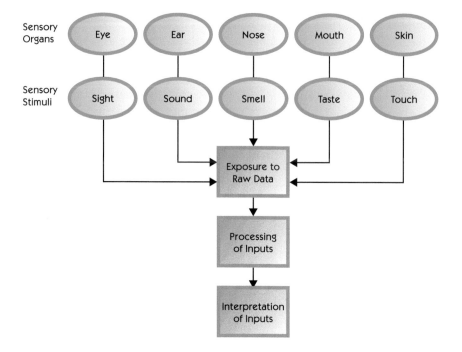

sensation
the responses of a person's sensory receptors to environmental stimuli and transmission of this data to the brain via the nervous system

EXHIBIT 3.1

An Overview of the Perceptual Process

CHAPTER 3 *Consumer Perception*

their fruits, and *feels* the weight and consistency of a melon as she examines it before purchase. The input picked up by her senses as she walks among the fruit stands is the raw data—ingredients in the initial step of information processing. Exhibit 3.1 depicts an overview of the perceptual process.

Just as the bright colors of the fresh fruits, their sweet scent, and their arrangement at the various stands aroused the shopper's desire to buy, so do the sensory qualities of nearly all products. These sensory qualities play an important role in enabling manufacturers to differentiate their products from those of competitors.

Vision

Researchers estimate that as much as 80 percent of what we receive from our environment is gained from vision. We tend to rely more on the other senses mostly when vision is unavailable (for example, in the dark).

The first impression that a product, ad, or store makes on us depends largely on its physical attractiveness; this fact explains why marketers rely heavily on visual appeals in product design, packaging, ad layout, and store decor.

Visual perception is a multidimensional phenomenon involving seeing a number of elements of the product, such as its color, size, shape, and movement. One of the most obvious visual qualities we experience in a product is its color. Not only does color help attract our attention, it also influences our emotions and affects our moods. An examination of the colors in a Crayola crayons box reveals that while the original crayons had only six colors (black, blue, brown, yellow, orange, and red), today Crayola offers 120 crayon colors, including such ones as purple heart, razzmatazz, tropical rain forest, and fuzzy wuzzy brown. These varied colors and names have been proliferating and are now appearing in all types of product categories, such as ice cream, juice drinks, and nail polish. Consider for a moment, how colors are also used in the decor of various commercial establishments. Nightclubs use red light to create an aura of arousal and romance. Hospitals use pale greens and blues to create a peaceful and relaxing environment. Mass-merchandisers use bright colors to attract shoppers' attention.

Sensory inputs are received through our five senses and play an important role in product differentiation.

Similarly, color expresses emotions. Red roses symbolize love and yellow ones represent friendship. In many cases, specific cultural values are associated with color. In the United States, white connotes happiness and purity, whereas black is linked with death and mourning. In some Asian countries, however, the opposite is true.

Research shows that package color is an important factor in grabbing consumer attention amid the clutter of competing products. For shoppers who are not loyal to a particular brand, a change in package color can win their attention and enhance their consideration of a brand.[3]

Creative use of color by manufacturers is important, particularly in the area of product design and packaging. Clothing and cosmetics exemplify product categories in which color plays a major role in determining consumers' acceptance or rejection.

Smell

Scents play an important role in our lives. Odors can stir emotions, elicit memories, produce hunger, induce relaxation, or even repel us. The smell of chocolate as we enter a confectionery or the scent of perfume as we pass through the cosmetics section of a department store entices many shoppers to stop and purchase. Humans, like all animals, quickly learn to assign values to different scents. They come to recognize that the unpleasant smell of spoiled food means harm, and thus the food should be avoided. On the other hand, they are attracted to the smell of a freshly baked cake due to the perceived promise of tasty ingredients such as butter, eggs, vanilla, and sugar.

The same effect of olfactory cues holds true in the case of human relationships. Both sexes are programmed to search for certain types of mates. One of the most primal determinants in this process is the sense of smell; that is, a desirable partner must smell right. Moreover, scientists have cited various cases of the invisible influence of scent in our daily lives. One of the best-known examples of this phenomenon is found in recent research regarding the effect of chemical communication via pheromones on human sexuality. Such influence has the ability of altering our hormone levels, accelerating our puberty, guiding our choice of mate, and even determining our sexual orientation.[4]

Responses to scents are culturally based. They result from prior associations between the scent and occasions or emotions that surrounded the presence of the scent. In the food category, for example, most people find the smell of fresh popcorn to be irresistible when they enter a movie theater. Garlic is viewed as delectable in Italy. Curry odors produce hunger sensations in India. Similarly, perfumes and colognes are capable of stirring up various feelings, emotions, or memories. The smell of someone's perfume or cologne, for example, is often a powerful enticement in a relationship—a theme that promoters of these products often utilize.

Realizing the positive effect of scent on consumption, some advertisers began using scented ads. In one type, a scented strip on the ad page releases a fragrance when the reader unfolds a crease (Figure 3.1). In another type, a scented spot produces a fragrance when the reader scratches it. Advertisers of a variety of products including perfumes, cosmetics, chocolates, and other foods and liquor have found that combining the scent with other elements of the printed ad tends to increase the effectiveness of their message.

Taste

Most scientists consider the sense of taste to be inseparable from the sense of smell. Receptors (taste buds) that reside on the tongue and palate combine with smell to produce familiar taste sensations such as saltiness, sweetness, bitterness, and sourness.

FIGURE 3.1

Ads for perfumes often contain a scent strip that allows consumers to sample the fragrance as an enticement to purchase the brand.

© Shutterstock.com

Taste has a significant effect on how foods and beverages fare in the marketplace—a fact that causes food and beverage processors to spare no cost or effort in ensuring that the taste of their products pleases consumer palates. Manufacturers of products ranging from cookies and snack foods to soft drinks, wines, and beers conduct taste tests either in an internal facility or through testing agencies such as Taste Test and St. Croix Sensory, Inc., which utilize professional sensory panelists who are trained to detect minute taste differences. Even schools such as Sensory Spectrum offer courses and seminars in taste perceptions.

An innovation in the sense of taste is the new electronic tongue, which was introduced a few years ago as a result of a joint Russian–Italian project. The electronic tongue, like its natural counterpart, can distinguish among a vast array of subtle flavors using a combination of the four elements of taste: sweet, sour, salty, and bitter. The electronic tongue is a silicon chip with small spherical beads a little wider in diameter than a hair. These beads act like test tubes, holding and analyzing liquid that is poured on them. The food and beverage industry uses the electronic tongue to monitor the flavors of existing products, and some have used the tongue to develop a digital library of tastes proven to be popular with consumers.

Acceptance of and preferences for new, unfamiliar taste sensations can be learned through familiarity. Many of us have developed an appreciation for foods that once were nontraditional to the American palate. Ethnic dishes, hot foods, and exotic spices are but a few examples of this phenomenon.

CONSUMER BEHAVIOR IN PRACTICE

No Plastic Surgeon Is Needed for This Nose

New electronic noses are now available. With these devices, researchers can perform a variety of functions that range from measuring and quantifying smell to designing a desirable aroma that can be added to a product. At General Motors, for example, researchers have used the electronic nose to pinpoint and simulate the *new car* smell that is so inviting to new car buyers. Similarly, Volkswagen engineers believe that they have isolated a *quality* smell that can be incorporated into new vehicles. Unilever uses the mechanical nose for sniffing people's armpits to design effective and pleasantly aromatic deodorant-antiperspirant products. Perfume makers use the new noses to defend their brands against counterfeit fragrances. Food and beverage producers find them valuable in choosing the perfect aroma to add to their products.

The new nose technology came about as a by-product of research on the stealth aircraft program conducted for the U.S. military. During that project, researchers were enamored of certain polymers, or chains of molecules, that had the characteristics of conducting electricity and producing definite reactions to smell. Even though polymers were never used in building stealth aircraft, the published research was enough to encourage scientists to use them in developing the electronic nose. At Warwick University in Britain, scientists used the technology to produce the first electronic nose prototype in the mid-1980s.

The principle on which these mechanical noses operate is the ability of polymers to absorb scent vapors and match them with models retained in computer programs. Thus, an electric nose can sniff a particular wine of a certain vintage, determine if it smells identical to another batch, and identify any existing differences.

Applications for this high-tech nose are virtually limitless. One application can be found in the food industry. The machine can verify or discredit superiority claims made by marketers on behalf of their products. For example, freshness claims for foods or beverages can now be verified. The U.S. Food and Drug Administration's fish inspectors currently utilize electronic sniffers to grade fish at dockside inspections. Using the new nose eliminates disagreements between fishers and inspectors regarding the grades assigned to commercial fish.[5]

Scent and taste are integral factors when marketing foods, beverages, cosmetics, and a host of other products. Visit Huber the Nose at www.thenose.ch. Enumerate some specific products in which scents play an important role. What other products might be created or improved by adding scents to them? Do scents of places (e.g., stores) or objects (e.g., new cars) influence your shopping and buying behavior? Why or why not?

Sound

Speech and music are two important weapons in the marketer's arsenal. Most marketing communications, including commercials, sales presentations, and stores' sound systems, employ speech or music. That is not to mention the extent of music as an industry in itself, with annual sales of music or music-related items amounting to hundreds of billions of dollars.

Making sense of speech is a cognitive process that involves our knowledge of meaning of words, how we string words together, our frame of reference, and the situation in which the speech is being presented. Music, on the other hand, has the ability to evoke feelings. In commercials, the choice of background music is a sensitive issue, because music can be used to set a desired mood, stir relevant emotions, or influence liking for the message. For example, research on the use of popular songs and song parodies in TV commercials for products including tennis shoes, soft drinks, and cookies revealed a positive effect of such music on consumers' recall of the ads.[6] Such recall is enhanced due to the emotional connections that many consumers have with a particular song or performer.[7] Likewise, advertisers have embarked on the music video approach popularized by MTV and VH1 and have used this format to build commercials and even entire campaigns.[8]

Research shows a positive correlation between music in retail settings and store sales. Morrison and colleagues conducted research on the effect of music (high or low volume) and aroma (vanilla scent present or absent) on young fashion shoppers in an authentic retail setting. Results showed that the volume of music and the presence of a vanilla scent both had a significant impact on shoppers' emotions and satisfaction levels. Additional analysis of the results revealed that the arousal generated by music and aroma resulted in heightened pleasure levels, that in turn positively influenced shoppers' behavior, including time and money spent, approach behavior, and overall satisfaction with the shopping experience.[9] In another study, research showed that in department stores where Top 40 music was played, shoppers over the age of twenty-five believed that they had spent more time at the site; where as in department stores that played easy-listening instrumental music, shoppers under the age of twenty-five felt that they had been in the store longer than they really were. These results confirm the notion that unfamiliar or less-preferred music tends to slow down perceived time for shoppers.[10] In still another investigation conducted in eating establishments, researchers found that restaurants in which slow-tempo music was played had longer waits for tables, as well as significantly higher bar tabs. Interestingly, although restaurant patrons did not eat more in the slow-music environment, they tended to consume more alcoholic beverages.[11]

Noise, on the other hand, is negatively correlated with retail sales. Levels of anxiety and stress increase with the amount of noise in the shopping environment. Thus, a noisy buying experience may adversely affect consumers' evaluations of stores and products.

Touch

Have you noticed how children show affection toward animals by touching and petting them or how mothers demonstrate love by caressing and hugging an infant? Touch, in this sense, communicates feelings.

Writers suggest there are two types of touch: active touch and passive touch.[12] In the first case, an individual touches to express a feeling or to initiate a reaction. In the second case, the receiver feels the experience of being touched, such as how we feel when we receive a massage.

Touch is a component in many consumer behavior situations. It is part of the exploratory nature of human beings. In shopping, people often squeeze a melon, feel the texture of a fabric, or run their fingers through a fur coat. Physical contact with products provides consumers with vital information that, in many cases, is a main ingredient in their choice among competing brands.

Some observers believe that one of the drawbacks of online shopping compared with traditional shopping is the fact that it neglects the importance of product exploration and active touching that many consumers feel is a necessary component in their shopping experience. Researchers have found that products with primarily material properties, such as clothing or carpeting, are more likely to be preferred in shopping environments that allow physical inspection and touching than products with geometric properties such as packaged goods for which marketing online or through direct mail would be appropriate strategies.[13]

Although the five human senses are presented here separately, in reality they are much more interrelated than we might suspect. Just as our sense of taste is highly dependent on the sense of smell, our human senses often work together in combination with one another. Many musicians and concert goers, for instance, report that they not only hear the music, they can actually *feel* it. For some people, the senses somehow fuse together and form a sort of sixth sense. This phenomenon is known as synesthesia. According to a recent report on CBS, some individuals report the ability to taste sounds or to *experience* colors.

synesthesia
the fusing together of the human senses

INPUT VARIATION AND ITS EFFECT ON SENSATION

Sensation depends on input variation. A more variable environment produces greater sensation than a constant environment, regardless of the strength of sensory input. Humans accommodate themselves to varying levels of environmental sensory input. When deprived of sensory stimulation for a time, we exhibit greater sensitivity to its return; hence the expression "It's so quiet, you can hear a pin drop." As sensory input decreases, our ability to detect change increases. We attain maximum sensitivity under conditions of minimal stimulation.

This fact has a number of important applications in marketing, particularly in the field of advertising. For example, consumers easily ignore ads when bombarded with a large daily dose of promotional messages. This tendency is a result of perceptual overloading, our inability to perceive all the stimuli that compete for our attention at any given moment. Humans also seem to have the ability to discard much of what they receive through their senses. This capability is referred to as perceptual vigilance. Perceptual vigilance has its roots in our tendency to be selective in what we perceive. Clearly, our senses are limited in their capacity to process all the stimuli in our surroundings. Hence, we attend to stimuli selectively.

perceptual overloading
the inability to perceive all the stimuli that compete for an individual's attention at a given moment

perceptual vigilance
an individual's ability to disregard much of the stimulation one receives through the senses

PERCEPTUAL SELECTIVITY

We are confronted daily with thousands of stimuli from our own environment. In the electronic media alone, we receive various types of online advertising including all sorts of banners, text messages, emails, in-game, and keyword ads on platforms such as Facebook and Twitter. We also are exposed to thousands of products in stores, ads in the media, as well as people, events, and situations. For example, retail stores such as Target carry 366,000 SKUs or product items, Walmart 200,000, and CVS 190,000. Because it is beyond a person's capability and interest to see everything there is to see, we screen out certain stimuli. This selectivity is of great concern to marketers, who attempt to communicate with their target audiences and surmount such blocking of information.

Selective Exposure and Attention

The selectivity process is like a series of filters or sieves that allows or disallows environmental stimuli to reach our consciousness. The first of these filters is called selective exposure. We exhibit selective exposure when we ignore media that address unimportant topics. Nobody pays attention to *every* ad, nor can anyone notice *all* the products in a supermarket.

selective exposure
a tendency of people to ignore media and ads that address topics that are unimportant to them

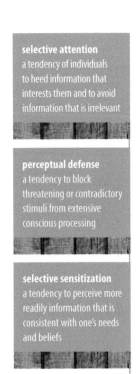

selective attention
a tendency of individuals to heed information that interests them and to avoid information that is irrelevant

perceptual defense
a tendency to block threatening or contradictory stimuli from extensive conscious processing

selective sensitization
a tendency to perceive more readily information that is consistent with one's needs and beliefs

selective interpretation
the act of combining relevant knowledge structures with expectations and intentions to derive meaning from a stimulus

Selective attention refers to our tendency to heed information that interests us; while at the same time we avoid information that is irrelevant, threatening, or contrary to our beliefs. Heavy smokers, for example, are unlikely to watch and attend to anti-smoking ad campaigns or read the affirmative disclosures (health warning labels) on cigarette packages. Exhibit 3.2 depicts the process of perceptual selectivity, indicating that perception occurs after environmental stimuli have been filtered through the processes of selective exposure and selective attention. Furthermore, the tendency of individuals to block threatening or contradictory stimuli from their conscious processing is known as perceptual defense. It serves as a defense mechanism to protect an individual's self-image and ego. We also more readily perceive information that is consistent with our own needs, beliefs, values, or attitudes. This tendency is known as selective sensitization. Sports fans, for example, are prone to keep up with their favorite teams and ignore others.

Selective Interpretation

Once an external stimulus attracts our attention, our perceptual system begins to consciously process it by means of selective interpretation. In interpreting a stimulus, we scan our memory for cues or relevant knowledge from prior learning and experience. We combine these cues with our expectations and intentions in order to interpret the stimulus and derive its meaning, which may or may not coincide with the intended meaning.

Marketers know that it is not what they say that matters, but rather what customers hear or want to hear that counts. A few years ago, G. Heileman Brewing Company, makers of Old Style Beer, ran a billboard ad in Chicago featuring infamous gangster Al Capone with the caption "Al persuaded all his friends to try Old Style." Although Heileman said the ad was one of a series designed to show how long Old Style had been available in Chicago, many viewers believed it perpetuated ethnic stereotypes. Heileman realized that viewer perceptions had distorted the intended meaning and promptly withdrew the ad in response to public outcry.[14] In another example, Nike a few years ago recalled 38,000 pairs of shoes bearing a logo that turned out to be inadvertently offensive to the Muslim community. The logo in question resembled the word *Allah*, which translates as "God" in Arabic. The notion that Nike would place the name of the deity on footwear was regarded by some to be a sacrilege. In response, Nike communicated sincere apologies for any unintentional offence. In addition to the recall, 30,000 pairs of shoes with the controversial logo were diverted from marketplaces such as Saudi Arabia, Kuwait, Indonesia, and Turkey to other markets.[15]

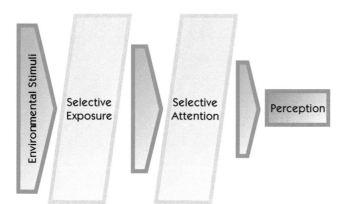

EXHIBIT 3.2

Perceptual Selectivity

Attention Stimulation

The phenomenon of perceptual selection poses a major challenge to marketers today. They must contend with the tech-savvy consumers of the day, such as users of smartphones, iPads, digital TVs, DVRs, and on-demand programming. This is particularly true today due to the availability of functions on these devices that allow users to delete, skip, clear, and cut promotional messages altogether when opening a site or viewing a program. Marketers must also deal with speed readers who seldom pay attention to print ads. In short, they must present messages to an audience that may not be interested in attending to them. On the other hand, many readers of special-interest publications read them cover-to-cover, ads and all, and even save them for future reference.

To combat selective exposure, marketers plan the placement of ads so that target consumers are most likely to be exposed to them. For example, some TV advertisers employ a tactic known as *roadblocking*. They arrange to air the same commercial on all networks at approximately the same time or during the same period, so that a person switching channels will still be exposed to the same commercial on whatever channel is being watched. To overcome selective attention, advertising appeals are designed to coincide with target consumers' lifestyles and needs. Another method is to address consumer fears or solve some problem, such as bad breath, hair loss, or dandruff. Choice of an appropriate medium is also important. Ads for expensive cooking utensils, fine wines, gourmet chocolates, and exotic desserts are more appropriate in *Bon Appetit* magazine than in *Business Week*. Because children influence the product choices their parents make, commercials for a kid's breakfast cereal are more effective during Saturday morning cartoons than on late-night talk shows.

Television advertisers employ a tactic known as *roadblocking*, so that a person switching channels will be exposed to the same commercial on whatever channel is being watched.

Adaptation Levels

Humans are able to adapt to a wide variety of physical, social, and psychological conditions and develop familiarity with stimuli, especially those they experience regularly, to the point where the presence of a stimulus fails to produce its characteristic sensation. While having lunch at the university cafeteria, you may be bombarded with sensory inputs such as noise generated by other students, background music, the smell of food, and the sight of people carrying trays. Yet you may still manage to read the assignment for an upcoming class without being bothered by the surrounding commotion.

adaptation
an indifference to a stimulus to which an individual has become overly accustomed

One method some TV commercials use to deviate from the audience's prior adaptation level is to create the impression of loudness by filtering out any noises that may drown out the ad's primary message. By removing low-frequency sounds that can mask higher frequencies, advertisers can ensure that sound in commercials is perceived at or near optimal levels. Departing from prior adaptation levels does not necessarily mean making clever, brilliantly executed presentations of stimuli. In some cases, monotonous or dull presentations can also be noticed, so long as they are different or unfamiliar.

STIMULUS AND INDIVIDUAL FACTORS OF PERCEPTION

As we discussed in the section on sensory systems, marketers attempt to design the physical attributes of products, brands, packages, ads, and stores to attract or direct consumer attention and entice prospects with merchandise offerings. The physical characteristics of objects are referred to as stimulus factors. They produce the physiological impulses that in turn produce a sensation. These factors (such as size, color, shape, taste, or smell) are the primary elements of the object that interact with our sensory systems to produce a sensation.

Just as the properties of one stimulus differ from those of other stimuli, human beings also differ from one another. Individual factors of perception are qualities of people that influence their interpretation of an impulse. Examples of individual factors include consumers' needs, interests, beliefs, goals, experiences, feelings, expectations, memories, personalities, self-perceptions, lifestyles, roles, risk tolerances, attention spans, and mental sets. Any of these may affect our perception of products, services, brands, stores, ads, or policies.

The needs of individuals influence their perception. Those who shop for food while hungry find everything appetizing. Consequently, they are prone to spend more on groceries. An individual's interests can determine whether or not he or she subscribes to specific magazines, watches particular TV programs, as well as how one uses his or her handheld electronic devices. A person's beliefs about various restaurants, prior experiences with them, and feelings toward them influence where he or she might take a friend for dinner. Our expectations about the future and tolerance for risk can influence our willingness to invest in the stock market or whether we are in the market for insurance. We tend to prefer products and brands that complement our personality, self-concept, and lifestyle. The type of car a person drives, for example, reflects his or her self-perception and communicates something about the person to others. The role we play at the moment also influences our perceptions. In the role of a busy student, we may eat fast-food lunches, but as a single parent, we may pack nutritious lunches for our school-age children.

Span of attention, another individual factor of perception, deals with limitations on a person's ability to process bits of information. Humans can attend to only a small number of items at any given time. This limit appears to range from five to seven chunks of information, where a chunk

stimulus factors
the physical characteristics of an object that produce physiological impulses in an individual

individual factors
the qualities of people that influence their interpretation of an impulse

chunk
an organized grouping of data inputs

is an organized grouping of data inputs. Social security numbers, for instance, are partitioned into three chunks—a three-digit number, two-digit number, and four-digit number. The length of time that stimuli can hold a consumer's attention also appears to be brief, often only a few seconds. Children, in particular, have very short attention spans.[16] Consequently, advertisers continuously provide appropriate cues in ads and commercials to recapture the audience's attention. For example, TV commercials for toys use special photographic angles, fast action, appealing colors, upbeat music, and other happy children to capture and hold kids' attention. Similarly, print ads for fast foods often depict mouth-watering close-up photos of a product to appeal to hungry consumers' taste buds.

An individual's mental set or perceptual style describes our tendency to process information and react in a certain manner under given circumstances. For example, an individual may be predisposed to consistently react positively to innovative ideas or to resist new ways of performing familiar tasks. People inclined to behave in particular ways often find it difficult to change.

Bottom-Up and Top-Down Processing

In the domain of research concerning how consumers process information to acquire meaning and form perceptions, a recent body of knowledge has emerged to explain two different pathways that sensory inputs can take before an individual formulates a perception. In the first pathway, which is known as bottom-up processing, features of the stimulus or stimulus factors of an object—such as its size, color, shape, taste, and smell—are the sensory inputs that become registered onto a sensory memory. These sensory inputs, in turn, get processed at a higher level of the brain. Finally, the view or a meaning of a stimulus becomes registered in our long-term memory. In this case, information processing has proceeded from the totality of the small parts (i.e., stimulus factors) to construct a view of the whole (i.e., the recognized pattern or perceptual image that has emerged). For example, consider the case of a consumer in a shopping mall who passes a pastry shop. She notices a delicious-looking chocolate cake, topped with frosting, fruit, and nuts, displayed in the window. Without hesitation, she enters the pastry shop and orders the cake. The stimulus factors of the object (i.e., the cake) in this case resulted in her positive perception and subsequent purchase action.

bottom-up processing
physical characteristics of the stimulus drive perception

In the second pathway, which is known as top-down processing, individual factors such as our needs, interests, goals, expectations, and experiences drive the extracted recognition pattern. Information processing, in this case, is based on our prior knowledge or schemata, which allows us to make inferences to perceive or see more than is contained in the stimulus itself. The resulting recognition, therefore, does not simply reflect a mere interpretation of a number of stimulus factors, but rather it represents a dynamic process of searching for the best meaning of the stimulus—given the individual characteristics and qualities of the perceiver. For instance, imagine a shopper who is looking to purchase a watch to replace her old one. In a jewelry store that carries watches, the shopper was shown two almost identical watches, indistinguishable in appearance and functions. The first is a Swiss watch, while the second is one made in China. After contemplating the alternatives for a moment, she chooses the Swiss-made watch—for which she pays a lofty price compared with the Chinese option. Her action can be explained by her preconceived beliefs regarding the high quality, precision, and dependability of Swiss-made watches compared with her lesser-quality perception of the Chinese import. Exhibit 3.3 depicts the two pathways of information processing known as bottom-up and top-down.

Although stimulus attributes and perceiver characteristics or conditions affect the way we perceive objects, the notion that perception can be explained solely in terms of stimulus and individual factors is debated, especially by Gestalt psychologists, whose views we discuss shortly.

top-down processing
individual experiences, goals, and expectations drive perception

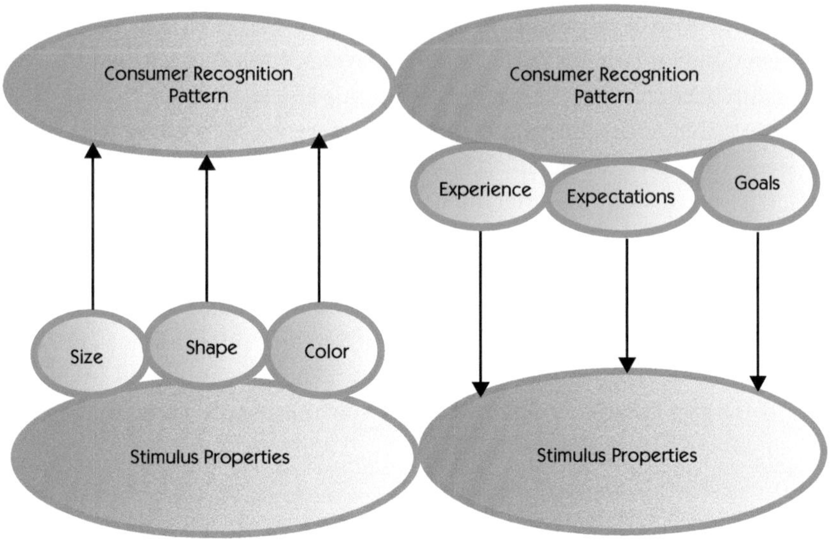

EXHIBIT 3.3

Bottom-Up and Top-Down Processing

Bottom-Up and Top-Down Processing

THRESHOLD LEVELS

Every human sensory process (sight, hearing, smell, taste, and touch) has an upper and lower limit of responsiveness. For example, humans cannot hear high-pitched whistles that dogs respond to easily. The study of the link between physical stimulation and resulting sensation is called *psychophysics*. It investigates the relationship between the psychological and the physical worlds.

There are three thresholds for each sense: an absolute threshold, a terminal threshold, and a differential threshold or just-noticeable difference (JND). The absolute threshold is the lowest level at which an individual can experience a sensation. It is the point below which the physical stimulus can no longer be detected. Absolute limits can theoretically be established for every type of sensation.

absolute (lower) threshold the lowest intensity level at which an individual can detect a stimulus

terminal (upper) threshold the point beyond which further increases in the intensity of a stimulus produce no greater sensation

differential threshold (JND) the smallest increment in the intensity of a stimulus that a person can detect

The terminal threshold is the point beyond which further increments in the intensity of a stimulus produce no greater sensation. Would adding a third scoop of raisins to Kellogg's Raisin Bran add to the taste? Would adding more perfume to a bottle of Hugo Boss aftershave improve its scent? Would mixing an added blend of coffee beans to Maxwell House Coffee improve the taste? Obviously, if such changes resulted in higher cost but had an undetected effect on quality or taste, they would be unwarranted.

The differential threshold or just-noticeable-difference (JND) is the smallest increment in the intensity of a stimulus that can be detected by an individual and still be perceived as an increase or decrease. In 1834 Ernst H. Weber, then a pioneer in the study of psychophysics, quantified the relationship between the intensity of a stimulus and the change in intensity that is required to produce a recognizable difference. According to Weber, the size of the least detectable change in the intensity of a stimulus, the JND, is a function of the initial intensity. For example, if the study lamp on your desk contains a 200-watt bulb, you are unlikely to notice an increase or decrease of a single watt in the intensity of light. However, if your room were illuminated by a single candle, you would immediately notice an additional candle's light. Similarly, a rebate of $200 for purchasing a $60,000 BMW would probably go unnoticed, but a $200 rebate offered by Sears toward the purchase of a $500 washing machine would immediately be detected by the marketplace.

What the JND Means to Marketers

A number of potential applications for the JND exist in marketing. These relate to pricing, product sizing, and packaging strategies. Whether marketers desire a change (such as altered package size, higher or lower price, or adjusted product quality) to be discernible by consumers or not, they need to estimate the JND.

Clothing retailers, for example, find that markdowns of less than 20 percent from the original price of a garment have little effect on enhancing sales. For consumers to believe they are getting a bargain, the markdown must be 20 percent or more. On the other hand, if the intention is to raise prices, marketers may want the effect to go undetected by the public. This is particularly true of manufacturers faced with rising costs of product ingredients. They debate whether to raise prices, with a possible negative effect on the company's competitive position, or alter ingredients (thereby reducing the quantity or quality of the product). In either case, the move is usually designed to be below the JND to produce the least disruptive effect on the company's competitive position.

ETHICAL DILEMMA

A Tarnished View of Gold

The adverse economic and political conditions that marred the first decade of the twenty-first century in the United States, including two wars, the housing meltdown, the subsequent financial crisis at home, a mounting national debt, recession, and falling value of the dollar, all took their tolls on consumer confidence, which plunged to historic lows. Consumers who lost a large portion of their investments during trying times rushed to protect whatever they had left of their nest egg.

For such persons, one attractive alternative to investing in the stock market was the opportunity to invest in gold. Gold, throughout history, has been perceived by people as a hedge or harbor against economic or political unrest, curren-

cy devaluation, inflation, and war. Bullish on gold, millions of Americans rushed to purchase the precious metal, armed with confidence in the soaring price of gold. For example, investors who purchased gold at $300 per ounce in the year 2002 increased the worth of their investment by a multiplier of 6 during the early 2010s. These consumers perceived gold to be a safe investment, capable of protecting them against inflation, as well as a tool to maintain or enhance the value of their investment portfolio.

Gold coins and bars, as well as gold accounts and certificates, were among the various ways consumers began to invest in gold. In their view, gold purchases provided safety under current volatile economic conditions and helped them diversify and protect their portfolios from fluctuations in value.

Overwhelming demand for gold by millions of speculators caused its price to skyrocket, reaching highs never before witnessed. For example, during August 2011, gold soared to a new record high of $1,908 per ounce at the London Gold Fixing.[17] Like most commodities, the price of gold is driven by supply and demand, as well as by speculation. Today, however, the price of gold has fallen to an average of $1,200 to $1,300 an ounce (as of this writing).

Under such unusual conditions of heightened demand for a commodity when consumers rush to buy as in the case of gold, billions of dollars exchange hands. Buyers can easily fall prey to unscrupulous vendors—particularly when many lack knowledge and expertise concerning their purchase. Scammers often overprice coins, lie about their bullion content, or attempt to pass off ordinary bullion coins as rare collectibles. Others may try to sell bullion pieces with the same design as coins from the U.S. Mint, but in different sizes—deceiving consumers into believing that the seller is affiliated with the federal government and is selling official U.S. Mint coins.

Unfortunate cases such as these prompted the FTC in 2011 to issue a Consumer Alert entitled "Investing in Bullion & Bullion Coins." This document covers such topics as tip-offs to rip-offs, hoping to arm consumers with sufficient knowledge to help them spot, stop, avoid, and report fraudulent and deceptive practices in the marketplace.

Just like any other commodity, the price of gold is driven by supply and demand. Hence, the price of gold will continue to soar to astronomic levels as long as investors, during these uncertain economic times, chase the bullion. Do you think that acquiring gold at these inflated prices represents a sound investment? Why or why not? Learn more about these issues by visiting www.consumer.ftc.gov/articles/0134-investing-gold. What precautions would you suggest that consumers should undertake in order to enhance their knowledge before making such a highly speculative investment decision?

Many companies use a strategy of downsizing (decreasing package size while maintaining the price) to combat rising costs. Philip Morris cut the weight of its Brim coffee from twelve to eleven and a half ounces but left the can size and price the same. Similarly, Kimberly-Clark cut the number of diapers in a package from eighty-eight to eighty. These moves in effect raised unit prices while not informing consumers that they were paying more.[18]

The same philosophy guides manufacturers and retailers who practice price lining, a strategy of offering a class of products for sale at only a few price levels. A women's clothing shop, for example, may carry three lines of comparable dresses at a low, medium, and high price. With this practice, marketers create the impression of distinct and noticeable differences between the lines by widening the price gap between them. In doing so, they ensure that consumers are unlikely to perceive the lines as similar, even if in reality they are very comparable.

Some JND tactics that involve making undetectable reductions in package contents have been questioned from an ethical perspective. M&Ms brand candy, on the other hand, occasionally sponsors sales promotions in which bonus-size packages boast of 10 percent more candy at the regular selling price, a difference that the firm expects consumers to notice.

SITUATIONAL INFLUENCES ON PERCEPTION

As consumers we are usually affected by the situation in which we buy and use products; that is, the factors above and beyond our own characteristics and those of a product or ad. We may feel exuberant or despondent, leisurely at ease or pressed for time.[19] We often tailor our purchases according to how we feel at any given time and the specific circumstances in which we find ourselves. Such behavior reflects our situational self-image, the physical and mental state we are experiencing at a specific moment in time.[20] For example, a person facing a frustrating situation may tend to smoke, drink, or overeat.

Situational variables are environmental circumstances that constitute the context within which purchases, product usage, and product-related communications occur. There are five classes of situational variables: (1) physical surroundings, (2) social surroundings, (3) task definition, (4) time, and (5) antecedent states. Like stimulus and individual factors, they influence the way we perceive an object or event as well as how we respond to it.

Physical Surroundings

Physical surroundings at any given site include its readily apparent properties, which act on our five senses. For example, Macy's department store in midtown New York, with its elegant fixtures and impressive displays, exemplifies a certain type of physical surrounding. Physical surroundings also include store location, parking facilities, and product assortment. Retailers orchestrate layout (the visible arrangement of merchandise and promotional materials), atmospherics (decor, sounds or music, lighting, aromas, temperature, humidity), customer services, and a variety of other factors including employees' dress, presentation, and demeanor to generate the desired perception of their stores. Clutter in the aisles, on-sale promotions, stock outs, and return policies, as well as some elements beyond a retailer's control such as the weather, can likewise influence shoppers' perceptions.

While this variable is obviously applicable to physical retail stores, similar principles apply to virtual stores visited by consumers who shop online. A

situational self-image
the physical and mental state a person is experiencing at a specific moment in time

situational variables
environmental circumstances that constitute the context within which transactions occur

creative and compelling website with a distinctive logo, digital photography, print collateral, rich interactive media presentation, music, and Flash as well as clever graphic design is necessary to create the desired positive effect in an online environment.

Social Surroundings

Social surroundings are a second set of situational factors. These include other persons present in the shopping environment, such as family members, store personnel and clientele, and the degree of crowding. For example, in a supermarket, parents are often pestered by their young children to buy junk food. Similarly, salespeople's characteristics and manners, as well as interpersonal interactions occurring in the vicinity, are all elements of the social surroundings.

Task Definition

Task definition, a third situational factor, reflects an individual's defined role in the shopping process. For example, one parent may assume the role of purchasing clothing for a family's young children. Task definition may also be the shopper's reason for engaging in a particular behavior. When invited to a dinner party, we may purchase a bottle of wine as a gift for the hosts that is markedly different from one intended for our own consumption. Marketers can build on the concept of task definition to enhance

Social surroundings may influence consumers buying.

© Monkey Business Images/Shutterstock.com

sales. Department stores, for example, encourage engaged couples to sign up for bridal registries. This service facilitates for a couple's friends and relatives the task of purchasing wedding gifts.

Time Perspective

Time perspective is a fourth situational factor. Time can be regarded absolutely or relatively. In absolute terms, time dimensions are, for example, hour of the day, day of the week, or season of the year. In relative terms, time can be regarded in relationship to some past or future event (such as time since or until meals or a paycheck). The appeal of many products rests on their ability to save time. Both the absolute and relative dimensions of time influence how consumers behave in the marketplace. For example, working consumers often shop evenings and weekends. People tend to spend more right after getting paid than later in the period between checks. Similarly, last-minute Christmas shoppers face a very different situation than individuals who complete their holiday shopping early.

Due to the immense growth in online buying, the element of shopping time has undergone drastic changes. Consumers can make purchase decisions more quickly, efficiently, and conveniently on the Web, where a great variety of products is available along with information about where to get the best deal. Moreover, there is no need for the shopper to go through the time-consuming efforts of traveling, dealing with salespeople, and waiting in line at checkout counters, as is the case in conventional retail stores.

Antecedent State

Antecedent state, a fifth situational factor, is the physical or psychological state of an individual immediately preceding his or her current state. Antecedent states are temporary. They can be classified as momentary conditions or momentary moods. Momentary conditions include such circumstances as having cash on hand or none at all. Momentary moods are states like being happy or sad, calm or angry, relaxed or excited. Momentary conditions and moods can influence whether or not consumers buy, what they buy, and how much they buy.

Situational factors, separately or in combination, can exert a direct impact on purchase choices. They can also combine with the characteristics of a product or a consumer to influence purchases. For example, an elated executive who has just been promoted may decide to buy her husband an expensive set of golf clubs rather than a simple shirt for their anniversary.

For marketers, knowing how a person feels and anticipating what is going on in the environment where a product is being purchased or consumed can help to better predict consumers' product and brand choices.

GESTALT PSYCHOLOGY

Gestalt psychologists suggest a different way of looking at perception. Unlike the traditional view, this perspective emphasizes perceiving cohesive wholes, recognizing meaningful patterns, and formulating total impressions rather than noting discrete elements of a stimulus.

Gestalt is a German word, roughly meaning *whole or total impression*. We do not notice or perceive solitary stimuli; rather, we perceive them as part of an overall pattern or Gestalt. In fact we strive to perceive cohesive wholes and meaningful patterns that are simple and complete rather than discrete components.[21]

To marketers, too, the total configuration of the marketing mix is more important than product design, price, distribution, or promotion considered separately. A brand, store, or company image is a total perception formed by processing information from many sources over time. Marketers also know that altering a seemingly minor element of a product, package, or ad sometimes alters its entire character. In a classic case that occurred in 1985, Coca-Cola attempted to change the formula of its flagship brand. In blind taste tests conducted on 190,000 consumers, subjects were asked their taste preferences for the traditional Coke formula, the new formula, and Pepsi. New formula Coke was found to be the consistent winner.[22] The public uproar that occurred when the traditional formula was withdrawn from the market forced the cola giant to bring back Coke Classic.

Consumers usually perceive environmental stimuli in a manner consistent with certain Gestalt principles—closure, grouping, proximity, context, and figure and ground. Let us see how these are relevant to marketing strategies and consumer perceptions.

Closure is our tendency to perceive a complete object even though some parts are missing. Upon experiencing an incomplete stimulus, we mentally bring it to completion. In so doing, our active involvement with this stimulus helps us remember it better. Closure, for example, explains the popularity of soap operas. Viewers become *hooked* on a show out of the need to complete the story line. Similarly, advertisers sometimes use incomplete illustrations, words, or jingles to attract attention and enhance recall.[23]

Several Gestalt principles relate to grouping. Grouping is the human tendency to perceive large data chunks rather than small units. We integrate bits of information into organized wholes, which enables us to evaluate brands over a variety of product attributes. When prospective students evaluate universities they might attend, their perceptions often involve grouping. The process of assessing these schools is often based largely on global evaluation and overall reputation rather than on specific characteristics of each school under consideration.

Proximity is a Gestalt principle that suggests an object may become associated with another because of spatial and temporal nearness to that item. Objects close together seem to belong together or appear related in some way. Nuts, when sold in supermarkets, could be displayed with snack foods or cake mixes and other baking-related items, in which case we mentally group them with these foods and perceive them as fattening. When they are shelved with health foods, however, we may perceive nuts to be nutritious items that are high in protein. Similarly, proximity relates to product-positioning strategy. Advertisers associate their brands with positive symbols, images, or situations during which the product is used. They also attempt to build associations between product purchase or use and some desirable outcome.

Likewise, the context or surroundings, circumstances, or setting in which stimuli occur affects the way we perceive them. For example, an article that appears in the *Wall Street Journal* would be perceived quite differently than the same story in a supermarket tabloid. The ruggedness of a four-wheel-drive vehicle may be expressed by picturing the vehicle against a mountainous terrain. Similarly, a hybrid, electric, or compact car is perceived as a desirable vehicle in an era of concern over pollutants in the air, fuel shortages, and rising gasoline prices.

Figure and ground suggests that objects or figures are perceived in relationship to their background or ground. Interaction between the object and its background is instrumental in creating a desired perception.[24] Gestalt psychologists note that in organizing stimuli into wholes, people tend to distinguish stimuli that are prominent (the figure that is generally in the foreground) from stimuli that are less prominent (those in the background). Both print ads and broadcast commercials, as well as websites,

grouping
the tendency to perceive data chunks rather than separate units

proximity
the tendency to assume relatedness due to spatial or temporal nearness

context
the setting in which a stimulus occurs affects how it is perceived

figure and ground
objects are perceived in relation to their background

are usually designed so that the figure dominates, while other elements recede into the background. If the figure is dominant, it is more likely that the eye will go directly to it, particularly if the background has a softer or fuzzier focus.

Up to this point we have discussed the physical and psychological processes that interact to produce a perception. Another area that merits exploration is broadly referred to as perceptual categorization—consumers' tendency to place products into logical categories or classes. In so doing, we simplify information processing and, consequently, the task of buying.

PERCEPTUAL CATEGORIZATION

We tend to group objects together and respond to their class membership rather than to their unique attributes. This enables us to process quickly and simply the large volume of stimuli to which we are exposed. For example, a customer notices an unfamiliar item in a supermarket. Based on cues from its whereabouts in the store and its package design, the consumer identifies the item as a pasta product. This process is called perceptual categorization. To categorize objects, we weigh cues from the stimulus item to possible matches in our long-term memory. We are likely to react to the item as we would to other elements within the same category. If we believe that pasta is a healthy and tasty alternative to high-fat meals, we may try the item; if we dislike spaghetti, we may avoid it.

perceptual categorization
the tendency to group
somewhat similar objects
together

Individuals formulate both generic product classes (detergents, snacks, cereals) and subgroups within broader categories (dishwashing detergents and laundry detergents). The more specific subgroups are often based on such factors as quality, durability, prestige, economy, and usage occasion. For example, consumers categorize both filet mignon and ground beef as food items. Filet mignon, however, is expensive and reserved for special occasions; hamburgers are ordinary-meal items. Marketers attempt to facilitate proper categorization of their products. For example, when Toyota introduced the Lexus and Nissan introduced the Infiniti, these two models were intended to be grouped with and compared to other expensive cars. To accomplish this objective, both companies produced a number of print ads and commercials that pictured the new models along with expensive, prestigious cars such as BMWs and Mercedes-Benzes in various settings. Similarly, when Honda introduced its hybrid Civic and Toyota its Prius, both were perceived as environmentally friendly vehicles.

As we saw in the previous chapter on segmentation, most marketers today do not try to make products all things to all people. Although it is essential that consumers recognize a brand as part of its appropriate product class, marketers do not want their brands to be perceived as duplicates of other brands. Rather, positioning strategies attempt to establish both correct brand categorization and brand uniqueness. For example, producers of analgesic products want consumers to classify their brands correctly as pain relievers, but not to think all pain medications are interchangeable.

Marketers attempt to understand how people make judgments about the properties they seek in products. They also try to provide clear, unambiguous cues that enable consumers to categorize products as intended. For example, the original Listerine's antiseptic color, medicinal taste, and tingling sensation suggest that the product kills germs. The swirl inside the top of a jar of peanut butter or tub of margarine suggests freshness. The sound of a new car door's slam suggests how well constructed it is.

Surrogate Indicators

Today, complexity among many consumer products, particularly high-tech items, has never been greater. Some of these products—Wi-Fi, HD, and 3D television; digital cameras; smartphones; and tablets—have tens or even hundreds of features or applications. Consumers, in many cases, struggle to appraise and evaluate the features of these devices and their uses. Keeping pace with such products' new attributes requires significant time and technical knowledge on the part of the consumer. However, since the majority of the consuming public often lacks both the technical expertise and the time required to understand, evaluate, and compare between these brands, consumers simplify their choice process by relying on substitute cues to categorize the brands or their features. For example, if a consumer is contemplating a purchase of a smartphone, the shopper may use cues such as price/brand as benchmarks to guide his or her choice. These cues—price and brand—are called surrogate indicators. We use surrogate indicators to place products into categories or discern uniqueness among brands within the same product class. For example, a recent study revealed that consumers rely on manufacturer reputation, the variety a brand offers, retailer reputation, and product warranty as useful surrogate indicators in selecting products. Other common surrogate indicators include brand name, price, and physical appearance.[25] Packaging and guarantee, when they serve as signals of product quality to consumers, are also surrogate indicators. Country of origin, in many cases, is also used by consumers as a substitute cue. Country of origin

surrogate indicators
the cues that consumers rely on to place products into categories

affects the perceived value of a product. A consumer's prior experience with a country's product, as well as his or her cognitions and feelings about that nation's image, has a major influence on that person's purchasing behavior. Just as Japanese autos, French perfumes, and Swiss watches are highly valued by many consumers, other countries' products, such as toys or seafood from China, may not fare so well.

As suggested by the adage "You get what you pay for," consumers often use price as a surrogate indicator. We tend to rely on price as an indicator of product quality when we face risky situations, when we lack confidence in our ability to assess quality directly, and when we suspect significant quality or price variations among brands. For different types of merchandise, we as consumers formulate notions of *expected price* that serve as reference points in judging the prices we encounter in the marketplace. Over time, these expected prices remain flexible. As selling prices rise and fall, we adjust our price expectations according to market realities and personal experiences.

Price, however, is not always the most important influence on our perception of quality. Other factors such as brand names, store images, prior brand experiences, and specific product-quality attributes can temper the impact of a price–quality relationship. Thus, our overall product perceptions blend information we derived from price, other external cues, and judgments of intrinsic product attributes.

Prototype Matching

A phenomenon closely related to perceptual categorization is known as prototype matching, our tendency to compare brands in a product category against the exemplar or ideal brand in that category. For example, various brands in the luggage category would likely be compared to a leading brand such as Samsonite. A given luggage piece, therefore, would be judged as acceptable or unacceptable according to how closely it matches the attributes of the category exemplar. Prototype matching explains the power of a brand leader to set the standards for the rest of the product category.[26]

PERCEPTUAL INFERENCE

Individuals form associations between stimuli. They develop beliefs about products, brands, stores, and companies based on previously acquired in-

Our overall product perceptions blend information from price, brand name, physical appearance, retailer reputation, and other judgments.

formation and their own experiences with the stimuli. Perceptual inferences are beliefs based on these forms of prior knowledge and experience that a person unconsciously or consciously comes to assign to products, brands, or stores.[27] For example, previous learning may cause consumers to associate high price with superior quality and, consequently, to anticipate a higher level of satisfaction when they select expensive brands and models.

perceptual inferences beliefs based on prior experience that a person assigns to products or stores

To prompt inferences concerning product quality, marketers may incorporate appropriate sensory cues into their product design. For example, Pine-Sol's strong antiseptic aroma implies that it disinfects as it cleans. Imperial Majesty perfume by Clive Christian of London comes in a Baccarat crystal bottle with an 18K gold-plated bottle collar adorned with diamonds, giving the perfume the prestige it deserves when it is sold at Nordstrom's for $869 an ounce.

There are three types of perceptual inferences. *Evaluation-based inferences* are judgments leading to a consistently positive or negative brand evaluation. Someone who has had a positive experience with a Magnavox TV may conclude that all Magnavox merchandise is good. This is called the *halo effect*. After a bad experience with the TV, the same person may conclude all Magnavox merchandise is inferior (a negative halo effect). Some inferences are *similarity based*. We may base our beliefs about a brand on its similarity to other products, simply by linking unfamiliar products to familiar ones. For example, a shopper may associate a new condiment packaged in a tall, slender bottle with ketchup. Still other inferences are *correlational*, based on drawing conclusions from the general to the specific. For example, a consumer may believe that the higher the dosage of pain reliever in a headache remedy, the more quickly the brand works. Thus, the brand containing the highest dose of medicine has to relieve pain the fastest.

Schema and Scripts

Consumers store in their memory categorized information about objects. As they gain shopping experience, they recall information in an orderly manner that permits them to buy more efficiently. A schema is an organizing framework, a set of expectations that provide a structure for understanding and interpreting new information. A major food processor spent heavily to develop a tastier ketchup with a process that preserved the tomato's aromatic qualities and natural flavor. Upon introduction in supermarkets, however, the ketchup flopped. Why? The new process had eliminated the overcooked, scorched flavor that seeps into ketchup made by conventional processing. Unfortunately, it was precisely this flavor that most consumers identify as the taste of genuine ketchup. The firm adjusted its equipment to overcook and successfully reintroduced an *improved* ketchup. The original ketchup simply didn't fit into consumers' schema of what *real* ketchup should taste like.

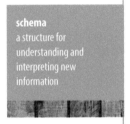

schema
a structure for understanding and interpreting new information

Consumers have general schemas and subschemas. An individual may, for example, have general schemas about automobile makes and subschemas about specific car features, such as four-wheel drive, convertible top, stick shift, and automatic transmission. Similarly, a person may have general schemas about retailers and subschemas about various types of stores, such as department stores, discount stores, supermarkets, and convenience stores.

script
the knowledge about procedures to follow in recurring situations

Scripts refer to our knowledge about the appropriate behaviors to perform in response to recurring events that we may encounter. For example, as we order a product online, return a purchased merchandise item to a store, or negotiate the purchase price of a new car, we act out a script, a behavior sequence appropriate for the situation. In buying a new automobile, for instance, we may (1) order the make, model, style, color, and various options; (2) agree on the delivery date; (3) negotiate a price; and (4) complete the details of a financing plan.

Scripts include our expectations about locations, situations, people, specific behaviors to perform, and outcomes of that behavior. They organize our knowledge about what to do in familiar situations and let us anticipate the outcome of our actions. Once activated, a script automatically guides most relevant behavior so that we don't have to make many deliberate, conscious decisions when faced with a similar situation. Scripts facilitate shopping. Rather than organizing information from scratch, we rely on experience to develop routines leading toward product purchase and use.

PERCEPTION AND IMAGES

Simply stated, image is a person's net impression of what a company, product, brand, or store is all about. Armani suits, for example, convey a different image from those purchased at Sears. Sources of images include sensory information from various sources such as advertising, personal experience, and symbols that people have come to recognize and respond to.

> **image**
> a person's view of what a company, product, brand, or store is

Martineau, based on the earlier work of Levy, characterized *image* as "the total set of attitudes, the halo of psychological meanings, the associations of feeling, the indelibly written aesthetic messages over and above bare physical qualities."[28] In other words, image invokes a functional and psychological portrait that a stimulus paints in consumers' minds.[29] It is the mental picture, personality, and feelings that an object conveys to consumers.

To attract customers, manufacturers and retailers must project an image that is acceptable to their target market. Consumers frequently form preferences for one brand or store over another because of its image. The way a brand or store is perceived and what it communicates about the consumer to others can be more important than how well a product works or how much a dealer charges. Thus, it is imperative that both manufacturers and retailers become cognizant of the many factors that contribute to brand and store images. The ad in Figure 3.2 depicts how Chanel uses an elegant image to promote its product line.

Image building presents a challenge for marketers because a mental image encompasses many facets, such as impressions of product attributes, types of people who use a brand, and situations surrounding brand use. Images can be built around notions of economy, safety, reliability, pleasure, status, distinctiveness, or other aspects of the product that may be of interest to the target market.

FIGURE 3.2

This photo from Chanel depicts the elegant styles the brand offers to affluent and fashion-conscious women.

A product's image can differ greatly from its physical attributes. For example, it is often the image we hold of food or beverage items that determines our preferences for them. Consumers frequently find it difficult to believe that brands in certain product categories are virtually identical. They come to insist on a particular brand largely due to image-building factors initiated by marketers such as branding, packaging, pricing, and promotion rather than due to physical product differences. The significance of brand image quickly becomes apparent in the case of a blind wine taste test performed at a winery in California. In that test, researchers gave respondents unidentified samples of red wines such as Merlot and Cabernet Sauvignon. Some of the samples were exclusive French brands; others were expensive competing California brands, as well as wines from Charles Shaw's own winery. To everyone's surprise, the inexpensive $2.49 bottle of Charles Shaw's wine was rated as high as or even higher than equivalent competing wines for which consumers pay significantly higher prices. The point is that both the famous labels and higher prices elevated consumers' perception of the taste and quality of the designer-brand wines.[30]

Like products and brands, stores also have images. Establishments such as Bloomingdale's, Saks Fifth Avenue, Nieman Marcus, and Crate and Barrel project very different images than Target, Kmart, Walmart, and Ross. In selecting stores, consumers look for those that match their self-concept. Some stores intimidate a shopper, whereas others are comfortable to patronize. For some consumers, the same store is regarded as an acceptable source for some types of merchandise but not for others. A shopper may perceive Sears to be a good place to buy appliances and housewares, but not clothing. However, as part of its strategy to overcome this less-than-glamorous perception of its fashions, Sears recently acquired Lands' End and started offering that line of clothing in its stores.

Because stores cannot be all things to all people, retailers attempt to create images congruent with the self-image held by the market segment they target. Store images are shaped by retailers' merchandise assortment, level of customer services, pricing policies, promotional activities, reputation for integrity, degree of community involvement, and atmospherics. Atmospherics entail all the various physical elements in a store's design, both inside and out, that appeal to customers' emotions and stimulate buying. Interior atmospheric elements include sensory factors such as layout (arrangement of departments, width of aisles, grouping of products, location of checkout areas), store fixtures, merchandise displays, wall and floor coverings, lighting, colors, sounds, scent, neatness, degree of crowding, personnel, and clientele. Exterior atmospheric elements include location, appearance of the storefront, display windows, entrances, and degree of traffic congestion.[31]

Interestingly, consumers formulate images of stores regardless of whether retailers deliberately attempt to convey a specific image.[32] Although brand name appeared to be the most important cue when consumers formed impressions about a store's merit, the number of salespersons per department seemed to most strongly influence customer images concerning its quality.

Imagery and Promotion

Imagery is a process by which we visualize sensory information in our working memory. Working memory refers to our ability to hold and manipulate information in the mind over short periods of time. For example, when we give directions to an out-of-town friend, we use mental imagery to picture the roads, exits, traffic lights, and stop signs to verbally express our memory of the route. Imagery is helpful to consumers in at least two ways. It helps them to recall and express information they have stored in their memory. It also facilitates consumers' comprehension when products or situations are presented in a pictorial or graphic form.

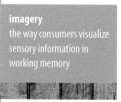

imagery
the way consumers visualize sensory information in working memory

Imagery is therefore important as a perceptual tool in promotion. In advertising, for example, imagery is created largely through illustrations. Pictures may be used to demonstrate how a product is used. Research shows that dually coded pictures (pictures that show the brand name along with the product) increase recall of the brand name.[33] This enhanced recall is thought to be the result of our seeing the information in two different forms—verbal and pictorial.

Together with the other ingredients of the marketing mix, promotion—and advertising in particular—plays an important role in establishing and enhancing favorable corporate, brand, and store images.[34] Because of advertising's ability to generate images, it has sometimes been referred to as the business of *image management*—creating and maintaining images and meanings in a consumer's mind.[35]

Image Change

The public's positive image of a firm is vital for its continued success. Images can range from clear to vague, from strongly positive to neutral or even negative. A favorable image virtually ensures continued attractiveness of the firm and becomes a valuable asset that is cherished and protected. A negative image, on the other hand, can seriously impair a firm's ability to do business and could even threaten its survival. As a result, image protection and restoration strategies may take the form of aggressive, reactive, or defensive moves.[36]

Management may take a firm's positive image for granted until something unfortunate occurs and executives are faced with a negative image to rectify. Because attitudes are slow to change, image correction is a time-consuming process. Examples abound in corporate history of companies that were faced with the challenge of changing negative images. Some of the most infamous incidents in recent times include Target's massive customer data security breach, Volkswagen's diesel emission scandal where the company intentionally masked true emission levels of diesel-powered cars, Johnson & Johnson Baby Powder containing talc for feminine hygiene that contributed to ovarian cancer in women, Takata's controversy over defective and potentially lethal airbags that inconvenienced millions of American car owners, Toyota's cover-up of vehicles' severe safety problem with unintended acceleration, and General Motor's faulty ignition switches.

GLOBAL OPPORTUNITY

What Do James Dean, Cowboys, and Latin Americans Have in Common?

Levi Strauss Company markets products in seventy countries around the world. The company owns and operates plants in twenty-five countries and has licensees, distributors, and joint ventures in many others. One of the pressing decisions the company faces in creating a uniform image throughout the world is whether to apply a worldwide strategy to all advertising or settle on localized campaigns for each country in which Levi's products are sold. By allowing the localization of Levi's advertising, the company fears that it may appear as separate and distinct firms in different nations. The fact that local advertising agencies in some countries are quite sophisticated whereas ad agencies in other nations lack expertise in creating and casting commercials would nurture such an impression. On the other hand, a uniform worldwide advertising strategy would tend to ignore differences that characterize consumers in various countries.

In determining which strategy is best, the company reviewed its current ads in various countries. For example, in European television, Levi's commercials project a super-sexy appeal. In the minds of at least some company executives, this is an objectionable personality for the brand. In Latin America, where Levi's ads addressed a family-oriented market, the advertising message was found to be substandard. In the United Kingdom, ads emphasized Levi's as an American brand starring a cowboy in a Wild West fantasy setting. In Japan, to overcome competition from other jean brands, Levi's positioned itself as legendary American jeans with commercials bearing the theme "Heroes Wear Levi's." Japanese Levi commercials featured clips of cult figures such as James Dean. In Brazil, where consumers are more strongly influenced by European fashion trends than by American trends, the French-filmed commercials featured cool young Parisians amidst a wild traffic scene. In Australia, creating brand awareness was the focus of Levi's advertising campaign. Commercials emphasized the brand name and Levi's quality image.

It appeared that while the advantages of employing a uniform advertising strategy in all markets were clear, the disadvantages are just as real. The unique needs of each market could not be met with a single worldwide advertising strategy. Moreover, implementation of a centralized advertising strategy would require an organizational structure that is considerably different from Levi's present one. Finally, local advertising agencies in different parts of the world often resist outside suggestions to change the way they conduct their business.[37]

Levi Strauss is a name known worldwide. The company's garments and jeans are popular in almost every country in the world. Learn about factors affecting standardization or adaptation of Levi's strategy and tactics in foreign countries by visiting the website http://www.academia.edu/386966/Levi_Strauss_And_International_Marketing_Investigation. *In your view, should Levi use an adaptation strategy to market its products in selected foreign countries based on the social, cultural, economic, competitive, and technological factors of the chosen nation? Why or why not?*

Brand Equity

The most successful brands within their product category develop brand equity. Brand equity is the added value a brand brings to a product beyond the item's functional value. For example, when brands like Nike or Reebok add value to athletic shoes and exercise gear, these brands are said to possess brand equity. Companies develop equity for their brands by consistently delivering high quality, building strong associations between a brand and a set of benefits (such as Sony's association with innovation and high quality), and developing a consistent image through sponsorship of humanitarian and environmental causes, the use of logos, trademarks, trade characters, or spokespeople.[38]

Brand equity increases profits and market share. It also enhances both customer and distributor loyalty to a brand. When firms apply brands with strong equity to new products or new lines of products, consumers are more apt to try them. Firms with brand equity may also allow other companies to license their brand for use on noncompeting products (such as Harley-Davidson sunglasses and beach towels).

RISK PERCEPTION

Perception of risk is a fact of life. Any task we undertake in performing our day-to-day activities involves some sort of risk or uncertainty. Whether you are driving your car, purchasing stocks through a broker, or online buying a product, you are taking a certain degree of risk.

Risk perception is a subjective judgment that we make about the characteristics and severity of uncertainties we face. Individuals confronted with the same decision perceive different degrees of ensuing loss or harm. Variations in the perception of risk are due to a number of individual factors that include a person's prior knowledge and experience, one's emotional state, his or her choice of exposure to the source of risk, degree of expected loss, whether or not the risk is within one's control, the level of uncertainty associated with the outcome, and the risk/benefit ratio of the consequences of an action. For example, a high sensation-seeking individual (i.e., one who craves challenges and thrills), such as a skydiver or mountain climber, perceives the risk of these activities differently than an acrophobic person.

Perception of risk is inseparable from any investigation of consumer behavior. Consumers incur various degrees and varieties of risk in the execution of every marketplace transaction. There are generally five types of risk that consumers experience. The first of these is *functional risk,* that is, whether or not the purchased product or service will perform as expected. A second type of risk is *financial risk,* that is, whether the product or service is worth the investment required. A third type is *physical risk,* which questions the danger the product or service poses to the individual or the environment. The fourth type of risk is *social risk,* which seeks to ascertain how significant others will perceive the purchase choice. The fifth type is *psychological risk,* the chance that a faulty choice may bruise the buyer's self-image.

Both consumers and sellers attempt to reduce the degree of risk perception in business transactions. Sellers, for example, adopt various risk-reduction strategies to aid buyers, including offering 100 percent satisfaction guarantees, free product returns, warrantees, refunds, samples, and free non-committing trial periods. They also enhance the benefits accrued from a purchase in order to equalize the relationship between risk/benefit paradigms. Consumers, on the other hand, attempt to reduce risk by comparing various competing offerings, acquiring product information from multiple sources, selecting reputable brands and vendors, and seeking endorsed brands, as well as relying upon other surrogate indicators like price.

Unfortunately, the concept of risk perception had become abused to some degree by less-than-scrupulous marketers. Some vendors have come to recognize the power of preying upon consumers' perceptions of risk and fears of uncertainty. Often, vulnerable consumers fall prey to tactics where marketers cite harm if purchase action is not taken. Examples abound in the fields of pharmaceuticals, insurance, health and beauty products, weight-loss clinics, and a host of home-security products and services.[39]

So far we have seen that consumers do not purchase objectively defined products. Rather, consumers buy products as they perceive them to be. They attend to only particular product attributes and process only a fragment of the advertising messages directed to them. What consumers learn about products, services, brands, and stores is largely an outcome of their experiences. What may seem obvious and critical for marketers may prove to be too subtle or even trivial for consumers. It is for this reason the study of consumer perception alone is insufficient to explain their behavior in the marketplace. It is equally important to understand how consumers *learn* about products, services, brands, and stores, which is the topic of the next chapter, dealing with consumer learning and memory.

SUMMARY

This chapter examines the physiological and psychological bases of perception and explains human perceptual processes. The process of perception begins with exposure to the abundant stimuli in the environment. Because perceptual processes are selective, some—but not all—stimuli may attract an individual's attention. Sensation occurs when an individual's sensory receptors transmit sensory data to the brain via the nervous system. Sensory systems include vision, smell, taste, sound, and touch. Perception occurs as individuals subjectively organize and interpret sensations.

A traditional notion views perception as the outcome of interaction between characteristics of stimuli, characteristics or conditions of perceivers, and situational factors. In this view, factors such as threshold levels (absolute, terminal, or differential) influence perceptual processes. The Gestalt view, on the other hand, emphasizes perceiving cohesive wholes, recognizing meaningful patterns, and formulating total impressions rather than noting discrete elements. Consumers usually perceive stimuli in their environment in a manner consistent with Gestalt principles, including closure, grouping, proximity, context, and figure and ground.

Individuals tend to group stimuli together into classes to facilitate dealing with them. This tendency is known as perceptual categorization. We consciously or unconsciously formulate beliefs about unfamiliar stimuli and assign meanings to objects based on other available information. This tendency is known as perceptual inference.

Schema are organizing frameworks that provide individuals with a structure for understanding new stimuli. Scripts suggest appropriate behavior sequences for particular environments and situations.

Image entails an individual's net impression of what a stimulus is all about. Product, service, and brand positionings must be appropriate for the particular market segment to which they are targeted. Firms may take proactive or reactive–defensive approaches to combat an unfavorable image. Among a firm's greatest assets is the ability of its brands to add value to products and services. This added value is known as brand equity.

Risk perception is a subjective judgment we make about uncertainties we face. Risk can take the forms of functional, physical, social, and psychological disposition.

CASE SYNOPSIS

Guns Anyone?

In the United States, the debate over availability of firearms to individuals has been going on for many years. On the two sides of the debate are gun rights supporters on one hand, and the gun control advocates on the other. The main issue underlying this debate boils down to the question of whether or not Americans would like the gun control laws—which were created to protect us—to take away our basic rights as citizens. This pro and con debate involves at least three entities who happen to have different interests and views regarding how to deal with the gun control issue. These three interested parties are the existing political regime, the citizens of the society, and the criminal element. Conclusions point out that it is primarily the criminal aspect that seems to cause the significant strife which motivates pro and con gun-control parties to require legislative action. Thus, it is safe to suggest that the interplay among these three entities works to prevent or promote passage of gun control laws.

Notes

1 Foreign versus American Cars: Is There a Difference?" *Quoted*, https://quoted.thezebra.com; http://www.msn.com/en-us/money/companies/gm-bets-americans-will-buy-cars-made-in-china/ar-CCIf7g; and http://www.cleanfleetreport.com/top-10-best-selling-mpg-cars-of-2015-first-half/.

2 Daniel Kahneman, *Attention and Effort* (Upper Saddle River, NJ: Prentice Hall, 1973).

3 "New Ideas MSI: Color Counts," *Marketing Management* 12, no. 4 (August 2003), p. 2.

4 Maureen Morrin and S. Ratneshwar, "Does It Make Sense to Use Scents to Enhance Brand Memory?" *Journal of Marketing Research* 40, no. 1 (February 2003), pp. 10–16; James V. Kohl, *The Scent of Eros* (San Jose, CA: Authors Choice Press, 2002).

5 Kyle Pope, "Technology Improves on the Nose as Scientists Try to Mimic Smell," *Wall Street Journal* (March 1, 1995), pp. B1, B8.

6 Gail Tom, "Marketing with Music," *Journal of Consumer Marketing* 7 (Spring 1990), pp. 49–53.

7 James Vail, "Music as a Marketing Tool," *Advertising Age* (November 4, 1985), p. 24.

8   Ibid.

9   Michael Morrison, Sarah Gan, Chris Dubelaar, and Harmen Oppewal, "In-store Music and Aroma Influences on Shopper Behavior and Satisfaction," *Journal of Business Research* (2011), pp. 64, 66, http://www.mendeley.com/research/instore-music-aroma-influences-shopper-behavior-sat . . .

10 Jennifer Copley, "Effects of Sound on Shoppers and Restaurant Patrons," *Music Psychology & Behavior* (May 8, 2008), http://jennifercopley.suite101.com/music-psychology--behavior-a53371.

11 Ibid.

12 George Gordon, *Active Touch* (Oxford, England: Pergamon Press, 1980).

13 Deborah B. McCabe and Stephen M. Nowlis, "The Effect of Examining Actual Products or Product Descriptions on Consumer Preference," *Journal of Consumer Psychology* 13, no. 4 (2003), pp. 431–439.

14 Raymond R. Coffey, "Advertisers Should Bury Old Gangsters," *Chicago Sun-Times* (June 7, 1994), p. 3.

15 Donna Abu-Nasr, "Nike Bows to Muslims, Will Recall 'Air' Shoes," *Chicago Sun-Times* (June 25, 1997), p. 59.

16 Andrew A. Mitchell, "An Information Processing View of Consumer Behavior," in Subhash C. Jain (Ed.), *Research Frontiers in Marketing, Dialogues and* Directions (Chicago, IL: American Marketing Association, 1978), pp. 189–190; Allan Greenberg and Charles Suttoni, "Television Commercial Wear-out," *Journal of Advertising Research* 13 (October 1973), pp. 47–54.

17 "Five Reasons to Invest in Gold (and Six Ways to Do It)," *The Christian Science Monitor, Christian Personal Finance, guest blogger* (April 29, 2010), www.csmonitor.com/ . . . /Christian . . . /Five/reasons/to/invest/in/gold/an . . .

18 J. Karremans, "Beyond Vicary's Fantasies: The Impact of Subliminal Priming and Brand Choice," *Journal of Experimental Social Psychology* 42 (2006), pp. 792–798; Anthony R. Pratkanis, "The Cargo Cult Science of Subliminal Persuasion," *Skeptical Inquirer* (2006), pp. 8–11.

19 Pradeep Kakkar and Richard J. Lutz, "Situational Influence on Consumer Behavior: A Review," in Harold H. Kassarjian and Thomas S. Robertson (Eds.), *Perspectives in Consumer Behavior*, 3rd ed. (Glenview, IL: Scott, Foresman, 1981), pp. 204–214.

20 Russell W. Belk, "An Exploratory Assessment of Situational Effects in Buyer Behavior," *Journal of Marketing Research* 11 (May 1974), pp. 156–63; U. N. Umesh and Joseph A. Cote, "Influence of Situational Variables on Brand-Choice Models," *Journal of Business Research* 16, no. 2 (1988), pp. 91–99; J. Wesley Hutchinson and Joseph W. Alba, "Ignoring Irrelevant Information: Situational Determinants of Consumer Learning," *Journal of Consumer Research* 18 (December 1991), pp. 325–345.

21 Harold H. Kassarjian, "Field Theory in Consumer Behavior," in Scott Ward and Thomas Robertson (Eds.), *Consumer Behavior: Theoretical Sources* (Upper Saddle River, NJ: Prentice Hall, 1973); David Horton and Thomas Turnage, *Human Learning* (Upper Saddle River, NJ: Prentice Hall, 1976); Mary R. Zimmer and Linda L. Golden, "Impressions of Retail Stores: A Content

Analysis of Consumer Images," *Journal of Retailing* 64 (Fall 1988), pp. 265–293; Gaetano Kanizsa, "Gestalt Theory Has Been Misinterpreted, but Has Also Had Some Real Conceptual Difficulties," *Philosophical Psychology* 7 (1994), pp. 149–162; Michael Stadler and Peter Kruse, "Gestalt Theory and Synergetics: From Psychophysical Isomorphism to Holistic Emergentism," *Philosophical Psychology* 7 (1994), pp. 211–226; Julius Harburger, "Concept Closure," *Advertising Age* (January 12, 1987), p. 18.

22 "In This Taste Test, the Loser Is the Taste Test," *Wall Street Journal* (June 3, 1987), p. 33; Robert F. Hartley, *Marketing Mistakes*, 4th ed. (New York: Wiley, 1989), pp. 221–236.

23 James T. Heimbach and Jacob Jacoby, "The Zeigernik Effect in Advertising," in M. Venkatesan (Ed.), *Proceedings of the Third Annual Conference* (Association for Consumer Research, 1972), pp. 746–758; Harburger, "Concept Closure."

24 Robin Pogrebin, "By Design or Not, an Ad Becomes a Fad," *New York Times* (December 24, 1995), p. E3.

25 Devavrat Purohit and Joydeep Srivastava, "Effect of Manufacturer Reputation, Retailer Reputation, and Product Warranty on Consumer Judgment of Product Quality," *Journal of Consumer Psychology* 10, no. 3 (2001), pp. 123–135; Niraj Dawar and Philip Parker, "Marketing Universals: Consumers' Use of Brand Name, Price, Physical Appearance, and Retailer Reputation as Signals of Product Quality," *Journal of Marketing* 58 (April 1994), pp. 81–95; William Dodds, Kent Monroe, and Dhruv Grewal, "Effects of Price, Brand, and Store Information on Buyers' Product Evaluations," *Journal of Marketing Research* 28 (August 1991), pp. 307–319; Kent Monroe, *Pricing: Making Profitable Decisions*, 2nd ed. (New York: McGraw-Hill, 1990); Tung-Zong Chang and Albert R. Wildt, "Price, Product Information, and Purchase Intention: An Empirical Study," *Journal of the Academy of Marketing* Science 22, no. 1 (1994), pp. 16–27; Donald R. Liechtenstein, Nancy M. Ridgway, and Richard G. Nitemeyer, "Price Perception and Consumer Shopping Behavior: A Field Study," *Journal of Marketing Research* 30 (May 1993), p. 242; Noel Mark Lavenka, "Measurement of Consumers' Perceptions of Product Quality, Brand Name, and Packaging: Candy Bar Comparisons by Magnitude Estimation," *Marketing Research* 3, no. 2 (June 1991), pp. 38–45; Rose L. Johnson and James L. Kellaries, "An Exploratory Study of Price/Perceived Quality Relationships Among Consumer Services," in Michael Housten (Ed.), *Advances in Consumer Research* 15 (1988), pp. 316–322; Durairaj Mahaswaron, "Country of Origin as a Stereotype: Effects of Consumer Expertise and Attribute Strength on Product Evaluations," *Journal of Consumer Research* 21 (September 1994), pp. 354–365; Jonah Berger et. al., "The Influence of Product Variety on Brand Perception and Choice" *Journal of Marketing Science* 26, no. 4 (July/August 2007), pp. 584–585; Peeter W. J. Verlegh et al., "Country of Origin Effects in Consumer Processing of Advertising Claims," *International Journal of Research in Marketing* 22, no. 2 (June 2005), pp. 127–139.

26 Mita Sujan, "Consumer Knowledge: Effects on Evaluation Strategies Mediating Consumer Judgments," *Journal of Consumer Research* 12 (June 1985), pp. 31–46; Eleanor Rosch, "Principles of Categorization," in E. Rosch and B. B. Lloyd (Eds.), *Recognition and Categorization* (Hillsdale, NJ: Lawrence Erlbaum, 1978).

27 Joseph W. Alba and J. Wesley Hutchinson, "Dimensions of Consumer Expertise," *Journal of Consumer Research* 13 (1987), pp. 493–498.

28 Pierre Martineau, *Motivation in Advertising* (New York: McGraw-Hill, 1957), p. 146.

29 Pierre Martineau, "The Personality of the Retail Store," *Harvard Business Review* 36 (JanuaryFebruary 1958),
    pp. 47–55.

30 Ron Kaspriske, "Uncorking a Few in the Wine Country," *Golf Digest* (September 2007).

31 Lil Berry, "The Components of Department Store Image: A Theoretical and Empirical Analysis," *Journal of Retailing* 45, no. 1 (1998), pp. 3–20; David Muzursky and Jacob Jacoby, "Exploring the Development of Store Images," *Journal of Retailing* 62 (Summer 1986), pp. 145–165.

32 Ibid.

33 "Exporting a Legend," *International Advertising* (November–December 1981), pp. 2–3; "Levi Zipping Up World Image," *Advertising Age* (September 14, 1981), pp. 35–36; "For Levi's a Flattering Fit Overseas," *Business Week* (November 5, 1990), p. 76.

34 Kenneth A. Hunt and Susan M. Keaveney, "A Process Model of the Effects of Price Promotions on Brand Image," *Psychology and Marketing* 11, no. 6, (November-December 1994), pp. 511–532; P. R. Dickson and A. G. Sawyer, "The Price Knowledge and Search of Supermarket Shoppers," *Journal of Marketing* 54 (July 1990), pp. 42–53; Joseph W. Alba, Susan M. Broniarczyk, Terence A. Shimp, and Joel E. Urbany, "The Influence of Prior Beliefs, Frequency Cues, and Magnitude Cues on Consumers' Perceptions of Comparative Price Data," *Journal of Consumer Research* 21 (September 1994), pp. 219–235.

35 C. Whan Park, Bernard Jaworski, and Deborah J. MacInnis, "Strategic Brand Concept Image Management," *Journal of Marketing* (October 1986), pp. 135–145; Thomas J. Reynolds and Jonathan Gutman, "Advertising Is Image Management," *Journal of Advertising* Research (February-March 1984), pp. 27–37.

36 Josee Bloemer and Ko Ruyter, "On the Relationship Between Store Image, Store Satisfaction, and Store Loyalty" European *Journal of Marketing* 32, no. 5/6 (1999), pp. 499–513.

37 Ama Carmine, "The Effect of Perceived Advertising Costs on Brand Perceptions," *Journal of Consumer Research* 17 (September 1990), pp. 160–171.

38 Don E. Schultz, "Brand Equity Has Become Oh So Fashionable," *Marketing News* (March 31, 1997), p. 9; Kevin Lane Keller, "Conceptualizing, Measuring, and Managing Customer-Based Brand Equity," *Journal of Marketing* 57

(January 1993), pp. 1–22; H. Shanker Krishnan and Dipankar Chakravarti, "Varieties of Brand Memory Induced by Advertising: Determinants, Measures, and Relationships," in David A. Aaker and Alexander L. Biel (Eds.), *Brand Equity and Advertising: Advertising's Role in Building Strong Brands* (Hillsdale, NJ: Lawrence Erlbaum, 1993), pp. 213–231; Peter H. Farquhar, "Brand Equity," *Marketing Insights* (Summer 1989), p. 59: Ama Carmine, "The Effect of Perceived Advertising Costs on Brand Perceptions," *Journal of Consumer Research* 17 (September 1990), pp. 160–171; Kenneth A. Hunt and Susan M. Keaveney, "A Process Model of the Effects of Price Promotions on Brand Image," *Psychology and Marketing* 11, no. 6 (November-December 1994), pp. 511–532.

39 Clinton M. Jenkin, "Risk Perception and Terrorism: Applying the Psychometric Paradigm," *Journal of Naval Post Graduate School Center for Homeland and Security*, no. 2 (July 2006); Jared Carbone et al., "Can Natural Experiments Measure Behavioral Responses to Environmental Risks?" *Environmental and Resource Economics* 33 (2006), pp. 273–297.

CHAPTER 4

CONSUMER LEARNING AND MEMORY

LEARNING OBJECTIVES

- To grasp the meaning and range of the consumer learning process.
- To develop a basic understanding of selected learning theories.
- To explore the concept of Neo-Pavlovian conditioning.
- To become familiar with the notion of hemispheric specialization of the brain.
- To gain insight into the phenomenon of vicarious learning.
- To comprehend the nature of memory and its structure.

KEY TERMS

learning
low-involvement learning
high-involvement learning
classical conditioning
repetition
contiguity
contingency
congruity
operant (instrumental)
    conditioning
positive reinforcement
negative reinforcement
reinforcement schedule
continuous reinforcement
intermittent reinforcement
massed (concentrated)
    practice

spaced (distributed)
    practice
behavior shaping
ecological design
servicescape
stimulus generalization
stimulus discrimination
cognitive learning
subjective experience
neo-Pavlovian
    conditioning
hemispheric specializa-
    tion of the brain
left hemisphere
right hemisphere
vicarious learning

learning curve
    (experience effect)
brand loyalty
inertia
brand parity
mnemonic devices
Google effect
sensory memory
short-term memory (STM)
encoding
long-term memory (LTM)
knowledge structures
information retrieval
retroactive interference
misinformation effect
proactive interference

One of today's persistent marketing problems is that consumers' purchasing habits are unpredictable. Consumers are too savvy to buy or stay with a brand on the strength of its name alone. They stray from their brands looking for alternatives that offer better price and value. The percentage of consumers who say they are loyal to well-known brand names has declined from a high of 82 percent in 1976 to around 50 percent today. This brand-switching trend is fueled by thousands of trading sites on the Internet, the availability of a gamut of private-label products, and the growing popularity of alternative retail outlets such as warehouse clubs and discount food and drugstores.

To businesses, brand loyalty translates into higher market share and profits. To enhance loyalty, various programs have been initiated by marketers to entice, reward, and maintain customers. According to the 2015 Colloquy Customer Loyalty Census, American households have membership in an average of twenty-nine loyalty programs. A glance at the various loyalty programs that businesses presently offer reveals the wide variety of reward systems. A common type of loyalty program employs a simple point system. Frequent customers earn points that translate into some type of reward, such as a discount, a freebie, or special customer treatment. Restaurants and supermarket chains often use such a system.

Another type uses a tier system to reward initial loyalty and encourage additional purchases. This system involves initiating small rewards as a base offering for being a part of the program, and then encourages repeat purchases by increasing the value of the rewards as the customer moves up the loyalty ladder. Virgin Atlantic Flying Club, for example, inducts members at the Club Red, then bumps them up to Club Silver, and then to Club Gold, with expanded benefits as they move up the ladder. These benefits range from discounts on rental cars, on airport parking, and on hotels, to check-in priority, double miles, and access to exclusive clubhouses.

A third type of loyalty program charges an upfront fee for VIP benefits. In this case, a one-time or annual fee lets customers bypass common purchase barriers. An example of this program is the Amazon Prime service, where for $99 a year, members get free two-day shipping on millions of products with no minimum purchase requirements, among other benefits.

Another type of loyalty program attempts to provide nonmonetary rewards structured around what the firms' customers value. These rewards may be in the form of company's support for an environmental, charitable, humane, or similar cause. For example, Patagonia, an eco-friendly outdoor apparel company, helps customers resell their used, highly durable Patagonia clothing online via the company's website.

Still another form of loyalty program is built around partnering with another company or companies that provide all-inclusive offers. American Express Plenty Program is a case in point that allows consumers to pool their rewards from various retailers, such as Macy's, AT&T, Rite Aid, Enterprise Rent-A-Car, Hulu, and more. Points earned for shopping at any of these retail outlets can be redeemed to pay for purchases made from the other participants in this program. For instance, Plenty points earned from renting a car from Enterprise can be applied toward payment of an AT&T phone bill.

Many companies today, such as phone companies, restaurants, car rental agencies, and hotels, realize the importance of such retention-intended frequent-shopper programs. Although such practices are expensive for participating companies, their cost is justified by the benefits of retained customers. They make good economic sense in light of the fact that the cost of retaining customers is minimal compared to the cost of acquiring new ones. In fact, it has been estimated that it costs a business between five to ten times as much to acquire a new customer as it does to sell to an existing one.[1]

Achieving customer loyalty is one of the foremost goals of marketing managers. Think of some programs that you personally have participated in (supermarket preferred-customer cards, frequent-flier miles) that are designed to enhance customer loyalty. Is the extent of your loyalty to a brand or store influenced by these programs? Visit Reward Credit Card at its website, www.rewardcreditcardsite.com and determine if, besides economic benefits, there are any psychological forces behind choosing a particular credit card.

This chapter discusses learning as it applies to consumer behavior. We introduce three major learning theories: classical conditioning, operant conditioning, and cognitive learning. Although the bases for these theories are different, they are complementary—not contradictory. Each theory explains different types of learning from different perspectives. Other forms of learning, such as vicarious learning and habit formation, are relevant, and we explore them as well. Finally, we discuss memory and forgetting.

WHAT IS LEARNING?

Learning infiltrates nearly all human behavior, and consumption of goods and services is no exception. Consumer behavior includes learning as both an adaptive and a problem-solving activity. Within economic, cultural, social, and psychological constraints, we exhibit behaviors that we anticipate will enable us to reach the various goals on which we focus. As we come to discover that certain behaviors produce results that are more satisfying than others, we reassess our decision processes and purchasing strategies accordingly.

Definition of Learning

learning
process by which changes occur in the content or organization of a person's long-term memory

Learning has been defined in a number of ways. In a broad sense, learning occurs when experience produces relatively lasting changes in a person's capabilities or behavior. More precisely, learning is any process by which changes occur in the content or organization of an individual's long-term memory.[2]

A few qualifications are in order. First, because learning frequently involves mental processes, it is not directly observable. Thus, we often measure it in terms of performance. Teachers measure student learning according to performance on exams; similarly, marketers may measure consumer learning as it is manifested in their shopping selections. Not all learning, however, produces immediate activity. Rather, it can offer information that may eventually lead to action. Whereas the majority of retail newspaper ads, many websites, and social media promotions seek prompt consumer responses, most manufacturer-sponsored TV, magazine, and online ads are image builders that are not expected to produce quick purchase reactions.

A second qualification governs the source of behavioral changes. Recall that our definition excludes behavior and ability changes that result from instinct and reflex, or growth and maturation of body tissues.

Third, the effects of learning are relatively long term. Learning is said to have occurred when a subject consistently responds in the desired manner. The definition excludes temporary changes precipitated by alcohol, drugs, or deprivation (hunger, thirst, fatigue).

Fourth, the term *behavior*, as employed in these definitions, covers both overt activities (such as shopping) and cognitive processes (such as prob-

FIGURE 4.1

Behavior change is the objective of this ad from the CDC, which presents facts regarding the dangers of smoking to one's health.

lem solving and information processing). The ad from the Center for Disease Control, shown in Figure 4.1, states facts pertaining to the health hazards of cigarette smoking. The goal of the ad is to get consumers to quit smoking.

Range of Learning Situations

Humans, throughout their lives, acquire numerous skills that enable them to manage their daily lives. They learn language skills to interact and communicate with others. They learn to recognize and respond to symbols encountered in the environment such as packages and brand names. They learn how to process information to solve problems. They learn to think by mentally manipulating symbols representing reality to form combinations of meaning. This thinking leads to insight and an enhanced comprehension of relationships in a problem. Through a process known as consumer socialization, they acquire the knowledge and skills necessary to function in the marketplace. For example, they learn to read the small print in a contract or negotiate the price of a new car. Through familiarity with objects over time and the influence of others, consumers learn tastes for specific products, styles, and brands.[3]

Applied specifically to the field of consumer behavior, learning occurs in situations ranging from low to high levels of consumer involvement. In low-involvement learning situations, consumers have little or no motivation to process the material to be learned. When consumers encounter ads in the media or on the web for products they do not use or stores where they do not shop, they may lack the incentive to attend to and process these messages.

In high-involvement learning situations, individuals are motivated to process the information to be learned. A consumer who plans to buy a new automobile is likely to navigate the Internet searching for and checking out automotive websites and/or seek advice from others to learn as much as possible about the car's features, performance capabilities, and gas mileage. The degree of consumer involvement is a function of the interaction between an individual, a stimulus, and a situation.[4] For instance, consumers who lack interest in automobiles might merely glance at car ads. However, if an automobile ad features an admired superstar, many of these same individuals might attend to the ad and read it carefully to learn what the celebrity has to say. Similarly, consumers who generally ignore car ads would likely become more involved with automobile advertising when the need to buy a car arises.

LEARNING THEORIES

A review of the literature on learning reveals a number of different learning theories.[5] These can be divided among two schools of thought: behavioral-associationist theories and cognitive-organizational theories. Three learning theories apply particularly well to the attempts of marketers to stimulate or change consumer behavior and are covered in this chapter. These theories are (1) classical conditioning and (2) operant conditioning, which fall under the behavioral-associationist heading, and (3) cognitive learning, which addresses the mental processes by which people acquire knowledge and form concepts.

low-involvement learning a case where individuals are less motivated to attend to and process material to be learned

high-involvement learning a case where individuals are motivated to process information to be learned

Classical Conditioning

The term *classical conditioning* elicits thoughts of the well-known experiments by Pavlov with dogs.[6] The process of classical conditioning involves forming a connection between a conditioned stimulus (in Pavlov's case, a bell) and an unconditioned stimulus (in Pavlov's case, food) to teach a desired reaction (salivation at the tone of the bell). To form the link between the bell tone and food, Pavlov sounded a bell just before the dogs were exposed to food. The bell tone was the conditioned stimulus (CS) and food was the unconditioned stimulus (US). Eventually, after many repetitions, hearing the bell tone caused Pavlov's dogs to expect food and to salivate. The bell had come to produce the same response, salivation (UR), originally produced only by food. A connection had been formed, and a primitive variety of learning had taken place. A schematic conceptualization of this process appears in Exhibit 4.1.

classical conditioning
a view that learning involves linking a conditioned stimulus and an unconditioned stimulus

Pavlov viewed conditioned responses as temporary and capable of being extinguished. The Russian word he used meant *conditional*, which suggests a temporary effect. Curiously, U.S. researchers assumed that Pavlov's interest was in the maintenance of responses and somehow translated his word as *conditioned*, which suggests the effects were permanent or final. Recognizing this departure from Pavlov's original intention, Krugman noted that long-term consumer likes and dislikes become part of an individual's personality in a way that briefly conditioned and easily extinguished conditioned responses do not.[7]

Classical Conditioning and the Formation of Associations

The traditional interpretation of classical conditioning views learning as forming connections or associations between environmental events.[8] Some psychologists consider these associations to be nothing more than linkages between two concepts. Other psychologists regard these associations as a fusing or blending so that two separate items are combined to form a larger unit that has no immediate resemblance to either item alone.[9] Associative learning via classical conditioning usually involves the organism's learning of an association between a conditioned (originally neutral) stimulus and an unconditioned stimulus, which could be biological (food, fragrance) or symbolic (the flag). In a consumer behavior context, conditioned stimuli include products, brands, and stores, whereas unconditioned stimuli might include celebrities, music, and humor. For example, studies have demonstrated that hearing music or humor we like or dislike while being exposed to products can directly affect our preferences for them.[10]

EXHIBIT 4.1

Schematic Presentation of
Classical Conditioning

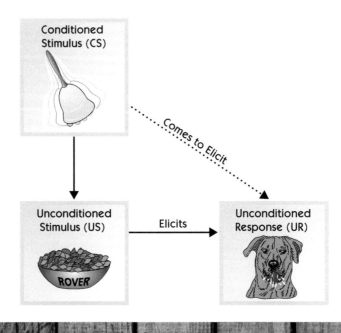

ETHICAL DILEMMA

Cause Behind Cause Marketing

Astute marketers have cleverly used the concept of classical conditioning to get consumers to reach for their brands. The ploy involves forming a connection between their brand and a particular charitable cause. American Express first came up with the idea back in 1983. Each time the cardholder charged an item, the company donated a penny toward restoring the Statue of Liberty. The result was a few million dollars to refurbish the Lady, plus the heightened goodwill for AMEX. Known as *cause marketing*, the practice is one of the fastest-growing and increasingly debated attempts by corporations to boost market share. Through the years, many examples of cause marketing were initiated, including the "Avon 39" walk in support of breast cancer research; Jet Blue's "Soar With Reading" campaign to donate books for kids who live in impoverished communities; TOMS with its "One For One" campaign, matching every pair of shoes purchased with a pair of new shoes given free to a child in need; Uber with its "No Kids Hungry" campaign to end childhood hunger; Kmart's campaign for supporting St. Jude's Research Hospital; Facebook's worldwide "Stop Ebola" campaign; Lush with its campaign "Charity Pot" to support nonprofits worldwide, including entities involved in animal welfare, environmental conservation, and humanitarian causes; Wendy's "Wonderful Kids" in support of foster care adoption; Safeway's "Hunger Is" campaign to provide full breakfasts for school kids; Costco's "Getting Vets Back to Work" campaign; Macy's "Buy One Coat & We'll Give One Coat" campaign; Sun Life Financial's "Team Up Against Diabetes" campaign; and Hanes with its "Hanes For Good" program to donate socks to shelters.

The purpose of these affiliations between businesses and charities is obvious. Although conveying a positive message to the company's audiences is an important objective, causes are instrumental in moving cases of merchandise. Such relationships get consumers emotionally involved, which encourages them to switch brands and retailers. When consumers were asked their feelings regarding charitable tie-ins, 40 percent of women and 30 percent of men reported that they were more likely to buy a product or service if they knew that a certain amount of the purchase price was going to be donated to a cause or campaign.

Critics argue that many companies are insincere in their claims of support for charities. Sometimes companies donate just a minuscule fraction of the funds they earn from the campaign to the chosen cause. Other firms promise to contribute "a portion of the proceeds" to some cause without stating how big that portion is, when the funds will be donated, or what the funds will be used for. In many instances, these programs lack transparency and specific information, which turns consumers into cynics, thereby defeating the very purpose for the cause marketing program. Critics suggest a number of factors for companies to consider in designing a good cause marketing program. They recommend that the program state exactly which charity will receive the funds in order to allow consumers to investigate the charity on their own. The program should also state why that specific charity was chosen, how much the charity will receive, when the funds will be re-ceived, and what the funds will be used for. With these standards in place, the initiating company stands a much better chance of attaining the program's stated objectives.

As instances of questionable cause marketing practices become increasingly commonplace, they could pose a threat to firms that run legitimate cause-related marketing campaigns. If consumers fall victims to cases of suspicious charitable solicitations, they could become turned off by such campaigns altogether.[11]

In your opinion, is cause marketing a desirable business practice? Discover why companies are interested in this endeavor by visiting www.tsaresearch.com/CRMFEATURE.html. For successful tie-ins between a brand and a charity, what prerequisites do you recommend? Is a natural fit between the product category and charity necessary? Why or why not? Learn about the importance of cause marketing as a business activity by visiting the site of the yearly awards forum for participating companies at http://www.causemarketingforum.com/site/c.bkLUKcOTLkK4E/d.9351101/k.33C5/2016_Halo_Awards.htm. Which cause marketing category (or categories) would you most likely tend to support? Why?

Research on the connection between music and sales involved the case of holiday music and holiday merchandise.[12] The study revealed that department stores which played Christmas music during the holiday season experienced on the average a 32.8 percent increase in sales volume of seasonal merchandise compared with stores that failed to play such music.[13] To summarize, through association, a product/brand (CS) can come to elicit liking/disliking (CR) analogous to the liking/disliking (UR) evoked by an ad's model, music, or humor (US).[14] According to one Coca-Cola executive, "Pavlov took a neutral object and by associating it with a meaningful object, made it a symbol of something else . . . that is precisely what we try to do in modern advertising."[15]

The traditional view of classical conditioning holds that conditioning represents the establishment of new reflexes (stimulus–response connections) that result from frequent pairings of a CS and US. In other words, classical conditioning is a low-level, mechanical process in which control over a response is passed from one stimulus to another.[16] From a consumer behavior perspective, this would suggest, for example, that if a particular piece of music emotionally excites the listener, then a brand paired with the same music should similarly stir the consumer.[17]

Learning Principles Under the Classical Conditioning Model

For connections to be formed under classical conditioning, four conditions must prevail—repetition, contiguity, contingency, and congruity. Repetition is the frequency of pairing the CS with the US. The more often the CS and US are coupled, the more quickly learning occurs.

Repetition is employed in scheduling media for a campaign. Advertisers reiterate their messages in many ads and commercials targeted to the same audience over a specified time period. Ad copy, especially in the broadcast media, repeatedly links the brand with its greatest benefit.[18] Figure 4.2 illustrates repetition by showing a series of photographs depicting various models of Mercedes-Benz automobiles.

Repeating advertising messages to an audience does, however, cause the impact of these messages to lessen. *Advertising wearout* is defined as diminished responsiveness of an audience to ads and commercials as a consequence of repeated exposure to them. Recently, new views regarding advertising wearout have appeared in the literature. For example, Hughes feels that wearout occurs when an ad no longer triggers recall of positive feelings from a viewer's long-term memory.[19] Wearout results, in part, from a viewer's adaptation to the ad as well as from lowered expectations of entertainment or new information from it.

Contiguity, a second principle, involves spatial and temporal nearness. Learning occurs more quickly when the CS is presented close to the US. In his experiment, Pavlov rang the bell (CS) at about the same moment he exposed the dog to food (US). If the bell were rung much earlier or later and in different surroundings, it would have been more difficult for the dogs to connect the bell tone with food. Marketers often try to associate products and product use with pleasant imagery through temporal or spatial proximity.[20] For example, sponsors advertise automobiles in luxurious surroundings, clothing and jewelry on attractive models, and beer and soft drinks in cheerful, party-like settings.

repetition
the frequency of pairing a conditioned stimulus with an unconditioned stimulus

contiguity
the spatial or temporal nearness of objects

©2004 Mercedes-Benz USA, LLC.   Please always wear your seat belt.   Call 1-800-FOR-MERCEDES or visit MBUSA.com/natgeogold

The most common photograph taken is with a loved one.

Unlike any other.   Mercedes-Benz

Mercedes-Benz USA, LLC.

To expedite learning via classical conditioning, stimuli should be presented in the proper order. A third principle known as contingency states that the CS should precede the US.[21] Research suggests the CS has predictive or information value. It signals that the US is about to occur. Thus, the conditioned response (CR) is anticipatory.[22]

contingency
the notion that the conditioned stimulus should precede the unconditioned stimulus

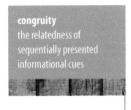

Finally, for associations to form between the CS and US, they must be related in some meaningful way. This principle is known as congruity, the consistency or relatedness of sequentially presented pairs of informational cues or concurrently encountered elements comprising a stimulus event.[23] Congruity and incongruity influence our processing and memory for events. Incongruent information tends to be more difficult to encode and retrieve. Irrelevant information tends to produce lower recall.

Operant (Instrumental) Conditioning

Operant or instrumental conditioning differs from classical conditioning in three significant aspects. First, unlike classical conditioning, operant conditioning is driven by the *consequences* of behavior, as subjects discover that certain actions produce more desirable outcomes than others. Second, in operant conditioning, learning occurs not through repetitive responses to contiguous stimuli but through trial and error. When a behavior is followed by a reward, the subject is more likely to repeat that behavior. In other words, he or she forms a *habit* or response tendency. On the other hand, when a person's behavior is punished, the subject tests new responses and engages in alternate activities until his or her actions are suitably rewarded.

The third difference is that whereas classical conditioning involves stimulus substitution, operant conditioning involves response substitution.[24] In other words, fruitless behaviors tend to be replaced with ones that are reinforced. Consumers who are unsuccessful in obtaining a pleasing resolution to a buying situation are likely to modify their solution until a subsequent response is found to be more satisfactory.

Classical and operant conditioning are similar in one significant aspect. Both models of learning ignore mental processes such as perception, thinking, and reasoning. Subjects are passive and make no attempt to assess the nature of the situation. Nor do they actively examine alternate response modes. In conditioning models, learners do not think; they simply behave.

Like Pavlov, U.S. psychologist B. F. Skinner used animal experiments to develop his operant learning model. In Skinner's conditioning exercises, hungry pigeons and rats were placed in so-called Skinner boxes equipped with special mechanisms such as pecking keys and levers designed to dispense food when touched. Initially the pigeons and rats wandered restlessly in the boxes, until they accidentally hit the special mechanism and food pellets rewarded them. Soon the test animals came to manipulate the food-dispensing mechanism continuously, seeking food pellets. Once the mechanism had been disconnected, however, their rate of manipulation decreased and eventually stopped. At that point, extinction had occurred. That is, the behavior ceased because key pecking and lever pressing were no longer instrumental in producing rewards.[25] The process of operant conditioning is depicted in Exhibit 4.2.

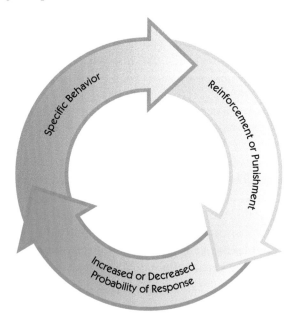

EXHIBIT 4.2

Schematic Presentation of Operant Conditioning

How Operant Conditioning Works

Operant conditioning alters the likelihood that a behavior will occur by changing the consequences of that behavior. Unlike classical conditioning, operant conditioning proposes a sequence in which behavior occurs first, perhaps in reaction to a cue. The behavior is then reinforced (or punished), and the result is an increase (or decrease) in the probability that the response will occur again. Reinforcement and punishment are, therefore, *instrumental* in bringing about a behavioral change.

Reinforcement is a reward given to acknowledge a desired behavior and increase the probability that it will be repeated in the future. It can be positive or negative. Positive reinforcement encourages behavior with pleasant consequences such as fun, enjoyment, relaxation, or savings. Marketers offer attractive benefits and other rewards to establish and bolster desired consumer behaviors. As we saw at the start of the chapter, many firms, such as airlines and credit card organizations, reward customers with frequent-flier miles as a bonus when they use the companies'

positive reinforcement an inducement to repeat a behavior to receive a pleasant consequence

services. Cosmetics companies often give customers free gifts when they purchase a designated item or spend a specified amount of money.

Negative reinforcement, on the other hand, offers the relief or removal of some adverse situation to increase the frequency of a behavior or to boost sales. For example, Bayer Aspirin, Tylenol, and Advil promise pain relief. Other products such as antibacterial soaps, antiperspirants, mouth-washes, anti-aging creams and treatments, as well as teeth-whitening strips are all positioned to lessen various consumer fears and anxieties. The term *negative reinforcement* must not be confused with punishment.

Punishment is an aversive or a repellent result that decreases the frequency of an undesirable response. Punishment can take two forms. Frequently it involves something that subjects perceive as painful or unpleasant. For example, motorists who exceed the posted speed limit may, if stopped by the police, be required to pay a hefty fine. Punishment may also take the form of the removal of something desirable or pleasant. Reckless drivers with numerous traffic violations may, as part of their penalty, have their driving privileges suspended. Marketers do not have the power to punish consumers for not taking a suggested action in any direct form, although some observers regard certain marketing practices, such as fear and guilt advertising, as falling under this label.

Reinforcement Schedules

The pattern in which reinforcements are given is known as the schedule of reinforcement. Different reinforcement schedules lead to different patterns of learning. There are two main types of **reinforcement schedules**: continuous (total) and intermittent (partial) schedules. **Continuous reinforcement** schedules reward a desired behavior every time it occurs. Under conditions of continuous reinforcement, learning occurs more quickly, but the sought behavior ceases shortly after the rewards stop. **Intermittent reinforcement** schedules, on the other hand, reward a desired behavior only occasionally. Although learning does not occur as quickly as under continuous reinforcement, intermittent reinforcement slows down the process of forgetting. In other words, when learned under conditions of intermittent reinforcement, behavior becomes more persistent. Many gamblers persevere, even after repeated losses, precisely because they do not expect to win every time and thus never know when the next win might occur. The *next time* may provide the coveted payoff. Hence the residual effects of learning persist. The effects of continuous and intermittent reinforcement on forgetting and behavior maintenance over time are depicted in Exhibit 4.3.

negative reinforcement
an inducement to repeat a behavior in order to remove an adverse situation

reinforcement schedule
the pattern in which reinforcements are given

continuous reinforcement
a reinforcement schedule that rewards a desired behavior every time it occurs

intermittent reinforcement
a reinforcement schedule that rewards a desired behavior only occasionally

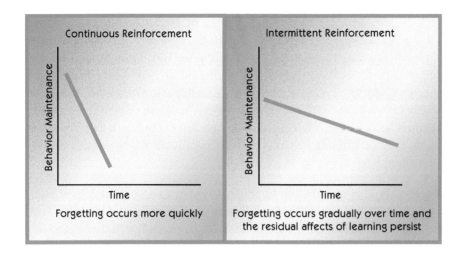

EXHIBIT 4.3

Rate of Forgetting

Continuous Reinforcement

Behavior Maintenance

Time

Forgetting occurs more quickly

Intermittent Reinforcement

Behavior Maintenance

Time

Forgetting occurs gradually over time and the residual affects of learning persist

Practice Schedules

Timing exerts important influences on learning. Massed (concentrated) practice condenses a learning schedule into a brief time span to accelerate learning. Spaced (distributed) practice, on the other hand, paces learning over a time interval to increase retention. Spaced practice typically involves several short learning sessions distributed over time with breaks or rest periods between them. Generally, massed schedules produce greater initial learning, but dispersed schedules produce learning that is more lasting. Traditional media schedules slot brief ads and commercials that recur over the duration of a campaign, approximating spaced learning. The *infomercial* phenomenon, on the other hand, might be compared to massed learning.

Challenges in Applying Operant Conditioning

One challenge that marketers face when applying operant conditioning concepts is that the desired behavior must occur first before it can be rewarded. For example, in the field of automobile sales, it is unlikely that prospects would be actively searching for a new car if their present vehicle were functioning well. Consequently, car dealerships need a strategy to entice prospects to visit their showrooms. Thus, where the probability that individuals will perform a desired behavior is small, marketers frequently rely on a process called behavior shaping. Behavior shaping is the process of breaking down a complex behavior into a sequence of simple component actions and then reinforcing the successive components to increase the probability that the final action will occur.

massed (concentrated) practice
lengthy learning sessions scheduled over a brief time period

spaced (distributed) practice
brief learning sessions intermingled with rest periods scheduled over a lengthy time period

behavior shaping
the process of breaking down a complex behavior into a series of simple stages and reinforcing the learner at each step

For example, an auto dealership can apply behavior shaping by mapping out a guided, step-by-step path that gradually steers prospects toward buying, rewarding them at each point along the way. First, the dealer may initiate a direct-mail campaign announcing the arrival of new models and offering visitors free refreshments, gifts, and opportunities to win prizes in hourly raffles. Second, the dealer may offer a $50 cash reward to test-drive a display vehicle. Finally, to encourage test-drivers to buy, a $1000 instant rebate may be extended to anyone who purchases a new car during the promotion period.

A second type of operant conditioning is known as ecological design. Ecological design is the calculated planning of physical space and other facets of the environment to modify human behavior or expedite a desired response. Studies in this field focus on what has been termed the symbolic servicescape. Rosenbaum, among others, postulated that servicescape frameworks serve as models for illustrating the factors that govern consumers' perceptions when they encounter consumption settings. The concept of servicescape proposes that a consumer interacts with the various elements—both physical and social—present in a service environment via matching such elements with his or her "place identity." In this sense, place identity refers to the congruity between a consumer's self-identity and the physical and social elements of the environment where the transaction is being conducted. A case in point is the promotional strategy employed by some upscale health clubs found in large metropolitan centers. Prospects tour the modern facility while listening to a carefully crafted presentation on the facilities and clientele. The tour guide shows them the sophisticated exercise equipment and yoga center, as well as the tennis and racquetball courts. They view the steam rooms, jacuzzies, and swimming pools, as well as shower rooms equipped with bathrobes, towels, and fancy toiletries. Finally, they visit the beautifully decorated juice bar. The presentation ends by offering the prospects an introductory discount and/or extra privileges, all making it virtually impossible for them to resist the temptation to join the health club.

Potential applications of ecological design are endless. Retailers seek convenient and accessible store locations with plenty of parking space to encourage shopping. They fashion selling-floor layouts and merchandise displays to expose customers to a wide variety of merchandise and trigger impulse buying. In one case, a firm that operates several 7-Eleven stores addressed the problem of loitering in store parking lots by installing exterior speakers and playing orchestral and easy-listening tunes. Kids, who composed a large percentage of the loiterers, hated the music and searched for different sites to congregate.[26]

ecological design
the planning of physical space and other facets of the environment to modify human behavior

servicescape
model for illustrating consumer perception patterns in specific consumption settings

Other applications of ecological design relate to the fields of information technologies and web design. Graphic artists employ animations, music, and color in order to reinforce the sponsor's image both online and offline and to make it easy to purchase the product with the click of a mouse. Similarly in the fields of interior design and home décor, marketers' ads usually depict attractive arrangements of home furnishings that reflect elegance and style. The photo in Figure 4.3 shows customers that appear highly satisfied with their purchase.

Applications of Conditioning Theories: Stimulus Generalization and Discrimination

Among the tendencies that we learn through classical and operant conditioning are the abilities to generalize and discriminate. Stimulus generalization means that once learners acquire a response to a particular stimulus, this response may be elicited by stimuli similar to the original one. For example, a person who is positively impressed by the quality of one German-made automobile may generalize this superior-quality perception to all cars made in Germany. Similarly, a consumer's negative reaction to a product of a particular brand can extend to all other products bearing the same brand name. Whether positive or negative, this tendency for a widely known brand to influence consumers regarding products bearing the same name is called a *halo effect*.

stimulus generalization
the tendency to assign commonality to similar stimuli

© Jack Frog/Shutterstock.com

FIGURE 4.3

This photo reflects the concept of ecological design. It shows the aesthetics and value of a stylish arrangement of furnishings that contemporary consumers crave for their modern homes.

Stimulus discrimination, in contrast, occurs when learners develop an ability to distinguish between, and respond differently to, similar—but nonidentical—stimuli. Even though research has shown that most consumers cannot distinguish between many brands of foods and beverages on the basis of taste alone, many people nonetheless develop a strong partiality for certain ones due to image-building marketing variables such as branding, packaging, pricing, and promotion. For instance, in a wine-tasting experiment reported on the ABC network, respondents were given two samples of wine representing the same brand. However, these subjects were told that the first wine sample came from a $5-per-bottle brand, and the second sample from a $45-per-bottle brand. As expected, respondents rated the second wine sample significantly better in taste and higher in quality than the first. Some consumers develop keener discriminating capacities within a particular product category than others. Stimulus discrimination based on physical or psychological product attributes is the foundation of positioning strategy, which attempts to establish a competitive advantage or unique image for a brand in consumers' minds. A brand has a high chance of success if consumers can be led to discriminate between that brand and its competition. This is especially true if the brand is noticeably better than other brands in some respect (Figure 4.4).

Cognitive Learning

Human learning ranges from simple and mechanical habit formation to complex information processing. Although we engage in considerable trial-and-error behavior, we are not locked into a ceaselessly repetitive stimulus–response behavior mode. We can and do readily modify our response tendencies when insight and understanding direct us to a different view of a situation or when our goals or motivations change. We are information processors who continuously alter our response tendencies. For example, in studies involving children, researchers such as Peracchio demonstrated that the ability of children to make mature consumer decisions increases with age.[27] According to this view, children can be segmented by age in terms of their stage of cognitive development or ability to comprehend concepts of increasing cognitive complexity.

Cognitive learning recognizes that we *think*, not just *do*. Cognitive learning pertains to changes in knowledge. It recognizes the active mental process through which people form meaningful associations among concepts, learn sequences of concepts, solve problems, and gain insights.[28] Cognitive learning theory evolved from Kohler's experiments on apes.[29]

FIGURE 4.4

Some airlines use images such as this to demonstrate that fliers can work, surf, text, tweet, and email while in flight.

© Matej Kastelic/Shutterstock.com

In one experiment, a chimpanzee was placed in a cage. Bananas hung from the roof and boxes rested on the floor. The chimp tried but could not reach the bananas, until it solved the problem by moving a box beneath the bananas. Learning resulted from insight; it was not an outcome of a mere stimulus–response–reinforcement pattern.

Cognitive theory emphasizes our capacity for problem solving and understanding relationships. Learners recognize a goal, engage in purposeful behavior to achieve the goal, apply insight to devise a solution, and accomplish their goal. Cognitive theory acknowledges the role and importance of reinforcement. Unlike the case in operant conditioning, however, where rewards are not evident until after behavior has occurred, in cognitive learning subjects understand and anticipate their goal (reward) from the start.

Cognitive learning theory also recognizes the role of subjective experience—our beliefs, values, attitudes, expectations, insight, understanding, and meaning. We synthesize our personal beliefs, attitudes, and prior experiences to produce insight into new situations. The brain or central nervous system dominates as we approach problems sensibly, interpreting new information to develop fresh beliefs and meanings. With goal orientation and perceptive thinking, learners can apply insight and reasoning abilities and draw from prior knowledge to understand current problem situations, even though there may be no historical precedents in their ex-

subjective experience
the notion that humans synthesize beliefs and experiences to gain insight into new situations

perience.[30] The ad from Bayer in Figure 4.5 employs cognitive learning concepts to convey to consumers the ability of Aleve to relieve pain for a much longer time period than Tylenol.

Cognitive learning theory also recognizes the role of information processing in attitude formation and change by consumers—what we think, feel, and do. Examples abound in this area. In the political arena, the accessibility and wide appeal of social media and television makes them effective media for providing prospective voters a convenient way to learn about political candidates and their stance on the key issues during an election year.[31] We can also envision how strategies such as persuasion can work effectively to promote various causes and issues, such as forwarding environmental concerns. Persuasion is a form of social influence that is accomplished more or less by guiding consumers toward accepting a new product, idea, attitude, or course of action by either rational or emotional means.[32] One recent application of an attitudinal model being applied is the recent rise in public outrage against alleged police brutality directed toward racial minorities, and the need to eliminate profiling and prejudice in the United States.[33]

Courtesy of Bayer HealthCare, Consumer Care LLC.

FIGURE 4.5

The illustration in this ad from Bayer shows just two tablets of Aleve compared with eight of Tylenol. The depiction quickly and effectively demonstrates Aleve's ability to provide longer-lasting pain relief.

Have A Pain-Free Holiday With Fewer Pills.

Switch and discover what 2 Aleve can do for your holiday. Unlike Tylenol,* Aleve can relieve pain all day with just 2 pills.

ALEVE

CONSUMER BEHAVIOR *AN APPLIED APPROACH*

CONSUMER BEHAVIOR IN PRACTICE

Our Era of Sensory Overload

Today we are witnessing a revolution in accessible knowledge. Our world has gone from one in which information was scarce and hard to find, to one where information is everywhere in staggering quantities. The massive volume of data that humanity generates is hard to fathom. Experts estimate that every two days, humans generate a quantity of data equivalent to the entire amount created from the dawn of time until the beginning of the twenty-first century. Consider for a moment the consequences of our daily activities. Every day we tweet 500 million times, share 70 million photos on Instagram, and watch 4 billion videos on Facebook. With the passage of every minute, 300 hours of new content is being uploaded on YouTube. Consider, in addition, the global "Internet of Things" that covers all objects from cars to baby food, and which is outfitted by sensors that communicate with the cloud and with one another. It has been estimated by IDC, a research firm, that by the year 2020 the volume of the world's digital data will grow to be a staggering 44 trillion gigabytes.

The ultimate force that came about in the current era of overwhelming knowledge is Google—the renowned entity that reconfigured our world. It empowers its billion-plus users with information of all types and forms, made available to them in 159 languages. It processes over 100 billion inquiries a month, and provides answers to every search no matter how trivial the subject happens to be. Yet Google is not just for curious minds. Google Scholar has been the cornerstone for academic research in all fields of science and arts. There is also Google Translate, which decodes 1 billion linguistic mysteries per day. With 25 million books already scanned, Google maintains the most comprehensive archive of the printed word.

Furthermore, Google Docs has changed the way we collaborate. It created a world where it is taken for granted that people can work together on virtually any type of document, whether for purposes of work or play. Additionally, Google Maps has become much more than a tool for figuring out best travel routes and times. It allows us to tour distant destinations without the bother of actual travel, to give our friends a virtual tour of our hometown, or to plan our vacations in advance. Consider, in addition, Google's Gmail, which allows us to maintain bottomless inboxes. The feature eliminates those times when storage space was sacred, and deleting old emails was a tedious but necessary periodic practice. Add to this Google Analytics, which helps marketers in the setting up and customization of tracking for websites and web mobile apps, as well as Internet-connected services. One application of Google Analytics is a custom dashboard to help drivers segment traffic from search engine optimization, social media, mobile, and other online marketing metrics. When we contemplate what Google has done to our present world, it's truly hard to remember what life was like before it.[34]

Even though Google has had a major impact on our daily life by facilitating the acquisition of information and knowledge about any topic, some critics point to a negative consequence of this incredible service. The 24/7 access to this limitless information source, they claim, is causing a tendency of mental laziness for many of us with regard to our willingness to remember things. Our brains instantly turn to the Internet to acquire the needed information for whatever question we need answered. Visit the website http://www.dailydot.com/technology/google-15-anniversary-search-maps/. Do you agree with the assessment that Google has simply become a collective mental crutch for the majority of the service users? Why or why not?

Neo-Pavlovian Conditioning

During the past two decades, some consumer researchers have begun to show renewed interest in classical conditioning. The traditional view of classical conditioning was of simple connections forming between stimuli and responses. The contemporary view, on the other hand, posits that learning is not simple, primitive, automatic, passive, or low involvement, but rather that it is a multifaceted process. Modern theorists no longer hold the notion that an organism's actions simply follow stimuli in a reflexive manner.[35]

neo-Pavlovian conditioning
a view that reshapes traditional classical conditioning into a fully cognitive theory

The modern view of classical conditioning, sometimes called neo-Pavlovian conditioning, reshapes traditional classical conditioning into a fully cognitive theory.[36] It holds that learned associations are rich, often complex, and may involve relationships among multiple objects and events in the environment. In other words, neo-Pavlovian conditioning emphasizes cognitive associative learning, which is not mere acquisition of new reflexes but rather procurement of new knowledge about the environment, where one stimulus provides information about another. This view is based on an assumption of intelligence and information-processing capabilities of the organism. The Metra ad in Figure 4.6 attempts to form a mental association between taking the train and driving one's own car.

Although the word *response* may suggest that what is conditioned in classical conditioning is overt behavior, a number of psychologists suggest that what is really conditioned is an *evaluative response* or attitude, and not overt behavior per se.[37] From marketers' point of view, attitudes that involve strong associations are highly functional. They free us from the effort required for deliberate reasoning and guide our behavior in a fairly automatic fashion. They serve to minimize information processing prior to initiating appropriate responses.[38] For example, consumers who associate the "Made in America" label with high quality and good workmanship tend to prefer to purchase products carrying this label over their imported counterparts.

WHICH LEARNING THEORIES DO MARKETERS EMPLOY?

Marketers approach the topic of consumer learning from a number of angles, employing concepts borrowed from classical and operant conditioning as well as from cognitive learning. Sometimes the emphasis is on the

FIGURE 4.6

This Metra ad, which draws a mental association between the train and a car, invites commuters to think of a train ride as a viable alternative to driving.

way consumers form habits and become loyal to a particular brand. At other times, marketers are interested in how attitudes develop and change. In still other cases, marketers are concerned with the manner in which consumers process information and arrive at decisions.

A glance at the field of advertising reveals that advertisers use a variety of strategies to convey their messages. Many ads are founded on classical conditioning concepts. For example, Walt Disney Company's affiliation with *Frozen* helps consumers and even toddlers to instantly recognize the sponsor of any promotion that employs the *Frozen* theme and the movie's characters. Other ads that emphasize product quality and positive product-use experiences draw from operant conditioning as well. Sony's ads, which emphasize the superior quality of its home electronics products, exemplify this approach. Still other ads present logical arguments supporting the choice of a specific brand or vendor. Every tax season, H&R Block runs ads that use this format, offering specific reasons why taxpayers should use the firm's services.

Thus, diverse perspectives such as habit formation *versus* problem solving and concept formation should not be considered contradictory, but rather complementary to one another.[39] No single theory completely explains learning. Rather, each view helps explain those aspects of learning that the other views neglect or have difficulty addressing.[40] Conditioning theories offer insights into low-involvement buying (such as in the case of products like detergents, paper towels, and toothpaste). Cognitive theories, on the other hand, relate to high-involvement purchasing (such as in the case of cars, furniture, and clothing), where problem solving involves information search and brand evaluation.

LEARNING AND HEMISPHERIC SPECIALIZATION OF THE BRAIN

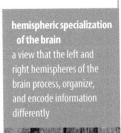

hemispheric specialization of the brain
a view that the left and right hemispheres of the brain process, organize, and encode information differently

During the past forty years or so, researchers have become interested in the topic of hemispheric specialization of the brain. The basic premise of this concept is that the right and left hemispheres of the brain are not identical in their anatomy or function. They process, organize, and encode information differently, and each is capable of functioning in a manner different from that of the other.[41]

The left hemisphere is considered to be a rational-linear part of the brain that specializes in sequential processing, logical and analytical thinking, and verbalization. Expressions of language through speech are exclusively processed in the left hemisphere.[42] The acquisition of new habit patterns is also considered a function of the left hemisphere, which has the ability to analyze the common aspects of a task and formulate logical and meaningful relationships among them. Reading, for example, is considered to be primarily a left hemisphere function.[43] Mathematics, and in particular calculations and algebra, are also postulated to be left hemisphere operations.

The right hemisphere, on the other hand, is capable of multiple processing of incoming stimuli. The interpretation of complex visual patterns is predominantly a right hemisphere function. The right hemisphere is much more effective in the recognition of faces, whereas the left hemisphere remembers the names that go with the faces. The retention of visual patterns, such as geometric designs and graphs, falls in the domain of the right hemisphere.[44] It is also believed that iconic (graphic) memory is primarily a function of the right hemisphere.[45] As a result, iconic presentation of information, in the form of graphic displays, diagrams, and flowcharts, greatly facilitates both comprehension and retention of information.

However, research reveals that for many individuals, the brain's right and left hemispheres do not operate independently of each other, but rather work together to process information. This view of hemispheric specialization suggests that both modes of consciousness and cognitive style complement each other. Whereas the left hemisphere tends to be logical, the right hemisphere tends to be creative. Because information processing requires interhemispheric organization, marketers often attempt to stimulate both hemispheres for maximum effect.

One application of hemispheric specialization lies in the selection of promotional media used by marketers. Because the left hemisphere is involved primarily with language and logic, it is credited with processing the kind of information consumers receive from copy-heavy Internet sites and from the print media. The right hemisphere, which houses spatial perception, holistic understanding, perceptual insight, sensation, artistic talent, and recognition of faces, is credited with processing the kind of information we receive from TV commercials, as well as from highly visual websites.[47]

left hemisphere
the area of the brain that specializes in analytical thinking, verbalization, and algebraic calculations

right hemisphere
the area of the brain that specializes in interpreting and recognizing visual patterns

In the first case, arguments, logic, and cues presented trigger left-brain processing and generate cognitive activity that encourages consumers to evaluate the pros and cons of the product or message.[48] But in the second case of television or highly visual Internet sites, both Hansen and Krugman suggest that the passive processing of images viewed on the screen falls in the domain of the right hemisphere, which deals with the visual and audible components of the commercial, including the creative use of symbols, music, and art.[49] Figure 4.7 from General Electric uses a cute analogy suggesting that the company merges high fashion (right brain) with high tech (left brain) to produce GE Profile appliances.

FIGURE 4.7

This ad from GE Profile addresses the roles of the right brain (high fashion) and left brain (high tech) in promoting its line of technically advanced, fashionably designed GE appliances.

LEARNING IN A SOCIAL CONTEXT: VICARIOUS LEARNING

Skinner, Tolman, Miller and Dollard, Bandura and Walters, and others have demonstrated that learning often occurs within a social context.[50] Consumer learning and behavior is largely social in nature and occurs within a social context.[51] The cultural socialization process and influence of reference groups, opinion leaders, family ties, and significant others are but a few among the many social forces that sway and reinforce consumers' choices and shape their response tendencies.

People often alter their behavior after viewing the behavior of others. Vicarious learning is behavior change that occurs as a result of observing the activity of others, called models, and the consequences of their behavior. An individual who watches others receive rewards for engaging in a behavior learns to imitate their actions. Similarly, someone who sees others receive punishment for their deeds learns to avoid them. For example, highway drivers tend to slow down when they observe a police vehicle with lights flashing that pulls over a speeding auto.

vicarious learning
behavior change due to observing others and the consequences of their actions

Advertisers apply vicarious learning concepts in several ways.[52] To develop a desired behavior, ads depict models (similar to the target audience) that use a sponsor's brand with satisfactory results. This approach suggests that the same rewards—in the form of benefits or compliments from peers—are forthcoming if viewers use the advertised brand. For example, an ad for a diet pill may show before and after photos of a consumer to illustrate the brand's effectiveness. To alter a behavior, ads may depict the mishaps that result from not using the sponsor's brand and suggest that the dire consequences can be avoided with the right product choice. Insurance companies often use testimonials from victimized customers whose polices from these firms spared their families from enduring devastating consequences and losses. To build on responses already learned, ads depict models using familiar products in innovative ways or on occasions other than those with which the items are usually associated. A commercial shows a tennis player, fatigued after a tough game, taking aspirin to relieve aching muscles and finding relief. Although viewers already know that aspirin abates headaches, getting people to perceive aspirin as a muscle pain reliever may create new sales opportunities.

Among the many ways that advertisers employ vicarious learning concepts is getting satisfied customers to offer testimony about the benefits or effectiveness of their brand.

LEARNING CURVES

As we continue to learn, we gain experience in the task being performed. The effect of experience, primarily due to dexterity derived from repetition, is embodied in the adages "Practice makes perfect" and "Experience is the best teacher." A task becomes easier as the number of repetitions increases. This concept is known as the learning curve or experience effect. It has been of great interest to industrial and strategic market planners, who apply it as a cost-reduction measure. Applications extend beyond manufacturing to activities such as sales, marketing, and distribution. The cost (or effort) of performing these tasks also falls appreciably as a consequence of accrued experience.

The same phenomenon holds true for purchasing behavior. Consumers accumulate experience in performing shopping tasks and develop strategies to streamline the process. They develop shopping routines requiring minimal thought, effort, or search and draw from their experiences with various brands. Brand loyalty is partly a manifestation of the learning curve. As they experiment with available brands, consumers adopt effort-reduction strategies to simplify their shopping.

Habit and Brand Loyalty

As a result of learning, we develop consistent patterns of behavior that we engage in repeatedly and without conscious thought. This phenomenon is known as habit. When applied specifically to consumer behavior, habits result from strong drive–response chains, brand–product category associations, and behavior-reward experiences with particular brands within product classes.

Brand loyalty is a consumer's consistent preference for and purchase of a specific brand within a given product category over time. Without information seeking or brand evaluation, brand-loyal consumers *automatically* tend to repurchase the same brand. Their commitment to a brand serves two purposes. In the case of high-involvement purchases with a strong degree of personal importance and relevance such as a car, brand loyalty reduces risk and facilitates selection. On the other hand, in the case of low-involvement purchases with a minor degree of personal importance and relevance such as a candy bar, routine purchasing saves time and effort.

learning curve (experience effect)
the notion that tasks become easier as the number of repetitions increases

brand loyalty
a consumer's consistent purchase of a specific brand within a product category

GLOBAL OPPORTUNITY

No Images of an Ugly American Here

Western images and lifestyles have become highly desirable models emulated by millions of consumers worldwide. Vicarious learning has resulted in a world where similarities seem to exist in its four corners. Our world today is characterized by a youth culture that has taken many of its cues from American pop culture. Kids in Hong Kong, Tokyo, Prague, and New Delhi are watching videos on YouTube, communicating on Facebook, surfing, tweeting, texting, and downloading the latest songs from iTunes. Fast-food restaurants and coffeehouses such as Mc-Donald's, Pizza Hut, and Starbucks have become favorite places where the young like to hang out. Colas and Baskin-Robbins ice cream have become staples in Cairo and Istanbul. American movies, TV soaps, and NFL games, as well as the Oscars and Grammies, have captured the interest of consumers in hundreds of countries.

Beyond goods and artifacts, the largest influence of such a transnational trend lies in the domain of values. Through the Internet and social media, as well as via movies, TV programs, and print media, America is sending its values of upward mobility and individualism to Taipei, Saigon, and Bombay.

There are many benefits as well as problems associated with this trend. Among the benefits, a borderless economy promotes allegiances to products not to countries. More understanding and cooperation between countries emerge as a result of trade. When a New Yorker buys a Mustang from Ford Motor Company, 60 percent of his or her money goes to South Korea, Japan, Germany, Taiwan, Singapore, Britain, and Barbados, as these regions supply parts and components for the automobile. Trade thus replaces war, and goods replace bullets.

On the negative side, however, are countries that are likely to remain separated from this transnational trend. Countries such as Afghanistan, Ethiopia, Rwanda, and some other less-affluent nations in Africa are likely to remain isolated—further widening the gap between the haves and have-nots. Beyond these few nations, however, the rest of the world continues to offer endless opportunities for marketers of many U.S. products and services.[53]

The past few decades have witnessed unparalleled trade cooperation between countries of the world. Visit www.census.gov/foreign-trade/top/index.html to learn which nations are the top trading partners of the United States. How do you explain the fact that so many products today have become "world products," regardless of where they originate? Does this trend mean that in due time, homogeneity may characterize all world cultures?

Marketers today attempt to develop brand loyalty through relationship marketing. *Relationship marketing* is a set of activities that marketers undertake to establish a positive tie with consumers. This bond encourages consumers to reduce their market choices voluntarily by engaging in an ongoing relationship with a marketer of a specific product, service, or brand or from a specific firm. Consumers may purposefully elect to reduce their choice options and maintain a continuing loyalty to a particular firm.[54] Activities such as diligently attending to consumers' needs, providing high-quality customer services, seeking consumer input for purposes of product design, and maintaining open and effective communication with them are among the methods marketers employ to build and solidify lasting trust relationships.[55]

To assess the extent of consumer brand loyalty, researchers no longer rely solely on survey data. In-store scanners and customer ID cards (or *preferred customer cards*) enable marketers to track customers' brand selections over time electronically. For example, to get a better understanding of their customers in real time, mall operators monitor shoppers' behavior with devices that track mobile phone signals. The goal is to ascertain how consumers roam about, which stores they visit, how long they pause in front of displays, and which products they pick up.

Brand loyalty is measured in terms of a subject's sequence or proportion of purchases within a product category. Some studies consider consumers to be *brand loyal* if they buy a given brand a specified number of times (typically three to five) in a row. In other studies, consumers are deemed *brand loyal* if a given brand constitutes a specified percentage of all purchases (typically 75 to 80 percent) in some product category within a stated period of time, such as three months.

Why Do Consumers Develop Brand Loyalties?

inertia
a pattern of repeatedly
buying a particular brand
merely because it is familiar

Some consumers repeatedly buy the same brand merely because it is familiar and doing so saves time and energy. They have no strong feelings about it one way or the other. This tendency is referred to as inertia and differs from genuine brand loyalty in that the former represents a case of low involvement. Such brand-purchase routines suggest arbitrary acceptance of a brand without any degree of commitment to it. Competitors who attempt to change consumer buying patterns based on inertia can often do so easily because they encounter little resistance to brand switching. In many but not all product categories, shoppers who find their usual brand to be temporarily out of stock or who come across price reductions, coupons, or point-of-purchase displays for competitive brands, are apt to switch.

In the case of true brand loyalty, on the other hand, repeat purchasing of a brand reflects high involvement and a conscious decision on the part of consumers to continue buying the same brand.[56] The pattern of repetitive behavior results from underlying positive attitudes toward the brand that are due to brand attributes, experience with the brand, or emotional attachment (such as congruence with a consumer's self-perception or associations with prior events).[57] *True-blue* buyers are not open to change and may rebel when their preferred brands are altered, redesigned, or eliminated.[58]

Why Do Consumers Switch Brands?

Consumers may switch brands for any number of reasons. Among these reasons are factors such as dissatisfaction with their current brand, recommendations from others, cues in the marketplace like price offers, or simply a desire to try something different and new. In our society, where almost all products face stiff and relentless competition, every brand category becomes subject to commoditization. That is, the differentiating benefit of one brand over other competing brands tends to diminish or disappear. Some consumers have come to believe that no significant differences exist among brands. This notion, known as brand parity, is reflected in a survey showing that worldwide, consumers who use products such as beer, cigarettes, paper towels, soaps, and snack chips believe all brands are more or less similar.[59] Interestingly, the same study found brand loyalty to be highest for cigarette purchases.

brand parity
a situation where many consumers come to believe that no significant differences exist among brands

What happens after once-loyal consumers switch from their regular brands? Four purchasing-behavior patterns have been identified.[60] The first of these is *reversion*, in which consumers switch back to their original brand. A second possible pattern is *conversion*, wherein consumers remain loyal to the new brand. A third possibility is *vacillation* or random switching between the new and old brands. The fourth pattern is *experimentation*, in which consumers engage in further systematic trial of other brands. A study by Mazursky, LaBarbera, and Aiello measured consumer response to various incentives to switch brands.[61] There was a difference in behavior depending on whether brand switching was induced by extrinsic incentives (price, coupon) or intrinsic ones (desire to try a new brand). Unlike intrinsic motives, extrinsic incentives motivate consumers to switch despite a high level of satisfaction with the last-purchased brand. Such switching behavior results in weaker intentions to repurchase the new brand.

MEMORY AND RETENTION

Maximizing consumer learning and curtailing their tendency to forget are primary objectives of marketers. Information storage and retrieval processes are therefore of particular concern to advertisers, who hope the campaigns they design will make lasting impressions on their audience. Consider what happens when you look up a telephone number in a phone directory or online. Your eyes selectively focus on the required information among an array of listings. An afterimage remains for a few moments—just long enough for you to dial the number. Unless you mentally rehearse the number or dial it frequently, however, you probably quickly forget it. In the process of seeking information, we all receive these kinds of stimuli and acquire much more than we need. Some of this data we remember, but the rest is forgotten.

In an effort to minimize forgetting, retention aids known as mnemonic devices have been developed to help people's retention processes. Mnemonic devices, which can be auditory or visual, promote retention of material by organizing it efficiently or identifying it with easily remembered symbols.[62] Advertisers frequently use music, rhyme, and rhythm to enhance memorability. Slogans and jingles, such as Ace Hardware's "Ace is the place with the helpful hardware man," is a case in point.

Marketers frequently provide word associations for telephone numbers. For example, a carpet retailer may pay a premium rate for the number corresponding to C-A-R-P-E-T-S or 1-800-M-A-T-T-R-E-S. Other commercials cheerfully sing sponsors' phone numbers to make them memorable. Trademarks such as Nike's swoosh and McDonald's Golden Arches, as well as trade characters such as the Snuggles bear and the Michelin tire man, use visible reflections of product attributes or benefits to enhance learning.

With the ever-expanding role of the Internet and social media in our life, the availability of search engines has reconfigured the way our brains process and retain information. A recent study by Dr. Betsy Sparrow, from Columbia University, together with her colleagues investigated the issue of whether or not our reliance on search engines makes it harder for us to recall information. The researchers tested how we retain information when it is stored somewhere that is easily accessible to us, such as online. Today, search engines—such as Google and Bing, where just about any piece of information can be retrieved in a matter of seconds—are being used by most of us as a personal memory bank or external hard drive for storing needed information. This phenomenon is known as the Google effect.

mnemonic devices
auditory or visual aids that promote retention of material by identifying it with easily remembered symbols

Google effect
information available online is less likely to be remembered than web-scarce information

The evidence, based on a series of four experiments, revealed that we are more likely to search for the information online. When the information is easy to find, we are more apt to remember where we found it rather than remember the information itself. Conversely, when the information is less accessible online, we tend to easily remember the information itself.

The Structure of Memory

Human memory is a complex mechanism. When information first enters our brain, it is directed through an area known as the hippocampus, which sorts it and directs it to other parts of the brain based on the information's importance or relevance. Memory consists of three storage systems: sensory memory, short-term memory, and long-term memory.[63] In sensory memory, incoming data undergo preliminary processing largely based on the physical qualities of a perceived object, such as its size, color, and volume. The instantaneous processing of visual and auditory data are referred to as iconic and echoic processing, respectively.[64]

After sensory processing, data input promptly passes into short-term memory (STM), called the *workbench* for information-processing operations. In STM, we categorize, process, and hold information for a brief period. If the information is significant to us, it may undergo a process known as rehearsal. Rehearsal is silent, mental repetition of the data and linkage of it to other information. Rehearsed data become transferred to long-term memory within two to ten seconds. Without rehearsal, we lose data inputs in thirty seconds or less.[65] STM's capacity to contain data is restricted to as few as four or five and perhaps up to seven items at a time.[66] Sometimes too much data competes simultaneously for our attention. This situation, called *information overload*, can reduce STM's capacity to only two or three bits of data. Much information may be lost. Knowledgeable advertisers, as a result, attempt to keep their messages simple and uncluttered without too much information.

Rehearsal keeps information in STM long enough to be encoded. Encoding is a process through which we select words or visual images to represent a perceived object. Trade characters and suggestive brand names such as Mr. Clean, Green Giant, and Endust are symbols provided by marketers to facilitate the encoding processes.

Both visual and verbal data are important in forming an overall mental image to encode. It requires less time to learn visual than verbal information, as we saw in the section on hemispheric specialization of the brain.

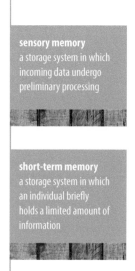

sensory memory
a storage system in which incoming data undergo preliminary processing

short-term memory
a storage system in which an individual briefly holds a limited amount of information

encoding
the process of employing symbols such as words or images to store a perceived idea

A print ad containing verbal information that is accompanied by an illustration is more likely to be encoded than verbal cues alone.

Long-term memory (LTM) is an information warehouse. Unlike STM, where information is held only momentarily, LTM retains information for a relatively longer span of time. Anderson, in what is known as the associative network model—a generally accepted representation of LTM—asserts that LTM can be represented as a network of nodes and connecting links, where nodes represent stored information or concepts, and links represent the strength of association between nodes.[67] For instance, consider the case of a consumer who ponders the purchase of an iPhone 7. She already owns a cell phone and is familiar with most of its functions. She feels its performance is satisfactory for use at home, as well as on her job as a sales rep. Her intrigue with the new iPhone 7 is strongly linked to its unique features, which make the functions of calling, text messaging, web browsing, checking email, navigation, playing music, taking photos, as well as watching movies and videos so much easier. She strongly dislikes the fact that her present phone lacks the majority of these features, which today any professional needs. Unlike her present cell phone, she is thrilled that the new phone allows her to download apps to support her professional and leisure activities as well as reduce her dependency on a desktop computer at home. Availability of future upgrades makes the phone even more enticing to her.

In LTM, information is organized and stored under cues or headings. If appropriate cues are present and if the setting and manner in which we process the information are suitable, then recall is simple.[68] If, however, appropriate or effective cues are absent, material cannot be recalled.[69] The more cues we use to store a piece of information in memory, the easier it is to retrieve it later on. For example, cues under which we may store aspirin in memory include usage occasions such as headaches and fever, brand names such as Bayer, and ad-photos of persons suffering from a cold or muscle pain.

Information stored in LTM is not passive. That is to say, we actively use knowledge structures, or arrangements of related bits of information, to store and organize information about products, brands, and retailers in memory. The way we interpret and respond to incoming messages depends on how the information fits into our knowledge structures. If new information coincides with stored information, the communication is more effective. On the other hand, if new information contradicts our stored information, we may become confused, and the incoming message will be less effective. Knowledge structures consist of more than just product types and brand names. They include our personal experiences as well as information we acquire from such sources as the media, salespeople, colleagues, friends, and family.

New information we gain also affects the structure of stored information. Information housed in LTM constantly goes through a process of reorganization, and new links between information chunks are always being formed. This process links fresh material to information already in storage in order to make new data inputs more meaningful. Impressive innovations in today's automobile models, such as using hydrogen and oxygen as fuel, have truly impacted consumers' decision process for purchasing a new car.

© Zavatskiy Aleksandr/Shutterstock.com

FIGURE 4.8

Innovations in new automotive models, particularly those relating to fuel, have impact our decision process for buying a new car.

INFORMATION RETRIEVAL

When we sift through our LTM to find the specific information we need, we engage in information retrieval. Information retrieval is the process of activating previously stored information from LTM. Contemplate a situation where a mother, on the occasion of her young daughter's birthday, decided to take her to a toy store in order to purchase a gift. As the two of them walked down an aisle in the doll section of the store, the daughter's attention was attracted by a popular doll, with which she immediately fell in love. In wanting to honor her daughter's request to buy the doll, the mother picked up the doll to examine it, only to recognize the brand name of the doll as one that had been reported in the media a few weeks earlier as the target of a possible recall due to the toxicity of the doll's materials. The mother's memory of this negative news—stored in her LTM—about the brand prompted her to direct the daughter's attention away from that doll and toward other possible alternatives. The doll's brand name served as a retrieval cue, which jogged the mother's memory of the product recall story.

Researchers, moreover, distinguish between information *availability* and *accessibility* in connection with information retrieval.[72] Even though information has been processed and stored in LTM, individuals are capable of retrieving only a small fraction of it.[73] Thus, availability of information in memory is a necessary but insufficient condition for its retrieval and subsequent use. Factors that influence information accessibility for retrieval purposes include (1) related learned information (in this case, that might be stored knowledge about toy recalls), (2) self- or externally generated retrieval cues (such as the doll's brand name), and (3) various encoding factors (family memories). When the retrieval procedure fails, it is an indication that extinction or forgetting has occurred.

EXTINCTION AND FORGETTING

Extinction and forgetting are opposites of learning. Both involve loss of responses, skills, or cognitive material that once was learned and entered into memory. Better initial learning, of course, reduces subsequent loss. For this reason, marketers spend generously on intensive advertising campaigns over many media types during the introductory stage of the product life cycle. Social media and television are particularly effective for such undertakings because they accommodate visual and auditory images that correlate and reinforce one another.

As we saw in the section on conditioning, *extinction* is one type of learning loss. A break in the link between behavior and expected reward leads to a rapid decline in the probability that a response will be repeated. Once a brand no longer satisfies consumers, the likelihood that they will repurchase it decreases dramatically. Eventually, they may stop buying it altogether. In the absence of reinforcement, behavior ceases to recur, and extinction ensues.

Forgetting also involves learning loss. When we forget, material that was once part of our conscious mind recedes into the mind's unconscious recesses and is no longer available for voluntary recall. Forgetting occurs when a stimulus is no longer repeated or perceived. Cessation of brand use or discontinuation of brand promotion can cause forgetting. For example, Ingersoll, which was once a popular brand of watch, is hardly remembered today.

Confusion makes learning more difficult and increases the likelihood of forgetting. Ad clutter and competitive advertising often interfere with message reception and cause confusion in a consumer's mind. A consumer exposed to a multitude of TV commercials promoting different brands of detergents, each having numerous features, can easily become confused. This, in turn, weakens the stimulus–reward connection.

Advertisers combat forgetting with media schedules that maintain a target level of advertising repetitions. Some messages, called *reminder* ads, are specifically designed to echo and reinforce earlier promotional efforts.

Mere reiteration of the same messages, however, is likely to irritate an audience. One of the best methods to help people form a concept is to demonstrate it in myriad diverse specific circumstances. Advertisers, therefore, create campaigns consisting of several ads or commercials, each of which echoes the same theme but presents it in a different setting. For example, separate ads for an all-purpose household cleaner might depict diverse applications ranging from washing kitchen floors and family room walls to disinfecting bathroom bowls.

Forgetting occurs very rapidly in the period immediately after learning. It then slows down as time passes.[74] No evidence supports the notion that mere passage of time causes forgetting. Rather, forgetting results from the active process of acquiring new responses that replace and interfere with earlier remembered patterns. Two obstacles hinder retention processes, retroactive and proactive interference.

In retroactive interference, recent learning interferes with our recollection of previously learned material. For example, on viewing two ads in succession, both for competitive brands, we may find our memory of the second ad interferes with recall of the first. For example, in viewing two successive shoe ads from Adidas and Nike, the resulting interference caused by the second ad would most likely affect consumers' memory of the first ad. This tendency is due to the functional similarity of the advertised products and the likeness of the two messages.

One type of retroactive interference, known as the misinformation effect, occurs when misleading details are suggested to a person after witnessing an event.[75] If an eyewitness to an incident is subsequently exposed to false details about it, the misinformation can impair the person's recollection of what really occurred and cause errors in his or her account of the event. The person may even come to believe the phony details if he or she has forgotten their source. This type of influence has often been applied by rival candidates during political campaigns. It usually takes the form of negative ads that provide false or misleading information about the other candidate's personality, views, or activities.

In proactive interference, prior learning interferes with recall of recently learned material. For example, in the breakfast cereal industry, familiarity with an established brand, such as Kellogg's, may overshadow a more recent and lesser known brand such as Nature Valley. The processes of retroactive and proactive interference are illustrated in Exhibit 4.4.

Message Interference and Likelihood of Recall

Forgetting that results from retroactive and proactive interference has important implications for marketers. Because we are exposed to such a large number of promotional messages daily, there exists significant potential for message interference. Confusion grows in proportion to the extent that competing ads push products from the same category or claim similar features and benefits.

Recent research findings indicate that interference effects occur only for unfamiliar brands.[76] Information about both familiar and unfamiliar competing brands was shown to have no effect on the recall of familiar brands.

retroactive interference
a case where recent learning interferes with recall of previously learned material

misinformation effect
a case where false assertions taint a person's recall of what *really* occurred

proactive interference
a case where prior learning interferes with recall of recently learned material

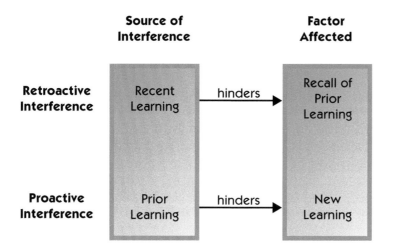

	Source of Interference		Factor Affected
Retroactive Interference	Recent Learning	hinders →	Recall of Prior Learning
Proactive Interference	Prior Learning	hinders →	New Learning

EXHIBIT 4.4

The Dynamics of Retroactive and Proactive Interference

Other recent research has found that a unique item in a series of relatively homogeneous items tends to be recalled easily, because the effects of retroactive and proactive interference are minimized in this situation.[77] A case in point is Geico, an auto insurance company that writes private passenger automobile insurance policies in all fifty states. Geico employs a direct-to-consumer sales model in its TV commercials, with several campaigns running simultaneously in national markets. The firm's mascot is a gold dust day gecko that speaks with a Cockney accent. Geico is well known in popular culture for its advertising, having made and aired a large number of commercials intended to amuse viewers.[78]

Learning is a major determinant of human behavior. Consumers are not born with brand preferences; they learn them over time by being exposed to advertising, interacting with significant others, as well as their own experience with products. Learning is critical to marketers, who are charged with the challenging task of getting consumers to learn about their brands, often amidst clutter initiated by competitive messages. In this sense, the marketer is a teacher aiming to facilitate learning through advertising, personal selling, or even through instructional manuals that accompany products.

Our perceptual processes are integral companions to the learning process. That is to say, learning does not occur in a vacuum. New data—once perceived—are cast against knowledge and experiences already in memory, causing the individual to form feelings or attitudes toward the incoming information. The next chapter addresses the topic of attitudes—how they form, how they can be strengthened, and how they change.

SUMMARY

The three major schools of learning theories are (1) classical conditioning, (2) operant conditioning, and (3) cognitive learning. Under classical conditioning, it is assumed that learning occurs as the result of connections formed between a conditioned stimulus and an unconditioned stimulus. The major learning principles include repetition, contiguity, contingency, and congruity.

Operant conditioning theory posits that learning occurs via trial and error, as consumers discover that certain behaviors produce more desirable outcomes. Marketers face the challenge of getting a desired behavior to occur so it can be rewarded. In this regard, behavior shaping and ecological design can prove to be helpful.

Cognitive learning emphasizes goal orientation, problem solving, and information-processing capabilities of consumers, who continually alter their response tendencies to adjust to varying circumstances.

Renewed interest in classical conditioning, interpreted in a neo-Pavlovian sense, has reshaped traditional classical conditioning into a fully cognitive theory.

Whereas the left hemisphere of the brain is considered to be the rational-linear part, the right hemisphere specializes in iconic types of information, such as diagrams, graphs, faces, and names. Knowledge about the brain may be useful to marketers when determining which types of media are appropriate for their promotions.

Vicarious learning occurs as a result of observing the behavior of others and the consequences of their behavior.

When people repeatedly perform a task, it becomes easier as they accumulate experience. This principle is known as the learning curve or experience effect. The learning curve phenomenon is exhibited when individuals develop consistent patterns in which they engage repeatedly and without thought. Such patterns are called habits. Habit is manifested in consumer behavior as buyers develop shopping routines and brand loyalties.

Memory consists of three storage systems: sensory, short-term, and long-term memory. Retrieval is the process of activating previously stored information from LTM. Both information availability and accessibility have a bearing on a person's ability to retrieve stored information. When the retrieval process fails, it is an indication that extinction or forgetting has occurred. Retroactive interference (perhaps due to the misinformation effect) and proactive interference can hamper a person's recall of information.

CASE SYNOPSIS

The Attractiveness of Lottery Tickets

The widely publicized January 2016 Powerball Lottery Drawing created the largest jackpot in the history of the world, totaling over $1.5 billion. As images and stories that accompanied this major event were covered in almost all media types, questions arose in the mind of many people as to the motives that lead others to go through the trouble of purchasing these tickets knowing the odds of winning are a mere 1 in 292 million. A number of academicians who were attending a business conference in a large metropolitan city held a discussion of the underlying psychological drives that compel individuals to purchase the tickets. A debate between conference attendees revealed a number of learning-related concepts that appear to explain why people participate in lotteries, such as reinforcement, loyalty and habit, heuristics, framing, the effects of prior memories, recouping prior losses, an addiction to gambling, and even a sense of unrealistic optimism.

Notes

1   Lindsay Kolowich, "7 Customer Loyalty Programs That Actually Add Value," *hubspot,* http://blog.hubspot.com/blog/tabid/6307/bid/31990/7-Customer-Loyalty-Programs-That-Actually-Add-Value.aspx; Ran Kivetz and Itamar Simonson, "The Idiosyncratic Fit Heuristic: Effort Advantage as a Determinant of Consumer Response to Loyalty Programs," *Journal of Marketing Research* 40, no. 4 (November 2003); Based on Shari Caudron, "Brand Loyalty: Can It Be Revived?" *Industry Week* (April 5, 1993), pp. 11–12, 14; "Credit Card Rewards Programs," *Creditor Web,* www.creditorweb.com/articles/credit-card-rewardsprograms.html; Hershey's Foods website, www.thehersheycompany.com/news/release.asp?releaseID=398319; Stephanie Clifford, "Linking Customer Loyalty with Social Networking," *The New York Times* (April 28, 2010), http://www.nytimes.com/2010/04/29/business/media/29adco.html?pagewanted=print.

2   A. A. Mitchell, "Cognitive Processes Initiated by Exposure to Advertising," in R. Harris (Ed.), *Information Processing Research in Advertising* (New York: Lawrence Erlbaum, 1983), pp. 13–42; M. L. Rothschild and W. C. Gaidis, "Behavioral Learning Theory: Its Relevance to Marketing and Promotions," *Journal of Marketing* (Spring 1981), pp. 70–78; J. P. Peter and W. R. Nord, "A Clarification and Extension of Operant Conditioning Principles in Marketing," *Journal of Marketing* (Summer 1982), pp. 102–107.

3   Morris B. Holbrook, "Nostalgia and Consumption Preferences: Some Emerging Patterns of Consumer Tastes," *Journal of Consumer Research* 20 (September 1993), pp. 245–256; Robert M. Schindler and Morris B. Holbrook, "Critical Periods in the Development of Men's and Women's Tastes in Personal Appearance," *Psychology & Marketing* 10, no. 6 (November–December 1993), pp. 549–564; Morris B. Holbrook and Robert M. Schindler, "Age, Sex, and Attitude Toward the Past as Predictors of Consumers' Aesthetic Tastes for Cultural Products," *Journal of Marketing Research* 31 (August 1994), pp. 412–422; Morris B. Holbrook and Robert M. Schindler, "Some Exploratory Findings on the Development of Musical Tastes," *Journal of Consumer Research* 16 (June 1989), pp. 119–124; Randall Rothenberg, "The Past Is Now the Latest Craze," *New York Times* (November 29, 1989), p. D1.

4   C. Huffman and M. J. Houston, "Goal-Oriented Experiences and the Development of Knowledge," *Journal of Consumer Research* (September 1993), pp. 190–207; S. A. Hawkins and S. J. Hoch, "Low-Involvement Learning," *Journal of Consumer Research* (September 1992), pp. 212–225; N. M. Alperstein, "The Verbal Content of TV Advertising and Its Circulation in Everyday Life," *Journal of Advertising* 2 (1990), pp. 15–22; D. D. Muehling, R. N. Laczniak, and J. C. Andrews, "Defining, Operationalizing, and Using Involvement in Advertising Research," *Journal of Current Issues and Research in Advertising* (Spring 1993), pp. 22–57; T. B. C. Poiesz and C. J. P. M. deBont, "Do We Need Involvement to Understand Consumer Behavior?" in F. R. Kardes and M. Sujan (Eds.), *Advances in Consumer Research* (Provo, UT: Association for Consumer Research, 1995), pp. 448–452.

5   Gordon H. Bower and Ernest R. Hilgard, *Theories of Learning,* 5th ed. (Upper Saddle River, NJ: Prentice Hall, 1981).

6   Ivan P. Pavlov, *Conditioned Reflexes: An Investigation of the Physiological Activity of the Cerebral Cortex,* G. V. Anrep (Trans., Ed.) (London: Oxford University Press, 1927); Peter C. Holland, "Origins of Behavior in Pavlovian Conditioning," in G. H. Bower (Ed.), *The Psychology of Learning and Motivation* 18 (Orlando, FL: Harcourt Brace Jovanovich, 1984), pp. 129–174; Kenneth Hugdahl, "Pavlovian Conditioning and Hemispheric Asymmetry: A Perspective," in G. Davey (Ed.), *Cognitive Processes and Pavlovian Conditioning in Humans* (Chichester, England: John Wiley, 1987), pp. 147–182; Walter R. Nord and J. Paul Peter, "A Behavior Modification Perspective on Marketing," *Journal of Marketing* (Spring 1980), pp. 36–47; Terence A. Shimp, "The Role of Subject Awareness in Classical Conditioning: A Case of Opposing Ontologies and Conflicting Evidence," in Rebecca Holman and Michael

Solomon (Eds.), *Advances in Consumer Research*, 18 (Provo, UT: Association for Consumer Research,1991), pp. 158–163; Elnora W. Stuart, Terence A. Shimp, and Randall W. Engle, "Classical Conditioning of Consumer Attitudes: Four Experiments in an Advertising Context," *Journal of Consumer Research* 14 (December 1987), pp. 334–349; Terence A. Shimp, Elnora W. Stuart, and Randall W. Engle, "A Program of Classical Conditioning Experiments Testing Variations in the Conditioned Stimulus and Context," *Journal of Consumer Research* 18, no. 1 (June 1991), pp. 1–12; Chris T. Allen and Thomas J. Madden, "A Closer Look at Classical Conditioning," *Journal of Consumer Research* 12 (December 1985), pp. 301–315; Lynn Kahle, Sharon Beatty, and Patricia Kennedy, "Comment on Classically Conditioning Human Consumers," in Melanie Wallendorf and Paul Anderson (Eds.), *Advances in Consumer Research* 14 (Provo, UT: Association for Consumer Research, 1987), pp. 411–413; Francis K. McSweeney and Calvin Bierley, "Recent Developments in Classical Conditioning," *Journal of Consumer Research* 11 (September 1984), pp. 619–631; Calvin Bierley, Francis K. McSweeney, and Renee Vannieuwkerk, "Classical Conditioning of Preference for Stimuli," *Journal of Consumer Research* 12 (December 1985), pp. 316–323; Terence A. Shimp, "Neo-Pavlovian Conditioning and Its Implications for Consumer Theory and Research," in Thomas S. Robertson and Harold K. Kassarjian (Eds.), *Handbook for Consumer Behavior* (Upper Saddle River, NJ: Prentice Hall, 1991), pp. 162–187; W. Jake Jacobs and James R. Blackburn, "A Model of Pavlovian Conditioning: Variations in Representations of the Unconditioned Stimulus," *Integrated Physiological and Behavioral Science* 30 (January 1, 1995), pp. 12–33; Arjun Chaudhuri and Ross Buck, "Media Differences in Rational and Emotional Responses to Advertising," *Journal of Broadcasting & Electronic Media* 39 (January 1, 1995), pp. 109–125; B. F. Skinner, "Some Responses to the Stimulus 'Pavlov,'" *Integrative Physiological & Behavioral Science* 31 (July 1, 1996), pp. 254–257.

7   Herbert E. Krugman, "Observations: Pavlov's Dog and the Future of Consumer Psychology," *Journal of Advertising Research* (November–December 1994), pp. 67–70.

8   Richard E. Petty and John T. Cacioppo, *Attitudes and Persuasion: Classic and Contemporary Approaches* (Dubuque, IA: Wm. C. Brown, 1981).

9   Bennett B. Murdock Jr., "The Contributions of Hermann Ebbinhaus," *Journal of Experiential Psychology: Learning, Memory, and Cognition* 11, no. 3 (1985), pp. 469–471.

10   Gerald J. Gorn, "The Effects of Music in Advertising on Choice Behavior: A Classical Conditioning Approach," *Journal of Marketing* 46 (Winter 1982), pp. 94–101; Chris T. Allen and Thomas J. Madden, "A Closer Look at Classical Conditioning," *Journal of Consumer Research* 12 (December 1985), pp. 301–315.

11   Cause Marketing Forum, *http://www.causemarketingforum.com/site/c.bkLUKcOTLkK4E/d.9351101/k.33C5/2016_Halo_Awards.htm*; Howard Schlossberg, "For a Good Cause," Promo 8, no. 3 (February 1994), pp.

38–50; John Graham, "Corporate Charity," *Incentive* (July 1994), pp. 51–52; Geoffrey Smith and Ron Stodghill, "Are Good Causes Good Marketing," *Business Week* (March 21, 1994), p. 64; "Cause-Related Fraud on the Rise," *Incentive* (August 1994), p. 8; Udayan Gupta, "Cause-Driven Companies' New Cause: Profits," *Wall Street Journal* (November 8, 1994), p. B1; Mary Rowand, "Shoppers Turn to Web for Holiday Wish Lists," *AMA* (November 15, 2007); "Think Before You Pink" (November 2007), www.thinkbeforeyoupink.org/Pages/InfoMktgCampaigns.html; Cone Communications, "Cone Report Benchmark Survey," www. msen.mb.ca/crm.html.

12 "The Effect of Music in a Retail Setting," University of Washington, www. faculty.bschool.washington.edu/ ryolch/Research/atmosphe.htm.

13 "Music Motivates Impulse Buyers, Not Thoughtful Shoppers," *Monitor on Psychology* 36, no. 10 (November 2005), www.apa.org/monitor/nov05/ music.html.

14 Shimp, "Neo-Pavlovian Conditioning and Its Implications for Consumer Theory and Research."

15 Ibid.

16 Robert A. Rescorla, "Pavlovian Conditioning: It's Not What You Think It Is," *American Psychologist* 43 (March 1988), pp. 151–160.

17 Shimp, "Neo-Pavlovian Conditioning and Its Implications for Consumer Theory and Research."

18 Chris Janiszewski et. al., "A Meta-Analysis of Spacing Effect in Verbal Learning: Implications for Research on Advertising Repetition and Consumer Memory," *Journal of Consumer Research* 30, no. 1 (June 2003), pp. 138–150.

19 G. David Hughes, "Realtime Response Measures Redefine Advertising Wearout," *Journal of Advertising Research* (May/June 1992), pp. 61–77.

20 Rebecca Gardyn and John Fetto, "Where's the Lovin?" *American Demographics* 23, no. 2 (February 2001), pp. 10–11.

21 John Kim, Chris T. Allen, and Frank R. Kardes, "An Investigation of the Mediational Mechanisms Underlying Attitudinal Conditioning," *Journal of Marketing Research* XXXIII (August 1996), pp. 318–328.

22 Robert A. Rescorla, "Pavlovian Conditioning and Its Proper Control Procedures," *Psychological Review* 74 (1967), pp. 70–71.

23 J. Meyers-Levy and A. M. Tybout, "Schema Congruity as a Basis for Product Evaluation," *Journal of Consumer Research* 16 (1989), pp. 38–54; T. K. Srull, M. Lichenstein, and M. Rothbart, "Associative Storage and Retrieval Processes in Person Memory," *Journal of Experimental Psychology: Learning, Memory, and Cognition* 11 (1985), pp. 316–345; James J. Kellaris and Susan Powell Mantel, "Shaping Time Perceptions with Background Music: The Effect of Congruity and Arousal on Estimates of Ad Durations," *Psychology & Marketing* 13, no. 5 (August 1996), pp. 501–515.

24 J. Charles Jones, *Learning* (New York: Harcourt Brace Jovanovich, 1967), pp. 28–29.

25 B. F. Skinner, *The Behavior of Organisms: An Experimental Analysis* (New York: Apple-Century-Crofts, 1938); Gordon R. Foxall, "Behavior Analysis

and Consumer Psychology," *Journal of Economic Psychology* 15 (March 1994), pp. 5–91; Blaise J. Biergiel and Christine Trosclair, "Instrumental Learning: Its Application to Customer Satisfaction," *Journal of Consumer Marketing* 2 (Fall 1985), pp. 23–28; Gordon R. Foxall, "The Behavioral Perspective Model of Purchase and Consumption: From Consumer Theory to Marketing Practice," *Journal of the Academy of Marketing Sciences* 20 (Spring 1992), pp. 189–198; Walter R. Nord and J. Paul Peter, "A Behavior Modification Perspective on Marketing," *Journal of Marketing* (Spring 1980), pp. 36–47; J. Paul Peter and Walter R. Nord, "A Clarification and Extension of Operant Conditioning Principles in Marketing," *Journal of Marketing* 46 (Summer 1982), pp. 102–107; Skinner, "Some Responses to the Stimulus 'Pavlov.'"

26 Dee Ann Glamser, "Mozart Plays to Empty Lot," *USA Today* (August 24, 1990), p. 3A; Mark S. Rosenbaum and Detra Montoya, "Exploring the Role of Ethnicity in Place Avoidance and Approach Decisions," *Journal of Business Research* 60, no. 3 (2007), pp. 206–214; Mark S. Rosenbaum, "Meet the Cyberscape," *Marketing Intelligence and Planning* 23, no. 7 (2005), pp. 636–647; Mark S. Rosenbaum, "The Symbolic Servicescape: Your Kind Is Welcomed Here," *Journal of Consumer Behaviour* 4 (2005), pp. 257–267; M. S. Rosenbaum and D. Y. Montoya, "Am I Welcome Here? Exploring How Ethnic Consumers Assess Their Place Identity," *Journal of Business Research* 60, no. 3 (2007), pp. 206–214.

27 Laura A. Peracchio, "How Do Young Children Learn to Be Consumers? A Script-Processing Approach," *Journal of Consumer Research* 18 (March 1992), pp. 425–440; Laura A. Peracchio, "Young Children's Processing of a Televised Narrative: Is a Picture Really Worth a Thousand Words?" *Journal of Consumer Research* 20 (September 1993), pp. 281–293; Carole Macklin, "The Effects of an Advertising Retrieval Cue on Young Children's Memory and Brand Evaluations," *Psychology & Marketing* 11 (May–June 1994), pp. 291–311; Jean Piaget, "The Child and Modern Physics," *Scientific American* 196 (1957), pp. 46–51.

28 Stephen J. Hoch and John Deighton, "Managing What Consumers Learn from Experience," *Journal of Marketing* 53 (April 1989), pp. 1–20.

29 Wolfgang Kohler, *The Mentality of Apes* (New York: Harcourt Brace & World, 1925).

30 Jennifer G. Paxton and Deborah R. John, "Consumer Learning by Analogy: A Model of Internal Knowledge Transfer," *Journal of Consumer Research* 24 (December 1997), pp. 266–284.

31 Chris Halt, "15 Ways Google Changed the World," *Daily Dot Tech* (September 4, 2013), http://www.dailydot.com/technology/google-15-anniversary-search-maps/; Susie Poppick, "10 Ways Google Has Changed the World," *Time* (August 18, 2014), http://time.com/money/3117377/google-10-ways-changed-world/; "Google (Alphabet) Knocking Down More Barriers to Knowledge," *Fortune* (June 1, 2015), p. 62; Lev Grossman, "What's This All About?" *Time* (July 6-13, 2015), pp. 42–44.

32 Mark Fitzgerald and Jennifer Saba, "Special Report: Outlook for Campaign Ad Revenue 2008," *Editor and Publisher* (December 18, 2007).

33 William D. Crano and Radmila Prislin, "Attitudes and Persuasion," *Annual Review of Psychology* 57 (January 2006), pp. 345–374.

34 Geoffrey Cowley, "The Wisdom of Animals," *Newsweek* (May 23, 1988), pp. 52–59.

35 Shimp, "Neo-Pavlovian Conditioning and Its Implications for Consumer Theory and Research"; Shimp, "The Role of Subject Awareness in Classical Conditioning: A Case of Opposing Ontologies and Conflicting Evidence."

36 Shimp, "Neo-Pavlovian Conditioning and Its Implications for Consumer Theory and Research."

37 Ibid.

38 Rom J. Markin Jr., *Consumer Behavior, A Cognitive Orientation* (New York: Macmillan, 1974), p. 239.

39 E. R. Hilgard and R. C. Atkinson, *Introduction to Psychology* (New York: Harcourt Brace Jovanovich, 1967), p. 306.

40 I. L. Sonnier, *Hemisphericity as a Key to Understanding Individual Differences* (Springfield, IL: Thomas Publications, 1992), p. 7.

41 C. W. Burklund and A. Smith, "Language and Cerebral Hemispheres," *Neurology* 27 (1977), pp. 627–633; B. Samples, "Education for Both Sides of the Human Mind," *The Science Teacher* 42, no. 1 (1975), pp. 21–23.

42 M. Hunter, "Right-Brained Kids in Left-Brained Schools," *Today's Education* (November–December 1976), pp. 45–48.

43 D. Hines, "Independent Functioning of the Two Cerebral Hemispheres for Recognizing Bilaterally Presented Tachistoscopic Visual Half-Field Stimuli," *Cortex* 11 (1975), pp. 132–143.

44 C. W. Taylor, "Developing Effective Functioning People: The Accountable Goal of Multiple Talent Teaching," *Education* 94 (1973), pp. 99–110; E. P. Torrance, "Emergence of Identity Through Expressive Activities," *Elementary English* (1973), pp. 849–852.

45 S. Weinstein, V. Appel, and C. Weinstein, "Brain Activity Responses to Magazine and Television Advertising," *Journal of Advertising Research* 20, no. 3 (June 1980).

46 M. B. Holbrook and W. L. Moore, "Feature Actions in Consumer Judgments of Verbal vs. Pictorial Presentations," *Journal of Consumer Research* 8 (June 1981), pp. 103–113.

47 Flemming Hansen, "Hemispheral Lateralization: Implications for Understanding Consumer Behavior," *Journal of Consumer Research* 8 (June 1981), pp. 23–36; Herbert E. Krugman, "The Impact of Television Advertising: Learning without Involvement," *The Public Opinion Quarterly* 29 (1965), pp. 349–56; Herbert E. Krugman, "Memory without Recall, Exposure without Recognition," *Journal of Advertising Research* 17 (1977), pp. 7–12; Herbert E. Krugman, "Sustained Viewing of Television," paper presented at the Conference Board, Council on Marketing Research, New York (1980).

48 B. F. Skinner, *Science and Human Behavior* (New York: Macmillan,1953); Edward Chance Tolman, *Purposive Behavior in Animals and Men* (New York: Appleton-Century-Crofts, 1932); N. E. Miller and J. Dollard, *Social Learning and Imitation* (New Haven, CT: Yale University Press, 1941); A. Bandura, "Social Learning Through Imitation," in M. R. Jones (Ed.), *Nebraska Symposium on Motivation* (Lincoln, NE: University of Nebraska Press,

1962), pp. 211–269; A. Bandura and R. H. Walters, *Social Learning and Personality Development* (New York: Holt, Rinehart and Winston, 1963).

49 Jagdish Sheth, "How Adults Learn Brand Preference," *Journal of Advertising Research* 8, no. 3 (September 1968), pp. 25–36.

50 Arjun Chaudhuri and Ross Buck, "Media Differences in Rational and Emotional Responses to Advertising," *Journal of Broadcasting & Electronic Media* 39 (January 1, 1995), pp. 109–125; Ross Buck, "Emotional Education and Mass Media," in R. P. Hawkins, J. M. Weimann, and S. Pingree (Eds.), *Advancing Communication Science: Merging Mass and Interpersonal Perspectives* (Beverly Hills, CA: Sage, 1989), pp. 44–76; C. Pechmann and D. W. Stewart, "The Multidimensionality of Persuasive Communications: Theoretical and Empirical Foundations," in P. Cafferata and A. M. Tybout (Eds.), *Cognitive and Affective Responses to Advertising* (Lexington, MA: Lexington Books, 1989), pp. 31–45.

51 "The Global Village Finally Arrives," *Time* 142, no. 21 (Fall 1993).

52 Jagdish N. Sheth and Atul Parvtiyar, "Relationship Marketing in Consumer Markets: Antecedents and Consequences," *Journal of the Academy of Marketing Science* 23, no. 4 (Fall 1995), pp. 255–271.

53 Regis McKenna, *Successful Strategies for the Age of the Customer* (Reading, MA: Addison-Wesley, 1991).

54 Jacob Jacoby and Robert Chestnut, *Brand Loyalty: Measurement and Management* (New York: John Wiley, 1978).

55 Anne B. Fisher, "Coke's Brand Loyalty Lesson," *Fortune* (August 5, 1985), p. 44.

56 Jacoby and Chestnut, *Brand Loyalty: Measurement and Management*.

57 Ronald Alsop, "Brand Loyalty Is Rarely Blind Loyalty," *Wall Street Journal* (October 19, 1989), p. B1; Andrew Greenfield, "Brands That Get Noticed," *Marketing Research* 15, no. 2 (Summer 2003), pp. 228–232.

58 Raymond J. Lawrence, "Patterns of Buyer Behavior: Time for a New Approach?" *Journal of Marketing Research* 6 (May 1969), pp. 137–144.

59 David Mazursky, Priscilla LaBarbera, and Al Aiello, "When Consumers Switch Brands," *Psychology & Marketing* 4, no. 1 (Spring 1987), pp. 17–30.

60 Naresh K. Malhotra, "Mnemonics in Marketing: A Pedagogical Tool," *Journal of the Academy of Marketing Science* 19 (Spring 1991), pp. 141–149.

61 Lyle E. Bourne, Roger L. Dominowski, and Elizabeth F. Loftus, *Cognitive Processes* (Upper Saddle River, NJ: Prentice Hall, 1979); Donald A. Norman, *Memory and Attention* (New York: John Wiley, 1969); Peter H. Lindsay and Donald A. Norman, *Human Information Processing* (New York: Academic Press, 1972); A. Newell and H. A. Simon, *Human Problem Solving* (Upper Saddle River, NJ: Prentice Hall, 1972).

62 Bourne, Dominowski, and Loftus, *Cognitive Processes*; Ulrich Neisser, *Cognitive Psychology* (New York: Appleton, 1966); Robert G. Crowsers, *Principles of Learning in Memory* (Hillsdale, NJ: Lawrence Erlbaum, 1976); Hershel W. Leibowitz and Lewis O. Harvey Jr., "Perception," *Annual Review of Psychology* 24 (1973), pp. 207–240.

63 Richard M. Shiffrin and R. C. Atkinson, "Storage and Retrieval Processes in Long-Term Memory," *Psychological Review* 76 (March 1969), pp. 179–193.

64   Herbert A. Simon "How Big Is a Chunk?" *Science* 183 (February 1974), pp. 482–488; George A. Miller, "The Magical Number Seven, Plus or Minus Two: Some Limits on Our Capacity for Processing Information," *Psychological Review* 63 (March 1956), pp. 81–97.

65   John R. Anderson, *The Architecture of Cognition* (Cambridge, MA: Harvard University Press, 1983).

66   Gabriel Biehal and Dipankar Chakravarti, "Consumers' use of Memory and External Information in Choice: Macro and Micro Perspectives," *Journal of Consumer Research* 12 (March 1986), pp. 382–405.

67   Kevin Lane Keller, "Memory Factors in Advertising: The Effect of Advertising Retrieval Cues on Brand Evaluations," *Journal of Consumer Research* 14 (December 1987), pp. 316–333; Kevin Lane Keller, "Memory and Evaluation Effects in Competitive Advertising Environments," *Journal of Consumer Research* 17 (March 1991), pp. 463–476; Fergus I. M. Craik, "Encoding and Retrieval Effects in Human Memory: A Partial Review," in A. D. Baddeley and J. Long (Eds.), *Attention and Performance* 9 (Hillsdale, NJ: Lawrence Erlbaum, 1981); Endel Tulving, "Relation Between Encoding Specificity and Levels of Processing," in L. S. Cermak and Fergus I. M. Craik (Eds.), *Levels of Processing in Human Memory* (Hillsdale, NJ: Lawrence Erlbaum, 1979), pp. 401–428.

68   John G. Lynch and Thomas K. Srull, "Memory and Attentional Factors in Consumer Choice: Concepts and Research Methods," *Journal of Consumer Research* 9 (June 1982), pp. 18–36.

69   *Ibid.*

70   H. Ebbinghaus, *Memory*, H.A. Ruger and C. E. Bussenius (Trans.) (New York: Teachers College,1913); Hubert A. Zielske, "The Remembering and Forgetting of Advertising," *Journal of Marketing* 23, (January 1959), pp. 231–243.

71   Kenneth R. Weingardt, Elizabeth F. Loftus, and D. Stephen Lindsay, "Misinformation Revisited: New Evidence on the Suggestibility of Memory," *Memory & Cognition* 23, no. 1 (1995), pp. 72–82; D. S. Lindsay, "Misleading Suggestions Can Impair Eyewitnesses' Ability to Remember Event Details," *Journal of Experimental Psychology: Learning, Memory, and Cognition* 16 (1990), pp. 1077–1083; Elizabeth F. Loftus, "Memory Malleability: Constructivist and Fuzzy-Trace Explanations," *Learning and Individual Differences* 7, no. 2 (1995), pp. 133–137; M. McCloskey and M. Zaragoza, "Misleading Postevent Information and Memory for Events: Arguments and Evidence Against Memory Impairment Hypotheses," *Journal of Experimental Psychology: General* 114 (1985), pp. 1–16; E. F. Loftus, H. G. Hoffman, and W. A. Wagenaar, "The Misinformation Effect," in M. L. Howe, C. J. Brainerd, and V. F. Reyna (Eds.), *Development of Long-Term Retention* (New York: Springer-Verlag, 1992).

72   Robert Kent and Chris T. Allen, "Competitive Interference Effects in Consumer Memory for Advertising: The Role of Brand Familiarity," *Journal of Marketing* 58 (July 1994), pp. 97–105.

73   "Geico Commercials 'about Geico,'" www.geico.com/aboutgeico

74   Ibid.

CHAPTER 5

CONSUMER ATTITUDES

LEARNING OBJECTIVES

- To define attitudes, ascertain their nature, and identify their sources.
- To recognize the ramifications of the four functions that attitudes serve.
- To become familiar with the tenets and applications of the traditional and multi-attribute attitude models.
- To develop a basic understanding of the theories of reasoned action as well as goal pursuit and trying.
- To learn about attribution theory as well as its behavioral implications.
- To investigate the roles of cognitive consistency and information processing theories in attitude change.
- To identify and comprehend the concept and application of the elaboration likelihood model.

KEY TERMS

attitudes	behavioral (conative) component	attitude change
attitude object		cognitive consistency
valence	multiattribute model	cognitive dissonance
intensity	attitude toward the object	theory
centrality		postpurchase dissonance
utilitarian function	theory of reasoned action (TORA)	information-processing approach
ego-defensive function		
value-expressive function	intention	elaboration-likelihood model (ELM)
knowledge function	attitude toward the behavior	
traditional model of attitudes		central route to persuasion
cognitive component	subjective norms	peripheral route to persuasion
affective component	goals attribution	

Mid-2015 news coverage reported that an estimated 3,400 Westerners had traveled to join ISIS in its quest to establish an Islamic State in Iraq and Syria. Among those, there are at least 200 American sympathizers who have gone to join the group. They run the gambit from rich to poor, educated to dropouts, male to female, teenaged to middle-aged. This portrait is nothing less than an illustration of the powerful role of human attitudes and feelings as major forces leading toward actions to support either a genuine or sinister cause.

The ISIS jihadist group burst onto the international scene in 2014, when it seized large territories in Syria and Iraq. No terrorist organization has been able to use the Internet as successfully when it comes to marketing itself and recruiting supporters as ISIS has been able to do. The group has the most sophisticated propaganda machine and global communication strategy that has stumped counterterrorism officials.

Just as Twitter and Facebook played a central role in the Arab Spring a few years ago, social media have been the power behind ISIS's propaganda success. In cyberspace, ISIS targets young people through high-quality videos, online magazines, the use of social media, and terrorist Twitter accounts. For example, the group has disseminated information almost exclusively via Twitter, where it can instantly share its views around the world and even enable supporters to participate in the process. ISIS also maintains Twitter feeds in various languages, including English. Some of those are "Al-Medrar," which publishes in a variety of tongues; "Platform Media," which primarily tweets news updates in Arabic; and "Al-Battar" media which has feeds that tweet news, graphics, official statements, and videos.

Supporters can sign up for an app from Android through Google Play called "Dawn of Glad Tidings" as a way of receiving information from ISIS on their smartphones. The group also organizes hashtag campaigns, skewing trending terms by encouraging supporters to repeatedly tweet various hashtags so that these terms would then trend on Twitter, vastly increasing the visibility of tweets bearing the group's messages.

Unlike Al-Qaeda recruitment efforts, which focused on attracting radicals who were motivated to join the fight, ISIS in contrast seeks to take a somewhat secular approach, portraying how much better life purportedly would be in the Caliphite state as compared to living in the corrupt West. The framing focus, in this case, is much more on "come and join us, and we will fight the good fight together" rather than on stressing hardship, gore, and suffering that turns off less radical, nonviolent individuals. The message, thus, appears to be relatable and inspirational. In terms of attitude formation and change, this strategy seems to be effective for reaching troubled individuals residing in Western countries and wanting to be part of something bigger. Such individuals are easily swayed by promises like free housing, ISIS-approved schooling for children, multiple wives, and attractive financial incentives.[1]

Noting the rapid spread of the wave of propaganda from ISIS and its effect on many people in Western countries, observers have been swift to claim that this movement demonstrates the fact that attitudes are contagious and can spread rapidly like viruses do. In such view, they claim that there isn't much we can do to prevent this propaganda from spreading. React to this claim and justify your answer. In the United States, there are many actions undertaken to fight this online recruitment effort. There is a belief that each of ISIS's propaganda goals is vulnerable to a messaging counteroffensive. Learn about this strategy to defeat ISIS in the propaganda war by visiting the site http://time/3751659/a-6-point-plan-to-defeat-isis-in-the-propaganda-war/. *Do you agree that such tactics can counter ISIS's messaging efforts? If not, what alternative courses of action would you suggest taking in order to defeat ISIS's sinister propaganda?*

This chapter examines factors that influence the formation and change of beliefs and attitudes. An understanding of these factors is imperative for both makers of public policy and marketers alike in their effort to anticipate and influence human behavior. If companies are to successfully develop and market innovative products that are on the leading edge, it is essential for them to analyze consumer behavior to understand the attitudes that drive it.[2]

WHAT ARE ATTITUDES?

Gordon Allport, an early researcher in the field of attitudes, suggested that the concept of attitude is probably the most distinctive, indispensable concept in social psychology. Current studies indicate that Allport's words are still true today. Some authors maintain that no other single influence is as important to the study of consumer behavior as the concept of attitude.

Attitudes are consistent inclinations—whether favorable or unfavorable—that people hold toward products, services, people, places, or events. They can be more formally defined as learned predispositions to respond in a consistent manner in respect to a given object.[3] Attitudes are thus *mental states* and part of our psychological makeup.

attitudes
learned predispositions to respond in a consistent manner to a given object

Let us look at the terms of our definition. Attitudes are *learned*. For example, media coverage or direct experience of the 9/11 attack on the United States resulted in overwhelmingly negative attitudes on the part of the public toward terrorists and terrorist groups such as Al *Qaeda and ISIS*. Similarly, from a marketing perspective, attitudes can be formed either as a direct result of experiences with a product or through information acquired from others, including the mass media. We are not born with attitudes; we develop them as we experience or learn about things surrounding us. Attitudes, however, are not synonymous with behavior. A person may hold a favorable attitude toward Porsche automobiles but may not purchase one due to the high cost.

Attitudes are characterized by *consistency*. This means that attitudes take time to develop and are stable and enduring. They are not cast in stone—they can be changed over a period of time, but this process is usually very slow. Consistency means that once negative consumer attitudes toward a product or corporation develop, marketers face difficulties in changing them.

Consumer attitudes are *responsive*. They form as we become able to judge a product or situation based on personal experience and acquired information or perhaps as we choose among a number of alternatives. For example, a positive experience with a Sony 3D HD television may lead us to believe this brand is superior to other sets on the market. We may insist on purchasing a Sony, even if less expensive alternatives are available. Our response does not have to be a purchase decision, however, and may simply entail recommending the brand to our friends.

attitude object
anything about which consumers can form an attitude

Anything about which we can hold an attitude is called an attitude object. People, products, services, brands, situations, companies, issues, and places are all examples. For example, the sport of golf can be an attitude object. Many people have positive feelings toward the game, whereas others find it boring. Each group will react to golf in its own way. Those with positive attitudes may play golf on a somewhat regular basis or watch golf tournaments on TV. Those with negative attitudes will likely avoid golf altogether. Of course, there are those who are indifferent about the game and hold neither negative nor positive attitudes toward it. Such individuals may or may not play the game or watch a tournament, depending on the degree of their social involvement with peers or family members who enjoy the game.

Although attitudes are well entrenched in the theory and practice of marketing, a major problem is that they are not directly observable. Attitudes must be inferred from what consumers say or do, and even then they may remain ambiguous. An observer who sees an individual attending a religious retreat might infer that this person is in favor of religion. In reality, however, the person may be attending the retreat because of a need for social interaction, to meet friends, or to find a marriage partner. Despite these types of ambiguities, understanding attitudes is essential to marketers because attitudes serve as a link between consumers' perceptions and their actual behavior.

VALENCE, INTENSITY, AND CENTRALITY OF ATTITUDES

Attitudes steer people in a particular direction with respect to an attitude object. This aspect of attitudes is called valence. Positive valence attracts individuals toward a stimulus object; negative valence repels them away from it. For example, Intel Corporation, maker of ultrafast computer chips, pays subsidies to computer advertisers who place "Intel Inside" slogans in their ads. This practice is an effective means of attaining positive valence for Intel.

Humans, in general, hold many attitudes with varying degrees of fervor, called intensity. For example, many consumers feel strongly about the brand of beer or wine they drink. The more strongly they feel about the product, the less likely they will be to change to another brand. Conversely, if an attitude is weak, the behavior can be changed easily. The probability of attitude change varies inversely with the intensity of the attitude.

Centrality of an attitude, on the other hand, refers to how closely an attitude reflects our core values and beliefs. Central values cover such things as patriotism, religion, ethics, political affiliation, and personal values and goals, all of which are resistant to change. A person who believes strongly in human rights will be critical of actions taken by countries that deny their citizens these rights. Consumers who are attracted to products such as Louis Vuitton purses or luggage, or Rolex watches and designer brands such as Yves Saint Laurent or Gucci exhibit a high level of attitude centrality because these items are psychologically important to them. Highly visible, expensive, and prestigious goods are often used as symbols to reflect one's self concept and feelings of self worth. People in many cases judge others' social worth based on their ownership of such possessions. However, in practice, most shopping-related attitudes are *peripheral*. For

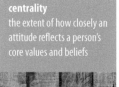

valence
an attraction or repulsion felt toward an attitude object

intensity
the extent of how strongly an individual feels one way or the other about an attitude object

centrality
the extent of how closely an attitude reflects a person's core values and beliefs

instance, attitudes toward the cell phone service provider we choose or the website from which we purchase products or services are usually somewhat easy to change because they do not relate to our central values and beliefs. As such, peripheral attitudes are susceptible to change.

SOURCES OF ATTITUDES

We learn, form, and acquire attitudes from many sources. The three major ones are personal experience with objects, social interaction, and exposure to mass media.

Personal Experience with Objects

We constantly touch, taste, feel, try on, or examine objects we encounter. Based on this contact, we evaluate objects in our environment and form attitudes toward them. Marketers induce trials so that we can experience products and their benefits firsthand before purchasing them. For example, most major automobile companies fight to get rental companies to use their cars in order to expose the public to a particular model. When renters drive a model and are impressed by its look or performance, they develop positive attitudes that may lead to increased sales or positive word of mouth.

Social Interaction

People tend to acquire, through social interaction, the attitudes of family members, friends, neighbors, and colleagues and perhaps online communities. Social groups, peer groups, and work groups are also influential in molding a wide range of product- and service-related attitudes. Many young people today choose to get a tattoo or have their body pierced largely to fit into and gain acceptance by their peer group.

Exposure to Mass Media, The Internet, and Social Media

No one has ever been exposed to so much information as the present generation. The multitude of social networks, websites, broadcast and cable networks, radio stations, newspapers, magazines, telephones, faxes, email, and traditional mail services have exposed us all to amounts of information no one ever thought possible. Events in other parts of the world are immediately communicated around the globe. With such an outpouring of information, the influence of mass media on attitude formation and change cannot be underestimated. Most products today have become equally universal; they are found in just about every country.

THE FUNCTIONS OF ATTITUDES

Attitudes serve four functions: utilitarian, ego-defensive, value-expressive, and knowledge functions.[4]

Utilitarian Function

When products help us gain rewards or avoid punishments, they perform a **utilitarian function**. Cosmetics, antiperspirants, and mouthwashes help us to either look good or avoid smelling bad. If a product helps us achieve a desired goal, our resulting attitude toward it will be positive. Conversely, our attitude would be negative if the product did not contribute to reaching our goal. For example, economically minded travelers may form positive attitudes toward airlines with low ticket prices, such as Southwest and JetBlue, because of the basic no-frills, low-cost transportation the firms provide. Fliers, on the other hand, may be negatively predisposed toward a particular airline that was responsible for lost baggage. To promote a product, marketers can emphasize a utilitarian purpose that the item can serve. For example, Procter & Gamble, Inc. may emphasize NyQuil's ability to relieve day and nighttime cold symptoms. By providing such facts, they highlight the utilitarian function of the brand and thus elevate the resulting attitudes toward it.

utilitarian function
the notion that some attitudes serve as a means to an end—gaining rewards or avoiding punishments

Ego-Defensive Function

These attitudes serve the social-adjustment function, which translates into a tendency to conform to expectations of others to permit social interactions to run smoothly and more efficiently. For example, humans are known to protect their egos and disguise their inadequacies. Consumers therefore often prefer particular products because of their compensatory value, such as Viagra (for sexual potency) and Botox (for enhancing appearance). Similarly, certain electronic keyboards compensate for players' lack of talent or training by automatically adding chords and rhythms that make inexperienced performers sound like professionals. Products such as these perform

an important ego-defensive function. When the external environment presents threats to the ego, internal anxieties arise, and defensive behavior commences to protect the ego's delicate sensitivities. Marketers recognize that some products are purchased to avoid anxiety-producing situations and offer reassurances of protection for consumers' ego states. For instance, in the case of brands of disposable adult incontinence briefs, the photo in Figure 5.1 could be used as a promotional appeal to encourage women to go ahead and dance without worries about bladder leaks. Similarly, Kellogg's Special K breakfast cereal is promoted as a means of improving health and achieving weight control through its low-carb weight-loss plan.

FIGURE 5.1

This photo depicts women dancing confidently without worries about bladder leaks.

© Pressmaster/Shutterstock.com

Value-Expressive Function

Attitudes serving the value-expressive function help consumers express their central values (such as patriotism) and idiosyncratic preferences (such as a preference for designer-label garments and expensive brands of home electronics), as well as assist them in conveying their self-perception to others. Patriotic feelings, for example, which resulted from the terrorist attack on Paris, France and San Bernardino, California had subsequent repercussions that affected our economy and generated significant changes in consumer attitudes toward a variety of domestic and foreign entities and issues. These attitudes had and will continue to have significant ramifications for our economy as a whole (such as the value of the dollar in foreign markets), and particularly for the dynamics of the marketplace.

Affected sectors, for example, include financial services, travel, hospitality, housing, energy, and security.

Another dimension of the value-expressive function of attitudes can be observed in our relentless effort to achieve self-enhancement, self-extension, and self-expression by communicating to others the values we revere, such as beauty, self-respect, freedom, pleasure, and accomplishment. Behavior stemming from such value-expressive attitudes demonstrates our core values. For example, some consumers prefer to purchase quality, expensive, prestigious, and distinctive products. Through such acquisitions, these consumers attempt to convey to others their accomplishments and success. Actions like this clearly demonstrate the potency of the **value-expressive function**. Capitalizing on these tendencies, marketers of consumer goods attempt to identify their brands with widely held or deeply seated values, portray their brands as means of expressing them, and surround their brands with symbols of them. Promotional strategies used by entities such as expensive automobile or motorcycle owners' groups, prestigious country clubs, and Ivy League colleges have been successful in attracting participants, members, or students by linking the advertiser to the values cherished most by these individuals. Luxurious automobiles are often promoted as self-expressive possessions due to their elegance and high price. The image in Figure 5.2 from Mercedes-Benz communicates the value-expressive qualities of owning this brand.

© Asier Romero/Shutterstock.com

By acquiring prestigious products, consumers attempt to convey to others their accomplishment and success.

© olgaru79/Shutterstock.com

FIGURE 5.2

This image communicates the self-expressive value of owning and driving this prestigious Mercedes-Benz automobile.

Knowledge Function

Most of us seek simplicity, stability, and predictability in our interaction with our environment. Knowledge helps us simplify and give meaning to what otherwise would be a complex and chaotic universe. Attitudes that serve the knowledge function help consumers organize, structure, and summarize large amounts of complex information about attitude objects so that decisions concerning them can be made quickly and easily. The knowledge function of attitudes reflects cognitive theories of learning and information processing, which portray humans as information seekers. Our knowledge quest is prompted by curiosity and the desire to deal competently and effectively with life's varied predicaments. Based on this function, we form our particular attitudes—positive or negative—regarding stimuli we encounter in our daily life.

The knowledge function offers insights for product-positioning strategies. Marketers must clearly and unambiguously position their brands and explain the benefits that differentiate a brand from its competition. For example, Apple's electronics are far more than a collection of innovative products. They are an ecosystem of interrelated devices that are ushering in a new era of computing. Apple's devices are examples of uncompromising industrial design, including the firm's iPhones and iPads, that are sold in hundreds of stores throughout the country. As such, Apple has become one of the most admired companies in the world, occupying the leadership position among competing brands.

The distinction we just drew between the various attitude functions (utilitarian, ego defensive, value expressive, and knowledge) helps marketers recognize that attitudes toward different product categories tend to be associated with different attitude functions.[5] For example, consumers tend to form utilitarian attitudes toward products such as kitchen disposal units or furnaces. Most people do not really care how a furnace looks versus how efficiently it operates. By contrast, attitudes toward perfumes, greeting cards, and designer-label clothing serve a value-expressive function. These products help us make favorable impressions on other people. Consequently, utilitarian ads are likely to be more effective in the case of the first type of products, whereas image-oriented ads are more suitable for the latter types.

DO ATTITUDES DETERMINE BEHAVIOR?

Decades of research show that we *sometimes* act in accordance with our attitudes. At other times, however, we behave in a manner quite inconsistent with them. For example, a Pew Research Center study in 2014 showed that 32 percent of American millennials see themselves as environmentalists and claim they are willing to make sacrifices for a better environment.[6] However, marketers have observed that when it comes to making concrete buying decisions, many are not the environmentalists they claim to be.

Researchers over the years have dealt with three fundamental issues: (1) *whether* a relationship between attitudes and behavior exists (that is, do attitudes influence behavior?), (2) *when* such a relationship is to be expected, and (3) *how* attitudes affect or guide behavior.

On the first point, *do attitudes relate to behavior*, researchers have found conflicting evidence. Corey, for example, examined the correlation between students' attitudes toward cheating and their actual cheating behavior and found it to equal zero.[7] Those who indicated negative attitudes toward cheating did cheat on a later test. Other evidence, however, shows a positive correlation between attitudes and behavior. For example, consumers who indicated having favorable attitudes toward coupons as a promotional practice tended to use them regularly when they shopped.[8]

Concerning the second point, *when a link between attitudes and behavior could be expected*, researchers have identified factors that are instrumental in determining whether the relationship between attitudes and behavior is strong or weak. Fazio and Ewoldsen cited a number of factors, called *moderating variables*, which govern this relationship.[9] These moderating variables include (a) qualities of the behavior (whether the behavior is general or specific), (b) qualities of the person (whether the person is inner or outer directed and whether or not the individual has a vested interest in the attitude issue), (c) qualities of the situation in which the behavior is exhibited (the physical and social surroundings, as well as the time context), and (d) qualities of the attitude itself (the apparent influence that the attitude exerts upon the individual).

To clarify, assume you enjoy sports, and tennis in particular. Assume further that a friend were to call you on a sunny Saturday morning with an invitation to play tennis at an exclusive country club. Most likely you would accept the invitation unless you had an important prior commitment. In this example, the relation between the positive attitude toward tennis and acceptance of the invitation is strong. In terms of the four moderating variables, (a) the attitude object is specific—playing tennis on a nice morning, (b) the outing offers an opportunity to socialize, (c) the game will take place at a fancy country club, and (d) the exercise will do

CONSUMER BEHAVIOR IN PRACTICE

A Whole New Me

In 2015, our youth-focused American society and the continued interest of people to enhance their physical appearance have managed to raise cosmetic surgery procedure market revenue in the United States to a staggering $17.5 billion. In addition to the desire of people to look young, other factors that fuel this growth are the increasing acceptance of cosmetic surgery, an aging U.S. population, competition for jobs at the workplace, and the popularity of weight-loss and reality TV programs.

Technological advances and cheaper cosmetic procedures have helped to initiate this growth. These advances made invasive procedures less painful, and nonsurgical techniques more effective. In terms of surgical and nonsurgical procedures, a 2015 GIA report on U.S. and European cosmetic procedures indicated that nonsurgical procedures, such as injectables, laser hair removal, microdermabrasion, chemical peel, among others, account for the higher share of the total procedure category in terms of number performed. However, even though these nonsurgical procedures are performed in large numbers—due to their lower cost, noninvasive nature, and quick treatment time—surgical procedures account for a larger share of consumer spending on cosmetic treatments and the related products.

Two of the leading surgical and nonsurgical cosmetic procedures that top the charts are breast augmentation and injectables (Botox and Dysport). However, in recent years, other types of corrective procedures, such as eyelid surgery, tummy tucks, buttock lifts, and buttock augmentation, have been gaining popularity. In the category of cosmetic surgery, injectables constitute the largest and fastest-growing segment of the U.S. cosmetic surgery product market. Factors that contribute to this growth are their noninvasive nature, prompt outcome, and minimal downtime. The category of implants represents the second major segment of that market, with breast implants claiming the lion's share of the implant market.

Regarding the gender makeup of the cosmetic surgery market, women have always been the dominant party in terms of total number of procedures performed. In 2015, over 90 percent of cosmetic surgery procedures were conducted on female patients. A study by Arnocky and Piche in 2014 found that women had more positive views on the subject of cosmetic surgery than males, and suggested that this discrepancy could be explained by differences in male and female mate choices. Males typically value physical attractiveness of females highly in their mate preferences; whereas females are more interested in the physical resources that a potential mate can offer them. Cosmetic surgery for males is usually motivated by a belief that a more dominant, attractive, masculine face can signal positive impressions, such as socioeconomic success and internal well-being, and can act as a visual marker for genetic quality.[10]

Recent research attempted to study factors that motivate people to undergo cosmetic surgery. One such investigation looked at factors such as self-esteem, life satisfaction, self-rated physical attractiveness, and media impact as major motivators for undergoing such procedures. Visit two websites that address these issues at http://www.ncbi.nim.nih.gov/pmc/articles/PMC3513261/ and http://dryoho.com/dr-yoho-book/chapter1-2.cfm. There are cases where cosmetic surgery is done for medical reasons, such as in cases of breast reconstruction due to cancer. In some states, insurance companies are reluctant to cover such procedures, claiming them to be cosmetic rather than therapeutic. Visit a site that touches on such issues at https://en.wikipedia.org/wiki/Plastic_surgery. What arguments would you present to such insurance companies to support a patient's claim for coverage? Explain.

you good. These types of factors moderate the relationship between attitudes and resulting behavior.

The third point, *how attitudes guide behavior*, has been the subject of a great deal of research. Many analysts and users of attitude responses in marketing research feel that it is essential to understand the attitudes that drive consumer behavior. Consequently, they frequently overrate the importance of reported attitudes. Most survey questionnaires fail to follow up attitude questions with an action question, such as: "OK, if that's how you *feel* about it, then what are you going to *do* about it?" In short, reported attitudes do not always equal action.[11] However, because attitudes often seem to guide behavior, a clear understanding of the role of attitudes in purchase situations can provide marketers with the means of dealing with issues of attitude creation and change.

In the following sections, we present basic attitude perspectives, starting with the traditional model of attitudes, followed by the multiattribute model, and then the theory of reasoned action.

THE TRADITIONAL MODEL OF ATTITUDES

A few years ago, after many years of stable sales, the purchase rate of aspirin suddenly skyrocketed. The explosion in sales was due to a report in a medical journal stating that daily doses of aspirin can lower the risk of heart attacks in healthy adults.[12] This example represents one approach to examining attitudes as a means of guiding behavior. Consumers originally knew that aspirin is useful for relieving headaches, colds, and fever. The new information about its ability to lower the risk of heart attacks, however, created a new belief and a positive feeling toward aspirin as well as an enhanced tendency among many people to use it for that purpose. The result was a sudden increase in demand for the product. The traditional model of attitudes, also called the tricomponent model, expresses this interrelationship and posits that attitudes consist of three components: *cognitive*, *affective*, and *behavioral* or *conative*.[13] A schematic diagram of the traditional model of attitudes appears in Exhibit 5.1. Each of these three components is described in the paragraphs that follow.

Cognitive Component

The cognitive component is what we think we know about an attitude object. Our beliefs could be based on *knowledge* (one's experience doc-

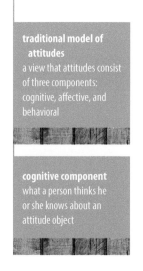

traditional model of attitudes
a view that attitudes consist of three components: cognitive, affective, and behavioral

cognitive component
what a person thinks he or she knows about an attitude object

EXHIBIT 5.1

Schematic Conception of
Attitudes: The Traditional
Model

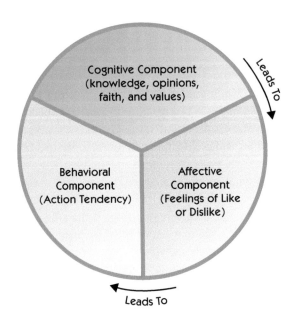

uments that aspirin relieves pain and reduces the risk of heart attacks),
opinion (inconclusive beliefs based on a medical journal's claims about the
significant health benefits of herbal remedies), *faith* (convictions about
the integrity of the researchers and their methods), or *value systems* (people should heed medical advice to maintain good health).

Affective Component

The affective component of an attitude includes feelings of like or dislike,
representing our reaction to the cognitive aspect of the attitude.[14] For example, after reading the medical journal's report about the way aspirin can
effectively reduce heart attack risks, an individual begins to form positive
feelings toward aspirin and commences to consider it as a viable treatment
for maintaining good health.

Behavioral or Conative Component

The behavioral or conative component of an attitude represents our tendency to respond in a certain way, as an expression of the favorable or
unfavorable feelings formed earlier. The behavioral component may take
the form of *overt behavior*. Consumers' rush to purchase and use aspirin after reading the medical report is a manifestation of the response to
the positive feelings generated by the article. However, others react to this

affective component
an individual's positive or
negative reaction to an
attitude object

**behavioral (conative)
component**
a person's action tendency
or intentions with respect to
an attitude object

new information by doing nothing. Researchers attempt to assess the *intentions* of consumers in such cases by asking about their possible future actions relating to the product under investigation.

ATTITUDE COMPONENTS AND MARKETING STRATEGY

When marketers use the traditional model to create or change attitudes, they appeal to consumers at the *cognitive* level with informative messages, at the *affective* level with emotionally toned messages, and at the *behavioral* level with incentives such as samples, coupons, or rebates. For example, one of the largest and more successful markets today is that for cosmetics and beauty products, which includes thousands of items from essential hygienic needs all the way to expensive and luxurious perfumes, colognes, and makeup. Effective product promotion is all the more important to the personal care industry, given the fact that people's needs and tastes differ widely. Hence, most well-known cosmetic companies, such as L'Oreal, Estee Lauder, MAC, Chanel, and Clinique, have adopted intensive promotional campaigns that include such elements as running attractive product ads in popular beauty magazines; incorporating scented strips allowing consumers to sample a fragrance; using glamorous models and celebrities as spokespersons; offering free makeovers in venues such as malls and department stores; establishing a presence on the web; harnessing the power of blogs to host product giveaways and promote their names; giving away free samples and gift packages to consumers who purchase specific beauty products; and distributing shirts and cosmetic bags bearing the name of the sponsoring firm. All of these are efforts designed to create and enhance favorable attitudes toward the cosmetic companies' lines.[15]

However, the traditional model of attitudes, despite its uses to explain attitude formation and change, tends to give the impression that overt behavior can be easily predicted from an individual's attitudes. In reality, as we've now seen, attitudes and accompanying behavior are often in obvious contradiction. This discrepancy renders false the notion that researchers can predict an individual's overt behavior through knowledge of that person's attitudes. Subsequent research efforts continued to address the issue of how attitudes guide behavior. One such effort by Martin Fishbein, a foremost researcher of attitudes, resulted in what is known as the multi-attribute model of attitudes. This model is briefly covered in the following section.

FISHBEIN'S MULTIATTRIBUTE MODEL OF ATTITUDES

multiattribute model
a view that attitude objects have a number of desirable or undesirable features that differ in importance to the same individual

attitude toward the object
an individual's overall appraisal (like or dislike) of an attitude object

The multiattribute model differs from the traditional model of attitudes in a number of respects. It recognizes that the attitude object can have a number of attributes that differ in importance to the same individual. It is possible for a consumer concurrently to hold strongly positive feelings toward some features of a product and less positive or even negative feelings toward other attributes of the same item. Consumers concerned about their diet may select a fat-free brand of ice cream even though they find the taste to be less appealing than traditional ice cream.

Fishbein hypothesized that an attitude toward the object is a function of (1) a person's beliefs about an object (the object's inclusion of a number of characteristic attributes) and (2) the person's evaluative aspects of those beliefs (that person's appraisal of the presence and desirability of each of these characteristic attributes in a brand). He proposed that through quantification of these two variables, it becomes possible to arrive at a numerical evaluation of attitudes toward a product. This, in turn, would allow marketers to use such knowledge in evaluating or comparing between a number of competing brands.[16]

To clarify, assume a study is conducted to compare three medium-priced brands of watches—Timex, Citizen, and Seiko. In this case, respondents are asked to identify the attributes they use to evaluate watches in actual purchase situations. Suppose the respondents identify four attributes: *attractiveness, brand reputation, price affordability*, and the watch's *special features*. Respondents are then asked to rate the importance of each of the four attributes by giving each a *numerical weight*. A six-point scale may be used for this purpose, where the higher number indicates greater attribute importance.

Further, respondents in the study are asked to rate the extent to which each brand possesses these same attributes; that is to say, to give *numerical ratings* (say from 1 to 7) to each of these attributes as it exists in each brand. These numerical ratings reflect respondents' perceived presence or absence of each attribute in each brand. For example, if a respondent feels that the Citizen watch has a better reputation than the other two brands, the respondent may give it a high rating of 7. Exhibit 5.2 depicts the case of a respondent in the process of evaluating the three brands of watches mentioned.

Through this process the respondent's scores can be calculated for each brand by multiplying each *attribute's numerical rating* times its corresponding *weight*. In this case, the respondent rated the Citizen watch to be best among the three choices, giving it a composite score of 104 compared to 96 for Seiko and 92 for Timex. By summing the scores for each brand from all the respondents comprising the study's sample, an overall numerical score emerges for each brand. The watch with the highest overall score is judged to be the most preferred (has the strongest positive attitude) from the standpoint of the study's respondents.

Perceive Attribute	Weight Assigned to Each Attribute (values range from 1–6)	Beliefs about Each Brand of Watch Numerical ratings (1–7) multiplied by weights (1–6)		
		Timex	Citizen	Seiko
Attractiveness	6	$\times 7 = 42$	$\times 6 = 36$	$\times 6 = 36$
Brand reputation	5	$\times 4 = 20$	$\times 7 = 35$	$\times 5 = 25$
Affordability	3	$\times 5 = 15$	$\times 6 = 18$	$\times 5 = 15$
Special features	5	$\times 3 = 15$	$\times 3 = 15$	$\times 4 = 20$
		92	104	96

EXHIBIT 5.2

A Respondent's Ratings of Three Brands of Watches Using Fishbein's Attitude-Toward-the-Object Model

Some researchers of consumer behavior believe that information obtained using Fishbein's multiattribute model is relevant to marketers from a strategic point of view. The model enables marketers to ascertain brand strengths and deficiencies relative to the competition by determining how consumers evaluate brand alternatives on critical attributes. Revealing the brand's perceived strengths and weaknesses has implications for both brand design and promotion. For design, product weakness may signal the need to undertake corrective brand reformulation.

Limitations of the Fishbein Model

Some consumer researchers contend Fishbein's model tends to assume that when consumers hold positive feelings toward most or even some features of a product, the positive attitudes toward these features will translate into a purchase.

Limitations of this type have led psychologists such as Ajzen and Fishbein to abandon the study of attitudes toward objects and focus instead on attitudes toward actions.[17] This revised view looks not only at the features of the object but also at the consequences of the purchase. Consider the case of a consumer contemplating the purchase of Apple's iPhone7 with hundreds of new software features. This individual may ponder such factors as screen size, increased productivity, information security, time required to learn, price, and many other aspects specifically relevant to that person. Therefore, from a consumer behavior point of view, it makes more sense to find out a prospective buyer's attitude toward the consequences of purchasing and owning the iPhone7 rather than merely to identify his or her attitude toward its features. In this case, despite the positive feelings about the phone's capability to communicate, access the Net, and secure personal information, the consumer may decide against the purchase due to perceived hindrances such as difficulty in mastering the new features and/or the lofty selling price.

Due to these concerns, Ajzen and Fishbein developed the theory of reasoned action to address the limitations of the previous view.

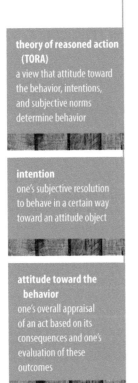

theory of reasoned action (TORA)
a view that attitude toward the behavior, intentions, and subjective norms determine behavior

intention
one's subjective resolution to behave in a certain way toward an attitude object

attitude toward the behavior
one's overall appraisal of an act based on its consequences and one's evaluation of these outcomes

THE THEORY OF REASONED ACTION

According to the theory of reasoned action (TORA), behavior is determined by a person's intention to behave.[18] Intention, in this sense, is a person's subjective resolution to behave in a certain way toward an attitude object. For example, women in Western societies buy cosmetic products with the intent of enhancing their natural beauty. Here, intention (looking attractive) determines the attitude toward the behavior (buying a brand of cosmetics, seeking Botox and Juvedurm treatments, and/or undergoing plastic surgery). Such behavior is also influenced by the social norm governing the action to be taken (the society admires and rewards good looks). By contrast, in some traditional Islamic countries, women's use of cosmetics and/or undergoing plastic surgery would be frowned upon, and purchase of such items or services is often discouraged. According to this view, in taking action, a person considers, weighs, and combines the following two factors: (1) attitude toward the behavior and (2) subjective norms regarding the behavior.

1. Attitude toward the behavior is the belief that our behavior leads to specific outcomes (positive or negative) and our evaluation of these

outcomes. For example, a couple contemplating adoption of a child would consider aspects of the adoption process such as going through a lengthy legal process, nurturing the child, forfeiting leisure time, incurring costs to raise the child, experiencing the pleasure of having the child, and anticipating love from the child, as well as their evaluation of these outcomes.

2. Subjective norms are our beliefs about what significant others think we should or should not do, as well as our inclination to comply with their specific desires. For a couple pondering adoption of a child, subjective norms would encompass their views regarding how their family and friends would perceive the action. Would these significant others be supportive, critical, or indifferent?

subjective norms
one's beliefs about what significant others think and inclinations to comply with their views

The more positively we view the outcome and the greater the approval from significant others we anticipate for the action, the more likely we are to arrive at the intention to undertake the action.

Although the views brought about by this theory may be plausible, the TORA fails to explain conditions where purchase situations are hindered by some adverse personal or environmental circumstances. The TORA presumes that if the consumer tries to act, no impediments are likely to stand in the way. That is to say, the formation of intentions in this case assumes the behavior is nonproblematic. In many instances, however, behavior can be impeded by real or imagined factors such as limits on consumers' ability, time constraints, and environmental contingencies. In the Apple iPhone7 example cited earlier, either external (environmental) or internal (personal) impediments, such as insufficient resources to buy the phone, unavailability of the device, or lack of self-confidence to understand the product's features, can thwart the action.

THEORIES OF GOAL PURSUIT AND TRYING

According to these theories, pursuits where an individual thinks impediments stand in the way of attaining a desired objective are termed goals. In this view, virtually all pursuits are seen as goals.[19] That is why we often hear people say, "I have a goal of trying to lose twenty pounds in the next six months," or say, "I have a goal of trying to learn skydiving this summer." Because most actions are forestalled by some unforeseen event, and

goals
pursuits where an individual thinks impediments stand in the way of attaining a desired objective

there is no certainty in goal achievement, behavior is reduced to merely *trying* to achieve the goal. That is to say, if consumers feel that a goal is too difficult to achieve, or a task is too complicated to handle, intentions to try it subside. This phenomenon may explain why more people are not skydivers or Ph.D. candidates.

GLOBAL OPPORTUNITY

A Chinese Cinderella

In the United States, parents who take their children to a Disney park know well that the stars of the show are the famous characters Mickey, Minney, and the Fairytale Princesses, which Walt Disney created and transformed into a perpetual cash flow machine. But as Disney was planning its massive $5.5 billion Shanghai Disney Resort (which opened in June 2016), cultural values were uppermost in the minds of the company's designers. These values require a thorough understanding of the Chinese culture and its nuances. Visitors to the new Shanghai Disneyland are wooed by a new cast of Chinese symbols and characters, such as the giant glass Peony blossom representing nobility and good fortune, erected at the center of a forty-bedecked fountain, or the "lucky" cloud patterns painted on some spires of the massive castle dwarfing the park.

Comic superheroes, including Superman and the Hulk, are presented along with a "Star Wars Launch Bay," where guests meet heroes and villains. Other distinctly Chinese attractions include the "Garden of the Twelve Friends," in which animals of the Chinese Zodiac are reinterpreted as Disney and Pixar animated characters. In addition, because the Chinese like large-scale visuals, Disney offers the "Enchanted Storybook Castle," the largest and tallest structure in any Disney park.

Chinese parkgoers also expect live entertainment—a desire that Disney fulfills via an adjacent Disneytown shopping plaza and its theatre where the Broadway hit show *The Lion King* is performed live in the Mandarin language.

The challenges that the project planners had to confront at the start touched on two values unique to the Chinese culture. The first related to China's previously-enforced one-child policy and its effect on the size of families visiting the facility. The average family, in this case, consists of three individuals, which would translate into at least two adults present for every child in the park. The second challenge revolved around the fact that Chinese companies do not typically offer paid vacation time. As a result, park attendance is expected to surge around a limited number of national holidays. This issue required that two actions be undertaken in order to deal with it effectively. The first dealt with reducing the waits at rides during peak times. For this concern, designers planned parades and street performances to draw attendees elsewhere in the parks, and added games, videos, and robots to distract and entertain customers while they wait in line. The second issue dealt with older family members, who will have to wait while their children go on the various rides. For this concern, operators designed plenty of seating, restaurants, viewing areas, and open space where older family members can spend time relaxing.

By expanding internationally, Disney admits that it had learned valuable lessons about the need to truly understand culture, respect its nuances, and ensure that people get what they expect.[20]

Disney, which already has five theme parks in Anaheim, Orlando, Paris, Tokyo, and Hong Kong, has now expanded its reach to Shanghai, China (with a total population of approximately 1.3 billion). This venture involved erecting a resort that exceeded $5.5 billion in investment. Learn more about this impressive venture by visiting http://thewaltdisneycompany.com/opening-date-set-for-shanghai-disney-resort-disneys-newest-world-class-destination/. *Considering the relatively modest incomes and low standard of living of the majority of Chinese families, versus the expected high fees for attending the park or spending a vacation at this new facility, do you envision that this venture will have a reasonable chance of success and profitability? Support your answer.*

The theory of trying proposes that there are three attitudes toward goals: (1) attitudes toward the consequences of *succeeding* to achieve a goal, (2) attitudes toward the consequences of trying but *failing* to achieve a goal, and (3) attitudes toward the *process* of striving to achieve a goal.[21] In applying the theory to purchase situations, it becomes evident that consumer attitudes toward the consequences of success and failure to achieve a goal, as well as their attitudes toward trying, influence the adoption process for new products.[22] Consider, for instance, the case of novice skiers who are unlikely to take up the sport and buy the necessary gear, unless they have both the desire to ski and the confidence in their ability to try and succeed in conquering challenging slopes.

Astute marketers recognize the importance of trials in getting consumers to buy their products. Because consumers, in this view, may perceive the purchase of a product as a goal, marketers can use strategies that enhance trial. They distribute free samples, allow product trials in the store, or place request cards for consumers to complete and receive free product samples.[23]

An example of such marketing strategies is evident in the arena of selling time-share or retirement community properties. Retiring couples who live in cold climates often contemplate a move to a warmer location where they hope to spend the rest of their lives in comfort. Such a desirable goal, however, is often hindered by impediments such as lack of knowledge regarding which area is more suitable for living, what choices exist in the various locales, and what types of property can be acquired at what price. Further impediments may also include the necessity of selling the present residence, leaving friends and acquaintances behind, disposing of many accumulated possessions, as well as the difficulty and cost of the physical move itself. As a result, many such couples delay their plans to pursue such a goal for years or even suppress the need to move altogether.

Many property developers have recognized these tendencies and have designed strategies to reduce or remove the impact of the aforementioned impediments. Programs such as offering prospects an opportunity to see and experience the property have been implemented through deals such as brief all-expenses-paid vacations to the property destination that prospects *win*. Other deals may involve offering valuable gifts just for visiting the property site. Those who accept these offers sit through a sales presentation designed to accomplish two objectives: first, to reduce the psychological impediment of fear associated with approaching an unknown investment, and second, advance the desirability of the present choice through witnessing the impressive amenities of the property firsthand, as well as taking advantage of the creative financial arrangements that facilitate immediate acquisition of the property. Such sales tactics have been highly successful in helping time-share and retirement property promoters to achieve admirable levels of sales.

All-expense-paid vacations to property destinations and valuable gift giveaways are successful sales tactics used to sell time-share and retirement properties.

© Martin Valigursky/Shutterstock.com

Other applications of this theory include the case of car dealerships that recognize the goal of many consumers to acquire new automobiles. However, the financial impediment frequently hinders fulfillment of this goal. To overcome this barrier, dealers often offer new cars with no down payment required at the time of purchase. Moreover, these dealers arrange for convenient monthly payments that commence after a grace period. The same strategy has been used by dealerships of home furnishings, allowing consumers to acquire their needed furniture while removing the associated financial impediments. Marketers of major appliances and home electronics go even a step farther. Not only do they remove the financial barriers, they further eliminate the physical impediments of delivering such heavy items to consumers' homes and ridding them of the old units. It should also be obvious that the success of the credit card industry was largely based on the same premise—eliminating financial impediments that most of us face as we attempt to fulfill our goals of product or service acquisitions.

The theory of goal pursuit and trying also addresses the role of significant others and social norms toward trying (i.e., how our neighbors, friends, and family would view an act, such as moving away from our present home to a distant retirement community). It further regards the *recency* and *frequency* of past trying, as well as the subjective norm toward trying, to be significant factors influencing our intentions to try, actual trying, and goal attainment. For example, consider the case of a couple who may have been contemplating a move to a warmer climate. If we were to learn that they had contacted and seriously explored four retirement communities in Florida, Arizona, Texas, and Tennessee over the past three months, this would be a positive indication revealing their serious intentions to achieve the goal of relocating. Accordingly, the frequency of past trial and recency of such trials exert significant influence on how available and accessible information about a goal (such as relocating) is. Furthermore, the intention to relocate would even be strengthened more if the couple knew that significant others, such as the family, were in approval and supportive of the move.

HOW ATTITUDES ARE FORMED

We form attitudes largely through association and learning, such as via classical and operant conditioning, as well as through cognitive learning.[24] (For a detailed discussion of these theories, see Chapter 4 on learning.) In *classical conditioning*, a positive attitude (conditioned response) can be elicited by presenting along with the brand (conditioned stimulus) an attractive unconditioned stimulus. An advertising manager may therefore pair the brand with an emotionally appealing stimulus in order to generate a desired consumer response. Many U.S. producers of cosmetics and perfumes use French-sounding brand names for their products to create the impression that they are exotic and desirable French creations. Through such a link, a positive consumer response is produced toward the brand. Similarly, associating a shampoo with proteins known to provide shiny and silky hair, or a facial cream with vitamin E known to restore health and radiance to the skin, brings about desirable linkages. In this manner, a positive attitude toward the shampoo or facial cream emerges. This strategy simply applies Pavlovian learning principles for purposes of attitude shaping.[25]

Similarly, the concept of family branding applies this classical conditioning viewpoint. Corporations such as Apple, Sony, and General Electric use the same brand name on every product they produce. The positive connotations that the well-known brand carries transfer to any new item these companies introduce.

Attitudes may also result from *operant conditioning*, in which learning occurs as a result of the consequences of the behavior itself. Rewards enhance attitudes toward a stimulus and increase the probability that a behavior will recur. During certain seasons of the year, such as the period before Christmas, many retailers open their doors early in the morning to accommodate shopping traffic. The first hundred or so customers, upon entering the store, may be given *early bird* gifts or discounts as rewards for shopping early. Such rewards are instrumental in developing positive attitudes toward the store as well as toward the shopping experience. Similarly, in view of the intense competition between cell phone companies such as Verizon, T-Mobile, and AT&T, among others, these service providers attempt to enhance favorable attitudes toward their particular brand by offering various deals and specials, such as free cell phones and accessories, as well as bundling packages at reduced rates.

In the context of *cognitive learning*, consumers form attitudes about products based on both exposure to information about them provided by marketers as well as through consumers' own cognitions (knowledge, experience, and goals). A number of recently developed models known as *attitude-toward-the-ad* models attempt to explain the way we may form attitudes, feelings, and judgments about products as a result of our exposure to ads about them. These models, which apply under low-involvement conditions, suggest that where, when, and in what context an ad is seen are among the variables that may shape the attitudes we form toward the ad and, in turn, toward the product.[26] Examples abound in the advertising field of instances where liking of the commercial translated into positive attitudes toward the product. Among these examples are the gecko commercials of GEICO automobile insurance company for the firm's low-cost policies. In such cases, it is clear that liking toward the ad may transfer to the brand. Conversely, if consumers dislike the ad, negative feelings toward the brand may result. The GEICO ad in Figure 5.3 applies the attitude-toward-the-ad model by depicting a popular trade-character presentation of a "Geckonomics" textbook for saving money on more than just car insurance.

All text and images are copyrighted with permission from GEICO.

FIGURE 5.3

In this ad from GEICO, popularity and liking for the gecko character are employed to enhance consumers' attitudes toward the brand.

ETHICAL DILEMMA

Lock Up the Treats

On New Year's Day 2014, it became legal in Colorado to sell marijuana in specially licensed dispensaries to adults age twenty-one and older. Much like shopping at a liquor store, a consumer can walk in a dispensary, show his or her ID, and make a purchase. These dispensaries, however, do not just carry marijuana for smoking, but also stock a wide variety of marijuana edibles, which come in forms such as cookies, gummies, brownies, carmels, hard candies, chocolate bars, Rice Krispies treats, among others.

In the first year of legalization in Colorado, 5 million edibles were sold. There are many companies that have jumped on the bandwagon, with names such as Dixie Elixirs, Incredibles, and Bluekudu, which have added many new items to the list of edibles. Also included among them is CanCor, the owner of Keef Cola, a soft drink line. Even a company such as Ben & Jerry stated that it would experiment with cannabis-infused ice cream if legal hurdles were removed.

Marijuana is legal for adult recreational use in such states as California, Alaska, Colorado, Oregon, Washington, the District of Colombia, and Guam. According to ArcView Market Research, U.S. sales of legal cannabis reached $5.4 billion in 2015. Edibles and other infused products make up at least half of the total figure, according to dispensary owners.

A major issue when ingesting marijuana is a person's inability to predict the right amount to consume. A number of factors affect a person's reaction to a dosage, which include the type of marijuana used in making the edible, the person's tolerance, body weight, gender, and age. And since the effect of edibles can take an hour or two to reach its height, the danger of impatient individuals ingesting more edibles can increase the likelihood of a negative reaction.

Despite a recent momentum for legalization of cannabis, the industry is still attempting to convince both lawmakers and the public that edible marijuana products are safe to consume. However, one major concern facing the industry is the obvious appeal of pot-infused candies, cookies, and soda pop to children. Children accidentally ingest edibles that look like their non-marijuana-infused counterparts. In the past couple of years, hospitals reported a significant increase in the number of children treated for unknowingly eating marijuana-laced treats. For example, the American Association of Poison Control Center filed 456 calls in 2014 about accidental exposure to THC, the active chemical compound in marijuana, among children under the age of twelve.

In the past couple of years, several states have taken steps to enact new marijuana laws in order to prevent or reduce such accidents. These laws require that marijuana edibles be sold in child-resistant packaging that is opaque so that the contents are not visible, free of cartoons or other images that may appeal to children, and constructed to be difficult for children under age five to open. Labels also must be informative and give warning regarding the package's contents.

Because edibles are in their own league for delivering a unique cannabis experience, regulations concerning edibles vary widely from state to state. Legalizing marijuana consumption, including these edibles, seems to present a new territory for both legislators and the public in general. Various states may follow suit and legalize marijuana consumption, while others may refrain to do so—resulting in a constantly evolving landscape of adopters.[27]

In the past few years, the cannabis industry faced a number of regulatory shifts, in particular regarding controversial pot-infused edibles. Various states, as well as their officials and constituencies, differ widely on this issue. Learn more about a state-by-state breakdown of cannabis-infused edible product laws by visiting http://ireadculture.com/cannabis-infused-edibles-laws-a-state-by-state-breakdown/. Further, some observers claim that tragedies surrounding edible-marijuana products could have been avoided if these regulations were initially set in place. Do you agree with this assertion? Why or why not? Speculate about the positive and negative outcomes that would be realized by legalizing marijuana altogether.

The role of cognition in attitude formation has stimulated research in yet another closely related area—our tendency to attribute causes to events we encounter. This tendency, known as attribution, has a bearing on the way we think of objects or situations around us and, in turn, how we coin our attitudes toward them.

ATTRIBUTION THEORY

According to attribution theory, we attempt to ascertain the causes of events in our daily lives. We make hypotheses about why things happen and who or what is responsible for their occurrence. We also try to discern whether incidents are caused by something internal or external to us. If a homemaker buys a new brand of cake mix and bakes a delicious dessert, the homemaker can attribute the positive outcome either to one's own baking ability or to the qualities of the cake mix. This process through which we determine causality exerts an effect on the attitudes we form.[28]

We make attributions in part to determine how to respond to occurrences now and in the future. Homemakers who attribute their cake's success to their own ability would not necessarily form positive attitudes toward the new brand, because in their view any brand would do. If, however, they attribute the cake's success to the new brand, homemakers are more likely to develop positive attitudes toward it and select it again.[29]

Attribution also provides insight for marketers in the area of promotional claims and how these claims affect the formation of consumers' attitudes. Prospects realize that some of the positive statements made by sellers about their offerings are ploys to generate purchases. Consumers in this case tend to discount such assertions as caused by the marketer's desire to promote their products—a feeling that reduces the effectiveness of the promotional effort. To avoid this possibility, researchers suggest the use of product disclaimers, or admission of some product limitations in comparison to the competition.[30] This strategy may enhance the credibility of the claims, creating a more favorable attitude toward a brand. Pharmaceutical companies' ads and commercials provide good examples of this strategy. The ads list the negative side effects associated with the medication being promoted and enumerate circumstances and patient conditions when the drug should not be taken.

attribution
efforts to ascertain the causes of events in our lives

HOW ATTITUDES ARE CHANGED

As was pointed out earlier in this chapter under the heading "Valence, Intensity, and Centrality of Attitudes," the likelihood that an attitude can be changed depends on its centrality and intensity. Attitudes are difficult to change, and the likelihood of their change varies inversely with their centrality and intensity; that is, the more central or extreme the valence of an attitude, the more difficult it is to modify or restructure it.

For many marketers and advertisers, attitude change is a primary goal. Attitude change shifts a negative valence to a positive one or vice versa. It requires a change in the organization or structure of a belief, or a change in the content of a belief itself.

The real challenge to marketers arises when the goal is to create favorable attitudes toward a company or its products among consumers who do not regard them favorably. A number of theories govern the approaches that marketers use to achieve attitude change. The most frequently employed are cognitive consistency and information-processing theories.[31] Let us look first at how cognitive consistency theories can help in this regard.

The Role of Cognitive Consistency in Attitude Change

The basic premise of cognitive consistency is that humans strive to maintain congruity between the three components of an attitude (cognitive, affective, and behavioral). Shoppers' purchasing behavior, for example, is expected to be consistent with their attitudes. The newly formed attitudes are also expected to be consistent with their values and personalities. Consistency theories actually encompass a large group of theories, including (1) cognitive dissonance theory, (2) balance theory, and (3) congruity theory.[32] These theories reiterate a recurring theme—a person's tendency to maintain harmonious relationships between the cognitive (belief), affective (emotional), and behavioral elements of an attitude. For the purposes of our present coverage, it suffices to view Festinger's cognitive dissonance theory to explain how creating a conflict (dissonance) can be instrumental in bringing about a desired attitude change.

Cognitive Dissonance Theory

Cognitive dissonance theory assumes that we seek consistency among the three attitude components, as well as congruity between our values

attitude change
a shift in the valence of an attitude from negative to positive or vice versa

cognitive consistency
a view that we strive to maintain congruity between beliefs, emotions, and behavior

cognitive dissonance theory
a view that inconsistency between a person's beliefs and behavior causes psychological tension

and the behavior we exhibit. Inconsistency among the components of an attitude produces psychological tension that motivates us to restore the balance. For example, individuals who go on a diet are much more likely to adopt foods that are made with various fat and sugar substitutes.[33] In so doing, such individuals maintain the psychological balance between beliefs (the need to lose weight) and actions (eating lower-calorie foods). If we experience dissonance between our beliefs and actions, we will either attempt to alter our behavior to be more consistent with our held beliefs or change our beliefs to become more consistent with our behavior.[34]

Festinger constructed cognitive dissonance theory within the confines of a free-will situation, where a person faces a free choice between a number of desirable alternatives. Dissonance occurs once the choice between alternatives has been made and, in this sense, is synonymous with postdecisional conflict. Suppose, for example, that an individual has to choose between two prestigious automobiles—a Mercedes-Benz and a BMW, for example. In resolving this conflict, the individual selects and purchases the BMW. Once an alternative has been chosen, the attractive features of the rejected alternative and unattractive features of the selected alternative start to become magnified in the consumer's mind. As a consequence, the consumer will experience postpurchase dissonance, a state of doubt regarding the wisdom of the purchasing decision. Because dissonance is felt as tension and psychological discomfort, the individual is motivated to resolve this condition by either revoking the decision (changing the behavior) or seeking out additional positive information to support it (reinforcing the original belief that led to the decision).

Marketers use dissonance to change attitudes. In creating a situation where information conflicts with beliefs, marketers hope that the resulting dissonant condition may lead to attitude or behavior modification. One popular strategy marketers use to conjure up dissonance is playing on consumers' fears. Insurance companies, pharmaceutical companies, medical centers, and investment consultants are among the many firms that use cognitive dissonance—precipitated by fear appeals—to change attitudes or improve feelings toward their products and services. For example, because many people do not like to think about death and the purchase of life (death) insurance, companies in this line of business attempt to overcome prospects' resistance by stirring their sympathy toward their family. Ads depict the bleak future that awaits a family's members if one were to die suddenly. Direct-to-consumer pharmaceutical ads are designed to raise consumers' fears regarding a variety of medical conditions. These commercials then encourage consumers to take the step of seeing their doctor and asking for the advertised drug. Figure 5.4 displays an ad from the Centers for Disease Control and Prevention in which imagery of the risky consequences of smoking are crossed with reasons to quit smoking in order to create dissonance.

Now let us turn our attention to the second approach to changing attitudes, known as information processing.

The Role of Information Processing in Attitude Change

Whereas the cognitive consistency approach emphasizes harmony among the components of an individual's attitudes, the information-processing approach emphasizes communicating relevant and appropriate facts to consumers. The underlying assumption is that consumers are rational and able to see the logic supporting an issue, causing them to adjust their behavior accordingly. This approach employs advertising and other forms of promotion specifically designed to produce the desired impact on the target audience.[35]

The information-processing model appears to be one of the most widely used strategies in marketing, largely because it lends itself well to the mass and social media. Its objective is to attain a change in the dynamics of an attitude through a change in its cognitive component. Because consumers are logical creatures capable of comprehension, data analysis, and problem solving to arrive at a goal-directed behavior, it follows that presenting them with persuasive communication should make behavior change possible. After processing the new information, the consumer may decide to change behavior toward an attitude object. For example, many consumers today prefer to purchase organic fruits and vegetables due to promotional efforts by Whole Foods and similar retailers to publicize the health benefits and superiority of organics over conventional produce.

If an individual is to be successfully persuaded, this person has to pass through a number of information-processing stages for maximum impact. McGuire, using an information-processing approach to explain attitude and behavior change, proposed a sequential series of six steps through which an individual passes in order to be effectively persuaded. Exhibit 5.3 illustrates them: presentation, attention, comprehension, yielding, retention, and behavior. Each of these steps can be assigned a certain probability of occurring, and the probability of an attitude change is the product of the probabilities of the individual steps.

As shown in Exhibit 5.3, a message intended to affect and persuade consumers must first reach them; it must also be presented in a way that wins

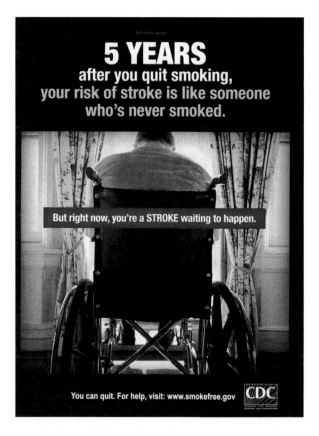

FIGURE 5.4

The illustration in this ad depicts a person in a wheelchair, along with the statement, "You're a STROKE waiting to happen." This message presents a powerful image likely to cause smokers to experience cognitive dissonance.

their attention. Further, receivers must comprehend the arguments and conclusions contained in the message and note their relevance to them. Yielding to conclusions largely depends on the persuasiveness of the arguments and their relevance to receivers' needs. Finally, consumers must retain the conclusions until an opportunity arises to act on them.[36]

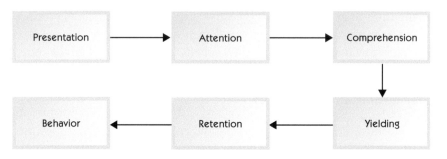

EXHIBIT 5.3

McGuire's Information-Processing Model

Source: William J. McGuire, "An Information-Processing Model of Advertising Effectiveness," a paper presented at the Symposium of Behavioral and Management Science in Marketing, Center for Continuing Education, University of Chicago, July 1969.

For marketers and advertisers, the result of persuasive communication depends on the degree of consumer involvement; that is, how important the attitude object is to the consumer. As we might expect, under conditions of *low involvement*, attitudes are less intense and are supported by less knowledge about the attributes of the stimulus. Such attitudes are more susceptible to change when individuals are exposed to persuasive arguments. For example, shoppers waiting in the checkout line at a grocery store may choose a brand of chewing gum that offers a two-for-the-price-of-one pack rather than their regular brand. For most consumers, chewing gum is a low-involvement product, and brand choice is not a significant issue. Promotional pricing strategies thus would likely affect brand selection.[37]

Under conditions of *high involvement*, on the other hand, consumers are motivated to think about the information presented. As a result, communication offering strong arguments and sound logic would likely be required to produce attitude change. For high-involvement situations, the persuasiveness of a message in the form of convincing evidence is critical if attitude change is to be achieved.

Marketers use a number of strategies that stem from the information-processing model to change consumer attitudes. These include making direct comparisons against competitive brands, highlighting present brand attributes, adding new attributes, providing knowledge of alternatives or consequences, and changing the relative values of brand attributes. You are probably familiar with many of these.

Making Comparisons Against Competition

The comparison strategy attempts to change consumer beliefs about the company's products in relation to those of competitors by emphasizing its advantages against competing brands. Comparative advertising, used in many cases to accomplish this objective, presents the company's product along with another competing brand mentioned by name; the message explains how the company's product is better in some way than the other brand.

Emphasizing Brand Attributes

The second strategy for changing attitudes centers on enhancing consumer knowledge of certain attributes or features of the brand. This communication strategy highlights less-familiar attributes to create a positive disposition toward the brand.

Adding New Attributes

Another strategy for changing attitudes is to add one or more new attributes to the product in an attempt to increase its attractiveness. Car models may include a number of extra options as standard equipment. Breakfast cereal may be promoted as containing fiber, lowering cholesterol, and being beneficial for the heart.

Providing Knowledge of Alternatives or Consequences

Providing consumers with evidence, facts, or figures that allow them to make an informed choice between existing alternatives is another strategy for changing attitudes. Through this exercise in logic, consumers can determine which alternative is best for them. Some Culligan ads, for example, explain to consumers the various impurities present in tap water and suggest a Culligan purification system as a solution to the problem. Competitors, such as Britta, offer self-monitoring water filters that, ads claim, remove lead and other contaminants, improve taste, and tell owners when the filter needs replacement.

Changing the Relative Value of Attributes

Still another approach to changing attitudes toward a product attempts to shift the relative values of specific attributes the product possesses.[38] For instance, how desirable is the decay-prevention attribute in toothpaste? Could fresh breath and whiter teeth be as important, or more important? How important is style or design to automobile buyers? Could gas mileage or protecting the fragile environment be a more powerful attribute?

Many of these strategies have been and continue to be successfully applied by marketers in their efforts to change consumer attitudes. Astute marketers have learned that attitude change is a slow, gradual, and difficult process, but in general it is more likely to occur (1) if consumers perceive greater benefit in a suggested course of action, (2) if consumers feel that their need has been satisfied more completely or easily by such an attitude realignment, (3) if a linkage has been formed between purchase of a brand and a specific consumer interest or cause, and/or (4) if incentives such as coupons, samples, rebates, sweepstakes, or giveaways have been made available by the seller.

CONSUMER REACTION TO MARKETERS' ATTITUDE-RELATED STRATEGIES

Up to this point, we have examined how marketers attempt to influence the formation or change of consumer attitudes as well as the strategies they use to accomplish these objectives. The other side of the coin, however, is the reaction of consumers as marketers seek to influence their attitudes. In other words, how do consumers react to these attempts, and how do they process the information marketers communicate to them? The elaboration-likelihood model addresses the ways consumers deal with these types of persuasive efforts.

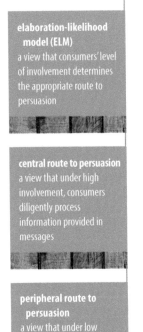

elaboration-likelihood model (ELM)
a view that consumers' level of involvement determines the appropriate route to persuasion

central route to persuasion
a view that under high involvement, consumers diligently process information provided in messages

peripheral route to persuasion
a view that under low involvement, consumers are less likely to process information provided in messages

The elaboration-likelihood model (ELM) proposes in general that an individual exposed to an ad will relate the information it contains to prior experiences, knowledge, and information to arrive at new ideas that were present neither in the ad nor in that person's previous knowledge set. This model also suggests that the degree to which a consumer *elaborates* on a message depends on its relevance to that person. The more relevant the message, the more elaboration occurs. The central route to persuasion requires greater elaboration; the peripheral route to persuasion requires less.[39] For example, a consumer who is experiencing symptoms of mild Alzheimer's disease would be more apt to elaborate on evidence provided in a message from Eisai and Pfizer regarding its prescription medicine ARICEPT for treating this condition than another individual who is not suffering such symptoms. Similarly, research has shown that when evaluating products, some consumers are particularly concerned about how their use of that product will affect the image they project, which would lead to central processing. For others, however, image is unimportant, which would lead to peripheral processing.[40]

The central route to persuasion is presumed to prevail under conditions of high involvement. Here, the message recipient has both the ability and motivation to process the information. An individual is likely to think about the evidence and arguments presented in the message, determine whether they are compelling, and then develop his or her position on the matter. For example, a prospective buyer may be exposed to an ad containing arguments supporting the purchase of a hybrid or electric automobile instead of a luxurious and expensive foreign car. The ad claims that by choosing the hybrid, the consumer would save money on gasoline and help protect the fragile environment. This prospect may find the evidence to be sufficiently compelling to select the hybrid instead of the foreign luxury car that was originally considered. Petty and Cacioppo suggest that the central route to persuasion can produce a lasting change in attitudes; however, they warn that this change may be difficult to accomplish. The ad in Figure 5.5 from ClimateMaster presents the claim that by using the company's geothermal heat pump systems, consumers can trim their heating and cooling costs by up to 80 percent, protect the environment, as well as benefit from new federal tax credits. By providing such facts about this innovative heating and cooling system, the ad employs the central route to persuasion.

CUT YOUR HEATING AND COOLING COSTS UP TO 80%.

Cut your energy bills. ClimateMaster geothermal systems tap the constant temperature of the earth to provide heating, cooling, and hot water. Your home stays comfortable year-round while trimming your energy use by up to 80%. And now with new federal tax credits, you will save an additional 30% on the total installation. Best of all, ClimateMaster systems are not only a good investment, they are a cleaner choice for the environment. To learn more about how the geothermal technology leader can help you cut your energy bills, visit climatemaster.com or call 877-436-6263 today.

CLIMATEMASTER
Geothermal Heat Pump Systems
An LSB Industries, Inc. Company (NYSE: LXU)

Ad courtesy of ClimateMaster Inc.

FIGURE 5.5

This ad from ClimateMaster provides solid reasons for installing this innovative geothermal heat pump system. Cost savings, protection of the environment, and tax credits are but three of the reasons emphasized in the ad to entice prospective buyers.

The peripheral route to persuasion, on the other hand, is likely to prevail under conditions of low involvement. Here message recipients are unlikely to have strong feelings about the issue or possess a great deal of prior knowledge about it. Nor would they devote a great deal of thought to the issues, evidence, or arguments presented in the message. The basis for this view lies in the observation that, in order to function in contemporary society, an individual must often act as a *lazy organism or cognitive miser*.[41] In many cases, people choose not to think a great deal about messages, issues, and arguments. Instead, they resort to some rudimentary means for deciding what is good or bad, desirable or undesirable. Individuals may simply respond to source cues (attractiveness, likability, credibility of a presenter) or apply uncomplicated rules of thumb (select the most advertised brand, choose the most expensive item, buy what happens to be on sale).

Recent research on the role of the elaboration-likelihood model in consumer processing of Internet advertising proposed a modified ELM that incorporates elements unique to the Internet environment.[42] Similar to the case of other media types, high involvement leads to click-through of banner ads via the central route. However, in low-involvement cases, factors such as larger-than-average ad size and dynamic animation tend to enhance click-through via the peripheral route. Other moderators of ad click-through were found to be product-category relevance, attitude toward web advertising, and consumers' experience with the Web.[43]

Because it would be impossible for most individuals to exert extensive mental effort to analyze all persuasive communications to which they are exposed, it may be sufficient in some cases for communicators to merely *expose* consumers to an issue or *remind* them of it, rather than present substantive arguments in order to achieve the desired attitude confirmation or change. By simply associating a product or issue with other positive information or desired goals the recipient may already hold, marketers could achieve their purpose of attitude change and behavior modification. The ad in Figure 5.6 from Light of Life Foundation applies the peripheral route to persuasion by means of the simplicity of its presentation.

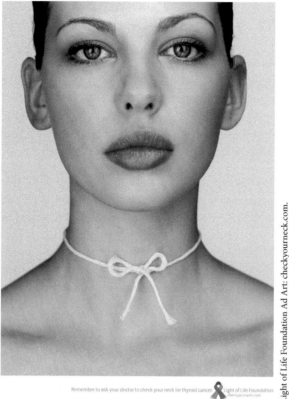

Remember to ask your doctor to check your neck for thyroid cancer. Light of Life Foundation checkyourneck.com

FIGURE 5.6

By minimizing verbal information about thyroid cancer, and utilizing a simple and attractive visual presentation, this Light of Life Foundation ad employs the peripheral route to persuasion.

At the heart of the study of consumer behavior is the notion that consumers attempt to accomplish some end result through the purchase and use of products or services. Through our discussion of the role of attitudes in shaping behavior, we have seen that the mechanisms by which attitudes influence actual behavior are quite varied. No simple relationship between attitudes and behavior applies to all products and situations. This realization brings to focus the need to understand other forces that impel our actions. The topic of motivation is presented in the next chapter to shed further light on the processes that underlie human behavior. In discussing motivation, the biological, social, and psychological bases for our actions will be examined along with an overview of the influence of emotions on our behavior.

SUMMARY

This chapter addresses the properties of attitudes; the relationship between beliefs, attitudes, and behavior; and the factors that influence attitude formation and change. Attitudes develop largely as a result of personal experience with objects, social interaction, and exposure to mass and social media. Attitudes can serve utilitarian, ego-defensive, value-expressive, and knowledge functions for an individual.

Individuals *sometimes* act in accordance with their attitudes. At other times they behave in a manner quite inconsistent with them. A number of theories address the impact of attitudes on behavior. One such theory is the traditional model, which suggests that attitudes consist of cognitive, affective, and behavioral components. Another view posits a multiattribute model in which individuals hold attitudes toward various facets of an attitude object. The theory of reasoned action distinguishes between attitude toward the object and attitude toward the behavior. It also recognizes the roles of intentions and subjective norms. The theories of goal pursuit and trying address individuals' attempts to reach a *goal* when real or perceived impediments stand in the way of attainment.

Attitudes are formed largely through association and learning, such as via classical and operant conditioning, as well as cognitive learning. Attribution is the process by which people hypothesize why things happen and who or what is responsible for various occurrences. Such attributions influence the way we perceive objects and, in turn, our attitudes toward them.

A cognitive consistency approach to attitude change posits that individuals strive for harmony between three components of an attitude (cognitive, affective, and behavioral). Cognitive dissonance theory assumes individuals seek consistency among the three attitude components, as well as congruity between their values and the behavior that stems from them. Inconsistency produces psychological tension that motivates a person to restore the balance.

An information-processing approach, on the other hand, emphasizes communicating factual, persuasive, and relevant messages to consumers in order to permit logical processing of ideas and, in turn, attitude or behavior change. This approach suggests five attitude change strategies for marketers: making comparisons against competition, emphasizing brand attributes, adding new attributes, providing knowledge of alternatives or consequences, and changing the relative value of attributes.

The issue of how consumers react to and process marketers' persuasive communications is addressed in the elaboration-likelihood model. In this view, the extent to which a consumer *elaborates* on a message depends on its relevance to that person. The more relevant the message, the more elaboration occurs. The central route to persuasion is presumed to prevail under conditions of high involvement. Under conditions of low involvement, the peripheral route to persuasion is likely to prevail.

CASE SYNOPSIS

Inside the War on Coal

Recently, the coal industry has been under siege from federal regulation due to President Obama's Clean Power Plan, which went into effect in October 2015. Calls from consumers and activists who support the plan to close aging coal-fired power plants resulted in forcing some coal producers to file for bankruptcy, and others to shut down altogether. In an effort to fight these restrictions, the coal industry is mustering all the weapons at its disposal—such as lobbying, legislation, litigation, and a multimillion-dollar advertising campaign—to highlight the benefit of "clean coal," as well as to point out the unfair loss of jobs for thousands of coal-industry workers. Furthermore, a group of coal-burning utility companies, along with twenty-nine states, filed a legal challenge against the Clean Power Plan and the EPA, a dispute that would almost certainly end up before the Supreme Court.

Notes

1   Evan Perez, "How ISIS Is Luring So Many Americans to Join Its Ranks," *CNN* (April 23, 2015), http://www.cnn.com/2015/04/22/politics/isis-recruits-american-arrests/; Faisal Irshaid, "How ISIS Is Spreading Its Message Online," *BBC News* (June 19, 2014), http://www.bbc.com/news/world-middle-east-27912569; Ray Sanchez, "ISIS Exploits Social Media to Make Inroads in US," *CNN* (June 5, 2015), http://www.cnn.com/2015/06/04/us/isis-social-media-recruits/; and "How ISIS Recruits Through Social Media,"

Fordham Political Review, http://fordhampoliticalreview.org/how-isis-re-cruits-through-social-media/.

2 Chet Kane, "Accessing Latest Trends? It's Attitude, Not Behavior," *Brandweek* (February 21, 1994), p. 15.

3 Martin Fishbein and Icek Ajzen, *Beliefs, Attitude, Intention, and Behavior: An Introduction to Theory and Research* (Reading, MA: Addison-Wesley, 1975), p. 6; Richard J. Lutz, "The Role of Attitude Theory in Marketing," in Harold Kassarjian and Thomas Robertson (Eds.), *Perspectives in Consumer Behavior, 4th ed.* (Upper Saddle River, NJ: Prentice Hall, 1991), pp. 317–339.

4 Rajdeep Grewal, Raj Mehta, and Frank R. Kardes, "The Timing of Repeat Purchase of Consumer Durable Goods: The Role of Functional Bases of Consumer Attitudes," *Journal of Marketing Research* 41, no. 1 (February 2004), pp. 101–115; Daniel Katz, "The Functional Approach to the Study of Attitudes," *Public Opinion Quarterly* 24 (1960), p. 170; see also S. Shavitt, "The Role of Attitude Objects in Attitude Functions," *Journal of Experimental Social Psychology* 26 (1999), pp. 124–148.

5 S. Arnocky and T. Piche, "Cosmetic Surgery as Intrasexual Competition: The Mediating Role of Social Comparison," *Scientific Research* 5 (May 2014), pp. 1197–1205; American Society of Plastic Surgeons, "2014 Plastic Surgery Report" (2014), http://www.plasticsurgery.org/news/plastic-surgery-statistics/2014-plastic-surgery-statistics.html; "Plastic Surgery Procedures Continue Steady Growth in US" (February 26, 2014), www.plasticsurgery.org/news/2014/plastic-surgery-procedures-continue-steady-growth-in-us.html; American Society for Aesthetic Plastic Surgery, "Cosmetic Surgery Statistics," http://www.surgery.org/media/statistics; "Plastic Surgeons in the US: Market Research Report," *IBIS World* (February 2015), http://www.ibisworld.com/industry/plastic-surgeons.html; "As Economy Grows, So Does the Plastic Surgery Industry," *ABC News*, http://abcnews.go.com/health/economy-grows-plastic-surgery-industry/story?id=12869991.

6 Shavitt, "The Role of Attitude Objects in Attitude Functions."

7 Aarthi Rayabura, "Millennials Most Sustainability-Conscious Generation Yet, But Don't Call Them Environmentalists," Pew Research Center (March 11, 2014), http://www.sustainablebrands.com/news_and_views/stakeholder_trends_insights/aarthi_rayabura/millennials_most_sustainability_conscious.

8 S. M. Corey, "Professed Attitudes and Actual Behavior," *Journal of Educational Psychology* 28 (1937), pp. 271–280; see also C. Seligman et al., "Predicting Summer Energy Consumption from Home-owners' Attitudes," *Journal of Applied Social Psychology* 9 (1979), pp. 70–90.

9 Laurie Peterson, "Get Ready for Global Coupon War," *Adweek's Marketing Week* (1991), in William D. Perreault Jr. and E. Jerome McCarthy (Eds.), *Applications in Basic Marketing*, 1993 ed. (Homewood, IL: Irwin, 1992), p. 151; Bill Wolfe, "Shoppers Save Coupons at a Healthy Clip," *Chicago Sun-Times* (October 18, 1998), p. 58A.

10 R. H. Fazio and D. R. Roskos-Ewoldsen, "Acting as We Feel," in S. Shavitt and T. C. Brock (Eds.), *Persuasion: Psychological Insights and Perspectives* (Boston: Allyn and Bacon, 1994), pp. 71–93.

11 Thomas T. Semon, "Knowing Attitudes Is Nice, but Not Enough," *Marketing News* (October 21, 1996), p. 6; Kane, "Accessing Latest Trends? It's Attitude, Not Behavior."

12 Laurie Freeman, "Sales of Aspirin Soar After Study," *Advertising Age* (March 28, 1988), pp. 3, 74.

13 Milton J. Rosenberg, "An Analysis of Affective–Cognitive Consistency," in M. J. Rosenberg, Carl I. Hovland et al. (Eds.), *Attitude Organization and Change* (New Haven: Yale University Press, 1960).

14 Joel B. Cohen and Charles S. Areni, "Affect and Consumer Behavior," in Thomas Robertson and Harold Kassarjian (Eds.), *Handbook of Consumer Behavior* (Upper Saddle River, NJ: Prentice Hall), pp. 188–240.

15 Gareth Parkin, "Promote Beauty with Promotional Products," *Article Dashboard,* www.articledashboard.com/Article/Promote . . . Promotional-Products/275350.

16 Martin Fishbein, "An Investigation of the Relationship Between Beliefs About an Object and the Attitude Toward That Object," *Human Relations* 16 (1963), pp. 233–240; Fishbein and Ajzen, *Beliefs, Attitude, Intention, and Behavior: An Introduction to Theory and Research*; Icek Ajzen and Martin Fishbein, *Understanding Attitudes and Predicting Social Behavior* (Upper Saddle River, NJ: Prentice Hall, 1980); William L. Wilkie and Edgar A. Pessemier, "Issues in Marketing's Use of Multi-Attribute Models," *Journal of Marketing Research* 10 (November 1973), pp. 428–441; James R. Bettman, Noel Capon, and Richard J. Lutz, "Multi-attribute Measurement Models and Multi-attribute Theory: A Test of Construct Validity," *Journal of Consumer Research* 1 (March 1975), pp. 1–14; Michael B. Mazis, Olli T. Ahtola, and R. Eugene Klippel, "A Comparison of Four Multi-Attribute Models in the Prediction of Consumer Attitudes," *Journal of Consumer Research* 2 (June 1975), pp. 38–52; David J. Curry, Michael B. Menasco, and James W. Van Ark, "Multi-attribute Dyadic Choice: Models and Tests," *Journal of Marketing Research* 28 (August 1991), pp. 259–267.

17 Fishbein and Ajzen, "*Beliefs, Attitude, Intention, and Behavior: An Introduction to Theory and Research.*"

18 Ajzen and Fishbein, *Understanding Attitudes and Predicting Social Behavior*; see also Michael J. Ryan and E. H. Bonfield, "Fishbein's Intentions Model: A Test of External and Pragmatic Validity," *Journal of Marketing* 44 (Spring 1980), pp. 82–95; Terence Shimp and Alican Kavas, "The Theory of Reasoned Action Applied to Coupon Usage," *Journal of Consumer Research* 11 (December 1984), pp. 795–809; Richard L. Oliver and William O. Bearden, "Crossover Effects in the Theory of Reasoned Action: A Moderating Influence Attempt," *Journal of Consumer Research* 12 (December 1985), pp. 324–340; Blair H. Sheppard, Jon Hartwick, and Paul R. Warshaw, "The Theory of Reasoned Action: A Meta-Analysis of Past Research and Recommendations

for Modifications and Future Research," *Journal of Consumer Research* 15 (September 1986), pp. 325–343; Richard P. Bagozzi, Hans Baumgartner, and Youjae Yi, "State versus Action Orientation and the Theory of Reasoned Action: An Application to Coupon Usage," *Journal of Consumer Research* 18 (March 1992), pp. 505–518.

19 Faryn Shiro, "Disney Shanghai: Go Inside $5.5 Billion Theme Park in China, *ABC News* (July 15, 2015), http://abcnews.go.com/Lifestyle/disney-shanghai-inside-55-billion-theme-park-china/story?id=32456306; Brett Nachman, "Disney in Depth," *Geeks of Doom* (March 3, 2016), http://www.geeksofdoom.com/2016/03/03/disney-in-depth-awaiting-shanghai-disneylands-majesty; Alejandro Alba, "Disney Reveals Concept Art for Shanghai 'Toy Story' Hotel," *NY Daily News*, http://www.nydailynews.com/news/world/disney-reveals-concept-art-shanghai-toy-story-hotel-article-1.2030820; "Disney Unveils Shanghai Disneyland Plans," *FOX News* (July 15, 2015), http://www.foxnews.com/travel/2015/07/15/disney-unveils-shanghai-disneyland-details/print.

20 I. Ajzen, "From Intentions to Actions: A Theory of Planned Behavior," in J. Kuhl and J. Beckmann (Eds.), *Action-Control: From Cognition to Behavior* (New York: Springer, 1985), pp. 11–39.

21 Richard P. Bagozzi and Paul R. Warshaw, "Trying to Consume," *Journal of Consumer Research* 17 (September 1990), pp. 127–140; Richard P. Bagozzi, Fred D. Davis, and Paul R. Warshaw, "Development and Test of a Theory of Technological Learning and Usage," *Human Relations* 45, no. 7 (July 1992), pp. 659–686; Richard P. Bagozzi, "Attitudes, Intentions, and Behavior: A Test of Some Key Hypotheses," *Journal of Personality and Social Psychology* 41 (October 1981), pp. 607–627.

22 Bagozzi, Davis, and Warshaw, "Development and Test of a Theory of Technological Learning and Usage"; Bagozzi and Warshaw, "Trying to Consume."

23 Maureen Milford (Gannett News Service), "New Policy for Stores: Please Try It," *Chicago Sun-Times* (July 28, 1997), p. 48.

24 John Kim, Chris T. Allen, and Frank R. Kardes, "An Investigation of the Mediational Mechanisms Underlying Attitudinal Conditioning," *Journal of Marketing Research* 33, no. 3 (August 1996), pp. 318–328.

25 John Kim, Chris T. Allen, and Frank R. Kardes, "An Investigation of the Mediational Mechanisms Underlying Attitudinal Conditioning," *Journal of Marketing Research* XXXIII (August 1996), pp. 318–328.

26 Terence Shimp, "Attitude toward the Ad as a Mediator of Consumer Brand Choice," *Journal of Advertising* 10, no. 2 (1981), pp. 9–15; Pamela M. Homer, "The Mediating Effect of Attitude toward the Ad: Some Additional Evidence," *Journal of Marketing Research* 27 (February 1990), pp. 78–86; Thomas J. Olney, Morris B. Holbrook, and Rajeev Batra, "Consumer Responses to Advertising: The Effect of Ad Content, Emotions, and Attitude toward the Ad on Viewing Time," *Journal of Consumer Research* 17 (March 1991), pp. 440–453; Stephen P. Brown and Douglas M. Stayman, "Ad: A

Meta-analysis," *Journal of Consumer Research* 19 (June 1992), pp. 34–51; Amitava Chattopadhyay and Prakash Negungadi, "Does Attitude toward the Ad Endure? The Moderating Effects of Attention and Delay," *Journal of Consumer Research* 19 (June 1992), pp. 26–33; Gabriel Biehal, Debra Stephens, and Eleonora Curlo, "Attitude toward the Ad and Brand Choice," *Journal of Advertising* 21 (September 1992), pp. 19–39.

27 Jessica McLaughlin, "Marijuana Edibles: A New Challenge for Regulators," *Law Street Media* (May 2, 2015), http://lawstreetmedia.com/issues/law-and-politics/marijuana-edibles-recent-laws-regulations/; Ricardo Baca, "New Rules in Effect for Colorado Marijuana Edibles," *The Cannabist* (January 29, 2015); Barcott, "Yasmin Hurd Raises Rats on the Upper East Side of Manhattan That Will Blow Your Mind," *Time* (May 22, 2015), pp. 40–45.

28 Valerie S. Folkes, "Recent Attribution Research in Consumer Behavior: A Review and New Directions," *Journal of Consumer Research* 14 (March 1988), pp. 548–565; Robert Baer, "Overestimating Salesperson Truthfulness: The Fundamental Attribution Error," in Marvin Goldberg et al. (Eds.), *Advances in Consumer Research* (Provo, UT: Association for Consumer Research, 1990), pp. 501–507; Valerie S. Folkes, "Consumer Reactions to Product Failure: An Attributional Approach," *Journal of Consumer Research* (March 1984), pp. 398–409; Richard W. Mizerski, Linda L. Golden, and Jerome B. Kernan, "The Attributional Process in Consumer Decision Making," *Journal of Consumer Research* (September 1979), pp. 123–140; Valerie S. Folkes, Susan Koletsky, and John L. Graham, "A Field Study of Casual Inferences and Consumer Reaction: The View from the Airport," *Journal of Consumer Research* (March 1987), pp. 534–539; Edward E. Jones et al., *Attribution: Perceiving the Causes of Behavior* (Morristown, NJ: General Learning Press, 1972); Jess Kellar Alberts, Yvonne Kellar-Guenther, and Steven R. Corman, "That's Not Funny: Understanding Recipients' Responses to Teasing," *Western Journal of Communication* 60 (September 1, 1996), p. 337; Steven G. Little, Robert C. Sterling, and Daniel H. Tingstrom, "The Influence of Geographic and Racial Cues on Evaluation of Blame," *The Journal of Social Psychology* 136 (June 1, 1996), pp. 373–379; Thomas Blass, "The Milgram Obedience Experiment: Support for a Cognitive View of Defensive Attribution," *The Journal of Social Psychology* 136 (June 1, 1996), pp. 407–410; John Maltby, "Attribution Style and Projection," *Journal of Genetic Psychology* 157 (December 1, 1996), pp. 505–506.

29 *Ibid.*

30 Robert B. Settle and L. L. Golden, "Attribution Theory and Advertising Credibility," *Journal of Marketing Research* 11 (May 1974), pp. 181–185.

31 Richard E. Petty, Rao H. Unnava, and Alan J. Strathman, "Theories of Attitude Change," in Thomas Robertson and Harold Kassarjian (Eds.), *Handbook of Consumer Behavior* (Upper Saddle River, NJ: Prentice Hall, 1991), pp. 241–280; Paul W. Miniard, Sunil Bhatla, and Randall I. Rose, "On the Formation and Relationship of Ad and Brand Attitudes: An Experimental and Causal Approach," *Journal of Marketing Research* 27 (August 1990), pp. 290–303; Carolyn Tripp, Thomas D. Jensen, and Less Carlson, "The Effects of

Multiple Product Endorsements by Celebrities on Consumers' Attitudes and Intentions," *Journal of Consumer Research* 20 (March 1994), pp. 535–547.

32 L. Festinger, *A Theory of Cognitive Dissonance* (Stanford, CA: Stanford University Press, 1957); Leon Festinger and Dana Bramel, "The Reactions of Human Cognitive Dissonance," in Arthur J. Bachrach (Ed.), *Experimental Foundations of Clinical Psychology* (New York: Basic Books, 1962), p. 254; J. W. Brehm and A. R. Cohen, *Explorations in Cognitive Dissonance* (New York: John Wiley, 1962), ch. 2; S. S. Komarita and Ira Bernstein, "Attitude Intensity and Dissonant Cognitions," *Journal of Abnormal and Social Psychology* 69 (September 1964), pp. 323–329; F. Heider, "Attitudes and Cognitive Organization," *Journal of Psychology* 21 (1946), pp. 107–112; C. E. Osgood and P. H. Tannenbaum, "The Principle of Congruity in the Prediction of Attitude Change," *Psychological Review* 62 (1955), pp. 42–55; C. E. Osgood and P. H. Tannenbaum, "The Nature and Measurement of Meaning," *Psychological Bulletin* 49 (1952), pp. 197–237.

33 Food and Drug Administration, "Olestra and Other Fat Substitutes," *FDA Backgrounder* (November 28, 1995), www.fda.gov/opacom/backgrounders/olestra.html.

34 Festinger, *A Theory of Cognitive Dissonance*; Festinger and Bramel, "The Reactions of Human Cognitive Dissonance"; Brehm and Cohen, *Explorations in Cognitive Dissonance*, ch. 2; Komarita and Bernstein, "Attitude Intensity and Dissonant Cognitions"; Chester A. Insko and John Schopler, *Experimental Social Psychology* (New York: Academic Press, 1972), p. 109; William H. Cummings and M. Venkatesan, "Cognitive Dissonance and Consumer Behavior: A Review of the Evidence," *Journal of Marketing Research* XIII (August 1976), pp. 303–308; Dieter Frey and Marita Rosch, "Information Seeking after Decisions: The Roles of Novelty of Information and Decision Reversibility," *Personality and Social Psychology Bulletin* 10, no. 1 (March 1984), pp. 91–98; J. Cooper and R. H. Fazio, "A New Look at Dissonance Theory," in L. Berkowitz (Ed.), *Advances in Experimental Social Psychology* (New York: Academic Press, 1984), pp. 229–266.

35 Durairaj Maheswaran and Brian Sternthal, "The Effect of Knowledge, Motivation, and Type of Message on Ad Processing and Product Judgments," *Journal of Consumer Research* (June 1990), pp. 66–73; Deborah Macinnis, "Characteristics of Music on High and Low Involvement Consumers' Processing of Ads," *Journal of Consumer Research* (September 1991), pp. 161–173.

36 William J. McGuire, "An Information-Processing Model of Advertising Effectiveness," a paper presented at the Symposium of Behavioral and Management Science in Marketing, Center for Continuing Education, University of Chicago (July 1969); G. S. Day, "Theories of Attitude Structure and Change," in S. Ward and T. Robertson (Eds.), *Consumer Behavior: Theoretical Sources* (Upper Saddle River, NJ: Prentice Hall, 1973), p. 326.

37 Michael L. Ray, "Marketing Communication and the Hierarchy of Effects," in Peter Clark (Ed.), *New Models for Mass Communication Research* 2 (Beverly Hills: Sage, 1973).

38 Ashesh Mukherjee and Wayne D. Hoyer, "The Effect of Novel Attributes On Product Evaluation," *Journal of Consumer Research* 28, no. 3 (December 2001), pp. 462–472.

39 Richard E. Petty and John T. Cacioppo, *Attitudes and Persuasion: Classic and Contemporary Approaches* (Dubuque, IA: Wm. C. Brown, 1981); John T. Cacioppo, Richard E. Petty, Chuan Feng Kao, and Regina Rodriguez, "Central and Peripheral Routes to Persuasion: An Individual Difference Perspective," *Journal of Personality and Social Psychology* 51, no. 5 (1986), pp. 1032–1043; Scott B. MacKenzie and Richard A. Spreng, "How Does Motivation Moderate the Impact of Central and Peripheral Processing on Brand Attitudes and Intentions?" *Journal of Consumer Research* (March 1992), pp. 519–529; Ronald C. Goodstein, "Category-Based Applications and Extensions in Advertising: Motivating More Extensive Ad Processing," *Journal of Consumer Research* (June 1993), pp. 87–99.

40 M. Snyder and K. DeBono, "Understanding the Functions of Attitudes: Lessons from Personality and Social Behavior," in A. R. Pratakins et al. (Eds.), *Attitude Structure and Function* (Hillsdale, NJ: Erlbaum, 1989), pp. 339–360.

41 R. E. Petty, "To Think or Not to Think, Exploring Two Routes of Persuasion," in S. Shavitt and T. C. Brick (Eds.), *Persuasion: Psychological Insights and Perspectives* (Boston: Allyn and Bacon, 1994), pp. 113–147.

42 Sanjay Putrevu and Kenneth R. Lord, "Processing Internet Communications: A Motivation, Opportunity, and Ability Framework," *Journal of Current Issues and Research in Advertising* 25, no. 1 (Spring 2003), pp. 45–59.

43 Chang-Hoan Cho, "How Advertising Works on the WWW: Modified Elaboration Likelihood Model," *Journal of Current Issues and Research in Advertising* 21 (Spring 1999), pp. 33–50; Gordon Bruner and Anand Kumar, "Web Commercials and Advertising Hierarchy-of-Effects," *Journal of Advertising Research* 40 (January/April 2000), pp. 35–42.

CHAPTER 6

MOTIVATION AND EMOTION

LEARNING OBJECTIVES

- To analyze and understand the concept of a motivated state as well as its arousal/direction prerequisites.
- To conceptualize five aspects of consumer motivation.
- To recognize the roles of needs, motives, goals, and desires in consumer motivation.
- To comprehend the sources, types, and resolution of motivational conflict.
- To explore the role of motivation research.
- To develop a basic understanding of the nature of human emotions and moods.
- To gain insight into how researchers measure human emotions.

KEY TERMS

motivation	instincts	avoidance–avoidance
arousal	homeostasis	conflict
direction	high sensation seekers	motivation research
intrinsic motivation	(HSS)	projective techniques
extrinsic motivation	low sensation seekers	association tests
rational motives	(LSS)	Zaltman Metaphor
emotional motives	optimal stimulation level	Elicitation Technique
needs	(OSL)	(ZMET)
physiological needs	general sensation-	focus groups
acquired needs	seeking scale (GSSS)	emotions
motive	motivational conflict	mood
goal	approach–approach	bonding
generic goals	conflict	
brand-specific goals	approach–avoidance	
desires	conflict	

Gambling, in one form or another, is presently within easy reach of nearly everyone. Lotteries, online gambling, legalized sports gambling, riverboat casinos, horse and greyhound racing, off-track betting, bingo lounges, and cruise ships are varieties of gambling that have become popular today with millions of people. In 2015, Americans wagered approximately $119 billion at land-based casinos, racetracks, legal and illegal sports gambling, as well as other types. Add to these the $70.15 billion that they spent on buying lottery tickets in the forty-three states in which lotteries are legal. Moreover, electronic gambling via online casinos and poker sites has grown significantly in the past couple of years, with wagers amounting to over $21 billion in 2015. This accelerated growth is due to the increased legalization trend in a number of states, as well as the convenience it provides to players. All that players have to do is log into their favorite website and participate in their preferred game. Betting on pro-football has also become a favorite kind of gambling. According to the American Gambling Association, U.S. participants wagered $4.2 billion on Super Bowl 50 in 2016.

Two factors have underscored the growth in legal gambling: public demand for gambling-style entertainment and states' need for new sources of revenue. Public officials view consumers' desire and attraction toward gambling as an excellent opportunity to provide much-needed funding for education and other publicly supported activities. For example, in the case of state-sponsored lotteries, approximately one-third of the proceeds help fund education. The prize percentage may run from 50 to 65 percent, while the remainder goes toward administrative expenses, retailers' commissions, and advertising costs.

From a behavioral point of view, studies show that gamblers tend to continue to gamble whether they are losing or winning. When losing, gamblers continue to place bets in order to recover losses. When winning occurs, bets are made to win more. In either case, it is hard for gamblers to stop gambling. Psychiatrists report seeing more and more patients with gambling-related problems. Lawyers assert that gambling is to be blamed for an increasing number of bankruptcies and divorces. Law enforcement officials indicate that some problem gamblers are turning to crime to pay their gambling debts. However, despite these ills, growth of the gambling industry continues.

We may wonder what motivates people to gamble. Is it the excitement, thrill, and high they get when they gamble? Is it the fun and entertainment involved? Is it greed to acquire easy money or something one has not worked for? Is it the challenge gambling generates? Or is it, like drugs and alcohol, a compulsive escape from reality? Regardless of the underlying motive, the growing trend for embracing and enjoying gambling seems to be a sign of the times.[1]

What do you think about gambling in general? In your opinion, what internal and external forces motivate people to gamble? Learn more about various states' involvement in lotteries by visiting the website www.mylottocorner.com. Also visit a site on federal gambling laws at www.gambling-laws-us.com/Articles-Notes/. What motivates the government of various states to sanction or sponsor gambling activities? Are such activities in the public's best interest?

This chapter emphasizes the importance of motivation and explains the various elements inherent in the motivational phenomenon. It then continues to briefly discuss theories of motivation and the role of emotions in determining behavior of consumers in the marketplace.

WHAT IS MOTIVATION?

It has been said that behind each human action lies a motive. If that motive could be understood, it would become possible to ascertain and even predict behavior. In solving criminal cases, detectives look for a motive to unravel the mystery. In industry, one of the major concerns is to motivate employees to work harder. In marketing, motivation is primarily an activity translated into the expenditure of billions of dollars spent annually on advertising and promotional campaigns designed to get consumers to buy.

Motivation underlies the reasons that encourage people to undertake certain actions. It is a state in which our energy is mobilized and directed in a selective fashion toward states of affairs in the external environment, called goals.[2] This view of motivation reveals that two conditions must prevail for motivation to occur. The first is a state of arousal or tension; the second is an impetus or direction for the behavior. Arousal is a tension state resulting mainly from unsatisfied needs. Direction, on the other hand, is an end toward which behavior is prompted. The state of tension that exists as a need arises activates or moves the individual toward purposeful behavior in the form of a goal. For example, dermatologists who use Allergan Company's Botox cosmetic injections typically promote this procedure by following this arousal-direction view of motivation. The theme of most of these ads depicts a "before" unflattering photo of

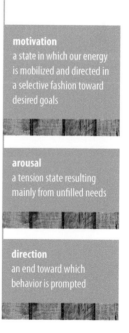

motivation
a state in which our energy is mobilized and directed in a selective fashion toward desired goals

arousal
a tension state resulting mainly from unfilled needs

direction
an end toward which behavior is prompted

women's or men's faces ravaged with wrinkles and lines, an image most consumers would find unappealing. The ads go on to show the "after" effect—how this highly successful, nonsurgical procedure can dramatically attain a desired facial rejuvenation and reduce wrinkles within days. This in-your-face approach, complete with unflattering images, is enough to create a tension level resulting in sales levels estimated to exceed 6.5 million injections in 2015 administered to 4.2 million patients nationwide.[3] The need-induced tension exerts a push on the individual to take the necessary action. This push gives both impetus and direction to the behavior. In this sense, tension is goal directing.

Various conditions can trigger arousal. *Physiological cues* such as stomach contractions, decreases in blood sugar levels, changes in body temperature, or secretion of sex hormones are a source of arousal. Arousal can also be generated by *emotional cues*. Fantasizing may stimulate latent needs. People who are bored or frustrated when trying to accomplish their goals may daydream about more desirable alternatives. Individuals can also become aroused when something lessens their freedom of choice.[4] For example, television cable customers, frustrated with their providers' limited channel offerings, have taken their business to other companies such as Direct TV or satellite dish networks that offer extensive channels at a reasonable cost. *Cognitive cue*s, such as personal accomplishments or even random thoughts, can similarly trigger arousal. Conscientious college students, for instance, may start to think about studying abroad for

An understanding of why people gamble can help either to cure a social problem or to capitalize on a business opportunity.

© Air Images/Shutterstock.com

a semester, doing an internship, or attending graduate school. Moreover, *environmental cues* such as aromas, ads, packaging, point-of-purchase displays, and price promotions may trigger arousal.

From a marketing and consumer behavior perspective, both arousal and direction are necessary prerequisites for a motivated state to exist. Promotions must both arouse prospects' desire for a product category and then clearly direct them to a specific brand. For example, a TV commercial by Pizza Hut shown during an evening talk show may depict a mouthwatering pizza being served at a social gathering. A couple watching the commercial suddenly develops hunger for a pizza. They respond to this hunger by picking up the phone and ordering a pizza from Pizzaria Uno, an Italian pizza parlor the couple prefers. In this case, it is easy to see that arousal succeeded, but direction failed. The couple's learned behavior (loyalty to Pizzaria Uno) altered the course of their direction. Pizza Hut created the motivation and paid for the commercial, but Pizzaria Uno reaped the benefits in the form of enhanced consumption of its pizzas.

CLASSIFYING CONSUMER MOTIVATIONS

Researchers focus on understanding the motives that activate human behavior. Motives are psychological constructs hypothesized to explain behavior. They cannot be observed, but the behavior that results from them can usually be witnessed. Motives in this sense are abstractions postulated to explain observable behavior. They are frequently classified as conscious–unconscious, high–low urgency, positive–negative polarity, intrinsic–extrinsic, and rational–emotional. Let us briefly examine these classifications and ponder their significance to the study of consumer behavior.

Conscious versus Unconscious

Motives can be *conscious* (sometimes referred to as manifest) or *unconscious* (sometimes referred to as latent). In many cases, a consumer's motives are conscious, and the reasons for an individual's behavior are clear to him or her. Hence, because consumers are aware of their conscious motives, these motives do not have to be aroused.

Sometimes, however, an individual's motives are unconscious, and the person does not know why a particular behavior was undertaken. Some gamblers become hooked on gambling. They risk losing their wealth, jobs, or even families over it. In most cases, they have no explanations for their destructive habit. A variety of reasons can cause motivations to be unconscious. First, needs themselves remain unconscious as long as they are being satisfied.[5] Unless an individual's sinuses are congested, he or she rarely thinks of the body's need for oxygen. Second, certain needs have such low priority for individuals that they are unaware of them. Third, needs may be repressed. That is, some individuals may avoid admitting the existence of a need. For example, celibate priests or monks, in a search for higher principles, choose to deny the presence of sexual needs.

From a consumer behavior perspective, because unconscious motives are dormant and unrecognized, they must be drawn to the consumer's attention by the promotional efforts of marketers. Reaching awareness of motivations we did not previously recognize can trigger purchase action. As an example, most people tend to regard themselves as invincible and fail to recognize the need to arrange for their death. The funeral industry, in response to this tendency, has developed promotions and offers that make the emotion-laden purchase of a casket more like buying a piece of furniture.[6]

High versus Low Urgency

Motives can exert either immediate or delayed impact on behavior. *High-urgency* needs require immediate attention and satisfaction. A consumer who needs to replace a furnace on a cold winter day or purchase a new suit for an upcoming job interview lacks the time needed to comparison shop and, consequently, may fail to get the best value. This urgency may in part explain why seasonal garments command their highest price at the start of the season. Consumers who need these seasonal products now are willing to pay whatever price it takes to acquire them.

The act of satisfying *low-urgency* needs, on the other hand, can be postponed. Consumers in this case have sufficient time to shop around and compare alternatives before buying. During periods of economic hardship or uncertainty, consumers tend to postpone the purchase of some durable goods (carpeting, furniture), because the purchase of these items is not urgent and can be delayed. Marketers, in this case, in order to stimulate purchase action and command better prices, attempt to create a sense of necessity and urgency for the products or services being promoted.

Positive versus Negative Polarity

Motives, in addition, display polarity. That is to say, they positively or negatively influence people's behavior. *Positive influences* lead individuals toward desired goals. For example, many people take daily vitamin supplements to enhance the nutritional value of their diet. They also may use colognes or aftershave lotions in order to smell good. Conversely, *negative influences* steer people away from adverse consequences. For example, some consumers may use gel toothpastes and mouthwashes to avoid bad breath, or they may use antibacterial soaps and antiperspirants to avoid body odor. Positively and negatively motivated groups of consumers may represent separate market segments. Although marketers usually employ positive brand benefits to entice consumers to follow a suggested course of action, they occasionally resort to negative motivating forces such as fear or guilt to bring about the desired change. The ad in Figure 6.1 from VPI PET Insurance Company employs the concept of negative polarity by depicting a dog in a dangerous situation in order to entice consumers to insure their pets.

Intrinsic versus Extrinsic

Behavior can be intrinsically motivated or extrinsically motivated. In the case of intrinsic motivation, an individual engages in behavior for the inherent pleasure of the activity undertaken; behavior *is* the reward. An

intrinsic motivation
behavior undertaken for the inherent pleasure of the activity itself

Behavior resulting from intrinsic motivation tends to be more enduring than behavior precipitated by extrinsic motivation.

© mimagephotography/Shutterstock.com

FIGURE 6.1

The dire outcome facing the dog in this depiction is designed to create sufficient motivation to steer pet owners toward insuring their pets.

Oh, no, he didn't.
Oh, yes, he did.

You can't explain risk to your dog.

VPI® Pet Insurance understands things happen, that's why we won't drop your pet's coverage no matter how many claims you make.

Compare rates today • 1-888-776-8328 • petinsurance.com/risk

Underwritten by Veterinary Pet Insurance Company (CA), Brea, CA; National Casualty Company (all other states), Madison, WI, an A+15 rated company. ©2011 Veterinary Pet Insurance Company. Nationwide Insurance is a service mark of Nationwide Mutual Insurance Company.

extrinsic motivation
behavior undertaken in order to acquire rewards

avid golfer, for example, may spend abundantly on golfing because of sheer enjoyment and pleasure in the game itself. Extrinsic motivation, on the other hand, moves an individual to acquire rewards that are independent of the activity. Golf pros may participate in tournaments to win trophies and large monetary prizes. Playing the game, in such cases, is not motivated by the mere fun of the activity itself but by the prospect of making money.

From a marketing perspective, behavior resulting from intrinsic motivation tends to be more enduring compared with that precipitated by extrinsic motivation. The pleasure of being involved in the activity itself ensures continued involvement and interest. Conversely, in the case of extrinsic motivation, once rewards cease, interest in the activity subsides. Marketers therefore try to create intrinsic motivation. Music and dance instructors; martial arts, yoga, and pilates trainers; and coaches who give tennis and swimming lessons are but some examples of entities that attempt to help people derive enjoyment from the activity itself and keep them interested through intrinsic motivation.

Rational versus Emotional

Motives have also been classified as either rational or emotional. Rational motives are aroused through appeals to reason and logic. They stress objective, utilitarian goals such as economy, durability, quality, and dependability. Rationally oriented advertising offers a straightforward, no-nonsense, factual message. It attempts to build a persuasive and credible argument in support of a brand by presenting relevant information and without necessarily being artistic or clever.[7] Fast-food franchises, for example, have advertised that their hamburgers are 100 percent pure beef. Phone companies and Internet service providers promote their services by stressing rational appeals such as better value through lower rates, broader coverage, and faster connections.

rational motives
those aroused through appeals to reason and logic

Emotional motives, on the other hand, entail goal selection that relies on subjective criteria. Emotional motives have their origin in human feelings and impulsive or unreasoned promptings to action.[8] In other words, emotional purchases are often whimsical rather than based on information and prepurchase deliberation. According to Holbrook and Hirschman, emotional consumption can be characterized by "pursuit of fantasies, feelings, and fun."[9] These passionate aspects of consumption focus on the "symbolic, hedonistic, and aesthetic" nature of consumption. Many emotional motives are linked to an individual's social and aesthetic requirements, as well as his or her self-concept. Such motives include status, belonging, beauty, pride, distinctiveness, and pleasure.

emotional motives
those aroused by stressing sentiments, fantasies, and feelings

Until recently, emotions were regarded as enemies of pure reason. Modern discoveries, however, reveal startling new images from MRI and PET scans showing that emotion is at the physical center of our brains. Emotion is not nature's afterthought; it is one of the primary regulators of health, happiness, reasoning, and human actions. In other words, emotions can help people be more efficient with their reasoning abilities. Although feelings sometimes derail thought, more often they point it in the right direction.[10] In the field of children's apparel, Gymboree Company, which operates hundreds of mall-based stores, has cleverly used emotions to influence what otherwise might be a rational purchase decision. Its reputation for producing and selling colorful clothes, reinforced by its multihued logo "Quality clothes, colorful kids" tagline, has given the company its strong competitive edge and enabled it to carve for itself a substantial niche in the highly competitive market for children's clothing.[11]

Most promotional campaigns fall somewhere along a continuum between purely rational and purely emotional. That is, they combine both rational and emotional motivations but may lean in one direction or the other. Exhibit 6.1 contains a sample listing of rational and emotional consumer motivations to which advertisers commonly appeal. Note that some appeals could be placed under both headings.

EXHIBIT 6.1

A Partial Listing of Rational and Emotional Motives and the Appeals Used to Stimulate Them

Rational Appeals	Emotional Appeals
Economy in purchase	Pride in personal appearance
Economy in use	Pride of ownership
Space saving	Ambition, competition, achievement, recognition
Labor saving	Religious conviction
Time saving	Approval from others
Labor saving	Status, prestige, esteem
Increased performance	Individuality
More efficient performance	Play, sport, physical activity
Simplicity in operation	Rest, relaxation
Durability (long product life)	Appetite, taste
Availability	Curiosity
Low maintenance cost	Guilt
Quality materials	Fear
Quality workmanship	Patriotism
Convenience	Love of family
Safety and security	Loyalty

ELEMENTS OF MOTIVATION

Four elements are inherent in motivation. They are needs, motives, goals, and desires. We discuss each briefly here in turn, but the separation is actually arbitrary because these concepts constantly overlap and interact. Motivation should be thought of as a dynamic process rather than as separate elements that make up the whole.[12]

Needs

Humans have diverse needs. Human requirements for food and drink, for safety, for social acceptance, and for achievement are but a few of the needs most of us are familiar with. Needs are internal forces that prompt behavior toward goal-oriented solutions. Unlike motives, needs do not necessarily trigger behavior. A person on a diet may, when feeling hungry, ignore the need for food. Similarly, a person who has recently quit smoking may suppress the desire for a cigarette.

Needs are usually treated under two broad categories, physiological needs and acquired needs.[13] Physiological needs are basic conditions that are required for the maintenance of life and the normal processes of health and growth. The human requirements for food, water, shelter, sex, and rest are examples. Acquired needs, on the other hand, are learned and conditioned by relationships with others in the environment and specific culture in which we are brought up. Consequently, these types of needs may vary cross culturally. What may be deemed desirable according to one set of cultural values may be regarded as undesirable according to the values of a different culture. Attitudes concerning what is beautiful, modest, or fashionable differ from one society to another. Thus, needs for cosmetics, jewelry, or diet foods and beverages are not universal. These are sometimes referred to as secondary needs.

Even though we distinguish between physiological and acquired needs, much behavior reflects an interaction between the two types. For example, a warm piece of clothing may suffice for a wintry day to protect an individual from the cold, fulfilling an important primary need for bodily protection. However, the person may opt for purchasing a fur coat because of a strong desire for status and prestige. Both primary and secondary needs interact in this case to influence the purchasing decision.

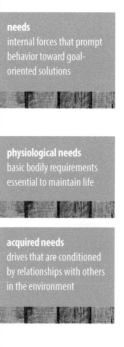

needs
internal forces that prompt behavior toward goal-oriented solutions

physiological needs
basic bodily requirements essential to maintain life

acquired needs
drives that are conditioned by relationships with others in the environment

Motives

Once a need has been activated, a state of tension exists that drives the individual to reduce or eliminate the need. In other words, the state of tension caused by an unfulfilled need creates a drive. A consumer who experiences such a state strives to reduce the tension by satisfying the need. For example, hunger is a basic need. When aroused in an individual, it becomes a motive for satisfying the need. The individual feeling the pangs of hunger may, for example, stop at Taco Bell to get a burrito. In this view, motives arise from states of imbalance or tension and carry out the function of energizing, activating, and directing the behavior toward desirable goals.

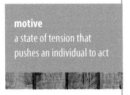

motive
a state of tension that pushes an individual to act

Motives, in the majority of cases, are directed toward reducing bodily deficiencies, whether biogenic or psychogenic. In addition, motives may direct behavior toward enhancing an individual's health, happiness, or well-being. They may also exist to push an individual away from dangerous places, situations, or harmful products. A motive, therefore, can direct us toward or away from some object, place, or situation. Motives, moreover, may be activated toward behaviors that are legal, moral, and ethical; or conversely, they may be activated toward illegal, immoral, and unethical actions. Motives, as you can see, are capable of accommodating an endless diversity of human needs.

Goals

Human behavior is not random or irrational, but goal directed. The sought-after result of motivation is some desirable goal.[14] The goal may be an object, an activity, or a situation toward which motivated behavior is directed. Goals *pull* individuals toward acquiring a reward. The challenge for marketers is to persuade consumers to perceive their product or service offerings as desirable goals that will satisfy their needs. Whereas needs and motives *push* the individual to correct a state of imbalance, goals *pull* the individual toward something perceived as desirable.

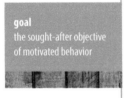

goal
the sought-after objective of motivated behavior

generic goals
nonspecific categories of products and services that can satisfy customer needs

Marketers differentiate between two types of goals, generic goals and product-specific goals. Generic goals refer to the general classes or categories of products and services that can satisfy certain consumer needs. For a commuter, automobiles (as opposed to using public transportation) may be considered one category among a number of alternative transportation means to fulfill daily travel needs. Automobiles, in this sense, comprise a generic class of products. Marketers are generally less concerned

230

with stimulating primary demand for an entire product category, except perhaps in such cases as ads by the American Dairy Association, Florida Orange Growers Association, California Raisin Growers' Association, and Almond Board of California, as well as other industrywide trade organizations. The generic ad for milk in Figure 6.2 promotes the consumption of milk to counteract the effects of eating spicy foods, without mentioning any specific brand.

FIGURE 6.2

In promoting the consumption of milk to counter the acidity of spicy foods, this ad from whymilk.com mentions no specific brand.

brand-specific goals
particular alternatives in a product category from which consumers can choose

Brand-specific goals, on the other hand, are the branded, identified, or labeled alternatives available in a category of products from which consumers select specific brands to satisfy their needs. In the commuter case mentioned earlier, the individual involved may decide to purchase an automobile and specifically choose a Ford Mustang to fulfill his or her travel needs. From a marketing point of view, the Ford Mustang is a brand-specific alternative. Mustang sales are most likely affected by the extent of promotional activities undertaken by Ford to stimulate demand for this model. So, unlike the case with generic goals for which needs may already exist, promotional programs are necessary to stimulate demand for product- and brand-specific alternatives. Every year, marketers allocate hefty sums of money to accomplish this objective. In 2016, the CBS TV network sold thirty-second ad spots during the Super Bowl at the incredible cost of $5 million per spot. Big advertisers such as Budweiser, Coca-Cola, Hyundai, LG, Colgate, Amazon, Doritos, TurboTax, McDonald's, Butterfinger, and Taco Bell were among the takers.[15]

The selection of goals by an individual depends on a number of factors that characterize the person or the situation at the time the need emerges. Factors such as this person's physical, financial, and emotional conditions affect goal selection. A graduating college student who is a first-time buyer of a new car may settle for a Hyundai rather than a BMW due to financial considerations. Cultural values and norms are another group of factors that influence goal selection. Whereas many people in the United States enjoy spending a sunny day on the beach, Middle Easterners avoid the sun due to a culturally based perception that dark skin is a sign of the working class and fair skin is a symbol of higher social stature.

In addition, products that consumers own or use such as the cars they drive, homes they buy, electronics they use, and clothes they wear convey something about themselves to people with whom they interact. The products consumers choose are, in reality, social symbols reflecting their self-image. They serve as a means of communication between an individual and his or her significant others. These symbols reflect images such as masculinity or femininity, ability, status, and success—self-image features an individual may desire to convey to others. Whereas many women in the United States aspire to lose weight, in some African countries, women prefer to gain weight, since a heavier body frame is deemed attractive. The ad from Raymond Weil found in Figure 6.3 uses the personal attribute of precision in musical performance as a motivator to own an elegant timepiece, such as the Maestro Collection.

Courtesy of Raymond Weil S.A.

FIGURE 6.3

The personal attribute of precision in musical performance that characterizes virtuoso musicians is employed in this ad from Raymond Weil as a motivator to acquire such a precision timepiece.

Desires

Recently, some researchers of consumer behavior have directed attention to the concept of consumer desires. They define consumer desires as belief-based passions that involve longing, yearning, and fervently wishing for something.[16] This perspective attempts to acknowledge products' rich symbolic meanings and consumers' emotional involvement with coveted goods.

desires
passions that involve longing, yearning, and fervently wishing for something

Desires involve an intensely passionate positive emotional attachment steeped in fantasies and dreams rather than based on reasoned judgments. Desires can be dangerous, because they often transgress the ordinary and border on being socially unacceptable. This transgressive character is part of their allure. Because of the dangers of losing control to a desire and the fear of appearing obsessed, consumers may try to tame and rationalize their desires so that they appear more socially acceptable. Ironically, however, doing so lessens the *mystical* power of current desires and leads toward developing new ones. Interestingly, once desired objects are ultimately obtained, consumers tend to become bored with them and desire new focal objects. The spectrum of human desires is endless. Desires vary by personality, gender, age, and culture. For example, when inquired about their desires, children in the United States tend to mention such things as toys, pets, candy, ice cream, and trips to an amusement park. Women often cite shoes, designer-label clothing, jewelry, cosmetics, and expensive perfume. Men, on the other hand, often report a desire for fancy cars, electronic gadgets, and unique collectibles. Seniors frequently speak of travel and visiting exotic places. These emotional urges bring about a desired state of affairs that help us experience life at its fullest.

Now that we have examined the four elements of motivation, let us look at the numerous theoretical attempts to conceptualize human motivation and explain its underlying causes.

THEORIES OF MOTIVATION

A glance at the literature on motivation reveals an abundance of theories attempting to conceptualize human motivation. Although each has its own merit, the discussion of all of them is beyond the scope of this book. These various theories, however, can be grouped under four main categories: (1) instinct theories, (2) drive theories, (3) arousal theories, and (4) cognitive theories. Each category warrants some explanation.

Instinct Theories

instincts
genetically transmitted physical and behavioral characteristics of a species that enable it to survive in the environment

Instinct theories of motivation suggest that behavior is innate. Humans, like all forms of animal life, are born equipped with instincts, the physical and behavioral characteristics of a species that enable it to survive. The origin of this approach to motivation dates back to the writings of the nineteenth-century naturalist Charles Darwin, who believed that instincts arise through a process of natural selection and are transmitted genetically to individual members of the species. Behavior and its underlying motivation reflect the process of adaptation of creatures to their environment.

Many theorists adopted this train of thought to explain various human tendencies. Freud's psychoanalytic theory viewed sexual instincts as a primary motivator of human behavior. Some of Freud's disciples, as well as others in disagreement with him, advocated that other human instincts supersede sexual impulses in directing behavior. Such impetuses include

ETHICAL DILEMMA

Challenging Children's Sensitivity to the Suffering of Others

Today, as many people seek to fill their leisure time with activities that involve adventure, promise fun, and provide a challenge, they find in electronic video games a practical venue to fulfill this need.

Video games in today's society have become extremely popular and are increasingly being allotted more time in the daily-life routine of many individuals. These games have been successfully marketed to and are easily obtained by both children and adults. It has been estimated that the average eight- to eighteen-year-old now spends nineteen hours per week playing these games. In 2015, Americans spent $25 billion on different types of video games.

Most of these games can be judged as having a positive influence on players, mostly through broadening their knowledge, improving their reaction time, and enhancing their creativity. As a learning tool for children in particular, these games may assist parents and educators in their mission to broaden a child's horizons and ensure the development of his or her ethical code, empathy, and concern for others. Through these games, children can also learn to take responsibility for their own actions.

One disturbing trend in this field, however, has been the proliferation of the violent variety of games. The content of this latter type has been claimed to encourage excessive aggression and cruelty among young people. Research has shown that such games may be more harmful than violent television shows and movies due to the fact that they are interactive, competitive, engrossing, and require the player to identify with the aggressor. As such, these games promote automatic aggression, and work to desensitize the players' reflective emotions, care for others, and responsibility for their behavior. The actions required from the players to successfully engage in the game involve a temporary yielding of the players' core values and moral judgement merely for the sake of winning.

The negative effect of these video games has raised major concerns of many groups, including parents, educators, law enforcement agencies, legislators, and mental health professionals. A Surgeon General's study along with a follow-up report by the National Institute of Mental Health identified three major effects of this type of violence on children's behavior: (1) Children may become less sensitive to the pain and suffering of others; (2) they may become fearful of the world around them; and (3) they become more likely to behave in aggressive and harmful ways toward others. In response to these concerns, some cities and states are now considering legislation designed to prevent the sale of mature-rated video games to children.[17]

The popularity of video games will continue to gain momentum as years go by. In your opinion, why are these games so popular among both the young and the old? How can society reduce the potential harm caused by certain types of these games? Do you think the benefits of the "good" games far exceed the social cost incurred because of the violent ones? For more information about the effect of violent games on children, visit http://www. news.iastate.edu/news/2014/03/24/violentgamesbehavior *and* http:// www.psychologymatters.org/mediaviolence.html. *Should legislation be enacted to restrict the sale and availability of such violent games? Defend your answer.*

belonging, engaging in social interaction, maintaining meaningful affiliations with others, surmounting perceived inferiorities, striving for superiority, and overcoming childhood insecurities in relationships with parents. Still other theorists presented a variety of biogenic and psychogenic instincts ranging from curiosity to self-assertion. Most perfume companies use a sexy model to create a desirable aura for the exotic brand of perfume (Figure 6.4).

Drive Theories

A motive, as was discussed earlier, is an internal state resulting from either biological or psychological disequilibrium. When a person's physiological or psychological equilibrium is disrupted, motives drive this individual to restore prior equilibrium or balance. Back in 1939, one of the pioneer biologists named William B. Cannon coined the term homeostasis to explain the self-regulating mechanism of the body that is hypothesized to maintain harmony of all bodily systems. Body chemistry and the sys-

homeostasis
a self-regulating mechanism of the body that maintains harmony of all bodily systems

FIGURE 6.4

The attractive model depicted in this photo is almost certain to attract readers' attention to the brand if it were used in an advertisement.

© Inga Ivanova/Shutterstock.com

236

tem's harmony are maintained in balance despite activities that may tend to change or alter their concentration or pattern. When this equilibrium is disturbed as a result of needs or external circumstances, the automatic homeostatic mechanism is no longer in harmony. This disequilibrium or imbalance causes the organism to be aroused to correct the deficit. Thus, tension reduction becomes the primary function of behavior. When homeostasis is restored, the internal stimulus subsides. In this event, motivation is seen as the driving force arising from homeostatic imbalance or tension.

Arousal Theories

Activation or arousal theories suggest that people often seek stimulation instead of trying to avoid it. In this view, consumers move from a neutral state to a more desirable enhanced state. Examples of arousal-seeking behaviors include traveling to exciting places, experiencing thrilling rides in amusement parks, sampling exotic foods, and participating in or viewing high-risk sports.

High sensation seekers (HSS) are individuals who have a stronger-than-average need to seek and approach activities, situations, and ideas that are novel, changing, complex, surprising, and more intense. For HSS types, tour operators provide trips that offer many exciting activities. These trips may include such physically demanding feats as mountain climbing, skydiving, and cave exploring. Adventurous vacationers are more likely than the population as a whole to be male, young, and have high household incomes. The ad in Figure 6.5 from the Marines appeals to adventurous recruits with a desire to lead and serve their country.

Some individuals, on the other hand, prefer to read a book, work on a computer, or watch TV in the comfort of their own home. Those persons who are less willing to seek and accept challenges are referred to as low sensation seekers (LSS). The tendency of people either to seek or to avoid thrilling, challenging activities has been called their optimal stimulation level (OSL).[18]

Researchers have attempted to develop various measures of the need for stimulation. For example, Zuckerman developed the general sensation-seeking scale (GSSS), which is designed to measure individual differences in sensation seeking along four dimensions:

1. Thrill and adventure seeking
2. Experience seeking

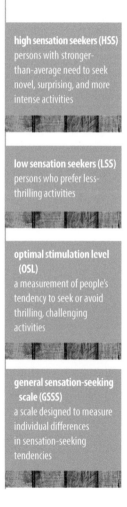

high sensation seekers (HSS) persons with stronger-than-average need to seek novel, surprising, and more intense activities

low sensation seekers (LSS) persons who prefer less-thrilling activities

optimal stimulation level (OSL) a measurement of people's tendency to seek or avoid thrilling, challenging activities

general sensation-seeking scale (GSSS) a scale designed to measure individual differences in sensation-seeking tendencies

3. Disinhibition
4. Susceptibility to boredom[19]

This scale allows researchers to divide respondents into high and low sensation seekers based on the research evidence that the OSL is constant within an individual, but varies from one individual to another.

Courtesy of the United States Marines.

Demanding outdoor sports have always been a favorite of many high sensation seeking individuals.

Cognitive Theories

Cognitive theories presume that human beings are rational, intelligent organisms who use their physical and intellectual capacities to fulfill their conscious desires. In this view, humans are not mechanically driven by internal needs and motives and by external stimuli. Rather, they are viewed as information processors and problem solvers who have the ability to deal effectively with their environment. This view of human behavior recognizes the interdependence between the mental processes of learning, feeling, thinking, performing, perceiving, remembering, and forgetting. Behavior is seen as a continuous interaction between these mental processes and an active process rather than an act that emerges only when a need arises. Behavior is purposeful and a means that humans use for controlling life events that surround them as well as for controlling their own states. People select goals to accomplish objectives (to learn, to dominate, to master the environment, to control their behavior) and consciously monitor their behavior to ensure the accomplishment of set goals.

Whereas the motivation theories covered so far in this chapter emphasize the roles of forces such as instincts, drives, arousal, and cognition in instigating or guiding human behavior, other views on a universal *need hierarchy* and *social motives* have also been advocated as dominant influences on human behavior. One such view is the familiar hierarchy of basic needs—physiological, safety, social, esteem, and self-actualization—which was proposed by Maslow. In this model, higher orders of needs emerge as motivating factors only after lower orders of needs are sufficiently satisfied. A second view, proposed by Murray, contains an alphabetical listing of social or instrumental motives, such as achievement, autonomy, dominance, harm-avoidance, and nurturance that are solicited in the service of our basic needs.

MOTIVATIONAL CONFLICT

Four of the motivational theories examined earlier—instinct, drive, arousal, and cognitive—emphasize different forces as an explanation of motivated behavior. However, such distinctions between the theories are largely artificial. Human motivation is complex and reveals the influence of varied forces driven by multiple causes. For example, the motivation to reproduce can be explained equally well in terms of instinct, drive, or arousal theories. In this sense, these theories are complementary rather than contradictory. They shed light on the diverse sources of human motivation and suggest that motivation is a complex, multifaceted phenomenon.

Life would be simple if consumers could deal with their needs, motives, and goals one at a time. Unfortunately, seldom is this the case. More often, a combination of forces, which differ in direction and strength, operate on an individual concurrently. Sometimes consumer motivations are complementary; at other times they clash. Take the case of satisfying hunger and pursuing a healthy lifestyle. Unfortunately, when a hungry individual is about to indulge in a rich pizza, a conflict arises. Although pizza is one of this person's favorite foods, it is also high in fat, cholesterol, and salt. Motivational conflict occurs when multiple needs function simultaneously and fulfilling one goal causes another to remain unsatisfied. The end result of such situations is *frustration*—an emotional state that arises when barriers interfere with goal-directed behavior.

motivational conflict
situations in which multiple needs simultaneously act on an individual

A widely accepted treatment of motivational conflict by Lewin proposes that some forces precipitate movement toward a goal (approach), whereas other forces deter such action (avoidance).[20] Consumer purchasing usually involves some degree of conflict between an individual's desire to acquire product benefits but resistance against spending money to acquire them. Knowledge of such consumer tendencies guides marketers in their quest for tactics designed to ease motivational conflicts in purchase situations. Tactics such as "buy now, pay later," "order through the Internet," and "return the product for a full refund" are but a few examples of tactics that marketers employ to reduce motivational conflicts for consumers.

Lewin identified three common types of motivational conflict. One type occurs when an individual must select between two attractive alternatives. A second type occurs when one's choice involves both positive and negative consequences. A third type occurs when a person must choose among two repulsive options. These are called approach–approach, approach–avoidance, and avoidance–avoidance situations, respectively. Exhibit 6.2 is a schematic diagram that summarizes these types of conflict.

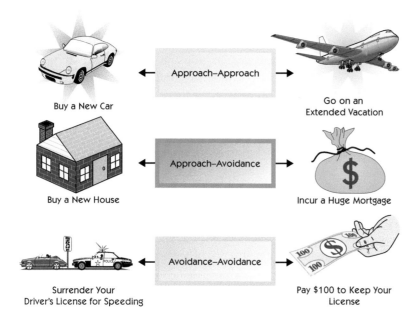

EXHIBIT 6.2

Schematic Diagram Summarizes the Three Motivational Conflicts

Approach–Approach

In **approach–approach conflicts**, consumers face a choice among desirable options. The more equal the attraction, the greater the conflict. For example, when browsing a restaurant's menu, we may find both steak and lobster appetizing. To help consumers resolve approach–approach conflicts, marketers may enable consumers to take advantage of multiple options simultaneously. Some restaurants, for example, offer surf-and-turf combination plates. Other businesses utilize strategically placed cues in the store to influence the brand selections of shoppers facing approach–approach conflicts. Such shoppers are quite susceptible to visual appeals,

approach–approach conflict
a situation in which a person faces a choice among two desirable alternatives

price offers, and other point-of-purchase enticements. Advertisers also often bundle multiple benefits in a single offer for the same reason. For instance, Verizon ads promise unlimited talk, unlimited texts, no annual contract, and discounts available for educators, government, and military personnel.

Approach–Avoidance

The most typical buyer behavior situation is approach–avoidance conflict because, in every case, consumers must surrender money and time, forego other opportunities, expend energy and effort, and incur risks to procure product benefits. Consumers purchase products and services only when their anticipated satisfaction exceeds the sacrifice of resources required. Thus, marketers must convince consumers that product rewards exceed their cost. In the food and beverage industry, new product opportunities have evolved out of approach–avoidance conflicts. For example, diet beverages and low-calorie, reduced-fat meals now enable weight-conscious consumers to both enjoy these products and lessen their caloric intake.

Avoidance–Avoidance

Avoidance–avoidance conflicts require consumers to choose one of two unpleasant alternatives and are thus difficult to resolve. For example, automobile drivers eventually face the choice of paying a huge bill to repair an old car or coming up with the necessary financing to buy a new one. Similarly, college students want neither to be without a computer nor to spend hundreds of dollars to buy one. Under such circumstances, marketers may attempt to reduce the negative aspect of spending the money by extending payment plans, offering trade-in allowances, or donating some portion of a product's selling price to a charitable cause. Marketers can also increase the negativeness of avoiding the purchase of a product or service. For example, ads for Jiffy Lube oil-change service remind drivers that failure to change a car's oil and filter regularly can cause expensive auto repairs later. In an alternative strategy, marketers restructure a negative situation into a positive one to make it more attractive. For example, most heads of households want neither to risk financial ruin for their loved ones in the event of death nor to pay the high costs of life insurance. Recognizing this, many life insurance firms create combination insurance and investment programs to shift the focus from policy costs and death to retirement income and return-on-investment.

MOTIVATION RESEARCH

Marketers and advertising agencies have become increasingly interested in why consumers behave as they do and why they select one product or brand instead of another. Motivation research explores the why aspects of human behavior with qualitative rather than quantitative research approaches.[21] This research is designed to delve below a subject's level of conscious awareness and uncover hidden motivations. Although such influences are difficult to determine, they may be central to understanding certain purchasing behaviors.

Motivation research employs a set of techniques, such as projective tests and depth interviews that were originally developed for use in clinical psychology and have been adapted for consumer research purposes.[22]

motivation research
the study of the why aspects of consumer behavior

One of the reasons behind the need for motivation research is variation in consumers' willingness and ability to provide the information that marketers require. Individuals may or may not know their motives, or they may be unwilling to reveal what they do know because they feel it is personal or fear that it is socially unacceptable. In other instances, consumers do not express their motives simply because they are unaware of the forces that underlie their behavior.

Consumers who are able and willing to discuss their buying motives when directly questioned represent the easiest situation for marketers to handle. Their motives often relate to aspects of products such as brand attributes, benefits, and image. Such motives are conscious, and subjects do not attempt to hide them.

However, even when consumers are aware of their basic motivations, they are often reluctant to admit or reveal information that is personal or unpleasant or shows them in an unfavorable light. Direct question-and-answer approaches are ineffective under such circumstances. To overcome consumer reluctance to cooperate, marketers rely on projective techniques, which are based on the idea of relieving subjects of direct responsibility for the feelings they express. These methods have subjects assume the role of someone else and speak on their behalf. In doing so, respondents reveal their own motives.

Consumers who are unaware of their motives and cannot directly report them present a challenge for researchers. In this case, projective techniques as well as association tests can be helpful.

Projective Techniques

Projective techniques are a set of specialized research tools that may be employed within the context of an in-depth interview to delve into a respondent's psyche and unravel the real reasons behind his or her consumption patterns.[23] Projective techniques take a variety of forms. For example, subjects may be shown ambiguous pictures or told about situations on which they are then asked to comment, thereby projecting themselves into the scene or predicament. Among the most popular projective tests employed for purposes of consumer research are the Thematic Apperception Test and cartoons.

Thematic Apperception Test

Some projective techniques are labeled storytelling techniques because they rely on pictorial stimuli such as photos, drawings, or cartoons that subjects are asked to explain. One such test is the Thematic Apperception Test (TAT). In marketing applications, researchers design ambiguous illustrations or photographs depicting some phenomenon of interest such as shopping and purchasing circumstances, product use, or social situations. Some pictures are clear representations; others are more obscure. The respondent is asked to explain what is going on and what the outcome might be or to tell a story about each picture. Because few clues are available in the picture, subjects draw from their own personality traits, experiences, motivations, feelings, and imagination and, by doing so, reveal something about themselves. Their responses are used to assess motives, beliefs, and feelings about the phenomenon under investigation.

Cartoons

In the cartoon variation of the TAT, empty balloons appear near the mouths or heads of characters in an illustration. Sometimes, one character is shown posing a question or statement to another. The respondent replies by providing the missing portion of the dialogue and in so doing, projects his or her own beliefs, feelings, or motives onto the characters in the picture. An example appears in Exhibit 6.3.

After a researcher shows a respondent this cartoon, the researcher asks the respondent, "What comment does the wife make in response to her husband's statement?"

The government is cracking down on the cigarette industry.

EXHIBIT 6.3

A Marketing Application of the Cartoon Technique

CONSUMER BEHAVIOR IN PRACTICE

Torture Those Creepy Males

A few years ago, McCann-Erickson, a large advertising agency, was approached by its client to determine why low-income women in the South, a key market segment, were not purchasing Combat, a new brand of roach killer in a plastic tray. Widespread household-infestation trouble indicated that tremendous sales potential existed among this group. However, women remained loyal to the traditional bug sprays they had used for years.

The agency knew that earlier advertising had been successful. Women knew about Combat and believed it killed roaches effectively, neatly, and inconspicuously. Nonetheless, they still weren't buying it.

Agency psychologists determined that conducting motivation research would help in this case, because they suspected that hidden motives were behind women's reluctance to accept Combat. As a result, they conducted in-depth interviews and asked women to sketch the roaches and compose brief stories to explain their drawings. It amazed researchers to discover that all the roaches drawn were males!

Women perceived roaches as sneaky male scavengers. They associated roaches with men who had abandoned them, left them feeling poor and powerless, or mistreated them in the past. The agency concluded that women prefer spray roach killers over products that do not permit users to see roaches suffer and perish.

According to Paula Drillman, the research director and agency's director of strategic planning, killing roaches with conventional bug sprays and watching them squirm and die allow women to express their hostility toward men and gain greater control over the roaches.[24]

Marketers sometimes attempt to discover hidden forces behind consumer acceptance or rejection of products. In the case of Combat, the roach killer, what hidden motives caused rejection of the product? To see an example of a site designed to promote understanding between the sexes, visit Balance Magazine at www.balancemagazine.com. *Can such sexist feelings be soothed?*

Association Tests

association tests
tests based on the immediacy of subject's responses to stimulus words or phrases

Association tests are based on immediacy of subjects' responses to a stimulus word or phrase that the interviewer poses. The immediate response is assumed to curtail self-censorship. That is to say, an individual lacks time to come up with logical or socially acceptable answers to the words or phrases provided. Responses, thus, are presumed to be a respondent's gut reactions to a stimulus. Commonly used association tests include free word associations and sentence completions.

Free Word Associations

In free word associations, a researcher dispenses a list of words one at a time to a respondent. Subjects are asked to respond immediately with the very first word that comes to mind for each. For example, in a study of cooking oil, key words in the list given to respondents might include cholesterol, fat, health, heart, margarine, butter, and cost. Responses are analyzed according to the frequency with which they are given as a reply, the average amount of time that elapses before a response is given, and the number of subjects who do not respond at all to a test word after a reasonable time. Free word associations have been used to test brand names for recognition, awareness, and recall as well as for possible negative connotations. They can also be used to uncover feelings about new products, and to identify key words for advertising and promotion.

Sentence Completions

Another popular variation of free word association is sentence completion. Sentence completions give subjects a more directed stimulus than simple word associations. Respondents are asked to complete each thought with the first phrase that comes to mind. The following phrases illustrate sentence completions.

> The average person considers rock-and-roll music . . .

> When you first get a new car . . .

> Housecleaning would be so much easier if . . .

> People who smoke cigarettes . . .

Other Motivation Research Techniques

A number of other techniques are also employed for purposes of conducting motivation research. They include the Zaltman Metaphor Elicitation Technique and focus groups.

Zaltman Metaphor Elicitation Technique (ZMET)

The Zaltman Metaphor Elicitation Technique (ZMET) is designed to elicit metaphors that can help researchers explore ideas that are deeply held by consumers regarding a variety of issues, such as brands, companies, purchase situations, product-usage patterns, or product concepts. In the ZMET, each participant is asked to collect a minimum of twelve images representing his or her thoughts or feelings about the research topic gathered from any source such as family albums, catalogs, or magazines. For example, in a study of women's thoughts and feelings about buying and wearing panty hose, twenty women were "Z-Metted." Each collected a dozen pictures from magazines, catalogs, and family photo albums. A review of these photos showed two types of images. The first consisted of pictures of steel bands strangling trees, twisted telephone cords, and fence posts encased in a tight plastic wrap. The second group of pictures was of flowers resting peacefully in a vase, a luxury car, and an ice cream sundae spilled on the ground.

The meaning of the first group of pictures is not hard to figure out. Many women view panty hose as hot, uncomfortable, and confining. However, the second group of pictures revealed a "like–hate" type of relationship. The flower vase picture indicated that wearing panty hose makes women feel thin and tall. The expensive car picture expressed a feeling of luxury felt when women wore panty hose. The spilled ice cream sundae represented embarrassment caused by stocking runs.[25] Such insights are important from a marketing standpoint because they provide a basis for understanding consumers and guide the manner in which marketers appeal to their diverse needs.[26] Findings from the panty hose study, for example, led hosiery manufacturers to alter their advertising appeals to include images reflecting luxury and allure.

Focus Groups

A focus group usually consists of eight to twelve people drawn from the population relevant to the issue under investigation. Unlike surveys, focus groups do not use structured questionnaires. The moderator of a focus group starts only with an explanation of the topic to be covered and mere-

Zaltman Metaphor Elicitation Technique (ZMET) a test where respondents provide images that represent their feelings about a topic

focus groups sessions where eight to twelve people—led by a moderator—freely discuss a topic

ly facilitates the respondents' flow of thought regarding the topic. Sessions usually last somewhere between ninety minutes and two hours.

The strength of the focus group method lies in its ability to acquire numerous and diverse views from respondents. It allows for spontaneity, and ideas may simply drop out of the blue during a focus group session. Furthermore, the group setting allows for idea generation and snowballing. A comment from one participant can trigger a chain of responses from the other members present.[27]

Focus groups are currently one of the most frequently used techniques in consumer research. They can be used to learn how consumers use a product or what a product means to them. Focus groups conducted by Nabisco, for example, revealed that many adults view Oreos as a cherished memory of childhood and perceive the cookie to be almost magical in its ability to make them feel good. This revelation led Nabisco to design its successful "unlocking the magic of Oreo" advertising campaign.

Similarly, focus groups can be used to find out consumer views about a product or brand as well as consumers' expectations of that product or brand. Ray-O-Vac found through a series of focus groups that consumers wanted brighter, more modern, and more dependable flashlights, and that they were willing to pay for the added durability. These insights led the company to develop its line of Workhorse flashlights, which regenerated a mature market.[28]

Recently, in order to offer clients a less expensive and quicker way to do consumer research, some consumer research firms have begun to conduct focus groups over the Internet.[29] Although capable of providing a speedy and low-cost means of acquiring data online, this technique is not without flaws. Critics of the approach contend that online chat sessions lack several critical components of genuine focus group research, such as authentic group dynamics and the inability to observe nonverbal or facial input of participants.[30]

However, it is important to recognize that because motivation research is exploratory in nature, it only offers insight and suggests hypotheses for more structured, quantitatively oriented investigations to be conducted with larger, more representative samples.

Now we shift our attention to a related and equally important topic in human motivation—that of emotions. We investigate the significant role they play in shaping our purchasing behavior as well as examine their influential place in the design of marketing strategy.

EMOTIONS

Humans are emotional creatures.[31] Our behavior is influenced to a great extent by emotions such as love, fear, anger, envy, surprise, loneliness, sorrow, and happiness. Even the goals we select are chosen in the context of our emotional states. Everybody has experienced emotional motivation. Emotions are evolutionary adaptations, as they enhance our ability to experience and evaluate our environment. We sometimes visit malls, department stores, and shopping websites to alleviate boredom.[32] At other times, we contribute to charitable causes out of compassion for the less fortunate.

The significance of the topic of emotions to marketers stems from the realization that stirring consumers' emotions can be a powerful strategy in product and service promotions. American Greetings, Inc. and Hallmark, the greeting card giants, successfully use emotional themes to sell their cards. Similarly, ads from florists such as FTD and 800-FLOWERS suggest sending flowers as a delightful means of expressing emotions. Music recording companies use the emotion of nostalgia to sell golden oldies. The movie industry stresses emotions to bring back older movies such as the original *Star Wars* and *The Wizard of Oz*. Carmakers such as Volkswagen have reintroduced popular older models such as the VW Beetle to capitalize on nostalgic feelings toward the original Bug. Advertisers have

emotions
feeling states such as joy or sorrow

Dire conditions depicted in tragedies such as this one stir powerful emotions, resulting in a stream of donations to help the victims.

© ChameleonsEye/Shutterstock.com

been known to recycle ads from the past. Retro campaigns have been run for brands such as Colonel Sanders on behalf of Kentucky Fried Chicken and E.T. for Reese's Peanut Butter Cup.[33] Other products or services for which emotions have successfully been tapped to enhance sales include Mickey Mouse pajamas, Superman t-shirts, and Strawberry Shortcake toys, among many others.

For many consumers, a major part of the appeal in product acquisitions is the emotional value the product offers. In purchasing or receiving a gift, for example, it is often not the monetary worth of the gift that determines its value, but the emotions that the gift conveys. Many of us also attach varied emotions to our possessions. For example, we may have a favorite pen, book, CD, or may keep some memorabilia of our favorite athlete or movie star. When we travel, we often buy souvenirs from the places we visit and tend to stay in accommodations where we have had fond memories. In realizing these tendencies, marketers attempt to establish connections between their specific product or service and emotions—a strategy known as *bonding*.[34] Through this strategy, it becomes possible to stimulate the need for a specific product or brand simply by stirring the emotions that the marketer has successfully connected to it.

The Nature of Human Emotions

For years, emotions were considered the base remnants of humans' animal selves imprisoned in primitive portions of the brain. Other thinkers have regarded emotions as ineffable ingredients of the human spirit, too elusive to capture. Recently, scientists have begun to capitalize on advances in brain scanning, pharmacology, and animal research. Their goal has been to trace feelings along their journey through the corporeal landscape and the brain's complex circuitry. They are shaking up centuries-old notions of how humans feel, why they differ from each other emotionally, and what makes them feel the way they do.[35] Biology does not always support traditional notions regarding how feelings fit together. Happiness, for example, is not the opposite of sadness, and depression is not simply exaggerated sadness.

Some scientists believe that emotions are mainly a physical reaction to environmental events and situational stimuli. Emotions can be accompanied by physiological changes such as eye-pupil dilation, increased perspiration, more rapid breathing, increased heart rate and blood pressure, and elevated blood sugar levels. Physical symptoms of anger, for example, may include accelerated heartbeat, change in the rate of breathing, blushing of the face, and shaking. Emotions can trigger specific behaviors. Fear may cause one to flee; anger may trigger striking; grief may precipitate crying. Strong emotional responses, such as intense anger or fear, can prevent one from thinking clearly. Emotionally charged states (happiness, surprise, rage, distress) can amplify positive and negative experiences. Later, recollection of these events can affect individuals' subsequent behavior.[36] Memories of a pleasant dinner with a close friend at a nice restaurant may cause an individual to frequent that place and recommend it to others.

Emotion versus Mood

Whereas emotions entail an individual's response to particular stimuli in the environment, mood entails a temporary feeling state or frame of mind.[37] Moods are already present when consumers experience ads, retail stores, products, services, and brands.[38] For example, a person can be in a good mood due to receiving a promotion or in a bad mood due to problems experienced at one's place of work. These moods could have a bearing on whether or not consumers shop, when and where they shop, and whether they shop alone or with others.

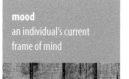

mood
an individual's current frame of mind

Mood also influences the way we respond to shopping environments and cues, such as point-of-purchase displays and how long we remain in a store.[40] Retailers often try to *create* a mood for shoppers, even though customers enter the store with preexisting moods. For example, fragrance counters in some department stores are sprayed with perfume scents to create a mood. Likewise, in an online environment, the use of color, music, and animation all combine to put visitors in a positive and receptive frame of mind. When selling homes, realtors have been known to ask current occupants to bake a batch of cookies in the oven before agents show the home to prospective buyers. The aroma of fresh-baked cookies can create a positive mood due to associations with fond childhood memories. Consumers in a positive mood tend to recall more information about a specific brand than those in a negative mood. However, it is unlikely that attempts to induce a positive mood toward that brand at the point of purchase via background music or other means would exert a noticeable impact on its selection by consumers unless a previously stored evaluation of it already existed.[41]

Research suggests that being in a good mood can facilitate flexibility in a person's thinking, enhance the recall of stimuli, encourage someone to seek variety, and increase his or her willingness to try new things.[42]

Online Shopping Invades India

For decades, American consumers have taken online shopping for granted. Not a day passes by without the majority of consumers using the Internet to make a purchase online. Internationally, however, this shopping convenience is hardly available in many countries. For most people in India, for example, with its population of 1.25 billion, such service would present an entirely new experience in their lives.

In 2012, Amazon sensed the huge potential of India as a ripe market for online shopping and decided to place the country as part of a crucial experiment in Internet buying and selling that may be expanded in the future to include other foreign countries. Amazon announced at that time that it is racing to piece together a plan to build from scratch an online shopping system where Indians can order anything they need—from clothing to electronics—with just a few mouse clicks.

In 2013, Amazon opened its experimental online shopping establishment in Govandi, one of India's poorest and most-sprawling suburbs, close to Mumbai. At this facility, customers can use the center's laptops to order any item they desire from sites that are connected to hundreds of thousands of merchandise items. These ordered items would be delivered to the establishment within a few days, at which time customers could come and pick them up. This system allows Indian shoppers to be exposed to millions of products available online, and purchase them usually at a much lower price than what they would have to pay at conventional retail stores.

Factors that encouraged Amazon to select India as one of the primary nations to initiate this experimental undertaking is the fact that English is the language of conducting business there. Unlike China, where Chinese dialects prevail, India, for this reason alone, is predicted to overtake China as the most investor-friendly country in just a few years. Another reason underlying India's huge potential for Amazon is that barely one-quarter of India's population has access to the Internet at home, whether on computer or smartphone; and only a small percentage of those currently ever shop online. Experts estimate that Amazon's revenue from this venture could exceed $137 billion by the year 2020.

Whether or not Amazon's plan for investment in this venture will be a success against the local rivals, who presently dominate the Indian market, remains to be seen. Yet Amazon's top management considers this move to be more than just another attempt to market goods online. Rather, it is a mandate for the company to build a whole e-commerce ecosystem that will make the world a better place to live for everyone, anywhere around the globe.[39]

When our mood is elevated, we tend to process information in detail, which leads to greater elaboration and recall.[43] Consumers engaged in the *internal search* stage of the decision process (sifting through memory for product knowledge) are likely to recall mood-compatible information, feelings, and experiences.[44] Consequently, marketers who put consumers in a good mood by using humor or pleasing visuals may enhance recall of positive product attributes. Isen and Means suggest that mood influences decision-making processes. They argue that when making purchase decisions, individuals who are in a positive mood tend to do so more efficiently.[45] For example, such persons are unlikely to waste time in reviewing information already examined.

From a consumer behavior perspective, some products seem to have mood-altering properties. Fragrances, alcohol, and tobacco are but some examples. It has also been observed that people sometimes use consumption to manage their moods. Fidel Castro, the former president of Cuba, is reported to have said that he smoked a cigar under two circumstances: to celebrate when he was in a good mood and to console himself when he was in a bad mood. People in elevated moods also report a greater willingness to spend. On the other hand, people in bad moods tend to be more willing to spend on items with mood-elevating properties, such as chocolates.

MARKETING AND PROMOTIONAL APPLICATIONS OF EMOTION

According to McClelland, emotional arousal is the primary energizing force behind consumer behavior.[46] Emotionally toned ads that attempt to stimulate a positive affective response rather than provide information or logical arguments can therefore be effective motivators in this view. Consumers seek products whose primary or secondary benefits are emotional. Many products and services (movies, TV programs, video games, electronic gadgets, and social media sites, as well as exotic travel destinations) offer emotion as a primary benefit. Other products offer emotion as a secondary benefit. Cars provide transportation and prestige; laptops offer productivity and convenience.[47] Acknowledging this fact, marketing communicators employ emotion within promotional campaigns in a variety of ways.

Ad campaigns frequently use emotions that directly relate to the product attributes and benefits. Many products offer emotional as well as utilitarian benefits. For example, most ads for reputable watch brands, such as Rolex, Bulova, and Mont Blanc, stress achievement and distinction, along with the utilitarian feature of superior accuracy in keeping time.

Other campaigns use emotions that do not directly relate to the product or its benefits. The goal of these remote emotional appeals is to increase the effectiveness of persuasive communications by increasing attention to the messages or making them more memorable. For example, humor has been used to sell products that aren't funny. Sex has been used to sell numerous products ranging from beverages and toothpastes to clothing and automobiles. Often, however, humor and sex have little or nothing to do with the goods being advertised.

How Emotional Ads Work

Emotional ads trigger physiological and psychological reactions that can be both positive and negative. The goal of marketers, of course, is to get consumers to attribute an experienced pleasantness—benefits and satisfaction—to brand attributes. Some evidence suggests that when viewing ads, consumers can experience and respond to very low, but detectable, levels of certain emotions.[48] The perception of these emotions, even at these minimal levels, may affect cognition and behavior.[49]

It has been proposed that the goal of emotional advertising is bonding. As mentioned earlier, bonding involves connecting the consumer and the product through an emotional tie.[50] Through this link, it becomes possible to activate the need for the product simply by stirring the relevant emotion. Consider, for example, the well-established tie between individuals, red roses, and love. Consumers are likely to purchase red roses when love emotions are stirred in certain circumstances or on special occasions such as Valentine's Day or Sweetest Day. Emotional appeals also appear to hold

bonding
the connecting of a consumer and a product through an emotional tie

the potential for enhancing the chance that a message will be perceived. Emotional ads can enhance attitude formation or change by increasing the marketer's ability to attract and hold attention. Viewers may be more apt to attend to ads that employ positive or even negative emotions than to neutral ads.

Similarly, emotional ads can amplify mental processing and increase consumer involvement with the product. For example, we are constantly exposed to ads and commercials that stimulate emotions, such as fear (e.g., of illness, identity theft, or injury); pity (e.g., for poverty, starvation, or victimization); sympathy (e.g., toward homelessness, old age, and victims of natural disasters); and pride (e.g., over patriotism, innovation, achievements). By heightening a viewer's state of physiological and psychological arousal, emotional ads may receive more thorough processing and be remembered better than neutral ads.[51]

Measuring Emotion

Researchers have been employing a variety of verbal, visual, and psychological response tools to measure consumers' emotional responses to advertising. There are verbal measurement scales that involve extensive adjective checklists that consumers complete. These types, however, are often viewed as lengthy and time consuming for attaining the desired results. Visual measurement tools are also available and are done via handheld dial-turning instruments that consumers maåœnipulate while watching the commercials being tested.

The PAD (Pleasure-Arousal-Dominance) Semantic Differential Scale devised by Mehrabian and Russell is currently the most widely used and validated instrument for measuring emotional response. The PAD Semantic Differential procedure is based on scales anchored by sets of emotion-denoting adjective pairs that tap into the intended emotion. For example, "Happy–Sad" is used to assess levels of *pleasure*.

The Self-Assessment Manikin (SAM) represents another method of measuring emotional responses. SAM depicts each PAD dimension with a graphic character arranged along a continuous nine-point scale. For *pleasure*, SAM ranges from a smiling happy figure to a frowning unhappy figure. For *arousal*, SAM ranges from sleepy with eyes closed to excited with eyes wide open. The *dominance* scale shows SAM ranging from a tiny figure representing a feeling of being submissive, to a large figure representing an in-control sort of feeling.[52]

In addition, BBDO Advertising Agency developed another method of gauging emotions based on facial expressions. This technique, known as the Emotional Measurement System (EMS), can be employed to gauge the emotions that an ad triggers. To test an ad, subjects are instructed to sort swiftly through fifty-three pictures and set aside those that reflect how they feel when viewing an ad under study. The percent of subjects that selects particular pictures yields a profile of viewers' emotional response to the test ad.[53] Four samples of facial expression photos from BBDO's EMS appear in Exhibit 6.4.

Throughout this chapter, we have seen that motivating consumers is a fundamental purpose of the marketing effort. The challenge for marketers lies in activating human motives and in getting consumers to perceive products and services as goals. Not all motivational appeals are equally capable of generating consumer response. Although the motivations underlying some purchases are quite simple, other purchases are influenced by more complex motivations.

One of the major factors that influences our tendency to respond to different motivational appeals is our personality. All of us have our own ways of dealing with the environment. These behavior patterns are unique to us. Whether or not motivational appeals such as fantasy, sex, wish fulfillment, escape, fun, fear, guilt, and so forth have an influence on us is governed to a large extent by our personality and how we give meaning to the world around us. The next chapter examines the way our personality develops and how personality, together with our lifestyle and self-concept, shapes our consumption patterns.

EXHIBIT 6.4

These four photos of facial expressions from BBDO's EMS depict the emotions of surprise, happiness–playfulness, disgust, and distraction. Respondents use these and other similar photos to express how they feel about an ad or a product.

SUMMARY

Motivation is a state of the individual in which bodily energy is mobilized and directed in a selective fashion toward states of affairs in the external environment, called goals. Motives can be conscious or unconscious. They can be based on needs that have a biological or psychological origin. In addition, motives can be classified as high versus low urgency, positive versus negative polarity, intrinsic versus extrinsic, or rational versus emotional.

Needs or requirements can become motives, which, in turn, lead individuals toward action. For marketers, it is necessary to both arouse consumers and direct them toward specific products, services, or brands, which consumers are persuaded to perceive as goals. Desires are steeped in fantasies rather than reasoning and refer to belief-based passions that involve longing, yearning, and fervently wishing for something.

A number of theories attempt to explain human motivation. These include instinct, drive, arousal, and cognitive theories. Instinct theories suggest that the origins of human motivation are innate and reflect adaptation of species to the environment. Drive theories suggest that disturbances, disharmony, or imbalances of an individual's body systems tend to be reduced or eliminated by means of an automatic and internal homeostatic mechanism, which seeks to rectify the disequilibrium. Arousal theory suggests that individuals seek stimulation instead of trying to avoid it. It also suggests that there exists an optimal stimulation level that individuals seek to maintain. Cognitive theories view humans as rational, intelligent creatures who have the mental capability to pursue goals they set for themselves. Other views of motivation include Maslow's self-actualization theory, which rank-ordered five basic human needs, and social motives theories, which list a number of social needs as the basis of human motivation.

As individuals attempt to satisfy their needs and attain their goals, motivational conflicts may arise.

Motivation research investigates the *why* aspects of human behavior. Consumers may be aware of the reasons behind their behavior and willing to discuss them, be aware of their motives but unwilling to discuss them, or be unaware of the internal forces that impact their behavior. Projective techniques such as the TAT and cartoons, along with associative techniques like word associations and sentence completions, as well as other procedures such as the ZMET and conducting focus groups can be employed to identify consumer motives.

Emotions are distinguishable, relatively strong, and largely involuntary feelings that arise in response to particular stimuli in the environment. Promotional strategies employ emotions in a number of ways. Although ads often use emotions that relate to product attributes and benefits, some ads attempt to increase the effectiveness of persuasive messages by using emotions that do not directly relate to the product, its features, or its benefits. Emotional ads not only try to trigger positive physiological and psychological consumer responses, they also attempt to achieve bonding; that is, to get consumers to somehow *connect* with the product or brand.

Emotions can be measured in a variety of ways. One method involves extensive adjective checklists that consumers complete. Another is accomplished by using visual measurement tools that allow consumers to manipulate a handheld dial to record their feelings while viewing ads or commercials. However, the PAD Semantic Differential Scale along with the Self-Assessment Manikin (SAM) are currently the most widely used tools to measure emotions. Emotions can also be measured by decoding facial expressions via use of the EMS Facial Photo System developed by BBDO Advertsing Agency.

CASE SYNOPSIS

You Have Nothing to Lose but Your Weight

Due to the overweight epidemic in our society, many individuals find a positive solution in joining one of the weight-management programs provided by a large number of competing services. Such facilities face two challenges in gaining and keeping customers. The first is the need to design an effective behavior modification system to ensure participants' persistence in the program; and the second is to create a weight-loss program that the participants find pleasing and easy to follow. Providers of such services, including Weight Watchers and Nutrisystem, have attempted to develop such programs.

Notes

1 Thomas Barrabi, "Legalized Sports Gambling? Americans to Bet $95 Billion on NFL, College Football This Season, Mostly Illegally, Group Says," *iB Times* (September 9, 2015), http://www.ibtimes.com/legalized-sports-gambling-americans-bet-95-billion-nfl-college-football-season-mostly-2089606; David McNew, "Americans Will Spend Over $4 Billion Gambling on Super Bowl 50," *Newsweek*, http://www.newsweek.com/super-bowl-gambling-las-vegas-panthers-broncos-421458; Casino Industry-Statistics & Facts, http://www.statista.com/topics/1053/casinos/; "Best US Online Gambling Sites," https://www.casino.org/us/gambling/; "Complete Guide to Casino Gambling for Americans," http://www.casino.org/us/guide/; Sean Flynn, "Is Gambling Good for America?" *Parade* (May 20, 2007); Richard K. Miller and Associates, "Casinos Gaming and Wagering 2011," *Research and Markets* (May 2011), http://www.reasearchandmarkets.com/reports/1803014/casinos_gaming_and_wagering_2011; Chad Hills, "Quick Guide: Articles on Gambling," *Citizen Link* (April 29, 2011), www.citizenlink.com/2011/04/29/quick-guide-articles-on-gambling.

2 Theodore M. Newcomb, Ralph H. Turner, and Philip E. Converse, *Social Psychology* (New York: Holt, Rinehart and Winston, 1965), p. 22.

3 "Botox Industry Statistics," Statistic Brain Research Institute (April, 2015), www.statisticbrain.com/botox-statistics/; Christine Bittar, "Allergan Set to Make Juvederm a Name," *MediaPost Publications* (January 25, 2007); "Plastic Surgery Guide" (January 16, 2012), http://www.plasticsurgeryguide.com/botox-prices.html.

4 Jack W. Brehm, "Psychological Reactance: Theory and Applications," in Thomas K. Skrull (Ed.), *Advances in Consumer Research* 16 (Provo, UT: Association for Consumer Research, 1989), pp. 72–75.

5 Wroe Alderson, "Needs, Wants, and Creative Marketing," *Cost and Profit Outlook* 8 (September 1955), pp. 1–3.

6 Gordon Fairclough, "Casket Stores Offer Bargains to Die For," *Wall Street Journal* (February 19, 1997), pp. B1, B10.

7 Scott Rockwood, "For Better Ad Success, Try Getting Emotional," *Marketing News* (October 21, 1996), p. 4.

8 Melvin T. Copeland, *Principles of Merchandising* (New York: A. W. Shaw Company, 1924), pp. 155–67; see also Carol Morgan and Doron Levy, "Why We Kick the Tires," *Brandweek* 38, no. 36 (September 29, 1997), pp. 24–28; Bill Bachrach, "How to Influence Human Behavior," *Executive Excellence* 12, no. 1 (January 1995), pp. 12–13.

9 Morris B. Holbrook and Elizabeth C. Hirschman, "The Experiential Aspects of Consumption: Consumer Fantasies, Feelings, and Fun," *Journal of Consumer Research* 9 (September 1982), pp. 132–140.

10 Dr. Henry H. Lodge, "Why Emotions Keep You Well," *Parade* (June 17, 2007), p. 17.

11 Becky Ebenkamp, "Color Coordination," *Brandweek* (January 12, 1998).

12 William N. Dember, "The New Look in Motivation," *American Scientist* (December 1965), pp. 409–427.

13 Chester R. Wasson, Frederick D. Sturdivant, and David H. McConoughy, *Competition and Human Behavior* (New York: Appleton-Century-Crofts, 1968), pp. 27–28.

14 Alain Jolibert and Gary Baumgartner, "Values, Motivations, and Personal Goals: Revisted," *Psychology & Marketing* 14, no. 7 (October 1997), pp. 675–688.

15 "Super Bowl Commercials 2016," http://www.superbowlcommercials2016. org/2016-advertisers/.

16 Russell W. Belk, Güliz Ger, and Søren Askegaard, "Consumer Desire in Three Cultures: Results from Projective Research," *Advances in Consumer Research* 24 (1997), pp. 24–28; Russell W. Belk, Güliz Ger, and Søren Aske-gaard, "Metaphors of Consumer Desire," *Advances in Consumer Research* 23 (1996), pp. 368–373.

17 Douglas Gentile, "Life Lessons: Children Learn Aggressive Ways of Think-ing and Behaving from Violent Video Games," *Iowa State University* (March 24, 2014), *http://www.news.iastate.edu/news/2014/03/24/violentgamesbe-havior;* "Violent Video Games—Psychologists Help Protect Children from Harmful Effects," wwwpsychologymatters.org/videogames.html; "Violence in the Media—Psychologists Help Protect Children from Harmful Effects," www.psychologymatters.org/mediaviolence.html; Jeanne B. Funk, "Chil-dren and Violent Video Games: Are There 'High Risk' Players?" http://cul-turalpolicy.uchicago.edu/conf2001/papers/funk1.html; Roni Caryn Rabin, "Videogames and the Depressed Teenager," *The New York Times* (January 17, 2011), http://well.blogs.nytimes.com/2011/01/18/video-games-and-the-depressed-teenager/.

18 George Kish and Gregory V. Donnenwerth, "Interests and Stimulation Seeking," *Journal of Counseling Psychology* 16 (1969), pp. 551–556; Nessim Hanna and John Wagle, "Who Is Your Satisfied Customer?" *The Journal of Consumer Marketing* 6 (Winter 1989), pp. 53–61; Richard Oliver, "Effect of Expectation and Disconfirmation on Post-Exposure Product Evalua-tions: An Alternative Interpretation," *Journal of Applied Psychology* 62, no. 4 (1977), pp. 480–486; Nessim Hanna, Rick Ridnour, and A. H. Kizilbash, "Optimum Stimulation Level: Evidence Relating to the Role of OSL in Predicting Sales Personnel Performance," *Journal of Professional Services Marketing* 10, no. 1 (1993), pp. 65–75; Jan Benedict, E. M. Steenkamp, and Hans Baumgartner, "The Role of Optimum Stimulation Level in Explorato-ry Consumer Behavior," *The Journal of Consumer Research* 19 (December 1992), pp. 434–448.

19 M. Zuckerman, "Development of a Sensation Seeking Scale," *Journal of Consulting Psychology* 28 (1964), pp. 477–482; Zuckerman, "Form V Sensa-tion Seeking Scale" (1979) in William O. Bearden, Richard G. Netemeyer, and Mary F. Mobley, *Handbook of Marketing Scales* (Newbury Park, CA: Sage, 1993), pp. 172–176; "Measuring Sensation Seeking," NIDA Notes

(July-August 1995), www.nida.nih.gov/NIDA_Notes/NNVoll0N4/Measure-Sens.html.

20 Kurt Lewin, *A Dynamic Theory of Personality* (New York: McGraw-Hill, 1935).

21 "Qualitative Research—A Summary of the Concepts Involved," *Journal of the Market Research Society* 21 (April 1979), pp. 107–124.

22 Dennis Rook, "Researching Consumer Fantasy," in Elizabeth C. Hirschman (Ed.), *Research in Consumer Behavior* 3 (Greenwich, CT: JAI Press, 1990), pp. 247–270; David Mick, M. De Moss, and Ronald Faber, "A Projective Study of Motivations and Meanings of Self-Gifts; Implications for Retail Management," *Journal of Retailing* (Summer 1992), pp. 122–144; Mary Ann McGrath, John F. Sherry, and Sidney J. Levy, "Giving Voice to the Gift: The Use of Projective Techniques to Recover Lost Meanings," *Journal of Consumer Psychology* 2 (1993), pp. 171–191; see also Barbara Stern's analysis of Dichter's Handbook—"Literary Criticism and the History of Marketing Thought: A NewPerspective on 'Reading' Marketing Theory," *Journal of the Academy of Marketing Science* 18 (Winter 1990), pp. 329–336.

23 Dennis W. Rook, "The Ritual Dimension of Consumer Behavior," *Journal of Consumer Research* 12 (December1985), pp. 251–264.

24 Ronald Alsop, "Advertisers Put Consumers on the Couch," *Wall Street Journal* (May 13, 1998), p. 17.

25 Daniel H. Pink, "Metaphor Marketing," *Fast Company* (April-May 1998), pp. 214–229.

26 Gerald Zaltman, "Metaphorically Speaking," *Marketing Research; A Magazine of Management and Applications* 8, no. 2 (Summer 1996), pp. 13–20; Gerald Zaltman and Robin Higie Coulter, "Seeing the Voice of the Customer: Metaphor-Based Advertising Research," *Journal of Advertising Research* 35, no. 4 (July-August 1995), pp. 35–51.

27 Thomas L. Greenbaum, *The Practical Handbook and Guide to Focus Group Research* (New York: Lexington, 1993); Jane Farley Templeton, *The Focus Group: A Strategic Guide to Organizing, Conducting, and Analyzing the Focus Group Interview* (Chicago: Probus, 1994); Jack Edmondston, "Handle Focus Group Research with Care," *Business Marketing* 79 (June 1994), p. 38; Thomas L. Greenbaum, "Who's Leading Your Focus Group?" *Bank Marketing* 25 (March 1993), p. 31; John Hoeffel, "The Secret Life of Focus Groups," *American Demographics* 16 (December 1994), pp. 17–19; Arch G. Woodside and Elizabeth J. Wilson, "Applying the Long Interview in Direct Marketing Research," *Journal of Direct Marketing Research* 9 (Winter1995), pp. 37–55.

28 Jennifer Riddle, "Complaining Customers Get Firms' Attention," *Wisconsin State Journal* (June 22, 1986), p. 2.

29 Thomas L. Greenbaum, "Internet Focus Groups: An Oxymoron," *Marketing News* (March 3, 1997), p. 35.

30 Kim Komando, "3 Reasons to Use Online Customer Surveys," Microsoft Small Business Center (2007), www.microsoft.coni/business/resources/marketing/small-business-rnarket-research.aspx.

31 Carroll Izard, *Human Emotion* (New York: Plenum Press, 1977); Marquis, "Our Emotions: Why We Feel the Way We Do; New Advances Are Opening Our Subjective Inner Worlds to Objective Study. Discoveries Are Upsetting Long-Held Notions."

32 R. A. Westbrook and W. C. Black, "A Motivation-Based Shopper Typology," *Journal of Retailing* (Spring 1985), pp. 78–103; T. C. O'Guinn and R. W. Belk, "Heaven on Earth," *Journal of Consumer Research* (September 1989), pp. 227–238; G. D. Mick, M. DeMoss, and R. J. Faber, "A Projective Study of Motivations and Meanings of Self-Gifts," *Journal of Retailing* (Summer 1992), pp. 122–144.

33 Karen Brooks, "Retro Hits and Myths," *Couriermail.com.au* (October 9, 2007), www.news.com.au/couriermail/story/0.23739.22557533-27197.00.html.

34 "Connecting Consumer and Product," *New York Times* (January 18, 1990), p. D19.

35 Marquis, "Our Emotions: Why We Feel the Way We Do; New Advances Are Opening our Subjective Inner Worlds to Objective Study. Discoveries Are Upsetting Long-Held Notions."

36 Joel B. Cohen and Charles S. Areni, "Affect and Consumer Behavior," in Harold H. Kassarjian and Thomas S. Robertson (Eds.), *Perspectives in Consumer Behavior*, 4th ed. (Upper Saddle River, NJ: Prentice Hall, 1991), pp. 188–240; Madeline Johnson and George M. Zinkhan, "Emotional Responses to a Professional Service Encounter," *Journal of Service Marketing* 5 (Spring 1991), pp. 5–16.

37 Kukil Bora, "Amazon Will Continue to Invest in India, Focus on Customers, Small Businesses: Jeff Bezos," *iB Times* (September 29, 2014), http://www.ibtimes.com/amazon-will-continue-invest-india-focus-customers-small-businesses-jeff-bezos-1696177; "Amazon Fuels India's Online Growth," *PlanetRetail, http://www.planetretail.net/news-and-events/amazon-fuels-indias-online-growth;* Jay Green, "How Amazon Flows Through India," *Seattle Times* (November 3, 2015), found in the *Cape Cod Times,* http://www.capecodtimes.com/article/20151103/NEWS/151109880.

38 Meryl Paula Gardner, "Mood States and Consumer Behavior: A Critical Review," *Journal of Consumer Research* 12 (December 1985), pp. 281–300; Robert A. Peterson and Matthew Sauber, "A Mood Scale for Survey Research," in Patrick E. Murphy et al. (Eds.), *AMA Educators' Proceedings* (Chicago: American Marketing Association, 1983), pp. 409–414.

39 Barry J. Babin, William R. Darden, and Mitch Griffin, "Some Comments on the Role of Emotions in Consumer Behavior," in Robert P. Leone, V. Kumor, et al. (Eds.), *AMA Educators' Proceedings* (Chicago: American Marketing Association, 1992), pp. 130–139; Patricia A. Knowles, Stephen J. Grove, and W. Jeffrey Burroughs, "An Experimental Examination of Mood Effects on Retrieval and Evaluation of Advertisement and Brand Information," *Journal of the Academy of Marketing Science* 21 (Spring 1993), pp. 135–142; Rajeev Batra and Douglas M. Stayman, "The Role of Mood in Advertising Effectiveness," *Journal of Consumer Research* (September 1990), pp. 203–214.

40 Gardner, "Mood States and Consumer Behavior: A Critical Review"; Ruth Belk Smith and Elaine Sherman, "Effects of Store Image and Mood on Consumer Behavior: A Theoretical and Empirical Analysis," in Leigh McAlister and Michael L. Rothschild (Eds.), *Advances in Consumer Research* 20 (Provo, UT: Association for Consumer Research, 1993), p. 631.

41 Knowles, Grove, and Burroughs, "An Experimental Examination of Mood Effects on Retrieval and Evaluation of Advertisement and Brand Information."

42 Alice M. Isen, Paula M. Niedenthal, and Nancy Cantor, "An Influence of Positive Affect on Social Categorization," *Motivation and Emotion* 16, no. 1 (1992), pp. 65–78; Alice M. Isen, "Some Ways in Which Affect Influences Cognitive Processes: Implications for Advertising and Consumer Behavior," in Alice M. Tybout and P. Cafferata (Eds.), *Advertising and Consumer Psychology* (Lexington, MA: Lexington Books, 1989), pp. 91–117; Barbara E. Kahn and Alice M. Isen, "The Influence of Positive Affect on Variety Seeking Among Safe, Enjoyable Products," *Journal of Consumer Research* 20, no. 2 (September 1993), pp. 257–270.

43 Isen, "Some Ways in Which Affect Influences Cognitive Processes: Implications for Advertising and Consumer Behavior," pp. 91–118.

44 Alice M. Isen, Thomas Shalker, Margaret Clark, and Lynn Karp, "Affect, Accessibility of Material in Memory and Behavior: A Cognitive Loop?" *Journal of Personality and Social Psychology* (January 1978), pp. 1–12; see also Edmund T. Rolls, "A Theory of Emotion and Its Application to Understanding the Neural Basis of Emotion," *Cognition & Emotion* 4, no. 3 (1990), pp. 182–184; Meryl Gardner, "Effects of Mood States on Consumer Information Processing," *Research in Consumer Behavior* 2 (1987), pp. 113–135; T. J. Olney, M. B. Holbrook, and R. Batra, "Consumer Responses to Advertising," *Journal of Consumer Research* (March 1991), pp. 440–453; S. P. Brown and D. M. Stayman, "Antecedents and Consequences of Attitude toward the Ad," *Journal of Consumer Research* (June 1992), pp. 34–51: G. Biehal, D. Stephens, and E. Curlo, "Attitude toward the Ad and Brand Choice," *Journal of Advertising* (September 1992), pp. 19–36; P. A. Stout and R. T. Rust, "Emotional Feelings and Evaluative Dimensions of Advertising," *Journal of Advertising* (March 1993), pp. 61–71; P. M. Homer, "The Mediating Role of Attitude toward the Ad," *Journal of Marketing Research* (February 1990), pp. 78–88; B. Mittal, "The Relative Roles of Brand Beliefs and Attitude," *Journal of Marketing Research* (May 1990), pp. 209–219.

45 Alice M. Isen and Barbara Means, "The Influence of Positive Affect on Decision-Making Stategy," *Social Cognition* 2, no. 1 (1983), pp. 18–31; Carlos A. Estrada, Alice M. Isen, and Mark J. Young, "Positive Affect Improves Creative Problem Solving and Influences Reported Source of Practice Satisfaction in Physicians," *Motivation and Emotion* 18, no. 4 (1994), pp. 285–299.

46 Weiner, *Theories of Motivation;* Agres and Bernstein, "Cognitive and Emotional Elements of Persuasion"; Jackson and Shea, "Motivation Training in Perspective"; McClelland, *Studies in Motivation*; McClelland, "Business Drive and National Achievement"; "Achievement Motivation Can Be Devel-

oped"; Korman, *The Psychology of Motivation*; McClelland, Atkinson, Clark, and Lowell, *The Achievement Motive*; McClelland, *Personality*.

47 C. Campbell, *The Romantic Ethic and the Spirit of Modern Consumerism* (Oxford: Blackwell, 1987).

48 Julie Edell and Marian Burke, "The Power of Feelings in Understanding Advertising Effects," *Journal of Consumer Research* 14 (December 1987), pp. 421–433; Robert A. Westbrook, "Product/Consumption–Based Affective Responses and Postpurchase Processes," *Journal of Marketing Research* 24 (August 1987), pp. 258–270.

49 Chris Allen, Karen Machleit, and Susan Marine, "On Assessing the Emotionality of Advertising via Izard's Differential Emotions Scale," in Michael Houston (Ed.), *Advances in Consumer Research* 15 (Provo, UT: Association for Consumer Research, 1988); Haim Mano, "Emotional States and Decision Making," in Marvin Goldberg et al. (Eds.), *Advances in Consumer Research* 17 (Provo, UT: Association for Consumer Research, 1990), pp. 577–584.

50 "Connecting Consumer and Product," *New York Times* (January 18, 1990), p. D19.

51 M. Friestad and E. Thorson, "Emotion-Eliciting Advertising," in R. Lutz (Ed.), *Advances in Consumer Research* 13 (Provo, UT: Association for Consumer Research, 1986), pp. 111–116.

52 John D. Morris, "Observation: SAM: The SelfAssessment Manikin," *Journal of Advertising Research* (November–December, 1995).

53 G. Levin, "Emotion Guides BBDO's Ad Tests," *Advertising Age* (January 29, 1990), p. 12.

CHAPTER 7

PERSONALITY, LIFESTYLE, AND SELF-CONCEPT

LEARNING OBJECTIVES

- To explore the various theoretical views of the meaning, nature, and development of personality.
- To grasp the basic tenets and marketing applications of a number of popular personality theories.
- To be able to compare and contrast selected basic personality theories.
- To recognize the role of lifestyle and psychographics in developing consumer typologies.
- To become familiar with the tools of AIO inventories as well as the VALS system for purposes of market segmentation.
- To analyze the importance of the self-concept and examine the way it influences consumer purchasing patterns.

KEY TERMS

personality	trait theory	VALS
id	traits	self-concept
superego	personality tests	extended self
ego	psychographics	possible self
neo-Freudian theory	AIO inventories	self-product congruence
compliance-aggressive-ness-detachment (CAD) scale		

From the dawn of history, physical beauty has been a valued goal. A variety of beauty practices have prevailed in various cultures over the ages, such as binding the feet; puncturing the ears, nose, and belly button; enlarging the lips; and tattooing the skin. Tombs in Egypt, for example, have revealed that women in the time of the Pharaohs used lip gloss, rouge, powder, eye shadow, nail polish, perfumes, and creams to enhance their natural beauty. Various cultures, as well as different periods of history, tend to subscribe to a desirable look or *ideal* of beauty. Present-day views regarding what is beautiful are very different from those of the past. In the United States, for example, the ideal figure of women has changed radically over the years. In contrast to the frail, underfed, and delicate look of women that prevailed in the nineteenth century, or the straight-laced look with corsets popular in the early twentieth century, today's beauty ideal is the healthy, vigorous, and relatively athletic look. By contrast, in the African country of Mauritania, being heavy is considered attractive. The heavier the woman is, the more desirable she is perceived by eligible men. Chances for marriage dramatically increase with gains in a woman's weight and size.

An individual's body image is an inseparable component of his or her concept of self. Body image is the subjective evaluation of one's physical appearance. In judging how attractive their physical self is, individuals compare how closely their look corresponds to the image that society values. Social comparison is a known human tendency. Consumers see idealized images in person, in advertising messages, in movies, and on television. Consciously or unconsciously, they compare themselves with these prototypes. The comparison often leads to dissatisfaction to the extent that self-perceptions do not match up with idealized images. Dissatisfaction has led, at least in our society, to the proliferation of products and services ranging from diet foods to exercise equipment, from cosmetics to plastic surgery, and from tanning salons to hairstylists. Many people willingly go to great lengths to change aspects of their physical selves. Recognizing this tendency, marketers frequently create insecurities in the minds of consumers regarding their appearance by emphasizing disparities between the real and the ideal self. Consequently, consumers become vulnerable targets for purchasing the recommended product or service offerings.

Because advertising generates social comparisons, and advertisers tend to portray *better-off* others as happy, beautiful, or wealthy people, it has been censured by critics as a major cause of consumer dissatisfaction. Advertisers argue that temporary dissatisfaction is beneficial and constructive. It motivates consumers and stimulates them to buy products or use services that improve their appearance and eventually enhance their self-image and satisfaction with themselves.[1]

Do you agree with the assertion that advertisers' depictions of thin and attractive models in ads are ineffective and undesirable today because the practice causes unhappiness in many less attractive women due to self-comparisons? Learn about models available for ads by visiting New Faces Models and Talent at the firm's website www.newfaces.com/ and Models.com at www.models.com. In your opinion, would consumers respond more positively to ads that depict more "typical" and not-so-glamorous models? Would you expect men and women to respond similarly to such ads? Explain.

Although it seems natural today to think about consumers in terms of having self-concepts that they attempt to protect and enhance through the purchase of products and services, this concept is a relatively recent view of people. The significance of this view lies in the observation that consumers' feelings about themselves shape their consumption practices. Many products from clothes to cosmetics are bought because a person is attempting to manifest a positive attribute or hide a negative aspect of self.

Personality has been investigated from many different points of view. Freudian theory, for example, emphasizes a conflict system between competing forces within an individual's psyche. The trait approach, on the other hand, hypothesizes that sets of inner personal attributes distinguish

© Monkey Business Images/Shutterstock.com

In our social interaction with others, we tend to automatically assign them certain personality traits that we presume they possess.

one individual from another. Many other explanations of personality also prevail.

This chapter examines personality from a number of theoretical vantage points while underscoring their marketing implications. We also examine consumer lifestyles as a basis for segmenting markets, targeting prospects, and positioning products. We conclude by addressing the self-concept and its impact on consumer buying tendencies.

WHAT IS PERSONALITY?

At one time or another, nearly everyone has gone on a blind date. Usually the first question posed to the matchmaker relates to what the prospective escort is like. "He [or she] has a great personality" is a frequent reply. After the date, however, one party may conclude that the companion had "no personality at all."

In casual conversations, the word *personality* often refers to whatever one individual observes in another person. In this sense, personality is the striking overall impression that a person leaves with others.[2]

The term *personality* is derived from *persona*, a Latin term for the masks worn by actors on stage in ancient Greek and Roman theaters. In the absence of a standard definition, the following represents the authors' view of personality's structure and functioning:

> *Personality* is the sum total of an individual's inner psychological attributes. It makes individuals what they are, distinguishes them from every other person, demonstrates their mode of adjustment to life's circumstances, and produces their unique, stable pattern of responding to environmental stimuli.

personality
the sum total of an individual's inner psychological attributes

This definition highlights a number of properties that characterize personality. First, it is unique. Personality is one among many internal properties of individuals that, together with environmental factors, shape human behavior. Individuals appear to possess distinctive qualities or unique clusters of attributes that distinguish them from others. Personality is unique to each individual, and no two people are identical. Second, personality is consistent. The preceding definition acknowledges that considerable stability, consistency, and predictability permeate a person's personality. The attributes that distinguish an individual are reasonably consistent across diverse sets of circumstances. Personality is not, however, fixed or rigid. Third, personality is not static. It evolves as part of a gradual maturing process and may be further altered by abrupt or pivotal life events such as a career change, the conception or birth of a child, divorce, a serious accident, or the passing of a loved one.

DIVERSITY OF PERSONALITY THEORIES

Although personality theories offer fascinating insights into human nature, little agreement exists about how the topic of personality should be approached. The number of personality theories is as impressive as the variation among them. Acknowledging that psychologists offer many and diverse opinions concerning personality formation, Hall and Lindzey submit that "no substantive definition of personality can be applied with any generality" and that "personality is defined by the particular empirical concepts which are a part of the theory of personality employed by the observer."[3]

One view of personality assumes that humans possess traits that determine their personality. In other words, if an individual behaves in a sociable, adaptable, achievement-oriented, or independent manner, it is so because that person possesses the corresponding traits. A second view postulates that an individual's personality is the result of events experienced in the past, especially during childhood. Freud, for example, believed that parent–child relationships during the first five years of life largely determine adult personality. A third view proposes that personality reflects striving on the part of an individual to acquire rewards and avoid punishments in the here and now. Safe driving, for example, has its rewards. Drivers who prudently obey traffic regulations and hope to arrive at their destination safely without getting a traffic violation are viewed as possessing cautious personalities. A fourth view speculates that personality unfolds in the quest to achieve goals and someday realize one's inherent potential. Conscientious students, for example, may have ambitious career plans. In a fifth approach, some researchers attempt to link personality to birth order (firstborn child, middle child, last-born child, only child).[4] According to this view, individual personality differences arise from the family setting, as siblings compete for parental attention.[5]

In recent years, personality research has taken a new direction. Many psychologists have come to reject the notion that there are cross-situational consistencies in behavior. In other words, they no longer propose that there exist broad patterns of behavior that permeate *all* the circumstances we encounter. Rather, many researchers today propose that behavior is situational, determined by the circumstances that surround a specific event. Studies investigate specific issues (such as problem solving, information processing, impulse buying, and bargain hunting) in specific situations and study how various personalities interact with the unique set of circumstances in order to produce behavior. In this view, behavior is governed not by all-determining personality traits but rather by personality *styles* that tend to be exhibited in particular situations. For example, individuals are not equally susceptible to persuasion on *all* topics or from *all* information sources. Similarly, individuals who shop compulsively in one product category (such as buying antique furniture) or shopping environment (such as buying at flea markets) may or may not do so in other product categories or buying environments.

Most psychologists do agree that personality is largely the social outgrowth of an individual's experiences with other people, events, and objects. These influences shape what and how people think, feel, act, communicate, desire, and dream. Marketers who understand the characteristics that consumers share in common and those that differentiate them may discover valuable insights for market segmentation, targeting, positioning, and design of promotional appeals. To investigate the relationship between per-

Many individuals enjoy frequenting flea markets, where a large variety of products and antiques can be found at bargain prices.

© Matej Kastelic/Shutterstock.com

sonality and purchasing behavior, this chapter briefly explores Freudian, neo-Freudian, and trait personality theories.

FREUDIAN THEORY OF PERSONALITY

From the dawn of history, humans have attempted to explain why behavior varies from one individual to another. Some researchers advocated that heredity underlies variations in human behavior, whereas others proposed physical features such as the size of a person's skull or skin color as the basis for these differences. Today, however, many believe that within the individual exists a segment of the mind, known as the *unconscious*, which has the power to affect feelings and behaviors. This approach has its roots in the theories of Sigmund Freud.[6]

Freudian psychoanalytic personality theory influenced our awareness of self and the understanding of our human makeup. It has been said that Freud invented psychoanalysis and propagated notions about the human mind. His wide-ranging collection of metaphors concerning the mental life of human beings has largely become common knowledge.[7] According to Freud, personality is a result of a dynamic struggle between inner psychological drives such as sex and aggression and social pressures such as moral and ethical codes. In addition, Freud believed that individuals are aware of only a limited number of the forces that truly drive their behavior.[8]

According to Freud, personality is a result of an interaction among the three components of personality: the id, the superego, and the ego. The id is an unconscious reservoir of human instincts that seeks pleasure and demands immediate satisfaction, and is not regulated by right or wrong. The superego is a largely unconscious repository of social, moral, and ethical codes that restricts how far a person can go to acquire goals and steers instinctive drives into acceptable avenues. The ego is the conscious control center that mediates the id's uninhibited impulses and the superego's constraints. Each person must achieve balance as the id's desires encounter the ego's logic and the superego's prohibitions. The ego pursues the goals of the id in a socially responsible manner. In the Freudian model, sexually related biological motivation and continual conflict between the id, superego, and ego permeate human personality. The way children manage conflict determines their adult personality, and unresolved childhood conflicts continue to affect adult behavior.[9]

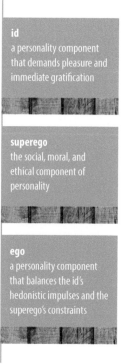

id
a personality component that demands pleasure and immediate gratification

superego
the social, moral, and ethical component of personality

ego
a personality component that balances the id's hedonistic impulses and the superego's constraints

Marketing Applications of Freudian Theory

Promotional appeals frequently address the id, ego, and superego components of personality. Advertisements frequently emphasize the pleasure and self-indulgent aspects of products. Whether the product depicted is a perfume or satin sheets, ads often attempt to address the pleasure principle of the id. Other ads employ sexual themes, sensuous illustrations or stories, and suggestive double meanings to promote various products and services. In still other applications of the id, ads often depict aggressive scenes or violent acts to promote sporting events, auto races, movies, and TV shows. Campaigns employing dream-sequence, fantasy, and wish-fulfillment themes are also sympathetic with the id's passionate cravings.

Sales promotion methods that address the ego or reality principle are also prevalent. Credit policies are often designed to appeal to the ego by glossing over the reality of spending money. Firms in many cases extend payment plans, buying incentives, or free goods or services to facilitate consumer purchases by temporarily underwriting some of the cost. Similarly, advertising occasionally appeals to an overburdened ego by offering consumers a way to escape from their conflicts. Advertising appeals, in such cases, stress the desirability of fleeing from life's troubles, pressures, and worries. Promotion for vacation resorts, pleasure cruises, and gambling casinos frequently employs escape, leisure, freedom, and fantasy appeals, but shows them reasonably priced to pacify the ego.

Promotional appeals also address the superego with references to social amenities, moral and ethical protocol, and tradition. Promotions frequently advance both legitimate and spurious arguments designed to help consumers surmount guilt feelings and rationalize or justify their purchases. De Beers uses the slogan "A diamond is forever," and Tesla Motors proudly claims that it is the most environmentally conscious auto company, as evidenced by its introduction of the first electric car in the United States. The photo in Figure 7.1 depicts the process of charging an electric car. The purchase of such a vehicle is driven by the desire to protect the environment, reflecting the influence of the superego.

neo-Freudian theory
a view that social variables rather than biological instincts and sexual drives underlie personality formation

NEO-FREUDIAN PERSONALITY THEORY

Four disciples of Freud developed their own psychoanalytic personality theories. Rather than focus on the significance and consequences of sexual conflicts, the ideas of neo-Freudians Adler, Horney, Fromm, and Sullivan

© Tom Wang/Shutterstock.com

FIGURE 7.1

Environmentally-conscious individuals who purchase an electric car are responding to the influence of the superego.

suggest that social variables and not biological drives underlie personality formation—hence the development of neo-Freudian theory.

Adler proposed that personality is the set of behaviors an individual employs in pursuit of superiority and perfection.[10] Humans are social beings motivated by urges to compensate for or overcome inferiority complexes. Feelings of inferiority often develop during childhood as a result of perceived physical, social, or psychological disabilities. These impediments may be real or imagined. By age four or five, and as a result of parent–child interactions, individuals choose and create their own unique style of life. This lifestyle is the basic character that defines and shapes their behavior and attitudes and that determines those aspects of the environment to which they will attend. According to Adler, individuals are conscious of the goals they strive to attain and the behavior they engage in to achieve their personal goals.

ETHICAL DILEMMA

Cosmetic Psychopharmacology and Designer Personalities

Depression strikes an estimated 20 million adult Americans each year. Studies reveal that regardless of race, depression seems to affect about twice as many women as men. This can be caused by a number of factors, such as postpartum depression, which can strike women who otherwise would have not suffered a depressive disorder.[11]

Many depressed individuals seek ways to reduce and manage stress. Although no drug can encapsulate happiness and provide solutions for all human problems, a number of by-prescription-only medications, such as Cymbalta, Zoloft, Lexapro, Paxil, Luvox, Remeron, and Effexor, as well as others, allow some persons to be the fully functioning individuals they could be if they were not troubled by depression, obsessive–compulsive disorders, or bulimia nervosa (an eating disorder).[12] In specific cases, some of these medications have also been used to treat phobias, mood swings, and premenstrual syndrome (PMS). These drugs relieve the symptoms of depression by increasing the availability of certain brain chemicals called neurotransmitters. It is believed that these brain chemicals can help improve patients' emotional state.[13]

Although the benefits of antidepressants are plausible, the media as well as pharmaceutical companies have heralded an era in which it would appear that altering an individual's personality might be as easy as changing one's hair color. Sensational journalism and advertising have left many people with the false impression that so-called *personality pills* or *happy drugs* can provide a quick pick-me-up and create

designer personalities. To some extent, drug companies themselves may have fostered this perception. For example, depressed Americans have been targeted with a number of direct-to-consumer (DTC) campaigns, the purpose of which is to offer help against depression. Commercials for Cymbalta tend to heighten awareness of depression by indicating a checklist of symptoms the company views as indicative of this condition. One such commercial enumerates where depression hurts, whom depression hurts, and how depression hurts. Another suggests physical or mental conditions that consumers should view as synonymous with depression. The commercial then directs consumers to ask their physicians about Cymbalta's role in overcoming these depressed feelings.[14] This elevated awareness has caused many to believe they suffer from depression.

Pharmaceutical companies have even gone a step further in promoting the use of antidepressants. There are now antidepressive medications for dogs and cats. Clomipramine, an antidepression medication, has already gained FDA approval for both human and canine use. It is currently being used for canines suffering from "separation anxiety" when a dog finds the absence of its owner too much to bear.[15]

To learn more about depression, visit www.upliftprogram. com/depression_stats.html. Some people believe that promotional campaigns to inform consumers about depression symptoms are merely self-fulfilling prophecies. By detailing the symptoms, many individuals come to identify with them and begin to feel they must be going through a state of depression. This self-assessment enhances the demand for and sales of antidepressant drugs. Do you agree or disagree? Why?

Horney suggested that personality develops as individuals attempt to deal with anxiety.[16] Humans are born helpless into a potentially hostile world; early anxieties stem from parent–child relationships. Horney hypothesized that people develop one of three behavior patterns to deal with their childhood insecurities and later anxieties. The *compliant personality* moves toward people when troubled. Compliant individuals seek affection, appreciation, acceptance, and approval from others. The *aggressive personality* moves against people when troubled. Aggressive individuals desire to stand out and excel; they seek admiration, power, and exploitation of others. The *detached personality* moves away from others when troubled. Detached individuals seek self-sufficiency, independence, and unassailability.

Fromm asserted that humans feel lonely and isolated because they have become separated from nature and other people.[17] Fromm emphasized humans' need for love, fellowship, and security in order to overcome feelings of loneliness, alienation, and insignificance.

Sullivan considered personality "a hypothetical entity that cannot be separated from interpersonal relations" and "the relatively enduring pattern of recurrent interpersonal situations which characterize a human life."[18] According to Sullivan, humans continually attempt to establish rewarding interpersonal relationships. Social associations, however, may threaten people's security and produce anxiety. Progression through a series of developmental stages leads individuals toward a mature repertory of interpersonal relations by adulthood (the early twenties).

Marketing Applications of Neo-Freudian Theory

Neo-Freudian personality theory directs marketers' attention to the social character of consumption. Many promotional campaigns emphasize social relationships and human interaction. The ad from EGG.LAND'S BEST in Figure 7.2 promotes the brand of eggs by depicting concern and care for members of one's family by wanting the very best for them. Similarly, purchase and use of personal-care products such as soaps, antiperspirants, and mouthwashes reflect consumers' concern for positive interpersonal relationships and anxieties over potentially offending others.

Cohen developed a compliance-aggressiveness-detachment (CAD) scale paradigm.[19] It was designed to classify subjects as high or low on Horney's hypothesized behavioral tendencies. The inventory asks respondents to finish thirty-five incomplete statements about various situations. On a six-point scale ranging from "extremely undesirable" to "extremely

compliance-aggressiveness-detachment (CAD) scale
a paradigm that classifies people based on how compliant, aggressive, and detached they are

desirable," subjects indicate their feelings about each situation. Specific statements measure compliance; others measure aggressiveness or detachment. Sample CAD statements appear in Exhibit 7.1.

	Extremely Undesirable	Extremely Desirable
Being free of emotional ties with others is:		
Giving comfort to those in need of friends is:		
To refuse to give in to others in an argument is:		

"FOR MY FAMILY, ONLY THE BEST IN NUTRITION."

Compared to ordinary eggs:
- 25% less saturated fat
- 10 times more vitamin E
- 3 times more vitamin B₁₂
- 2 times more vitamin D
- Double the Omega 3
- 38% more lutein
- 175 mg cholesterol (58% DV)
- Good source of vitamin B₂
- 125 mg choline

Eggland's Best eggs are different. As soon as you open a carton of EBs, you see that red EB stamp on every egg—the sign that you're getting the very best in freshness and quality.

Besides giving your family superior nutrition, EBs also give them more of the farm-fresh taste they love. Better taste and better nutrition also add up to better value—which is something all families are looking for these days.

So, why give your family ordinary when you can give them the best? Eggland's Best.

Also available in cage-free and organic varieties

EGG-LAND'S BEST

Better taste. Better nutrition. Better eggs.™

www.EgglandsBest.com
facebook.com/EgglandsBestEggs @EgglandsBest

Courtesy of Eggland's Best LLC.

Using a sample of undergraduate male university students, Cohen administered the CAD inventory and asked brand preferences in fifteen product categories where Horney's social traits seem to operate. Finding that personality differences had a generally small—but significant—effect on purchase patterns in seven of the fifteen product categories, Cohen suggested the link between personality and consumer behavior merits further investigation. Social-approval appeals, social-conquest themes, and individualistic or nonsocial-context promotional approaches could prove useful in targeting compliant, aggressive, and detached personality types, respectively. Since Cohen's study, CAD scales have been further tested and applied by marketers in a variety of studies covering topics such as purchase involvement, product evaluation, and social influences on buying.[20]

Although Freudian and neo-Freudian theories were useful to gain insight about the motivations that direct consumers' behavior, many researchers were uncomfortable with them largely because they lacked a quantitative dimension. Their usefulness depended on the researcher's interpretative skill. For this reason, interest grew in using standardized personality tests that are reliable and valid psychological measurements designed to identify and quantify personality traits. The relationship of these traits to consumer preferences and purchases can then be further examined. In the following section, let us examine trait theory and identify the role personality traits play in shaping consumption behavior.

TRAIT THEORY

The trait approach to personality study, known as trait theory, classifies people according to their dominant characteristics or identifiable traits, which are manifested in the form of consistent responses toward environmental stimuli. Traits are thus characteristics that distinguish individuals from one another and that translate into relatively permanent and consistent response patterns. The trait approach to personality attempts to identify, through factor analysis and other statistical techniques, the predominant characteristics of human personality. Through standard psychological inventories, personalities are described and classified in terms of such traits as dominance, sociability, self-acceptance, responsibility, and so forth.

From a marketing perspective, the value of trait theory stems from the fact that because traits are considered to be attributes of the person and not of

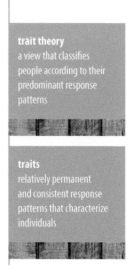

trait theory
a view that classifies people according to their predominant response patterns

traits
relatively permanent and consistent response patterns that characterize individuals

the situation, similar environmental stimuli or situations generally elicit a consistent response pattern from a particular individual. For this reason and because of the ease with which the trait approach can be applied, trait theory has been extensively utilized in marketing. A number of traits have been used as correlates in consumer behavior studies. *Innovativeness*, for example, is the extent to which an individual enjoys trying new things.[21] *Materialism*, a second trait, refers to the degree of importance that a person attaches to procuring and owning products.[22] *Self-consciousness*, a third trait, entails the extent to which a person deliberately monitors and controls the image of the self that he or she projects to others. *Need for cognition* is the degree to which someone is inclined to think about things.[23] Additional traits that have been frequently used in consumer behavior studies include *tolerance for ambiguity, dogmatism, category width, social character, compulsiveness, variety seeking, tendency to conform*, and *the need for emotion*. These traits are discussed in Exhibit 7.2.

One well-known instrument for measuring an individual's personality traits or psychological type is the Myers-Briggs Type Indicator.[24] The four scales that the instrument measures are (1) extroversion/introversion, (2) sensate/intuitive, (3) thinking/feeling, and (4) judging/perceiving. The various combinations of these preferences result in sixteen personality types that are denoted by four letters, such as INTJ (which stand for introversion, intuition, with thinking and judging), to represent a person's tendencies on the four traits. This instrument has been widely used for purposes of recruitment, career counseling, occupational choices, market segmentation, and dating services.

Recent research has found a strong relationship between personality traits and the biology of the brain.[28] For example, if two people were to experience a similar crisis (such as divorce, loss of a job, or death of a family member), one individual may appear to fall apart while the other glides through it, seemingly in control. Why might they react so dissimilarly? The biology of the brain appears to play an essential role, contributing to an understanding of the individual differences in personality traits. Compelling evidence suggests that 50 to 70 percent of individual variation in personality trait scores is related to genetic influence, but the remaining 30 to 50 percent can be attributed to environmental influences.[29]

Tolerance for ambiguity is a personality trait that refers to how individuals tend to react in situations that are novel, complex, or insoluble. Those with high tolerance for ambiguity deal with inconsistency in a constructive way. Those with low tolerance for ambiguity view it as undesirable or threatening.

Dogmatism is a personality trait that measures how rigid or not rigid a person is toward unfamiliar objects, individuals, or situations. Highly dogmatic individuals are less likely to be accepting of other views that are contradictory to the ones they hold.

Category width is a trait that measures to what degree an individual is likely to tolerate risk. It addresses the extent to which an individual is willing to accept poor or negative consequences or outcomes of decisions one makes.

Social character is a trait that identifies where an individual belongs on the continuum that ranges from being inner directed to being other directed. Inner-directed consumers tend to be more independent in their thoughts and behavior. Other-directed individuals, on the other hand, tend to look to others for direction as to what course of action is appropriate.

Compulsiveness is a trait that amounts to a form of addiction to a particular behavior. Compulsiveness extends beyond mere fixations of stamp, coin, and record collectors to include consumers with uncontrollable urges to shop, gamble, smoke, drink, abuse drugs, or indulge in sex.[25]

Variety seeking is a trait that distinguishes between people in terms of the extent to which they seek challenge, excitement, and variety in their lives.[26] Low sensation seekers prefer a quiet, calm, undisturbed existence. High sensation seekers, on the other hand, become bored if their lifestyle is void of challenge, excitement, and action.

Tendency to conform is a trait that distinguishes people based on their proclivity to conform to social pressures when making purchases. Individuals with a low tendency to conform go ahead with their intended purchases whether they shop alone or with a group. Those who exhibit a high tendency to conform tend to make many more changes in purchase plans when shopping with a group than when shopping alone.[27]

Need for emotion is a trait that distinguishes between people in terms of their degree of emotionality. Highly emotional individuals react more sensitively to objects and situations, whereas those who rank low on this trait react in an indifferent manner more frequently and to a wider range of events.

Innovativeness is a trait that reveals the extent to which individuals sense excitement and stimulation upon experiencing new opportunities, objects, or situations. They savor the new, the offbeat, and the risky. An emphasis on this trait of innovation could be demonstrated by using the photo in Figure 7.3 to highlight a company's efforts to bring tomorrow's technology and innovation into today's classrooms.

FIGURE 7.3

The sense of excitement reflected on the faces of students and teacher in some ads reveals the power of innovative technology to stimulate learning in the classroom.

© Monkey Business Images/Shutterstock.com

Recently, a study addressed the issue of whether personality traits are genetically determined. The study provided the first confirmed association between a specific gene and a normal personality trait called *novelty seeking*.[30] Whereas previous studies have shown more generally that genes affect personality, as do an individual's life experiences, this discovery provided the first missing link between genes and personality by implicating a particular communication system within the brain. Such findings represent a possible step toward unraveling the genetics of personality. Perhaps with future advances in gene detection technology, it may become possible and useful for marketers of services such as insurance, investments, and travel to gauge the novelty-seeking tendencies of their clients in order to offer them programs specifically designed for their personality types.[31]

Measuring Traits

Trait theory is built on a number of assumptions:

- Traits are identifiable, and a limited number of traits are common to most individuals.
- Traits are relatively stable and, regardless of specific environmental circumstances, exert fairly pervasive effects on behavior.
- Traits vary in intensity among different people, and the degree to which individuals possess various traits is measurable via questionnaires or other behavioral indicators.

- People who possess similar traits and trait intensities have similar goals and tend to behave alike.

Advocates of trait theory speculate that if researchers can identify the particular combination of traits that an individual possesses and uncover the consistencies in his or her behavior, then it should be possible to make predictions concerning this person's behavior. Personality trait assessment relies on personality tests, questionnaires designed to measure one or more personality traits. To develop personality tests, researchers often start with subjects' replies to a number of questions that attempt to reveal their response tendencies (such as rigidity or openness). Respondents may be requested to agree or disagree with statements such as "There is usually only one best way to solve a problem" or "Most people don't know what's good for them." Likewise, respondents may be asked to respond to questions designed to express their likes or dislikes for particular situations or types of people.

personality tests
questionnaires designed to measure personality traits

Results of these tests produce trait profiles of participating individuals that are then correlated with data on their product purchases. The main purpose of this procedure is to identify behavioral patterns that can be generalized to an entire market segment. For example, researchers may seek answers to such questions as, "What is the trait profile of consumers who purchase convertible automobiles?" or "What traits identify those who purchase environmentally friendly products?"[32] As can be seen, the value of trait theory to marketing stems from the possibility of treating consumers who display similar personality traits as market segments and then, developing appropriate appeals for such groups of consumers based on their distinguishing traits.

In order to apply standardized personality tests in marketing investigations, marketers and researchers must first speculate which specific traits are likely to influence brand preference before choosing a particular personality test.[33] Merely borrowing standard personality inventories designed for clinical purposes and attempting to discover useful relationships between personality and shopping behaviors or brand preferences frequently produces poor results.[34] Clinical multitrait personality inventories were not designed to investigate consumer behavior.[35] Tailor-made personality inventories or modified personality tests that focus on specific constellations of traits that researchers suspect to be related to product use, are more likely to be useful for purposes of consumer research than are standardized clinical tests.[36]

CONSUMER BEHAVIOR IN PRACTICE

A Cheerful and Good-Natured Stove

Is your refrigerator sensitive, gentle, and faithful? Is your wine loving and friendly? Is your microwave oven a male or female? Is your blender a teenager or a senior citizen? If these questions seem strange, they are considered very useful by many companies today that attempt to discover what human personality traits consumers assign to brands. In the minds of many consumers, products and brands take on personalities of their own. This *brand personality* is a valuable tool for both marketers and consumers alike. Marketers have long realized that consumers buy products and brands with personalities that match their own. Product personalities give consumers confidence in their purchase decisions, facilitate the choice process when selecting among competing brands, and enhance their loyalty to the chosen brand.

In a recent study by Whirlpool Corporation, researchers attempted to identify the personality traits that consumers assign to Whirlpool's brands. In one phase of the study, Whirlpool researchers asked respondents first to select adjectives from a list to describe familiar Whirlpool brands. Listed adjectives included such human personality traits as dependable, strong, independent, hardworking, trustworthy, and faithful. Second, respondents were instructed to indicate whether the brand is masculine or feminine.

The results were interesting. Whirlpool brands were viewed as gentle, sensitive, quiet, good natured, flexible, modern, cheerful, and creative. Personified, Whirlpool brand was perceived as a modern, family-oriented woman who lives the best of suburban life and is considered a good friend and neighbor.

KitchenAid was perceived as a modern professional woman who is competent, aggressive, and smart and who works hard to acquire the better things in life. She is sophisticated, glamorous, wealthy, elegant, fashionable, and innovative.

What is the value of all this? Companies say that this knowledge helps them to concisely establish the brand personality in all communications directed toward the market. Product personality also facilitates the creation of differences between brands for the purpose of attaining greater brand loyalty and gaining an advantage over the competition.[37]

The goal behind building a brand personality is to create a match between the personalities of customers and those of the brand. Visit the website of General Motors Corporation at www.gm.com. Consider several models of GM automobiles such as Chevrolet, Buick, Cadillac and Saturn. What type of brand personality does the company aspire to build for each model? What marketing strategies and tactics are employed in building unique personalities for each model?

Marketing Applications of Trait Theory

Trait theory is one of the most often used methods for researching the link between personality and consumer behavior. As mentioned earlier, studies frequently search for correlations between a set of specific personality traits and consumer behaviors such as product purchases, brand choice, retail store selection, online shopping, media selection, and a variety of other factors. For example, one recent study found a measurable link between the personality traits of extroversion and neuroticism and postpurchase processes such as consumer satisfaction/dissatisfaction, loyalty, complaining, and word of mouth.[38]

Another study correlated the variety-seeking trait to consumption behavior and found interdependence between this trait and product choice, store choice, and susceptibility to advertising appeals.[39] The study reported that high sensation seekers, as a result of being intrigued with the prospect of *newness*, were more likely than low sensation seekers to be consumer innovators. As to store choice, the study reported that high sensation seekers tended to prefer shopping at downtown stores because they enjoy the noise and bustle of downtown. Low sensation seekers, on the other hand, were found to be typically mall and online shoppers who try to avoid the exciting but stressful downtown atmosphere. Reaction to advertising and susceptibility to different advertising appeals also varied between high and low sensation seekers. High sensation seekers were more likely to react favorably to informative advertising that appealed to their curiosity and tended to evaluate the merits of the advertised product on the basis of their own experiences. Low sensation seekers, on the other hand, were less apt to evaluate product merits on their own, except within the confines of reference group settings and the presence of a trusted celebrity or expert.

It has also been observed that consumers with opposite traits may still display the same purchase behavior. Two consumers on opposite ends of a personality-trait continuum, such as aggressiveness, may purchase the same sports car. The first may do so to express and match an outgoing self-image. The second may do so to offset or overcome feelings of insecurity.

Of course, marketers who plan to use personality traits as a basis for market segmentation have to make sure that groups of consumers possessing common personality traits are sufficiently large to offer genuine potential. They must further be demographically homogeneous or geographically clustered so that they can be economically reached through the mass media. Those traits that form the basis for segmentation should then serve as a guide in developing the appropriate marketing mix.[40]

Early researchers were able to devise instruments that combined the quantitative aspect of personality inventories with the qualitative information offered by psychoanalytic procedures. The result was an approach that was called psychographics—the science of measuring and categorizing consumer lifestyles. Psychographics offers insight into what goes on in the consumer's mind and seeks to identify individual consumption-related activities, interests, and opinions. The following section is devoted to a discussion of psychographics.

PSYCHOGRAPHICS

psychographics
a segmentation approach that classifies consumers based on their lifestyle

Psychographics, which investigates consumer lifestyles, differs from trait theory in that it explores the possibility of developing meaningful categories out of the infinite range of activities, interests, and opinions that characterize consumers. Psychographics is a research approach rather than a personality theory, whose aim is to assess consumers' lifestyles so that meaningful consumer typologies can be identified.

Marketers have long realized that, in many cases, demographic dimensions alone—such as age, education, income, occupation, sex, and marital status—fail to explain certain consumer behavior tendencies. For example, there is no relationship between demographics and smoking, drinking, preference for sports, going to movies, choosing music, and liking the outdoors. These tendencies reflect lifestyle preferences, which vary dramatically between people.

AIO inventories
questionnaires designed to reveal consumers' activities, interests, and opinions

Psychographics uses statements designed to reveal the activities, interests, and opinions of consumers, commonly referred to as AIO. AIO inventories are constructed specifically for each study to assess the lifestyles of a target group in order to link AIO with a specific consumption behavior or preference, such as purchase and use of a certain product, service, or brand.

AIO inventories typically contain a large number of statements. Respondents are instructed to express their degree of agreement or disagreement with each. *Activity* statements, for example, may include phrases describing what individuals do, what they buy, and how they spend their time. *Interest* statements may cover subjects' preferences, priorities, and concerns. *Opinion* statements may solicit respondents' views and perceptions on a variety of aspects related to their social, cultural, or economic surroundings as well as on the products or services that constitute the subject of the investigation. Exhibit 7.3 shows part of an AIO inventory designed to reveal store patronage patterns and preferences of a group of consumers.

Data obtained from AIO inventories are then analyzed using statistical techniques such as factor analysis, cluster analysis, and cross-tabulation. This analysis reveals meaningful groupings that seem to share a particular consumption tendency or that form a distinguishable profile. For example, data on attitudes of adults toward animal welfare, animal rights, animal experiments, animal testing, animal hunting, animals as pets, and animals as a source of food are usually obtained through AIO inventories. The Roper Center for Public Opinion Research and the National Opinion Research Center at the University of Michigan conduct such surveys and provide comprehensive data on distinguishable groupings within the public and their attitudes on these issues. Marketers then correlate these findings with consumer behavior and tendencies such as consumption of meat, purchase of cosmetics that have been tested on animals, acquiring pets and feeding them, as well as buying gear related to hunting for recreation and sport.

	Definitely Disagree			Definitely Agree		
I like to have a salesperson assist me in making a selection.	1	2	3	4	5	6
I like to stick to well-known brand names.	1	2	3	4	5	6
I shop a lot for specials.	1	2	3	4	5	6
I like to be considered a leader.	1	2	3	4	5	6
I like to feel attractive to the opposite sex.	1	2	3	4	5	6
I buy a lot of goods on impulse.	1	2	3	4	5	6
I like to go shopping with friends.	1	2	3	4	5	6
Good grooming is a sign of self-respect.	1	2	3	4	5	6
When buying clothing, I am more concerned with style than price.	1	2	3	4	5	6
Weekends are my favorite time to shop.	1	2	3	4	5	6
Store brands are just as good as nationally advertised brands.	1	2	3	4	5	6
I pay a lot more attention to prices now than I ever did before.	1	2	3	4	5	6

EXHIBIT 7.3

AIO Questionnaire: Sample Items

AIO inventories vary in the degree of their specificity. Researchers may aim at obtaining highly specific types of information that can be valuable in revealing consumption patterns for specific product categories such as pet food. On the other hand, AIO inventories may be designed to collect broad and general types of information in order to identify meaningful consumer typologies or market segments. Typologies based on lifestyle can be useful in a variety of ways such as defining new-product targets, positioning products through advertising, designing campaign themes or appeals, and determining which media to use to reach various prospect groups.

A landmark effort in this area of segmentation, developed by the firm now known as Strategic Business Insights (SBI), is VALS™. VALS™ examines the intersection of psychology, demographics, and lifestyle. VALS™ asserts that people buy products and services and seek experiences that fulfill their characteristic preferences and give shape, substance, and satisfaction to their lives. An individual's primary motivation determines what in particular about the self or the world is the meaningful core that governs his or her activities. VALS™ identifies the patterns that reinforce and sustain a person's identity as the person expresses it in the marketplace.[41]

THE VALS™ SYSTEM

VALS™ asserts that the majority of consumers are driven by one of three primary motivations: ideals, achievement, and self-expression. Ideals-motivated consumers are guided in their choices by abstract, idealized criteria, rather than by feelings, events, or a desire for the approval and opinion of others. Achievement-motivated consumers look for products and services that demonstrate success to their peers. Self-expression-motivated consumers are guided by a desire for social or physical activity, variety, and risk-taking.

In addition to segmenting by primary motivation, the VALS™ typology also segments by resources. The resources dimension, depicted as a continuum ranging from minimal to abundant, refers to the full range of psychological, physical, demographic, and material means and capacities that are available to consumers.[42] Two groups operate outside the motivations dimension due to very abundant or very constrained resources.

Using a survey and proprietary algorithm, VALS™ identifies eight consumer segments. Each segment has a unique combination of primary motivation and resources that underlie consumer decision making. As a result, each segment is distinct. VALS™ explains why different consumers exhibit different behaviors and why different consumers exhibit the same behavior for different reasons. Exhibit 7.4 is a depiction of the eight VALS™ segments classified on the two dimensions of primary motivation (the horizontal dimension) and resources and innovation (the vertical dimension).

Exhibit 7.5 further clarifies the composition of each of the eight VALS™ segments and reveals particular and distinctive behavioral tendencies, attitudes, lifestyles, and decision-making patterns characteristic of individuals who fall into each segment.

VALS™
a segmentation approach that classifies consumers according to primary motivations and resources/innovation

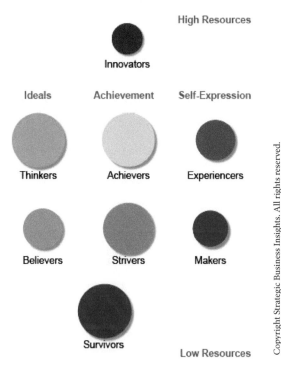

US VALS™ Framework

High Resources

Innovators

Ideals   Achievement   Self-Expression

Thinkers   Achievers   Experiencers

Believers   Strivers   Makers

Survivors

Low Resources

EXHIBIT 7.4

VAL™ Configuration of Consumer Categories.

Marketing Applications of VALS™

VALS™ has helped marketers develop strategy, select target consumer groups that represent the best prospects, develop effective media plans, and construct messaging that will make an emotional connection with the target. Successful VALS™ clients include business categories such as real-estate development, vehicles, packaged goods, financial services, and environmental organizations.

Believing that a single segmentation system cannot be applied cultural-ly, Strategic Business Insights has country-specific frameworks for China, the Dominican Republic, Japan, Nigeria, Venezuela, and the United Kingdom.

VALS™ is a widely used tool for assessing consumer groups to identify best prospects. Experienced firms subscribe to VALS through an annu-al license; however, SBI conducts the majority of VALS work on a pro-prietary-project basis.[47] Recent work includes projects for a global auto manufacturer to increase sales for one of their brands (*Achievers*); media planning for one of the largest U.S. banks (*Experiencers* and *Achievers*);

EXHIBIT 7.5

The Eight VAL™ Segments

Innovators are take-charge people with enough confidence to try, fail, and try again. They are information ready and future focused. Because they have the most abundant resources. Innovators may exhibit all three primary motivations depending on the situation. Receptive to new ideas and technologies Innovators are self-directed consumers and early adopters.

Thinkers are motivated by ideals; they have "ought" and "should" benchmarks for social conduct. Thinkers are the center of the old guard. They are mature, satisfied, comfortable, and reflective. They are not influenced by what's hot. For example, they use technology in functional ways.

Achievers are motivated by achievement. They are anchors of the status quo with a me-first, my-family-first attitude. Achievers follow a traditional life path—marriage, home, family, and career. They believe that money is the source of authority. Achievers are politically conservative, and value consensus, predictability, and stability over risk, intimacy, and self-discovery.

Experiencers are motivated by self-expression. Young, enthusiastic, and optimistic, Experiencers want everything. They see themselves as spontaneous and very sociable. They are the first in, first out of trend adoption because they are easily bored—they seek the next new thing. Experiencers' high energy finds outlets in physical and online activities.

Believers, like Thinkers, are motivated by ideals. They believe in right and wrong to guide them to live a good life. They are not looking to change society. Believers have no tolerance for ambiguity. Conventional, they are loyal consumers who find advertising a legitimate information source. Their lives are organized around home, family, community, and social or religious organizations to which they belong.

Strivers, like Achievers, are motivated by achievement. The center of street culture, Strivers live in the moment. Although money defines success, lack of higher education means that most experience revolves around employment. Strivers are fun loving, but constrained finances and low self-confidence result in more solitary pursuits, such as gaming and reading romance novels, than social pursuits.

Makers, like Experiencers, are motivated by self-expression. They express themselves and experience the world by working on it; they have enough skill and energy to carry out their projects successfully. Makers are practical people who value self-sufficiency. They believe in sharp gender roles and protect what they think they own. They may be perceived as anti-intellectual.

Survivors have the fewest resources of the eight groups. As a result they live narrowly focused lives. They often believe that the world is changing too quickly. Survivors take comfort in routine and the familiar. Cautious and risk averse, survivors are the last to adopt new products, services, and technology.

to increase U.S. sales of an international cosmetics brand (*Thinkers* and *Achievers*); an environmental organization promoting the harmful effects of climate change (*Innovators* and *Achievers*); and a state department of health on a smoking-cessation campaign (*Experiencers* and *Strivers*).

VALS is especially useful for technology and telecommunications companies to identify early adopters and plan for product diffusion in the consumer space. For example, prospective buyers of various technological devices, such as smart phones and smart phone brands, as well as tablets (as shown in Figure 7.5) are not the same. As in the case of new communications technology, target consumers for in-vehicle technology (such as hands-free parking, in-lane warning systems, and automatic braking) as well as interest in driverless vehicles, has different appeals to different consumer groups.

FIGURE 7.5

The allure of technology that gives users the whole Internet for a better Web experience is an effective appeal designed to stimulate action from Innovators.

THE SELF-CONCEPT

Each of us has attitudes, feelings, perceptions, and evaluations of ourselves in terms of physical appearance, attractiveness, mental aptitude, capabilities, roles, and so on. Some of these attributes we like and others we deplore. The overall image that a person holds of him or herself is referred to as that individual's self-concept. The self-concept is the sum total of an individual's beliefs and feelings about him or herself.

self-concept
the overall image that a person holds of him or herself

Although the self-concept is closely associated with personality, the concept of self is a narrower approach to the study of consumer behavior than the broader field of personality. It permits the specific focus on the individual and allows the measurement of conscious determinants that shape a person's behavior. The importance of the self-concept stems from the observation that consumers' feelings about themselves shape their consumption practices. Many products from clothes to cosmetics are bought because a person is attempting to manifest a positive attribute or hide a negative aspect of self.

The self-concept is a complex structure that can be described along many dimensions including both our self-assessment and the way others perceive us. We evaluate ourselves in relation to others as we go through life

GLOBAL OPPORTUNITY

Those Irresistible Classic Cars

A trend that appears to be sweeping affluent consumers in many European countries today is the growing flirtation with classic American muscle cars, as well as old American vehicles that drivers in the United States have long since forgotten. An increasing number of enthusiastic Europeans are flaunting their wealth and high status in their communities by shunning the latest prestigious European car models and driving American vintage automobiles, such as the Buick Regal, Skylark, Cadillac El Dorado, Caprice, as well as many other U.S.-made models.

Driving an old American car in any of these countries, including Germany, Switzerland, the United Kingdom, France, and Italy, is not easy or cheap. Parts are hard to find and are very expensive, the price of gas is three times higher than that in the United States, and mechanics who know how to repair vintage models are a rarity.

For example, in Germany, young enthusiasts prefer the American automobile forerunners over their own powerful and prestigious domestic cars. And just like any car-collector market, Germans are divided into two niches: the hotrod customizers and the old classic lovers (e.g., the old Chevrolet, Impala, and Dodge Coronet Wagon). The first group takes over an airfield in the city of Hunxe every summer for *Bottrop Kustom Kulur,* the largest show of its kind in Germany; and the second group keeps these cars in pristine condition, taking them out for Sunday morning rides to flaunt their beauty in downtown areas.

It is not just the high cost of owning and maintaining these cars that makes possession of such oldies a burden, but also maneuvering them on the narrow streets in most European cities. The roads of many of these older countries were designed for much smaller vehicles. Attempting to pilot these eighteen-foot oversized American gas guzzlers, such as a Grand Torino station wagon, seems like trying to navigate an oceanliner along a narrow river.

Today, such enthusiastic collectors are able to access the latest information about such vehicles from various websites devoted to classic American automotive memorabilia and social media that reach other like-minded individuals, as well as through various exhibitions of vintage autos that spring up in the capitals and major cities of most of these countries.

American tourists who visit Europe are often amazed when they observe the presence of these vintage American classic cars and the trouble their owners willingly endure when attempting to navigate and park them in downtown areas. From your perspective, what psychological concepts—such as personality traits, self-concept, and lifestyle—are at play in explaining this type of fascination or behavior? Visit a German website that is devoted to classic American automotive memorabilia at https://chromjuwelen.com/. *In your estimation, is the attraction to old American classics among affluent Europeans likely to endure and grow or perhaps fade away in coming years? Explain your answer.*

experiences. Starting with childhood, we begin to develop self-aware-ness—that is, awareness of the extent to which we are similar to or dis-similar from others. We learn our strengths and weaknesses and develop positive or negative feelings about what we are as a result.[43]

Self-concept also emerges from other people's opinions of us. We learn to per-ceive ourselves as others perceive us. Relationships with other people play a significant role in forming the self. We are constantly interpreting how others perceive the symbols we surround ourselves with. We adjust and pattern our behavior based on others' expectations, meeting some and failing others.

The self-concept is thus the outcome of a comparison between our actual standing on some attribute and an ideal. The ideal is our conception of how we would like to be. People often experience discrepancies between their ac-tual and desired selves. For some individuals, this gap is wider than for others. Such individuals are particularly suitable targets for ad campaigns that use fantasy appeals as ways to cope with problems in the real world or to com-pensate for boredom.[44] Campaigns for Disney theme parks, films, videos, and related merchandise offer examples of ads that employ fantasy appeals.

Variety of Self-Concepts

A variety of self-concepts have been identified in consumer behavior liter-ature. Early work by Carl Rogers, a pioneer in the field of the self-concept, identified a number of components of the self such as the real self (the individual as an objective entity), the ideal self (what the individual would like to be), the self-image (how individuals see themselves), the apparent self (the self that others see), and the reference-group self (the self one imagines that others see).[45]

Newer research has added other concepts such as the extended self and the possible self. The extended self is the self defined in terms of an individual's more important possessions.[46] The extended self includes the home, clothing, car, and furnishings a person owns. Possessions, in this sense, are perceived as a confirmation or extension of the self-image. Such goods are said to pos-sess *badge value* because they communicate something about their owners or users and how they feel about themselves. For instance, the J. Crew label on a pair of jeans suggests something different about the person wearing them than does Wrangler (the popular brand for rodeo riders and cowboys).

The possible self, on the other hand, refers to an individual's perceptions concerning what he or she would like to become, what one could become,

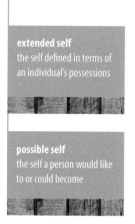

extended self
the self defined in terms of an individual's possessions

possible self
the self a person would like to or could become

or what one fears becoming. The notion of possible selves conveys a stronger future orientation than the other self-concept types.[47]

These different types of self-images manifest themselves in different buying situations. Because many consumption activities are related to self-evaluation, consumers reflect their values through the products they buy and activities they undertake. To be congruent with the reference-group self, for example, an individual may take up golf and buy all the necessary gear for the game to be accepted into a group. Deep inside, however, he or she may not really care for the game.

Measuring the Self-Concept

A popular method of measuring the self-concept involves use of the Q-sort technique. Q-sorting is a sophisticated form of rank ordering. It involves giving the respondent a number of cards, usually somewhere between 60 and 120, where each card contains a statement or a situation for the respondent to evaluate. Each respondent is asked to sort these cards into a number of piles arranged by the researcher to reflect the degree of the respondent's personal assessment of each statement.

In using Q-sorts to measure the self-concept, a number of statements addressing various elements of the self are developed by the researcher. Each statement is then printed on a card. Respondents are given these cards and instructed to sort them into a predetermined number of piles (such as seven piles), based on how each respondent assesses these statements. The following is an example of a typical set of statements on a Q-sort designed to measure the self-concept:

Definitely me					**Definitely not me**	
1	2	3	4	5	6	7

I feel I am a bit of a risk taker.
I feel more sophisticated than most people around.
I enjoy being alone.
I favor medical procedures to improve one's looks.
I always like to impress others.
I often fantasize about winning the lottery.
I usually take the initiative when meeting others.
I'm good at giving people advice.

The reason for having an odd number of piles in the Q-sort is to allow for a neutral position. Respondents are instructed to place into the neutral pile (pile 4 in the preceding example) those cards that are left over after other choices have been made. These are the statements toward which the respondent is indifferent. The number of cards to be placed in each pile is often designed to approximate the distribution of the normal curve. Data from the Q-sort are then analyzed through statistical techniques that may include factor analysis and cluster analysis.

A person's role as teacher in a classroom can be completely different than his or her role in other aspects of life.

Measurement of the self-concept via Q-sorting helps marketers identify clusters of individuals that exhibit similar concepts of self. The assumption is that people with similar self-concepts tend to exhibit similar consumption habits; hence, such identification would help marketers decide on the appropriate strategies to target them.

Self-Concept and Social Roles

As consumers assume diverse social roles, they put on different selves like actors who perform in a theater. Each role requires its own script, props, and costumes.[48] A person learns what others expect from the role and develops the behaviors necessary to meet these expectations. Whether the role be that of husband, parent, boss, or student, different aspects of the self come into play and are manifested in a person's behavior. Some components of the self are more active in one role than in another. As a parent, the individual may be caring, affectionate, and giving—characteristics that may not be apparent in the same person's role as a boss. Some identities are more central to the self than others. An individual's identity as a parent can be more central than that as a tennis player. The degree of centrality of the identity (or lack thereof) is instrumental in determining the seriousness an individual places on performing what is expected from the role.

The importance of role recognition to marketers lies in the observation that people are often concerned about the impression they make on others. An elevated level of sensitivity about the image that a person communicates to those around him or her results in heightened concern about the appropriateness of one's consumption-related behaviors. Those who demonstrate greater public self-consciousness are sometimes referred to as *high self-monitors*. High self-monitors are intensely attuned to the way they present themselves within social environments. In contrast to *low self-monitors*, high self-monitors are more apt to select products based on their estimates of how these items will be perceived by others.[49] Such persons tend to be more interested in clothing and heavier users of cosmetics.[50] The degree to which a consumer is a high or low self-monitor can be gauged by the extent to which he or she agrees or disagrees with statements such as "I guess I put on a show to impress or entertain others" and "I would probably make a good actor."[51]

Self-Concept and Consumption

Consumption of products and services contributes to the definition of the self. It has been said that you are what you consume. In other words, the products and services that people consume help them define their self-concept and social identity.[52] In addition, an individual's consumption of products and services affects other people's perceptions of him or her.[53]

People, more often than not, use another individual's possessions or consumption behavior to help them make judgments about who that person is. They often consider a person's clothes, make of automobile, dwelling, home decoration, and leisure activities to make inferences about that person's personality. Grubb and Grathwohl believe that one meaningful way of understanding the role of goods is to view them as symbols serving as a means of communication between individuals and their significant others.[54] In the same way that the use of certain products and services influences other's perceptions of who we are, these same products are instrumental in determining our own concept of self.

Many studies support the view that congruence exists between product usage and self-concept.[55] Self-product congruence refers to the tendency of individuals to select and use products that match some aspect of the self. Brands have personalities or images, and consumers seek those brands that match their self-image or the image they would like to project to others. These brand personalities can be more enduring and influential than the product's functional attributes. Differentiating brands can thus become possible through attaching emotional values into a brand to reflect a unique brand personality.[56] A recent study by Kressmann and colleagues tested the effect of self-image congruence on loyalty for car brands. Six hundred car owners were surveyed. The results documented the paramount importance of self-congruity in predicting brand loyalty.[57] Another study found that employed females were likely to shop for and wear those outfits that

self-product congruence
a tendency to select products that match some aspects of the self

match their ideal career self-image. The more upward the career anchorage, the greater the preference among such employees for wearing businesslike outfits.[58]

Certain properties tend to characterize the products that consumers use as symbols. To qualify, the products must be visible in use—that is, conspicuous products that are readily apparent to others. Products such as automobiles, clothing, and furnishings are examples. The product class must also carry a distinctive brand name, steep price tag, or prestigious origin so as to allow formation of a stereotypical image of the user. One can easily see in Figure 7.5 how a familiar product, such as an automobile, can become a symbol of success and prestige.

FIGURE 7.5

Based on a global reputation for performance, innovation, and design, many drivers and affluent consumers crave Porsche as a symbol of distinction.

© Gyuszko-Photo/Shutterstock.com

SUMMARY

For purposes of the study of consumer behavior, personality can be defined as the sum total of an individual's inner psychological attributes. Personality makes individuals what they are, distinguishes them from every other person, demonstrates their mode of adjustment to life's circumstances, and produces their unique, stable pattern of responding to environmental stimuli. Personality theories that are particularly relevant to the study of consumer behavior include Freudian, neo-Freudian, and trait theories.

Psychographics, which is employed to investigate consumer lifestyles, is related to trait theories. Psychographics is not a personality theory. Rather, it is a research approach whose aim is to assess consumers' lifestyles so that meaningful consumer typologies can be identified. Unlike trait theories, which classify people according to their dominant characteristics using personality tests, psychographic research employs AIO inventories. AIO inventories are constructed specifically for each study to assess the lifestyles of a target group. The objective is to link AIO with specific consumption behaviors or preferences, such as purchase or use of specific products, services, and brands. The VALS program is a landmark effort in the field of psychographic research.

Consumers simultaneously hold a number of images of themselves. The self-concept is a complex structure that includes both an individual's self-assessment *and* the way one is perceived by others. A number of self-concepts are possible, including the real self, the ideal self, the self-image, the apparent self, and the reference-group image. The extended self includes some of an individual's most important possessions, especially those with badge value. The possible self includes an individual's perceptions concerning what he or she would like to become, could become, or fears becoming.

Product, brand, and service consumption contribute to an individual's definition of self. Consumers tend to choose products, brands, and stores that match some aspects of their self; to protect their self-images; and to buy products whose images correspond to, enhance, and communicate their self-concept, a notion known as self-product congruence. Goods often serve as social tools or symbols by which individuals disclose something about themselves to others.

CASE SYNOPSIS

Beauty for Billions or Billions for Beauty?

Welcome to a trend we cultivate in our contemporary society today—the pursuit of beauty and captivating appearance. Reasons behind this phenomenon are numerous. Researchers have found that human beings are hard-wired to respond more favorably to attractive people and that good-looking individuals are generally regarded to be more talented, kind, honest, and intelligent than their less-attractive counterparts. Research has also revealed that companies which place a premium on hiring attractive individuals earn, on the average, higher revenue than similar firms that do not.

Beauty in our society has become a coveted goal for which people spend dearly on products and services in search of captivating looks. Beauty is celebrated throughout the world. Beauty pageants have become annual traditions in almost all nations. International pageants are significant undertakings, with billions of dollars spent on items ranging from wardrobes and cosmetics to coaches who teach the contestants how to walk and talk.

Critics and supporters prevail in this arena. Supporters argue that beauty boosts the confidence of and self-concept of participants, as well as enhances their chances of success in life. Critics, on the other hand, claim that emphasis on mere physical beauty creates a powerful drive for many women to conform to conventional glamour standards glorified by the media and by such shows as beauty pageants.

Notes

1   Marsha L. Richins, "Social Comparison and the Idealized Images of Advertising," *Journal of Consumer Research* 18 (June 1991), pp. 71–82; Lois W. Banner, *American Beauty* (Chicago: University of Chicago Press, 1980).

2   Calvin S. Hall and Gardner Lindzey, *Theories of Personality,* 2nd ed. (New York: John Wiley, 1970), pp. 7–9.

3   Ibid.

4   Barbara Dominguez, "Enlightening New Science of Birth Order," *The Daily Sundial, in Northern Star* (May 1, 1997); Cheryl Russell, "What Your Birth Order Says About You," *USA Weekend* (May 9–11, 1997), p. 16.

5   "Can Birth Order Predict Your Personality?" *EEO BiMonthly, Equal Employment Opportunity Career Journal* (February 28, 1997).

6   Paul Gray, "The Assault on Freud," *Time* (November 29, 1993), pp. 47–51; "Sigmund Freud," www.wynja.com/giganto/
psych/freud.html; Dr. W. Boyd Spencer, "Sigmund Freud" Outline, www.oldsci.eiu.edu/psychology/Spencer/Freud.html; Austrian National Tourist Office, "Sigmund Freud's Biography," www.austria-info.at/personen/freud/freud1_e.html; Austrian National Tourist Office, "The Epochal Significance of Sigmund Freud's Work, www.austria-info.at/personen/freud/freud2_e.html; Austrian National Tourist Office, "Freud's Followers and the Impact of His Theories," www.austria-info.at/personen/freud/freud3_e.html; "Freud: The Master . . . or a Has-Been?" www1.rider.edu/suler.freud.html.

7   Paul Gray, "The Assault on Freud," *Time* (November 29, 1993), pp. 47–51.

8   Spenser Rathus, *Psychology* (New York: Holt, Rinehart and Winston, 1981).

9   Hall and Lindzey, *Theories of Personality*; Duane Schultz, *Theories of Personality* (Monterey, CA: Brooks/Cole, 1976).

10   Hall and Lindzey, *Theories of Personality*, pp. 134–137; Schultz, *Theories of Personality*, pp. 68–83.

11   Hall and Lindzey, *Theories of Personality*, pp. 130–134; Schultz, *Theories of Personality*, pp. 86–101.

12   Hall and Lindzey, *Theories of Personality*, pp. 137–157; Schultz, *Theories of Personality,* pp. 104–116; Harry Stack Sullivan, *The Interpersonal Theory of Psychiatry* (New York: Norton, 1953), p. 111.

13   Joel B. Cohen, "An Interpersonal Orientation to the Study of Consumer Behavior," *Journal of Marketing Research* 4 (August 1967), pp. 270–278; Joel B. Cohen, "Toward an Interpersonal Theory of Consumer Behavior," *California Management Review* 10 (Spring 1968), pp. 73–80; Jon P. Noerager, "An Assessment of CAD—A Personality Instrument Developed Specifically for Marketing Research," *Journal of Marketing Research* 16 (February 1979), pp. 53–59.

14   Jerome Kernan, "Choice Criteria, Decision Behavior, and Personality," *Journal of Marketing Research* 5 (May 1968), pp. 155–164; Joel B. Cohen and Ellen Golden, "Informational Social Influence and Product Evaluation," *Journal of Applied Psychology* 50 (February 1972), pp. 54–59; Noerager, "An Assessment of CAD—A Personality Instrument Developed Specifically for Marketing Research"; Arch Woodside and Ruth Andress, "CAD Eight Years Later," *Journal of the Academy of Marketing Science* 3 (Summer–Fall 1975), pp. 309–13; Michael Ryan and Richard Becherer, "A Multivariate Test of CAD Instrument Construct Validity," *Advances in Consumer Research* 3 (1976), pp. 149–154; Pradeep K. Tyagi, "Validation of the CAD Instrument: A Replication," *Advances in Consumer Research* 10

(1983), pp. 112–118; Mark E. Slama, Terrel G. Williams, and Armen Tashchian, "Compliant, Aggressive, and Detached Types Differ in Generalized Purchasing Involvement," *Advances in Consumer Research* 15 (1988), pp. 158–162.

15   Gordon R. Foxall, "Cognitive Styles of Consumer Initiators," *Technovation* 15, no. 5 (June 1995), pp. 269–288.

16   Marsha L. Richins and Scott Dawson, "A Consumer Values Orientation for Materialism and Its Measurement: Scale Development and Validation," *Journal of Consumer Research* 19 (December 1992), pp. 306–316; Marsha L. Richins, "Special Possessions and the Expression of Material Values," *Journal of Consumer Research* 21 (December 1994), p. 531; Richard G. Netemeyer, Scot Burton, and Donald R. Lichtenstein, "Trait Aspects of Vanity: Measurement and Relevance to Consumer Behavior," *Journal of Consumer Research* 21 (March 1995), pp. 612–626; Susan Schultz Kleine, Robert E. Kleine III, and Chris T. Allen, "How Is a Possession 'Me' or 'Not Me'? Characterizing Types and an Antecedent of Material Possession Attachment," *Journal of Consumer Research* 22 (December 1995), pp. 327–343.

17   Ronald E. Goldsmith and Charles F. Hofacker, "Measuring Consumer Innovativeness," *Journal of the Academy of Marketing Science* 19, no. 3 (1991), pp. 209–221; Curtis P. Haugtvedt, Richard E. Petty, and John T. Cacioppo, "Need for Cognition and Advertising: Understanding the Role of Personality Variables in Consumer Behavior," *Journal of Consumer Psychology* 1, no. 3 (1992), pp. 239–260; Richard Petty et al., "Personality and Ad Effectiveness: Exploring the Utility of Need for Cognition," in Michael Houston (Ed.), *Advances in Consumer Research* 15 (Ann Arbor: Association for Consumer Research, 1988), pp. 209–212; John T. Cacioppo, Richard Petty, and Katherine Morris, "Effects of Need for Cognition on Message Evaluation, Recall, and Persuasion," *Journal of Personality and Social Psychology* (October 1993), pp. 805–818; James W. Peltier and John A. Schibrowsky, "Need for Cognition, Advertisement Viewing Time, and Memory for Advertising Stimuli," in Chris T. Allen and Deborah Roedder John (Eds.), *Advances in Consumer Research* 21 (Provo, UT: Association for Consumer Research, 1994), pp. 244–250.

18   Zorika Petic Henderson, "Neurobiology's Role in Personality and Emotion," *Human Ecology Forum* 23 (March 1, 1995), pp. 8–11.

19   Ibid.

20   Richard P. Ebstein et al., "Dopamine D4 Receptor (D4DR) Exon III Polymorphism Associated with the Human Personality Trait of Novelty Seeking," *Nature Genetics* 12, no. 1 (January 1996).

21   Ibid.

22   Joseph D. Brown and Russell G. Wahlers, "The Environmentally Concerned Consumer: An Exploratory Study," *Journal of Marketing Theory & Practice* 6, no. 2 (Spring 1998), pp. 39–47.

23   Todd A. Mooradian and James M. Olver, "I Can't Get No Satisfaction: The Impact of Personality and Emotion on Postpurchase Processes," *Psychology & Marketing* 14, no. 4 (July 1997), pp. 379–393.

24   N. Hanna and J. S. Wagle, "Who Is Your Satisfied Customer?" *The Journal of Services Marketing* 2, no. 3 (Summer 1988), pp. 5–13; Wann-Yih Wu, "The Role of Risk Attitude on Online Shopping," *Social Behavior and Personality* 35, no. 4 (May 2007), pp. 453–468.

25   James F. Engel, Roger D. Blackwell, and Paul W. Miniard, *Consumer Behavior*, 7th ed. (Fort Worth: Dryden Press–Harcourt Brace Jovanovich College Publishers, 1993), pp. 358–359.

26 William Bearden and Randall Rose, "Attention to Social Comparison Information: An Individual Difference Factor Affecting Conformity," *Journal of Consumer Research* 16 (March 1990), pp. 461–71.

27 "MBTI Basics," The Myers-Briggs Foundation, www. myersbriggs.org/my-mbti-personality-type/mbti-basics/.

28 Zorika Petic Henderson, "Neurobiology's Role in Personality and Emotion," *Human Ecology Forum* 23 (March 1, 1995), pp. 8–11.

29 Ibid.

30 Richard P. Ebstein et al., "Dopamine D4 Receptor (D4DR) Exon III Polymorphism Associated with the Human Personality Trait of Novelty Seeking," *Nature Genetics* 12, no. 1 (January 1996).

31 Ibid.

32 Joseph D. Brown and Russell G. Wahlers, "The Environmentally Concerned Consumer: An Exploratory Study," *Journal of Marketing Theory & Practice* 6, no. 2 (Spring 1998), pp. 39–47.

33 Tim Triplett, "Brand Personality Must Be Managed or It Will Assume a Life of Its Own," *Marketing News* 28 (May 9, 1994), p. 9.

34 Hans Baumgartner, "Toward a Personology of the Consumer," *Journal of Consumer Research* 29, no. 2 (September 2002), pp. 286–293.

35 Raymond L. Horton, "The Edwards Personal Preference Schedule and Consumer Personality Research," *Journal of Marketing Research* 11 (August 1974), pp. 335–37; Harold H. Kassarjian and Mary Jane Sheffet, "Personality and Consumer Behavior: An Update," in Harold H. Kassarjian and Thomas S. Robertson (eds.), *Perspectives in Consumer Behavior*, 4th ed. (Glenview, IL: Scott, Foresman, 1991), pp. 291–353; Jennifer L. Aaker, "Measuring Brand Personality," unpublished manuscript, Stanford University (September 1994).

36 William D. Wells and Arthur D. Beard, "Personality and Consumer Behavior," in Scott Ward and Thomas S. Robertson (eds.), *Consumer Behavior: Theoretical Sources* (Upper Saddle River, NJ: Prentice Hall, 1973), pp. 141–99.

37 Kathryn E. A. Villani and Yoram Wind, "On the Usage of 'Modified' Personality Trait Measures in Consumer Research," *Journal of Consumer Research* 2 (December 1975), pp. 223–26.

38 Todd A. Mooradian and James M. Olver, "I Can't Get No Satisfaction: The Impact of Personality and Emotion on Postpurchase Processes," *Psychology & Marketing* 14, no. 4 (July 1997), pp. 379–93.

39 N. Hanna and J. S. Wagle, "Who Is Your Satisfied Customer?" *The Journal of Services Marketing* 2, no. 3 (Summer 1988), pp. 5–13; Wann-Yih Wu, "The Role of Risk Attitude on Online Shopping," *Social Behavior and Personality*, vol. 35, no. 4 (May, 2007), pp. 453–468.

40 James F. Engel, Roger D. Blackwell, and Paul W. Miniard, *Consumer Behavior*, 7th ed. (Fort Worth: Dryden Press–Harcourt Brace Jovanovich College Publishers, 1993), pp. 358–59.

41 SRI Consulting Business Intelligence, http://www.sric-bi.com/ VALS/

42 Ibid

43 "What is VALS," http://www.mediamark.com/ memri/quicksheets/ VALS_Quick_Sheet.pdf

44 SRI Consulting Business Intelligence, "VALS Applications," http://www.sric-bi/VALS/applications.shml

45   Lewis C. Winters, "International Psychographics," *Marketing Research: A Magazine of Management and Applications* (September 1992), pp. 48–49.

48   Marsha L. Richins, "Social Comparison and the Idealized Images of Advertising," *Journal of Consumer Research* 18 (June 1991), pp. 71–83.

49   Harrison G. Gough, Mario Fioravanti, and Renato Lazzari, "Some Implications of Self Versus Ideal-Self Congurence on the Revised Adjective Check List," *Journal of Personality and Social Psychology* 44, no. 6 (1983), pp. 1214–20; Steven Jay Lynn and Judith W. Rhue, "Daydream Believers," *Psychology Today* (September 1985), p. 14.

50   A. Ben Oumil and Orhan Erdem, "Self-Concept by Gender: A Focus on Male–Female Consumers," *Journal of Marketing Theory & Practice* 5, no. 1 (Winter 1997), pp. 7–14; Ibrahim Hafedh, "A Multi-Dimensional Approach to Analyzing the Effect of Self-Congruity on Shoppers' Retail Store Behavior," *Innovative Marketing*, vol. 3, no. 3 (2007).

51   Russell W. Belk, "Possessions and the Extended Self," *Journal of Consumer Research* 15 (September 1988), pp. 139–68; Russell Belk, "My Possessions Myself," *Psychology Today* (July–August, 1988), pp. 50–52; Amy J. Morgan, "The Evolving Self in Consumer Behavior: Exploring Possible Selves," in Leigh McAlister and Michael L. Rothschild (eds.), *Advances in Consumer Research* 20 (Provo, UT: Association for Consumer Research, 1993), pp. 429–32; Raj Mehta and Russell W. Belk, "Artifacts, Identity, and Transition: Favorite Possessions of Indians and Indian Immigrants to the United States," *Journal of Consumer Research* 17 (March 1991), pp. 398–411; Marsha L. Richins, "Special Possessions and the Expression of Material Values," *Journal of Consumer Research* 21 (December 1994), pp. 522–33; Kleine, Kleine, and Allen, "How Is a Possession 'Me' or 'Not Me'? Characterizing Types and an Antecedent of Material Possession Attachment."

52   Morgan, "The Evolving Self in Consumer Behavior: Exploring Possible Selves."

53   Erving Goffman, *The Presentation of Self in Everyday Life* (Garden City, NY: Doubleday, 1959).

54   Morris B. Holbrook, Michael R. Solomon, and Stephen Bell, "A Re-Examination of Self-Monitoring and Judgments of Furniture Designs," *Home Economics Research Journal* 19 (September 1990), pp. 6–16; Mark Snyder, "Self-Monitoring Processes," in Leonard Berkowitz (ed.), *Advances in Experimental Social Psychology* (New York: Academic Press, 1979), pp. 851–928.

55   Arnold W. Buss, *Self-Consciousness and Social Anxiety* (San Francisco: Freeman, 1980); Lynn Carol Miller and Cathryn Leigh Cox, "Public Self-Consciousness and Makeup Use," *Personality and Social Psychology Bulletin* 8, no. 4 (1982), pp. 748–51; Michael R. Solomon and John Schopler, "Self-Conciousness and Clothing," *Personality and Social Psychology Bulletin* 8, no. 3 (1982), pp. 508–14.

56   Mark Snyder and Steve Gangestad, "On the Nature of Self-Monitoring: Matters of Assessment, Matters of Validity," *Journal of Personality and Social Psychology* 51 (1986), pp. 125–39.

57   Michael R. Solomon, "The Role of Products as Social Stimuli: A Symbolic Interactionism Perspective," *Journal of Consumer Research* 10 (December 1983), pp. 319–29; Robert E. Kleine, Susan Schultz-Kleine, and Jerome B. Kernan, "Mundane Consumption and the Self: A Social Identity Perspec-

tive," *Journal of Consumer Psychology* 2, no. 3 (1993), pp. 209–35; Newell D. Wright, C. B. Claiborne, and M. Joseph Sirgy, "The Effects of Product Symbolism on Consumer Self-Concept," in John F. Sherry Jr. and Brian Sternthal (eds.) *Advances in Consumer Research* 19 (Provo, UT: Association for Consumer Research (1992), pp. 311–18; Susan Fournier, "A Person-Based Relationship Framework for Strategic Brand Management," Ph.D. dissertation, University of Florida (1994).

58 Jack L. Nasar, "Symbolic Meanings of House Styles," *Environment and Behavior* 21 (May 1989), pp. 235–57; E. K. Sadalla, B. Verschure, and J. Burroughs, "Identity Symbolism," *Housing, Environment, and Behavior* 19 (1987).

59 E. L. Grubb and L. Grathwohl, "Consumer Self-Concept, Symbolism, and Market Behavior: A Theoretical Approach," *Journal of Marketing* 31 (October 1967), pp. 22–27.

60 Sak Onkvisit and John Shaw, "Self-Concept and Image Congruence: Some Research and Managerial Implications," *Journal of Consumer Marketing* 4 (Winter 1987), pp. 13–24; George M. Zinkhan and Jae W. Hong, "Self-Concept and Advertising Effectiveness: A Conceptual Model of Congruency, Conspicuousness, and Response Mode," in Rebecca H. Holman and Michael R. Solomon (eds.), *Advances in Consumer Research* 18 (Provo, UT: Association for Consumer Research, 1991), pp. 348–54; C. B. Claiborne and M. Joseph Sirgy, "Self-Image Congruence as a Model of Consumer Attitude Formation and Behavior: A Conceptual Review and Guide for Further Research," (a paper presented at the Academy of Marketing Science Conference, New Orleans (1990); Marsha L. Richins, "Special Possessions and the Expression of Material Values," *Journal of Consumer Research* 21 (December 1994), pp. 522–33; Kleine, Kleine, and Allen, "How Is a Possession 'Me' or 'Not Me'? Characterizing Types and an Antecedent of Material Possession Attachment"; Mary K. Ericksen, "Using Self-Congruity and Ideal Congruity to Predict Purchase Intention: A European Perspective," *Journal of Euromarketing* 6, no. 1 (1996), pp. 41–56; Michael Lynn and Judy Harris, "The Desire for Unique Consumer Products: A New Individual Differences Scale," *Psychology & Marketing* 14, no. 6 (September 1997), pp. 601–16; Susan Fournier, "Consumers and Their Brands: Developing Relationship Theory in Consumer Research," *Journal of Consumer Research* 24, no. 4 (March 1998), pp. 343–73; Mark P. Leach and Annie H. Liu, "The Use of Culturally Relevant Stimuli in International Advertising," *Psychology & Marketing* 15, no. 6 (September 1998), pp. 523–46.

61 Rajagopal, "Impact of Advertising Variability on Building Customer Based Brand Personality under Competitive Environment," *Latin American Business Review*, vol. 6, no. 3 (2005), pp. 63–84.

62 Frank Kressmann, et. al., "Direct and Indirect Effects of Self-Image Congruence on Brand Loyalty," *Journal of Business Research*, vol. 59, no. 9 (September 2006), pp. 955–964.

63 Mary K. Ericksen and Joseph Sirgy, "Employed Females' Clothing Preference, Self-Image Congruence, and Career Anchorage," *Journal of Applied Social Psychology*, vol. 22, no. 5, (March 1992), pp. 408–422.

CHAPTER 8
CONSUMER DECISION MAKING

LEARNING OBJECTIVES

- To understand the factors at play in the process of consumer decision making.
- To conceptualize the difference between programmed versus nonprogrammed buying decisions.
- To gain insight into Dewey's five-stage problem-solving process as applied to consumer purchasing decisions.
- To recognize the importance of postpurchase feelings and their effect on the behavior of consumers.
- To ascertain the causes of consumer satisfaction/dissatisfaction.
- To identify the reasons for and causes of consumer behavior as well as recognize methods to maximize consumer satisfaction.

KEY TERMS

constructive processing	brand loyalty	prospect theory
involvement	internal search	framing
low involvement	sharpening	decision rules
high involvement	leveling	compensatory decision
nonprogrammed decision	external search	rule
extended problem	evoked set	noncompensatory
solving	heuristics	decision rule
limited problem solving	evaluative criteria	instrumental performance
impulse purchases	salient attributes	expressive performance
programmed decisions	determinant attributes	consumer satisfaction

Daily, as consumers, we face an overwhelming number of decisions ranging from those related to our home and job to others, such as buying a car or deciding on a vacation destination. In earlier times, arriving at informed decisions was simple. Asking friends, looking up facts in reference materials, and conversing with sales staff at stores were the usual methods for seeking information. Today, with Twitter and Facebook, the countless apps fed into our smartphones, as well as the significant role of the Web, the flow of facts and opinions never ceases. Information today finds more ways to reach us, more often, and more instantly.

While this avalanche of information can be viewed as a positive factor for our informed decision making, recent research has shown that excessive information can lead to objectively poorer choices or even to choices that people come to regret later on. The reason is that the unconscious system that guides many of our decisions is sidelined by too much information, hindering our ability to make smart, creative, and successful decisions.

Researchers have learned that decisions requiring creativity benefit from letting the issue gestate below the level of conscious awareness. The key reason for this is the limited capacity of our brains' working memory. It is common knowledge that the brain can roughly hold up to seven items at a time. Anything beyond seven must be processed into our long-term memory—a process that requires additional conscious effort. In this case, the brain struggles to figure out which information to keep and which to disregard. This process requires still further cognitive resources—particularly when the amount of information is overwhelming. Moreover, it is not only the *quantity* of information that hampers information processing, but also the *rate* at which information is coming. A ceaseless influx of information impels us to respond instantly, detracting our brain's ability to observe logical connections. Today, we have been programmed to respond instantly, sacrificing thoughtfulness and accuracy for the sake of prompt decisions.

Sound decisions, therefore, may require that we pull back from this constant barrage of facts to allow the brain to subconsciously synthesize new information with our existing experience and knowledge. Such allows the new to integrate with the old, below the conscious level, forming novel connections. In fact, *sleeping* on a decision helps us to differentiate between the vital and the irrelevant facts, leading to sound decision making. Hence, one often hears the adage "let me sleep on it," which is commonly used when we face major decisions that need to be made.[1]

So much for the ideal of making well-informed decisions via the plethora of information that surrounds and confounds us today. Although we give lip service to preferring more information, the fact is excessive information can be debilitating to our decision-making processes. With too much information, poor decisions are likely to be made since a dormant brain's active process that weighs the pros and cons of relevant decision attributes is hindered. What are the ramifications of these new findings to consumers in general? Also, what are the implications to businesses that include both social and cyber media in their promotional strategy? Learn more about the counterintuitive approach to making decisions by visiting the Harvard Business Review blog article at http://blogs.hbr.org/cs/2011/05/a_counter-intuitive_approach_t.html. What do you think are the best ways to approach complex decisions? What are some of the methods of "sleeping on it"?

This chapter addresses consumer decision-making processes. We begin by differentiating between nonprogrammed and programmed decision processes. Next, we analyze the stages that comprise the decision-making process, from the problem-recognition phase through postpurchase evaluation. Finally, we examine determinants of consumer satisfaction or dissatisfaction with a purchase.

THE DECISION PROCESS

The U.S. consumer today is simply one of the most cared for and pampered in the world. There is significantly more product selection, more product information, and more places at which to shop than in any other country in the world. A multitude of suppliers offers a complex mix of products and services. They utilize highly sophisticated pricing, distribution, and promotional strategies in a continuous race to please finicky consumers.

We have only to consider the variety of alternatives available to a new car buyer to realize the complexities of choice. A bewildering array of automobile makes, both domestic and foreign, with dozens of models available within each make and diverse features, power ranges, and options, present buyers with a true challenge.

Although a wide range of choices represents a positive sign of progress and reflects a society's high standard of living, it nevertheless complicates the choice process. When confronted with an excessive number of alternatives from which to select, consumers may become perplexed and bewildered. They may simply patronize their usual brands and stores, or information overload may lead them to arrive at a product selection based on gut feeling.

One of the assumptions made in consumer behavior research is that most purchases are preceded by a decision process. A decision is an act that prevails only if the consumer is faced with two or more alternative courses of action, all of which have good probabilities of bringing about a desired end result. Decision making is the process of considering, evaluating, and choosing between these alternatives. Consumers who face a no-choice buying situation are simply not exercising decision making.

Consumers make many types of decisions. One type relates to whether they should buy a product under consideration. A recent college graduate commencing a new job in a large city mulls over a decision about the practicality of commuting to and from work via public transportation versus purchasing a new automobile. Assuming the consumer elects to purchase a new car, a further issue relates to the type of vehicle—gasoline powered, hybrid, or electric. Once that decision has been made, the make of the car, specific model, color, and options package remain to be decided. The graduate must still decide on the dealership from which the auto will be purchased, how the new car purchase should be financed, and whether extended warranty coverage is desirable.

When faced with two or more options in relation to any given problem or need, we tend to subjectively evaluate the alternatives, pondering the available information in light of our present and future expectations. We establish an order of preference among the alternatives that may shape the outcome of the final purchase selection.

The many and varied options available to new car buyers illustrate the complexity of choice.

ARE CONSUMERS RATIONAL?

Classical economic theory painted a picture of consumers as rational decision makers. Consumers are assumed to attempt to maximize their utility or satisfaction (supposing they can measure it) continuously within the constraints of limited resources. It further presumes that this rational consumer is able to select from among all possible alternatives a combination of products and services that will provide the greatest total utility given his or her limited resources.[2]

This view suggests that the consumer is knowledgeable about all the possibilities or alternatives available in the marketplace, their features, their qualities, their prices, and the utilities that can be extracted from acquiring and using them. It ignores the socio-psychological factors that influence human behavior, and the effect of family members and friends, as well as information from the traditional and electronic media on consumer preferences.

Thus the traditional portrait of the rational, objective, utility-maximizing, information-processing, decision-making consumer is greatly simplified. Consumers are unlikely to be computing, calculating entities that mathematically gauge the outcome of each alternative considered. For example, a consumer may consult scores of travel websites to choose a vacation destination, only to be overwhelmed with information that may cause that person to opt for a stay action. Similarly, a student choosing a college gets close to selecting a specific school based on an intensive online search of possible institutions. Suddenly, friends drench her inbox with reasons to go elsewhere, causing her to abandon her original "informed" choice.[3]

Studies have provided evidence concerning the way brand purchases occur without prior consideration of alternatives. Impulse and compulsive buying represent specific cases of purchasing where emotionality overcomes rationality. Impulse buying represents around 40 percent of all consumer spending, including money spent on e-commerce sites.[4] A positive mood at the time of shopping, social interaction with others, and presence of irresistible bargains are among the reasons for this tendency. In the case of electronic media purchases, research identified the design elements of the website itself as a major factor that drives shoppers to make these impulse purchases.[5] In terms of who buys on impulse, research indicates that categories vary by age, income, and specific products/services purchased. For instance, younger consumers with high incomes represent a large percentage of impulse buyers. In terms of gender, statistics show that a higher percentage of females (60 percent) tend to buy on impulse.[6]

Researchers have come to realize that decision makers may engage in a variety of shortcuts in making choices. This is particularly true when they feel that the effort of systematic search and information processing is not justified, given the outcomes. A consumer may use what is known as constructive processing by evaluating the effort required to make a particular choice, then choosing an effort level best suited to the task. In this sense, consumers are tailoring their degree of cognitive effort to the task at hand.[7]

constructive processing
a tendency of consumers to tailor their cognitive effort to suit the task at hand

EFFORT VARIATIONS IN CONSUMER DECISION MAKING

The decisions consumers make vary widely in importance and so require different amounts of effort.[8] The amount of effort consumers expend when buying products or services is often a function of their degree of interest in and involvement with a particular purchase. Involvement depends on the degree of personal relevance that a product or service holds for the consumer and on the extent to which it serves as a vehicle of personal identification. In the case of low involvement, a consumer views a purchase as unimportant and regards the outcome of his or her decision as inconsequential. Because the purchase carries a minimal degree of personal relevance or identification, the individual feels there is little or nothing to be gained from attending to the details of a purchase. For example, a purchase of a candy bar requires minimal or no premeditation and planning.

involvement
the degree of personal relevance that a purchase holds for the consumer

low involvement
a case in which consumers attach minimal personal relevance to a purchase

High involvement purchases are those that are important to the consumer either from a financial, social, or psychological point of view. The purchase is characterized by personal relevance and identification with the outcome. An individual anticipates a potentially significant gain from expending time and effort in comparison shopping before buying. A wine connoisseur purchasing an expensive bottle of wine to give as a house gift perceives the brand choice as having a high degree of personal identification. A high level of felt involvement can increase an individual's willingness to search for, process, and transmit information about a purchase.[9]

high involvement
a case in which consumers attach elevated relevance to a purchase

One way of looking at a classification of the decision-making process is to think of it in terms of a continuum, anchored at one end by programmed decisions and at the other extreme by nonprogrammed decisions. Many decisions fall somewhere between these two extremities.

NONPROGRAMMED DECISIONS

When a purchase decision involves products or services that are financially, socially, or psychologically important, consumers are likely to diligently seek out information from many sources, take time to analyze the information, and methodically sift through all the details before arriving at a final purchase decision. Such would be the case when consumers buy a new home or make a major investment in the stock market. Nonprogrammed decisions are either novel to consumers or are infrequently encountered, and experience appears to be of little value in reaching a decision. No standardized solution for handling the problem exists. A customized, tailored approach seems to be required in order to handle the situation.

Such cases are likely to activate a variety of cognitive processes. The consumer is willing to expend major cognitive effort, is more receptive to information sources, and is more inclined to process the acquired information. Evaluation of the acquired information is conducted in view of consumers' lifestyles and self-images, as well as against present and future needs and anticipated resource availability.

Marketers recognize consumers' need for detailed information when nonprogrammed decisions are being made. Marketers who provide such information are likely to receive favorable responses from consumers who would otherwise, in the absence of such information, feel skeptical and

nonprogrammed decision a case in which a novel or infrequently encountered situation requires a customized solution

For most families, the purchase of a new home is a nonprogrammed decision entailing significant financial, social, and psychological consequences.

© michaeljung/Shutterstock.com

ambivalent about specific product and brand offerings and drop them from active consideration.

Nonprogrammed decisions include a range of decision process possibilities. As in the case of purchasing a new home, extended problem solving is a decision situation characterized by a high degree of perceived risk. Decisions, in this case, may require significant financial commitments, involve social or psychological implications, and entail symbols that communicate an image of the owner to others. In such cases, internal and multiple external information sources are sought. Information is likely to be processed actively and carefully. Alternatives are meticulously evaluated, and their attributes are painstakingly matched and compared.

In the case of limited problem solving, consumers have some experience in dealing with the purchase situation. They have already established criteria for evaluating products, services, or brands within the choice category. It is unlikely, for example, that a consumer whose wristwatch needs replacement would systematically search for information and rigorously evaluate each available alternative. A simpler approach, such as buying the same watch brand used previously or purchasing a well-known brand, may work well.

Impulse purchase situations are quite common. Impulse purchases, which are considered special cases of nonprogrammed decisions, involve little deliberation and limited or no external search. Cues such as price deals, special offers and targeted messages on the Internet, point-of-purchase displays, advertising messages, or a salesperson's comments, strategically situated by marketers, frequently trigger such purchasing responses. The purchase takes place within a short time span, and limited or no cognitive effort is allocated to the decision process. Emotional appeals usually play a major role in such purchases.[10]

PROGRAMMED DECISIONS

At the other end of the continuum are decisions made with little or no conscious cognitive effort. Purchases of many products, such as soft drinks, toothpaste, coffee, or the daily newspaper, are repetitive and routine. Such programmed decisions require no special thought on the part of the consumer and are performed with minimal effort and conscious control.

Much consumer behavior can be classified as programmed decisions. The habitual or routine nature of many purchases allows consumers to minimize the time and effort spent on purchasing familiar, frequently bought, and often-used goods. Brand loyalty represents a special case of habitual purchasing behavior. Repetitive purchasing of brands that have proven satisfactory in the past is an effort-minimization strategy that speeds the shopping experience and eliminates the risk of selecting an unsatisfactory alternative.

brand loyalty
an attachment to brands that have proven satisfactory in the past

From the perspective of brand managers, routine purchasing of a given brand by loyal consumers is a coveted accomplishment. However, such good fortune is not necessarily permanent. Programmed decisions are not irrevocable and can be reprogrammed at some point in the future. Customer loyalties are fickle. They can change at any time if the product fails to provide the desired benefits or a competitor succeeds with price or promotional tactics to uproot the previous purchasing routine.

THE NATURE OF THE CONSUMER DECISION PROCESS

Consumer decision processes can be characterized as a form of problem solving. When consumers perceive a discrepancy between an actual state of affairs and a desired or ideal state of affairs, problem recognition arises. Individuals then become involved in a problem-solving process. This process entails a sequence of activities designed to arrive at a decision leading to a satisfactory solution to the perceived problem.

John Dewey identified five stages in problem solving.[11] In a slightly modified and adapted form, they are as follows.

1. Problem recognition
2. Search activity
3. Identifying and evaluating alternative solutions
4. Purchase or commitment
5. Postpurchase considerations

Although these steps are suggestive, shoppers may proceed directly from problem recognition to purchase. In some instances, a problem may not even exist before the purchase occurs, such as in the case of impulse purchases. The mental or physical activity associated with each stage may vary significantly based on the cost of the product or service. The following sections of this chapter explain each of Dewey's stages as they relate to consumer decision processes. Exhibit 8.1 is a depiction of these stages.

EXHIBIT 8.1

Stages of the Consumer
Decision Process

PROBLEM RECOGNITION

A problem exists when an individual is enticed by a goal but lacks certainty about the best solution for the specific dilemma that he or she faces. A young man experiencing hair loss perceives this predicament as a major problem. Desiring to appear attractive, he feels threatened that hair loss will reduce his attractiveness and limit his ability to socialize. The consumer, in this case, perceives a variance between an actual and a desired state of affairs. The result is a form of incongruity or dissonance that triggers behavior.

From a consumer behavior point of view, the chance of buying a product or service is enhanced when marketers successfully create a tension state for the consumer. If the disturbance in an individual's psychological field is strong enough, a problem surfaces at the conscious level. The tension may be sufficiently intense to arouse motives or reasons that impel the consumer to think about the problem and trigger a need for him or her to take corrective measures. One form of treatment is the purchase of a product or service as a solution to the problem. For example, today many individuals worried about facial age lines resort to treatments such as Botox injections to alleviate their concerns over looking older. However, unfortunately, not every problem is solvable through product purchase and use. In some instances, individuals process information or engage in physical or mental activity that leads only to frustration or further anxiety. Consumers may discover that there is no viable, simple, or instant solution to their problem. They may even discover that a course of action they hoped would bring their problem to a satisfactory resolution has failed to provide the anticipated end result. For instance, a consumer may come to realize that the promised loss of weight from a certain diet pill may never materialize.

Problem recognition is not merely an outcome of marketing efforts aimed at making consumers aware of product groups or brands. It is, in many instances, the outgrowth of consumers' striving to fulfill the demands of everyday life.

Consumer problems can be the result of *assortment depletion*, wherein individuals experience inadequacies in their stock of goods. A family can run out of milk, breakfast cereal, aspirin, soft drinks, or some other commodity. At other times, *changes in consumers' life circumstances* may cause them to need something they never had occasion to need or use before. Career changes may require that individuals purchase a variety of electronic items to maintain an up-to-date home office. Retirement causes some to search for hobbies to occupy their newfound free time. *Product acquisitions* frequently require the purchase of further products such as supplies, accessories, and energy sources. Consumers who buy an *iPhone* may soon add an iCloud as well as other related apps and accessories to use in conjunction with their iPhone. *Product obsolescence* may cause individuals to replace goods, such as a smartphone in place of a traditional flip cell phone. Some products break or wear out; others go out of fashion. *Expanded means*, financial or otherwise, may lead to expanded desires and higher levels of aspiration. A promotion and corresponding pay raise may translate into a desire for more possessions, expanded roles, or changes in lifestyle—causes for generating new consumer problems. Similarly, *contracted means* (such as a job layoff) may cause someone to cancel a planned vacation. Finally, *expanded awareness* can also be a source of problem recognition. Consumers constantly receive new information about their surroundings, largely through marketing stimuli such as advertising and other promotional activities, as well as from the Internet. Discoveries of *new* and *improved* products create cognitions that may alter consumers' satisfaction with their present state of affairs.

SEARCH ACTIVITY

Problem recognition is followed by search activity. The objective of search activity is to identify and familiarize oneself with the courses of action available to solve the perceived problem. A patient who was advised by a physician to exercise daily may look at alternative fitness-equipment choices, such as a treadmill, Step Master, rowing machine, or Nordic-Track. Later in the decision process, a consumer will examine the relative merits of the various options and contemplate the consequences of selecting one of them.

The amount of search activity undertaken varies greatly from casual to systematic, based on a number of factors such as the importance of the problem, the urgency of the purchase, the degree of involvement with the product or service, and the availability of such alternatives.[12] For example, a consumer who discovered a dandruff problem may do nothing more to find a solution than consider the experience of friends or family members who had a similar problem. On the other hand, a novice investor in the stock market may spend a great deal of time and effort to learn about the various companies listed on the NASDAQ.

TYPES OF SEARCH

Information search can be internal, external, or a combination. An internal search entails scanning one's memory for product-related information, and an external search involves physical (and perhaps mental) efforts to solicit and gather information from outside sources.

Internal Search

Internal search is the mental activity of retrieving information that has been stored in long-term memory and deals with products or services that can help an individual solve a problem. Past experiences, positive or negative, with products, services, stores, salespeople, or other aspects of the purchase situation as well as ads or conversations with friends may be recalled. Consumers may recollect previous experiences such as how nicely they were treated by a waitress at a particular restaurant, how wonderful the entrées were, and how delicious the desserts tasted.

Consumers' memory structure has profound implications to marketers. Because of the extensive amount of sensory stimulation that strikes the consumer almost daily, sharpening and leveling, both simplification strategies, take place. Sharpening is a process of changing stimuli from ambiguous forms to more conventional ones as people attempt to make a complex situation consistent with preexisting simple schemas. Sharpening deals with encoding and categorizing redundant or confusing information into chunks that are meaningful to a person. For example, we often hear people say that they take Centrum vitamins daily to enhance

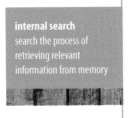

internal search
search the process of retrieving relevant information from memory

sharpening
a process of changing stimuli from ambiguous forms to more conventional ones

their health and vigor. Similarly, because of the numerous attributes of a product such as a headache remedy (pain relieving, gentle, fast acting, easy to swallow, long lasting, etc.), people use sharpening as a shortcut to abbreviate the product selection process. Evidence points to the fact that as consumers become familiar with a product category, they tend to evaluate the alternatives in it by *brand* rather than by *attributes*, and they tend to make more global evaluations of brands.[13] In the headache remedy example, a consumer may simply select a well-known brand such as Excedrin for headaches and another like Bayer for colds.

Leveling, on the other hand, is a process of generalization, wherein details are omitted in order to simplify the memory structure. Leveling also occurs when information about one object can be transferred or generalized to another object. For example, the generic term "hybrid cars" has been used to indicate energy-saving vehicles regardless of their make or model.[14]

Sharpening and leveling often promote brand loyalty and hinder the marketing efforts of a newcomer into a product category. From the perspective of the consumer, making global evaluations based on *brand* is a preferred strategy, because it offers a shortcut compared with the effort-laden process of considering and evaluating products in terms of their attributes.

Stimulating consumers' memory is a necessity for marketers who stand to benefit from a simplified consumer evaluation process. Brand advertising, point-of-purchase materials, hang tags, store shelf talkers, kiosks, slogans, and other materials are designed to jog consumers' memories and prompt global and effortless evaluations.

External Search

External search seeks out new information through a variety of avenues that may include *market-oriented sources* such as advertising, promotional materials, packaging, and web shopping search engines; as well as *interpersonal sources*, such as talking with salespeople and peers, or email and participation in online communities, like Facebook.

The Web facilitates consumers' access to a wealth of consumption-related information. For example, Google recently surveyed the usage and behavior of U.S. consumers in regard to their smartphone habits and how the smartphone has influenced their search behavior, shopping, and response to mobile advertising.[15] The report found that 81 percent of smartphone owners used their phone to browse the Internet. Search sites proved to be the number-one type

Today, the shopping experience has been greatly simplified and enhanced as the Web has provided both the convenience and wealth of information needed for consumers to make wise choices.

© goodluz/Shutterstock.com

of website visited, accessed by 77 percent of smartphone users. Consumers turned to search sites to help them access a wide variety of information, including news (57 percent), dining (51 percent), entertainment (49 percent), shopping (47 percent), technology (32 percent), travel (31 percent), finance (26 percent), and automotive (17 percent). The survey further revealed that nine of ten smartphone searchers took action as a result of mobile search, with over half (53 percent) leading to a purchase. Search also influences other types of buyer behavior. For example, 40 percent have recommended a product or brand to others as a result of smartphone search, and 53 percent continued to research online by seeking additional information on their computers.

Further, it has been observed that consumers use Internet search in a variety of ways. They may search for information through the Internet and end up buying the product online. Alternatively, they may search the information on the Internet, but then buy the product through traditional channels. In a third case, they may search the information through traditional channels, and then buy the product online.[16]

Recognizing that consumers use search throughout the multichannel shopping process, retailers now incorporate *search marketing* into their overall multichannel strategy. Brick-and-mortar chains are realizing that they need technologists more than ever as they upgrade their web operations and compete with websites such as Amazon.com as well as other online retailers. Online sales become more important to the bottom line every year, especially as many U.S. chains continue to close stores. With ever-changing consumer lifestyles and shopping habits, physical retail stores find themselves in greater need of programmers and designers to improve websites, launch mobile apps, and integrate technology into physical stores. A 2015 survey by the Federal Reserve on consumers' use of smartphones while shopping at a store found that among smartphone owners, 47 percent used their mobile phone to comparison shop on the Internet; and 33 percent used a barcode scanning application for price comparisons. Also, the survey revealed that 31 percent scanned a quick response (QR) code in a newspaper, magazine, or billboard advertisement to obtain information about a product; and 42 percent used their phone to get product reviews or product information while shopping at the retail store. Recognizing this trend, savvy retailers such as Sephora are using mobile to deliver in-store experiences to consumers. Sephora found that its customers rely on their smartphones while shopping in the store to help them find the right products. It designed a Sephora app to assist shoppers, giving them direct access to product ratings and reviews. [17]

Researchers suggest that consumers tend to adapt and modify their external search effort to match the significance of the specific decision-making problem at hand. In this view, the research strategy for a specific decision-making problem is contingent upon a number of personal factors that characterize an individual decision maker. A study by Compete, Inc. surveyed 2 million Internet users regarding their search activity during the automobile purchase process. Approximately 70 percent of them stated that they searched the Web throughout the entire procedure. Over half of the buyers indicated that web search helped them narrow the list of vehicles they were originally considering, a procedure known as *winnowing*, and helped them evaluate the few surviving options side by side, a process known as *comparison*.[18] The four factors that appear to be significant in determining the amount of external search undertaken are:

- *Individual learning style:* Not all consumers have the same ability to explore, search, and process information. For example, novelty- and fashion-conscious consumers are likely to be passive learners, willingly accepting new things with little concern for outcomes and implications of their actions.[19]
- *Product involvement:* The higher the degree of involvement, the more likely a consumer will seek and systematically process information. For example, for most people, the decision to purchase a new automobile involves deliberate and exhaustive search for and processing of external information.

- *Experience:* Consumers facing new or unfamiliar purchase situations are likely to expend more search time and exert greater effort than experienced buyers. A novice investor in the stock market is more apt to seek advice from investment counselors than veteran investors.
- *Risk perception:* The amount of external search positively correlates with the degree of perceived risk. In general, the higher the perceived risk, the greater the time and effort expended on external search. For example, when purchasing toys or garments for children, many parents attempt to learn about their safety before purchasing. The topic of risk perception is discussed in detail at the end of Chapter 3 on Consumer Perception.

IDENTIFYING AND EVALUATING ALTERNATIVE SOLUTIONS

The third step in the consumer decision process is the evaluation of alternative resolutions to the perceived market-related problem. This process may be executed simultaneously with the search process, or it may emerge only after the consumer identifies and acquires sufficient information on the available alternatives. The goal of this step is to determine a choice set and compare the attributes of alternatives that fall within it. Two activities are involved in this evaluation process. The first is to narrow product alternatives to a manageable number. The second is to evaluate the attributes of each alternative in order to choose the best option.

Identifying Alternatives

At this point in the decision process, the consumer has a pool of alternatives that he or she has become aware of through advertising, peer influences, previous experiences, or visits to stores and websites. However, the consumer is unlikely to consider all these. More often, consumers consider a modest subset of alternatives and tend to obtain information about that restricted set of options. The small set of brands that come to mind when one contemplates buying a product is known as the evoked set. Contrary to the traditional notion that consumers engage in an effortful, systematic search for information on a large number of alternative products, recent research suggests that such incidents are rare, even when decisions involve major purchases. In most cases, consumers tend to reduce alternatives in the evoked set to a manageable number in order to save time and effort. The *consideration set* is composed of those brands the

evoked set
those few brands that come to mind when one thinks of a product category

CONSUMER BEHAVIOR IN PRACTICE

Decision-Enticing Games

The past few years have witnessed the rise of a number of skillful online sites, such as Groupon, LivingSocial, and Kgbdeals, which are designed to appeal to our desire for entertainment, recreation, and just plain having fun. A number of these sites have achieved overwhelming popularity, with Groupon being the favorite among the completing online sites.

These ingenious marketing operations employ the power of social networking both on- and offline to attract customers' business. With the use of collective buying power, these sites are able to offer significant discounts for "deals" involving any number of products or services ranging from food and beverages to trips and spas.

The secret of these sites' success rests on operators' ability to adopt four creative strategies that reflect the firms' deep understanding of consumers' psyche and how they make purchase decisions. The first strategy takes the form of creating a gamelike setting for the site. The site's homepage displays a "primary deal" with a ticking countdown timer, where the number of people who purchased is displayed on the page next to the bargain price. The user, in this case, is challenged to participate in the game by completing a "now or never" transaction. Users are induced to act promptly in order to beat the hypothetically fleeting deal, motivated by the anticipated satisfaction of landing a desirable product or service transaction at a bargain price.

The second creative strategy is based on carefully selecting products and services that are of interest to the specific user group. By following a localization approach, the product/service offer is matched with users' characteristics and interests. In this case, simplicity is further enhanced by focusing the selling effort on only a single product/service at a time. A single item, "the primary deal," takes up most of the homepage, thereby focusing users' attention on one object.

The third strategy focuses on the visual aspects of the site. Directing users' eyes to the main feature on the homepage is the key objective behind sites, the largest and brightest elements on the home-page are the title, photo, and "buy" button.

The fourth motivator in the site's strategy is the intimate feelings that users have toward the social group. Social media have magnified the sense of belonging between users of such social sites by creating a space where people feel closer to others, even though they do not know them personally. This feeling encourages users to take up activities and purchase products or services that peer group members sign up for. A sense of identification with members of one's group thus plays a significant role in prompting the choice to close the deal.

It is not surprising, therefore, to note the continued success of these sites. In this game there seems to be no losers. The three parties involved—the site, the deal provider, and the consumer—all end up as winners.[20]

Marketers have a choice between selecting traditional advertising media to promote their product/service sales or using the services of sites such as Groupon. If you knew that Groupon usually offers users significant discounts reaching up to 50 percent or more off regular prices, and further keeps a share of 50 percent of the discounted deal price (i.e., the seller ends up with only 25 percent of its regular price), how would you justify a company's decision to select this alternative? Learn more about the workings of such sites by visiting http://wheredoigetajob.com/tag/selling-groupons/. *Are the services of these sites as effective in promoting large business operations as they are in promoting small businesses? Why or why not?*

consumer would actually contemplate purchasing (such as those brands that an individual is favorably impressed with and may indeed buy).

Consumers use simple rules of thumb or heuristics to reduce the effort involved in the decision-making process. Chaiken suggests that over time, consumers attempt to automate their decisions by seeking shortcuts to the extent that their decisions become programmed.[21] For example, research has revealed that consumers under conditions of time constraint were more likely to choose (1) higher-quality, higher-priced brands; (2) higher-quality brands over low-quality brands; and (3) top-of-the-line products. One possible explanation for these time-constraint effects is that consumers used a "brand-name" heuristic. Heuristic processing entails following simple practices, such as *always buy the brand on sale, buy a well-known brand, buy the store brand, buy what the family uses, buy what a neighbor recommends, buy the most expensive model*, or other similar routines.

Marketers must ensure that their brands are included in the evoked sets of target consumers. This becomes particularly crucial at those points in time when these consumers are actually considering the purchase of brands within a particular product category. It is essential that marketers' brands be well publicized both off- and online, be made readily available both in stores that carry the product category and on their websites, and be supported with promotion, service, financing options, and warranty coverage. Such tactics are effective and necessary means to achieve brand inclusion in the consumer's evoked set.

Evaluating Alternatives

Once alternatives representing possible solutions to the perceived problem have been assembled, evaluation of these options commences in order to arrive at a choice among them. Recall that decision rules which guide this selection process can range from systematic information search (which considers many alternatives and the various attributes of each) to simple and quick choice strategies. The choice can be effort laden in the case of systematic processing or effortless in the case of heuristic processing.

In contemplating the various alternatives, consumers may focus on particular product features and ignore others. The product characteristics or features that consumers use to judge the merits of the competing options are known as the evaluative criteria. How individuals evaluate alternatives is influenced by both individual and environmental factors. In this sense, evaluative criteria become a product-specific manifestation of an

heuristics
simple rules of thumb consumers use as shortcuts to reduce shopping effort

evaluative criteria
product characteristics consumers use to judge the merits of competing options

individual's needs, values, lifestyle, and roles. Consumers employ these evaluative criteria to decide both what to buy and where to buy it.

Consumers' evaluative criteria are not static. These criteria vary from one individual to another; and in different situations, certain criteria become more important than others. For example, when eating at a fast-food restaurant, how important are criteria such as food preparation, freshness of ingredients, and speed of service to patrons? Beyond the client's goal of consuming a filling meal at a reasonable price, how do diners trade off taste versus fat content or speed versus ambiance? This understanding of how important certain criteria are to the patrons of an establishment can help the firm develop effective internal and external marketing strategies.

Some attributes upon which alternatives are evaluated are salient in nature, while others are determinant. Both types, however, affect the marketing and advertising strategies of firms. In a purchasing situation, consumers would normally consider salient attributes first. In the case of buying a new automobile, salient attributes include the vehicle's make, price, model, gas mileage, and quality ratings. However, it is the determinant attributes, such as the vehicle's color, display panel, seating capacity, comfort, roominess, and wheel design that usually determine which brand or dealership buyers frequent, especially when the alternatives are equivalent on salient attributes.[22]

Assessing the Positivity or Negativity of Alternatives

Three factors appear to impact individuals' judgment concerning the positivity or negativity of potential consequences of their decision. The first is how a person values the alternatives; the second is how a decision is framed; and the third is how the outcomes of these alternatives relate to that person's memories.

Prospect theory attempts to explain how decision makers under risk conditions value different options (prospects) and assess the positiveness or negativeness of their outcomes.[23] According to prospect theory, an individual's perceptual apparatus is attuned to the evaluation of changes or differences rather than the evaluation of absolute magnitudes. For example, an object at a given temperature may be judged as hot or cold to the touch, depending on the temperature to which one has adapted. The same principle applies to nonsensory attributes such as quality, value, and prestige. Thus, the method that a decision maker uses to evaluate the positivity or negativity of options (prospects) does not necessarily coincide with their objective or *actual* value, but rather with their *psychological* valuation.

salient attributes
important aspects of a product that affect the choices consumers make

determinant attributes
those features on which alternatives are believed to differ

prospect theory
a view of how decision makers, under risk conditions, value different options and assess their outcomes

Prospect theory explains the difference between actual and psychological valuation through the use of a *hypothetical value function*, a depiction of the relationship between the *psychological* valuation of gains and losses resulting from a course of action and the actual value of those gains and losses.

In Exhibit 8.2, the horizontal axis represents the actual value of an alternative, whereas the vertical axis represents the psychological value of that alternative. It has been observed that in decisions involving risk taking, losses loom larger than gains. In a betting situation, for example, the anguish an individual experiences in losing a sum of money appears to be greater than the pleasure associated with winning the same amount. Thus, the value function (*VL*) for losses in the graph (the lower-left quadrant of the diagram) is steeper than the value function (*VG*) for gains (the upper-right quadrant of the diagram). The graph reflects this tendency by showing that the value function for gains (*VG*) is concave above the reference point A and convex below it.

This analysis points to the conclusion that in decision-making situations that involve assumption of risk, increasing gains have decreasing psychological value. This tendency is consistent with the economic concept of diminishing marginal utility, which proposes that each additional unit of an item obtained by a consumer results in proportionately lower utility or

EXHIBIT 8.2

A Hypothetical Value Function

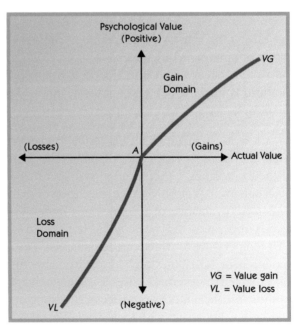

Source: Daniel Kahneman and Amos Tversky, "Prospect Theory: An Analysis of Decision Under Risk," Econometrica 47, no. 2 (March 1979), p. 229. Reprinted with permission.

satisfaction for each subsequently added unit. Conversely, in the domain of losses, additional losses are weighted more heavily than gains. For example, gamblers in the loss domain who have already squandered large sums of money are prone to take further risks to recoup losses and break even. On the other hand, a gambler in the gain domain is likely to act more conservatively, because each additional gain is perceived as having less and less psychological value.

Framing of Decisions

Prospect theory also incorporates the concept of framing, which posits that the same decision can be viewed from either a gain or a loss perspective, depending on the reference point an individual applies.[24] It is analogous to describing a drinking glass as half full or half empty. In one experiment, for example, subjects were asked to give their impressions of ground beef.[25] Identical product information was provided, but the descriptions were framed positively (75 percent lean) or negatively (25 percent fat). Ratings were taken on four scales: good–bad tasting, greasy–greaseless, high–low quality, and fat–lean. When the evaluation was framed positively, subjects rated the ground beef as significantly better tasting, less greasy, higher quality, and more lean.

Another type of framing effect can be observed in regard to price cuts and sales promotions that accomplish a similar purpose. A price reduction framed as an adjustment from a product's base price seems smaller than if it were framed from a zero point. Assume that a $100 product is reduced to $90. Outright price cuts and coupon offers usually amount to a small change in the overall appraisal of price. On the other hand, a rebate for the same amount—if perceived independently of the product's base price—would make a larger psychological impact on the consumer and represent a gain. For example, automobile pricing is often done using rebates rather than outright discounts from the original price because selling prices of $22,000 and $21,250 are not that different. By contrast, when we get a $750 rebate check in the mail, it seems as if we have gained a large sum of money compared to receiving nothing at all.

Similarly, when customers receive a free gift or an opportunity to win a prize, they would likely frame the outcome as a gain rather than a price reduction. For instance, assume a customer buys an iPhone for $600. The retailer tosses in a free phone case. In such a situation, the iPhone's case would be valued independently of the price paid for the phone. In other words, the consumer would perceive the $30 value of the phone case as a

framing
a view that a given decision can be structured from either a gain or a loss perspective

gain rather than as a reduction in the iPhone's selling price. As a consequence, the gift or prize would have greater psychological value.[26]

The time interval between a decision and the onset of gains or losses also affects perceived valuation. For instance, credit customers take immediate possession of a product and defer payment. Those who incur interest charges prefer having an item now (gain) and discount the psychological value of future payment (loss). The further into the future a cost will be experienced, the less psychological impact it tends to have.[27] Consequently, some people lose self-control when buying on credit.[28]

Linkages to Memories When consumers evaluate the possible consequences of a decision, they may recollect the outcomes of similar incidents. Linkages that a person makes between prior events and the alternatives currently under scrutiny can precipitate positive or negative evaluations of these options. For example, an athlete shopping to replace tattered sports gear may reminisce about winning or losing previous tournaments as that athlete tries on or tests out new goods. One's feelings about a brand worn or used during a winning season are likely to be positive. Conversely, brands that kindle memories of a losing season may be viewed negatively.

PURCHASE OR COMMITMENT

The purchase decision is the outcome of the search and evaluation process. As we discussed earlier, the degree of ease or difficulty associated with making a purchase commitment is a function of the financial, social, and psychological importance placed on the outcome.

Choosing Among Alternatives

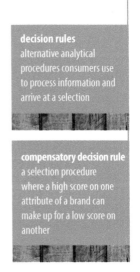

decision rules
alternative analytical procedures consumers use to process information and arrive at a selection

compensatory decision rule
a selection procedure where a high score on one attribute of a brand can make up for a low score on another

Consumers use a number of decision rules to reach a choice among alternative courses of action. These decision rules specify how consumers combine and process information in order to compare product alternatives. Decision rules can be divided into two broad categories—compensatory and noncompensatory rules. Compensatory decision rules involve simultaneously evaluating available alternatives on a number of product attributes. Such an evaluation procedure enables a high standing on one of a brand's attributes to make up for other perceived shortcomings. A car buyer may still contemplate a hybrid vehicle by Honda even though it does not offer the attractive sporty design of other alternatives, provided that the Honda hybrid does offer other features that the car shopper considers desirable, such as economy and environmental friendliness.[29]

Noncompensatory decision rules, on the other hand, evaluate alternatives one at a time, eliminating all the alternatives that fail to meet specific attribute requirements. In this evaluation procedure, a brand's high standing on some attribute cannot offset a poor standing on another attribute. A homemaker who purchases breakfast cereal for family members may eliminate any sugar-coated cereals from the evoked set, even though these sweetened cereals may be preferred by her children over other brands. Descriptions of the decision rules appear in Exhibit 8.3.

Compensatory: a high score on one attribute of a brand can make up for a low score on another

- To preserve the environment, a consumer acquires solar panels for her home, even though her investment in this technology far exceeds the cost of relying on traditional energy sources.
- A consumer patronizes a pricy department store due to the fact that the retailer supports a charitable cause that the consumer strongly endorses.
- In the search for financial security, a consumer chooses a bank's CDs offering relatively low interest rates rather than opting for the significantly higher returns offered by other more-aggressive types of investments.

Noncompensatory: a high score on one attribute of a brand cannot offset a low score on another

- In her effort to protect her children from lead poisoning, a mother refrains from purchasing reasonably priced toys made in China due to fear that the toys' paint may be tainted with lead.
- A consumer stops dining at his favorite restaurant due to perceived indifference on the part of the establishment's waiters.
- A supporter of animal rights ceases to purchase her favorite makeup from a well-known cosmetics firm upon learning that the company runs cosmetics tests on animals.

EXHIBIT 8.3

Decision Rules

The Selection Process

In selecting a product or brand from a host of competing alternatives, consumers follow a number of decision-making patterns in order to arrive at their ultimate choice. For example, they may simply select the brand or model that offers the greatest number of positive attributes. They may also arrange the attributes they desire according to their order of importance, and then select the brand that ranks the highest on the most critical features. Consumers may also use global or holistic evaluations (e.g., brand image or reputation) to determine the brand or model to be chosen from among a list of competing options. Alternatively, they may establish a minimal acceptable quality or performance standard for each attribute, and then require that the chosen brand surpasses those minima in order to be selected (e.g., seeking a house with no less than two bedrooms and a minimum of the two baths). The selection process, of course, may vary among different individuals according to their reason for purchase (e.g., for themselves or as a gift), the level of involvement (high or low consequences of the purchase), as well as how much time and effort the particular consumer is willing to spend in the selection process.

POSTPURCHASE CONSIDERATIONS

The act of purchasing does not conclude the decision-making process. For progressive marketers today, it is considered the first step toward building a coveted long-term relationship with the prospect-turned-customer. The outcome of postpurchase evaluation is a critical factor in this process. Feelings of satisfaction or dissatisfaction are instrumental in determining whether consumers will repeat the act of purchasing the brand, recommend it to others, and form positive attitudes toward the brand and the company that sponsors it.

Today, in order to establish firms as service leaders—those that offer improved customer experiences and relationships—companies are adopting the concept of customer touchpoints management (CTM). These touchpoints are the various stages constituting the totality of a customer's experiences with the firm during all interactions, human or mechanical, that occur during a customer's relationship lifecycle with the firm. This relationship spans the gambit from prospect, to buyer, to user, to repeat buyer, to a switcher or disposer, and even to a returning customer. At each one of these lifecycle touchpoint stages, the goal is to design and implement procedures and protocols whose primary objective is to attain the highest possible level of customer satisfaction. By improving customer relationships, organizations can improve market share, sales, and both customer and employee loyalty.

Swan and Combs propose that consumers evaluate products based on a limited set of attributes.[30] Some of these determinant attributes are relatively important to consumer satisfaction. Other factors, although not critical to determining satisfaction, can still relate to dissatisfaction when their performance is deemed unsatisfactory. In this regard, two facets of product performance can be identified. Instrumental performance refers to product performance as a means to a set of ends. In other words, instrumental performance involves the utilitarian performance of the physical product per se. Expressive performance, on the other hand, entails performance that a consumer considers as an end in itself. Expressive performance pertains to social or psychological attributes—that is, stylistic and self-expressive aspects of a product, rather than its functional characteristics.

Sometimes the determinant attributes for a specific purchase are the product's expressive performance rather than its instrumental performance. Nevertheless, inferior instrumental product performance may lead to consumer dissatisfaction with the purchase, even though its expressive performance happens to be superior.[31] For instance, an individual may buy a jacket because of its fashionable styling (an expressive attribute). This person may later become dissatisfied with the jacket if it fails to provide warmth, the seams tear, or the zipper breaks (instrumental attributes).

Determinants of Consumer Satisfaction

Consumer satisfaction is an attitude formed toward a purchase. Research suggests that customer satisfaction is influenced by both the level of *effort* expended by consumers and their level of *expectations*. The level of effort

instrumental performance
product performance as a means to a set of ends

expressive performance
performance that a consumer considers as an end in itself

consumer satisfaction
an attitude formed toward a purchase

The pleasant and respectful treatment customers receive from sales personnel in a store is often a major reason for consumer satisfaction with that store.

© Dragon Images/Shutterstock.com

expended mediates product evaluation and the resulting degree of satisfaction. Effort is a flexible, highly unstable, and individual yardstick. Equal amounts of effort extended by different individuals may be perceived by each as an investment or sacrifice of different magnitude and, as such, may yield different amounts of reward or satisfaction.[32]

Effort is often equated with sacrifice. Wasson asserts that every exchange in the marketplace can be viewed as a combination of some sacrifices.[33] Almost always, some relinquishing of financial resources, some loss of time in searching for the product and in consummating the purchase, and commitment to spend time and effort necessary to learn the product's use system are required. In this sense, effort can be measured in financial, physical, or mental units.

Satisfaction, on the other hand, has been described by Howard and Sheth as a mental state of feeling adequately or inadequately rewarded in a buying situation for the sacrifice a buyer has undergone.[34] Reward is meant to include not only those benefits resulting from consumption of a brand, but also any other satisfactions received in the purchasing and consuming process.

GLOBAL OPPORTUNITY

Fast-Food Rulers in China

As U.S. fast-food chains look toward foreign markets for growth, they face a typical decision-making question concerning which fast-food model to employ abroad. The issue centers around whether a chain should follow its U.S. model and offer its core products much like it does at home, or alternatively, whether it should adapt its organization and offerings to suit the local tastes of residents in the host country. The answer to the question concerning which of these two philosophies is "right" presents a dilemma to managers of fast-food organizations in their efforts to expand globally. Consider two success stories: those of KFC and McDonald's in China.

The first case involves the Yum Corporation. In 1987, when Yum brands, the holding company of KFC and Pizza Hut, faced falling revenues in the United States, it started to investigate the possibility of expanding overseas. Location studies at that time revealed that China was a promising market due to its sheer size and large expanding population. By entering that market, Yum realized that due to distinct local taste preferences, the company needed to adapt its product offerings to local palates and lifestyles. The menus, therefore, were reconfigured to add dishes similar to the foods that millions of Chinese grab from street-stall restaurants. Food items such as a bowl of congee (a rice porridge), a dragon twister (a chicken wrap), or a spicy tofu chicken rice were added to the usual fried chicken bucket menu items. The company hired Chinese managers for advice on food tastes, built partnerships with local companies, and trained other Chinese to operate the new branches that the company continued to add almost daily. The company, in 2015, commanded a 40 percent market share of China's $121.7 billion fast-food market. Starting with just a single restaurant in 1987, Yum now operates 5,003 KFCs in 650 Chinese cities. McDonald's, on the other hand, which is a competitor in fast-food industry in China, holds a 16 percent market share. Unlike KFC's policy of menu adaptation to suit local tastes, McDonald's opted to follow the same core strategy used in the United States by offering its familiar menu items. The restaurants' layout, décor, and atmosphere also followed the familiar format used at home. In this manner, McDonald's franchises were marketed as sophisticated venues for legions of increasingly affluent and status-conscious Chinese, who seek to emulate the admired American way of life.

To maintain this image, McDonald's restaurants feature bright, warm colors along with soft, comfortable seating within fashionable interiors. In addition, new restaurants feature drive-through facilities to appeal to China's increasingly mobile population. Over the next five years, McDonald's plans to add more than 1,000 restaurants in China (that is, 250 restaurants per year). In March 2016, McDonald's operated more than 2,200 restaurants.[35]

The depiction of both KFC and McDonald's reveals contrasting cases for global executives seeking to determine which business model should be followed in an emerging market. Should the home-base model be kept intact, modified, or discarded altogether? Such a decision is obviously a correlate between three main factors: the product, the host country, and the management philosophy. Learn more about KFC and McDonald's by visiting http://hbr.org/2011/11/kfcs-radical-approach-to-china/ar/pr *and* http://www.reuters.com/assets/print?aid=USTRE-6BE0VJ20101215. *Which of these two alternative strategies would you suggest for a fast-food company pursuing global expansion in India? Similarly, which of these two strategies would you suggest for Campbell's Soup Company in Canada? Support your answers.*

As mentioned earlier, customer satisfaction is an evaluative judgment related to the level of consumer *expectations* rather than to *actual* product performance. Satisfaction is a function of the discrepancy or contrast between obtained and expected outcomes. If expectations are high and performance falls below one's expectations, dissatisfaction arises. If, on the other hand, actual performance meets or exceeds expectations, the consumer is delightfully pleased. Consequently, a major concern of many marketers today is the ability to create realistic consumer impressions in order to avert disappointment due to elevated expectations. For example, auto manufacturers in the United States continue to express concern over how long it will take public perceptions to catch up with objective improvements in the industry. Similarly, airlines engaged in reducing service levels to control costs long for a quick match between passengers' expectations and the reduced service level necessitated by these cost-reduction measures.

The promotional strategy used by a firm and the claims it makes can influence the level of formed expectations. Overstated product claims raise very high expectations. A recent Federal Express ad promised users of the firm's services second business day delivery to Europe. Such promises produce expectations of very high service quality. If actual experience with the service is disconfirmed, the resulting consumer dissatisfaction would most likely be higher than it would have been had the claims not been made. On the other hand, slightly understating product claims may in fact lead to higher satisfaction. Understated product claims generate moderate expectations that can then be surpassed by actual product performance and lead to a higher level of satisfaction.

CONSUMER COMPLAINT INTENTIONS AND BEHAVIOR

Even a single dissatisfied consumer means a loss to an organization. Customer dissatisfaction is of great concern to marketers because it is more cost effective to keep existing customers than try to win new ones. Dissatisfaction is a potential source of negative word-of-mouth communication. For example, today a dissatisfied consumer may post a petition on a website such as Change.org, watch it quickly rack up thousands of signatures, and force the company to correct a situation or even change a policy. Today, customer service has become one of the major concerns of business firms. Social media has both driven and ushered the dramatic change in the ways customers and businesses interact. Customers now demand a high level of speed, convenience, and transparency—factors that placed social media as an essential component of businesses' customer service strategies.

Displeased customers have a variety of social media types, such as Facebook and Twitter on their side, to air their frustrations in dealing with businesses. In addition to individual efforts to publicize their grievances, a number of sites such as Gripevine.com, wacktrap.com, and yelp.com offer assistance in widely disseminating customer complaints. Gripevine.com, for instance, which provides a mobile app for the iPhone, makes effortless the task of posting a complaint simultaneously to one's Facebook friends and Twitter followers. According to company executives' estimates, the complaint message reaches in excess of a startling 1,644,483 people. In this case, a consumer's gripe goes to Facebook, Twitter, and to the named company's customer service department. The firm is invited to remedy the problem, and would earn a viral "cheer" for having done so.[36] Wacktrap. com, on the other hand, is a social network built around sharing and exchanging complaints and life experiences. The site enables customers of any firm to connect and directly communicate over similar experiences in order to find solutions to company-related customer service issues. Other customer protection entities include the Bureau of Consumer Protection (a branch of the FTC), Consumer Protection Agency, Consumer Financial Protection Bureau, as well as various state consumer protection offices.[37]

In a recent survey conducted by SmartBrief on Social Media, which tracked feedback from leading marketers regarding social media practices and issues, respondents' views revealed the following:

- 34.5 percent indicated that social media forces companies to respond, follow up, and resolve complaints immediately.
- 31 percent felt that social media increases awareness of consumer complaints.
- 17.7 percent reported that while registering complaints in social media can elicit a quick response, doing so does not necessarily result in a prompt resolution of the issue.
- Over 13.2 percent stated that social media gives consumers more control over their messages.[38]

Consumers today are cognizant of the fact that companies are becoming more proactive in monitoring online communication on blogs, social networks, and forums. They believe, as a result, that complaints appearing in social media platforms are given more attention by company executives due to their potentially damaging effect on a firm's reputation, if those grievances are not resolved in a timely manner.

Many firms today have started to look at complaints as an opportunity rather than as a liability.[39] The value of complaints lies in their ability to reveal to the firm what consumers do and do not want. An effective complaint handling system is vital today in view of the emphasis on customer service quality. Such systems should allow for both prompt handling of individual complaints and for aggregate complaint analysis.[40]

Research has shown that negative emotion decays slowly. However, by providing factual, objective, and counter-attitudinal information from credible sources (such as positive word of mouth, blogs on the Internet, and testimony from expert sources like *Consumer Reports* magazine), attitudes may change in the direction of the new information and lessen the likelihood of negative behavior.

MEASUREMENT STANDARDS FOR CUSTOMER SATISFACTION

A number of measures were recently developed by academic and business entities that are designed to capture consumers' attitudes (likes/dislikes) toward a brand or establishment. These measurements basically reflect an appraisal on how a product's or firm's performance compare against consumers' expectations (exceed or fell short of expectations). Among these are the following measurements:

- American Customer Satisfaction Index (ACSI) is a scientific standard of customer satisfaction. ACSI scores reflect and predict loyalty and word-of-mouth communication, as well as purchase and repurchase intentions. It has been used to measure customer satisfaction annually for more than 200 companies in forty-three industries and ten economic sectors. Two companies, CFI Group and Foresee Results, have been licensed to apply the methodology of the ACSI for both the private and public sectors.[41]
- The Kano Model is a measure of customer satisfaction developed by Professor Noriaki Kano. It classifies customer preferences into five categories: Attractive, One-Dimensional, Must-Be, Indifferent, and Reserve. The model sheds light on the product attributes in terms of which attributes are perceived as important to consumers and which are not.
- SERVQUAL or RATTER is a service-quality framework that has been incorporated into customer satisfaction surveys. It is mainly used to reveal a gap between customer expectations and their actual experience with a product or an establishment.

- J.D. Power and Associates constructed a popular measure of customer satisfaction, which is known for its ratings and rankings of prestigious companies and brands, including the automotive industry. The company's market research consists primarily of consumer surveys and is publicly known for the value of its product awards.
- Other research companies involved in either consumer or business-to-business surveys are also available. These include A.T. Kearney's Customer Satisfaction Audit process for consumer related product/companies, as well as InfoQuest box for business-to-business studies.[42]

TO WHOM DO CONSUMERS COMPLAIN?

Consumers can direct their complaints to a variety of places. Individual consumers can circulate complaints by posting them onto a company's Facebook page, Twitter account, or other popular forums monitored by businesses. Alternatively, they can use the services of social networks such as Gripevine.com and wacktrap.com mentioned earlier. Another possibility is to go even further and organize petitions on a website such as Change.org and have thousands of consumers sign on to the cause. In addition, consumers can submit their complaints directly to firms' customer service departments, state agencies (such as the state attorney's office), the Federal Trade Commission, the mass media, credit card companies, and the Better Business Bureau (BBB).[43]

Firms need to assemble all dissatisfied customers' complaints, wherever consumers may have directed them. The company's customer service department or web-based service center is a logical starting point. In the case of third-party complaints made against the firm to other entities, such as virally to the fore-mentioned websites, to state agencies, the Better Business Bureau, the FTC, the media, or credit card companies, extra effort is required to locate and diligently address them. Such complaints are especially important because they are potentially more damaging to the firm's reputation than those addressed directly to the firm. Negative publicity in the conventional and social media, legal actions against the firm, or charge-backs from credit card companies as a result of third-party complaints place the firm in a compromising position.[45]

ETHICAL DILEMMA

Congratulations . . . You Have Won a Dream Vacation

The tourism industry is one of the largest in the United States, serving the recreational, leisure, and business needs of millions of domestic and foreign travelers. In 2015, the industry made a total contribution of $1.5 trillion to the gross domestic product (GDP), and is forecast to contribute more than $2.5 trillion by the year 2025.

A frugal attitude that has prevailed over the past few years has led many travel service marketers, such as tour operators, airlines, and hospitality and leisure industries, to slash prices in order to stimulate travelers to take action. Consumers have received offers known as "flash sales," which are unsolicited emails promoting rock-bottom leisure travel deals.

In this vast and somewhat perplexing environment, a number of fraudulent travel clubs and operators have found conditions ripe for offering deceptive vacation packages, designed to lure unsuspecting victims. A number of such schemes are involved. One of these entails the use of consumers' business cards or names that have been unsuspectingly placed into a drawing for a free vacation. Alternatively, names can be lifted from a list of frequent travelers. These consumers receive notices from such operators congratulating them on "winning" a fabulous vacation for a very attractive price. All they are asked to do is to immediately "secure" or "register" the vacation with a major credit card, make a deposit, and select the preferred travel dates. The dream trip, however, turns out to be a complete fabrication, due to many hard-to-meet rules or hidden and expensive conditions that a person's schedule cannot accommodate.

A second deceptive scheme uses the allure of "all-inclusive" discount packages to get buyers to take the bait. The surprise occurs later, when consumers realize that they are expected to pay exorbitant prices for "uncovered" parts of the deal, such as extra airfare or hotel charges, handling, membership, and processing fees, or expensive charges for upgrades.

A third format for these so-called "deals" is found in the sphere of timeshare sales. Consumers are led to believe they've won a great vacation at a rock-bottom price. Once consumers reach their destination, however, they are required to spend a large part of their vacation trapped listening to lengthy, high-pressure sales pitches concerning the benefits of investing in time-share properties.

Similarly, students during spring breaks often sign up and pay for vacation packages offered by low-cost operators. The companies that offer these "deals" normally use charter flights, which are not covered by the same laws that govern commercial airlines. Charter flights can be cancelled for any reason by the operator, leaving students in many cases stranded at airports. Furthermore, the travel agency's contract often includes a clause stating that their agent has the right to postpone the departure flight by as many as three days without providing any advance notice to travelers.

To add to the misfortune of victims of such scams, attempts to cancel the trip are flatly met with a typical "no-refund policy" statement, leaving the consumer with no recourse. Perhaps learning the vocabulary of such operators, verification of arrangements before making payment, and checking an agent's service record are sound steps we as consumers can take to avoid becoming victims of fraudulent operators.[44]

Although there is truth to these incidents of scams conducted by some unscrupulous travel operators and telemarketers, there are many other reputable companies that provide quality vacation packages at reasonable prices. Today, distinguishing the good from the bad rests with travelers themselves. Learn how to protect yourself against scams by visiting the FTC website http://www.ftc.gov/bcp/edu/pubs/consumer/telemarketing/tel11.shtm and discover what others are saying about any travel company by visiting the TrustLink website at http://www.trustlink.org/Ask-The-Community/Question/Business/IS-THIS-A-SCAM-1854. Because the role of protecting against such scams rests with the consumer, would you recommend increasing the role of the government in identifying and prosecuting fraudulent operators? If so, what could and should the government do to halt public deception efforts?

WHAT CAN BE DONE?

Most consumer-oriented firms today take matters of customer disputes and complaints seriously and make systematic efforts to learn the degree of consumer satisfaction or dissatisfaction with their products and services. Since most online firms establish web-based customer service centers to deal with customer comments and complaints, experience has shown that the major causes of online customer complaints are the unsatisfactory responses provided by these centers.

To improve these centers' operations, progressive online firms today establish technologically advanced customer service centers, referred to as *web-enabled customer contact centers*, which provide online chat services to the firm's customers and include efficient customer self-help centers, or a combination of several customer communication channels. Further, to overcome delayed responses to customers, firms like www.neimanmarcus.com now offer real-time customer service.

Another inexpensive method used to facilitate complaint handling is a toll-free consumer hotline that offers consumers a way to air their disputes. They encourage dissatisfied consumers to conveniently voice their concerns rather than become angry and cease to purchase the brand altogether. Customers whose problems are promptly brought to satisfactory resolutions are likely to be pleased and continue to be loyal customers.[46]

A third way to handle customer complaints is to establish consumer affairs offices. These offices, headed by a top-level executive of the firm, are assigned responsibility for collecting complaints, analyzing their nature, contacting complainants, suggesting corrective actions, and following up with the suggested solutions. In some firms, consumer affairs offices are given responsibility for *aggregate complaint analysis*, which tracks complaints based on numbers, trends, and major sources of dissatisfaction. This type of analysis allows firms to establish complaint benchmarks against which they monitor the effectiveness of service quality over time. In some instances, this department also conducts periodic surveys to ascertain customer attitudes.[47]

Consumer education programs constitute a fourth method employed by some firms to reduce the occurrence of consumer complaints. The philosophy behind this method is the proposition that knowledge is a vital ingredient in forming expectations. Because consumer expectations are the

basis for their satisfaction or dissatisfaction, knowledge enhances awareness and thus influences expectations. Some pharmaceutical companies,
for example, go beyond the requirements of the law and make an extra
effort to publicize the negative side effects of their medications in order
to influence consumer expectations. Such knowledge can be disseminated
through advertising (pamphlets and package inserts), speakers, ads, and
videos.

In the last six chapters, we have examined in detail the way consumers
perceive, learn and remember, form attitudes, and come to need and
want. We have also investigated how consumers' personalities, lifestyles,
and self-concepts influence what they choose to buy. In addition, we have
studied how consumers process information and seek solutions to their
problems. However, consumer behavior does not occur in a vacuum. We
exist in the context of a larger population, where our actions are influenced
by others around us. From the very moment of our birth, we are subject
to social factors that play a major role in shaping our values, aspirations,
and purchasing patterns. In the remaining chapters, we cover such topics
as group, family, and personal influences, social class, and culture. We also
investigate the role of marketing communication in enhancing the spread
of innovations across a society. Herein lies its important role in the diffusion process. Diffusion is the process by which a new idea—be it a product
or service, a practice, or a belief—spreads throughout the marketplace.
The topic of diffusion is covered in the next chapter.

SUMMARY

This chapter deals with the decision-making process. It starts with a discussion of the degrees of cognitive effort that are employed by consumers in the decision-making process. These efforts can range from significant to minimal, depending on whether a decision is nonprogrammed or programmed. Some nonprogrammed decisions—such as those that are financially, socially, or psychologically important—occur after intense deliberation and cognitive effort. Some nonprogrammed decisions entail limited problem solving on the part of consumers, because buyers have some prior experience with the product. Still other nonprogrammed purchases are impulsive. Programmed decisions are usually made with little or no cognitive effort, such as when consumers have become loyal to a particular brand.

Dewey identified five stages of the consumer decision process. Specifically applied to the study of consumer behavior, these stages are (1) problem recognition, (2) search activity, (3) identifying and evaluating alternatives, (4) purchase or commitment, and (5) postpurchase considerations.

In the problem-recognition stage, marketers attempt to establish conscious awareness of a problem. If consumers become cognizant of a problem that can be lessened or eliminated through purchase behavior, the second stage—search activity—begins. Search can be either internal (consumers draw from information stored in memory) or external (consumers visit stores, speak to salespersons, and read promotional materials as well as package information). Several factors influence the extent of search activity, such as consumers' learning style, product involvement, experience, and risk perception.

Once consumers acquire needed information, the evaluation stage emerges. Consumers narrow down the number of product alternatives they actually consider to a manageable number. Various heuristics or simple rules of thumb may be used to reduce the effort one expends. Consumers may evaluate both the salient and determinant attributes of each alternative under serious consideration. They may also contemplate the potential outcome (positive or negative) of selecting a particular option. In this regard, prospect theory is discussed, including concepts such as the hypothetical value function, framing, and linkages to past memories.

In the process of choosing a particular alternative, consumers may apply various compensatory and noncompensatory decision rules by which they compare alternatives and arrive at a selection.

The act of committing to a particular alternative—purchasing—does not terminate the decision-making process, because postpurchase considerations arise. The satisfaction or dissatisfaction consumers experience from their product choice largely relates to the product's instrumental or expressive performance, the amount of effort or resources consumers expend to obtain the product, and consumers' level of product expectations.

It is more cost effective for marketers to satisfy and retain existing customers than to try to win new ones. Dissatisfied consumers are a potential source of negative word of mouth. Many firms now view complaints as valuable feedback about what consumers do and do not want. Well-handled complaints may alter consumers' final disposition toward the complaint encounter in a positive direction. Because consumers may complain via the social media as well as to firms' customer service departments, web-based service centers, state agencies, the FTC, the mass media, credit card companies, and the BBB, firms must assemble complaints, wherever customers may have directed them, to avert negative publicity or even the possibility of a boycott.

CASE SYNOPSIS

An Inquiry into the College Choice Process

Recent changes taking place in our society today, including the rise in student debt and failure of many students to graduate in four years, have raised major concerns among college administrators regarding future trends of student enrollment. This case reports on a meeting between the admissions director at a well-known Ivy League school and her staff to assess the decision-making process that students pass through in arriving at their final choice of a school. Other factors considered by the committee included published statistics on the expected number of students graduating from high school in upcoming years, the share of these planning to go on to college, and the rise of the population within the traditional college age range of eighteen to twenty-four years. A major component of the discussion, however, was analyzing and understanding the issue of how today's students go about making a college-choice decision. Such understanding would help schools design strategies to attract future enrollees.

Notes

1   Maarten Vos and Amy Cuddy, "A Counter-intuitive Approach to Making Complex Decisions," *Harvard Business Review* (May 16, 2011), http://blogs.hbr.org/cs/2011/05/a_counter-intuitive_approach_t.html; Society for Neuroscience, "Decision-Making," *SFN Brain Briefings,* (October 2009), http://www.sfn.org/index.aspx?pagename=brainBriefings_09_decisionmaking&print-on; Sheena Iyenger, "*The Art of Choosing,*" *Abacus* (July 2011); and Joanne Cantor, Ph.D., *Conquer Cyber Overload* (Cantor Books, 2011).

2   Paul J. H. Schoemaker, "The Expected Utility Model: Its Variants, Purposes, Evidence and Limitations," *Journal of Economic Literature* 20 (June 1982), pp. 529–563.

3   Verena Veneeva, "Consumers' Decision Making-Preeminent Tool to Analyze Consumer Behaviour," *Ezine Articles,* http://ezinearticles.com/?Consumers-Decision-Making-Preeminent-Tool-to-Analyze-Con. . .

4   "What Causes Consumers to Buy on Impulse? User Interface Engineering: E-commerce white paper," www.*uie.com/publications/whi.*

5   "The Truth About Impulse Buying," *C&E Vision's Industry News Feed—Marketing Practice Management* (March 14, 2011), http://blog.isurf,info/?p=2727; Donald Black, "A Review of Compulsive Buying Disorder," *World Psychiatry* (February 2007), http://www.ncbi.nlm.nih.gov/pme/articles/PMC1805733/.

6   Helen Liggatt, "Women Are Likely to Impulse Buy Online," *BizReport* (December 10, 2007), http://www.bizreport.com/2007/12/women_more likely to impulse buy online.html.

7   John W. Payne, James R. Bettman, and E. J. Johnson, "Behavioral Decision Research: A Constructive Processing Perspective," *Annual Review of Psychology* 4 (1992), pp. 87–131.

8   Judith Lynne Zaichkowsky, "The Personal Involvement Inventory: Reduction, Revision, and Application to Advertising," *Journal of Advertising 23, no. 4* (December 1994), pp. 59–70; Edward F. McQuarrie and J. Michael Munson, "A Revised Product Involvement Inventory: Improved Usability and Validity," in John F. Sherry Jr. and Brian Sternthal (Eds.), *Advances in Consumer Research* 19 (Provo, UT: Association for Consumer Research, 1992), pp. 108–115; William C. Rodgers and Kenneth C. Schneider, "An Empirical Evaluation of the Kapferer-Laurent Involvement Profile Scale," *Psychology & Marketing* 10, no. 4 (July–August 1993), pp. 333–345; Deborah J. MacInnis, Christine Moorman, and Bernard J. Jaworski, "Enhancing and Measuring Consumer's Motivation, Opportunity, and Ability to Process Brand Information from Ads," *Journal of Marketing* (October 1991), pp. 332–353; J. Craig Andrews, Srinivas Durvasula, and Syed H. Akhter, "A Framework for Conceptualizing and Measuring the Involvement Construct in Advertising Research," *Journal of Advertising* (December 1990), pp. 27–40; Sharon Shavitt, Suzanne Swan, Tina M. Lowrey, and Michaela Wanke, "The Interaction of Endorser Attractiveness and Involvement in Persuasion Depends on the Goal that Guides Message Processing," *Journal of Consumer Psychology* 2 (1994), pp. 137–162.

9   Richard L. Celsi and Jerry C. Olsen, "The Role of Involvement in Attention and Comprehension Processes," *Journal of Consumer Research* 15 (September 1988), pp. 210–224; Marsha L. Richins, Peter H. Bloch, and Edward F. McQuarrie, "How Enduring and Situational Involvement Combine to Create Involvement Responses," *Journal of Consumer Psychology* 1 (September 1992), pp. 143–154.

10 Dennis W. Rook and Robert J. Fisher, "Normative Influences on Impulsive Buying Behavior," *Journal of Consumer Research* 22 (December 1995), pp. 305–313; Francis Piron, "Defining Impulse Purchasing," in Rebecca H. Holman and Michael R. Solomon (Eds.), *Advances in Consumer Research* 18 (Provo, UT: Association For Consumer Research, 1991), pp. 509–514.

11 John Dewey, *How We Think (Boston:* D. C. Heath, 1910), ch. 8.

12 Gordon C. Bruner II, "The Effect of Problem-Recognition Style on Information Seeking," *Journal of the Academy of Marketing Science* 15 (Winter 1987), pp. 33–41.

13 James R. Bettman and C. Whan Park, "Effects of Prior Knowledge and Experience and Phase of Choice Process on Consumer Decision Processes: A Protocol Analysis," *Journal of Consumer Research* 7 (December 1980), pp. 234–248; Philip A. Dover and Jerry C. Olsen, "Dynamic Changes in an Expectancy-Value Attitude Model as a Function of Multiple Exposures to Product information," in Barnett A. Greenberg and Danny N. Bellenger (Eds.), *Contemporary Marketing Thought* (Chicago; American Marketing Association, 1977), pp. 455–460; Jacob Jacoby, Robert W. Chestnut, and William A. Fisher, "A Behavioral Process Approach to Information Acquisition in Nondurable Purchasing," *Journal of Marketing Research* 15 (November 1978), pp. 532–544.

14 Peter R. Dickson and Alan G. Sawyer, "The Price Knowledge and Search of Supermarket Shoppers," *Journal of Marketing* 54 (July 1990), pp. 42–53.

15 Leena Rao, "Google Survey: 39 Percent of Smart Phone Owners Use Their Devices in the Bathroom," *TechCrunch,* (April 26, 2011), http://techcrunch.com/2011/04/26/google-survey-39-percent-of-smartphone-owners-use-t...

16 Byeong-Joon Moon, "Consumer Adoption of the Internet as an Information Search and Product Purchase Channel: Some Research Hypotheses," *International Journal of Internet Marketing and Advertising* 1, no. 1 (2004).

17 "How Mobile Phones Affect Shopping Behavior," Federal Reserve (March 2015), http://www.federalreserve.gov/econresdata/mobile-devices/2015-how-mobile-phones-affect-shopping-behavior.htm; "How Consumers are Using Their Smart Phones in Stores," Google, (2015), https://www.thinkwithgoogle.com/articles/how-digital-connects-shoppers-to-local-stores.html; Leena Rao, "Google Survey: 39 Percent of Smart Phone Owners Use Their Devices in the Bathroom," *TechCrunch* (April 26, 2011), http://techcrunch.com/2011/04/26/google-survey-39-percent-of-smart-phone-owners-use-t. . .

18 Yahoo and Compete, Inc., "Find Internet Search Plays Key Role in Automotive Research and Purchase Decisions," *Yahoo Media Relations,* http://docs.yahoo.com/docs/pr/release1264.html.

19   Elizabeth K. Sproles and George B. Sproles, "Consumer Decision-Making Styles as a Function of Individual Learning Styles," *The Journal of Consumer Affairs* 24, no. 1 (1990), p. 145.

20   Todd W., "Understanding Groupon and How It Can Help Your Business," *Where Do I Get a Job?* (July 26, 2011), http://wheredoigetajob.com/tag/selling-groupons/.

21   Shelley Chaiken, "The Heuristic Model of Persuasion," in M. P, Zanna, J. M. Olson, and C. P. Herman (Eds.), *Social Science: The Ontario Symposium* 5 (Hillside NJ: Lawrence Erlbaum, 1986).

22   Stephen M. Nowlis and Itamar Simonson, "Attribute-Task Compatibility as a Determinant of Consumer Preference Reversals," *Journal of Marketing Research* 34, no. 2 (1997), pp. 205–218.

23   Daniel Kahneman and Amos Tversky, "Prospect Theory: An Analysis of Decision Under Risk," *Econometrica* 47, no. 2 (March 1979), pp. 263–291.

24   Alice A. Wright and Richard J. Lutz, "Effects of Advertising and Experience on Brand Judgments: A Rose by Any Other Name," in Leigh McAlister and Michael L. Rothschild (Eds.), *Advances in Consumer Research* 20 (Provo, UT: Association for Consumer Research, 1992), pp. 165–169; Donald J. Hempel and Harold Z. Daniel, "Framing Dynamics; Measurement Issues and Perspectives," in Leigh McAlister and Michael L. Rothschild (Eds.), *Advances in Consumer Research* 20 (Provo, UT: Association for Consumer Research, 1992), pp. 273–279.

25   Irwin Levin, "Associative Effects of Information Framing," *Bulletin of the Psychonomic Society* 25 (1987), pp. 85–86.

26   William D. Diamond and Abhijit Sanyal, "The Effects of Framing on the Choice of Supermarket Coupons," in Marvin E. Goldberg and Gerald Gorn (Eds.), *Advances in Consumer Research* 17 (Provo, UT: Association for Consumer Research, 1990), pp. 488–493; John Mowen, Alan Gordon, and Clifford Young, "The Impact of Sales Taxes on Store Choice: Public Policy and Theoretical Implications," *Proceedings of Summer Educators' Conference* (Chicago: American Marketing Association, 1988).

27   John C. Mowen and Maryanne M. Mowen, "Time and Outcome Valuation: Implications for Marketing Decision Making," *Journal of Marketing* (October 1991), pp. 54–62; Joan Meyers-Levy and Durairaj Maheswaran, "When Timing Matters: The Influence of Temporal Distance of Consumers' Affective and Persuasive Responses," *Journal of Consumer Research* 19 (December 1992), pp. 424–433.

28   Stephen J. Hock and George F. Lowenstein, "Time-Inconsistent Preferences and Consumer Self-Control," *Journal of Consumer Research* 17 (March 1991), pp. 492–507.

29   C. Whan Park, "The Effect of Individual and Situation-Related Factors on Consumer Selection of Judgmental Models," *Journal of Marketing Research* 13 (May 1976), pp. 144–151.

30   J. E. Swan and L. J. Combs, "Product Performance and Consumer Satisfaction: A New Concept," *Journal of Marketing* 40 (April 1976), pp. 25–33.

31 J. E. Swan and L. J. Combs, "Product Performance and Consumer Satisfaction: A New Concept," *Journal of Marketing* 40 (April 1976), pp. 25–33.

32 Nessim Hanna, "Can Effort/Satisfaction Theory Explain Price/Quality Relationships?" *Journal of the Academy of Marketing Science* 6, no. I (Winter 1978), pp. 91–100.

33 C. R. Wasson, *Consumer Behavior: A Managerial Viewpoint* (Austin, TX: Austin Press, 1975), p. 256.

34 J. A. Howard and J. Sheth, *The Theory of Buyer Behavior* (New York: John Wiley, 1967).

35 Subrat Patnaik, "McDonald's to Add More Than 1,000 Outlets in China" (March 31, 2016), http://www.reuters.com/article/us-mcdonalds-china-idUSKCNOWX16M; "Fast-Food Restaurants in China: Market Research Report," *IBIS World* (October 2015), http://www.ibisworld.com/industry/china/fast-food-restaurants.html; Adam Minter, "Fast Food Loses Its Sizzle in China," *Bloomberg View* (October 22, 2015), http://www.bloombergview.com/articles/2015-10-22/u-s-fast-food-chains-lose-their-sizzle-in-china; Laurie Barkett, "China Isn't the Easy Market It Once Was for Fast-Food Chains," *The Wall Street Journal* (October 20, 2015), http://www.wsj.com/article/china-isnt-the-easy-market-it-once-was-for-fast-food-chains-1445359105; Maggie Starvish, "KFC's Explosive Growth in China," *Harvard Business School Working Knowledge* (June 17, 2011), http://hbswk.hbs.edu/cgi-bin/print/6704.html; William Mellor, "McDonald's No Match for KFC in China as Colonel Rules Fast Food," *Bloomberg Business Week* (June 28, 2011), http://www.bloomberg.com/news/print/201l-01-26/mcdonald-s-no-match-for-kfc-in-china; "Kentucky Fried Chicken Banks on China," *The New York Times* (May 5, 2008), http://www.nytimes.com/2008/05/05/business/worldbusiTiess/05iht-kfc, 1.l2567957,html?p...

36 Randall Stross, "Consumer Complaints Made Easy, Maybe Too Easy," *The New York Times* (May 28, 2011), http://www.nytimes.com/20ll/05/29/technology/29digi.html?_r=1&pagewanted=print; "Gripevine.com Launches First Social Media Network for Consumer Complaint Resolution," *Yahoo Finance* (February 6, 2012), http://finance.yahoo.com/news/gripevine-com-launches-first-social-150000282.html.

37 Joe Manna, "5 Ways to Complain Through Social Media" (May 12, 2010), https://blog.joemanna.com/5-ways-to-complain-through-social-media/; "Network Making Consumer Complaints Social Has Customers Talking about the Company They Keep," *PR Web* (February 29, 2012), http://www.prweb.com/releases/20l2/2/prweb9213550.htm.

38 Mirna Bard, "Does Social Media Affect Consumer Complaints?" *Smart Brief Jobs* (January 5, 2011), http://smartblogs.com/social--media/2011/01/05/does-social-media-affect-consumer-complai..,

39 Sweta Chaturvedi Thota, "Do Consumers Hold Grudges and Practice Avoidance Forever?" *Journal of Consumer Satisfaction, Dissatisfaction, and Complaining Behavior* (January 2006), http://findarticles.com/p/articles/mi_qa5516/is_200601/ai_n21406176/print.

40 John A. Schibrowsky and Richard S. Lapidus, "Gaining Competitive Advantage by Analyzing Aggregate Complaints," *Journal of Consumer Marketing* 11, no. 1 (1994), pp. 15–26.

41 Alexander Serenko, "Student Satisfaction with Canadian Music Program," *Assessment and Evaluation in Higher Education* (2010), p. 35.

42 Kevin Dow et. al, "Antecedents and Consequences of User Satisfaction with E-mail Systems," *International Journal of E-Collaboration* 2, no. 2 (2006), pp. 46–64.

43 "Complaint Procedure Assists in Resolutions," *Chicago Sun-Times (Special Advertising Supplement)* (October 27, 1996), p. E7.

44 "FLA.tourism industry sees modest growth in 2011," foxnews.com (December 12, 2011), http://www.foxnews.com/us/201l/12/12/fla-tourism-industry-sees-modest-growth-in-20l1...; "Telemarketing Travel Fraud," Federal Trade Commission, http://www.flc.gov/bcp/edu/pubs/consumer/telemarketing/tell1.shtm; "Fraudulent Travel Clubs/Deceptive Vacation Packages/Holiday Timeshare Traps," www.crimesofpersuasion.com, http://www,crimes-of-persuasion.com/Crimes/Telemarketing/Outbound/Minor/vacations.h..,

45 Ron Kurtis, "Dealing with Customer Complaints," *School for Champions,* www.school-for-champions. com/tqm/complaints.htm.

46 A. F. Wysocki et al., "Consumer Complaints and Types of Consumers," *University of Florida* (May 2001), http://edis.ifas.ufl.edu/HR005.

47 Mary Gardiner Jones, "The Consumer Affairs Office," *California Management Review* 20 (Summer 1978), pp. 63–73.

PART 3

SOCIAL AND CULTURAL INFLUENCES ON BEHAVIOR

© megallopp/Shutterstock.com

CHAPTER 9

DIFFUSION OF INNOVATION

LEARNING OBJECTIVES

- To understand the diffusion process and identify its four basic components.
- To become familiar with the process, forms, and categories of innovation.
- To conceptualize what constitutes a "new" product.
- To examine aspects of new products that enhance their chances of acceptance in the marketplace.
- To recognize and distinguish between five categories of adopters.
- To examine the adoption process as well as its stages.
- To recognize the functional and psychological sources of consumer resistance to adopting innovations.

KEY TERMS

diffusion	trialability	knowledge
adoption	divisibility	persuasion
discontinuous innovations	mass communication	decision
	personal communication	implementation
dynamically continuous innovations	rate of adoption	confirmation
	frequency of purchase	discontinuance
continuous innovations	innovators	value barrier
symbolic innovations	early adopters	usage barrier
relative advantage	early majority	risk barrier
compatibility	late majority	tradition barrier
simplicity	laggards	image barrier
observability	S-shaped diffusion curve	

When the motorcycle was introduced in the United States around the late 1800s, it was merely a motorized bicycle. A feeble internal combustion engine strapped to the frame powered the rear wheel by means of a belt. Almost all of the 4,000 cycles registered in the United States in 1900 were used solely for transportation rather than recreation.[1] From the very outset, Harley-Davidson envisioned an opportunity in this market. The first Harley-Davidson motorcycle was built in 1903 in Milwaukee, Wisconsin. William Harley, together with the Davidson brothers, designed and built high-quality motorcycles from scratch. At that point of operations, the entrepreneurs' goal was simply to develop technically superior motorcycles that would sell themselves. To bikers of the era, reliability was a most salient feature. Cyclists depended on a bike's ability to withstand the poor road conditions that prevailed at that time.

Following the Industrial Revolution, the United States was evolving quickly. Harley-Davidson at the time foresaw the potential for growth and profits ahead. The firm, at that point, was one of more than 100 U.S. motorcycle manufacturers. When Ford Motor Company first introduced its Model-T car in 1908, the motorcycle market was devastated. Most motorcycle companies folded as a result. Harley-Davidson, however, thrived due to its popularity with the public and contracts to equip the government (military) with specially designed motorcycles. This trend continued during World War I and helped the firm to survive the Great Depression.

In the 1950s, many factors helped enhance the motorcycle's popularity. New roads across the United States were being constructed, and existing roadways were being improved. In addition, family income rose after World War II. Discretionary income had made it possible for people to buy products they could not purchase during the war years. Because purchasing an automobile was still beyond most people's means, many bought a motorcycle instead.

By 2010, the company had increased its motorcycle heavy-bike market share for white males age thirty-five and older to over 60.9 percent, and for men and women between the ages of eighteen and thirty-four to a whopping 48.6 percent, a figure four times the share of its closest competitors in the latter segment.

The company's core customers—white males age thirty-five and older—continue to be the primary market segment for Harley-Davidson motorcycles. Lately, however, the company decided to aggressively pursue "outreach" customers who can be described as young individuals, ages eighteen to thirty-four, women, African-Americans, and Hispanics.

Today, nationwide, 39 percent of motorcycle owners are fifty-one to sixty-nine years of age, according to the Motorcycle Industry Council. Therefore, in order to appeal to the older riders and others who spend plenty of time in the saddle, comfort features—such as wider and deeper passenger seats—have been added to the design. Harley-Davidson, in addition, introduced the "Trike"—a three-wheel motorcycle that has become popular with older riders, since it is easier to handle than a big two-wheel bike, particularly in stop-and-go traffic.[2]

Certain makes of bikes, such as Harley-Davidson, have taken on a distinguished personality of their own and have created an image that far transcends the bike's functional or utilitarian value. Learn about Harley-Davidson by visiting www.harley-davidson.com. *How does this site promote the "Harley lifestyle"? Is this lifestyle an integral part of the brand? What motivates the brand's "cult" of followers?*

This chapter focuses on two closely related processes. The first of these is the subject of how innovations spread within a social system. Afterward, the chapter takes up the topic of the way consumers decide to accept or reject an innovation. Comprehension of both processes is critical for marketers striving to introduce new products into the marketplace successfully.

WHERE DID IT ALL BEGIN?

The origins of research in diffusion can be traced back to the nineteenth century in the fields of anthropology, sociology, and religion. Initially, German and British anthropologists and sociologists investigated the spread of ethnic traditions and religious doctrines, transfer of technology, expanse of political beliefs, and spread of commerce among nations. By the early twentieth century, marketers in the United States began to apply this type of research to the issue of new-product acceptance. During the 1920s, the study of diffusion accompanied the introduction of hybrid seeds, which held the potential for significantly increasing agricultural yields. The U.S. Department of Agriculture conducted extensive research concerning those farmers who adopted hybrid seeds, those who were reluctant to do so, and the reasons behind both decisions. Other diffusion-related studies soon followed and addressed such varied topics as insurance purchases, voting tendencies, and new-product acceptance.

The study of diffusion addresses two main issues. First, these studies explore how acceptance of a *new product* or *new idea* spreads within the

diffusion
the spread of a new product or idea within the marketplace

adoption
the decision-making stages an individual goes through before accepting a product

marketplace. This is termed diffusion. Second, these studies probe into the decision-making process that leads toward a consumer's acceptance or rejection of a new product or idea. This is termed adoption. The *diffusion process* is a macroprocess concerned with the spread of a new product or idea from its original source to and throughout the general public. In contrast, the *adoption process* is a microprocess dealing with the stages that an individual goes through before accepting a product. In the following sections of the chapter, we examine the process of diffusion and explain its four components. We then shift our attention to a discussion of adoption.

THE DIFFUSION PROCESS

The word *diffusion* is derived from a Latin word meaning "to spread out." Thus, scientists may speak of gaseous vapors that diffuse or gradually unfurl through the expanse of available space. In a marketing sense, diffusion deals with how an innovation spreads within the marketplace by means of communication (which may include the mass media, sales representatives, opinion leaders, and members of a social system) over a period of time. Diffusion is simply the sum total of many individual adoption decisions. There are four basic components in the diffusion process:[3]

- Innovation
- Channel of communication
- Social system
- Time

Let us clarify the role played by each of these four components in the diffusion process.

THE INNOVATION

New-product development is big business. Although consumer product firms tend to derive a slightly greater percentage of sales from new products than do business product firms, the introduction of new products has been and continues to be a critical activity for all companies.[4] In the food industry alone, around thirty-four new food products are launched every day.[5] More than ever, existing products can be expected over the course of time either to be preempted by new and improved products or to degenerate to a position where profits are nonexistent.[6] Think of the fate of products such as Burma Shave, Brylcream, Hai Karate, and Beanie Babies which were once widely recognized and frequently purchased.[7] Today, however, many of them have either disappeared from the marketplace or at least reached the end of their lifecycle.

Without a doubt, the long-term health of most organizations is tied to their ability to provide existing and new customers with an ongoing stream of new products.[8] Over 10,000 new products are marketed in the United States every year, and hundreds of thousands of people make their living producing and marketing new products.[9] Almost 3 percent of this country's gross national product (GNP) is spent on the technical phase of new-product development; this percentage represents research and development (R&D) only, not manufacturing and marketing costs.[10] The ad in Figure 9.1 not only emphasizes frequency of innovations being introduced to the marketplace today, but also highlights the role DHL plays in the prompt delivery of these advances to the global community.

Classifying Innovations

Innovations take a variety of forms. Some innovations represent genuine technological advances that become embodied into new-to-the-world products (e.g., iPhone, WiFi, Blackberry, GPS navigation systems). More commonly, innovations involve modifications or improvements to existing products, such as adding a new feature, ingredient, color, or scent to a product. Still others involve symbolic representations that alter the social and psychological meaning of products (new car designs or hairstyles).

Robertson identified three classes of new products: discontinuous, dynamically continuous, and continuous innovations. His distinction between these three classes of products is founded on two elements: the extent to which they represent changes in technology and the extent to which the innovation requires changes in established consumption or usage patterns of adopters.[11] From a consumer behavior perspective, the greater the required change in established consumption habits resulting from the innovation, the less the chance that the innovation will gain quick acceptance. Conversely, the less disruptive the innovation is to these patterns, the greater the likelihood that it will gain widespread adoption. This section explains Robertson's threefold classification of innovations.

FIGURE 9.1

An innovation such as the affordable 3-D printed artificial limb represents a recent breakthrough in medical science. This ad for DHL highlights the firm's critical role in the swift delivery of these advances worldwide.

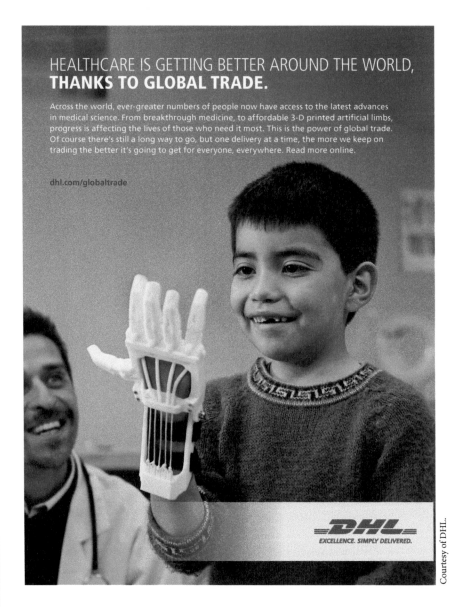

HEALTHCARE IS GETTING BETTER AROUND THE WORLD, **THANKS TO GLOBAL TRADE.**

Across the world, ever-greater numbers of people now have access to the latest advances in medical science. From breakthrough medicine, to affordable 3-D printed artificial limbs, progress is affecting the lives of those who need it most. This is the power of global trade. Of course there's still a long way to go, but one delivery at a time, the more we keep on trading the better it's going to get for everyone, everywhere. Read more online.

dhl.com/globaltrade

DHL
EXCELLENCE. SIMPLY DELIVERED.

Courtesy of DHL.

Discontinuous Innovations

discontinuous innovations unique products that significantly alter established consumption routines

Discontinuous innovations are unique pioneering products that significantly disrupt and alter established purchasing and consumption routines. Discontinuous innovations involve major technical advances on the part of their creators. As a result of this striking newness, learning of new consumption or usage patterns is required.

CONSUMER BEHAVIOR IN PRACTICE

Get 'Em While They're Still Young

Many marketers consider college students to be a fertile and desirable market to pursue. One reason is that they represent a good-sized market. In 2011, the number of students enrolled in institutions of higher education reached 17.6 million; it is projected to reach 20 million by 2020. A second reason for this market's attractiveness is that today's college students have more money than their predecessors, and they don't mind parting with it.

Companies that target the college student market use a variety of appeals. Realizing that this market is composed of a varied mix of high and low sensation seekers, these firms develop strategies to appeal to the whims of these various segments. There are companies such as tour operators and beer distributors that still cater to the spring break crowd and participate in rowdy contests, promotional beach games, and product giveaways during gatherings where surfing, romance, drinking, and wet t-shirt contests are the norm. Other companies, however, take a more responsible approach to reaching students. Ford Motor Company, for example, generates collegiate sales by offering students $500 cash incentives plus Ford's best credit rates when the student purchases or leases a new car. Verizon's tactics to lure college students include no security deposit for up to three lines, unlimited talk and text, unlimited international messaging, plus Mobile Hot Spot on capable devices.

Similarly, alcoholic beverage companies spend millions of dollars to promote their products to college students. For example, Anheuser-Busch targets college students on various campuses by engaging students with "combat" marketing tactics—that is, placing beer in front of students at various venues, such as tailgating during college games and free bar events. During these events, the company gives away promotional items such as t-shirts, inflatable chairs, concert tickets, and even scooters. Anheuser-Busch further utilizes Facebook and Twitter, as well as its own website, to promote upcoming events and their location. It documents these events by taking a large number of photos and posting them to the various websites.

Based on their realization that 84 percent of college students carry at least one credit card, these companies continue to vigorously pursue the collegiate market. Their arsenal includes t-shirts, iPods, and other gifts plus a host of benefits such as zero interest for a grace period as well as no annual fee. The goal behind all these efforts is obvious—by getting students to use their brands while in college, companies hope to create customers for life.[12]

Are the benefits to companies of using come-ons to attract college students worth the effort and cost invested? Visit www.free2tlk.com to learn how Verizon appeals to college students. Do you think that most college graduates maintain their college "product and brand relationships" in later years? In your opinion, what types of products can benefit most from this early familiarity?

Because discontinuous innovations require learning of new behavior patterns on the part of consumers, marketers must first sell prospective customers on the concept behind the innovation before they can sell the product. In other words, they need to educate consumers to respond to the new idea and then supply the product. Once the concept has gained acceptance, selling the product is relatively easy. This fact may explain the reason why it is often difficult for truly new products to gain quick acceptance in the marketplace. For example, it took many years for products such as the facsimile (fax) machine or contact lenses to become accepted by the masses.[13]

Discontinuous innovations are rare. Early examples include automobiles, airplanes, and telephones as well as more recent ones such as smartphones, MP4 players, portable video gadgets, and GPS navigation devices. Innovations of this type have changed and will continue to change the way we live and conduct business.

Dynamically Continuous Innovations

Dynamically continuous innovations are new-product creations or alterations in existing products that entail minor technical advances and do not strikingly alter established consumer buying and usage patterns. Dynamically continuous innovations include adaptations of, replacements for, or improvements to existing products. Such innovations are new in some respects; in other ways, however, they are just slightly different or are simply minor modifications of existing products. Dynamically continuous innovations have some disrupting influence on customary consumption practices and require some new learning on the part of consumers. Examples include digital cameras, laptop computers, voice-activated electronics, new computer operating systems, and conventional cell phones.

Continuous Innovations

Continuous innovations are extensions or modifications of existing products with little or no change in technology. Continuous innovations are low-learning cases and require minimal, if any, adjustments in conventional consumption routines. Continuous innovations frequently take the form of imitative products. That is, they are new to the sponsoring company but perhaps not new to the marketplace, such as organic foods, high-pixel resolution digital cameras, or a diet or low-fat product extension to an existing food line. Other continuous innovations incorporate very slight changes, such as those related to appearance, packaging, size, color, new flavors, or style and fashion. Examples include new automobile models, new styles of clothing, whitening-formula toothpastes, flavored dental floss, liquid hand soaps, and moisturizing hand sanitizers. Continuous innovations may also incorporate new uses or applications of a familiar product. The present popularity of iced teas and coffees stands as a case in point. Another example of a successful modification of an existing product was the introduction of an odor-free cat litter. The ad for Fresh Step in Figure 9.2 informs pet owners of the odor-free feature of this new product.

Extending Robertson's work, subsequent researchers have expanded the list of innovation classes to include what they have labeled symbolic innovations.[14] Symbolic innovations are those that convey new social or psychological meanings. In marketing, a classic example of symbolic innovation involves designer mineral water, which takes an existing product and gives it a new social meaning. Water, in this case, is repositioned as a purifying body cleanser (as in Evian ads) or as a fashionable alternative to alcohol (as in Perrier ads).

Although innovations can be either symbolic or technological or even both, their effect on established consumer behavior patterns varies widely.

symbolic innovations
cases where a product conveys new social or psychological meanings

"GREEN WORKS" is a registered trademark of The Clorox Company. Used with permission." © 2012 The Clorox Company. Reprinted with permission. Photo copyright Jill Greenberg.

FIGURE 9.2

This eye-catching Fresh Step ad from the Clorox Pet Product Company reflects the concept of continuous innovation. The ad highlights the odor-eliminating feature of this new product.

Smartphone, iPod, and video game technologies, for example, have considerably altered social patterns of communication and recreation. However, most symbolic innovations, such as those related to style and fashion, are continuous in nature and involve minimal change to consumption habits.[15]

What Is a "New" Product?

Whereas, in the eyes of the Federal Trade Commission, use of the word *new* in advertising is restricted to products distributed and made available in the marketplace within a time span of less than six months, the very notion of innovativeness, novelty, or newness is subjective and relative. In fact, time may or may not have anything to do with newness. For example, products qualify as new if consumers within a particular market lack awareness of or experience with them. In other words, that which is old to some may be brand new to others and vice versa. While smartphones, PCs, and tablets are standard household items within developed nations, they remain unavailable to millions of people in Third World countries.

New, therefore, may be thought of as anything that consumers perceive as new. Perception of newness, in many cases, can result from changes to packaging, price, distribution, and promotional strategies. In the same sense, newness of a product to the firm that manufactures or distributes it does not necessarily constitute novelty to the marketplace and consumers. From the perspective of newness, products enhanced by high-technological breakthroughs may excite product engineers, but it still remains to be seen whether they will do so for consumers.

Multiplicity of New-Product Strategies

Firms do not restrict themselves to any single type of new product. Rather, organizational efforts tend to emphasize a variety of endeavors. In both consumer firms and business firms, line extensions, which add related products to the current line, are the most common way of generating new products. Examples include Kellogg's introduction of Smart Start Antioxidants breakfast cereal, Jello Gelatin's creation of Jello Pudding Pops, or Dannon's launch of Activia yogurt.[16] After line extensions, in decreasing order of importance, consumer product firms tend to focus on totally new products; efforts to improve existing product quality; adding features to current products; adding value to current products through distribution, price, and promotion; and finding new uses or markets for existing products. Business product firms, on the other hand, exhibit a somewhat different order of emphasis. After line extensions, they tend to focus on adding features to current products, developing totally new products, improving the tangible quality of current products, finding new uses or markets for current products, and adding value to current products through distribution, promotion, and price.[17]

These facts reveal that a good number of organizations are deemphasizing truly innovative products and are relying instead on defensive approaches such as flooding markets with line extensions. This trend has been confirmed by a study of the U.S. consumer products field that revealed that only about 5.7 percent of all new products introduced during a half-year period could be considered innovative.[18] This result does not compare favorably to findings of a study of British and Japanese firms, which revealed that approximately 80 percent of these foreign competitors were developing radically new products as part of their development efforts.[19] In one investigation, a disappointingly low share of U.S. business product firms—just over one-third—engaged in the development of totally new-to-the-world products.[20]

FACTORS THAT INFLUENCE CONSUMER ACCEPTANCE OF NEW PRODUCTS

Some new products meet with instant success, such as the iPhone, iPod, and tablet, whereas others such as solar-energy-powered heating and cooling systems are taking many years to gain acceptance. Certain features of product innovations appear to contribute to their success, whereas others seem to have no effect whatsoever on that success.[21] At the Marketing Science Institute, a research group backed by giants such as Procter & Gamble and Apple Computer, the first priority of business is improving new-product development procedures. Companies as diverse as Apple, Yahoo, Google, Hewlett-Packard, Motorola, Colgate-Palmolive, Honda, and Toyota are all tackling new-product issues in order to learn what contributes to the success of new products and how to keep flops to a minimum. When executives at Hewlett-Packard's Medical Product Group studied ten of their new-product failures along with ten of their successful products, they were able to identify a number of factors that determined which products flourished and which did not—information that led to future successes.

Based on studies of the adoption of new products and practices, Rogers identified five product characteristics that seem to influence consumer acceptance of new products. These characteristics are:

1. Relative advantage
2. Compatibility
3. Simplicity–complexity
4. Observability
5. Trialability and divisibility[22]

Relative Advantage

Consumers are more inclined to purchase a new product when it offers a relative advantage over alternative merchandise. Relative advantage is the degree to which consumers perceive a new product as different from, and better than, its dated substitutes. For example, Dean Food Company has introduced a new package concept to enhance milk consumption. Instead of the square wax-lined cartons that were used before, single servings of chocolate milk are now packaged in attractive plastic bottles with screw-on caps called TruMoo Chugs.[23] The greater the advantage, the greater the new product's chance of selection and the sooner the innovation will be adopted. ATMs achieved quick acceptance because they made banking transactions available around-the-clock, a highly perceived advantage to consumers. On the other hand, although debit cards and POS (point-of-sale) cards offered advantages to banks and retailers, consumers perceived little relative advantage over credit cards or personal checks, and they thus had significantly lower usage rates.

A good example of relative advantage is found in the competitive floral industry. FTD offers floral arrangements and specialty gift items, including boxed flowers, plants, dried flowers, gourmet food selections, holiday gifts, bath and beauty products, jewelry, wine and gift baskets, and stuffed animals.[24] FTD was established in 1910 by a few florists who agreed to exchange orders for out-of-town deliveries via telegraph. Today, FTD encompasses 20,000 independent florists in the United States and is linked by state-of-the-art technology to 50,000 florists in 154 countries around the world. FTD was both the first floral wire service made available to the public and the first among such services to publish a selection guide containing photos of hundreds of floral arrangements to help consumers make appropriate choices. A few years ago, FTD added a toll-free number—800-SEND-FTD—making it still easier for consumers to send flowers. In addition, FTD has its website—www.ftd.com—which offers 1,000 floral arrangements and specialty gifts for holiday and special occasions. Convenience and speed of sending flowers to anyone, anywhere, anytime offers customers a genuine relative advantage. Similarly, in the case of paint, manufacturers originally packaged paint in metallic cans, which caused the paint to spill while pouring. New and improved plastic containers that are designed to prevent spills were introduced to the market in the past few years.

Compatibility

A new product should be consistent with consumers' existing needs, beliefs, values, attitudes, experiences, and habits. The better the compatibility of a new product with consumers' lifestyles and established practices, the more quickly the innovation will be adopted. The success of Oscar Mayer's Lunchables is a case in point. It is a meal-in-a-box that parents of school-age children love. It solves the parents' problem of what to make for lunch every day, and at the same time, provides an expanded choice of lunch items kids enjoy.[25]

In March 2016, Apple released its compatible and user-friendly iOS 9.3 Night Shift new Quick Action app, representing the third significant update to the iOS 9 operating system since it was launched in September 2015. This new version—which added new features, refinements, and bug fixes—became available on the date of release to all iOS 9 users as an over-the-air update. It can also be downloaded through iTunes on the Mac and PC. This new update was welcomed by users of the iPhone 6s and 6s Plus, where several apps are gaining new Quick Actions. Weather, Settings, Compass, Health, App Store, and iTunes Store all offer new or improved features when pressed on the Home Screen.[26]

Simplicity–Complexity

Simplicity is the extent to which consumers perceive a new product as easy to understand, assemble, and operate. The simpler an innovation is to comprehend and use, the greater its chance of being selected and accepted by consumers. Conversely, the more complex an innovation is, the less likely it is to find favor among the public. In 1998, Apple Computer introduced the Apple Puck Mouse, a puck-shaped mouse, along with its introduction of iMac G3. This odd device was one of Apples most dubious creations. The device had a single button that was difficult to find without looking for it, and made the experience of "mousing" totally impractical

compatibility
the perceived property of a new product as being consistent with consumers' beliefs, values, experiences, and habits

simplicity
the perceived property that an innovation is easy to understand, assemble, and operate

due to the fact that users could not figure out which direction the mouse was pointing.

With the sweeping technological advances of the day, some products have become so complex that consumers continue to shy away from them. Observing this trend, camera manufacturers—both still and video—were among the first to realize the importance of simplicity. Modern cameras are now all digital, where any of their advanced features can be activated by a simple push of a button. Similarly, think of the millions of life-simplifying apps that consumers download from the App Store. They run the gamut from news to business to entertainment.

Observability

observability
the perceived property that an innovation is visible and communicable to potential adopters

Observability is the extent to which an innovation is visible and communicable to potential adopters. Highly visible products, such as automobiles and fashions, are more quickly adopted and diffused than, say, headache remedies or soaps, which are used in private. Studies of adoption of solar power panels by consumers in the United States show that acceptance often occurred within concentrated areas, such as California, Arizona, and Oregon, rather than throughout the entire country, and within certain concentrated neighborhoods within each one of these states.[27] Neighbors, once exposed to the comfort of air conditioning, wanted a unit for themselves. Manufacturers of sporting goods such as Wilson and athletic footwear such as Nike or Reebok frequently induce professional athletes to use their equipment or wear their shoes in order to enhance brand visibility. Use of a new product by talented heroes at sporting events and celebrities in movies or on TV can enhance the speed of adoption.

The case of AriZona iced tea offers a good example of the importance of observability. The tea comes in a bottle that is so well designed many consumers buy it just for the container. Each new variety of AriZona iced tea is anxiously awaited by collectors. As a result, AriZona iced tea stands out in a busy product category of soft drinks, replete with hundreds of other competing brands.

Trialability and Divisibility

trialability
the perceived property that a new product can be experienced before purchase

When consumers can experiment with a new product on a limited basis and evaluate its merits before making a purchase commitment, adoption occurs more quickly. This property of a product is known as its trialability. When consumers can be given a free sample of a new product to test, achieving trial is simple. Toward this end, Procter & Gamble spends millions of dollars annually to distribute free *trial-size* new-product samples to households throughout the United States. Such mini-specimens are sent directly to consumers' homes or handed out inside retail stores to allow consumers to try new products that few would have ventured to try otherwise. Although this practice is relatively easy in the case of sampling consumer goods, such as foods, soaps, or toothpaste, the case of durable goods presents a challenge. Limited trial of these types of goods, however, may be possible via tactics such as demonstrations in retail showrooms or consumers' homes, trial in-home placements, lease-with-option-to-buy plans, and 100 percent satisfaction guarantees. For this reason, most automobile companies, such as Ford and General Motors, woo car rental companies to get them to carry their recent models. The objective is obvious—when drivers try a new-car model, they are often impressed with its performance and frequently become potential buyers.

In recent years, trialability has also been enhanced electronically through virtual reality. Recent developments in this technology have enabled consumers to experience a product before making a purchase choice. The use of web-based virtual reality (VR) technology has been an effective way to facilitate shopping for many products, including furniture and clothing. VR offers consumers realistic product trials in cyberspace without the temporal and physical constraints of brick-and-mortar stores. In the case of furniture, VR technologies offer dynamic interaction with pieces of furniture by allowing users to zoom-in, zoom-out, move, or rotate an ob-

The attractive packaging of AriZona iced tea makes this brand stand out among the many other soft drink brands in the marketplace.

ject. Among the biggest problems that furniture buyers face has been their inability to view the product in their home setting and to match choice alternatives with their currently owned pieces of home decor. However, realistic trialability—including close inspection of individual items and combinations of items—can be attained when the furniture and the environment for which it is intended are all generated in three-dimensional real-time interactive computer graphics. Similarly, in the marketplace for clothing, VR has made and will continue to make the shopping experience practical and convenient. A consumer looking for a dress will soon be able to step into a fitting room online, try it on, view herself from all angles, adjust the lighting and dress color, and send a snapshot to family members or friends for their opinion. Through virtual shopping, she will also be able to use an avatar, a virtual representation of herself, to shop with friends in a three-dimensional online environment in real time, and try on virtual merchandise, as well as make purchases.

divisibility
the perceived property that a new product can be sampled in small quantities

Divisibility is also an important factor in encouraging adoption. If consumers can try new products in small quantities, achieving trial is relatively easy. In a study of five packaged goods by Shoemaker and Shoaf, nearly two-thirds of consumers were found to make trial purchases of new brands in quantities smaller than those they usually purchased.[28] Realization of this tendency, in part, prompted Campbell's to introduce individual servings and smaller-sized packages of its soups and other ready-to-eat meals.

THE CHANNEL OF COMMUNICATION

Communication is essential for widespread acceptance of innovation. Communication enables marketers to promote their brands and thus sell their products or services. Without communication channels, consumers would remain largely unaware of new goods and services available in the marketplace. Diffusion researchers focus their attention on the process of transmitting product-related information through various channels of communication. Their objective is to understand the relative impact of messages and channels employed on new-product acceptance or rejection.

Marketing communication can be divided into two major types: mass communication and personal communication. Mass communication relies on the mass media to disseminate information to a target audience. Mass-media vehicles include the Web, magazines, newspapers, television, and radio, as well as many of today's electronic technologies, such as smartphones, tablets, and pocket PCs. Personal communication, on the other hand, involves two or more persons interacting directly with each other either face-to-face, person-to-audience, or over conventional phone lines.

mass communication relies on the mass media to disseminate information to a target audience

personal communication involves two or more persons interacting directly with each other

Over the years, diffusion researchers have argued that personal communication is the major key to persuasion. They further supported the contention that mass-media channels are merely effective in creating awareness and knowledge concerning innovations, while interpersonal channels are the force in forming and changing consumer attitudes regarding a new product or idea. According to this view, it is the influence of personal communication that brings about the decision to adopt or reject an innovation.

Today, however, with the recent overwhelming advances in technology, the Internet—which is considered a mass medium—has the ability to reach an unlimited number of audience members without many of the limitations that characterize other forms of mass media, such as absence or delay of feedback as well as restrictions in the amount of information communicated. Through interactivity, consumers can receive information on any topic upon demand and respond to messages they receive instantaneously. In fact, no mass medium can match the Internet's ability to convey as much specific, up-to-date, and detailed information.

With the present accessibility of the Internet for most consumers, information on virtually any topic, product, service, or company imaginable is just a few keystrokes away. The Web has taken on the role of an interpersonal medium. Internet blogs, online communities, social networks, virtual worlds, photo galleries, and email are but a few of the vehicles that have helped to fuel the diffusion and adoption of present-day products and ideas.

New avenues of communication make possible the transfer of information with simple strokes on a keyboard or flips of a switch. Through interactive TV, consumers can receive any type of programming or information upon demand, ranging from educational programming and news broadcasts to product lists and grocery services. Via interactivity, direct-mail campaigns that used to cost advertisers thousands of dollars in the not-so-distant past can now be accomplished electronically for pennies per contact.

Beyond methods of reaching likely consumers through traditional media types such as newspapers, magazines, television, and radio, the rapid growth of interactive technology has prompted many companies to re-think the way they can reach prospects. Now, companies are increasingly running online ads that focus less on pitching their products or services than promoting their Facebook pages and Twitter accounts. Such ads, which have menu tabs and resemble mini-websites themselves, permit users to click within the ad to see a brand's Twitter messages or Facebook wall posts in real time. Alternatively, consumers are able to watch a brand's video content from YouTube. They can do all of this without leaving the webpage where the ad appears. A number of digital advertising formats are currently available. One approach infuses ads with live content from other sites, including Facebook and Twitter. Another format used with in-text advertising—where advertisers pay for keywords to be hyperlinked within an article or blog post—causes ads to pop out in a window on the same page when viewers click on the hyperlinked keywords.[29]

No matter how large a company's promotional budget may be, marketers of new products stand to benefit greatly from positive word-of-mouth communication. With the declining trust in advertising, word of mouth has become the most influential communication channel. Online consumer reviews provide a trusted source of new-product information for consumers. Therefore, they are considered potentially valuable assets for generating sales. Positive word-of-mouth communication occurs when satisfied adopters of an innovation recommend the new product to their friends or relatives. Although the marketer of an innovation can control new-product advertising, word-of-mouth cannot be controlled by the firm. Consequently, it may be positive and helpful, or negative and harmful.[30] Both exposure to advertising in the media and hands-on product experience can have the effect of precipitating word of mouth among consumers. Word of mouth is considered more effective than advertising due to the credibility and trustworthiness of the source. Diffusion largely depends on a chain of positive interpersonal communications, whereby successive layers of consumers adopt a new product upon the advice of slightly more venturesome acquaintances.

THE SOCIAL SYSTEM

Humans do not exist in a social vacuum. Rather they are members of social systems. A social system is a physical, social, or cultural environment to which individuals belong and within which they function. Social systems unite groups of persons who interact, at least occasionally, because they share certain common needs, problems, activities, interests, places of residence or employment, and the like. Members of a social system have at least one characteristic in common (same sex, similar age, same occupation), which makes them potential buyers of or influencers for a marketer's product. In the case of men's cordless electric shavers, the social system consists of males who are old enough to grow unwanted facial hair.

For a suntan lotion, the social system includes all individuals, male or female and young or old, who are exposed to UVA rays.[31]

Within a social system, each member possesses a particular status and plays a specific role. Positive and negative sanctions are in place to ensure that behavior complies with group expectations. The social system serves as a reference group as individuals carry over its norms and values into their purchase decisions. Keep in mind, however, that individuals exist at the intersection of multiple social systems (personal, familial, social, and professional) and frequently face inter-role conflicts that must somehow be resolved.

The specific norms, values, traditions, standards, attitudes, and expectations of the social system are instrumental in influencing the acceptance of innovative products and ideas. These can make or break a new product. Traditional versus modern, religious versus secular, or adventurous versus cautious cultural orientations can influence an innovation's acceptance or rejection. New, revealing styles of swimsuits may be quickly endorsed in liberal, secular societies but may be swiftly shunned by more conservatively aligned social systems.

Not only do norms, values, attitudes, and expectations vary between social systems, but the expanse of specific orientations can vary between societies. The varied degree of diffusion of innovation across cultures is a fact of life. The World Bank report entitled, "Global Economic Prospects January 2016: Technology Diffusion in the Developing World," finds that the rate of diffusion of innovation in various cultures is a function of a number of factors, including socioeconomic differences, the availability of a critical mass of technological competencies in a country, as well as the affordability of the particular technology. For example, the Internet economy metric combines three factors at economy level: the number of Internet users, the average per capita income, and an adjustment factor reflecting the economy's income disparities. The World Bank Report indicated that the pace of technological progress in developing countries has been much faster recently than in high-income countries—reflecting the increased exposure to foreign technology as a result of the opening of these markets to international trade and foreign direct investment.[32]

Some of the documented cases of cross-cultural diffusion stand to clarify the varied degrees of speed at which innovation spreads within different cultures, and to pinpoint the factors that underlie the associated diffusion rate. Such cases include, for example, the way in which Ebola, Zika, and

AIDS awareness and treatments differ from one country to another, due to factors such as socioeconomic conditions in each nation and differential access to patient care.[33] Another example includes the case of the rapid pace of diffusion for cell phones in many areas of the world, including sub-Saharan Africa, among other places without landlines.[34] Still other cases include the $100 laptop project, which remained in place for a number of years until 2014, and that was initiated by the One Laptop Per Child Association (OLPC), and the degree to which coverage was achieved in various countries. This level of success was influenced by the extent of each country's governmental interest and willingness to cooperate with OLPC. Further, the recent cases of the quick diffusion of automobiles in both China and India stand to confirm the positive association between the rate of diffusion and cross-cultural socioeconomic conditions, especially the gains in the income level of the middle class in these two countries.

Three aspects of the social system have been found to influence the speed of diffusion:

- The greater the degree of compatibility between the innovation and values held by a social system's members, the more brisk the pace of diffusion.
- The more homogeneous (nonsegmented) the social system, the quicker the diffusion process. Homogeneity maximizes interpersonal contact.[35]
- The diffusion of innovations across cultures depends largely upon the distance between the countries and the social similarity of their cultures.[36]

The acceptance of new products is both shaped and emulated by interaction among the people who belong to a particular social system. Huge multinational corporations have been known to falter occasionally in global markets when attempting to introduce domestically successful products. Why? They simply fail to adjust the product or its supporting marketing strategy to accommodate the dissimilar social systems in host countries. For example, Crest toothpaste initially failed in Mexico. When Procter & Gamble tried to use its U.S. campaign, Mexicans appreciated neither its promised decay-prevention benefit nor its scientifically oriented copy.[37] On the other hand, 3M's successful introduction of Post-it notes into Japan is due, at least in part, to recognizing the need to use long, narrow paper shapes suited to the vertical character of Japanese writing.[38]

TIME

The inclusion of time as a variable in diffusion research serves a number of important functions. Knowing the *rate of adoption* or relative speed with which consumers adopt an innovation is vital in planning production schedules and inventory requirements. Initial overproduction of an innovation as a result of high sales expectations can be financially devastating for a business. If the rate of adoption turns out to be slow, the excessive production ties up capital in unsold goods, causes overstocks in distribution outlets, and forces lower prices in order to move excess goods. Similarly, knowledge of the *frequency* with which consumers purchase a new product is an important factor in streamlining distribution practices. Scheduling new-product deliveries to dealers is founded on knowledge of the frequency with which consumers repurchase that product. The two time-related factors in the diffusion process can thus be identified as the rate of adoption and the frequency of purchase.

rate of adoption
the relative speed with which consumers adopt an innovation

The rate of adoption refers to the length of time it takes a new product to become accepted by potential adopters within a given social system.[39] This rate is measured by the time span it takes consumers to adopt an innovation. In the field of electronics, we all have witnessed the astonishing adoption rate of the iPad, which was first introduced in April 2010 and was met with overwhelmingly positive reception. Apple sold over 3.2 million iPads in its debut third quarter of 2010, which far exceeded analysts' expectations of 1 million units. Apple then followed its debut quarter with an additional 4.2 million iPads sold in the fourth quarter, resulting in $2.8 billion in revenue. In 2011, sales skyrocketed by 75 percent, with volume surpassing 7.3 million units, and recorded an additional $4.6 billion in revenue.[40] Once again, Apple followed its blockbuster with an iPad2, with sales amounting to over 7 million units. In March 2012, Apple introduced the "New iPad," which continued the success story of its predecessors.[41] The most recent iPad models are the iPad Mini 4, released on September 9, 2015; and the 9.7-inch iPad Pro, released on March 31, 2016. As of January 2015, there have been over 250 million iPads sold. iPad tablets are second most popular, in terms of sales, against Android-based units.

frequency of purchase
the rate at which consumers purchase a product after the initial purchase

Frequency of purchase refers to the rate with which a consumer purchases the product after the initial purchase—sometimes referred to as the repurchase rate. This measurement differentiates between heavy users (who buy more of the product and do so frequently), moderate users (who display an average usage and purchase rate), and light users (who buy less of the product and do so infrequently). For manufacturers of new products, frequency of purchase represents valuable information in directing distribution schedules. Failure to identify this rate can result in stockouts for dealers if mammoth demand for the new product materializes or overstocks if demand is slow to come about.

Time and the Adopter Categories

Consumers exhibit individual differences in their readiness and willingness to try and accept new products. In other words, whereas some people test and accept an innovation soon after its introduction, others wait for additional information or rely on learning about the experiences of persons who are more venturesome than themselves when deciding whether to try or adopt. Some people delay longer than others before adopting a new product, and still others may never adopt altogether. As a result, marketers are interested in learning how long after product introduction various consumer groups adopt, how long adoption takes, reasons for time differences among consumer groups, and which individual and environmental variables distinguish earlier adopters from later adopters.

Marketers of new products recognize the important role of more innovative individuals in gaining new-product acceptance. As opinion leaders, they pass along information about the new product to others—a concept referred to as *word of mouth*. Marketers often research the demographic and psychographic characteristics as well as the media habits of these more venturesome consumers so that promotion and distribution can be first targeted to them. This is no small task, because researchers have yet to prove the existence of a general personality trait among consumers known as *innovativeness*. Rather, individuals tend to be venturesome in some product categories and more traditional in others. A sales professional, for example, may dress conservatively yet might drive the latest new model of automobile, loaded with all the options. Similarly, one who relishes sampling new and exotic cuisines may be politically quite conservative. Marketers of new products face the challenge of identifying the characteristics of those consumers who are likely to be venturesome in a specific product category.[42]

Rogers conceived a classification consisting of five adopter categories based on innovativeness as manifested by the length of time it takes consumers to adopt an innovation.[43] His model, depicted in Exhibit 9.1, follows the normal (bell-shaped) distribution. In other words, after a slow start, increasing numbers of people adopt the new product as it becomes

Adopter Categories Based on Innovativeness

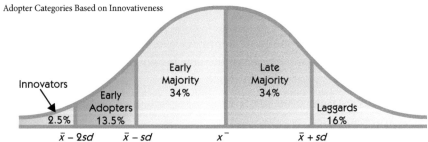

Source: Everett M. Rogers, Diffusion of Innovation, 4th ed. (New York: Free Press, 1955). Copyright ©1955 by Everett M. Rogers.

more apparent. The number of adopters eventually reaches a peak and then gradually drops off as fewer potential adopters remain. Rogers assumes that eventually there will be 100 percent adoption and thus excludes nonadopters from his groupings and percentages. This is a bold assumption because, regardless of their merit, few innovations ever achieve universal acceptance. The following paragraphs provide a brief profile of the types of individuals who make up each of the five categories proposed by Rogers.

Innovators

Representing 2.5 percent of the market, innovators are venturesome individuals and the first to adopt a new product, even at some risk.[44] Innovators tend to have higher social status and enjoy higher incomes. They tend to be younger, better educated, more cosmopolitan and mobile, more self-confident, and more reliant on their own values and judgment than

innovators
the first 2.5 percent of the market to adopt a new product

Innovators tend to be younger, better educated, more cosmopolitan and mobile, more self-confident, and more reliant on their own values and judgment.

© Stock-Asso/Shutterstock.com

CONSUMER BEHAVIOR *AN APPLIED APPROACH*

on group norms. Innovators are more likely to obtain information from nonpersonal sources, scientific sources, and experts. Promotional appeals targeted to innovators frequently use factual appeals that emphasize product attributes and corresponding customer benefits. Innovators tend to be less brand loyal and more attracted to products or situations that provide diverse challenges.

Early Adopters

Early adopters represent the next 13.5 percent of the market to adopt a product. Although early adopters are not the first to adopt, they adopt early—but carefully—during the product's lifecycle. Unlike innovators who are characterized by broad involvement outside the local community, early adopters tend to be socially integrated and involved within their local community. They are more reliant on group norms and values and are most likely to be *opinion leaders or influencers* in their community. Because they are likely to transmit word-of-mouth influence to their acquaintances and colleagues, and because other people are interested in and influenced by their opinions, early adopters are probably the most important group in determining whether a new product will succeed. Early adopters play critical roles as trendsetters and tastemakers. Consequently, they are largely responsible for determining which new products will be deemed acceptable by future adopters.

In the diffusion process, *agents of change* (parties who seek to accelerate the spread of a given innovation) usually focus their initial persuasive efforts on early adopters. When marketers succeed in attracting early adopters to an innovation, the broader market eventually follows, due to the respect other consumers have for early adopters' opinions. For example, in the wine industry, marketers attempt to attract early adopters by holding wine-tasting events where guests taste new wines and learn about each variety from hosting reps. Promotional messages targeted to these early adopters frequently employ factual appeals. In addition to their dependence on mass media to acquire knowledge about new products, early adopters rely on sales personnel as an important information source. They tend to display high usage rates in the product category in which the innovation falls. Marketers of new products are keenly interested in identifying and reaching these early adopters. They are an important target for ads and other promotions aimed at creating a market where none previously existed.[45]

early adopters
the second tier of consumers (after the innovators) to adopt an innovation

The Early Majority

The early majority represents the next 34 percent of the market to adopt. Although the early majority adopts just before the average consumer in a social system, they deliberate their decision carefully. Members of the early majority are likely to gather more information and evaluate more brands than early adopters and are likely to be opinion leaders' friends and neighbors. This group is slightly above average in social and economic standing. The early majority tends to rely considerably on ads, salespeople, and contact with early adopters as information sources. Promotional appeals targeting the early majority frequently employ expert appeals and celebrity endorsements.

The Late Majority

The late majority represents still the next 34 percent of the market to adopt. The late majority is skeptical. They may lack the financing to purchase the innovation, or they at least feel that the new item is not worth its cost. Members adopt an innovation to save time or effort or in response to social pressure to conform, but only after most acquaintances have already done so. The late majority tends to be below average in income and education level. Trusting group norms, the late majority relies primarily on word-of-mouth communication from peers—the late or early majority—rather than on the mass media as a source of information. Advertising and personal selling are less effective with this group. Promotional appeals targeting the late majority frequently employ conformity appeals ("Everyone else does, why not you?").

Laggards

The laggards are the last 16 percent of the market to adopt. Laggards tend to fall at the low end of the socioeconomic scale and, like innovators, do not rely on group norms. Laggards are independent and tradition bound. Feeling estranged in a progressive marketplace, laggards are suspicious of change and resist adopting an innovation until it has become something of a tradition itself. By the time laggards adopt an innovation, it has probably been superseded and abandoned by the innovators in favor of more recent models. Promotional efforts targeted to laggards may suggest that a new product does what familiar products do, only better.

Given the preceding classification, the obvious question concerns how marketers can identify innovators and early adopters among personal and business consumers in order to focus early marketing attention and efforts toward them. A review of the literature suggests five traits that often differentiate innovators and early adopters from the masses:[46]

1. *Venturesome:* an obvious need to be daring and different
2. *Socially integrated:* extensive and frequent contact and interaction with others in one's community or profession
3. *Cosmopolitan:* interest in world affairs and perspectives that extend beyond the immediate locale
4. *Upwardly mobile:* capable of moving upward along the social scale
5. *Privileged:* wealthy (or at least possessing adequate resources) and financially independent

The S-Shaped Diffusion Curve

Studies suggest that as diffusion progresses, a fairly predictable path of dissemination is followed. For marketing managers, this pattern, called the S-shaped diffusion curve, holds forecasting implications. Strategists can anticipate that cumulative adoption effect of an innovation, if successful, will likely proceed as follows.

- Initially, market acceptance for an innovation increases rather slowly.
- Then, after a rather lethargic beginning, market acceptance for an innovation accelerates more rapidly.
- Finally, market acceptance continues to grow but at an increasingly sluggish pace, because nearly all candidates for adopting the innovation have already done so.

In other words, the *S-shaped diffusion curve* concept holds that the probability of purchase at any point in time is directly related to the number of previous buyers. The rationale is that among consumers, two groups can be identified: early buyers who provide initial sales growth for an innovation, and followers who require broader distribution, more industry advertising, and word-of-mouth exposure before they become sufficiently confident to make the decision to purchase a new product.[47] Eventually, the pool of potential adopters becomes increasingly exhausted, and the growth rate decelerates as a sort of *glass ceiling* is approached. For example, the traditional landline home phone, which was invented by Alexander Graham Bell in 1876, is a case in point. In the early years after its introduction, market acceptance of the home phone was slow due to a lack of landlines and the high cost of their installation. By the year 1880, there were only 30,000 phones in use. However, within a matter of thirty years, this number had soared to 7 million by the year 1910, and further to 30 million by 1948. The acceleration in demand continued until a peak was reached in 2003, with roughly 268 million home phones in use. Today, however, due to the popularity and spread of wireless technology,

S-shaped diffusion curve a pattern of market acceptance for an innovation that begins with a slow start, followed by more rapid acceptance, and then a slowdown.

EXHIBIT 9.2

A Modified S-Shaped
Diffusion Curve for
Landline Phones Allowing
for the Phenomenon of
Discontinuance in Future
Years

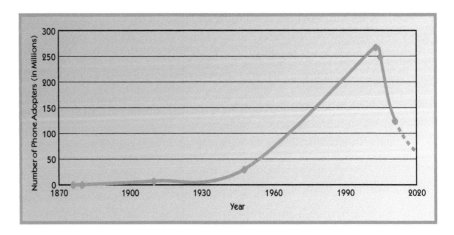

a notable change in the demand for and use of landlines has occurred. According to a recent survey by the National Institute of Health, many U.S. households have ditched their landline and rely solely on cell phones. Back in 2005, approximately 7 percent of consumers had given up their home phone. By 2015, a mere 8 percent of households had maintained just landline phones, more than 47 percent of American homes used only cell phones, while 42 percent had both cell phones and landlines.

The graph in Exhibit 9.2, which is a modified S-shaped diffusion curve, illustrates this effect. In this depiction, the course of time (by year—1876 through 2020) is plotted across the horizontal axis, and the number of landline phone adopters in the United States is plotted along the vertical axis. Notice how the resultant curve approximates the shape of an elongated letter *s*. This curve depicts a slow start in the initial years, followed by a period of rapid growth through the year 2003, and a steady decline since then.

It should be noted here that diffusion patterns can vary from a curve that extends for many years to a rapidly declining curve of short duration. For example, today's popularity of many successful products and services such as movies, computer software, and game software shows a quick diffusion at first, followed by a rapid decline occurring within a brief time span.

THE ADOPTION PROCESS

In order to improve the probability of success for a new product, marketers must understand the adoption process. The more innovative the new product, the more important at first this knowledge becomes. Simply stated, adoption entails a sequence of stages that an individual passes through along a road leading toward the acceptance of new products, services, or ideas. Marketers who develop insights into how and why products or ideas spread, how and why they are accepted or rejected, and the types of consumers who are most likely to purchase or embrace them soon after their introduction, are in a better position to design effective introductory marketing strategies.

STAGES OF THE ADOPTION PROCESS

Adoption requires a series of successive judgments in an individual's decision process regarding acceptance of a new-product offering. The adoption process begins when a consumer or other adopter unit (a family, community, organization) first learns of a new product and ends when that unit finally decides to adopt or reject it. Rogers proposed a decision-making model for adoption of innovations. His original model depicted six stages of the adoption process: awareness, interest, evaluation, trial, adoption, and confirmation. However, his revised model defines the innovation-decision process as consisting of five stages: knowledge, persuasion, decision, implementation, and confirmation.[48] We discuss each in turn.

Knowledge

In the knowledge stage, a consumer is exposed to an innovation's existence and obtains some understanding of how it functions. At this point, consumers are aware of the innovation but have made no judgment concerning its relevance to a recognized problem or need. A family, for example, may learn from ads about a new home security system. Knowledge is largely the result of selective perception and occurs via social media, mass media, or a combination of both. Prior conditions (such as felt needs or problems) and characteristics of the decision-making unit (such as socioeconomic status) can influence the reception of information about the new product.

knowledge
a state of being exposed to and aware of an innovation's existence

Persuasion

At the persuasion stage, the prospect formulates a favorable or unfavorable attitude toward the new product. A consumer may mentally imagine how helpful or satisfying the product might be in some anticipated future-use situation. The perceived risk associated with buying and using the new home security system, for example, may cause the family to weigh the potential value of state-

persuasion
a stage where a prospect formulates a favorable or unfavorable attitude toward an innovation

of-the-art home protection against the potential costs involved. Communications (such as websites, advertising, catalogs, in-store materials, talking to other people) and the perceived characteristics of the innovation (such as its relative advantage and cost) influence this process of attitude formation. In the realm of persuasion, companies attempt to reduce consumers' perceived risk associated with new-product acquisitions. This goal is usually accomplished by allowing consumers to sample or try a product before purchase. Computer and automobile companies, as mentioned earlier, offer lease contracts with the option for purchase to reduce risk perceptions.

Decision

decision
a stage where a prospect makes a choice to either adopt or reject an innovation

Decision occurs when the prospect engages in activities that lead to a choice to adopt or reject the new product. Adoption is a decision to make full use of an innovation as the best course of action. According to Antil, adoption involves both a psychological and a behavioral commitment to a product over time.[50] In other words, we decide to continually use the product unless situational variables (such as lack of resources or product unavailability) prevent usage. In the example of the home security system, the family may conclude that due to an escalating crime rate in the neighborhood, the protection is well worth its cost. As a result, the decision is made to adopt. Rejection, on the other hand, is a decision not to adopt. Rejection can be either active or passive. In the case of active rejection, a prospect considers product adoption (perhaps including even its trial) but then decides not to adopt. Passive rejection, on the other side, consists of never really considering use of the innovation. By presenting facts about its features and benefits, marketing communications help consumers to evaluate an innovation and decide whether to accept or reject it.

Implementation

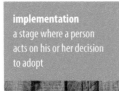

implementation
a stage where a person acts on his or her decision to adopt

Implementation occurs when a prospect puts the adoption idea into action. At this point, the innovation-decision process shifts from a mere mental exercise to one that entails actual behavioral change. Active information seeking addresses such questions as where to obtain the new product, how to use it, what operational problems the user is likely to encounter, and how to solve them. Agents of change dispense technical assistance to clients as these clients begin the process of implementation to help them with various aspects of product use, maintenance, or service. A marketer's introductory strategies relating to financing, delivery, installation, and service are usually designed to make consumer purchasing easy.

ETHICAL DILEMMA

A Sparkle of Youth . . . In a Bottle

Herbal supplements such as ginkgo biloba, echinacea, St. John's wort, burdock root, and ginseng are the fastest growing herbal remedies that the market has witnessed in recent years. Consumer adoption of herbs and supplements has gained vast momentum since Congress ruled that manufacturers could make health claims for nutritional supplements and that the Food and Drug Administration couldn't treat them like drugs. Sales of these natural remedies as a result have grown over 25 percent annually. Annual sales in the United States for 2015 were $33 billion, with an estimated projected sales in 2016 to reach $35 billion.

Presently, more than 1,500 companies compete in this promising field. Companies such as Warner-Lambert, Pharamanex, Celestial, and Bayer offer a variety of products ranging from cholesterol-lowering herbal remedies to vitamins and minerals designed to enhance health, treat tension, and permit mood control.

Observing consumers' enhanced interest in these new herbs, many beverage companies have jumped on the bandwagon and have introduced new drinks laced with a variety of these herbs. Some of these drinks contain beta carotene, ginseng, aloe vera, and high doses of chromium. However, unlike sports drinks such as Gatorade that are formulated to replenish body nutrients, the makers of the new beverages claim that these drinks can bring back youth, improve health, and result in a longer, happier life.

Similarly, operations that market Chinese herbal supplements in the United States often claim that the products they sell treat or cure diseases. For example, a vendor of a pill called Dia-Cope claimed that the pill prevents, treats, and cures diabetes. Another supplier claimed that "Sagee," a Chinese herbal supplement, could improve memory and concentration, repair damaged brain cells, slow the aging of the brain, and increase the learning ability of people with mental handicaps including Alzheimer's disease. These sellers often advertise their products on websites available in multiple languages, including English, Chinese, Japanese, Korean, Indonesian, Spanish, and Russian.

Such claims are questionable at best because no scientific proof exists to support them. This may explain the twenty-first century terminology and jargon used by marketers of these products to appeal to the same basic human dreams that have existed since the dawn of history.[49]

In the past few years, many consumers have come to believe in the benefits of herbal remedies. Visit the website of GNC at http://www.gnc.com/Default.aspx?lang=en and the site of the Mayo Clinic at www.mayoclinic.com/health/herbal-supplements-SA00044. What do you think about the health claims made by makers of these herbal remedies and beverages? Who are the most likely prospects for consuming these products? Should legislation be passed to regulate and monitor such health claims?

Confirmation

Even after a consumer makes the decision to accept a new product, the newly converted customer may perceive some degree of postpurchase doubt. That is, an individual may seek reassurance that the decision to purchase and use the product was appropriate or correct. In the confirmation stage, the consumer

> **confirmation**
> a stage where an adopter experiences postpurchase doubt and seeks reassurance for the decision made

assesses his or her satisfaction with the product and decides whether to continue to purchase and use it. As a result of confirmation or disconfirmation, adopters may strengthen their commitment to a new product or cease to utilize it altogether, a phenomenon known as discontinuance. Discontinuance refers to the reversal of a consumer's decision to adopt a product or service and his or her choice to cease using it. For example, in some cases, consumers may reverse their adoption decision after being exposed to conflicting messages about the new product, or when using the innovation conflicts with established habits. In the case of the home security system, family members may find that too many false alarms are being accidentally triggered by children in the house to the point of aggravating the parents, the neighbors, and the police—a situation that may lead them to discontinue the service.

HOW TYPICAL ARE THE STAGES OF ADOPTION?

From the preceding, we should not suppose that all consumers pass through all stages of the adoption process each and every time they purchase goods and services. The adoption process specifically addresses the individual's deliberation about whether to accept new, previously unfamiliar products and services. The more novel, complex, expensive, or potentially risky the innovation is perceived to be, the more likely an individual is to systematically progress through the entire process or spend more time at any given stage. The duration of the time interval spent at any given stage or between stages varies among different individuals. For example, innovators and early adopters are less likely to go through a lengthy deliberation process compared with other adopter categories. Also, the stages leading up to adoption may not always occur in the specific order proposed, some stages may be omitted, and multiple stages may occur simultaneously. It is conceivable, for example, that upon becoming aware of a new product such as Ginkgo health supplement, a prospect may instantaneously become interested in it, mentally evaluate it, and arrive at an intention to adopt it. In another instance, a prospect may reject an innovation at one stage of the adoption process but resume the process at a later date. Thus, an individual could eventually adopt a product or service that he or she had previously rejected.

RESISTANCE TO ADOPTION

Some obstacles create serious barriers to new-product adoption and may cause consumers to reject an innovation altogether. A model proposed by

Ram and Sheth identified three functional obstacles (value, usage, and risk barriers) and two psychological obstacles (tradition and image barriers) that serve as sources of consumer resistance to adopting innovations.[51]

Value Barriers

A value barrier is any potential lack of product performance relative to its price compared to that of substitute goods. A new technologically advanced smartphone may carry a hefty price tag of $700, where as other more-conventional cell phones may be available for less than $150. A number of avenues are open to marketers in this case in order to overcome a perceived value barrier. First, marketers may explore technological advances that lower production costs and, in turn, the innovation's selling price (as has been the case for PCs). Second, marketers may significantly improve product performance and, ultimately, utility to prospective adopters. Third, marketers may improve the new product's positioning and sponsor informative advertising to convince prospects of the innovation's merit. For example, a new smartphone's advanced digital technology and unique features may be presented to the public as major improvements over conventional cell phones and well worth the investment.

Usage Barriers

A usage barrier exists when an innovation is not a part of prospects' routines. Marketers in this case may attempt to boost usage by identifying and cultivating markets that are unfamiliar with the product. The global expansion of American fast-food establishments, for instance, gave many of these companies' unlimited opportunities in new markets all over the world. Second, marketers may follow a systems perspective. That is, they may coordinate the new product with a network of other interlocking products and activities. Horizontal cooperative advertising between complementary products (electronics and add-ons) or services (airlines, car rental companies, and hotels) are prime examples in point.[52]

Third, marketers may utilize change agents, such as opinion leaders, to actively endeavor to switch peoples' mindsets and habits. In the fashion industry, for example, designers sponsor well-publicized fashion shows attended by the elite as a means of creating opinion leaders who, when they adopt, spread the fashion to others.[53]

value barrier
a perceived lack of product performance relative to its price compared to that of substitute brands

usage barrier
a condition where an innovation is not part of a prospect's routines

Cheers to the Wines from California

The U.S. wine industry has gone through a radical transformation, from being a largely domestic industry to a globally respected wine exporter. Until the 1980s, the wine market was largely a domestic one, with imports mostly arriving from France, Italy, and Spain. Today, the situation has changed dramatically, and California has risen as one of the most productive regions of superior wines.

Historically, it wasn't until the repeal of Prohibition in 1933 that Napa Valley's wine industry began its renaissance. During the years of World War II, a group of vintners came together to share the ideas of growing grapes and making wine. They laid the foundation for the Napa Valley Vintners, a dynamic trade organization dedicated to advancing the valley's wines. As time went by, the ingenuity, inventiveness, and free thinking of these pioneers came to bear fruit. First, they embarked on the issue of obtaining grape vines from Europe. This was followed by adopting creative methods of making these vines put out huge amounts of fruit. And instead of using the tradition-driven, old-world ways of winemaking, they created modern approaches that were developed in California. These approaches were based on tinkering, cloning, cataloging, and earth-science experimentation in order to give California wines their desired properties. By so doing, the vintners were able to produce high-quality wines that are full of character and distinctiveness—equal to those from Europe.

During the 1950s and 1960s, Napa Valley continued to gain notoriety in wine circles. It attracted a whole new generation of winemakers. A unique group of human resources came to age in the 1970s due to a success story generated by a public victory for the small California wine region at an international wine-tasting competition in Paris. Napa Valley wines went head to head with the legendary French Bordeaux in a blind taste test and won critical acclaim.

Today, there are over 400 California wineries, and many of them export to over 165 markets worldwide. The United States now ranks as the fourth leading wine producer in the world. The United Kingdom is the premier customer of the California wines internationally.

U.S. wine exports, 90 percent from California, reached $1.5 billion in winery revenues in 2014. Volume shipments were 443 million liters or 49.3 million cases. The European Union was the top destination for U.S. wine exports, accounting for $518 million; followed by Canada, $487 million; Japan, $101 million; China, $71 million; Hong Kong, $69 million; Mexico, $24 million; and South Korea, $22 million. This impressive trend is expected to persist as California wines continue to invade markets traditionally held by older winemaking countries such as France and Italy.[54]

From the dawn of history, wine has been produced by various regions in the world. Some of the countries that traditionally dominated the making and exportation of wine include France, Italy, Spain, Portugal, Greece, and even Australia. The United States is actually a newcomer to this industry, but the quality of its wines has equaled or even surpassed that of those other regions. To what factors do you attribute this success story, particularly in the international market? Would you expect this successful trend to continue in the future if you knew that other low-cost producers of wine in some foreign countries, such as China, are already becoming formidable producers and aggressive marketers of their low-price wines globally? To learn more about California wines, visit the California Wine Institute at www.wineinstitute.org/resources/statistics/article122. Do you think that the growth of demand for domestic wine will eventually help reduce American wine imports—positively influencing the balance of trade for the United States? Explain.

Risk Barriers

A **risk barrier** occurs when uncertainty lingers concerning the economic-value, functional-performance, safety, social, or psychological aspects of adoption. Marketers can surmount such reservations among consumers via strategies such as reducing price, increasing consumers' product education, and expediting experiences with and trials of a product. Marketers can also elicit product endorsements and testimonials from product authorities, celebrities, and ordinary satisfied customers. Advertisers frequently use seals of approval from respected associations to support their claims. This has been proven to be a successful strategy used by many firms in order to reduce risk barriers. For this reason, many household products bear the Good Housekeeping Seal of Approval; and many automakers proudly tout the J.D. Powers quality ratings of their cars.

risk barrier
a condition where uncertainty lingers about adopting an innovation

Tradition Barriers

A **tradition barrier** exists when cultural norms and values hamper product adoption. For example, life insurance is frowned upon in some fundamentalist Islamic countries on the basis that it is unthinkable to insure against the will of *Allah* (God). To surmount such obstacles, marketers must be sensitive to social mores and customs. Under such conditions, marketers should promote the service in a way that ties in with widely held cultural values rather than in a manner that abruptly alters established traditions. By utilizing appropriate agents of change over time, marketers may successfully reshape consumer ideas, opinions, and practices.

tradition barrier
a condition where cultural norms and values hamper product adoption

Image Barriers

An image barrier exists when a product or brand is unknown by the public or suffers from a relatively unfavorable image. In this case, marketers may be able to use well-known spokespersons to draw positive attention to the brand and boost its image, license a brand name with a solid image, or initiate an image-building ad campaign to enhance the firm's reputation. A few years ago, Hyundai automobile company suffered from a low-quality image compared to Japanese cars such as Toyota, Honda, and Mazda. As a result, Hyundai initiated a comprehensive and costly ad campaign that appeared in most U.S. media. The message highlighted the quality, design, safety, warranty, and economy of the firm's vehicles, and significantly enhanced the image of the brand.

As a new idea or product becomes available, information about it spreads from its source to receivers in the marketplace. This process may involve the mass media, word of mouth, observation of the new product in use, or any of a variety of other vehicles that help bring about widespread adoption of the product or idea in a social system. Diffusion of an innovation is therefore a part of the collective behavior of a group. Information about a product or an idea flows within and between the tiers of a social system. Group influence within the society functions as a powerful force leading toward final acceptance or rejection of an innovation. Group influence and its ramifications for marketers and researchers of consumer behavior is the topic of the next chapter.

SUMMARY

Diffusion is a macroprocess concerned with the spread of a new product or idea from its original source to and throughout the general public. There are four basic components in the diffusion process: the innovation, the channel of communication, the social system, and time.

Innovations or *new* products are any products, services, or ideas that consumers perceive as new. New products can result from changes in technology and production processes, from changes in a firm's marketing strategy, or from a combination of these. One classification of new products distinguishes between discontinuous, dynamically continuous, and continuous innovations. Five product characteristics influence consumer acceptance of new products: relative advantage, compatibility, simplicity–complexity, observability, and trialability–divisibility.

Communication of product-related information is essential for the widespread acceptance of an innovation across the marketplace. Without communication, consumers would remain largely unaware of new products. Channels of communication include the mass media, interpersonal communication, and interactive technologies. Diffusion depends on a chain of interpersonal communications, whereby successive layers of consumers adopt a new product upon the recommendation of slightly more venturesome acquaintances.

Diffusion occurs within the context of a social system in which individuals play specific roles, adhere to group norms and values, interact with others, and influence others as well as receive influence from them.

The time dimension includes such aspects as the *rate of adoption and frequency of purchase.* Consumers exhibit individual differences in their readiness and willingness to try and accept a particular new product, service, or idea. Thus five adopter categories can be identified: innovators, early adopters, early majority, late majority, and laggards. The S-shaped diffusion curve depicts the fairly predictable pattern of market acceptance for new products over time—slow at first, then more rapid, then at an increasingly sluggish pace.

Adoption is a microprocess dealing with the stages that an individual goes through before accepting a new product. Stages of the adoption process, which Rogers termed the innovation-decision process, are knowledge, persuasion, decision, implementation, and confirmation. In some cases, an innovation fails to become integrated into an adopter's life routine.

Five types of barriers—value, usage, risk, tradition, and image—serve as sources of consumer resistance to adopting innovations.

CASE SYNOPSIS

Drones: The Pros and the Cons

Drones are now playing an increasingly important role in businesses, including agriculture, engineering, and real estate, in addition to many other applications. Millions of consumers today are buying the machines and taking to the sky. There are now hundreds of drone models available in the marketplace, ranging in price from $100 to $7,000 or more, depending on the specific features requested by the buyer.

Safety and privacy remain in the forefront of the drone debate. In one respect, incidents of "potentially unsafe" drones have increased dramatically, where drones are flown at high altitudes invading the paths of passenger aircraft. Most observers believe, however, that consumers will eventually adapt to drones, and predict that the public's fear as well as safety and privacy concerns about drones will disappear. On the other hand, drones also represent an economical weapon offering terrorists a means to accomplish their sinister plans in support of their criminal or political ideologies.

Notes

1   T. Bolfert et al. (Eds.), *Harley-Davidson, Inc: Historical Overview, 1903–1993* (Milwaukee, WI: Harley-Davidson, Inc., 1994).
2   Rick Barrett, "Harley-Davidson Seeks to Move Throttle to Meet Changing Demographics," *Journal Sentinel Online* (March 21, 2015), http://www.jsonline.com/business/harley-davidson-seeks-to-move-throttle-to-meet-changing-demographics-b99464795z1-297125131.html; Thomas Gelb, "Overhauling Corporate Engines Drive Winning Strategies," *Journal of Business Strategy* 19, no. 6 (November–December 1993), pp. 6–12; Milia Boyd, "Harley-Davidson Motor Company," *Incentive* (September 1993), pp. 26–31; John D. Stoll, Kyle Peterson, and Nick Zieminski, "Legend Rolls On with Newer Looks to Lure Younger Riders," *Chicago Tribune Business Report,* sec. 2 (December 8, 2011), p. 3; "Harley-Davidson Motorcycle Sales, Shipments, and Revenues," http://knol.google.com/k/harley-davidson-motorcycle-sales-shipments-and-revenues.
3   Vijay Mahajan, Eitan Muller, and Frank M. Bass, "New Product Diffusion Models in Marketing: A Review and Directions for Research," *Journal of Marketing* 54 (January 1990), pp. 1–26; for a model of diffusion processes in developing countries, see Eric J. Arnould, "Toward a Broadened Theory of Preference Formation and the Diffusion of Innovations: Cases from Zinder Province, Niger Republic," *Journal of Consumer Research 16 (September 1989),* pp. 239–267.
4   Nessim Hanna, Douglas Ayers, Rick Ridnour, and Geoffrey Gordon, "New Product Development Practices in Consumer Versus Business Products Organizations," *The Journal of Product & Brand Management 4, no.* 2 (1995).
5   Marcia Mogelonsky, "Product Overload," *American Demographics* (August 1998), pp. 65–69.
6   T. D. Kuczmarski, *Managing New Products: The Power of Innovations* (Upper Saddle River, NJ: Prentice Hall, 1992).

7   Brian Wansink, "Making Old Brands New," *American Demographics* (December 1997), pp. 53–58.

8   E. Yoon and G. L. Lilien, "New Industrial Product Performance: The Effects of Marketing Characteristics and Strategy," *Journal of Product Innovation Management* 2, no. 3 (1985), pp. 134–144.

9   C. M. Crawford, *New Products Management* (Boston: Irwin, 1994).

10 Hanna, Ayers, Ridnour, and Gordon, "New Product Development Practices in Consumer Versus Business Products Organizations."

11 Thomas S. Robertson, "The Process of Innovation and the Diffusion of Innovation," *Journal of Marketing* 31 (January 1967), pp. 14–19.

12 "Kick Off Your New Adventure Covered by the Best Network" (2016), http://www.verizonwireless.com/landingpages/international-student/; Peter Piazza, "Microsoft Will Lure Students with Free Software," *Data Storage Today* (February 18, 2008); Becca Madder, "Wireless Companies Boost Efforts to Lure Young Buyers," *Business Journal* (November 30, 2001); Jessica Silver-Greenberg, "College Students Majoring in Credit Card Debt," *Business Week* (September 5, 2007); Beth Marklein, "For Profit Colleges See Major Gains in Past Decade," *USA Today* (June 2, 2011), http://www.usatoday.com/news/education/2011-05-26-for-profit-college-undergraduate-enrollment_n.htm; Gina Damato, "Students Targeted During Promotional Campaigns of Energy Drinks, Beer," *da* (October 29, 2010), http://www.thedaonline.com/news/students-targeted-during-promotional-campaigns-of-energy-drinks-beer-1.1735591.

13 Page C. Moreau, Donald R. Lehmann, and Arthur B. Markman, "Entrenched Knowledge Structures and Consumer Response to New Products," Journal of Marketing Research 38, no. 1 (February 2001), pp. 14–16.

14 Elizabeth C. Hirschman, "Symbolism and Technology as Sources for the Generation of Innovations," in Andrew Mitchell (Ed.), *Advances in Consumer Research* 9 (Ann Arbor, MI: Association for Consumer Research, 1982), pp. 537–541.

15 Rosella Capetta et al., "Convergent Designs in Fine Fashions: An Evolutionary Model for Stylistic Innovation," *Research Policy* 35, no. 9 (November 2006), pp. 1273–1290.

16 "Good Food, All Day Long," Kelloggs, www2.kelloggs.com/Product/Product.aspx.

17 Hanna, Ayers, Ridnour, Gordon, "New Product Development Practices in Consumer Versus Business Products Organizations."

18 C. Miller, "Little Relief Seen for New Product Failure Rate," *Marketing News* 27, no. 13 (1993), pp. 1, 18.

19 S. Edgett, D. Shipley, and G. Forbes "Japanese and British Companies Compared: Contributing Factors to Success and Failure in NPD," *Journal of Product Innovation* Management 9, no. 1 (1992), pp. 3–10.

20 Hanna, Ayers, Ridnour, Gordon, "New Product Development Practices in Consumer Versus Business Products Organizations."

21 Lee Eun-Ju, Lee Jinkook, and David Eastwood, "A Two-step Estimation of Consumer Adoption of Technology-Based Service Innovations," *Journal of Consumer Affairs* 37, no. 2 (2003), pp. 256–282.

22 Everett M. Rogers, *Diffusion of Innovations,* 4th ed. (New York: Free Press, 1995).

23 Mogelonsky, "Product Overload," p. 69.

24 "Enlighten Me: What Is an FTD Florist," https://enlightenme.com/ftd-florist/; "FTD Group Inc.," Yahoo Finance Site, http://finance.yahoo.com/9/pr?s=ftd.

25 Mogelonsky, "Product Overload," p. 68.

26 Juli Clover, "Apple Releases iOS 9.3 with Night Shift New Quick Actions App Improvements, '1970' Bug Fix and More,"*Macrumors* (March 21, 2016), http://www.macrumors.com/2016/03/21/apple-releases-ios-9-3/.

27 "To Cut Price, SolarCity Leases Solar Panels," C/netNews.com (April 1, 2008), www.news.com/8301-11128_3-9907982-54.html.

28 Robert W. Shoemaker and F. Robert Shoaf, "Behavioral Changes in the Trial of New Products," *Journal of Consumer Research* 2 (September 1975), pp. 104–109.

29 Andrew Newman, "Brands Now Direct Their Followers to Social Media," *The New York Times* (August 3, 2011), http://www.nytimes.com/2011/08/04/business/media/promoting-products-using-social-me . . .

30 Michael J. Etzel, Bruce J. Walker, and William J. Stanton, *Marketing*, 11th ed. (New York: McGraw-Hill, 1997), p. 211; Peter L. Sher and Sheng-Hsien Lee, "Consumer Skepticism and Online Reviews: An Elaboration Likelihood Model Perspective," *Highbeam Business* (February 1, 2009), http://business.highbeam.com/407739/article-1G1-195982392/consumer-skepticism-and-o . . .

31 Hubert Gatignon and Thomas S. Robertson, "A Propositional Inventory for New Diffusion Research," *Journal of Consumer Research* 11, no. 4 (March 1985), p. 859–867.

32 World Bank Group, "Global Economic Prospects January 2016," http://elibrary.worldbank.org/doi/abs/10.1596/978-0-8213-7365-1; Yoram Wind, Thomas S. Robertson, and Cynthia Fraser, "Industrial Product Diffusion by Market Segment," *Industrial Marketing Management* 11 (1982), pp. 1–8; Enrique Rueda-Sabater and John Garrity, "The Emerging Internet Economy: Looking a Decade Ahead," The Global Information Technology Report 2010-2011World Economic Forum.

33 Stephen Crystal, "The Diffusion of Innovation in AIDS Treatment: Zidovudine Use in Two New Jersey Cohorts," *BNET.com* (October, 1995), http://findarticles.com/p/articles/mi_m4149/is_n4_v30/ai_17635052/print.

34 Joel Garreau, "The Fastest Global Diffusion of Any Technology in Human History," 12 Degrees of Freedom (March 1, 2008), http://12degreesoffreedom.blogspot.com/2008/03/fastest-global-diffusion-of-any.html.

35 Gatignon and Robertson, "A Propositional Inventory for New Diffusion Research"; Frank M. Bass, "A New Product Growth Model for Consumer Durables," *Management Science* 15 (January 1969), pp. 215–227.

36 Gatignon and Robertson, "A Propositional Inventory for New Diffusion Research"; Kristiaan Helsen, Kamel Jedidi, and Wayne S. DeSarbo, "A New Approach to Country Segmentation Utilizing Multinational Diffusion Patterns," *Journal of Marketing* 57 (October 1993), pp. 60–71; Robert Fisher and Linda Price, "An Investigation into the Social Context of Early Adopter Behavior," *Journal of Consumer Research* 19 (December 1992), pp. 477–486.

37 Philip Kotler, *Marketing Management,* 8th ed. (Upper Saddle River, NJ: Prentice Hall 1994), p. 412.

38 William G. Zikmund and Michael d'Amico, *Marketing, 4th ed.* (Minneapolis: West, 1993), p. 301.

39 Scott Roberts and Rajiv Dant, "Socioeconomic, Cultural, and Technical Determinants of Contemporary American Consumption Patterns," in Stanley Shapiro and A. H. Walle (Eds.), *1988 AMA Winter Educators'* Conference (Chicago: American Marketing Association, 1988), p. 321.

40 Andy Zaky, "Zaky: 2011-2012 iPad Sales Estimates," *Seeking Alpha* (May 27, 2011), http://seekingalpha.com/article/272181-zaky-2011-2012-ipad-sales-estimates.

41 "The iPad's 5th Anniversary: A Time for Apple's Category-Defining Tablet," *The Verge* (April 17, 2015); "Garner Says Worldwide Tablet Sales Grew 68 Percent in 2013, With Android Capturing 62 Percent of the Market," *Garner* (March 3, 2014); "Apple Reports First Quarter Results," *Apple Press Info* (January 24, 2012), http://www.apple.com/pr/library/2012/01/24Apple-Reports-First-Quarter-Results.html.

42 Kotler, *Marketing Management,* pp. 348–349.

43 Rogers, *Diffusion of Innovations.*

44 Gatignon and Robertson, "A Propositional Inventory for New Diffusion Research"; David Midgley and Grahame Dowling, "A Longitudinal Study of Product Form Innovation: The Interaction Between Predispositions and Social Messages," *Journal of Consumer Research* 19 (March 1993), pp. 611–625; Ronald E. Goldsmith and Charles F. Hofacker, "Measuring Consumer Innovativeness," *Journal of the Academy of Marketing Science* 19 (Summer 1991), pp. 209–221.

45 William G. Zikmund and Michael d'Amico, *Basic Marketing* (Minneapolis–St. Paul, MN: West, 1996), p. 170.

46 C. Merle Crawford, *New Products Management* (Burr Ridge, IL: Irwin, 1994), p. 292.

47 Edwin E. Bobrow and Dennis W. Shafer, Pioneering New Products: *A Market Survival Guide* (Homewood, IL: Dow Jones–Irwin, 1987), p. 139; Vijay Mahajan, Eitan Muller, and Frank M. Bass, "New Product Diffusion Models in Marketing: A Review and Directions for Research," *Journal of Marketing* 54 (January 1990), pp. 1–26; Mike Stobbe, "Nearly Half of US Homes Use Cell Phones Only, Shun Landlines" (December 1, 2015), http://phys.org/news/2015-12-homes-cellphones-shun-landlines.html.

48   Rogers, *Diffusion of Innovations.*

49   "Retail Sales of Vitamins and Nutritional Supplements in the US," Statista. com, www.statista.com/statistics/235801/retail-sales-of-vitamins-and-nu-tritional-supplements-in-the-us/; Stephen Daniells, "Herbal Supplement Sales to Hit $93.15 Billion by 2015: Report" (January 13, 2011), http://www. nutraingredients/usa.com/Markets/Herbal-supplement-sales-to-hit-93.15-billion-by-2015-Report; D. Kirk Davidson, "Products New, but Puffery Same as Always," *Marketing News* 28, no. 23 (November 7, 1994), p. 14; David Vaczek, "Herbal Effervescence," *Promo* (November 1998), pp. 37–41; John Greenwald, "Herbal Healing," *Time* (November 23, 1998), pp. 59–69.

50   John M. Antil, "New Product or Service Adoption: When Does It Happen?" *Journal of Consumer Marketing* 5 (Spring 1988), pp. 5–15.

51   S. Ram and Jagdish N. Sheth, "Consumer Resistance to Innovations: The Marketing Problem and Its Solutions," *Journal of Consumer Marketing* 6 (Spring 1989), pp. 5–14.

52   Zikmund and d'Amico, *Basic Marketing,* p. 301.

53   Kotler, *Marketing Management,* p. 412.

54   "2014 California Wine Sales Grew 4.4 Percent by Volume and 6.7 Percent by Value in the U.S.," *Wine Institute* (May 19, 2015), https://www.winein-stitute.org/resources/pressroom/05192015; "California Vintners Step Up Marketing Efforts," Beach California.com, www.beachcalifornia.com/wine2. html; "California Wineries," Beach California.com, www.beachcalifornia. com/wine.html; "2007 California Wine Sales," Wine Institute, wineinstitute. org/resources/statistics/article122; Marc Lifsher, "California Wine Exports Heading Toward a Record Year," *Los Angeles Times* (December 13, 2011), "2011 U.S. Wine Exports, 90 Percent from California, Reach New Re-cord of $1.4 Billion," *Yahoo News* (February 16, 2012), http://news.yahoo. com/2011-u-wine-exports-90-percent-california-reach-140213522.html

CHAPTER 10

GROUP INFLUENCE

LEARNING OBJECTIVES

- To grasp the meaning and nature of social groups.
- To identify various types of social groups.
- To distinguish between roles and status within the context of a group.
- To explore five types of social power as well as the way marketers employ them.
- To comprehend the nature, types, and influence of reference groups.
- To identify the levels of conformity to group mandates.
- To conceptualize the impact of reference groups on consumer behavior.

KEY TERMS

group	role-related product	anticipatory aspirational
norms	cluster	reference groups
primary groups	status	symbolic aspirational
secondary groups	conspicuous consumption	reference groups
formal groups	reward power	negative reference
informal groups	coercive power	groups
planned groups	legitimate power	disclaimant reference
emergent groups	referent power	groups
social networks	expert power	compliance
consumption subcultures	reference groups	reactance
brand communities	membership reference	classical identification
brand tribes	groups	reciprocal identification
roles	aspirational reference	internalization
	groups	

Black Lives Matter (BLM) is a freedom rights movement that was formed during the protest surrounding George Zimmerman's arrest and trial. It started in July 2013 as a result of the acquittal of neighborhood watch coordinator George Zimmerman by a Stanford, Florida jury for the murder of seventeen-year-old Travon Martin. Angered and deeply disillusioned by the verdict, members of the Black Organizing for Leadership & Dignity (BOLD) group began asking the organization's leaders how they were going to respond to the assault on and devaluation of Black lives. A post on Facebook written by Alicia Garza, a domestic worker-rights organizer, entitled "A Love Note to Black People" called on them to "Get active" and "Fight back," ending her post with the words "Our Lives Matter, Black Lives Matter." With that in the summer of 2013, the movement with the hashtag #BlackLivesMatter was born in the social media.

Unlike most other freedom rights groups, BLM immediately recognized the value of social media in developing a political agenda and mobilizing Black people for action. By using Facebook, Twitter, and Tumblr, participants created a movement unlike most Black freedom campaigns that preceded it. The new movement was powerful, yet diffused, linked not by physical proximity of participants but by the mobilizing force of social media. A hashtag on Twitter linked the fates of millions in a way that transcended geographic boundaries and time zones.

BLM embraced a number of tactics, such as using the slogan, "Shut it down." But beyond rhetorical slogans, activists by the dozens marched onto highways disrupting traffic, linking arms across railroad tracks to stop trains, sitting down in urban intersections, delaying sporting events, and temporarily occupying shopping malls, major retail stores, police departments, and city halls. Political slogans used during the demonstrations included arousing phrases such as "Black lives matters," "Hands up, don't shoot," and "I can't breathe."

BLM incorporated individuals on the margins of traditional Black freedom movements, including women, the working poor, the disabled, undocumented immigrants, atheists and agnostics, and those who self-identify as gay and transgender. Such marginalized Black individuals played a major role in the formation of the group and in its ongoing community activities and protests.

By early 2015, the BLM slogan had become a most recognized symbol against what many individuals called an unjustifiable killing of unarmed Blacks as well as police brutality against persons of color. It also advanced the idea that action is needed on behalf of all who have been ignored or marginalized in earlier freedom campaigns.

By February 2015, the movement's influence had reached the national popular entertainment media. TV shows, as well as magazines—such as *Essence*—profiled and supported the movement. At that same time, BLM had initiated another new tactic by publicly challenging politicians, including 2016 political candidates to state their positions on BLM issues, as well as to declare their envisioned policies on that topic. As a consequence, most major Democratic presidential candidates stated that they were developing new special policy agendas that would specifically address policing reform and racially disproportionate incarceration. Thus, by employing cyber activism, the BLM movement was able to bring public attention to race, class, gender, nationality, sexuality, disability, and state-sponsored violence into focus. As a consequence, millions of people are now aware of the ongoing impact of police brutality on Black lives, and the need to confront prevailing racism in our society.[1]

The power of the dominant social platforms—such as Facebook, Twitter, Tumblr, and You-Tube—has been demonstrated in the BLM movement. Social media have also clearly altered virtually all aspects of group behavior today. Such media have provided a voice to communicate with activists, a forum to influence Blacks and others, and a pad from which to launch marches and demonstrations. Learn more about the role of social media and educational institutions in the rise of the BLM movement by visiting https://www.washingtonpost.com/national/how-black-lives-matter-born-on-the-streets-is-rising-to-power-on-campus/2015/11/17/3c113e96-8959. *While there are many advantages of the social media for marketers, there are also a number of limitations. Cite the benefits and drawbacks of social media, and comment on their expected positive and negative roles in influencing group behavior within our society.*

This chapter explores how groups attain conformity to their expectations, why individuals comply with group standards, and what forms of power are at play in group interaction. The powerful impact of groups on consumers, particularly the effect of those social networks with whom individuals interact frequently, mandates that marketers examine their characteristic relational processes. Such knowledge can then be applied to guide the formation of effective marketing strategies.

THE MEANING AND IMPORTANCE OF GROUPS

group
people who share beliefs, have role relationships, and experience interdependent behavior

The term group refers to two or more individuals who share a set of norms, values, or beliefs; have certain role relationships; and experience interdependent behavior.[2] Based on this definition, a group is not merely a collection of individuals who happen to be at the same place at the same time. People attending a show, patronizing a shopping mall, or riding a bus do not constitute a group. A group is a social system with its own shared beliefs, norms, and values concerning areas of common interest. Ideally, within this structure, group members interact with one another and share a common goal and sense of belonging.

norms
shared guidelines to accepted and expected behavior

As mentioned, group norms are legitimate, shared guidelines to accepted and expected behavior.[3] They specify proper and improper actions under particular circumstances and serve as standards against which members evaluate the appropriateness of their own behavior and that of others. Norms stipulate what is required, acceptable, and prohibited. They may cover such issues as styles of dress, table etiquette, roles assumed, manner of speech, personal hygiene, and other recommended modes of behavior for members of the group. Some group norms apply equally to all members. Other sets of norms apply only to those persons who occupy specific roles within a group (doctors, lawyers, judges, professors, or clergy).

Rarely, if ever, does a single group provide for all human needs and wants. Thus, there are many groups to which people may belong. Family and friendship groups, Internet community groups, work groups, religious groups, civic groups, athletic groups, charitable groups, and educational groups are among the most familiar. As evidenced by their diverse names and labels, different groups exist for different purposes. The common purpose that binds group members together may, however, hold higher priority for some members than for others. Similarly, the purpose for joining the group can vary, depending on an individual's priorities. For example, an individual may join a social network to share ideas with other members, while another may join the same group in search of friends.

The significance of a group rests in its ability to influence thoughts, feelings, and behaviors of individual participants, whether the group is traditional or online, actual or even imagined. This influence may include social perception and social interaction, as well as other effects on members' cognitions and affective states.

From a marketing point of view, it is important to understand groups' influence on members' perceptions, behavior, and ultimately decision making. In addition, it is equally important to understand that groups themselves are behavioral entities characterized by interlocking relationships between members. Such knowledge is helpful when marketers design promotional strategies, such as those that firms use today to appeal to influential consumer tribes and to establish powerful brand communities.[4]

SELECTED TYPES OF SOCIAL GROUPS

Groups can be classified based on a number of variables, such as regularity of contact, size, availability of membership, and degree of intimacy within the group. For our purposes, however, it is sufficient to classify groups on the basis of *intimacy* (primary versus secondary), *formality* (formal versus informal), and *purpose* (planned versus emergent).

PRIMARY VERSUS SECONDARY

Primary groups are usually small and intimate groups whose members come together on a regular basis, exhibit spontaneous interpersonal behavior, communicate face-to-face, and maintain commitment of self and concern for others in the group. The family represents an important primary group. Other examples of groups with close ties include athletic teams, local chapters of fraternities or sororities, monasteries, and convents.

primary groups
small, intimate groups
that meet regularly and
communicate face-to-face

secondary groups
groups in which regular,
face-to-face contact is
lacking

Secondary groups, on the other hand, are teams where intimacy and personal interaction are less evident than in primary groups. Secondary groups lack the regularity of contact and personal commitment or concern for other members that characterize primary groups. Although communication may still involve face-to-face interaction, other communication efforts are impersonal in nature and occur via the mass media, such as in the case of virtual or online communities. Examples of other secondary groups may include professional organizations, religious denominations, alumni associations, labor unions, and similar groups.

FORMAL VERSUS INFORMAL

formal groups
highly organized groups with an explicit structure and specified goals and procedures

Formal groups are highly organized hierarchical groups in which the structure is explicitly defined, objectives are clearly specified, roles and statuses are clearly delineated, and procedures and responsibilities are strictly observed. In the business world, major corporations within practically every industry have formal organizational structures that ensure the continuity of their mission, objectives, operational strategies, and policies, regardless of the specific individuals that occupy various positions in these groups.

informal groups
groups in which structure, goals, and procedures are less explicit

Informal groups, on the other hand, frequently emerge within the formal group. Informal group relationships, for example, emerge between people working together as they socialize. This socialization provides a setting for exchange of ideas, viewpoints, and behavior patterns that may add to the efficiency of the organization structure or, as is the case in many present-day corporate structures, may impede its functioning. For example, workers on an assembly line in a factory may have an unspoken informal rule restricting their output to a slower pace than would otherwise be possible. A system of informal rewards and punishments guarantees persistence of these rules.

Informal groups, which have their own centers of power and systems of rewards and punishments, often emerge within formal organizational structures.

© Monkey Business Images/Shutterstock.com

PLANNED VERSUS EMERGENT

Planned groups are specifically formed for some purpose—either by their members or by some external individual or organization. For example, clubs, schools, and churches as well as virtual communities (such as Facebook, and YouTube) constitute various forms of this classification. Members, in such cases, share close relationships and camaraderie with other members.

Emergent groups, on the other hand, come into being spontaneously, either where a set of individuals find themselves together with others in the same place, or come to know each other through interaction over the Internet via virtual communities, blogs, or message boards, and the like. For instance, in the first case, participants in a marathon or walk for breast cancer could constitute such a group. The second case might include people who happen to post on our Facebook wall.

planned groups
groups formed by persons or organizations for some specific purpose

emergent groups
groups that spontaneously come into being

ONLINE COMMUNITIES AND SOCIAL NETWORKS

An online site is a platform that focuses on building social relationships among individuals who share similar interests, backgrounds, or activities across political, economic, and geographic borders. These interactions can take place in various forms. The main types of social networking interactions are those that contain category places (e.g., former school classmates, means to contact with friends, self-description pages) and a recommendation system linked to trust. Today, sites such as Facebook, Google+, and Twitter combine all these features.

Social networking sites share a variety of technical features. A basic feature is the presence of visible profiles of "friends," who are also users of the site. A profile is generated by users when they answer a number of questions, such as education, interests, and occupation. To such profile, users may be allowed to upload photographs or multimedia content. Many sites, moreover, allow users to post blog entries, search for others with similar interests, and share lists of contacts with others. User profiles often include a section dedicated to comments made by other users.

social networks
online groups that serve to build relationships among individuals across political, economic, and geographic borders

In this sense, social networks have the ability to create groups that share common interests or affiliations. In such groups, research has shown that groups' effect on individual members is dependent on the *structure* of the network. Smaller, tighter networks can be less useful to or less influential on their members than networks characterized by many loose or weak ties with individuals outside the main network. More-open networks, with many weak ties and loose social connections, are more likely to introduce new ideas, perspectives, and behaviors to their members than closed networks with many redundant ties. Stated differently, a group of individuals who do things only with each other tends to share the same pattern of thought and behavior. However, when group members form connections with other individuals from diverse social spheres, they become exposed to a new and broader range of information and perspectives. Such influence is valuable for the diffusion of innovation process, which today is largely dependent on the important role of social networks in promoting new products, ideas, and practices among members. An emerging trend that is expected to further enhance social networks' influence on groups is the rapid spread of mobile social networks and their ability to reap the combined benefits of real time and location-based communication, eliminating time and space barriers.[5]

CONSUMPTION SUBCULTURES

consumption subcultures
distinguishable subgroups of society that share a strong commitment to a product, brand, or activity

Consumption subcultures are distinctive subgroups of society that self-select on the basis of a shared commitment to a particular product class, brand, or consumption activity. Examples of such groups include Harley-Davidson Motorcycle Owner Group (HOG)[6] and the Deadheads. They also include bodybuilders and the Weider Brothers empire, NASCAR and rodeo fans, and—to some extent—groups such as surfers and skateboarders. These are usually characterized by their identifiable, hierarchical social structures, unique ethos, shared beliefs and values, as well as distinguishing jargon and rituals. The basis for the rise of these subcultures is their members' ritualistic consumption of certain products and brands or involvement in activities that distinguish them as cohesive groups. The unifying force, in this case, is the shared interest in the unique consumption pattern or the involvement in the singular activity.

Such subcultures are usually assessed through ethnography, which is the study of human behavior in its natural context. Ethnography involves observation of consumers' purchase behavior and/or activities in the physical settings in which they naturally occur. Depth interviews are also conducted to obtain participants' perspectives.

Due to the ritualistic devotion of members of these subcultures to certain products, brands, or activities, marketers can take active roles in inducting and socializing new members as well as cultivating the commitment of current members of such groups. Harley-Davidson, for example, has been highly successful in creating and maintaining a powerful and committed subculture of Harley owners by strategically supplying a steady stream of information geared to the needs of present and new members, as well as by providing a full range of clothing accessories and services that function to enhance members' pride and involvement. In return, Harley-Davidson receives the enviable benefits of steadfast customer loyalty, positive word of mouth, and a flow of highly beneficial feedback.

BRAND COMMUNITIES

A brand community is one that is formed on the basis of a strong attachment to a company and its products. It reflects a solid connection between a brand and the consumers of that particular brand. Consider, for example, products such as Jimmy Choo's illustrious shoes, the Porsche automobile, Apple electronics, Harvard University, or even Starbuck's coffee, and how these organizations have succeeded in attracting loyal and enthusiastic fans who truly believe in and advocate their brands. Such fans have not only made their chosen brand an integral part of their lives and opted to actively seek out and interact with others who share the same interests, but they are willing to go out of their way to promote the company and its products.

Muniz and O'Guinn presented a definition of the term *brand community* and laid out a description of the common characteristics inherent in such groups. They defined brand communities as "a specialized, non-geographically bound community that is based on a structured set of social relations among admirers of a brand."[7] This definition paints a portrait of brand community as a self-selected group of individuals who share strong commitment toward a brand's value, voluntarily act as representatives of that brand, and display a tendency to maintain close relationships with other members of the group.

brand communities
groups that are formed on the basis of a strong attachment to a firm or its products

In terms of the defining aspects of brand communities, Muniz and O'Guinn further identified three characteristics that distinguish brand communities: consciousness of a kind (i.e., the connection that members feel toward one another); shared rituals and traditions (i.e., customs that provided legitimacy to community membership); and moral responsibility (i.e., sense of duty or obligation to the community).

The creation and development of brand communities have become key tasks for marketers. The fact that nearly half of all people make their purchases based on recommendations from their online friends tends to place brand communities in a prime position to enhance the value of a company or its brand.[8]

BRAND TRIBES

In the postmodernity period, which advocated a move away from individualism in search for group relationships involving strong social bonds with others, the concept of tribes has entered the vocabulary of marketers. According to Simmons, a tribe is a network of people gathering homogeneously together for social interaction, often around consumption activities and brands.[9] Members of a brand tribe are not simply consumers, they are also believers in and promoters of a brand. These tribes are formed through self-identification with a brand. The emotional connection they have toward a firm or its products has been shown to be linked to the individual's social identity. The tribe, in effect, represents an expression of an individual's self-identity. According to Cova and Cova, consumer tribes differ from historical tribes by exhibiting a new social order, wherein status within a tribe is achieved by a different and specific set of values.[10]

Examples of tribes may include NFL fans; coin, music, and art collectors; devoted followers of a celebrity; a religious sect; a fraternity; a garden club; and wine aficionados. Tribal relationships, which connote bonded loyalty and trust, can be an asset to firms. Marketers can use this concept to foster and nurture a close-knit group of loyal fans to enhance a brand's standing in the marketplace.

brand tribes
networks of people gathering homogeneously around consumption activities or brands

While brand tribes and brand communities constitute two similar concepts, there is a major difference between them. While brand communities are explicitly commercial, brand tribes represent relationships between individuals and center around ties between consumers. This relationship can be expressed in terms of consumer-to-consumer links compared to the business-to-consumer ties that characterize brand tribes.[11]

ROLES

Roles are major determinants of groups' expectation from their members. Role patterns as well as role-related expectations have major effects on consumer behavior. Shakespeare adeptly summarized role theory when he wrote:

> All the world's a stage,
> And all the men and women merely players.
> They have their exits and their entrances;
> And one man in his time plays many parts.

Just as a playwright's script calls for actors to wear indicated costumes, speak assigned lines, handle certain props, and perform designated actions, specific functions are assigned to or voluntarily assumed by persons who occupy particular positions within groups. Roles are patterns of behavior performed by individuals within a given social context. Such behavioral patterns may derive from formal role definitions prescribed by the group, from informal rules of the group, or from a history of prior experiences. For example, in virtual communities, individuals' patterns of participation in an online interaction vary significantly. Research has revealed at least fifteen role types played by participants. A sample of these roles includes *core participants* who provide a large proportion of an online group's activity, *readers* who are not comfortable in posting but mainly read, *dominators* who post frequently and influence the space of an online interaction, *flamers* who send hostile and unprovoked messages, *actors* who develop different online personas, and *spammers* who post the same thing over and over again.[12]

Roles in which people serve greatly influence their consumption behavior. In a study by Rassuli and Harrell, a predominantly male sample composed of professionals and skilled workers was asked to create sets of living room furniture.[13] It was found that the members of each occupational group had similar notions regarding what constituted an appropriate cluster of furniture. In other words, physicians in the sample tended to select similar items, as did a subsample of firefighters and a subsample of professors.

Certain products are essential to meeting the requirements associated with specific roles. A consumer's role-related product cluster is the set of goods necessary to play a given role competently.[14] Products can be functionally or symbolically imperative to meeting role-related expectations.

roles
patterns of behavior performed by individuals within a given social context

role-related product cluster
the set of goods necessary for a person to play a given role competently

Today, corporate sales reps cannot function without electronic devices such as smartphones and pads, among others, to satisfy the requirements of their job. Role-related product clusters define both appropriate and inappropriate products for a given role. The tuxedo required of instrumentalists performing with an orchestra would be unsuitable when flipping hamburgers at McDonald's.

As the environment changes over time, definitions of the behavior befitting to a role and pertinent product clusters also change. In many business offices, paper files have been replaced by a virtual office where innovations including the latest word processors, links with information networks, and mobile communications have become the norm. Similarly, within the American family, a number of role changes have been taking place in recent years. Included in these are the emerging role of men as helpmates with babies, as well as those where couples take on the task of caring for their elderly parents.

The criteria that consumers use to evaluate products and services when occupying one of their roles may be quite different from the criteria they would use when serving in another capacity. Consider the case of a consumer who is both parent and purchasing agent for a corporation. Such a person would seek different features in a smartphone bought for personal use than one purchased for use in business.

Within a group or a society as a whole, the role an individual plays or the position he or she occupies carries with it a certain degree of importance, influence, and prestige. Think of the stature associated with a position such as the CEO of a major corporation or the power held by a governor of a state. Such status is an inseparable component of group functioning and merits mention in the following section.

STATUS

Status represents the relative position a person occupies along a specific group's social continuum. Stated differently, status is one's rank within a group's power or prestige hierarchy. Status materializes in different ways; it can be either achieved or ascribed. *Achieved status* within a group reflects an individual's efforts, accomplishments, or contributions to the group. For example, individuals who earn an MBA degree and have several years of business experience possess credentials that qualify them for a highly paid managerial position in a major corporation. In such cases, individuals are said to possess achieved status. *Ascribed status*, on the other hand, can be a result of factors such as social class, wealth, age, gender, and ethnicity. For example, a person who is born into an affluent, aristocratic family may have ascribed status as part of the elite upper class.

Generally, higher status implies greater power and influence within the group. Furthermore, the range of acceptable behavior to which individuals must conform varies according to their status in the group. Higher-status members are permitted a wider range of acceptable behavior than are other group members. A company's president, for example, can arrive late to a meeting with subordinates; subordinates, however, would risk penalties if they were to arrive late for that same meeting.

Consumers frequently purchase products, services, and brands suggestive of their elevated status in a group. They do so because prestigious products, services, and brands communicate a desirable image of them to others. Massive, elegantly furnished homes built on several acres of wooded land and luxurious automobiles, as well as hired household help (butlers, maids, cooks, gardeners, and chauffeurs), exemplify status symbols. The term conspicuous consumption has been applied to the acquisition and prominent exhibition of these extravagant luxuries in order to provide evidence of the ability to afford them. Although such items in reality possess little in common, many consumers tend to group them together as a symbolic unit.[15]

conspicuous consumption
the acquisition and exhibition of extravagant luxuries to portray one's ability to afford them

Conspicuous consumption refers to the acquisition and exhibition of extravagant luxuries to prove one's ability to afford them.

© Visionsi/Shutterstock.com

Due to adverse economic conditions in recent years, many consumers have moved from conspicuous to rational consumption. Such individuals are frugal and crave good value.[16] A number of companies such as Subaru (the Japanese auto manufacturer), Ross, Target, and Walmart, as well as many known merchandisers' "outlet stores," are examples of firms that have identified value-driven consumers as their target customer profile.

SOCIAL POWER

The ability of a group to influence the beliefs, attitudes, and behavior of individuals stems from the power it possesses over them. Marketers, as influencing agents, have at their disposal a number of power bases to influence consumer behavior. Although the extent to which marketers possess these power bases varies, a combination of them can often bring about desired changes in consumer behavior and consumption patterns.

TYPES OF SOCIAL POWER

French and Raven identified five types of social power.[17] These include reward, coercive, legitimate, referent, and expert power. This section explains each.

Reward Power

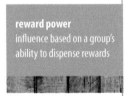

reward power
influence based on a group's ability to dispense rewards

Reward power is based on the ability of the group to dispense rewards. Rewards offer reinforcements that are instrumental in influencing or altering behavior. The greater the reward a group can administer, the stronger its power to attain compliance with group norms.

Rewards occur in many forms. They can be tangible (gifts, monetary compensation, awards for achievement) or intangible, such as those that are psychological in nature like praise and recognition. Marketers employ a variety of methods to reward consumers. Perhaps the most important of these is satisfaction of consumer needs offered by marketers' products or services. Other forms of reward include price deals, coupons, premiums, rebates, sweepstakes and contests, as well as corporate sponsorship of popular entertainment programming in the media or cause-related marketing efforts. Such rewards provide an incentive for prospects to select a particular brand or patronize a particular retailer.

Coercive Power

Coercive power involves the power of a group to punish members, with the goal of obtaining compliance with norms and expectations. A new army recruit quickly learns to obey officers' orders to avoid harsh sanctions. The impact of coercive power on compliance is a function of the magnitude of the sanction. The more severe the threatened punishment, the greater the degree of conformity.[18]

Flora Nuit, the latest and most-intimate way to shop for lingerie, is an example of an in-home party, where a coercive sales strategy is employed. At such events, a friend hosts a group, lays out appropriate snacks and beverages, and then a brand ambassador arrives at the party with lingerie in different styles and sizes for everybody to try on, all in the comfort of the friend's home.[19] Guests at such in-home sales events tend to feel that because their peers are buying, failure to place at least a token order would be embarrassing and disappoint the hostess. Group pressure creates a social obligation for guests to purchase an item or two in order to save face.

In general, marketers do not possess coercive power. They cannot reprimand or discipline consumers for failure to follow a recommended course of action. However, marketers frequently employ a modified type of coercive power in the form of fear or guilt appeals used in ads. Crusades against drug abuse warn against the destruction of the human mind and body. Antismoking campaigns frequently focus on cancer and heart or lung disease. Mothers Against Drunk Driving (MADD) emphasize death or disablement due to accidents caused by intoxicated drivers.

In other instances, advertising emphasizes the negative consequences that can result if consumers fail to use the product. Condom advertisers, for example, build on the public's anxiety over catching sexually transmitted diseases (STDs) as a consequence of engaging in unprotected sexual activity. Ads sponsored by *Milk Life* may warn women that lack of calcium, a prime nutrient found in milk, can lead to osteoporosis. Sales reps for firms selling home security systems may describe dire consequences faced by the victims of home intruders.

Unfortunately, elements of this power base have occasionally become the tools of intimidation employed by unscrupulous salespersons, particularly when dealing with the elderly and other unsuspecting, vulnerable consumers.

coercive power
influence based on a group's ability to administer punishments

Legitimate Power

In any group there are norms, values, roles, and expectations, as well as pressures to uphold the principles that the group endorses. It is anticipated that each member's attitudes and behavior will coincide with these standards. Eventually, group members internalize feelings that they *should, ought to,* or *must not* undertake certain actions or support particular views. These feelings of propriety may originate from mandates of one's parents, religion, patriotism, or other groups. Individuals, over time, adopt these standards of conduct as their very own.

The feeling of legitimacy created through internalized norms and values has the same property as power. It engenders the same response as that created through reinforcing or punitive actions. Such influence is known as legitimate power. Individuals in a group sense a personal obligation to think or act in accordance with group expectations. Doctors and lawyers adopt a code of professional ethics that includes a responsibility to protect the confidentiality of their patients or clients. Members of MADD would not drink and drive because of internalized beliefs regarding such irresponsible behavior.

legitimate power
influence that occurs as a result of individuals' feelings of obligation

Marketers sometimes employ legitimate power to promote products or concepts. Campaigns founded on themes of patriotism or environmentalism as well as those that make references to propriety and tradition employ legitimate power. Ads stressing the *buy American* principle, for instance, exemplify the assumption that patriotic citizens should possess a desire to protect and help American industry and labor. Such consumers would prefer products manufactured in the United States over imported goods.

Referent Power

A group's referent power is manifested through an individual's desire to identify with a group and to share a sense of oneness with it. For example, a study dealing with parental influence on their children's selection of a college major revealed that parental encouragement had a significant positive influence on their children's choice of major.[22]

We can think of reference groups as sources of referent power. No one can deny the influence of professional athletic teams on sports fans, music groups on music lovers, or the Boy Scouts or Girl Scouts on participating youth. The greater the attraction of the referent, the greater the identification and consequently the more powerful the referent influence. Marketers find referent power valuable in product and service promotions.

Consumers crave a sense of belonging to and identification with a group or structure that can offer them feelings of security and belonging. Consequently, advertisers spend handsomely to secure well-known and liked characters, such as movie superstars, sports heroes, public figures, and TV personalities to help promote their brands, boost awareness of their companies and brands, strengthen their image, or increase attention to their messages. Many sponsors feel that the payback in terms of product recognition and image enhancement justifies the cost incurred.[23]

A study by Agrawal and Kamakura suggests that using celebrities in ads may increase a firm's value.[24] Celebrity endorsers can affect attitude formation and change because they may attract more attention or possess more credibility than noncelebrities. Furthermore, consumers may identify with or want to emulate celebrities. Consumers may also relate traits of celebrities with product attributes in a way that coincides with their own personal wants. A number of recent studies have shown that celebrity endorsers are most influential when their image matches the personality of the product and the actual or ideal self-concept of the target market.[25]

Expert Power

Expert power is derived from an influencing agent's possession of specific knowledge or skills in which an individual is lacking. The wisdom or ability the expert exhibits in a specific area is sufficient to induce compliance. Legal counsel provided by an attorney and medical advice given by a physician exemplifies cases of expert power. The scope of expert power is restricted to the specific area in which the expert possesses extraordinary knowledge or ability. In the pet food field, for example, companies that sell "designer" chow are borrowing a strategy from pharmaceutical companies, which routinely persuade doctors to prescribe their drugs. Marketers of pet foods reportedly spend hundreds of thousands of dollars to get veterinarians to recommend their premium-priced products to pet owners.[26]

Advertisers frequently use experts such as engineers, doctors, scientists, researchers, and financiers to present an objective evaluation of a product or service. The audience's acceptance of claims made by such experts is a function of how credible they are perceived to be.

SOCIAL POWER USED BY MARKETERS

Although marketing strategies may use one or more of the various types of social power, those employed most frequently are reward, referent, and expert power. Psychological sanctions (coercive power), when used, tend to decrease the attractiveness of the source and may elicit the opposite reaction of the response desired. In addition, their effect is often short lived, because sanctions fail to produce permanent attitudinal or behavioral change. Likewise, marketers' use of legitimate power is limited. Its effect is confined to those cases where consumption of a product or a stand on an issue can be cleverly linked to some socially prescribed behavior, where a person ought to do or should refrain from performing some act.

Now, let us turn our attention to another aspect of group influence that deals with the consequences of group interaction. As social beings, humans tend to model their beliefs, attitudes, and behaviors after those of other members of the groups with whom they affiliate. Most individuals relate to particular groups and exhibit a great deal of concern over how they are perceived by other people whose opinions they value and whose acceptance they seek. The specific groups individuals identify with and emulate, or whose approval is of concern to them, are called reference groups. In the following section, we investigate some aspects of reference groups such as their composition and types, as well as their influence on us and on our behavior.

REFERENCE GROUPS

Reference groups are any sets of people that provide individuals with a standpoint or perspective for evaluating or patterning their own beliefs,

reference groups
groups that provide a perspective for evaluating or patterning one's own behavior

values, attitudes, goals, or behavior. Thus, any group that influences consumer purchase decisions can be considered a reference group. Our desire to identify with and emulate admired groups underlies the purchase of many products as well as the specific brands that we select. Advertisers, as a result, often show products used and enjoyed within group settings. Such groups can exert an influence on information processing, attitude formation, and purchase behavior.[27]

In most cases, reference groups do not dictate what individuals must do. Rather, individuals are influenced by actions of these groups, by respect for the group's opinion, or by concern for the group's feelings. Reference groups take various forms. Private online communities represent one such form. As an example, in one online community devoted to weight loss and sponsored by Glaxo-SmithKline, women dieters meet other like-minded women who support their dieting struggles through instant messaging and chat discussions. Realizing the power of online communities to influence target groups, a growing number of companies such as Glaxo, Kraft, Hewlett-Packard, and Coty are learning how to use the Web to harness such power by teaming up with Communispace Corp., a startup that hosts private online communities.[28]

Popularity among reference groups is one major reason why a sport like golf has an army of faithful followers.

© bikeriderlondon/Shutterstock.com

Reference groups play a pivotal role in shaping consumer decisions by pressuring individuals to conform to group norms, providing believable information, and offering a set of values to identify with and express.[29] One's family and peers are prime examples of groups that serve as models in this way. Recently hired employees of a firm, for example, use their new colleagues as a reference group when making decisions about styles of clothing to wear at work, appropriate topics for conversation, and acceptable viewpoints to express.[30] In this situation, normative influence occurs as these recently hired employees apply group norms and values to define the new situations they encounter.

Similarly, reference groups frequently serve as credible sources of potentially useful information for uncertain or uninformed consumers.[31] A person who observes others using a given brand or acting in a particular way in an ambiguous situation may emulate that behavior simply because it seems to be the right thing to do. Teens, for example, often look to their peers to determine which brands of jeans or shoes to purchase. Consumers may select a brand because its widespread use in the group suggests that it is indeed good. Studies have revealed that insurance and medical services were susceptible to reference group influence due to the fact that individuals lack confidence when purchasing such services and, as a result, are open to group influence in the form of peer recommendations.[32]

Individuals also tend to make self-appraisals, compare their behavior, and gauge the outcomes of their actions against those of like-minded others of equivalent standing. We frequently appraise our own status, measure our accomplishments, and verify our ideas against those of our peers.[33] Then we pattern our beliefs, feelings, or actions accordingly. This process of social comparison is especially strong when no tangible, objective yardsticks are available.[34] For example, stylistic preferences for music are largely a matter of personal taste. However, when selecting the right mix of music for a party, hosts often assume that the types liked by their guests are more appropriate choices to play.[35] As such, reference groups set standards for self-evaluation or serve to validate one's personal beliefs, attitudes, and behavior.[36]

Reference groups vary in size, structure, and composition. Consequently, individuals can be influenced in dissimilar directions by different reference groups. The following section addresses the different types of reference groups.

TYPES OF REFERENCE GROUPS

Individuals may belong to a group they feel offers them a model or guide. Sometimes they merely aspire to membership in a group they admire, but for some reason, cannot join. In other cases they may even shun membership in a certain group they feel offers them a negative frame of reference. In general, reference groups can be classified as membership, aspirational, and dissociative reference groups.

Membership

Membership reference groups are those to which an individual currently belongs or qualifies for membership. Family, friends, fraternities, church-

membership reference groups
groups to which a person currently belongs or qualifies for membership

es, and work groups are examples of membership reference groups. Similarly, individuals who reach fifty-five years of age can join the American Association of Retired Persons (AARP), and those who contribute to a public TV channel are members of its supporting group.

Within membership reference groups, a person has been accepted and is perceived by others as belonging to the group. Whereas membership in some groups is automatic, such as being an alum when a person graduates from a university, membership in some others—such as a political party—is voluntary. Individuals are free to join, refrain from joining, or withdraw from the group after joining.

Aspirational

Individuals need not be members of groups that offer them a frame of reference. Individuals may seek membership in a group for which they lack the needed qualifications or abilities. Such groups are called aspirational reference groups. For example, an individual may seek entry into a prestigious country club. However, the club's hefty annual membership dues and the person's social standing may prevent him or her from joining. Individuals generally try to emulate the beliefs, values, attitudes, and behavior of members of those groups that they aspire to join.

Aspirational reference groups can be anticipatory or symbolic. Anticipatory aspirational reference groups are those with which an individual has at least some direct contact and somewhat reasonable expectations of joining at a future time. A middle manager may aspire to move up an organizational hierarchy to a top management position.

Symbolic aspirational reference groups, on the other hand, are groups in which individuals' chances of achieving membership are remote at best, regardless of their sincere desire to join and their willingness to adopt and emulate group beliefs, norms, values, attitudes, or behavior. Few aspiring, talented individuals ever become professional athletes, famous recording artists, or movie superstars even though, as fans, they pattern their lives after highly successful role models. The influence of well-known symbolic groups, such as sports teams or rock groups, have a great influence on consumer behavior as can be observed in fans' imitation of group members' appearance, mannerisms, or behavior.

aspirational reference groups
groups in which a person seeks membership but lacks the qualifications to join

anticipatory aspirational reference groups
groups a person has reasonable expectations of joining in the future

symbolic aspirational reference groups
groups in which one's chances of gaining membership are remote at best

Dissociative

Not all groups provide consumers with a positive frame of reference. Some offer individuals a negative reference point.[37] Consumers may wish to differentiate themselves from or establish distance between themselves and certain undesirable groups. In some cases, individuals simply reject the objectives, agenda, or methods of the negative group. In other cases, however, a disassociation with a particular group is based largely on the biases of those outside the negative group (rather than on the group itself).

There are two types of dissociative reference groups: negative and disclaimant. Negative reference groups are groups with which individuals wish to avoid association or identification. Individuals may go out of their way to avoid contact with members of certain groups such as the KKK, street gangs, cults, skinheads, and drug abusers. Disclaimant reference groups, on the other hand, are those that individuals may have previously joined or otherwise belonged to, but whose values they later rejected. A person who registers as a member of a political party may later switch to another party because of disagreement with the party's stand on particular issues. The ad in Figure 10.1 depicts individuals that most people would regard as members of a negative or dissociative reference group.

negative reference groups groups with which individuals wish to avoid association or identification

disclaimant reference groups groups to which a person previously belonged, but whose values one later rejects

The intensity of group influence on beliefs, attitudes, and behavior is a function of individuals' willingness to accept the mandates of the group.

© Syda Productions/Shutterstock.com

FIGURE 10.1

This ad from PARENTS., theantidrug.com, contrasts our conventional image of drug dealers with modern abusers of prescription drugs currently sitting in our medicine cabinet.

Courtesy of DraftFCB.

Negative reference groups can affect consumption behavior. Some consumers, for example, regard censorship advocates as negative reference groups. Attempts by certain organizations to purge the sexually explicit and violent lyrics of particular rap artists' music or ban their hits altogether only cause some fans to crave them more. Similarly, some moviegoers who consistently disagree with particular critics' movie reviews are attracted to those films that such commentators dislike. However, marketers rarely appeal to the desire to avoid or disclaim a group. Rather, advertisers attempt to ensure that targeted consumers do not link their products to dissociative groups. In this vein, Honda motorcycle ads have depicted "you meet the nicest people" (rather than hair-raising Hell's Angels) riding Honda cycles. In many cases, marketers' appeals to nonconformity tend to take on a positive rather than a negative tone. Some campaigns, for example, encourage consumers to flaunt their individuality and dare them to be a bit different compared to other group members.

DEGREES OF REFERENCE GROUP INFLUENCE

The intensity of group influence on beliefs, attitudes, and behavior is a function of individuals' willingness to accept the mandates of the group. Three degrees of group influence have been identified.[38] In the first case, an individual merely goes along with group mandates. In the second case, which reflects a more intimate relationship, the individual identifies with the group. In the third case, which is more of a union between the individual and the group, the person professes group norms and values as his or her own. These degrees of influence, which have been labeled compliance, identification, and internalization, are briefly explained in the following paragraphs.

Compliance

Compliance, the weakest degree of reference group influence, occurs when a person goes along with a group to obtain approval or avoid disapproval. The person adopts group dictates not out of genuine belief in their content or worth, but rather because they are instrumental in producing a satisfying social effect. An individual learns to do or say the expected things in public, regardless of what his or her private convictions may be. Behaviors adopted via compliance are expressed only when a person's behavior is visible to the influencer.

A number of studies have confirmed this tendency.[40] For example, a study by Lascu, Bearden, and Rose investigated the effect of group size and expertise on subjects' susceptibility to social influence.[41] In their experiment, a number of students were asked to evaluate a liquid diet drink, and as-

compliance
the act of going along with a group to obtain approval

ETHICAL DILEMMA

Electronic Town Halls for Political Campaigns

The Internet has become an integral element of political campaigns in the United States. It has forever changed American presidential campaigns and has brought back the roots of American politics, where communities got together and discussed public issues in town halls. Being a form of electronic town hall, the Internet allows people to communicate directly with elected officials via their online presence. From websites and Twitter accounts to YouTube videos, voters can discuss issues in real time with the candidates as well as with each other. In the 2016 presidential campaign, the town-hall format has become increasingly popular on cable news networks. As of this writing, there have been twenty-four town-hall events across CNN, Fox News, and MSNBC, up from just a handful in the entire 2012 campaign. While town-hall events lack impressive Nielsen ratings, as do debates, they give TV news a chance to probe more deeply into the candidates' policy positions, as well as allow for audience participation and questions.

Today, candidates, political parties, fund raisers, lobbyists, and legislators all have online strategies for advocating their goals. Politicians on the Left and Right alike use the Internet to spread their message by means of videos, disseminated primarily on YouTube, as well as by maintaining active campaign blogs.

When it comes to where voters get their political news, a 2015 Pew Research Center analysis shows that in a given week, 61 per-cent of the millennial generation reported turning to Facebook in order to receive their political and government news. Similarly, roughly half (51 percent) of Gen Xers reported getting their political and government news on Facebook. In this sense, the Internet has become a valuable—yet inexpensive—medium that promotes grassroots democracy, and allows true communication among people who exchange views on matters of common concern in a rational process of debate. Likely voters can thus form opinions that would shape the important political decisions.

The growing importance of the Internet in the political arena, however, does not necessarily mean that the medium fosters greater democracy. On one side, many households lack Internet access. Furthermore, the vast nature of the Internet makes finding authoritative, factual, trustworthy, and objective information difficult. The big media channels that currently dominate the Internet, as well as any antidemocratic force, can circulate materials and views that may sway public opinion in a direction that is harmful to the free election process."[39]

The digital age has forever changed the way presidential campaigns are run globally and in the United States. Learn more about the major role of the Internet in world politics by visiting http://www.people-press.org/2012/02/07/cable-leads-the-pack-as-campaign-news-source/2-... What social forces are at play in political campaigns conducted over the Web? Do you think that the Internet as a medium for political campaigns promotes or hinders the democratic process? Explain your answer. What are the drawbacks, if any, of this medium in the political arena?

sistants were planted to influence student ratings of the drink. The results revealed that not only did conformity to group pressure exist in the case of less-knowledgeable students, but conformity equally prevailed even when the group members were highly knowledgeable about dietary products.

Occasionally, group pressures to conform become too intense and seem to violate people's freedom. Evidence exists that pressure to conform works only up to a point and that excessive pressure may lessen the degree of compliance. In such cases, consumers may reject the group or its norms altogether and demonstrate independent behavior. This tendency is known as reactance. For example, in our society, deliberate and intense pressures placed by the public and the government on getting smokers to kick the habit has prompted some to become more adamant about smoking than otherwise would have been the case. Similarly, teenagers who face parental disapproval regarding tattooing or body piercing often engage in such practices as a form of reactance to such pressure.

Reactance becomes increasingly likely as individuals encounter restrictions on their rights to choose and the attraction of the proscribed behavior option increases.[42] A study by Lessne and Notarantonio concluded that soft drink ads that restricted the quantities customers could purchase had the effect of increasing the brand's attractiveness to shoppers.[43]

Identification

Identification denotes a somewhat closer and more dependent relationship with the group than suggested by compliance. *Identification* occurs when a person accepts influence because doing so is associated with a satisfying self-defining relationship with the influencer.[44] It serves to validate our connection to a group in which our self-identity is anchored. We model our behavior along particular lines to meet the expectations of fellow group members. Children, for example, take on parental beliefs, attitudes, and behaviors. Similarly, physicians who join the AMA or attorneys who join the bar association take on many of the group's conventions as part of their socialization into it. Identification differs from compliance in that the identifier actually believes in the attitudes or behaviors adopted. They are accepted both publicly and privately.

At least two forms of identification can be distinguished: classical and reciprocal. In the case of classical identification, accepting influence is a means of establishing or maintaining one's self-image or relationship to the group. The identifier desires to be like (or even to be) the influencing agent and takes on part or all of the influencer's role. An actor in a supporting role in a movie often yearns to play the role of the leading star. Those who occupy a role desired by the identifier or who possess attributes he or she lacks tend to be attractive influencers. In the case of reciprocal identification, a person may be involved in a complementary

reactance
a situation in which one resists pressure to conform and behaves independently

classical identification
the case where one accepts influence in order to establish or maintain one's self-image within a group

reciprocal identification
the case where a person accepts influence due to playing a complementary role with another individual

relationship with another individual (friend or spouse) or enact a social role defined with reference to the influencing agent, such as in the cases of interactions between doctors and patients or lawyers and their clients. The identifier and influencer share expectations of each other's behavior. The identifier empathically reacts in terms of the influencer's expectations, views, or recommendations. The image in Figure 10.2 could be used in an ad to build on the fact that many golfers who identify with pros, like Phil Mickelson, would like a chance to seek his professional advice on how to be prepared for the game.

FIGURE 10.2

In their effort to become better players, golfers tend to admire and emulate the pros with whom they identify.

© Mitch Gunn/Shutterstock.com

Internalization

Internalization occurs when an individual accepts group influence because the induced behavior is intrinsically rewarding, congruent in some way—rationally or otherwise—with the person's own value system. Behavior adopted via internalization tends to become integrated with the individual's existing values. Consumers may adopt the recommendation of a credible group such as Greenpeace because they find its views regarding environmental issues to be relevant to their perceptions and congruent with their values.

Here, the individual accepts the values and norms of the group as his or her personal values and norms. For example, consumers who prefer to purchase environmentally friendly products do so because of their inherent belief that such actions are necessary to protect the fragile environment. Similarly, vegetarians abstain from consuming meat due to personal convictions concerning the rights of animals. In Figure 10.3, the catch phrase "Girl Power" inspires women to embrace and live by the concept of equality of the genders.

internalization
influence that occurs when individuals accept group norms and values as their own

FIGURE 10.3

The slogan "Girl Power" in this depiction expresses solidarity with and internalization of the gender equality concept.

REFERENCE GROUP INFLUENCE ON CONSUMER BEHAVIOR AND MARKETING STRATEGY

A survey of the literature reveals that a number of factors such as consumers' demographic characteristics and personality traits, as well as group characteristics, situational factors, and product types, affect the likelihood that group influence will occur.[45] Among these influences, it appears that the main determinant of whether or not consumer purchases are influenced by reference groups is a product's social value. Products that are conspicuous, such as homes, automobiles, clothing, jewelry, and luggage, possess a high level of social value. As such, their purchase is much more likely to be influenced by reference groups. On the other hand, products like salt, waxed paper, and antifreeze have little or no social value. Consequently, their purchase is less susceptible to group influence.

Marketers who intend to employ reference group influence as part of their strategy must realize that consumers have multiple reference groups. Different groups are known to influence different types of people and different purchase decisions. Individuals may look to reference groups in their community, on the Internet, at work, at school, and at the gym. They may look to a neighbor for recommendations regarding lawn-care products, to a business colleague for advice concerning their car, and to a virtual community on the Web for ideas about sporting apparel or equipment.

It follows that marketers who employ group influence as part of their strategy face multiple tasks. First, they must determine the types of groups that various kinds of people are likely to refer to when making decisions about the specific product class. Having identified the groups that are truly germane to the purchasing situation, marketers are in a position to choose pertinent emissaries to deliver their messages and plan their campaign strategy.

Groups influence many aspects of our lives. We use groups as reference points against which we measure our own behavior or accomplishments. Groups also influence our consumption behavior as we tend to emulate the consumption behavior of others. Similarly, views and opinions of groups around us significantly affect how we feel about the issues and occurrences in our environment.

CONSUMER BEHAVIOR IN PRACTICE

Plastic Symbols of Affiliation

If you are a student, you are likely to own a sweatshirt, jacket, duffel bag, or coffee mug with your school's logo on it. You may even carry plastic money or have a license plate bearing your university's name. Affinity marketing, which identifies a person with a particular group, offers an excellent example of how marketers creatively synthesize both reference groups and referent power in order to influence consumer behavior. Affinity marketing enables consumers to flaunt their identification with some membership group (school, church, corporation), symbolic group (NFL team, rock group), or cause (animal rights, environmental protection).[46] Affinity marketing capitalizes on the allegiance that many people feel to the organizations they belong to or the causes they believe in. It attaches symbols of consumers' group affiliations to the tools of their daily life.

The premise behind affinity marketing is that when offerings within a product or service category are all basically similar, consumers would prefer to support the specific groups or causes with which they are personally associated. In what has become an extremely pervasive variety of affinity marketing, many financial institutions now offer distinctive affinity credit cards. Here's how the arrangement works. A bank and an organization, such as a college alumni association, form an alliance whereby the bank promotes its credit cards to the school's faculty, staff, and current as well as former stu-

dents.[47] The charge card identifies the school rather than the bank as the card's sponsor (State College Visa card rather than Citibank Visa card). The arrangement benefits both partners. The school receives a percentage of all ensuing credit card charges. The bank, in return, acquires access to a special-interest market niche.[48]

A distinction, however, should be made between an *affinity* card and a co-branded card. An *affinity* card carries the name of an organization, school, sports team, or a hobby that generally benefits from each purchase a consumer makes using the card. The objective in this case is to tap into consumers' desire to support an organization or a cause. *Co-branded* cards, on the other hand, carry the name of a for-profit partner, such as an airline or store. They promote brand loyalty by offering rewards of free miles, gifts, or discounts.[49]

Currently, approximately 53 percent of the cards in the wallets of U.S. consumers are co-branded or affinity cards.[50]

The success of affinity credit cards has led banks, nationally and internationally, to offer them to various groups. Learn more about affinity and co-branded credit cards by visiting http://www.marketing-schools.org/types-of-marketing/affinity-marketing.html. What are the underlying forces behind individuals' attraction to affinity credit cards? Other than financial advantages, what social or psychological benefits do groups or individuals obtain through these cards?

Group membership and participation often yield tangible as well as psychological benefits; such is the case with the family group. The family is an extremely influential social group that dramatically shapes our beliefs, views, behavior, and consumption patterns due to the close contact and the length of time we spend with this social group. The family as well as significant age groups are the topics covered in the next chapter.

SUMMARY

Groups are defined as two or more individuals who share a set of norms, values, or beliefs; have certain role relationships; and experience interdependent behavior. True groups cooperatively interact with one another and share a common goal, common norms, and a sense of belonging.

Groups can be classified as primary or secondary, formal or informal, and planned or emergent. Beyond these basic types of groups, consumption subcultures are distinguishable subgroups of society that share a strong commitment to a product, brand, or activity. Brand communities are groups that are formed on the basis of a strong attachment to a firm or its products. Brand tribes are networks of people gathering homogeneously around consumption activities or brands.

Members occupy specific roles, which are valid only within the context of the group. Role-related product clusters are sets of goods necessary to play a given role competently. Members hold a specific status within the group. Conspicuous consumption entails the use of goods as status symbols.

There are five types of social power: reward, coercive, legitimate, referent, and expert power. Three of these—reward, referent, and expert power— are particularly useful in designing marketing strategy.

Reference groups are sets of people that provide individuals with a perspective for evaluating or patterning their own beliefs, values, attitudes, or actions. Reference groups exert normative, informational, or comparative influence on individuals. Reference groups can be classified as membership, aspirational, and dissociative types. The degree of reference group influence can be classified as compliance, identification, and internalization.

Reference groups can influence consumers' product or brand choices. Marketers who employ group influence as part of their strategy must identify the groups that are looked to by their target consumers, determine the nature and degree of influence these groups exert, and select effectual representatives of influential groups to deliver their messages.

Teen Peer Pressure

This case addresses types of peer pressure that high school students in our society face today. The case narrates a meeting between three students who volunteered to speak to school officials about the problems of violence, drug abuse, and increased sexual activity that prevailed in the school environment. School officials sought to determine the likely causes of these problems in order to figure out how to deal with them. Among the solutions under consideration was adopting a student-run drug-free program that relies heavily on peer pressure to keep members of the student body off drugs.

Notes

1   Janell Ross, "How Black Lives Matter Moved From a Hashtag to a Real Political Force," *The Washington Post* (August 19, 2015), https://www.washingtonpost.com/news/the-fix/wp/2015/08/19/how-black-lives-matter-moved-from-a-hashtag-to-a-real-political-force/; The Rachel Maddow Show, MSNBC, "'Black Lives Matter' Builds Power Through Protest" (October 8, 2015), www.msnbc.com/rachel-maddow/watch/-black-lives-matter--presses-equality-demands-501828675508; Alexandra Seltzer, "Corey Jones' Brother, 'Black Lives Matter. All Lives Matter,'" *My Palm Beach Post.com* (October 22, 2015), http://www.mypalmbeachpost.com/news/news/corey-jones-brother-black-lives-matter-all-lives-m/nn7k8/; Stephen Hegg, "Tactics of Black Lives Matter," http://kcts9.org/programs/in-close/tactics/black-lives-matter.

2   D. Cartwright and A. Zander, *Group Dynamics* (New York: Harper & Row, 1968).

3   Arnold Birenbaum and Edward Sagarin, *Norms and Human Behavior* (New York: Praeger, 1976).

4   "How Groups Influence Their Members," *Psychological Resources* (February 6, 2011), http://psychological resources.blogspot.com/2011/02/how-groups-influence-their-members....

5   John Scott, *Social Network Analysis* (London: Sage, 1991); Stanley Wasserman and Katherine Faust, *Social Network Analysis: Methods and Applications* (Cambridge: Cambridge University Press, 1994); "What Is the Value of Participating in an Online Community?" *Full Circle Associates* (December

2000), www.fullcirc.com/community/whyparticipateonline.htm; Robin B. Hamman, "Cybersex Amongst Multiple Selves and Cyborgs in the Narrow-Bandwidths Space of America Online Chatrooms," www.greenlloyd. com/bodyincyberspace.htm; Julian Dibbell, "Where Do We Actually Go When We Go Somewhere in Cyberspace?" www.greenlloyd.com/bodyincyberspace.htm; Sue Boetcher et al., "What Is a Virtual Community and Why Would You Ever Need One?" *Full Circle Associates* (January 2002), www. fullcirc.com/community/communitywhatwhy.htm.

6   John W. Schouten and James H. McAlexander, "Subcultures of Consumption: An Ethnography of New Bikers," *Journal of Consumer Research* 22 (June 1995), pp. 43–61.

7   Albert M. Muniz and Thomas C. O'Guinn, "Brand Community," *Journal of Consumer Research* 27 (March 2001), pp. 412–432.

8   Nielsen, "Online Shopping Trends," *USA: The Nielsen Company* (2010); Albert M. Muniz and Thomas C. O'Guinn, "Brand Community," *Journal of Consumer Research* 27 (March, 2001), pp. 412–432.

9   G. Simmons, "Marketing to Post Modern Consumers: Introducing the Internet Chameleon," *Journal of Marketing* 42, no. 3, pp. 299–310.

10 Bernard Cova and Véronique Cova, "Tribal Marketing: The Tribalisation of Society and Its Impact on the Conduct of Marketing," *European Journal of Marketing* 36, no. 5/6 (2002), pp. 595–620; Bernard Cova and Véronique Cova, "Tribal Aspects of Postmodern Consumption Research: The Case of French In-line Roller Skaters," *Journal of Consumer Behaviour* 1 (2001): 67–76, doi:10.1002/cb.54; see also Cova and Pace, "Products: New Forms of Customer Empowerment–The Case 'My Nutella The Community,'" *European Journal of Marketing* 40, no. 9/10 (2006), pp. 1087–1105; Bernard Cova, "Community and Consumption: Towards a Definition of the "Linking Value" of Product or Services," *European Journal of Marketing* 31, no. 3/4 (1997), pp. 297–316; Bernard Cova, Robert V. Kozinets, and Avi Shankar, *Consumer Tribes* (Oxford, UK: Elsevier, Butterworth-Heinemann, 2007); Bernard Cova, Stefano Pace, and David J. Park, "Global Brand Communities Across Borders: The Warhammer Case," *International Marketing Review* 24, no. 3, (2007), pp. 313–329; Bernard Cova and D. Dalli, "Community Made: From Consumer Resistance to Tribal Entrepreneurship," *European Advances in Consumer Research* 8, in S. Borghini, M. A. McGrath, and C. Otnes (Eds.), Proceedings of the 2007 European ACR Conference, Milan, July 3–5, 2007; Bernard Cova and D. Dalli, "Building Blocks for a Theory of 'Working' Consumers," 3rd CCT Conference, Boston, June 2008; Bernard Cova and S. Pace, "Tribal Entrepreneurship: Consumer Made and Creative Communities as Market Makers," in K. Tollin and A. Carù (Eds.), *Strategic Market Creation. A New Perspective on Marketing and Innovation Management* (Chichester: John Wiley, 2008), pp. 313–336.

11 Cleo Mitchell and Brian Imrie, "Consumer Tribes, Membership, Consumption, and Building Loyalty," *Asia Pacific Journal of Marketing and Logistics* (June 24, 2009), http://www.scribd.com/doc/56446623/Consumer-Tribes;

Bernard Cova, Robert V. Kozinets, and Avi Shankar, *Consumer Tribes* (Oxford, UK: Elsevier, Butterworth-Heinemann, 2007); Albert M. Muniz and Thomas C. O'Guinn, "Brand Community," *Journal of Consumer Research* 27 (March, 2001), pp. 412–432, E. O. Wilson, "What's Your Tribe?" *Newsweek* (April 9, 2012), pp. 43–46; Cova and Cova, "Tribal Marketing: The Tribalisation of Society and Its Impact on the Conduct of Marketing"; Cova and Cova, "Tribal Aspects of Postmodern Consumption Research: The Case of French In-line Roller Skaters."

12 Nancy White, "Community Member Roles and Types," *Full Circle Associates* (January 12, 2001), www.fullcirc.com/community/memberroles.htm.

13 Kathleen M. Rassuli and Gilbert D. Harrell, "Group Differences in the Construction of Consumption Sets," in Kim P. Corfman and John G. Lynch (Eds.), *Advances in Consumer Research* 23 (Provo, UT: Association for Consumer Research, 1996), pp. 446–453.

14 M. R. Solomon and B. Buchanan, "A Role-Theoretic Approach to Product Symbolism," *Journal of Business Research* (March 1991), pp. 95–109; Rassuli and Harrell, "Group Differences in the Construction of Consumption Sets."

15 James H. Leigh and Terrance G. Gabel, "Symbolic Interactionism: Its Effects on Consumer Behavior and Implications for Marketing Strategy," *The Journal of Consumer Marketing* 9, no. 1 (Winter 1992), pp. 27–38; Dong H. Lee, "Symbolic Interactionism: Some Implications for Consumer Self-Concept and Product Symbolism Research," in M. E. Goldberg et al. (Eds.), *Advances in Consumer Research* 17 (Provo, UT: Association for Consumer Research, 1990), pp. 386–393; Marsha L. Richins, "Social Comparison and the Idealized Images of Advertising," *Journal of Consumer Research* 18, no. 1 (June 1991), pp. 71–93; Irfan Ahmed, "The Role of Status in Service Interactions," *AMA Winter Educators' Proceedings* 3 (1992), pp. 142–143; Elizabeth C. Hirschman, "Cocaine as Innovation: A Social-Symbolic Account," in John F. Sherry and Brian Sternthal (Eds.), *Advances in Consumer Research* 19 (Provo UT: Association for Consumer Research, 1992), pp. 129–139; Eva M. Hyatt, "Consumer Stereotyping: The Cognitive Bases of the Social Symbolism of Products," *Advances in Consumer Research* 19 (1992), pp. 299–303.

16 Howard Schlossberg, "Conspicuous Consumption Is a Thing of the Past for 'Relaxed' Consumers," *Marketing News* (January 4, 1993), pp. 7, 16.

17 J. R. P. French Jr. and B. Raven, "The Bases of Social Power," in D. Cartwright (Ed.), *Studies in Social Power* (Ann Arbor MI: Institute for Social Research, 1959), pp. 150–167.

18 A. Gaviria and S. Raphael, "School-Based Peer Effect and Juvenile Behavior," *The Review of Economics and Statistics* 83, no. 2 (2001), pp. 257–268.

19 Kate Hakala, "Lingerie Parties Are Going to Become the New Tupperware Party," nerve.com (February 10, 2014), http://www.nerve.com/love-sex/underwear-parties-are-going-to-become-the-new-tupperware-parties; Ellen Graham, "Tupperware Parties Create a New Breed of Super-Saleswoman," *Wall Street Journal* (May 21, 1971), pp. 1, 18; Flavia Krone and Denise Smart, "An Exploratory Study Profiling the Party-Plan Shopper," in Robert

H. Ross, Frederick B. Kraft, and Charles H. Davis (Eds.), 1981 Proceedings, Southwestern Marketing Association, Wichita State University (1981), pp. 200–203; Manli Ho, "Peddling Naughty Lingerie . . . in Suburban Living-grooms," *Boston Globe* (March 2, 1976); J. K. Frenzen and H. L. Davis, "Purchasing Behavior in Embedded Markets," *Journal of Consumer Research* (June 1990), pp. 1–12.

20   "What Percentage of Your Car Was Made in America?" *ABC News*, abcnews.go.com/WN/MadeInAmerica/page/made-america-car-ameri-can-made-13795239; "Made in American," Automotive Addicts.com (April 10, 2012), http://www.automotiveaddicts.com/inthenews/07-10-06.html; Jim Mateja and Rick Topely, "Made in America? Hard to Tell," *Chicago Tribune* (September 24, 2006).

21   Kelsey Mays, "The 2015 American-Made Index," Cars.com (June 28, 2015), https://www.cars.com/articles/the-2015-american-made-in-dex-1420680649381/; Kelsey Mays, "The Cars.com American-made Index," cars.com (December 28, 2007), www.cars.com/go/advice/Story.jsp?sec-tion=top&subject=ami&story=amMade1207.

22   Cathy Pearson and Mary Dellmann-Jenkins, "Parental Influence on a Student's Selection of a College Major," *College Student Journal* (September 1997), pp. 301–313.

23   Kevin Goldman, "Year's Top Commercials Propelled by Star Power," *Wall Street Journal* (March 16, 1994), p. B1.

24   J. Agrawal and W. A. Kamakura, "The Economic Worth of Celebrity En-dorsers," *Journal of Marketing* (July 1995), pp. 56–62.

25   M. A. Kamins, "An Investigation into the 'Match-up' Hypothesis in Celebri-ty Advertising," *Journal of Advertising,* no. 1 (1990), pp. 4–13; S. Misra and S. E. Beatty, "Celebrity Spokesperson and Brand Congruence," *Journal of Business Research* (September 1990), pp. 159–173; J. Lynch and D. Schuler, "The Matchup Effect of Spokesperson and Product Congruency," *Psychol-ogy & Marketing* (September 1993), pp. 417–445; M. A. Kamins and K. Gupta, "Congruence Between Spokesperson and Product Type," *Psychology & Marketing* (November 1994), pp. 569–586; C. Tripp, T. D. Jensen, and L. Carlson, "The Effects of Multiple Product Endorsements by Celebrities on Consumers' Attitudes and Intentions," *Journal of Consumer Research* (March 1994), pp. 535–547; M. F. Callcott and W. N. Lee, "Establishing the Spokes-Character in Academic Inquiry," in F. R. Kardes and M. Sujan (Eds.), *Advances in Consumer Research* 22 (Provo, UT: Association for Con-sumer Research, 1995), pp. 144–151.

26   Tara Parker-Pope, "Why the Veterinarian Really Recommends That 'De-signer' Chow: Colgate Gives Doctors Treats for Plugging Its Brands, and Sees Sales Surge," *Wall Street Journal Eastern Edition* (November 3, 1997), p. A11.

27   William O. Bearden, Richard G. Netemeyer, and Jesse E. Teel, "Measure-ment of Consumer Susceptibility to Interpersonal Influence," *Journal of Consumer Research* 15 (March 1989), pp. 473–481.

28 Heather Green, "It Takes a Web Village," *Business Week* (September 4, 2006), p. 66.

29 Terry L. Childers and Akshay R. Rao, "The Influence of Familial and Peer-Based Reference Groups on Consumer Decisions," *Journal of Consumer Research* 19 (September 1992), pp. 198–211; William O. Bearden and Michael J. Etzel, "Reference Group Influences on Product and Brand Purchase Decisions," *Journal of Consumer Research* 9 (September 1982), pp. 183–194; C. Webster and J. B. Faircloth III, "The Role of Hispanic Ethnic Identification on Reference Group Influence," in C. T. Allen and D. R. John (Eeds.), *Advances in Consumer Research* 21 (Provo, UT: Association for Consumer Research, 1994), pp. 458–463.

30 Bearden, Netemeyer, and Teel, "Measurement of Consumer Susceptibility to Interpersonal Influence"; W. O. Bearden, R. G. Netemeyer, and J. E. Teel, "Further Validations of the Consumer Susceptibility to Influence Scale," in M. E. Goldberg et al. (Eds.), *Advances in Consumer Research* 17 (Provo, UT: Association for Consumer Research, 1990), pp. 770–776; O. A. J. Mascarenhas and M. A. Higby, "Peer, Parent, and Media Influences in Teen Apparel Shopping," *Journal of the Academy of Marketing Science* (Winter 1993), pp. 53–58.

31 Childers and Rao, "The Influence of Familial and Peer-Based Reference Groups on Consumer Decisions."

32 R. C. Becherer, W. F. Morgan, and L. M. Richard, "Informal Group Influence among Situationally/Dispositionally Oriented Customers," *Journal of the Academy of Marketing Science* (Summer 1982), pp. 269–281; Bearden and Rose, "Attention to Social Comparison Information: An Individual Difference Factor Affecting Consumer Conformity"; D. N. Lascu, W. O. Bearden, and R. L. Rose, "Norm Extreme and Interpersonal Influences on Consumer Conformity," *Journal of Business Research* (March 1995), pp. 201–213; L. R. Kahle, "Role-Relaxed Consumers," *Journal of Advertising Research* (May 1995), pp. 59–62; B. G. Englis and M. R. Solomon, "To Be and Not to Be," *Journal of Advertising* (Spring 1995), pp. 13–28; see also P. Choong and K. R. Lord, "Experts and Novices and Their Use of Reference Groups," *Enhancing Knowledge Development in Marketing* (Chicago, IL: American Marketing Association, 1996), pp. 203–208.

33 Jay C. Wode and Charles J. Gelso, "Reference Group Identity Dependence Scales: A Measure of Male Identity, Male Reference Group Identity Dependence," *The Counseling Psychologist* 26, no. 3 (1998), pp. 384–411.

34 Leon Festinger, "A Theory of Social Comparison Processes," *Human Relations* 7 (May 1954), pp. 117–140; George P. Moschis, "Social Comparison and Informal Group Influence," *Journal of Marketing Research* 13 (August 1976), pp. 237–244; Robert E. Burnkrant and Alain Cousineau, "Informational and Normative Social Influence in Buyer Behavior," *Journal of Consumer Research* 2 (December 1975), pp. 206–215; M. Venkatesan, "Experimental Study of Consumer Behavior Conformity and Independence," *Journal of Marketing Research* 3 (November 1966), pp. 384–387; Childers

and Rao, "The Influence of Familial and Peer-Based Reference Groups on Consumer Decisions"; M. Deutsch and Harold B. Gerard, "A Study of Normative and Informational Social Influences upon Individual Judgment," *Journal of Abnormal and Social Psychology* 51 (1955), pp. 624–636.

35   Chester A. Insko, Sarah Drenan, Michael R. Solomon, Richard Smith, and Terry J. Wade, "Conformity as a Function of the Consistency of Positive Self-Evaluation with Being Liked and Being Right," *Journal of Experimental Social Psychology* 19 (1983), pp. 341–358.

36   Childers and Rao, "The Influence of Familial and Peer-Based Reference Groups on Consumer Decisions"; Bearden and Etzel "Reference Group Influence on Product and Brand Purchase Decisions."

37   Englis and Solomon, "To Be and Not to Be."

38   Herbert C. Kelman, "Processes of Opinion Change," *The Public Opinion Quarterly* 25, no. 1 (Spring 1961), pp. 57–78; Herbert C. Kelman, "Compliance, Identification, and Internalization: Three Processes of Attitude Change," *Journal of Conflict Resolution* 2, no. 1 (1958), pp. 51–60.

39   Amy Mitchell, "Millennials and Political News," *Pew Research Center* (June 1, 2015), http://journalism.org/2015/06/01/millennials-political-news/; Amy Mitchell, "Media Sources District Favorites Emerge on the Left and Right," *Pew Research Center* (October 21, 2014), http://www.journalism. org/2014/10/21/session-1-media-sources-distinct-favorites-emerge-on-the-left-and-right/; "Reputations Changer Reviews," *Mehr Nachrichten von FinazNachrichten.de* (March 20, 2012), http://www. finaznachrichten. de/ausdruck/2012–03/23033546-reputation-changer-reviews- . . .; Vanessa Fox, "Super Tuesday, Internet Style: How We're Using the Web in the 2008 Elections," *Search Engine Land* (February 5, 2008), http://searchengineland. com/080205–190713.php; Merlyna Lim and Mark E. Kann, "Politics: Democratic Deliberation and Mobilization on the Internet," *Networked Publics*, http://networkedpublics.org/book/politics; Jake Tapper, "Clinton Launches Obama Attack Websites," *ABC News* (December 20, 2007), http://abcnews. go.com/print?id=4032659; "Cable Leads the Pack as Campaign News Source," *Pew Research Center* (February 7, 2012), http://www.people-press. org/2012/02/07/cable-leads-the-pack-as-campaign-news-source/2- . . .

40   Jennifer D. Campbell and Patricia J. Fairey, "Informational and Normative Routes to Conformity: The Effect of Faction Size as a Function of Norm Extremity and Attention to the Stimulus," *Journal of Personality and Social Psychology* 57 (March 1989), pp. 457–468; Barbara C. Perdue and John O. Summers, "Checking the Success of Manipulations in Marketing Experiments," *Journal of Marketing Research* 23 (April 1986), pp. 317–326.

41   Lascu, Bearden, and Rose, "Norm Extreme and Interpersonal Influences on Consumer Conrmity": P. F. Bone, "Word-of-Mouth Effects on Short-Term Product Judgments," *Journal of Business Research* (March 1995), pp. 213–223.

42   R. D. Ashmore, V. Ramchandra, and R. Jones, "Censorship as an Attitude Change Induction," a paper presented at meetings of the Eastern Psychological Association, New York, 1971; R. A. Wicklund and J. Brehm, *Perspec-*

tives on Cognitive Dissonance (Hillsdale, NJ: Lawrence Erlbaum, 1976); see also Michael B. Mazis, Robert B. Settle, and D. C. Leslie, "Elimination of Phosphate Detergents and Psychological Reactance," *Journal of Marketing Research* 10 (1973), pp. 390–395; Snyder and Fromkin, *Uniqueness: The Human Pursuit of Difference.*

43 Greg J. Lessne and Elaine M. Notarantonio, "The Effect of Limits in Retail Advertisements: A Reactance Theory Perspective," *Psychology and Marketing* 5, no. 1 (1988), pp. 33–44.

44 Aida Hurtado, Patricia Gurin, and Timothy Peng, "Social Identities—a Framework for Studying the Adaptations of Immigrants and Ethnics: The Adaptation of Mexicans in the United States," *Social Problems* 41 (1994), p. 129.

45 Donald W. Hendon, "A New Empirical Look at the Influence of Reference Groups on Generic Product Category and Brand Choice: Evidence from Two Nations," in *Proceedings of the Academy of International Business: Asia-Pacific Dimension of International Business* (Honolulu, Hawaii: College of Business Administration, University of Hawaii, December 18–20, 1979), p. 757; Robert T. Green, Joel G. Saegert, and Robert J. Hoover, "Conformity in Consumer Behavior: A Cross-National Replication," in Neil Beckwith et al. (Eds.), *1979 Educator's Conference Proceedings* (Chicago, IL: American Marketing Association, 1979), pp. 192–194; Lyman O. Ostlund, "Role Theory and Group Dynamics," in Scott Ward and Thomas S. Robertson (Eds.), *Consumer Behavior: Theoretical Sources* (Upper Saddle River, NJ: Prentice Hall, 1973), p. 245; Harold H. Kassarjian, "Riesman Revisited," *Journal of Marketing* 29 (April 1965), pp. 54–56; Richard W. Mizerski and Robert B. Settle, "The Influence of Social Character on Preference for Social Versus Objective Information in Advertising," *Journal of Marketing Research* 16 (November 1979), pp. 552–558.

46 Judith Waldrop, "Plastic Wars," *American Demographics* (November 1988), p. 6.

47 P. Rajan Varadarajan and Anil Menon, "Cause Related Marketing: A Coalignment of Marketing Strategy and Corporate Philanthropy," *Journal of Marketing* 52 (July 1988), pp. 58–74; Scott M. Smith and David S. Alcorn, "Cause Marketing: A New Direction in the Marketing of Corporate Responsibility," *Journal of Services Marketing* 5, no. 4 (Fall 1991), pp. 21–37.

48 Terry Lefton, "Discovery Channel's Credit Card Includes Animal Protection Hook," *Brand.week* 39, no. 26 (June 29, 1998), p. 12.

49 "Popular, Personalized Credit Cards Losing Punch in Saturated Markets," *The Clarion Ledger Business* (December 23, 2002).

50 Robin Sidel, "Credit-Card Firms Reap Rewards of Consumer Brand Loyalty," *The Wall Street Journal* (May 13, 2015), http://www.wsj.com/articles/credit-card-firms-reap-rewards-of-consumer-brand-loyalty-1431551439; "In a Maturing US Co-branded and Affinity Credit Card Market, Growth Remains for Issuers Exploring Untapped Segments," Reuters (November 5, 2009), http://www.reuters.com/article/2009/11/05/idUS183916+05-Nov-2009+MW20091105; "Co-branded and Affinity Credit Cards in the US," the-infoshop.com (May 2007), www.the-infoshop.com/study/pf51662-co-branded.html.

CHAPTER 11

THE FAMILY AND GENERATIONAL COHORTS

LEARNING OBJECTIVES

- To ascertain the role of the family in the process of consumer socialization.
- To become cognizant of family consumption roles.
- To explore the dynamics of the family decision-making process.
- To learn how children influence the process of family decision making.
- To understand the concept of the family life cycle.
- To review nontraditional living arrangement patterns prevalent in contemporary society.
- To comprehend the concept of generational cohorts and its implications for market segmentation.

KEY TERMS

family	boomerang children	Boomers II cohort
enacted role	sandwich generation	Generation X cohort
perceived role	generational marketing	Generation Y cohort
prescribed role	cohort	(Millennials)
family lifecycle	Boomers I cohort	Generation Z cohort

The roles of men and women in the family, as well as in society, have changed drastically over the last few decades. Traditional households headed by male wage earners have waned, giving way to a variety of living arrangements that range from single-person households to cohabitating couples to families of mixed races.

One of the most notable trends in this social evolution has been the rise of what has been termed the "unmarriage revolution," which is the decoupling of formal man/woman legal ties. In 2015, according to the Bureau of Labor Statistics, single adults in the United States outnumbered their married counterparts for the first time since 1976. There are now 124.6 million single Americans, accounting for 50.2 percent of the U.S. population, age sixteen and older, who are experimenting with new ways to organize their lives and relationships.

The cultural change that occurred during the Vietnam War resulted in revolutionary ways of thinking and behaving, altering the public's view of government, institutions, media, and marriage. This change fostered the emergence of female sexual freedom and economic power. It led many women to postpone marriage and invest in education without having to worry that remaining single might derail their pursuit of professional goals. In fact, women today constitute over 60 percent of all college students and earn the majority of doctorate and master's degrees. As a result, women now fill a majority of jobs in the United States, including over half of all managerial and professional positions, according to U.S. Department of Labor data. Furthermore, 38 percent of wives now outearn their husbands, according to a recent study by the Pew Research Center. The impact of the newfound power of women is felt everywhere, from the classroom to the boardroom, affecting matters that range from dating to managing household operations.

Increased earnings have enhanced women's economic influence both at home and in the work- and marketplace. The Pew Research Center also found that in households where the wife earns more, she typically makes twice as many buying decisions as the male partner. Sectors benefitting from this augmented influence of women include food, healthcare, education, childcare, apparel, consumer durables, and financial services. Another consequence of this shift lies in the area of responsibilities for childcare, where men have become more hands-on over the past generation.[1]

The impact of women's power today is being felt everywhere, from the classroom to the boardroom, and in how men and women interact in society. To learn more about the rising economic *status of women, visit the website of Nielsenwire at* http://blog.nielsen.com/nielsenwire/global/below-the-topline-womens-growing-economic-power/ *and also the site of author Liza Mundy at* http://huffingtonpost.com/liza-mundy/sex_b_1367092.html. *In what ways do women's financial and professional empowerments affect relationships within the family? Enumerate a number of financial and relational decision areas within the family that may be impacted. Do you think that the role of men is being compromised as a result? Explain your answer.*

This chapter deals with the family and significant age groups. The first half addresses consumer socialization, family consumption roles and decision processes, the family lifecycle, and recent household trends. The second half covers generational marketing, or market segmentation by life experiences.

THE FAMILY

The mere mention of the word *family* conjures up a host of images ranging from warmth, love, sharing, and caring to instances where neglect and physical abuse may prevail. Whichever is the case, the family context of interpersonal communication is believed to have the greatest influence on consumer socialization.

The Census Bureau defines family as "two or more persons, related either through birth, marriage, or adoption, living under one roof." This definition gives rise to the conventional image of family consisting of a mother, father, and two children. However, the reality may be quite different. Contemporary families come in different forms and sizes. These include traditional families, stepfamilies, blended families, single-parent households, childless couples, and extended families, as well as other possibilities. Thus, the definition of family has become almost personal, taking in those to whom we are connected in a fundamental way.

> **family**
> two or more persons, related either through birth, marriage, or adoption, living under one roof

Communication among family members plays a significant part in shaping a family's consumption behavior. Family influence emerges as a result of the frequency and impact of contact within the household. In this section, let us consider the forces that underlie this influence and observe how the roles played by various family members determine the extent of that influence.

SOCIALIZATION

Socialization is the process by which individuals develop, through interaction with others, specific patterns of socially relevant behavior and experience. The socialization of today's adolescents occurs within the confines of the technological revolution that has swept their lives and influenced their learning, recognition, and consumption behavior. Through online communities, virtual realities, text messaging, and the various electronic gadgets they possess, most of them are continuously in touch with and affected by other people with whom they communicate.

Most children today have Internet and video game access; many also have a smartphone as well as an iPod and iPad. The number of children joining social networking websites such as Facebook and Twitter is growing daily. Technological advance has enabled 'tweens to access the same content from different media, often from mobile ones, as well as access the Internet through their smart phones.

A recent report from DataBank indicated that 60 percent of children between the ages of three and seventeen use the Internet at home. This is due to the fact that in-home Internet access has soared dramatically over the past few years, with the help of additional technologies. These entail Internet-enabled devices, including not only the computer itself, but also TVs, e-books, and handheld devices, such as music players and smartphones.[2]

Parental influence is another important factor in the development of various dimensions of children's consumption patterns. A study by Moore and Moschis found that the family affects the development of adolescents' materialistic orientation.[3] A separate longitudinal study by the same researchers investigated the effects of the family on adolescents' consumption learning, in both the short and the long run. This study found that parent–child interaction has some long-run influence on development of brand preferences as well as on ability to distinguish facts from exaggerations in ads as the child reaches adolescence.[4]

In addition, many studies confirm the family's influence on the development of children's decision-making patterns. For example, a cross-sectional study of the development of an adolescent's decision-making process confirmed that parents are more likely to be influential at the information-seeking stage than at the product-evaluation stage.[5] However, the development of the child's consumer decision-making patterns appears to be based on

As children grow older, they begin to acquire greater independence in purchase decisions, partially because of their age and partly due to earning their own money outside the family.

certain parent and child characteristics such as age, social class, sex, and family characteristics.

As far as *age* is concerned, children generally attain greater family independence in decision making as they grow older, although the degree of independence varies with the extent of parental permissiveness and the product type. Further, once the children begin to earn money outside the family, they are less subject to parental control through manipulation of resources.

Independence in decision making can also be a function of *social class*. For example, middle-class children appear to attain less independence in purchasing as they grow older than do children in lower and upper social classes. This tendency is due to middle-class families' greater consciousness of the normative standards of their class and their subsequent greater desire to supervise their children's activities closely in an effort to socialize them into the class norms.[6] Alternatively, this phenomenon may be attributed to the possibility that children from working classes need to work and earn money to support the family, thus attaining greater independence from their parents. Middle-class children, on the other hand, whose parents have long-range plans for them (such as attending college), are likely to display less independence because their parents are able to continue to exercise influence through control of resources.[7]

Sex of the child also affects parental influence on the child's consumption behavior. Studies show, for example, that female adolescents display a greater need for conformity to peer group norms. As a result, they have purchasing patterns that reflect greater family independence, particularly in purchasing products relevant to physical appearance such as healthcare products and clothing.[8]

Finally, *family characteristics* are also likely to affect parental influence on children. Aldous, for example, concluded that children of working mothers are likely to be socialized better or faster because they are often expected to take on more consumer responsibilities than children of non-working mothers.[9]

Studies indicate that although the family plays an important role in consumer socialization of the young, parental influence is often casual and can hardly be characterized as premeditated or deliberate consumer training. Research reveals that parents often expect their children to learn through observation.[10] Parent–child discussions about consumption are most likely to take place when the child requests a product seen via advertising.

FAMILY CONSUMPTION ROLES

Each member of a family plays a role. This role specialization affects the decision-making process as well as what is or what is not purchased. In most purchase situations, it is individuals (rather than entire families) who buy products. A consumer analyst must be able to identify such role specialization because of its impact on how marketers should target their efforts and to whom, as well as on where products should be offered for sale. For example, wives and girlfriends purchase 70 percent of the fragrances and colognes used by men, 90 percent of all greeting cards are purchased by women, and it is usually parents who purchase school supplies for young children, not the children themselves.[11] This realization, even though logical, eluded Crayola, the maker of children's drawing and coloring instruments. At first, the company targeted only children with advertising shown on Saturday morning TV programs. Later, however, realizing that it is usually mothers who actually purchase the product, the company shifted a portion of its advertising to mothers by placing ads in women's magazines. Figure 11.1 is an example of an ad from Crayola directed toward parents of young children.

Family consumption involves at least eight definable, sometimes overlapping roles. These roles, described in Exhibit 11.1, can be assumed by a man/woman or child, or they can be performed by more than one person.

The term *role* has at least three meanings. The enacted role is the actual overt behavior displayed by an individual in a particular situation. The perceived role is what an individual interprets his or her obligations or behavioral patterns to be. The prescribed role is the set of expectations held by others as to what modes of behavior should be displayed by an individual in a situation.[12] The concept of prescribed role is usually the most evident in family role structure, because culture prescribes what is appropriately masculine and feminine and who is responsible for what. However, recent trends show a blurred image of family role structure as a result of the social changes that are taking place in contemporary society. For example, the present generation of fathers is more involved in childcare than ever before.[13]

Family buying roles, in this sense, can affect every aspect of the marketing strategy for a product. Marketers need to be mindful of buying roles when

enacted role
the overt behavior displayed by an individual in a particular situation

perceived role
an individual's perceived obligations

prescribed role
the set of expectations held by others as to what modes of behavior should be displayed by an individual in a situation

FIGURE 11.1

Recognizing that adults are equally part of the decision process when buying art supplies for children, Crayola directs this ad to parents of young children.

Image provided courtesy of Crayola LLC and used with permission. © 2012 Crayola. Crayola Oval logo and Everything Imaginable are trademarks of Crayola. Photography by Luca Zordan.

they design products and packages, set prices, select distribution channels, choose media, and create advertising appeals.

Eight Family Consumption Roles

1. *Influencers:* those family members whose opinions or requests lead to making a product or service selection.
2. *Gatekeepers:* those family members who control the flow of product or service information into the household.
3. *Deciders:* those family members with the authority to make the final purchase decision.
4. *Buyers:* those family members who act as the purchasing agent, visiting the store or placing a phone or online order.
5. *Preparers:* those family members who ready the purchased item for consumption.
6. *Users:* those family members who consume the product or service purchased and readied.
7. *Maintainers:* those family members who attend to various tasks related to keeping the household functioning.
8. *Disposers:* those family members who are assigned authority to terminate the use of specific products or services.

THE FAMILY DECISION PROCESS

The relative influence of husband, wife, and children in decision making has been a topic of great interest in the study of consumer behavior. Although information about it is clearly very important from a marketing perspective, research in this area remains most challenging. Families differ significantly from each other in terms of wealth, social status, lifestyle, age, number of children, and other variables. They also vary regarding the personalities of family members. Furthermore, specific types of products or services under consideration for purchase must be taken into account.

Decisions in the family range from individual choices made by each member separately to joint decisions involving two or more members. Decision patterns can be classified into four categories:

1. *Autonomic,* in which each spouse independently makes about half the decisions
2. *Husband dominant*
3. *Wife dominant*
4. *Syncretic,* in which decisions are made jointly by the husband and wife[14]

CONSUMER BEHAVIOR IN PRACTICE

The Multiple Roles of Working Mothers

Today, millions of women with children are working outside the home to cover the rising costs of running a household. This shift in roles has resulted in fewer mothers (less than one-third) who remain at home and provide full-time care for their children. It has been reported that half of all preschoolers spend at least part of the day in the care of adults other than their parents. This change in the lifestyle of many women has resulted in rapid growth in the number of daycare centers and other forms of nonparental care for children.

Childcare arrangements take different forms. According to the National Center for Educational Statistics, the most common form of childcare was center-based programs, accounting for approximately 55 percent of children, with 35 percent left in the care of Head Start, and 10 percent in home-based relative and nonrelative care.

A number of factors affect the choice of childcare arrangements used by mothers. Among the more important influences are age of the child, family income, marital status, and cost. Regarding age of the child, childcare centers are used more frequently for two- to four-year-olds than for infants. This may be attributable to parental preference as well as to the fact that many childcare centers do not accept infants.

Income also affects the type of childcare that mothers use. Families in the higher-income category are more likely to use childcare centers than are families in lower-income groups. However, as family income increases, the use of public childcare centers declines while use of private centers increases. This is due to the fact that upper-income families can more easily afford the private centers. In addition, dual professional couples may use a nanny or *au pair* to provide full-time in-home childcare and support.

Marital status is another factor affecting the choice of childcare arrangements. Younger single women usually turn to their relatives and childcare centers more often than do married women, who receive some childcare help from the child's father. Older single women do not use childcare centers as often as married women do. They find it more economical to rely on relatives or have the children care for themselves.

Cost is a factor in the choice of childcare arrangement. The cost of childcare is staggering. Year after year, it is the largest annual household expense, averaging $18,000 for families in the United States. In 2015, a Care.com report states that the average weekly cost of a daycare center is $188 for one child, and $341 for two children. A family daycare provider (also called in-home daycare) is the least expensive option, at $140 for one child, and $267 for two children. Younger mothers utilize childcare services an average of forty hours per week, compared with around twenty-five hours for older women. The reason may be that older mothers tend to have more children, and older children can care for younger ones.

One of the most frequently cited problems relative to the childcare issue is that the lack of affordable quality childcare hinders the careers of many women. Even if the mother is employed, tardy arrivals to or absences from a job due to childcare problems could delay advancement. A catch-22 situation exists: without childcare women could not seek work, and without work they could not afford the costs of childcare.[15]

One of the major problems facing women with children today is the ability to maintain a balance between their family role on one hand and their professional role on the other. Learn more about childcare services by visiting http://government.cce.cornell.edu/doc/reports/childcare/websites.asp. *Although the human resource policies of many companies and organizations accommodate family obligations, others still lag behind. In your opinion, what types of policies or actions should firms undertake to help women with children maintain this balance? In your opinion, is the cost of such programs justifiable? Why?*

During the past two decades, the study of marital roles in the decision-making process has evolved from a focus on stereotypical depictions of these roles in a family setting to investigations of changing roles in our contemporary society. More recent research has focused on investigating how roles vary across product categories and across decision phases. These studies typically rely on respondents' perceptions, impressions, or recollections of their involvement in decisions that occur within the confines of the family and whether they acted autonomously or jointly. The Allstate ad in Figure 11.2 depicts the added role of fathers as providers of care and protection for their family and young children.

An early study by Davis and Rigaux pointed out that the dominant marital roles in family decision making varied according to the phase of the decision process (information-search stage versus purchase-decision stage).[16] Subsequent studies by others confirmed this tendency. For example, Putnam and Davidson found that the tendency toward autonomic decisions was predom-

FIGURE 11.2

This ad from Allstate reflects the added roles played by fathers within the contemporary American family. The ad emphasizes the need to provide sufficient insurance coverage to protect the future of both family and children.

7 LBS. 2 OZ. CAN FEEL
LIKE THE WEIGHT OF THE WORLD.

Did you know most people need around 7 times their annual income in life insurance to help provide for their family? At Allstate, we can help you with your changing protection needs. From auto to home to life, even planning for your child's education. Are you in Good Hands®?

LIFE CHANGES. YOUR INSURANCE SHOULD KEEP UP. THAT'S OUR STAND.

Call your local Allstate Agent, 1-800-ALLSTATE® or Allstate.com.

Allstate.
You're in good hands.

inant in the information-search stage; however, there appeared to be an obvious shift toward joint decisions in the final stage of purchase.[17] They also found less sex-role dominance and more autonomic decision making for less-risky purchases. The tendency toward joint final decisions makes intuitive sense when we view the final decision as a culmination of the purchase process—a most important stage for accenting the individual roles of each spouse. This tendency is particularly prevalent when the decision concerns a high-involvement item and when the couple is concerned about living with the consequences of a poor autonomous decision.

Several factors have been suggested by researchers as significant in influencing the relative roles of husband and wife in family decisions. These factors can be summarized as follows.

Egalitarianism

Egalitarianism can be defined as a general value system stressing equality in marital relations.[18] The degree of influence attributed to either the husband or the wife in a family decision is thought to be a function of the level of "traditional marital values" present in the family. For example, in households where *traditional* marital-role values exist, the husband would be expected to make the majority of the decisions whereas the wife's role would be limited to domestically oriented tasks.[19] One study compared two samples from the United States and China.[20] The less-egalitarian, more patriarchal Chinese culture was found to foster less joint decision making and more husband dominance. Some observers attribute this pattern in part to China's former one-child policy, which seems to have reinforced China's male-dominant attitude.

Several factors influence the level of egalitarianism manifested within the family. As the level of education, income, and occupational prestige experienced by the wife increases, so also does her input into the family decision-making process.

Involvement

Involvement is the degree of relevance an individual assigns to an object or issue. A spouse's level of involvement depends on the degree of personal significance that the product or service holds for that individual. For example, when investigating spousal purchase patterns for consumer products and professional services, studies reveal some differences in the types of decisions undertaken by either the husband or the wife. A study by Cosenza showed that purchase of women's clothing tended to be wife dominant, whereas purchase of life insurance and homeowners' insurance tended to be husband dominated.[21]

Empathy

The degree to which spouses exhibit *empathy* toward each other's preferences is an important influence on family decision making. The empathic response is a reaction in which one spouse feels as if he or she were a participant in the sensations and feelings of the other spouse. In households where empathy projection exists between the spouses, joint decision making is more likely to occur. In this case, joint decisions are not simply made to avoid the risk of a negative long-term reaction from the other spouse where a poor autonomic decision was made. Rather, they reflect a spouse's willingness to participate in the feelings of the other and a desire to go along through sharing his or her view regarding the issue.

Recognized Authority

Recognized authority is a mutually agreed-upon or culturally recommended and socially acceptable right to decide, assigned to one spouse. In family decision making, this recognized authority may result from a deliberate division of functions or roles between the husband and the wife. Each spouse is perceived to possess different talents, interests, and functions, many of which are complementary to those of the other spouse. Such recognized authority is not usually perceived as threatening. Instead, it promotes and enriches the common family well-being.

Recognized authority varies among different households and between cultures. What constitutes a husband's or wife's domain within one household or culture may not be the same in another. However, research indicates that general patterns do exist with regard to the types of recognized authority. Wives, for example, have more recognized authority in caring for young children, whereas the husbands' sphere may include taking care of the mechanical aspects of the family's automobile. Conflict arises when a couple fails to agree on recognized authority, where one spouse is less empathic to the preferences of the other, or where an egalitarian atmosphere is lacking within the family.

Now that we have briefly reviewed consumption roles and the factors at play in the family decision process, let us examine the increasingly important role that children play in household decision processes.

CHILDREN'S INFLUENCE ON FAMILY DECISION MAKING

In 2016, there were 73.7 million children at or under the age of seventeen in the United States. In that year, teens along with 'tweens reportedly spent around $159 billion of their own money on products and services. In addition, children under age twelve as well as teens influenced parental purchases totaling over $500 billion.[22] According to C&R Research, 'tweens and teens spend their money on many products and services including beverages, candy, clothing and shoes, eating out, going to movies, music, snacks, toys, and video games. However, these tech-savvy kids still spend most of their money on food and drinks, followed by toys, clothing, and social outings. Add to these figures the goods and services that college students spend their money on, which include music, theater and concert tickets, games, movies bought, as well as alcohol, travel, entertainment, and automotive.[23]

Children make their biggest impact in the food and beverage category. Products such as candy, soft drinks, and cereals account for a good share. It is here that they spend approximately 40 percent of their own money, and influence a substantial share of family purchases on food and drinks.

The second category of expenditure for kids is electronic items, such as games, music and movie downloads, as well as theater and concert tickets, and toys. Approximately 30 percent of their own money is spent on this class of goods and services every year. Once again, kids also influence a hefty share of their family's expenditures on electronics and various forms of entertainment.

The third category on which children spend heavily is apparel. Expenditures in this category amount to about 40 percent of their own money. Kids in the ten- to thirteen-year-old age bracket make more than two-thirds of their own apparel decisions.

The fourth category of expenditure for kids, children's personal care products (which could be purchased by family members or by the children themselves), represents 10 percent of children's resources in 2016. This category includes items such as oral hygiene, facial creams and medications, soap and bath products, shampoos and conditioners, as well as sunshield products.

For children, the primary source of income is their parents. Much of this money comes in the form of allowances. In addition, kids receive money as gifts for birthdays, holidays, and other occasions. They also earn money for performing some household chores and for doing occasional jobs outside the home, such as babysitting.

Regarding their shopping behavior, children prefer stores that play popular music and incorporate an element of theater into their environment.[24] Kids ages eight to twelve like mass merchandisers because of these stores' breadth of product offerings, including such items as electronic gadgets, games, toys, clothes, school supplies, and snacks.[25]

Characteristics of Childrens Shopping

Kids prefer shopping with other kids and, unlike their parents, this group is largely unconcerned with price. They tend to spend between $39 and $69 on an average purchase. Cash is the usual method of paying for their purchases. However, a whopping one-third of them have use of a credit card.

Children today are shrewd. In addition to being tech savvy, they get much of the information they need from their smartphones. Their shopping behavior is characterized by having disposable cash, buying on impulse, and visiting multiple stores.

Children's influence on their parents' purchasing behavior has been the subject of many studies. Children attempt to manipulate parents to get them to yield to their requests. A number of factors seem to have a bearing on the degree of children's impact on their parent's purchase decisions. The age of the child and personality of the parents, as well as the specific product being purchased, are important factors that determine the extent

Children's influence on their parents' purchasing behavior has been the subject of many studies.

© Hteam/Shutterstock.com

CONSUMER BEHAVIOR *AN APPLIED APPROACH*

of that influence. In general, the younger the child, the less the influence. Strict versus permissive parental personalities also affect the child's role in a family's decision-making style. Recently, many parents started ceding unprecedented decision-making power to their kids—perhaps due to changes in family lifestyles as well as to the rising number of dual-income parents. For example, in the area of the family car, children as young as eight have been reported to influence the car-buying selection process.[26] This trend of children's influence is largely due to the tendency of parents to include the children in a family's leisure and recreation travel episodes. In so doing, the kids play the consumption role of *influencers*.

Children affect parental spending through either direct or indirect types of influence. *Direct influence* occurs in the form of children's requests, demands, and hints directed toward their parents in a purchase situation. A child, for example, may specifically ask for a bag of M&M candy. *Indirect influence*, on the other hand, occurs when the parents know the brands their children prefer and buy them without being asked to do so.[27]

It is anticipated that the market potential for kids will continue to grow at the same double-digit annual rate that characterized its growth during the past decade. The importance of children's purchasing power and their influence on parents can be observed in the variety of products offered to them. Kids' versions of many adult products find their way to the marketplace every day. Virtually every adult consumer product, from books to foods, shoes, clothes, medications, music, and video games, has been scaled down and dolled up to suit children. The increasing attractiveness of the youth market is due to a number of factors, such as the extra money that kids have today, their unlimited access to media, and the fact that they are more savvy and informed than their predecessors. Today's youth seek any number of adult products, such as smartphones and iPads.[28]

Marketers have coined a name for their strategy of getting kids to buy adult merchandise. This tactic is known as "age compression," which involves pushing adult products and attitudes on young children. In many cases, the strategy merely involves extending an already existing adult product to this market by scaling it down and adding youth appeal to its package and/or brand name. In this sense, the "new" product targeted to children is merely a slight variation of the adult version, sometimes with a modified brand name or package, which is merely a miniature of the adult item.[29]

One major advantage of the age compression strategy is the fact that through this early targeting, a brand can increase its chance for a greater share of each customer's business in later life. Brand preference is more lasting when formed in childhood years, resulting in greater lifetime revenue for a firm. It has been suggested, for instance, that lifetime revenue from one customer of a hamburger chain might be $12,000. Since it is relatively possible for a hamburger chain to develop a relationship with children, this target of $12,000 should be manageable.[30]

In recent years, marketers' efforts to reach children through electronic media have gone through dramatic changes. The world of media, particularly TV, which for many years dominated the children's field, has given way to a new arena crowded with smartphones, iPads, video games, instant messaging, virtual reality websites, online social networks, and email.

A number of laws have been enacted to protect the vulnerability of children from various abusive tactics. Among these are the Telecommunications Act of 1996, which requires TV sets to include a V-chip to block programs with content parents find objectionable; the Communications Decency Act of 1996, which imposes criminal sanctions on those who knowingly transmit obscene materials to children under the age of eighteen; and the Children's Online Privacy Protection Act of 1998, which requires operators of websites and online services directed to children to obtain verifiable parental consent and to keep confidential any information disclosed from others, including parents. In addition, the Children's Advertising Review Unit (CARU) of the Council of Better Business Bureau provides guidelines and evaluates consumer complaints regarding advertising that targets kids.

© Alena Ozerova/Shutterstock.com

ETHICAL DILEMMA

Wombs for Rent

The primal drive to have children has prompted many couples in our society who are unable to conceive on their own to seek the services of artificial insemination clinics, invitro fertilization, and gestational surrogacy procedures. There are two reasons for the overwhelming rise in demand for such reproductive assistance services: first, infertility affects more than 6 million women and their partners in the United States; and second, major advances in medical technology have significantly enhanced the success rate of invitro fertilization.

In the case of commercial surrogacy, the practice of having "wombs for rent" has been growing steadily over the past few years. The idea of a woman bearing a baby for another is as old as civilization itself and was even regulated in the Code of Hammurabi in 1800 BC. Surrogates are impregnated in vitro with the egg and sperm of couples unable to conceive on their own. The surrogates carry the baby full term, undergoing any hardships, pain, and risks of labor. Industry experts estimate that there were 2,000 surrogate births within the United States in 2010, and that number is expected to surpass that figure threefold by 2016.

The motivations of gestational carriers vary widely. Some perform this service because they believe that one of the greatest rewards surrogate mothers experience is the sense of self-worth and empowerment gained by helping others. Other surrogates also feel that performing this service is equivalent to offering an organ transplant to someone who truly needs it. However, many surrogates perform this service to earn fees, where the compensation usually amounts to over $20,000, plus $10,000 to cover attorney's fees, insurance, and contract-drafting costs. Surrogate mothers and the parents sign a contract that specifies, among other things, the couple's responsibility for all the medical expenses and the surrogate's fee, as well as arrangements for receiving the baby at birth.

Surrogacy is not just an American phenomenon. It has spread globally to a large number of foreign countries. In India, for example, baby-making comes at the intersection of high productive technology and a plentiful cheap labor market. At a clinic in Kaival Hospital in the town of Anand, a number of women carrying children for infertile couples from many countries, including the United States and the European Union, are kept in the clinic throughout the months of pregnancy, are provided with medical care, and are paid more than many of them would have earned in fifteen years. This form of womb outsourcing has flourished in India and has become a viable growth industry.

Surrogacy is viewed by some as a creative method of assisting reproduction that benefits individuals who cannot conceive or carry a pregnancy to term. Ethically, such programs raise a host of questions that touch on the values of society, tampering with the miracle of life, the morals of modern science, exploitation, and globalization. One concern, for instance, is the fear that wealthy, self-obsessed, and shallow women may decide to have their babies via surrogates merely to avoid stretch marks.[32]

Learn more about surrogacy by visiting the Human Rights Campaign website at http://www.hrc.org/resources/entry/overview-of-the-surrogacy-process. *Learn about the pros and cons of this practice by visiting* http://www.positive-parenting-ally.com/ethics-of-surrogacy.html. *Do you think that surrogacy is an ethical solution for family building? Why or why not?*

THE FAMILY LIFECYCLE

For years, sociologists and marketers have recognized the fact that most families tend to pass through a fairly steady and predictable series of stages as household members grow older. These stages constitute what has become known as the family lifecycle (FLC). The stages of the FLC model are primarily based on four characteristics:

- Age
- Marital status
- Employment status of the head of household
- The absence or presence of children and their ages

Marketers usually deduce the ages of the parents and the relative amount of disposable income from the household's stage in the FLC. At each stage, there are unique needs, differences in earning power, and specific demands placed on household resources.

Traditionally, starting with *bachelorhood*, most individuals move on to form a family unit by marriage. *The honeymooner* stage ends when the first child is born. The *parenthood* stage continues as long as at least one child resides in the married couple's home. Eventually, in the *post-parenthood* stage, the mature children depart from their parent's home, leaving behind an "empty nest." Finally, the *dissolution* stage occurs when one of the spouses dies. Figure 11.3 depicts a situation where a mother and daughter share an online educational experience.

As people move from one FLC stage to the next or as they assume different life roles, various types of products and services increase or decrease in importance. Young bachelors and newlyweds, for instance, are likely to purchase electronic devices, to exercise, to consume alcohol, and to frequent bars, concerts, and movies. Families with young children are major purchasers of health foods and fruit juices, whereas many single-parent households and those with older children tend to buy more junk food. Home-maintenance services are likely to be used by older couples ("empty nesters"), bachelors, and families with children. An understanding of such consumption patterns coupled with knowledge of demographic trends in the marketplace can help marketers forecast demand for specific product and service categories over time. Monitoring changes over time in needs, preferences, and priorities of consumers is essential for segmenting markets, targeting prospects, and positioning

FIGURE 11.3

In contrast with traditional educational methods of prior generations, instilling knowledge to the young is now facilitated via the most advanced technologies.

products. For example, Folger's Singles, Starbuck's Via, and Nescafe's Tasters Choice as well as Keurig coffeemakers are intended for people who live alone and who do not need to brew a full pot of coffee at a time.[31]

A MODERNIZED FAMILY LIFECYCLE

Not long ago, this traditional FLC model typified the overwhelming majority of U.S. households. In recent years, however, a number of cultural, socio-demographic, and lifestyle trends in the United States, as well as technological advances, have reconfigured the structure and profile of the U.S. family. For instance, significant increases have occurred in the number of singles, unmarried cohabitants, same-sex unions, dual-career couples, childless couples, single-parent households, adoptions by single persons, late-in-life marriages, blended families, children living with their grandparents, as well as divorces and separations. There has also been a notable increase in the number of extended families.[32] This diversity coupled with other developments such as changing roles of men and women, spousal abuse, family planning, artificial insemination, and legalized abortion strongly suggest that the contemporary notion of the family must be expanded to include such multiform situations.

Although many people still maintain the traditional view of marriage for themselves and others, some individuals contend that social changes such as these necessitate updating standard terminology. In particular, the definitions of single and married persons require revision. Perhaps *singles* should include anyone who is presently unmarried, regardless of past marital status. Perhaps *married* should embrace any couple that resides together and intends to share an extended relationship. In this view, a man and woman living together with or without formally exchanging vows would fall into the married category, and same-sex couples would qualify as married if they contemplate a long-term partnership. These are but a few of the departures from the traditional family lifecycle concept that realistically reflect metamorphoses occurring in modern society.[33]

To compensate for the limitations of the traditional model, researchers of consumer behavior have sought out expanded FLC models that better reflect today's heterogeneity of households and living arrangements.[34] Nontraditional households include both family and nonfamily types. *Nontraditional family households* include childless couples, same-sex unions, career-oriented couples who delay having children until later in life, couples who enter into marriage with a child, single parents (widows or widowers, persons with custody of a child after divorce, persons who have children out of wedlock, singles who adopt a child), and extended families. Today, the range of extended families includes single adults who return home to their parents to lessen the expenses of living alone while establishing a career, divorced sons and daughters who return to their parents' home (perhaps with grandchildren), infirm elderly parents who move in with their children, and newlyweds who live with their inlaws. *Nonfamily households*, on the other hand, include single persons (most of whom are young), unmarried couples, divorced persons without children, and widowed persons.

In view of these social changes, researchers such as Gilly and Enis as well as Murphy and Staples, among others, have proposed redefined family lifecycles. Gilly and Enis proposed a FLC that depicted three age groups (under 35, 35–64, and 65 and over) and divided these age groups into fourteen categories.[35] Murphy and Staples, on the other hand, developed a model that depicted fourteen FLC categories and divided heads of households into separate categories of young, middle-age, and older life phases.[36]

Let us now consider some of the forms of nontraditional living arrangements that have recently emerged in our society and that reflect a marked deviation from the traditional FLC.

NONTRADITIONAL LIVING-ARRANGEMENT PATTERNS

Nontraditional households are supplanting conventional family units as the norm. In fact, according to the Pew Research Center, fewer than half (46 percent) of U.S. children today live in a so-called "traditional" family. In 2015, data reflect a significant shift in the American family. While the "ideal" involved couples marrying young, then starting a family, and staying married "'til death do they part," the present family has become more complex and less traditional. Today, 46 percent of families consist of two married partners in their first marriage, 15 percent entail two married partners with one or both remarried, 34 percent involve single parents, with 5 percent having no parent at home.[37] Since the last half of the twentieth century, marketers have become increasingly aware of and responsive to various nontraditional living-arrangement patterns, such as boomerang children, single-parent families, single-person households, as well as same-sex households. Ramifications of these trends extend to many areas of consumer behavior. For example, the rise in the number of single-parent families impacts various facets of consumer behavior such as the number of meals eaten out; consumption of convenience foods; eating meals on the run; and use of smartphones to keep track of kids as well as monitor the household.

Boomerang Children

Today, one in five people in their twenties and thirties is presently living with his or her parents.[38] These so-called boomerang children include in-

boomerang children
grown children—now adults—who continue to live in or return to their parents' home

creasing numbers of college graduates who have headed home after facing a disappointing job market and expensive housing, weighed down by the highest school debt burden of any graduating class. Such young people seem to abound, particularly if they happen to be in low-paying creative careers such as acting, publishing, and music. They try to maintain the amenities of their affluent upbringings. Studies show that return-home rates tend to rise during periods of high unemployment, but long job searches, low pay for entry-level jobs, and student debt, as well as high housing costs, are also factors. Whereas some return out of economic necessity, others reappear because they have been spoiled by their parents' affluence and feel disinclined to accept a lower standard of living if they were to reside on their own.[39] Evidence suggests that men are more likely than women to reappear on parents' doorsteps, due in part to the fact that the median age at which men marry is twenty-seven—more than two years later than the average for women. Although boomerangers are largely single, statistics reveal that many married couples with children also return to their parents' home. The length of stay, in most cases, ranges between six months and two years.[40] Boomerang children tend to spend more on discretionary purchases such as entertainment, clothing, and personal-care items.[41]

It is interesting to note that many families with a boomerang child at home are simultaneously providing some form of financial assistance to an elderly parent, which places a heavy burden on the family's resources. Demographers refer to such families as a segment of the sandwich generation, which includes any household with children and parents who concurrently provide assistance to their *own* aging parents.

sandwich generation
parents who simultaneously support both their kids and their elderly parents

Single Parenthood

Over the last few decades, the proportion of traditional two-parent families has been declining while that of single-parent households has been on the rise. According to the Custodial Mothers and Fathers Report released by the U.S. Census Bureau in 2015, there were 13.6 million single parents in the United States, who were raising 23 million children. The report revealed that 84 percent of these single-parent households are headed by mothers, and only 16 percent by fathers. Many single-parent families are low-income households. Around 27.7 percent of households headed by a custodial single mother with children live in poverty, compared to only 11.1 percent of households headed by a single father with children.[42] Three major subgroups of one-parent families can be identified:

- Displaced homemakers (i.e., a person who works for her family at home but does not earn a paycheck)
- Adolescent mothers
- Single fathers

In the first subgroup, the *displaced homemakers*, marital dissolution drastically reduces the new single-parent family's available income. Displaced homemakers are at a disadvantage because they often lack an employment and credit history, training, and marketable job skills. Concerning the second subgroup, *adolescent mothers*, the Centers for Disease Control and Prevention as well as the Office of Adolescent Health report that in the year 2014, there were 24.2 births for every 1,000 adolescent females between the ages of fifteen and nineteen, or 249,078 babies born to females in this age group. Nearly 89 percent of these births occurred outside of marriage. The 2014 teen birth rate reveals a decline of 9 percent from the year 2013, when the birth rate was 26.5 per 1,000, which means that the teen birth rate has declined almost continuously over the past twenty years. Still, the U.S. teen birth rate is higher than that of many developed countries, including Canada and the U.K. The third subgroup, consisting of *single fathers,* tends to have a more healthy economic status compared with its female single-parent counterpart. However, single fathers often find their sole child-rearing role conflicting with work expectations and often feel that they are filling social roles for which they are unprepared.[43]

More than one in four U.S. children are being raised in a single-parent household.

The Live Alones

Marketers are just beginning to realize the buying power of the live-alone market.[44] Men and women who live alone can and do spend heavily—any way they please. In the year 2015, estimates reveal that live alones in the United States constitute 28 percent of all households, which means that they are now tied with childless couples as the predominant residential category. Live alones are primarily women, about 18 million of them, compared with 14 million men. The majority, more than 16 million, are middle-aged adults between the ages of thirty-five and sixty-four. The elderly account for about 11 million of the total figure. Young adults between the ages of eighteen and thirty-four number more than 5 million.[45]

Those who live alone constitute an attractive market in certain product and service sectors. Recent reports from market analyst Datamonitor indicate that single-person households spend around 150 percent more per person on rent than those who live in households of two people or more. They also account for 41 percent of the personal-care market and tend to spend more on alcohol. In addition, they lay out more per person for reading materials, tobacco products, and smoking supplies.[46]

A number of traits characterize the live-alone market. Singles tend to be self-reliant and gravitate toward products that are low maintenance, affordable, quiet, and safe.[47] Because they prefer living close to where they

Singles tend to be among the best customers for restaurants.

© Syda Productions/Shutterstock.com

work, they are willing to move into the dense, attached homes as well as lofts and condos that most families with children tend to avoid. Singles also tend to be among the best customers for restaurants. They tend to spend more on travel, convenience foods, and sporty automobiles than married adults. This segment constitutes a lucrative market for many items ranging from dating services to fashionable clothing.

GENERATIONAL MARKETING

Generationally defined lifestyles and social values exercise as much influence on buying as more commonly known demographic factors such as income, education, and gender.[48] Marketers are discovering how to exploit the life experiences that define each generation of consumers. This practice is known as generational marketing. Unlike a mass-marketing strategy, where consumers—regardless of their demographics—are viewed as a whole, generational marketing identifies and addresses smaller segments of the market based on the significant experiences they share.[49] Whereas a generation is usually defined by dates of birth, a cohort catalogs each generation in terms of external events that occurred during its members' formative years.

A cohort is an aggregate of people who have undergone similar experiences, passed through cultural milestones and historical events, and shared common memories of events that transpired during a particular time frame. Because members of a cohort share common recollections, it is possible to appeal to them through symbolism meaningful to each cohort. Feelings of nostalgia could be created by using familiar appeals based on prior experiences. The success of the revived Volkswagen Beetle is largely due to nostalgia for the old Bug. Clothing fashions and music keep coming back in cycles, fueled by generations that are emotional about things they experienced when they were children. Similarly, commercials for many products today, such as cars, soft drinks, and financial services, borrow hits from the 1960s and classic rock era in an effort to stimulate sales among the Boomers.[50]

generational marketing
the cataloging of generations in terms of external events that occurred during their members' formative years

cohort
an aggregate of people who have undergone similar experiences and share common memories

CLASSIFICATION OF CONSUMERS BY LIFE EXPERIENCES

A contemporary glance at the lifestyles of the present-day generations in our society reveals a need to update the classification of cohorts that prevailed in the 1990s and that were suggested by authors such as Meredith and Schewe.[51] Today's generations have expanded, and may be classified into five major cohort types. These are labeled the Boomers I cohort, the Boomers II cohort, the Generation X cohort, the Generation Y cohort (also known as the Millennials), and the Generation Z cohort. It is worth noting that demographers disagree about each of these groups' exact parameters, and certainly these classifications overlap to some extent.

Boomers I Cohort

Boomers I cohort
individuals age sixty-two
through seventy (in 2016)

Also called the Woodstock generation, the Boomers I cohort consists of individuals who, as of this writing (2016), are ages sixty-two through seventy. Boomers I were born between 1946 and 1954. Brought up with the experience of the Vietnam War, the assassinations of John F. Kennedy and Martin Luther King Jr., and the first moon walk, this group embraces the values of youthfulness, invincibility, and freedom. The hippie movement was a natural outcome of this orientation. They created a new meaning of the youth culture, popularizing blue jeans, rock music, and sexual permissiveness. They vowed to stay forever young, but at the same time exhibit concerns about health, old age, and retirement. Boomer I members are dissimilar to their parents in that they like to spend, borrow, and, in many cases, live beyond their means. They enjoy owning conspicuous products. The Beatles, Elvis Presley, and the Grateful Dead are among their favorites. Baby Boomers will reconfigure the aging picture in America over the next decade or two, as this generation faces both opportunities and potential crises.

Boomers II Cohort

Boomers II cohort
individuals age fifty-one
through sixty-one (in 2016)

Also called zoomers, the Boomers II cohort embraces individuals who, as of this writing (2016), are fifty-one through sixty-one years of age. Boomers II were born between 1955 and 1965. The Watergate era took its toll on this group, resulting in a loss of faith in the existence of an idealistic political system. Their ingrained sense of entitlement has been overtaken by unmet expectations. They tend to be somewhat self-absorbed, pursuing personal goals and instant gratification.[52] In order to have a lifestyle as good as that of their predecessors and to flaunt their success, they like to spend and will go into debt to acquire material possessions. Concerned about the environment, they tend to prefer environmentally friendly products. They like rock and roll and have a permissive view of sex.

Generation X Cohort

Also called baby busters, the Generation X cohort consists of individuals who, as of this writing (2016), are thirty-nine through fifty-one years of age. They were born between 1965 and 1977.[53] The Generation X cohort grew up in the era of X-rated movies, legalized abortion, and the information superhighway. They are the first to have grown up with computers and, perhaps more importantly, the first to play video games. Unhappy about the environmental and economic problems they inherited, they are cynical and display seemingly contradictory behavior. They tend to be antihype and reject the concept of conspicuous consumption. Products that hype their own success with copy points such as upscale or bestselling are unlikely to persuade Generation Xers, whose money motto was once "Spend, spend, and spend." They are now worried about the debt being loaded into their future. Their political views are colored by the principle of "What's in it for me?" It is interesting to note that improving public education is one of the highest public policy priorities for Xers.[54]

Generation Y Cohort (The Millennials)

The group within the ages of twenty-two and thirty-eight is dubbed the Generation Y cohort or the Millennials.[55] They were born between 1978 and 1994. Members of this segment constitute the most ethnically and racially diverse cohort of youth in the nation's history. They are starting out as the most politically progressive age group in modern times. They constitute the first generation in human history that regards behaviors like tweeting and texting, along with using social media sites like Facebook, YouTube, Google, and Wikipedia to be everyday parts of their social life and their search for understanding. This group is the least religiously observant generation of youth since survey research began charting religious behavior. This segment is more inclined toward trust in institutions compared with either of its two predecessor generations. It is the cohort that witnessed events such as the attack on the World Trade Center and the cloning of human cells. Many use extreme fashions, such as body piercing, dyed hair, and tattoos. When it comes to loyalty, the companies they work for are last on their list of priorities, behind their families and friends. Their favorite music is grunge, retro, and rap.

Generation Z Cohort

Generation Z cohort chronologically follows Generation Y. Members of Generation Z are mostly in their teens and early twenties, as of this writing

Generation X cohort individuals age thirty-nine through fifty-one (in 2016)

Generation Y cohort individuals age twenty-two through thirty-eight (in 2016)

Generation Z cohort individuals age birth to early twenties (in 2016)

(2016). They were born after 1995. These young adults of today are primed to become the dominant influencers tomorrow. Generation Z witnessed the attack on the World Trade Center, the Great Recession, the era or war on terror, as well as the election of President Barack Obama. They are the children of older and wealthier parents who have fewer siblings, so they are privileged with parental spending power in the billions. From a materialistic point of view, they constitute the most supplied generation of children ever. Technologically, no other generation before them could claim its exposure to or experience with the digital world. They have unlimited access to information through the Internet and social media, as well as from other forms of mobile technology. As such, access to information has become an integral part of their existence. They pioneered anonymous social media platforms, such as Secret, Whisper, and SnapChat, where incriminating images disappear almost instantly. Recent reports reveal that before they can even read, almost one in four children in nursery school is learning the skill of using the computer. According to the Department of Education, about one-quarter of children ages three to five who attend such schools have gone online. By kindergarten, a third of them were reported to have used the Internet, typically under adult supervision.[56]

Members of Generation Z are children of older, wealthier parents. They tend to have unlimited access to information through the Internet and social media, as well as other forms of mobile technology.

© Phovoir/Shutterstock.com

GLOBAL OPPORTUNITY

Study Abroad Programs . . . A Window of Opportunity

In today's increasingly interdependent global environment, where many U.S. firms operate overseas or serve global accounts, the need for a globally savvy workforce has become essential. In searching for new hires, U.S. companies, particularly those that have operations overseas, require evidence of a well-developed international perspective and exposure to other countries. This is particularly the case when these employees must deal with people from other cultures.

In order to prepare such a culturally savvy workforce, innovative educational programs had to be designed to allow for the training of students to gain this new global perspective. One avenue that has proven to be effective in incorporating global awareness within the university curriculum is the study abroad program. Such programs, which usually span one or two academic terms, are being offered at many colleges and universities today. They allow students to travel and experience foreign cultures firsthand, while fulfilling course requirements and earning credit hours. Study abroad programs cover a wide variety of topics, extending from business classes to courses in archeology and the arts.

For many, this overseas student experience is truly valuable. To them, it represents the first time they leave their home country. Living in a different country for a semester or two tends to increase students' tolerance and cultural awareness, which are essential traits in today's diverse workforce. Those who study abroad are also likely to gain perspective on how it feels to be an outsider in a foreign environment. They also gain cultural sensitivity toward minority and foreign colleagues in the workplace. In addition to the multicultural outlook they acquire, there are the added benefits of mastering a second language, the opportunity for travel, and establishing connections with other fellow students.

Against these benefits, there are a few limitations to participating in study abroad programs. Among these are the hindrances of both financial ramifications and the challenges that parents face when their child leaves home to go abroad. For most families, the financial requirements of sending a child abroad are so large that many families dismiss the idea quickly. Fortunately, however, solutions exist in the form of obtaining student loans as well as educational grants and scholarships from various governmental or nongovernmental sources. The second obstacle is parental concern and apprehension that is experienced when their son or daughter leaves home for a foreign country. Such emotions can be easily understood in light of their young adult living alone for an extended time in an unfamiliar place. However, the multicultural outlook the student acquires and the enhancement of his or her future employment prospects as a result of participating in such a program far exceed the drawbacks that may be envisioned by some overly protective parents.[57]

MARKETING APPLICATIONS OF GENERATIONAL COHORTS

Generational marketing systems hold high promise for marketers of many products and services. The power of this system lies in its ability to categorize consumers into groups of individuals with homogeneous life experiences. Common experiences of a generation create a specific sensibility that touches all its members in some way. Through these experiences, individuals' views are formed regarding what is funny, what is stylish, and what is taboo. It directs them to what is appropriate and what is not. Consequently, those who have similar life experiences are most likely to be similar with respect to other behavioral characteristics, such as product purchase, motivations, and media behavior. This implied psychological coherence of these segments allows marketers to use language and symbols and to make offers that are meaningful to them and likely to produce a desired response.

Cohort segmentation, for example, allowed Weber Company, the maker of grills, to profile the buyers of its products.[58] The company's executives determined that generational cohort differences are useful to identify who is buying their grills and to ascertain the type of grills they are most likely to purchase. The company produced a twenty-minute video that dramatized the lifestyles of cohorts and made it available to its distributors and sales staff. Each cohort vignette pictured its home environment, complete with appropriate lifestyle items. The vignette portrayed the typical cohort family, their guests, their food preferences, and the type of grill its members are most likely to purchase.[59]

The cohort approach to understanding consumer tastes has helped many marketers select appeals—whether through music, images, jokes, or values—that evoke the shared experiences of people belonging to the same generation. Companies such as Jaguar Cars Ltd., Volkswagen, and Levi Strauss & Co. have similarly reported they have successfully used this approach to design products or services that suit particular cohorts or create appeals that win their favor.[60]

As we have seen while investigating the process of decision making within a family setting, decisions can range from individual choices made by a single family member to joint decisions that entail input from multiple parties, including husband, wife, and/or children. In these cases, each member of the family influences others, and is influenced by others. The family, in this sense, is but one example of social groups in which personal influence plays an important role. Personal influence describes the process by which others influence us either verbally (friends, neighbors, or colleagues) or virally (through communication on the Internet). The significance of personal influence lies in its credibility as a source of product-related information due to perceived objectivity of the source. The topic of personal influence is covered in detail in the next chapter.

SUMMARY

The U.S. Census Bureau traditionally defined *family* as "two or more persons, related either through birth, marriage, or adoption, living under one roof." Nevertheless, contemporary families or households come in myriad forms, sizes, and compositions. The family plays an integral role in the process of consumer socialization—the process by which individuals acquire the knowledge, skills, and attitudes relevant to their effective functioning as consumers in the marketplace.

At least eight family consumption roles can be identified. These include influencers, gatekeepers, deciders, buyers, preparers, users, maintainers, and disposers. The family decision process can be classified into four categories: autonomic, husband dominant, wife dominant, and syncretic. The relative roles of the husband and wife in family decisions are impacted by such factors as egalitarianism, involvement, empathy, and recognized authority.

The family lifecycle refers to the series of stages through which households pass as their members grow older. The stages of the FLC model are primarily based on age, marital status, employment status of the head of household, and the presence or absence of children as well as their ages. At each stage, there are unique needs, differences in earning power, and specific demands placed on household resources. Five distinguishable stages of the traditional FLC are bachelorhood, honeymooner, parenthood, post-parenthood, and dissolution. Modernized family lifecycle models recognize the diversity of contemporary households and societal trends, such as increases in the number of singles, unmarried cohabitants, dual-career couples, childless couples, single-parent households, adoptions by single persons, late-in-life marriages, blended families, children living with their grandparents, as well as divorces and separations. Accompanying such increases is a notable growth in the number of extended families.

Generational marketing targets segments of the population based on external events that occurred during the formative years of a generation. Whereas a generation is defined by dates of birth, a cohort catalogs each generation in terms of external events that occurred during its members' formative years. Generational cohorts include the Boomers I, Boomers II, Generation X, Generation Y (Millennials), and Generation Z cohorts.

Generational marketing systems can help marketers of many products and services identify groups of consumers with homogeneous life experiences. Those who have similar life experiences are likely to be similar with respect to other behavioral characteristics, such as product purchase, motivations, and media behavior. The implied psychological coherence of such segments allows marketers to use language and symbols, select appeals, and make offers that are meaningful to them.

CASE SYNOPSIS

The Issue of Employing Older Workers

Today, the United States is undergoing a major demographic shift in the age structure of its population. The average and median age of Americans is rising and affecting the composition of the workforce. For example, by the year 2020, 55 percent of the civilian labor force will be fifty-five and over, up from only 13 percent in the year 2000. Recognizing these shifts in our society, both the U.S government and many private firms and industries have initiated steps to help accommodate this new trend.

A closer look at the prevailing attitudes of firms regarding the issue of employing older workers reveals two distinct managerial views concerning such a policy. On one side, successful employers of older workers provide a number of advantages to this practice, such as wider experience and greater loyalty of such workers to the firm. On the other side, however, there are some recruitment managers who perceive risks in employing older workers. This is due to assumptions that such workers have lower productivity, cost more to maintain, and exhibit less flexibility than younger workers.

Notes

1   David K. Li, "Single Adults Now Outnumber Married Adults," *The New York Post* (September 9, 2014), nypost.com/2014/09/09/single-adults-now-outnumber-married-adults/; Nora Daly, "Single? So Are the Majority of U.S. Adults," *PBS NewsHour* (September 11, 2014), www.pbs.org/newshour/rundown/single-youre-not-alone/; U.S. Department of Labor Statistics, "America's Young Adults at 29" (April 8, 2016), www.bls.gov/news.release/nlsyth.nr0.htm; Liza Mundy, *The Richer Sex* (New York: Simon & Schuster, Inc., 2012); Donna St. George, "More Wives Are the Higher-income Spouse, Pew Report Says," *Washington Post* (January 19, 2010); Hanna Rosin, "She Makes More Money Than He Does. So?" *Slate* (February 16, 2011), http://www.rolereboot.org/archives/details/2011-02-she-makes-more-money-than-he-does-so.

2   "Home Computer Access and Internet Use," *Child Trends DataBank* (2013), childtrends.org/wp-content/upload/212/07/69_Computer_Use.pdf; http://childtrends.org/?indicators=home-computer-access.

3   R. Moore and G. P. Moschis, "Role of Mass Media and Family in Development of Consumption Norms," *Journalism Quarterly* 80, no. 1 (Spring 1983), pp. 67–73.

4   R. Moore and G. P. Moschis, "The Effects of Family Communication and Mass Media Use on Adolescent Consumer Learning," *Journal of Communication* 31, no. 4 (Fall 1981), pp. 42–51.

5   G. P. Moschis and R. Moore, "A Longitudinal Study of the Development of Purchasing Patterns," in P. Murphy (Ed.), *Proceedings of the Educators' Conference* (Chicago: American Marketing Association, 1983), pp. 114–117.

6   G. P. Moschis et al., "Mass Media and Interpersonal Influences on Adolescent Consumer Learning," in B. Greenberg (Ed.), *Proceedings of the Educators' Conference* (Chicago: American Marketing Association, 1977), pp. 68–71.

7   J.A. Clausen, "Perspectives on Childhood Socialization," in J.A. Clausen (Ed.), *Socialization and Society* (Boston: Little Brown, 1968).

8   Moschis et al., "Mass Media and Interpersonal Influences on Adolescent Consumer Learning."

9   J. Aldous, "Commentaries on Ward, Consumer Socialization," *Journal of Consumer Research* 1 (September 1974), pp. 15–16.

10   S. Ward, D. B. Wackman, and E. Wartella, *How Children Learn to Buy: The Development of Consumer Information Processing Skills* (Beverly Hills, CA: Sage, 1977).

11   P. Sloan, "Matchabelli Name Readied for Men's Fragrance Line," *Advertising Age* (September 18,1978), p. 3; B. Voss, "Selling with Sentiment," *Sales & Marketing Management* (March 1993), pp. 60–65.

12   J.W. McDavid and H. Harari, *Social Psychology* (New York: Harper and Row, 1968), pp. 268–269.

13   Bernice Kanner, "Toplines: Are You Normal?" *American Demographics* (March 1999), p. 19.

14   H. L. Davis and B. P. Rigaux, "Perception of Marital Roles in Decision Processes," *Journal of Consumer Research 1* (June 1974), pp. 51–62; M. A. Straus, "Conjugal Power Structure and Adolescent Personality," *Marriage and Family Living* 24, no. 1 (February 1962), pp. 17–25.

15   "How Much Does Child Care Cost?" (2015), https://www.care.com/a/how-much-does-child-care-cost-1406091737; U.S. Department of Education, National Center for Educational Statistics (2011); Digest of Educational Statistics (2010), (NCES 2011-015), Chapter 2; Molly Henneberg, "Child-care Cost Skyrockets: Costs More Than College in Some States," *FOX News* (August 30, 2011), http://www.foxnews.com/politics/2011/08/30/child-care-cost-skyrockets-costs-more-than-college-in-some-states/.

16   Davis and Rigaux, "Perception of Marital Roles in Decision Processes."

17   M. Putnam and W. R. Davidson, *Family Purchasing Behavior II: Family Roles by Product Category* (Columbus, OH: Management Horizons, 1987).

18   L. H. Rogler and M. E. Procidano, "Egalitarian Spouse Relations and Wives' Marital Satisfaction in Intergenerationally Linked Puerto Rican Families," *Journal of Mar*riage *and the Family* 51 (February 1989), pp. 37–39.

19   W. J. Qualls, "Household Decision Behavior: The Impact of Husbands' and Wives' Sex Role Orientation," *Journal of Consumer Research* 14 (September 1987), pp. 264–279.

20   J. Ford, M. S. LaTour, and T. L. Henthrone, "Perception of Marital Roles in Purchase Decision Processes: A Cross-Cultural Study," *Journal of the Academy of Marketing Science* 23, no. 2 (Spring 1995), pp. 120–131.

21   Robert M. Cosenza, "Family Decision Making Decision Dominance Structure Analysis—An Extension," *Journal of the Academy of Marketing Science* 13, no. 1/2 (Winter–Spring 1985), pp. 91–103.

22   "Marketing to Children Overview," CCFC (Campaign for Commercial Free Childhood), http://www.commercialfreechildhood.org/resource/mar-

keting-children-overview; ChildStats.gov, "POP1 Child Population: The Number of Children (In Millions) Ages 0 to 17 In the United States," http://www.childstats.gov/AMERICASCHILDREN/tables/pop1.asp.

23 Via Zaarly, "What College Kids Spend Their Money On," *Alltop* (September, 2011), http://holykaw.alltop.com/what-college-kids-spend-their-money-on-infogr.

24 Liebeck, "The Consumer Connection: Children under 13."

25 Datamonitor, "Best Practices in Teen and Tween Personal Care 2002," http://www.marketresearch.com/map/prod/829427.html; David G. Kennedy, "Coming of Age in Consumerdom," *Am. Demographics* (April 2004), p. 14.

26 "Kids Now Have a Bigger Say in the Car Buying Decision," *Easier Motoring* (August 11, 2006), www. easier.com/view/News/Motoring/articles-64579.htm/.

27 "Children as Consumers," *Global Issues* (January 8, 2008), www.globalissues.org/TrendRelated/Consumption/Children.asp.

28 "Selling to Kids: Kid-Sizing Adult Products by the Book," *BNET.com's Find-Articles* (March 7, 2001), http://findarticles.com/p/articles/mi_m0FVE/is_4_6/ai_71352186/print.

29 James U. McNeal, *The Kids Market: Myths and Realities* (Ithaca, NY: Paramount Market Publishing, Inc.).

30 "The ABCs of Adult Marketing to Children," *PR Watch* (July 7, 2006), www.prwatch.org/node/4957.

31 "24 Rare Surrogate Mother Statistics," BrandonGaille.com (October 26, 2014), http://brandongaille.com/24-rare-surrogate-mother-statistics/; Helier Chevng, "Surrogate Babies: Where Can You Have Them And Is It Legal?" *BBC News* (August 6, 2014), www.bbc.com/news/world-28679020.

32 U.S. Census Bureau, "Households and Families 2010," http://www.census.gov/prod/cen2010/briefs/c2010br-14.pdf; Christy Fisher, "Census Data May Make Ads More Single-Minded," *Ad Age* (July 20, 1992), p. 2.

33 U.S. Census Bureau, "Households and Families 2010," http://www.census.gov/prod/cen2010/briefs/c2010br-14.pdf; Sam Roberts, "Report Finds Shift Toward Extended Families," *The New York Times* (March 18, 2010), http://www.nytimes.com/2010/03/19/us/19family.html?_r=1.

34 Based on data from the U.S. Census Bureau, "Households and Families 2010," http://www.census.gov/prod/cen2010/briefs/c2010br-14.pdf.

35 Charles M. Schaninger and William D. Danko, "A Conceptual and Empirical Comparison of Alternative Household Life Cycle Models," *Journal of Consumer Research* 19 (March 1993), pp. 580–594.

36 Schaninger and Danko, "A Conceptual and Empirical Comparison of Alternative Household Life Cycle Models"; Patrick E. Murphy and William A. Staples, "A Modernized Family Life Cycle," *Journal of Consumer Research* 6 (June 1979), pp. 12–22.

37 Jennifer Hickey, "Pew: Only 46 Percent of U.S. Families Are 'Traditional,'" *Newsmax* (January 16, 2015), http://www.newsmax.com/US/Family-single-parent-children-Pew-Research/2015/01/16/id/619047/.

38 Adam Davidson, "It's Official: The Boomerang Won't Leave," *The New York Times* (June 20, 2014), www.nytimes.com/2014/06/22/magazine/its-official-the-boomerang-kids-wont-leave.html?html?_r=0.

39 Jay MacDonald, "How to 'Gently' Toss Your Boomerang Kid," *Bankrate* (September 9, 2005), www.bankrate.com/brm/news/pf/20050909a1.asp.

40 Gary Picariello, "They're Back: Boomerang Kids," *Associated Content* (June 1, 2007), www. associatedcontent.com/article/259628/theyre_back_boomerang_kids.html?cat=12.

41 Pamela Paul, "ecoboomerang," *American Demographics* (June 2001), pp. 44–49.

42 Jennifer Wolf, "Single Parent Statistics," *About.com* (2007), http://single-parents.about.com/od/legalissues/p/portrait.htm; "Custodial Mothers and Fathers and Their Child Support: 2009," *U.S. Census Bureau* (2011).

43 "Trends in Teen Pregnancy and Child Bearing," Office of Adolescent Health (2014), http://www.hhs.gov/ash/oah/adolescent-health-topics/reproductive-health/teen-pregnancy/trends.html; "Teen Pregnancy in the United States," Centers for Disease Control and Prevention (2014); Genaro Armas, "Single-Father Homes on the Rise," *ABC News* (May 18, 2015), http://abcnews.go.com/US/story?id=93279&page=1; Kim Parker, "5 Facts About Today's Fathers," *Factank* (June 18, 2015), www.pewresearch.org/fact-tank/2015/06/18/5-facts-about-todays-fathers/; Lisa Belkin, "Single Fathers: Pew Research Reports Number of Single Dads Has Jumped in the U.S." (July 2, 2013).

44 Maria Popova, "Going Solo: A Brief History of Living Alone and the Enduring Social Stigma Around Singletons," *Brain Pickings* (May 9, 2012), http://www.brainpickings.org/index.php/2012/05/09/going-solo-klinenberg/.

45 Tim Henderson, "Growing Number of People Living Solo Can Pose Challenges," *The Pew Charitable Trusts Research and Analysis* (September 11, 2014), http://www.pewtrusts.org/en/research-and-analysis/blogs/stateline/2014/09/11/growing-number-of-people-living-solo-can-pose-challenges.

46 "People Living Alone Account for 41 Percent of the Personal Care Market," *Goliath* (2008), http:// goliath.ecnext.com/coms2/gi_0199-3010729/ People-living-alone-account-for.html.

47 Sara Hammes and June Fletcher, "Selling to Singles and Couples," *Builder* 17, (February 1994), p. 52.

48 Jock Bickert, "Waging War on the 98%," *Direct Marketing* (February 1996), pp. 40–43; Jock Bickert "Cohorts II: A New Approach to Market Segmentation," *Journal of Consumer Marketing* 14, no. 5 (1997), pp. 362–379.

49 Geoffrey Meredith and Charles Schewe, "The Power of Cohorts," *American Demographics* 16, no. 12 (December 1994), pp. 22–27, 31; Faye Rice, "Making Generational Marketing Come of Age," *Fortune* (June 26, 1995), pp. 110–114.

50   Tony Laidig, "Using the Power of Nostalgia as a Marketing Strategy," *Scribd* (2007), www.scribd.com/doc/3192077/Using-the-power-of-nostalgia-as-a-marketing-strategyLAIDIG; Nedra Weinrich, "Harnessing Nostalgia," *MarketingProf Daily Fix* (June 1, 2007), www.mpdailyfix.com/2007/06/harnessing _nostalgia.html.

51   Meredith and Schewe, "The Power of Cohorts," summarized in Rice, "Making Generational Marketing Come of Age," pp. 110–114.

52   J. Walker Smith and Ann Clurman, "Generational Marketing," *Inc.* (April 1997), pp. 87–88, 91.

53   "Toplines: Conflicting Signals," *American Demographics* (November 1998), p. 19.

54   William J. Schroer, "Generation X, Y, Z, and Others," *The Social Librarian*, http://www.socialmarketing.org/newsletter/features/generation3.htm; Laura Barcella, "Generation X's Debt Headache," *Alter Ne* (May 31, 2006), www.alternet.org/workplace/36658/.

55   William J. Schroer, "Generation X, Y, Z, and Others," *The Social Librarian*, http://www.socialmarketing.org/newsletter/features/generation3.htm; and Generation Y: Today's Teens—the Biggest Bulge since the Moomers—May Force Marketers to Toss Their Old Tricks," *Business Week* (February 15, 1999), www.businessweek.com/1999/99_07/b36/6001.htm.

56   Alex Williams, "Move Over, Millennials, Here Comes Generation Z," *The New York Times* (September 18, 2015), http://www.nytimes.com/2015/09/20/fashion/move-over-millennials-here-comes-generation-z.html; William J. Schroer, "Generation X, Y, Z, and Others," *The Social Librarian*, http://www.socialmarketing.org/newsletter/features/generation3.htm; Susan Walsh, "Kids as Young as 2 Using Internet," *Chicago Sun-Times* (June 5, 2005).

57   "Study Abroad—The Advantage of Going Global," *Education Corner,* http://www.educationcorner.com/study-abroad-going-global.html.

58   Bickert, "Cohorts 11: A New Approach to Market Segmentation."

59   Ibid.

60   Michael M. Phillips, "Demographies: Selling by Evoking What Defines a Generation," *Wall Street Journal* (August 13, 1996).

CHAPTER 12

PERSONAL INFLUENCE AND WORD OF MOUTH

LEARNING OBJECTIVES

- To examine the nature of personal influence and opinion leadership.
- To comprehend the power and vividness of word-of-mouth communication.
- To develop a basic understanding of models of the personal influence process.
- To gain insight into the methods of identifying and/or creating influencers.
- To examine the three personal influence strategies that marketers use to benefit their firms.
- To review how marketers combat negative word of mouth.

KEY TERMS

personal influence	hypodermic needle	shopping pals
word of mouth (WOM)	model	market maven
opinion leaders	trickle-down model	surrogate consumer
brand advocates	trickle-up model	teaser campaigns
opinion leadership	trickle-across model	product placement
agents of change	two-step model	testimonials
availability-valence	multistep model	
hypothesis	influencer	

On one Tuesday morning in October 2015, an unusually large volume of chatter appeared on celebrity pages, and an equal explosion on Twitter occurred. This massive online movement was caused by a single tweet from celebrity TV host, Oprah Winfrey, regarding her decision to join the diet company Weight Watchers International. Oprah, on that day, had tweeted a video celebrating the fact that she had lost twenty-six pounds by following the Weight Watchers diet while she was still eating bread every day.

The overwhelming reactions of the public and media to Oprah's tweets came as no surprise. In our contemporary society, such reaction by the general public to the views of celebrities has been common, whether these individuals are movie stars, athletes, politicians, or others of similar stature in the public eye. For example, in the case of Oprah, who was ranked by *Forbes Magazine* as the World's Twelfth Most Powerful Woman, she has been successful in shifting people's views and attitudes toward firms, products, or other individuals. A case in point was her well-known book club, in which fifty-nine out of seventy books that received her seal of approval made it onto the *New York Times Magazine* bestsellers list.

Therefore, it was a sound strategic move for Weight Watchers to look to Oprah for help in turning around the firm's fading image and subsequent declining profitability. Before her decision to join, the number of the company's subscribers and attendance at meetings had noticeably declined. The goal that Weight Watchers had in mind was that Oprah's empowerment would reverse the company's poor performance record and place the company on a more profitable track. Such actually occurred in the first few months following the commencement of Oprah's tweets. For example, within just a few months, the value of Weight Watchers stock continued to climb from a mere $2.17 per share to $25 by December.

However, once the exciting news about Oprah's involvement had quieted down, the company's stock prices started to fall gradually, with the decline trend continuing through February 2016 and beyond, at which point Weight Watchers announced a 41 percent drop in profitability. It was only natural that investors would ponder the reasons behind such poor market performance, especially when they had observed the miraculous Oprah effect work so well on previous occasions. They wondered whether Oprah's "halo effect" had lost it glitter.

A few reasons come to mind that would explain Oprah's short-lived influence in this particular case. Once the brief endorsement rally had ceased, investors and admirers started to realize the broad benefits that Oprah received in exchange for her endorsement. Fans found out that for every pound of weight that she had lost, Oprah earned $2.4 million, and that figure did not even include the value of her option grants and her 10 percent stake in the company. Oprah was also appointed as a member of the Weight Watchers Board of Directors and as a consultant to the firm.

Another reason for the abbreviated period of influence was the hefty cost of signing up and maintaining membership status with Weight Watchers. Unlike the meager cost of purchasing a typical bestseller paperback that Oprah had endorsed in her book club, Weight Watchers was pushing members to agree to lengthy membership terms and pay their dues up front—a hefty investment and a long-term commitment in the view of many who are not sufficiently motivated to emulate her or who are conveniently accustomed to forget their pledges to lose weight.

In addition, Weight Watcher's declining membership numbers and fading image was, to some degree, due to increased competition. This competition came from online weight-loss devices and services, as well as smartphone diet apps, such as activity tracker Fitbit and MyFitnessPal. These aides were available at no charge, and—as such—had affected the demand for the services of Weight Watchers, as well as other diet centers.[1]

Our society has become obsessed with the culture of celebrities. Actors, athletes, politicians, among others have strongly influenced our beliefs, interests, and behavioral patterns. The domain of their impact ranges from trends in fashion to political preferences. Learn about how celebrities influence the masses by visiting the website http://www.ehow.com/about_6675427_do-celebrities-influence-people .html. *What are the social and psychological phenomena that underlie our obsession with celebrities? Is their influence mostly beneficial or detrimental? Why do the masses heed their advice? To what extent are you personally influenced by celebrities? Explain how and why.*

We begin this chapter by exploring the dynamics of personal influence and word-of-mouth communications, as well as by ascertaining the role played by opinion leaders in disseminating product and service information to others. We then examine the characteristics of influencers and cite strategic marketing implications of these concepts to the field of consumer behavior.

PERSONAL INFLUENCE

Our purchasing behavior is frequently affected by the people with whom we intermingle. Just as reference groups and family members shape our beliefs, attitudes, and behavior, so also do other individuals with whom we interact. These interactions between two or more persons frequently influence the ideas, feelings, or conduct of one or more participants in the dialogue. This phenomenon is known as personal influence.

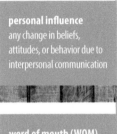

personal influence
any change in beliefs, attitudes, or behavior due to interpersonal communication

word of mouth (WOM)
sharing of an opinion about a product, service, or company between an independent source and a receiver

Personal influence refers to any change, whether deliberate or inadvertent, in an individual's beliefs, attitudes, or behavior that occurs as the consequence of interpersonal communication. Word of mouth is one of the means through which personal influence can occur. Word of mouth (WOM) is communication between a source and a receiver, where the receiver perceives the source as independent regarding a product, service, or brand. Such communication may be personal or may alternatively occur online through the use of preexisting social networks. WOM is originated by a third party, transmitted spontaneously in a way that is somehow autonomous of the party being talked about. In this sense, in WOM, both the message and the medium are independent.[2] People generally think of WOM in terms of advice given and received within the context of face-to-face communication. In reality, WOM recommendations of products, services, brands, and stores can be transmitted either in person, over the phone, through the mail, or online through social networks, buzz, viral grassroots campaigns, brand advocates, cause influencers, review sites, blogs, and forums. In this sense, WOM is the actual sharing of an opinion about a product or service between consumers. As such, it should be distinguished from viral marketing, which is typically reserved for programs where the advertising is talked about as opposed to the product itself. For example, viral videos, where the humor overshadows the brand, represent a case in point. The ad in Figure 12.1 from Allianz, a global financial network, stresses the value of verbal word of mouth spoken by a father to his son regarding selection of the right network to accelerate financial growth.

The effects, as well as the form, of WOM vary with the blend of industries, products, and services to which the WOM pertains. In research specific to healthcare marketing, for example, studies conclude that personal influence has a more decisive effect on the purchase decision than do commercial sources of information.[3] For example, in the selection of obstetric-gynecologist health professionals, friends, family, and other doctors and nonphysician healthcare providers were found to be important

FIGURE 12.1

The tagline and illustration in this ad for Allianz Financial Network reflects the notion that word of mouth is an effective medium for communicating financial advice.

word-of-mouth sources. Similarly, family and other doctors were found to be important word-of-mouth sources in the selection of an internist.[4] Personal influence, in these cases, was the main determinant of the choice of physician.

The increasing popularity of hybrid and electric cars at the present time is largely due to both word of mouth concerning energy costs and visual influence, as this type of car continues its debut on the nation's highways.

Personal influence can be verbal, visual, or both.[5] Consumers may track product, service, and store comments from blog postings, forums, and message boards, or simply overhear other peoples' opinions about them. In other cases, consumers observe what other people are doing, wearing, or using and may even ask them what an item is, how much it costs, and where it was purchased. The consequence of these information-sharing exchanges is influence that can be either one way or mutual. In the area of clothing, for example, visual influence can be so dramatic that a new style becomes fashionable across the entire nation in a matter of just a few weeks.

WHO ARE THE OPINION LEADERS?

opinion leaders
knowledgeable, influential persons who casually provide advice

When confronting unusual circumstances, unfamiliar issues, or challenging decisions, individuals in search of pertinent information frequently turn to others within their social sphere who are better informed on the subject. Those more-knowledgeable persons who casually provide advice are known as opinion leaders. Opinion leaders play a key communications role by conveying credible information via WOM and influencing the viewpoints or actions of others.

Many products and services that are an integral part of our lives today get their initial boost from opinion leaders. These individuals are the experts, gurus, and mavens. Their sphere of influence may be global, national, or local in nature. The attribute that gives them their influence is the trust that consumers place in their recommendations. They are perceived as objective evaluators of the overwhelming amount of information with which consumers are faced. They process marketers' communications and translate the messages for the rest of us. They spread marketers' information to us by conspicuously displaying their recent purchases, vocalizing their thoughts, or urging us to try something unfamiliar and new by means of instant messaging, video chat, Facebook, Twitter, email, VoIP, videoconferencing, Skype, blogs, among others. According to a recent Nielsen Global Online survey of 25,000 Internet consumers, 90 percent of those responding noted that they trust recommendations from people they know, while 70 percent trust consumer opinions posted online.[6]

These tiers of advocates and influencers are the ones who start the chain reaction of WOM and give the products, services, or ideas they support their initial jumpstart. Examples of opinion leaders abound. Simply think of recommendations provided by movie critics or food gurus on websites such as Zagat's Guide to Restaurants and Hotels, or tech buffs for the latest models of home electronics.

Progressive companies have come to realize that in order to run a successful word-of-mouth marketing campaign, they have to reach and maintain relationships with highly effective groups of influencers. Due to their use of both online and offline media channels, influencers are able to provide a communications shortcut—thereby helping companies effectively and inexpensively reach their intended market.

To reach a broad base of consumers, marketers in today's viral society use a variety of means to enhance the power of word of mouth. Among these methods is the brand advocate. Brand advocates are individuals that companies effectively use in order to spread word of mouth about their products, services, or firms. A brand advocate is a customer who has been officially commissioned to speak on behalf of a company's brand without compensation. Even though they are not monetarily rewarded, they often receive incentives in the form of discounts, free merchandise, t-shirts, and pens, as well as other perks. A recent survey of the attributes of advocates reveals that such individuals create and curate more than twice as many communications about brands as the average web user. They are savvy, in writing meaningful content and sharing it on highly visible sites. They reportedly reach 82 percent of consumers, and the majority of those consumers are influenced by the online reviews they read from these advocates. Brand advocates are 2.5 times more likely to use social networks to expand their circle of friends and share product information with them than average web users. Their top three topics of discussion are food, personal-care items, and household products. Moreover, 54 percent of advocates report that they view information-sharing with others as a form of relaxing hobby. Their pride in helping others is an important motivator for them, but the main drive for their contribution is the recognition they receive from others as a valuable and helpful source of information.[7]

brand advocates
consumers who speak on behalf of a company without monetary compensation

From the perspective of social scientists, opinion leadership is the extent to which an agent is informally able to incline the beliefs, attitudes, or behaviors of other people in some desired way. In a marketing sense, however, opinion leadership refers to the influence that individuals conversant with a product, service, or company exert on the minds and actions of other consumers. A distinction, however, must be drawn between unpretentious opinion leaders and those individuals or organizations that actively seek to change other people's minds. Parties, whether political, religious, or commercial, whose personal or collective agendas entail active

opinion leadership
an agent's ability to informally incline the beliefs, attitudes, or behaviors of others

attempts to modify other people's beliefs, attitudes, or behaviors are more correctly termed agents of change.

Opinion leadership is an inherent and indispensable element in the give-and-take of interpersonal relationships. It is not a personality trait that some people possess and others don't. In fact, most people would qualify as opinion leaders in some subject or product category.

UNLEASHING THE POWER OF PERSONAL INFLUENCE AND WORD OF MOUTH

Powerful personal influence and word of mouth can be created in a variety of ways. In addition to the efforts of brand advocates, companies can use the following means as well.

- *Soliciting the help of key individuals and parties with clout:* The popularity of individuals such as celebrities, TV personalities, athletes, high-profile corporate executives, and members of the press enables them to influence others and enhance publicity for a firm's activities or products. This is usually accomplished through television shows, sponsoring special events, movies, print articles, and endorsements. For example, the late Steve Jobs's close relationships with journalists netted Apple hundreds of positive articles appearing in the media about Apple and its innovative products. Talk-show hosts, such as Oprah Winfrey, Ellen DeGeneres, and Whoopi Goldberg, can create a great deal of buzz. For example, in the case of Oprah's final few shows, she gave her audience the keys to their own brand new 2012 VW Beetles (with Volkswagen being the sponsor and beneficiary of this word-of-mouth event); and she flew the entire audience of her last show to Australia (with Tourism Australia and Qantas being the beneficiaries). Similarly, reality TV shows can publicize products and services used by program participants. Likewise, product placements in movies, TV shows, and video games are effective methods of creating publicity for many products that appear casually in such media.
- *Initiating buzz in the social sphere:* This strategy can be accomplished via promoting a newsworthy event or providing an unusual offer to the public.
- *Generating online personalized or tailored consumer experiences:* This technique has been one of the most popular methods responsible

mainly for the success of a site such as Amazon.com, among others. Today, a clear trend expressed by consumers is their need for greater personalization of products and services.

- *Capitalizing on online sites and services:* Such sites may include Twitter, Facebook, and YouTube. A company may be able to interact with prospective customers through a "Facebook Fan Page," which offers a venue for the firm's fans to interact, participate, and stay informed about the company and its operations. For example, Best Buy's Fan Page lets the consumer shop and read reviews from shoppers about products right on Facebook. If the consumer is unsure regarding, say, which smartphone to buy, he or she can get feedback from over millions of fans online.

- *Broadcasting ads that create buzz:* Creative advertising campaigns can trigger a great deal of interest and generate significant word of mouth. A recent U.K. Cadbury confectioner's advertising campaign presented a TV commercial featuring a gorilla playing drums to an iconic Phil Collins song. The bizarre juxtaposition was an immediate hit, causing 6 million consumers to go online in order to view the commercial. Cadbury, in return, gained positive consumer perception and escalated sales.[8] The same concept is being employed by companies in the United States as they create innovative commercials broadcast during the Super Bowl.

- *Using search engine optimization methods (SEO):* This is the practice of trying to get the company's website, blog, or other page ranked highly in search engines for a particular keyword or phrase. The ultimate goal is to drive free traffic to the company's website when visitors conduct a search on a particular keyword.[9]

Needless to say, there are unlimited possibilities a company may pursue to enhance the power of word of mouth. Companies are constantly searching for new and innovative ways to extend their reach online though word of mouth.

VIVIDNESS AND IMPACT OF WORD-OF-MOUTH COMMUNICATION

Compared to pallid messages carried by the conventional mass media, verbal or viral WOM information tends to be more vivid and salient, largely because it emanates directly from another individual who person-

Drug Reps Power . . . Indian Style

Today, India's rising incomes and surging rates of medical problems, such as heart disease, diabetes, and cancer, have opened the door for many American pharmaceutical companies to expand their operations in that country. India's pharmaceutical market is dominated by ten large companies, including Pfizer, GlaxoSmithKline, Merck, and Johnson & Johnson. Together, these pharmaceutical companies maintain an army of 100,000 drug reps, who visit doctors to promote their company's specific brand. The main reason for the arsenal is to maintain face-to-face contact with doctors in India.

The Indian government has traditionally placed a ban on advertising and promotion of prescription drugs, as well as prohibited pharmacists from substituting one maker's pills for those made by other companies. To bolster sales of their brands, the only strategy left for these companies is to maintain a large number of drug reps to visit doctors on a regular basis to inform them about drugs in their company's line. Those visits usually occur once a week. A drug rep's quota is to visit, on the average, eleven doctors per day. A major problem confronting these reps, however, is the fact that doctors who see an average of fifty patients per day have limited time to allocate for such visits—limiting the duration of a typical visit to approximately twenty to sixty seconds. These circumstances often cause reps to wait for an hour or more to see a doctor.

Nevertheless, despite such difficulties, pharmaceutical companies that produce name brands are performing exceptionally well in India against the myriads of generics, which constitute a large portion of the drugs prescribed in that country. Studies undertaken by consultant McKinsey have indicated that the annual growth of pharmaceutical sales in India rose significantly since 2010, amounting to over $27 billion in 2016.

India's restrictions on drug promotion and advertising would appear to have been designed to protect the public against self-medication and the perils of direct-to-consumer advertising. Nevertheless, they limit India's more than 800,000 practicing doctors to sales pitches coming from drug reps as the sole source of updated medical information to which they are exposed. This move affirms the notion that the personal influence method is the preferred strategy of the Indian government for marketing and selling pharmaceuticals in that country.[10]

The growth of the Indian economy and rise in the income of the country's middle class has result-ed in greater concern about matters of health. Increasingly, consumers in India are visiting doc-tors and taking more medications. Learn more about the pharmaceutical industry in India by visiting India in Business at http://www.indiainbusiness.nic.in/industry-infrastructure/industrial-sectors/drug-pharma.htm. *Do you think the role of drug reps in educating doctors in India is sufficient to create a pool of sufficiently knowledgeable physicians with regard to medications for various ailments? What are the negative consequences of restricting advertising and promotion for pharmaceuticals, and leaving the educational aspects for medications in the hands of company-sponsored drug reps?*

ally recounts his or her own experiences. WOM has been described as "live," not canned like most other company's communication.[11] It is live because it is custom tailored to the people who are participating in it. Consumers are not receiving a sales pitch, but are getting answers to their important questions. As such, consumers pay more attention to word of mouth because it is more relevant and complete compared to any other form of communication.

Word of mouth is limitless in the sense that it would take only a few influencers to ignite a chain reaction, where successive tiers of receivers influence the next tier. In a successful campaign, recipients of a message become powerful carriers spreading the word to still more carriers, much like a virus rampages a given population. Since the receiver of advice determines what to ask, whom to approach, in what forum, and whether to continue the dialogue or drop it altogether, the custom-tailored nature of WOM is paramount.

As a consequence of its vivid character, WOM information is more accessible in memory and exerts a relatively greater impact on consumers.[12] A number of reasons explain why WOM appears more vivid than messages received via the conventional mass media. First, WOM has personal relevance, which increases receivers' involvement levels and, consequently, its impact. Second, WOM is concrete, containing detailed facts about specific people, situations, actions, and outcomes. Third, WOM testimony occurs in close temporal, spatial, and sensory proximity to receivers. The story is fresh and new, its setting and context are local and recognizable, and the account describes the narrator's firsthand experience, to which listeners can likely relate.

Messages that are vivid and concrete tend to wield greater influence on receivers than does more abstract information.[13] Vivid information tends to attract and hold receivers' attention, to stimulate their imagination, to make its way into their long-term memory, and to be recalled longer and more easily. Highly vivid messages can conjure up positive or negative impressions among receivers because of what has become known as the availability-valence hypothesis. The availability-valence hypothesis states that vivid information tends to be stored in semantic memory with more links to other concepts. This more elaborate mode of storage can make vivid information more accessible for retrieval. Our product judgments depend on the nature of the information available in memory.[14] If this information is positively valenced, judgments tend to be positive. If, on the other hand, the information is negatively valenced, judgments tend to be negative.

availability-valence hypothesis
a view that vivid information tends to be stored in memory with more links to other concepts

MODELS OF THE INFLUENCE PROCESS

Over the years, a number of models were coined to explain the manner in which people are influenced by marketers' communication efforts. Whereas one model advocated that it was the media that exerted direct influence on their audiences, alternative models presented opinion leaders as the most important influencers in the communication process. Let us now consider these varied perspectives and examine the role of opinion leaders in human interactions.

THE HYPODERMIC NEEDLE MODEL

One communication approach is the so-called hypodermic needle model. The term conjures up an image of a huge syringe with which a communicator injects the public with a message. Through the needle flows a one-way stream of ads directed to target consumers. The hypodermic needle model speculates that the media have an immediate, direct, and forceful impact on new-product acceptance by a mass audience. Following this approach, huge advertising budgets and effective, cost-efficient (in terms of cost-per-thousand impressions) mass-media strategies are assumed to expedite new-product introductions as well to create demand for established products. An example of such a strategy is used by advertisers who spend $5 million for a thirty-second commercial during the Super Bowl. In addition, marketers attempt to reach their target market through advertisements in a variety of media types using precision targeting methods. More precise targeting is made possible by today's network, magazine, and newspaper regionalization efforts to localize ad reach.[15]

The basic assumption of the hypodermic needle model (Exhibit 12.1) is that messages will reach and influence captive audiences. The drawback of this model, however, lies in the selective perception processes of consumers, where many of them tend to tune out promotional messages or disregard them due to lack of interest, disagreement with the messages, or based on a belief that they are biased and untrustworthy.[16]

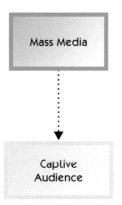

EXHIBIT 12.1

The Hypodermic Needle
Model: Influence Flow

THE TRICKLE-DOWN MODEL

The traditional version of the trickle-down process states that personal influence passes from higher social classes to classes below them. That is to say, the upper class and the elite in society hold a position of power in influencing the rest of the general public. However, a new view of the trickle-down model (Exhibit 12.2) greatly extends the circle of those high-status influencers to include others who are prominent in a society. This updated concept recognizes the power and influence of those who are in the media spotlight and for whom the public holds affection, admiration, or fascination. This group may include public figures, celebrities, professional athletes, movie stars, and TV personalities. For example, no one can deny the influence of public figures and celebrities like William Shatner who speaks for priceline.com, Oprah Winfrey for Weight Watchers, Angelina Jolie for Louis Vuitton, Jennifer Aniston for Smart Water and Aveeno products, and Jennifer Lopez for Gillette shavers.

trickle-down model
a view that influence flows from celebrities and elite influentials to emulating recipients (the general public)

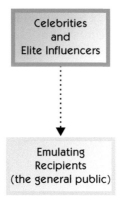

EXHIBIT 12.2

The Trickle-Down Model:
Influence Flow

The growth of the mass and electronic media and their use by many people, particularly the young, has opened the floodgate to a highly exclusive circle of influential figures. A study by Boon and Lomoroe into admirer-celebrity relationships among young people reported that 75 percent of young adults at some time in their life had a strong attraction to a celebrity, and 59 percent of them stated that their idols had influenced many aspects of their attitudes and behavior.[17] In the updated trickle-down model, influence flows downward from both the elite and celebrities to the emulators. Celebrities can play a key role in influencing others, since they offer a variety of possible selves that individuals may wish to test. They provide living examples of how to dress and to behave.[18] In a recent *Newsweek* poll, for example, 77 percent of respondents stated that young female celebrities have too much influence on young girls in our society today.[19] The influence may be more negative than positive, as these celebrities' haircuts, tattoos, smoking habits, dating, and manner of dress are imitated by adoring young women and men.[20]

British academicians studied the manner in which celebrities influence young people and their social networks. They reported that in the past, it was parents, teachers, and friends who were the key influencers. However, the overwhelming growth of the mass and electronic media today coupled with their constant campaigns to make celebrities bigger than life have helped compound people's attachment to media figures, including pop stars, actors, and sports heroes. This sense of attachment underlies and helps explain much of the attitudes and behavior of their fans.[21]

trickle-up model
a view that influence flows upward from usual recipient emulators to the general public as well as to celebrities and elite influencers

On occasion, influence has been known to follow a vertical upward path. The trickle-up model, an exception to the general rule, refers to cases where a product or style originating among those who are typically emulators or influence-recipients eventually gains acceptance and popularity among the elite and celebrity influencers. In cases of trickle-up, grassroots pioneers less inclined to closely conform to the dominant culture's norms constitute the innovators. Eventually, the novel product or style disseminates upwards to the elite and celebrities who find the novelty appealing. Products and services that have benefitted from trickle-up processes include jeans, athletic footwear, Timberland boots, many ethnic foods, tattoos, body piercings, and various styles of music, including jazz, blues, country, heavy metal, and rap.

THE TRICKLE-ACROSS MODEL

Due in part to the widespread popularity of social networking sites, such as Facebook, LinkedIn, and Twitter, millions of consumers communicate daily with members of their real-world communities. The result of using these technologies enhances the power of horizontal influence between individuals. In fact, recommendations from peers and acquaintances, as well as opinions posted online by other community members, have become the most-trusted forms of advice that influence consumer purchase decisions.[22] Consider, for instance, the influence of advice sites such as Angie's List, which have become popular in recent years. In the trickle-across model, therefore, influence follows a horizontal pattern, where consumers emulate the beliefs, attitudes, and behaviors of people just like themselves. In this view, new technologies have given everyday people the ability to influence or be influenced by others who they may never have seen or met. As a result, consumer power shifts from the "expert" to everyone, giving everyday individuals the ability to shape, make, and share news and information, as well as give and receive advice. This type of influence is known as the trickle-across model (Exhibit 12.3).

trickle-across model
a view that influence flows horizontally among peers

EXHIBIT 12.3

The Trickle-Across Model: Influence Flow

THE TWO-STEP MODEL

The two-step model (Exhibit 2.4) advocates that it is the opinion leaders who have greater topic-bound exposure to the mass and electronic media than those they influence, and that it is these individuals who mediate the flow of message content to a large number of passive information recipients. These opinion recipients constitute the majority of consumers.

According to the two-step model, many consumers in their purchasing behavior do not rely on firsthand exposure to ads run in the media nor

two-step model
a view that it is opinion leaders who receive messages first from the mass media and then pass them on to others

EXHIBIT 12.4

The Two-Step Model

do they require personal experience with products before buying them. Rather, they learn a great deal from the experiences and opinions of other people around them—the influencers. In this view, the role of mass media is to transfer information to those influencers who, in turn, transfer product information or advice to others via WOM. As a consequence, those influencers or opinion leaders informally shape other people's consumption-related beliefs, attitudes, and behaviors. For example, wine-tasting events are sponsored by wineries, distributors, and liquor stores. These occasions are advertised to wine opinion leaders through wine-related magazines and direct mail or wine-related websites. Wine opinion leaders, as a result of knowledge gained from these events, pass this information along to others. Likewise, the travel and hospitality industries have raised this technique to a fine art. Las Vegas hotels such as Luxor, Caesar's Palace, and Bally's, for instance, successfully attract millions of visitors every year based on WOM received from influencers.[23]

In its time, the two-step theory was a significant contribution because it countered a then-accepted view that the mass media were consumers' primary information sources. In contrast, it proposed that interpersonal communication, not advertising, carried the greater influence. Today, however, many marketers discern shortcomings in the two-step model. First, seldom do opinion leaders simply propagate mass-media dispatches to a set of inert followers. Second, opinion leaders often base their opinions on product trial rather than views injected by marketers through the mass media.

Today, marketers are cognizant of the fact that advice seekers frequently initiate WOM exchanges. Ads carried by the media sometimes prompt fact seekers to approach opinion leaders for advice. Thus, influence from the mass and social media extends beyond opinion leaders to information seekers as well.[24]

THE MULTISTEP MODEL

multistep model
a view that mass-media messages reach both opinion leaders and followers who then share that information with others

The multistep model is largely an elaboration and extension of the two-step model. It postulates that information transmitted through the mass media reaches opinion leaders as well as opinion followers. A distinguishing characteristic of this model is the assumption that opinion followers are not passive. Rather, they are active seekers of information from both opinion leaders and media sources.

In the multistep model, nearly everyone is potentially reachable through mass communication. Although both opinion leaders and opinion followers may receive product news from the mass and electronic media, this information is more apt to reach opinion leaders and influencers first. They, in turn, pass along this information to others. It should be noted here, however, that in some instances, gatekeepers—individuals who have the power to forward or restrict messages—may choose to block messages' availability to others. Examples include parents who restrict their children's exposure to certain Internet sites and TV programs or government censors who prevent certain news or facts from reaching the general public.

Opinion followers, according to this model, actively seek information regarding products, services, and stores from online, the media, and interpersonal sources. They also may receive unsolicited advice from various sources. In this sense, bidirectional influence can flow between opinion providers and opinion receivers. In other words, roles of opinion leader and opinion follower may reverse, depending on the specific situation or product of interest.[25]

Exhibit 12.5 illustrates the multistep model. In this depiction, movement downward (following the solid arrows) involves advice giving, which can be initiated as a result of a situation causing one to seek advice or a conversation that triggers giving the advice. The model shows that information

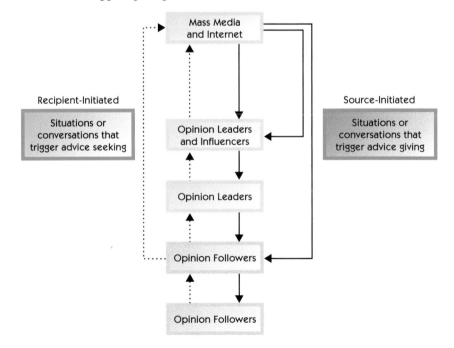

EXHIBIT 12.5

The Multistep Model: Influence Flow

Because pharmaceutical firms identify physicians as opinion leaders, their sales staff visit physicians and distribute drug samples and supporting literature.

© Dmitry Kalinovsky/Shutterstock.com

from the media or the Internet can reach both opinion leaders and opinion followers at the same time. However, due to opinion leaders' greater interest in the product or service, they frequently externalize this information and share it with other opinion leaders or opinion followers, who in turn may share the information with others like themselves.

In this depiction, movement upward (following the dashed arrows) entails information acquisition, which can similarly be initiated by advice-seeking situations or conversations. Opinion followers may actively seek advice from persons like themselves, from opinion leaders, or from the media. Opinion leaders may also seek information from other opinion leaders or from the media.

For example, motion picture studios regard critics as important sources of information for moviegoers. Consequently, studios invite critics to sneak previews and expend considerable effort to befriend and cajole them. At preview events, movie studios wine and dine the critics. Critics in attendance also discuss the film among themselves. Sometimes, studios bring out the stars so critics can meet and interview them, all in an effort to promote positive reviews that can then be quoted in movie ads. Critics' influence is likely to be greatest when a film first opens and little other information about it is available. Later on, critics exert a lesser influence on box office revenues; as more people view the film and as WOM from other moviegoers becomes increasingly available, the influence of critics is likely to wane.[26]

CONSUMER BEHAVIOR IN PRACTICE

Power of the Word

No other business in the history of the United States has yet been able to dramatically use the powers of personal influence and word of mouth to enhance its competitive market position as Apple has done. The late Steve Jobs, as well as his successor CEO Tim Cook, always believed that the public's perception and support for a product or firm is inherently based on its emotional attachment and sense of belonging to a firm as could be expressed as a member of a tribe or community.

Recalling Apple's strategy when the firm's first iPhone was about to be introduced in 2007 reveals a portrait of Jobs's intention to announce to the world the new generation of smartphones. He shrouded his announcement with mystery, and coined the innovation as a life-changing tool. His action drove the firm's customer base into frenzy, creating overwhelming press attention. This resulted in thousands of articles appearing in over fifty major publications, all discussing and speculating about the features of the new iPhone.

In a similar fashion, Apple employed this strategy to introduce every iPhone the firm has put out since then, with Cook following the same strategy as Jobs in publicizing Apple's new devices. By harnessing the powers of personal influence and word of mouth, Apple succeeded in masterfully manipulating public eagerness for its innovative devices, as well as enhanced the anticipation and excitement that surrounded these products' release—actions that resulted in unparalleled levels of sales. Apple's success story for the firm's iPhone is, and will continue to be, a unique case about which marketers will marvel for many years to come.[27]

Online social networks have greatly enhanced the power of word of mouth. Thousands of comments, stories, compliments, and/or complaints in blog postings change the narrow meaning of "word of mouth" from verbal face-to-face communication between two individuals to a massive phenomenon that shares information among millions of consumers. Learn more about word of mouth by visiting the website from the Word of Mouth Marketing Association at http://www.womma.org/about/. To what extent should marketers encourage such online chatter? What are the ramifications of ignoring the things that consumers say?

INFLUENCER IDENTIFICATION

In today's virtual marketplace, the ability to attract, nurture, and retain influential consumers has become a core competitive advantage that companies strive to attain. While influencer marketing is not synonymous with word-of-mouth marketing, WOM is a core component of the mechanics of influencer marketing.

An influencer can be thought of as a third party who significantly shapes other consumers' purchasing decisions. The Word of Mouth Association defines an influencer as "a person who has a greater than average reach or impact through word of mouth in a relevant marketplace."[28] Targeting influencers is receiving more emphasis now as a means of amplifying mar-

influencer
a person with above-average reach or impact via word of mouth in a relevant marketplace

keting messages in order to counteract the growing tendency of customers to ignore traditional marketing efforts.

Targeting influencers involves indentifying the individuals who have gained influence over potential buyers, then orienting the firm's marketing activities around these influential parties. These influences may be buyers of the company's products, but also be third parties such as the firm's employees or suppliers, journalists, academicians, industry analysts, or other professionals and community leaders.

OBJECTIVES OF INFLUENCER IDENTIFICATION

Objectives of identifying influencers in a commercial context include the following: (1) *which tools* marketers can use to identify influencers, (2) company programs designed to *engage* influencers, and (3) *measuring* of the effectiveness of influencers.

Identifying Influencers

There are at least seventy companies offering online influencer measurement tools. Companies such as BuzzLogic and Nielsen BuzzMetrics offer services that can provide a client with the knowledge of who is talking about its brands, as well as enable the company to pinpoint the most influential communities in its case. Other companies including Ammo Marketing, Liquid Intelligence, and DesignKarma, Inc. have developed their own proprietary methodologies for identifying and targeting influencers for a market or a market sector. In addition, the Avant-Guide Institute, a New York-based trends-forecasting firm, has for its clients maintained a large proprietary network of influential early-adopters, dubbed "trendsformers" numbering in the thousands, including journalists, bloggers, academicians, industry analysts, and professional advisors. Furthermore, there are a number of free tools available for companies interested in developing their own system of influencer identification. A sample of these includes:[29]

- Google Blog Search: Since blogs often become hubs of conversation and communication, tools such as Google Blog Search provide a good place to start for influencer identification. The tool's advanced search feature allows a company to find out what consumers are saying online about the company.

- BlogPulse: This tool is an automated trend-discovering system for blogs and is best used as a blog search engine. This tool can help a company in the process of influencer selection, since it provides highly detailed data on blogs.
- Ice Rocket: Originally a blog search engine, this has recently been updated to incorporate several social networks into its searches. It permits the user to identify those talking about the firm and its brands.
- Blogrolls: Once a list of blogs has been identified, bloggers are then scanned to identify the websites peers recommended to them. This type of peer-to-peer endorsement reveals to the user who the bloggers find influential within their peer group.
- Boardreader: This tool is a forum and a message board search engine. It is useful in guiding a company to places where conversations about the firm are taking place.
- TouchGraph Google Browser: This tool allows the user to learn how topics, people, and organizations are connected through networks. It demonstrates the sphere of influence in such interactions and enables a company to accurately pinpoint relationships between chunks of information in a simple and clear way.
- HootSuite: This tool has an outstanding search facility allowing a company to see in real time what customers are saying. It thereby enables a firm to identify influencers, answer queries, rectify problems, or close sales.
- Facebook Search: Since millions of users frequently post status updates on Facebook, this tool is a valuable method for identifying people who are talking about a company, product, or brand at the grassroots level.

In addition to these, many other similar tools are available to help firms identify influencers. These include Technorati, a search engine for bloggers based on keyword search; PostRank Connect, which links brands and individuals; Buzzstream, which provided detailed influencer profiles; Attensity, which monitors 37 million blogs and forums; Teramatic, which provides a sense of *who* should be considered a specific firm's influencer; and Twend, which identifies Twifolk who talk about the firm's brand.

It is necessary, however, to recognize that influencers play a variety of roles at different points in a decision process. Indentifying how and when particular types of influencers affect the decision process enables the company to selectively target influencers, depending on their specific profile of influence.

Engaging influencers

Once a firm has been able to identify its influencers, the next step is to attempt to engage them. This strategy requires that the firm commits to a long-term engagement relationship, since by definition, influencer programs are long-term, multiyear commitments designed to build a relationship between the firm and its customers.

By directly engaging influencers with executive contact opportunities, special offers, and unique content, a company can directly engage members of influencers' social sphere. Specific strategies can be used for this purpose. These strategies may vary depending on the type of industry initiating the influence, its audience, and its business objectives. The following are a number of practices that companies presently use to influence engagement of influencers and help spread WOM.

To initiate a relationship with influencers, the company may engage with them in conversations and mutual exchanges in order to gain their trust and possibly their collaboration. For example, the company may ask the influencers to review or test one of the company's products or experience one of its services and write a guest blog regarding their views about the experience. The requests may be as simple as asking for a brief mention in a link back to the company's website. Such action generates faith and interest in the company's activities and products.

- *Connecting with influencers offline:* Reaching influencers through online sources misses the personal touch that offline contacts provide. Many influential exchanges of information still occur offline. In fact, it has been claimed that over half of WOM episodes still occur face-to-face in interpersonal settings.[30] Providing influencers with opportunities for meeting others like themselves, chatting with executives, seeing for themselves how and where products are being manufactured, can be a significant factor in enhancing their enthusiasm. Meeting events may include providing guest speakers, conducting brainstorming sessions, arranging conferences, conducting conference calls, and running focus groups, among others.
- *Focusing on providing influencers with relevant content:* This is the type of news or information that influencers need in order to republish and share with their audience. While most influencers create their own content, in many cases they are content curators. The company, therefore, must provide engaging content that is readymade to help influencers with their mission. Many companies, for this purpose, com-

bine long form content—including blogs, videos, how-to's, tips and tricks, webinars, and Q&As—with short content—such as Tweets, Facebook posts, and LinkedIn discussions.

- *Rewarding influencers:* For most influencers who spend time and effort creating content and sharing it with others, it is not all about financial rewards. Their efforts of sharing give them feelings of importance and pride. Rewards in such cases can be in the form of allowing influencers private access to company facilities, executives, and important people; deals; or inside information that is usually restricted to a select few. These opportunities to connect behind-the-scenes are perceived by the influencer community as "social currency," giving them a sense of stature and connection with the firm.
- *Closing the loop with feedback:* Since influencers are a good source of product feedback, the firm's marketing program must be designed to close the loop back to the influencers in regard to what the firm is doing with their feedback and suggestions. Without that attention and care given to influencers' comments and suggestions, influencers' enthusiasm is likely to wane.
- *Recognizing those who influence the influencers:* It is not enough for a company to maintain relationships with the influencers. It is important to remember that influencers have their own trusted networks of individuals and experts to whom they turn for information and recommendations. Recognizing and seeking this important group of people and attempting to initiate relationships with such key enablers can help the company in its efforts to expand its domain of influence.

Measuring the Effectiveness of Influencers

In an effort to ascertain the effectiveness and impact of influencers' efforts on enhancing the company's bottom line and shareholders' return on investment, a number of measurements have been developed. Most of these measures are similar to programs that broadcasters and publishers of printed media, as well as social media professionals, have been using to evaluate and estimate the success rate of their various programs or publications. A set of tools already available online can help firms in this endeavor. Presently, there are web applications with content management, measurement tools of engagement and influence in social media. These tools are quickly becoming popular as means of measuring the effectiveness of influencers and gauging their reach through the various social networks. Users now can access more than thirty different platforms and tools for measuring the effectiveness of social media influencers.[31]

Alternatively, a company that prefers to find out for itself how much the influencers are engaging the online community can ask the influencers to try the firm's products or services, and then discuss them under respective social networks. The firm can then observe, through an enhanced digital dashboard, applying metrics that measure the dissemination of brand mentions across numerous web platforms, to find out how much online interaction has been created.

Now let us turn our investigation to other matters of interest to marketers. These include sources of personal influence other than traditional opinion leaders and influencers, and what motivates these individuals to communicate the information received to others.

ARE THERE OTHER SOURCES OF PERSONAL INFLUENCE?

In addition to influencers, three other types of influencers can be identified. These sources include shopping pals, market mavens, and surrogate consumers.

Shopping Pals

shopping pals
other persons who accompany a consumer on a shopping trip

Sometimes another person physically or "electronically" (via smartphone) accompanies a consumer on his or her shopping trip and acts as a source of information, advice, influence, and support. Such individuals are called shopping pals. In a study by Harman and Kiecker, shopping pals were used 25 percent of the time by purchasers of electronic goods.[32] In that study, male and female shopping pals tended to serve different roles for the shoppers they accompanied. Male shopping pals tended to be used as sources of product-category expertise, product facts, and retail store and price information. Female shopping pals, on the other hand, provide moral support and boost other female friends' confidence in their decisions, especially when they shop for apparel.

Market Mavens

In your daily interaction with other people within the face-to-face domain, you may have encountered friends, colleagues, or neighbors who appear to be sensitive to their shopping experiences and tend to be highly motivated to talk about products, services, stores, events, and prices.

This type of individual belongs to a consumer category known as market mavens. Market mavens are not necessarily authorities in any particular product category. Rather, they are a sort of generalized opinion leader in the sense that they display interest in diverse types of marketplace information. Market mavens tend to be sociable and enjoy talking to others about their knowledge and experiences. They feel confident about their overall understanding of how and where to procure products and in their ability to help others find the best prices and places to shop.

market maven
a person who actively transmits marketplace information

Shopping pals often accompany consumers to help them with their merchandise choices.

Surrogate Consumers

Sometimes consumers lack the know-how, time, or ambition to personally search for information, evaluate alternatives, and arrive at a decision. They may detest particular shopping chores and prefer to employ an intermediary who will gather and evaluate information, narrow down their options, or make a purchase selection. Such go-betweens are called surrogate consumers. A surrogate consumer is "an agent retained by a consumer to guide, direct, or transact marketplace activities."[33] Surrogate consumers can play a wide variety of roles, including tax consultants, lawyers, wine stewards, interior decorators, financial managers, stockbrokers, professional shoppers, wedding planners, and reunion planners.

surrogate consumer
an agent who a consumer retains to guide, direct, or transact marketplace activities

ETHICAL DILEMMA

A Tale of a Green Car

For over seven years, Volkswagen initiated overwhelming promotional and buzz campaigns, both in print and electronic media, boasting of a new addition to its line of vehicles—an ecofriendly automobile that fulfilled the dreams of many for a car with better fuel economy and glowing environmental protection credentials. This long-awaited star was the 2009 Volkswagen Jetta TDI. Commenting on this newcomer, the *Green Car Journal* in 2008 published an article in which it compared the five finalists of its annual "Green Car of the Year" award. In this article, the journal reported that rising to the top of its list was the 2009 Volkswagen Jetta TDI. The journal went on to state that the car was a winner because of its groundbreaking clean diesel, stringent tailpipe emission standards, extraordinary fuel efficiency, and reasonable price. Impressed with these specifications, consumers in the United States, as well as abroad, rushed to acquire this new ecofriendly car, resulting in sales figures of over 0.5 million vehicles in the United States alone, and over 10 million worldwide.

As time passed, the public in September 2015 began to learn some disturbing news about these VW diesel cars. At that time, the U.S. Environmental Protection Agency (EPA) issued a notice of violation to the Volkswagen Corporation, stating what while the vehicles met emission standards for dangerous nitrogen oxides (NOx), the vehicles met these standards only while running their paces in an artificial, indoor laboratory setting. However, the report pointed out that once these cars were driven on the road, the software in the engine that turned on emission-reduction equipment self-readjusted, and the car on the road started to emit forty times the permissible levels of NOx.

Volkswagen has already made public announcements that came close to admitting liability. The firm acknowledged and apologized for the fact that its diesels used dual-strategy software to manipulate emissions. In the United States, the reaction of both government and the general public to this obvious case of fraud was harsh. In addition to a civil suit filed by the U.S. Department of Justice and the EPA, subjecting VW to up to $45 billion in fines, and ordering criminal inquiry into the case, there were more than 500 class action suits filed on behalf of owners and lessors of the VW diesel cars. Additional class action suits were also filed by used-car dealers handling competing American and foreign automobiles, who claimed unfair competition.

All in all, an estimate of the funds that VW has to surrender in order to comply with the government rulings, such as car "fixes" or buying back the defective units, as well as to pay the fines, compensation, restitution, and attorneys' fees, will eventually reach a staggering $100 billion—a hefty fine for an action VW thought would be too minor to be noticed.[34]

The auto industry in Germany is crucial to that nation's economy. Volkswagen is a quasi-state entity that has controlled government regulators there due to the huge labor force of over 500,000 that the firm employs as well as VW's auto exports all around the world. Based on European law and its soft interpretation of the questionable software that Volkswagen used for emission purposes, the company refused to extend its offer of any compensation to the firm's millions of European customers, a tactic that generated a significant amount of negative word of mouth. Learn more about how foreign regulators reacted to the VW emissions scandal by visiting http://fortune.com/2015/09/26/heres-how-regulators-around-the-world-have-reacted-to-the-vw-emissions-scandal/. In Europe, some maintain that American reaction to the scandal is overblown, driven by greedy lawyers and politicians eager to help domestic automakers gain ground against European rivals. Do you support such claims? How would you respond to such criticism?

Surrogates tend to be utilized for high-involvement purchases (expensive furniture, complex investment securities) by persons willing to delegate a task to a more competent external agent—frequently a paid professional. Essentially, surrogate consumers become an extra tier in the distribution channel between manufacturer and final consumer, charged with performing all or part of a decision process. Although the extent of surrogates' influence varies, marketers cannot ignore it. Rather, marketers should assess the extent to which surrogates influence purchases of their firm's products or services by final consumers. Marketers should then target promotional materials to surrogate consumers as well as direct ads to end users.

STRATEGIC APPLICATIONS OF PERSONAL INFLUENCE AND WORD OF MOUTH

Personal influence can often be used as an element of a company's marketing strategy. As mentioned earlier, favorable WOM is a valuable supplement to any size promotional budget. Strong positive WOM enables many companies such as Apple, Walmart, and Harley-Davidson to decrease their advertising budgets.[34] delete this duplicated endnote number In some instances, firms have been known to omit advertising and sales efforts completely and to rely solely on personal influence and word of mouth.[35]

When deciding whether and how to utilize personal influence, marketers must ascertain the extent to which personal influence is likely to affect prospective purchasers of their products or services. Products in some categories stand to benefit more from operative personal influence than others. Within some merchandise categories, consumers derive personal satisfaction or opportunities for self-expression from product ownership and use. Influencers are more apt to actively disseminate, via traditional and viral WOM, product information related to conspicuous products like automobiles and fashion merchandise. However, in our technologically sophisticated environment, we also tend to seek advice for just about everything we buy. WOM is an important means of acquiring this information. In general, three approaches are available to marketers who wish to capitalize on personal influence as a promotional strategy. These methods are:

1. creating various types of influencers,
2. stimulating influencers, and
3. simulating influencers.

CREATING VARIOUS TYPES OF INFLUENCERS

Marketers can employ a number of strategies to create various types of influencers. These strategies may vary based on the type of industry or business the firm is in. Companies that market products may find certain strategies more effective than others employed in the service domain. For example, whereas Ford Focus loaned cars to customers to initiate buzz, the company Shortcuts, an online grocery coupon service, used a flurry of blog posts following the firm's launch. In addition to identifying and engaging brand influencers, which were discussed earlier in this chapter, the following strategies are among those that have proven effective in enhancing WOM:

- *Using seeding agencies to help plant viral WOM:* Companies such as BzzAgent and SheSpeaks work with consumers who like to try new products and services. If those consumers like the product, they are encouraged (but not required) to spread the word about it.
- *Reaching community experts (who influence the influencers) through personal means or via social media and the company's website:* Newsworthy information about the company can be directed to community experts in order to enhance their awareness of a firm's products, policies, and events. The purpose, of course, is to help experts spread the news to the group of influencers they are in contact with.
- *Working with promotion agencies that target local grassroots organizations:* Such social networks as parent teacher associations (PTAs) provide excellent grounds for viral buzz.
- *Creating and implementing events that foster WOM:* Such efforts include holding seminars, conferences, and swap meets where customers and prospects can be brought together.
- *Gaining media coverage of a company's newsworthy activities or creating stories pertaining to the company's line and how it relates to consumers' lifestyle and emotions:* Hallmark generated a great deal of WOM when the company asked customers to relay personal experiences relating to the firm's line of greeting cards. The company made and aired brief videos of some of these experiences. One particularly successful video that brought tears to the eyes of viewers and created a significant amount of buzz centered on the mother of a young girl whose husband had passed away. Her little girl wanted to send her daddy a message of love and farewell. The segment showed the young girl and her mother tying a Hallmark greeting card bearing the emotional message to a helium-filled balloon and releasing it into the heavens.
- *Using canned WOM methods:* Canned WOM tactics may include audio, video, and the Web, as well as brochures that are designed to de-

liver customer recommendations and positive WOM about the firm's products and services.

- *Establishing affiliation programs by formally joining customers and the company together in a mutually beneficial manner:* Harley-Davidson created a successful nationwide affiliation "family" program that brings satisfied customers together with each other, as well as with the top executives of the firm.

Creating influencers in the print media has also been a popular strategy to initiate the flow of personal influence. Popular personalities and celebrities are frequently pictured along with the promoted product to enhance the item's appeal.

STIMULATING INFLUENCERS

Marketers can also *stimulate* or encourage consumers to discuss a product, brand, or company.[36] One such approach entails running teaser campaigns. Teaser campaigns are promotions that drop bits of information and withhold the particulars. Motion picture and TV show producers have effectively used this technique by releasing advance teaser ads about a movie or upcoming program that arouse audience interest and heighten its anticipation. Teaser campaigns release just enough details about the movie or show to arouse audience curiosity and get people talking.

teaser campaigns
promotions that drop bits of information while withholding the particulars

Similarly, clever and imaginative campaigns may entice a desire on the part of the audience to comment on them. One such example of imaginative campaigns is that recently initiated by British Petroleum (BP) to overcome the negative effect of the infamous oil spill. The company's intensive advertising campaign overemphasized its present environmental concerns and the multiple steps it has been taking to clean and protect the environment, as well as to compensate the people affected. Such messages initiated an avalanche of articles, discussions, and conversations both in the media and among the public.

Inaugurating activities around a product can help marketers increase brand awareness and stimulate WOM. Some firms sponsor events such as parades, open houses, sweepstakes, contests, or athletic tournaments to gain public exposure and generate talk. Others arrange for product demonstrations or sample giveaways at strategic visible locations like shopping malls and airports. Still other companies employ a tactic known as a product placement, where branded merchandise appears in movie scenes, TV programs, or video games. Firms frequently approach movie studios to publicize their brand within motion pictures and television shows.[37]

product placement
display of branded merchandise in movie scenes or TV shows

SIMULATING INFLUENCERS

In addition to stimulating opinion leadership, advertisers use a variety of formats that *simulate* impartial persons informally giving and receiving information via WOM. Slice-of-life, hidden camera, and testimonial ad formats employ simulated influence. *Slice-of-life* commercials allow the audience to eavesdrop on an exchange. These mini-skits depict a troubled individual encountering another person who spontaneously proposes a solution. A physician, for example, can be shown to recommend an over-the-counter stomach antacid to a patient. In other ads, the simulated opinion leader reiterates what a real opinion leader had previously advised, as in the "My doctor said Mylanta" commercials. *Hidden-camera* commercials portray individuals going about the task of buying a product without suspecting that they are being recorded. For example, a recent commercial from Pizza Hut depicted a hidden camera rolling in a well-known New York restaurant. The ad showed fifty New Yorkers immensely enjoying dishes of Tuscany-style pasta, supposedly prepared by a famous chef. After commenting about superior flavor of the dish, members of the group were surprised to learn that the pasta had been actually prepared by Pizza Hut, and that dish was a new addition to the firm's menu.

testimonials
ads that depict a celebrity, expert, or ordinary consumer who endorses a brand

Ads frequently employ testimonials in which relevant celebrities, experts, or other ordinary consumers endorse a brand. Celebrities are effective givers of testimony, particularly when they have some believable connection with the advertised product. Testimony from experts enhances the credibility of advertising claims, and is effectual when a purchase involves financial, functional, or physical risk. Testimony and reviews from ordinary consumers are effective because people tend to identify with others like themselves.

Occasionally, advertisers use their own current or former corporate executives as spokespersons, such as Steve Jobs for Apple. Present or past company owners, CEOs, or presidents speaking on behalf of their firms appear to be highly credible and good sources for buzz.[38]

COMBATING NEGATIVE WORD OF MOUTH

As shown earlier in this chapter, word of mouth is far and away the most powerful force in the marketplace. It has been described as the proximal cause of purchase—the most recent encounter that happens just before buying and a powerful purchase trigger.[39]

Three situational factors seem to increase the likelihood that word-of-mouth communication will take place: (1) when consumers who enjoy talking about purchase alternatives become familiar enough with a company's products or services that they can discuss them, (2) when consumers of a product or service experience an emotional reaction—favorable or unfavorable—to it, and (3) when dissatisfied consumers of a product or service find it difficult to complain to the party that caused the dissatisfaction. Regarding this last point concerning consumer complaints, the prevalence of present-day tools that simplify WOM exchanges have forever changed the playing field. Today, popular social networks, review sites on the Internet, blogs, and forums have become powerful tools in the hands of consumers to communicate their dissatisfaction with businesses. According to a recent study by the Society for New Communications Research, 59 percent of consumers use social media to vent their frustrations about customer service. In addition, 74 percent choose companies or brands based on online shared experiences from others, and 72 percent search companies' online customer service records prior to purchasing products and services from them.[40]

Three dimensions of consumer complaint behavior can be identified. The first is formal complaints that involve complaining directly to the seller. The second is private complaints that are sent to friends, family members, and online. The final is third-party complaints that consist of formal complaints directed to the media, to consumer groups, to the Better Business Bureau, or to government agencies. Researchers have suggested that complaint behavior may be sequential in nature; that is, certain complaint actions are taken only after other avenues have been exhausted.[41]

It appears that both the nature of the firm's response (product replacement, repair, or refund) *and* the speed of that response (days versus weeks) compared to consumers' redress expectations are the key factors in determining how consumers will react toward the company. To avoid incidents of consumer dissatisfaction and probable negative WOM, progressive marketers have adopted measures to *exceed* consumers' redress expectations. Such companies attempt to learn about consumer dissatisfaction at the individual level *before* it surfaces. Their reasoning is that to restore satisfaction and its favorable effect on repurchase intention, the company should find out about product failures ahead of time.

Companies can take several steps to prepare for and protect themselves against negative WOM. This is particularly true since negative comments on popular social networks and review sites, as well as blogs and forums, can rank in the top ten results when consumers enter the company's name in a search. This convenience allows a consumer to easily find such information. First, the company can establish a crisis-watch program to monitor, assess, and regularly check what is being communicated about it online. Monitoring feeds allows the company to immediately respond to negative WOM posts. This objective can be attained by monitoring Read-WriteWeb, which has a good roundup of tools that companies can use to check their online reputation, including Google Alerts, Traker, Naymz, Monitor This, Technorati, and Rapleaf.

Second, the company can be proactive in building relationships with the WOM community in which it operates. For example, the company can respond, without delay, to a negative posting directly in the blog comments, since most blogs have a comment feature enabled. The company can also establish its own blog, so that consumers can easily send and receive communication relating to their concerns. In so doing, the company can come to understand its customers' needs and be able to spot market opportunities.

Third, the company should provide truthful facts whenever any event touching the company threatens to turn into a public controversy. Honest information disclosure has the power to neutralize the potential negative effect of WOM that can harm the firm.[42]

In this chapter, we have seen how influence travels between and within the various layers of a society. Influence flow depends on who occupies the roles of influencers and receivers. The roles of influence provider and influence receiver, in turn, are largely determined by demographic characteristics and behavioral patterns that distinguish between individuals. Such characteristics, in the final analysis, constitute the grounds for assigning a particular social standing to each individual within a particular society.

Thus, the cumulative social standings of individuals in a culture constitute the basis for identifying tiers that sociologists have labeled social classes. Social class studies are deemed valuable to marketers because the different consumption and behavior patterns of these societal tiers hold significant implications to practitioners and researchers in the field of consumer behavior. The following chapter deals with the topic of social class and its many implications for segmenting, targeting, and positioning strategies in the disciplines of marketing and consumer behavior.

SUMMARY

This chapter covers the topic of personal influence, which refers to any change in a person's beliefs, attitudes, or behavior that results from interpersonal communication. Personal influence is transmitted both verbally and virally. WOM is personal communication between a receiver and a source that the receiver perceives as independent regarding a product. In a marketing sense, opinion leadership refers to the influence that individuals conversant with a product or service category exert over the minds and actions of other consumers. Verbal or viral WOM is powerful. Compared to messages carried by the media, WOM information tends to be more vivid, more salient, and more accessible for retrieval from memory.

When consumers lack product knowledge, they often turn to more knowledgeable acquaintances as credible sources of counsel. The passage of product-related information to others tends to be incited by situational or conversational circumstances and normally occurs within the context of casual interaction or through planned or unplanned use of the Internet. A number of models have been proposed to explain the flow of messages from message sources and target audiences. These models include the hypodermic needle model; trickle-down, trickle-across, and trickle-up models; the two-step model; and the multistep model.

Marketers attempt to identify and target opinion leaders and influencers, then orient the firm's marketing activities around these influential parties. Objectives of influencer identification within a commercial context deal with (1) learning which tools marketers can use to identify influencers, (2) designing company programs to engage influencers, and (3) measuring the effectiveness of influencers.

When deciding whether and how to use personal influence as part of their strategy, marketers may elect to create various types of influencers. In this regard, strategies that have proven to be effective include (1) using seeding agencies to help plant viral WOM, (2) reaching community experts (who influence the influencers) through personal means or via social media and the company's website, (3) working with promotion agencies that target local grassroots organizations, (4) creating and implementing events that foster WOM, (5) gaining media coverage of a company's newsworthy activities or creating stories pertaining to the company's line, (6) using canned WOM methods, and (7) establishing affiliation programs that link customers with the company in a mutually beneficial manner. Marketers may also stimulate influencers (e.g., via teaser campaigns, clever and imaginative messages, and product placements) or simulate influencers (e.g., via slice-of-life, hidden camera, and testimonial ad formats).

Occasionally marketers find themselves in situations where they must combat negative WOM. Negative WOM may result from consumer dissatisfaction and resulting unredressed complaints. Among the strategies that marketers employ to reduce dissatisfaction and combat negative WOM are establishing a crisis-watch program, being proactive in building relationships with the WOM community in which the company operates, and promptly providing facts when a crisis threatens the firm's operations.

CASE SYNOPSIS

Obesity . . . and the Expanded Role of Healthcare Providers

The problem of obesity has hit epidemic proportions in the United States. Many consumers experiencing weight-related issues attempt to reduce their waistline by simply taking diet pills and various herbal supplements, rather than consulting with a healthcare provider. Consumers often learn about these pills and supplements through ads in the media or via recommendations from their friends. They self-prescribe these medications without fully understanding their potency or negative side effects. This action is usually taken as an alternative to paying fees to healthcare providers—out-of-pocket costs that insurance companies traditionally did not cover. This dilemma was partially resolved when the CMS announced in 2011 that Medicare would begin paying for obese patients to undergo physician-supervised treatment for weight loss. The effect of face-to-face treatment by a qualified healthcare provider not only protects overweight patients from the potential dangers of self-diagnosis, but serves to enhance the success of the regimen recommended by a healthcare provider in achieving the desired weight-loss goal.

Notes

1   Michael Hiltzik, "So Much for the 'Oprah Effect,' as Weight Watchers Stock Fails," *LA Times* (February 1, 2016), http://www.latimes.com/business/hiltzik/la-fi-mh-so-much-for-the-oprah-effect-20160131-column-html; Paul R. La Monica, "Oprah Just Lost $27 Million on Weight Watchers," *Money.CNN* (February 26, 2016), http://money.cnn.com/2016/02/26/investing/weight-watchers-oprah-winfrey-earnings-stock/; Paul R. La Monica, "Oprah May Not Save Weight Watchers After All," *Money.CNN* (January 11, 2016), http://money.cnn.com/2016/01/11/investing/weight-watchers-oprah-winfrey/; and Weight Watchers, "Are You Ready to Join Me?" Weight Watchers, https://www.weightwatchers.com/uk/how-it-works/oprah.

2   Paula Fitzgerald Bone, "Determinants of Word-of-Mouth Communication During Product Consumption," in John F. Sherry and Brian Sternthal (Eds.), *Advances in Consumer Research* 19 (Provo, UT: Association for Consumer Research, 1992), pp. 579–583; W. R. Wilson and R. A. Peterson, "Some Limits on the Potency of Word-of-Mouth Information," in T. K. Srull (Ed.), *Advances in Consumer Research* (Provo: UT: Association for Consumer Research, 1989), pp. 23–29; J. E. Swan and R. L. Oliver, "Postpurchase Communication by Consumers," *Journal of Retailing* (Winter 1989), pp. 516–533; P. M. Herr, F. R. Kardes, and J. Kim, "Effects of Word-of-Mouth and Product-Attribute Information on Persuasion," *Journal of Consumer Research* (March 1991), pp. 454–462; C. Walker, "Word-of-Mouth," *American Demographics* (July 1995), p. 38.

3   Betsy Gelb and Madeline Johnson, "Word of Mouth Communication: Cases and Consequences," *Journal of Health Care Marketing* 15, no. 3 (Fall 1995), pp. 54–58.

4   Ibid.

5   Thomas S. Robertson, *Innovative Behavior and Communication* (New York: Holt, 1971), p. 170; Deborah Sue Yeager, "Markdown Mecca," *Wall Street Journal* (July 6, 1976), p. 1

6   "Global Advertising: Consumers Trust Real Friends and Virtual Strangers the Most," *NielsenWire* (July 7, 2009), http://blog.nielsen.com/nielsenwire/consumer/global-advertising-consumers-trust-real-friends-and-virtual-strangers-the-most/.

7   Phil Mershon, "9 Reasons Your Company Should Use Brand Advocates: New Research," *Social Media Examiner* (June 13, 2011), http://www.socialmediaexaminer.com/9-reasons-your-company-should-use-brand-advocates-new-research/.

8   Jacques Bughin, Jonathan Doogan, and Ole Jergenvetik, "A New Way to Measure Word-Mouth Marketing," *McKinsey Quarterly* (April, 2010), http://www.scribd.com/doc/46913890/A-New-Way-to-Measure-Word-Of-Mouth-Marketing.

9   Lauren Dugan, "Does Word of Mouth Marketing Work Better on Social Media? *Media Bistro* (August 19, 2011), http://www.mediabistro.com/alltwitter/tag/influencers.

10 "Pharma Sales in India to Touch $27 Billion by 2016: Deloitte," *Economic Times, India Times* (February 16, 2014), http://articles.economictimes.indiatimes.com/2014-02-16/news/47379629_1_chronic-therapies-heath-awareness-life-sciences; ITP Division, Ministry of External Affairs, Government of India, "India in Business" (2006), *http://www.indiainbusiness.nic.in/industry-infrastructure/industrial-sectors/drug-pharma.htm.*

11 Silverman, "How to Harness the Awesome Power of Word-of-Mouth."

12 Herr, Kardes, Kim, "Effects of Word-of-Mouth and Product-Attribute Information on Persuasion: An Accessibility-Diagnosticity Perspective."

13 Richard Nisbett and Lee Ross, *Human Inference: Strategies and Shortcomings of Social Judgment* (Upper Saddle River, NJ: Prentice Hall, 1980).

14 Jolita Kisielius and Brian Sternthal, "Examining the Vividness Controversy: An Availability-Valence Interpretation," *Journal of Consumer Research* 12 (March 1986), pp. 418–431.

15 Elihu Katz and Paul F. Lazarsfeld, *Personal Influence: The Part Played by People in the Flow of Mass Communication* (Transaction Publishers, 2005).

16 "Mass Media: Types and Influences," *Word Press* (October 23, 2007), http://maxibona.wordpress.com/2007/10/23/mass-media-types-and-influences/.

17 S. D. Boon and C. D. Lomore, "Admirer-Celebrity Relationship Among Young Adults: Explaining Perceptions of Celebrity Influence on Identity," *Human Communication Research* 27 (2001).

18 D. C. Giles and J. Maltby, "The Role of Media Figures in Adolescent Development: Relations Between Autonomy, Attachment, and Interest in Celebrities," *Personality and Individual Differences* 36 (2004).

19 "Britney Spears Shaven 'Hair Cut': Is It Worth the Media Buzz?" *Huliq News* (February 18, 2007), www.huliq.com/11471/brittney-spears-shaven-haircut-is-it-worth-the-media-buzz.

20 "Long-Term Harmful Effects of Britney, Paris, and Lindsay's Bad Behavior on Young Women," *Huliq News* (February 17, 2007), www.huliq.com/11469/long-term-harmful-effects-of-brittney-paris-and-lindsays-bad-behavior-on-young-women.

21 Sarah Cassidy, "Celebrities Now More Influential on Young People Than Parents," BNET.com (March 1, 2004).

22 Tom Pick, "Best Social Media Stats and Market Research of 2010," *Social Media Today* (September 8, 2010), http://socialmediatoday.com/tom-pick/176932/best-social-media-stats-and-market-research-2010-so-far.

23 Thomas W. Valente and Rebecca L. Davis, "Accelerating the Diffusion of Innovations Using Opinion Leaders," *Annals of the American Academy of Political and Social Science* 566 (November 1999), pp. 55–67.

24 P. H. Reingen and J. B. Kernan, "Analysis of Referral Networks in Marketing," *Journal of Marketing Research* (November 1986), pp. 370–378.

25 L. F. Feick, L. L. Price, and R. A. Higie, "People Who Use People," in R. J. Lutz (Ed.), *Advances in Consumer Research* 13 (Provo, UT: Association for Consumer Research, 1986), pp. 301–305; P. H. Reingen, "A Word-of-Mouth Network," in M. Wallendorf and P. Anderson (Eds.), *Advances in Consum-*

er Research 14 (Provo, UT: Association for Consumer Research, 1987), pp. 213–217; L. J. Yale and M. C. Gilly, "Dyadic Perceptions in Personal Source Information Search," *Journal of Business Research* (March 1995), pp. 225–237.

26 "Film Critics: Influencers or Predictors?" *Marketing News* (April 28, 1997), p. 18.

27 Adam Lashinsky, "How Tim Cook Is Changing Apple," *Fortune* (June 11, 2012), pp. 110–118; Andy Ihnatko, "Speculating on next *i*Phone via secret video," *Chicago Sun-Times* (June 8, 2012); Dave Balter, *The Word of Mouth Manual 2* (Print Matters, Inc., 2008); Stephen H. Waldstrom, "A Stroll Through the *i*Phone App Store," *Business Week* (July 28, 2008), p. 74.

28 Word of Mouth Marketing Association, "WOMMA's Influence Handbook," http://womma.org/influencerhandbook/2/.

29 Word of Mouth Marketing Association, "How to Work Effectively with Influencers," WOMMA, http://womma.org/influencer/howto/; Ben Cotton, "10 Free Tools to Identify Online Influencers," *Adelman Digital* (September 20, 2010), http://www.adelmandigital.com/2010/09/10-free-tools-to-identify-online-influencers/.

30 W. J. Carl, "What's All the Buzz About? Everyday Communication and the Relational Basis of Word-of-Mouth and Buzz Marketing Practices," *Management Communication Quarterly 19, no. 4* (2006), pp. 601–634.

31 Jo Startmann, "Finding 30 Free Tools for Social Media Influencers," *Freshnetworks* (November, 2010), http://www.freshnetworks.com/blog/2010/12/free-tools-for-finding-social-media-influencers/.

32 Ibid.; Leisa Reinecke Flynn, Ronald E. Goldsmith, and Jacqueline K. Eastman, "Opinion Leaders and Opinion Seekers: Two New Measurements," *Journal of Academy of Marketing Science* 24 (Spring 1996), pp. 137–147.

33 Michael R. Solomon, "The Missing Link: Surrogate Consumers in the Marketing Chain," *Journal of Marketing* 50 (October 1986), pp. 208–218.

34 Trefis Team, "Here's Why the Market Reaction to Volkswagen's Emissions Scandal Is Justified," *Forbes*, (October 1, 2015), Christiaan Hetzner, "German Industry's Reaction to VW Scandal Is Another Scandal," *Auto News*, (December 3, 2015), http://www.autonews.com/article/20151203/BLOG06/312039945/german-industrys-reaction-to-vw-scandal-is-another-scandal; Paul Horrell, "Here's How VW Is Responding to Its Big Diesel Emissions Scandal," *Top Gear*, (October 30, 2015), http://www.topgear.com/car-news/insider/heres-how-vw-is-responding-to-its-big-diesel-emissions-scandal; and "How Did People React to VolksWagen Scandal?," *Quora*, (November 5, 2015), https://www.quora.com/How-did-people-react-to-VolksWagen-Scandal.

35 Christy Fisher, "Wal-Mart's Way," *Advertising Age* (February 18, 1991), p. 3; "Viral Advertising Spreads Through Marketing Plans," *US Today* (June 23, 2005); Manohla Dargis, "We're All Gonna Die! Grab Your Video Camera," *New York Times* (August 1, 2008), movie review of *Cloverfield*.

36 R. L. Bayus "Word-of-Mouth: The Indirect Effects of Marketing Efforts," *Journal of Advertising Research* (June–July 1985), pp. 31–35.

37 "Films Ruling the Box Office This Week," Brandchannel 2011 Brandcameo Product Placement Awards (2012), http://www.brandchannel.com/brandcameofilms.asp; Katherine Neer, "How Product Placement Works," *Howstuffworks* (2008), http://money.howstuffworks.com/product-placement.htm/; "Product Placement Growth Fueled by Increase in Channels," *Howstuffworks* (June 9, 2008), http://howstuffworks.com/framed.htm?parent=product-placement.htm&url=http://www.productplacement.biz1.

38 Judith Dobrzynski and J. E. Davis, "Business Celebrities," *Business Week* (June 23, 1986), pp. 100–107; Leslie Schultz, "Not Quite Ready for Prime Time President," *Inc.* (April 1985), pp. 156–160.

39 Silverman, "How to Harness the Awesome Power of Word-of-Mouth."

40 Linda Bustos, "Negative Word of Mouth: Crisis or Opportunity?" *Get Elastic* (May 7, 2008), www.getelastic.comreputation-management-damage-control/.

41 Diane Halstead, "Negative Word of Mouth: Substitute for or Supplement to Complaints?" *Journal of Consumer Satisfaction, Dissatisfaction, and Complaining Behavior* (January 2002).

42 Paul Rand, "Understanding and Managing Negative Word of Mouth," *Ketchum* (September 28, 2005), www.ketchum.com/paul_rand_managing_negative_word_of_mouth_article; Glen Allsopp, "How to Deal with Negative Blog Posts," *Viper Chill* (February 19, 2008), www.viperchill.com/how-to-deal-with-negative-blog-posts/.

CHAPTER 13
SOCIAL CLASS

LEARNING OBJECTIVES

- To examine the concept of social class and the way our society regards the class issue.
- To gain insight into the multitiered class structure of the United States.
- To ascertain patterns, causes, and ramifications of the evolving social class structure in contemporary society.
- To probe the criteria and methods used in measuring social classes.
- To identify and examine five relevant issues associated with the concept of social class in contemporary society.
- To review the impact of social class membership on various aspects of consumer behavior.

KEY TERMS

social class	subjective measures	composite-variable
stratification	reputational measures	indexes
egalitarianism	objective measures	status crystallization
social mobility	single-variable indexes	overprivileged
nonproductive reach		underprivileged

Even though Americans are not all equal in status, most of us perceive ourselves as members of a huge middle class. This belief stems largely from an ingrained self-perception of being average, normal, and about equal in stature to everyone else. Within this theme of equality that runs through American social relationships, being on par with everybody else seems to be the "right thing to say and do" socially.

However, in many other societies, class is a more prominent issue, and social rankings bestow different degrees of importance, influence, and prestige to specific members of a society. In few other places is this social demarcation more evident than in Great Britain, where royalty and aristocracy have been the foundations of this country throughout its history. The recent massive celebration in June 2012 of Queen Elizabeth II's Sixtieth Diamond Jubilee is a case in point. Although some may wonder why the British are still fascinated by such relics of the past, the fact remains that these inherited traditions are the very backbone of England.

Only about one-third of British aristocracy is honored with noble titles such as sir, lord, or knight. Traditionally, aristocrats did not work for a living. They inherited their money, which was usually spent on elegant homes, horses for hunting or racing, gaming, fine wines, and exquisite possessions.

Foremost among characteristics that distinguish British aristocrats is a deeply ingrained sense of duty, coupled with impeccably good manners. This sense of duty is manifested in deep involvement with charity events and needy causes. Because aristocrats have a supreme sense of self-confidence, they do not care what other people think of them. They tend, as a result, to be unimpressed by the achievement of others. They are preoccupied with the countryside and country sports, such as cricket, rugby football, polo, and croquet. During winter evenings, favorite pastimes include billiards, bridge, and backgammon. Most of them dislike living in cities and prefer out-of-the-way country homes, which they seldom name, believing that the people who matter would know where they live.

In Ireland and Scotland, many aristocrats live in old castles, adorned with furniture that is inherited, never bought, and that rarely matches. Walls are decorated with an abundance of portraits of ancestors. The more portraits a castle has, the greater the prestige and honor accredited to its occupants.

British aristocrats tend to send their children to be educated at Eton, the top British public school established in 1440 by Henry VI. Annual tuition there exceeds £30,000. This was the school chosen by the Royal Family to complete Prince William's education. Old Etonians hold a great deal of power and prestigious posts in Britain. Exclusively male at one time, the school today accepts a limited number of women.

British aristocrats have their own mode of speech. They sit not in the lounge but in the drawing room. They do not go to the toilet, but to the lavatory. To avoid attention in public eating places, British aristocrats seldom dine in restaurants. They prefer the privacy of their own homes or a friend's dinner table, where good plain English food and fine wines from personal cellars are served. Along with this love of home is a significant attachment to the club—an aristocrat's inviolable refuge from reality. Most prestigious London clubs have changed very little over the years. In these for-men-only clubs, the staff upholds old traditions with great pride, only whispering as they talk, and making sure that members are elegantly served. Business discussions in the club are rarely heard. They are simply not allowed.[1]

Values and traditions in any culture dramatically influence how the society is stratified, as well as how people in each stratum live, what they like, and what interests them. Find out more about the British culture by visiting www.geocities.com/TheTropics/2865/index.htm. Compared to our seemingly classless society in the United States, what factors account for the permanent, formal caste system that characterizes British society? In your opinion, are the modern social–economic realities likely to change the way the British feel regarding their present rigid class structure?

In this chapter, we examine the impact of social class on consumer behavior and the implications of class differences for marketers when designing strategies. Specifically, we cover the concept of social class, the U.S. class structure, class measurement, and the influence of class on purchasing and consumption patterns.

INTRODUCTION TO SOCIAL CLASS

Marketers are keenly interested in the distribution of wealth across the marketplace, because this phenomenon largely demarcates which groups of people exhibit the greatest purchasing power. The marketing literature clearly establishes that income—the amount of resources an individual or household earns—exerts a major impact on consumer purchases. Some companies, such as Rolex and Bentley Motors, vie for the upper, more affluent levels of society. Others firms, such as Walmart, successfully target less opulent, working-class consumers.

The less opulent consumers constitute the main target of box stores like Walmart and K-Mart.

Although income and social class are related, they are not synonymous. Social class refers to the overall rank assigned to large groups of people, according to the values held by a particular society. From a marketing perspective, social class identifies large groups of people who share common ideas about how life should be lived. Whereas income influences purchasing behavior through availability of resources, social class affects how consumers spend that income. This may include where they live, what recreational activities they pursue, how they decorate their home, and the types of products and services they acquire.

© Dmitri Ma/Shutterstock.com

Socioeconomic status and lifestyle are, to a great extent, inseparable.[2] Social class membership and relative standing within a class impact people's beliefs, values, and behaviors.[3] People's lifestyles and tastes, as well as their consumption patterns, can be viewed largely as expressions of their socialization into a particular class. People learn the values and behaviors appropriate to their class formally via schooling as well as vicariously by observing their peers.

THE CONCEPT OF SOCIAL CLASS

Many species of animals, such as wolves and chickens, arrange themselves into multitiered or stratified societies in which the most aggressive creatures command the first pick of food, mating partners, and living space.

A study by Schjelderup-Ebbe described a barnyard community where each hen held its own definite position in the pecking order of the group.[4] Within the brood, each hen was found to dominate those of lesser standing and acquiesce to those of higher stature. Broadening the notion of a dominance–submission hierarchy to apply to humans, Ries and Trout noted, "Consumers are like chickens. They are much more comfortable with a pecking order that everybody knows and accepts."[5]

All but the smallest and most primitive societies have demonstrated stratification, or formal systems of economic and social inequality.[6] Social identity comes about when a culture establishes limits on interactions between people of unequal status. The existence of deference (social honor paid to members of higher classes by those of lesser social stature) is well accepted among social scientists. According to Weber, social class demarcates individuals' future opportunities and possibilities.[7] Furthermore, both social class and relative standing within a class are considered important sources of consumer beliefs, values, and behaviors.[8]

stratification
a system of classifying members of a population based on economic and social characteristics

HOW U.S. CONSUMERS VIEW SOCIAL CLASS

It is a common belief that compared to the class system in Europe the United States does not have a rigid and clearly defined class system. Class distinctions in the United States are so subtle that foreign observers—especially those accustomed to a rigid caste system like that of India—often miss class nuances.

Many people associate the word *class* with unpleasant connotations. For many, particularly those who harbor deep feelings of egalitarianism, the idea of typing people is disturbing. Such persons feel that the United States was founded on a principle of equality, and people should be measured by their own accomplishments, not by who their families happen to be. As a consequence, most U.S. citizens feel they belong to a massive middle class that seems, at the first glance, to engulf everyone around. However, no one can deny that in the eyes of others, all of us are defined, at least in part, according to an elaborate system that includes our occupation, education, income, family standing, type of residence, possessions, appearance, and manner of speech. These distinctions between people who otherwise are assumed to be equal not only occur on an interpersonal basis, but also abound in every aspect of the business world. Examples include major airlines' three-tiered categorization of fliers, theaters with graded sections, and manufacturers' *good, better*, and *best* product gradations. Similarly, corporate, government, and ecclesiastical organizational structures are based on rigid *clan* hierarchies and various employment cadres.

FACTORS OBSCURING THE RECOGNITION OF SOCIAL CLASS IN THE UNITED STATES

A number of factors obscure the recognition of divergent social classes in the United States. These include the doctrine of egalitarianism, the size of the middle class, the possibilities for mobility in an open-class system, and confusion between social class and income.

Egalitarianism

Whereas very few Europeans, especially among the British, would offer apologies for their country's social hierarchy, the United States was founded on the principle of egalitarianism, which advocates equality among people. Egalitarian beliefs run counter to any idea implying that some members of society are more privileged and, in some way, superior to others.

Size of the Middle Class

The size of the middle class in the United States to some extent hides the existence of a social class structure. Unlike many societies in which there are the very rich, the very poor, and only a few in-between, the United States still has a comparatively large middle class. However, current adverse economic conditions and job losses have resulted in many middle-class households shrinking into the ranks of the underprivileged.

Social Mobility

Social mobility is a third factor that plays a significant role in the failure to recognize class distinctions. The Horatio Alger story, a partly real and partly mythical tale about a penniless young orphan who became successful in business and in life, has made a strong and lasting impression on the U.S. consciousness. Similarly, anecdotes about Mark Zuckerberg (Facebook), the late Steve Jobs (Apple), and Bill Gates (Microsoft), as well as Commodore Vanderbilt (the skipper of a Staten Island garbage scow), Swift (a pushcart meat peddler on Cape Cod), and a host of other rags-to-riches narratives, have served to inspire many people in the United States with dreams of climbing the social ladder.

Social Class versus Income

Finally, many people confuse social class with income. Income is a gauge of the amount of money that individuals or families have available to spend, but income figures can obscure the many factors that truly differentiate between classes such as occupation, education, lifestyles, values, and attitudes. Although jobs that rank relatively low in social prestige may earn as much or even more than jobs that rank relatively high, the reverse also frequently occurs. With the downturn in our country's economic activities that started in 2007, some highly qualified individuals have been marginalized and are underemployed or working for lower pay and fewer benefits.[9]

WHY LEARN ABOUT SOCIAL CLASS?

The benefit of social stratification lies in its ability to provide a basis for market segmentation. Although social classes are tremendously large social aggregates containing vast differences in individual behavior and great diversity of life circumstances, the presence of certain shared values, attitudes, behavioral patterns, and lifestyles among members of each social class can facilitate the targeting process.

Marketers can now pinpoint the class status and buying patterns of just about everyone in the market. As we mentioned in the segmentation chapter, PRIZM from Nielsen Claritas Inc. broke down the entire United States into geodemographic clusters, to allow for more precise targeting. For example, according to Nielsen Claritas, a person at the highest level of the suburban elite class would most likely live in Upper Crust or Blue Blood Estate territories like Scarsdale (outside New York), Winnetka (outside Chicago), or Atherton (south of San Francisco). That person would probably own a prestigious brand automobile, read one or more business magazines, and patronize a full-service brokerage firm. If that person were an Urban Gold Coaster, he or she would be likely to live on the Upper East Side in Manhattan, along Lake Michigan in Chicago, or in the Pacific Heights section of San Francisco. This person's inclinations would likely include sailing, use of advanced electronic devices, and investing in the stock market.

Beneficiaries of such targeting efforts include direct marketers and advertisers—in both traditional and viral media—who use precision targeting through the localization strategies of these media types. Dividing consumers into groups with common demographic, lifestyle, or behavioral characteristics allows the firms to zero in on minute niches of the population whose characteristics are known. Members of these niches thus are most likely to respond to particular offerings crafted specifically to suit their particular needs and interests.

The intention is to eliminate nonproductive reach, otherwise known as the junk mail or spam phenomenon. Conventional promotion aimed at broad audiences usually translates into waste. Disinterested consumers who receive web communications, ads, or unsolicited items in the mail usually ignore them or discard them without even a second glance. To overcome this problem, database marketing came to the rescue. Marketers are now able to identify and reach clusters of consumers who share common characteristics, interests, incomes, professions, lifestyles, and preferences. By knowing the characteristics of a group, marketers can design messages precisely calibrated to get members to act. For example, using its database, Hilton Hotels Corporation designed award-winning programs for business executives, such as its Hilton Meetings product for business travelers, Hilton HHonors, and its frequent guest programs.[10] Similarly, companies such as Groupon, LivingSocial, and kgbdeals use their sites to offer services and products specifically chosen to match the profiles of their clientele. Among

nonproductive reach
the effort wasted on contracting consumers who are unlikely prospects

Ownership of expensive "toys" such as this yacht is among the characteristics of PRIZM's Upper Crust cluster.

© SNEHIT/Shutterstock.com

the many users of database marketing are credit card companies, banks, food and nonfood companies, pharmaceutical firms, as well as liquor, travel, and recreation establishments.

Advertising agencies that operate in both the traditional and viral spheres are also avid users of this type of focused data. Advertisers today are forced to cater precisely to specific groups as a result of the present highly fragmented class structure in the United States. Whether the appeals are subtle or blatant, they are designed with class characteristics and aspirations in mind. Ads for domestic beer versus French wines, and for Hyundai versus Bentley, are designed to touch off a personal response and signal to a specific class that the product is appropriate for its tastes and social status.

CLASS STRUCTURE IN THE UNITED STATES

Most highly industrialized nations exhibit neither strict and tightly defined class systems nor pure social strata. Rather, in countries like the United States, a series of *status continua* can be identified.[11] These status continua reflect various factors that the society as a whole values. In achievement-oriented cultures like our own, income, occupation, education, residence, and possessions would be more likely to endow us with status than factors unrelated to accomplishment like family heritage, race, or gender. By contrast, more traditional societies such as China, India, and to some extent Great Britain might ascribe greater importance to such factors as ancestry or the social status of one's parents.

Researchers of the social class phenomenon differ with regard to the number of classes that exist in the United States. Estimates vary from as few as two classes to as many as nine. Those who propose a two-tiered society believe that the distinction between classes lies in the domain of ownership of the means of production. The *haves* own the means of production and employ the *have-nots*. The have-nots, on the other hand, sell their labor power to the haves in order to survive. This situation, inevitably, leads to antagonism between the two classes, which, in turn, is the main driving force in the system.[12]

Other authors such as Paul Fussell, for example, identified nine distinct classes that range from an elite class, virtually invisible behind the tall walls of their mansions, all the way to an underclass, equally invisible in their hovels. Still others, such as William Thompson, Joseph Hickey, and

© Mikael Damkier/Shutterstock.com

In the year 2015, 564,708 persons were homeless on any given night in the United States.

Dennis Gilbert, proposed a six-class structure that ranges from high-level executives, celebrities, and heirs at the top all the way down to others who occupy poorly paid positions, who lack job skills and have little or no participation in the labor force, or who rely on government support for survival.[13]

MULTITIERED SOCIAL CLASS STRUCTURE OF THE UNITED STATES

In recent years, particularly since the Great Recession (2007 through 2009) and subsequent recovery, Americans have experienced economic turmoil that has affected our class categories. Taking these major socioeconomic changes into consideration, in combination with classifications by contemporary sociologists such as William Thompson, Joseph Hickey, Leonard Beeghley, Dennis Gilbert, and others, the social class structure in the United States can be summarized in the following manner.[14]

The Upper Class

A recent report by a team of sociologists indicated that the upper class currently accounts for approximately 3 percent of the population. It is divided into two subgroups: the upper-upper, constituting 1 percent of the population and including blue bloods who inherited their wealth, top executives, celebrities of superstar stature, high-rung politicians, and multimillionaires; and the lower-upper class accounting for 2 percent of the population and including the corporate elite, who own or control America's corporations, as well as those who earn exceptionally high incomes through boardroom memberships. For this second group, income and wealth statistics serve as the standard for placing them into this subcategory. There remains, however, disagreement over the inclusion of those "*nouveau riche*" as members of the upper class.

The Middle Class

The middle class has fallen behind financially over the past decade. Due to the housing market crisis, job losses, and other consequences of the Great

Recession, its median wealth (assets minus debt) fell sharply. According to analysis of government data, this group, whose income falls between $76K to $126K constituted 40 percent of the U.S. adult population in the year 2015. Based on this range of income, the middle class can be divided into two distinct subgroups, the upper-middle (about 15 percent of the population, earning between $96K and $126K) and the lower-middle (about 25 percent of the population, earning between $76K and $95K per year).

The upper middle class consists of highly educated, salaried professionals and managers with above-average income, mostly in the six-figure range. Many of these individuals hold graduate degrees, enjoy greater work autonomy, and are often members or officers of professional organizations. Examples include physicians, lawyers, executives, scientists, esteemed authors, and journalists.

The lower middle class, on the other hand, consists of semiprofessionals and craftspeople that have some degree of work autonomy. Most of the members of this group have at least some college education and mostly occupy white-collar positions.

However, it should be noted that the distinction between the two segments of the middle class based on income levels alone could be misleading. Household income distribution can neither reflect the standard of living for a household nor its class status with complete accuracy.

The Working Class

Sociologists estimate the size of the *working class* to be approximately 45 percent of the population. This group also consists of the two subgroups known as the working class (about 30 percent of the population, earning between $45K and $75K per year) and the working poor (about 15 percent, earning between $19K and $44K per year).

The first subgroup includes individuals who occupy clerical jobs that normally carry minimum job security. These positions entail routinized work schedules and processes, and require no decision-making capabilities. Members of this group usually hold a high school degree. Once again, it should be noted here that the standard of living of households within this category varies widely based on the number of wage earners within the household. For instance, husband–wife households with no children where both spouses work have been observed to enjoy a higher standard of living than other households with a single wage earner and a number of children to support.

The working poor segment, on the other hand, is made up of individuals holding retail, service, and low-rung clerical jobs. Those who occupy such positions are characterized by low levels of education often gained in substandard school systems. The types of jobs they hold offer little security, low chances for advancement, and minimal protection from poverty—conditions that create feelings of vulnerability and susceptibility to changing economic circumstances.

The Under Class

Located at the very bottom of the social hierarchy, the *underclass* accounts for about 15 percent of the population and consists of individuals who either occupy poorly paid positions, are infrequent participants in the labor force, or rely on government support or charity for survival. In 2015, reports indicated there were 46.7 million individuals living in poverty in our society. Due to low educational level of some high school or less, their chances of acquiring or maintaining well-paying jobs are severely restricted. Many members of this group live below the poverty level, with food insecurity present among one-third of them.

THE EVOLVING SOCIAL CLASS STRUCTURE OF THE UNITED STATES

Today, new social trends continue to alter the profile of social classes in the United States. The growing gap between those who are well off and everyone else is among the more troubling phenomena of our time. For example, in the past few years, the concentration of wealth among a handful of people at the top has set new records. According to market research and consulting from Spectrum Group in 2015, there were 10.1 million households in the United States with $1 million or more in investable assets, excluding the value of their primary residence. Despite ongoing concerns about market volatility and direction of the economy, the United States added 300,000 new millionaires in 2016, bringing the total to 10.4 million. Furthermore, the number of households worth $5 million or more also grew to reach 1.3 million, compared with 1.24 million in 2013. The number of households worth $25 million or more also increased and exceed 145,000, up from 132,000 in 2013.

As these figures indicate, the wealth gap between the rich and the poor grew wider in the past decade. According to a recent Pew Research Center report, the wealth of the top 10 percent of Americans grew, while that of the bottom 90 percent declined. In fact, the top 0.1 percent of the population are now worth more than the entire bottom 90 percent of the population. This fact is confirmed in a 2015 World Wealth Report, which showed that the number of American High Net Worth Individuals (HNWI) now exceeds 4.68 million individuals, with total wealth amounting to $16.2 trillion.[15]

Against this glamorous picture of the rich lies another gloomy image of the poor. The U.S. Census Bureau reports that in 2015, the official poverty rate was 13.5 percent, with 46 million people living in poverty. In terms of race, the poverty rate for non-Hispanic whites was 10.1 percent, which is lower than the poverty rates for other racial groups. For Blacks, for example, the poverty rate was 26.2 percent, with a total of 10.8 million black people living in poverty. Among Hispanics, the poverty rate was 23.6 percent, with over 13 million Hispanic people living in poverty. Among Asians, the poverty rate was moderately low at 12 percent, with 2.1 million Asians living in poverty.[16]

In terms of age and gender for the same year, one-third (33 percent) of adults sixty-five and older had incomes below twice the poverty household levels. The poverty rate was even higher among women ages sixty-five and older than for men in this same age group. Among individuals ages eighty and older, 23 percent of women lived below the poverty thresholds compared to 14 percent of men in the same age category.

This dire situation has resulted in many calls for a national effort to cut the poverty rate in our society. Suggested remedies include government-initiated public projects, raising the minimum wage rate, granting an income tax credit for the poor, investing more in rural communities, supporting education and training for the less fortunate, expanding family literacy programs, implementing universal healthcare coverage, and strengthening labor laws to protect the rights of workers.

IMPLICATIONS OF EVOLVING SOCIAL CLASS TRENDS

Recent changes in the profile of the social class structure in our society are affecting where and how consumers shop. For example, high prices and low personal income have driven more people to shop at dollar stores, discount supercenters, warehouse stores, and thrift shops. In the case of the

ETHICAL DILEMMA

Ego or Hard-Work Driven CEO Pay?

Everyone today realizes that the gap between the rich and the poor is widening. The concentration of financial resources at the top of the economic ladder has left average families with inadequate income to maintain a decent standard of living. In the past few years, the nation's aggregate household income has substantially shifted from middle-income to upper-income households, driven by the increasing size of the upper income tier and more-rapid gains in income at the top. In the case of the middle class, for example, the median wealth has plunged by 28 percent over the last decade, while that of the upper class has soared by 7 percent. As a consequence, many families now face difficulties in maintaining their former levels of consumption.

Against this bleak backdrop, a 2015 report by Glassdoor Economic Research regarding the average CEO pay in companies listed on the S&P 500 was $13.8 million. However, for all major corporations in the United States, the overall pay for CEOs ranged from $7.3 million near the bottom to over $400 million at the top—a figure that may include bonuses and profit sharing in exceptional cases. Such high pay can be observed in the cases of Viacom's CEO who received $431.1 million in 2011, as well as Apple's CEO who was paid $378 million in that same year.

At the center of the controversy lies the question of the fairness of CEO pay levels compared with those of average workers. A recent Pew Research Center report found that Americans drastically underestimate the CEO-to-worker pay gap. Respondents estimated the average CEO earned thirty times as much as the average unskilled worker. In actuality, the CEO-to-worker pay ratio is 354-to-1. At present-day rates, a minimum wage earner would have to work 636 years to earn the same as a CEO's median salary for a single year. Fortunately, however, public outcry and media coverage of such income inequalities have resulted in a number of measures being undertaken by the government, as well as by other entities such as shareholders, to address this issue. For example, in July 2010, the Dodd-Frank Wall Street Reform and Consumer Protection Act was passed, which among its many financial regulatory reforms, provided shareholders with a nonbinding so-called "say-on-pay" vote to approve or disapprove the firm's executive compensation—the level of which must be disclosed according to existing SEC rules. In addition, in 2011, the IRS was given the charge of enforcing "The Federal Private Inurement Prohibition," which strictly forbids a tax-exempt organization's managers from receiving unreasonable benefits from the nonprofit's income or assets. In August 2015, new rules were adopted by the Securities and Exchange Commission (SEC) requiring that with the start of 2017, public companies will be required to disclose the ratio of CEO pay to median worker pay. This rule will provide transparency into the pay scale within some of the largest corporations, all the way to the top.

The exceptionally high income of CEOs consists of a number of components. In addition to their salaries and bonuses, CEOs receive stock-based pay and profit sharing. This means that the executives are also owners of the corporation for which they work.

A number of factors help preserve this unusual high CEO-pay practice. A large portion of the benefits that top executives receive are hidden. The law does not require that they be disclosed. A second factor entails compensation consultants' drive to encourage CEOs to reach for the sky in their salary negotiations in order to surpass the pay of their peers. Nevertheless, the forementioned regulatory actions have served to sound a warning to corporate governance that excessive compensation practices will face heightened scrutiny and enhanced regulatory oversight.[17]

Reactions concerning the inequity of the income issue in our society have risen dramatically in recent times. Learn more about this topic by visiting the AFL-CIO Executive PayWatch website at www.paywatch.org. Examine a few case studies the site provides, such as CitiGroup and Hewlett Packard, and the success of these firms' shareholders to curb their companies' excessive CEO compensation. Beyond the steps already initiated by the government, what actions would you suggest to curtail the excessive compensation packages offered to CEOs in the United States?

dollar store, firms such as Dollar General, Family Dollar, and Dollar Tree have done exceptionally well in the past few years. During and after the Great Recession, customers mobbed low-end stores seeking deals on everything from food, clothing, and decorations to health and beauty items. People who had never shopped at such stores before suddenly began to trade down from luxury and mid-level retail establishments.[18]

Some of the biggest marketers in the United States are adopting a two-tiered strategy, tailoring their products and pitches to two different Americas. Companies from AT&T through Disney to General Motors now openly embrace this two-tier marketing strategy, which deliberately polarizes products and services as well as their sales pitches to the two market segments of the rich and the poor.[19]

In the same vein, Paine Webber, Inc. has advised investors to follow a Tiffany/Walmart strategy and avoid companies that serve the middle of the consumer market. Some companies try to attract customers on both sides of the divide with an upstairs–downstairs approach. For example, at Gap's Banana Republic stores, denim jeans sell for roughly $79. Gap's Old Navy stores sell a similar version for about $29. Both chains are thriving.[20]

A glance at the changes just described reveals an evolving marketplace. On one side, the shrinking income of many households translates into frugality that will characterize their buying patterns. On the other side, the *selectively affluent* offer excellent opportunities. They are the consumers whose incomes may not qualify them for entrance into exclusive country clubs or gated communities, but who have an affluent mindset and sufficient discretionary income to satisfy their aspirations. This newly emerging class, which is well educated and generally highly paid, provides a market for many quality and prestigious products and services, such as expensive cars, jewelry, and vacations. Figures 13.1 and 13.2 are aimed at selectively affluent audiences.

MEASURING SOCIAL CLASS

We informally apply a variety of criteria to judge the social status of other persons around us, to classify or grade other people in terms of the location of their residence and their possessions. Criteria may include such things as the other party's ancestry, occupation or income, education or intelligence, authority or influence, associations, behavior, speech, tact-

© Darren Brode/Shutterstock.com

© sippakorn/Shutterstock.com

fulness, and grooming. In fact, the specific yardsticks we employ to rank other people along some sort of social scale reflect, to a large extent, the norms, values, and ideals of the society in which we live.

More formally, social scientists have applied three basic techniques to research the topic of social class. In one approach, individuals rate their own social standing. Second, individuals can be requested to evaluate the social position of others. In still another technique, impartial measurement criteria are applied as indicators of the particular social class to which an individual belongs. These procedures, known respectively as subjective, reputational, and objective measures, are discussed in paragraphs that follow.

Subjective Measures

subjective measures
ways of determining social
class membership based on
individuals' classification of
themselves

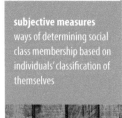

Subjective measures of social class probe individuals' class-consciousness or sense of belonging and identification with others. When employing these measures, researchers give participants an opportunity to classify themselves, based largely on their self-images, in order to determine the social class structure. Although this method of measuring class offers simplicity and convenience, it can lead to an erroneous profile of the social classes. Some respondents over- or understate their class standing, thereby causing over- or undercounts of various class memberships. For example, according to a recent Pew Research Center survey, nine of every ten people in the United States labeled themselves as "middle class." Approximately 50 percent believed they were simply "middle class," 18 percent claimed to be "upper-middle class," and 21 percent felt they belonged to the "lower-middle class." Only 2 percent labeled themselves as "upper class," and 8 percent called themselves "lower class." Demographically, the self-described middle class covered the entire spectrum of the population. The survey sited contradictions, where a couple making $70,000 a year in one state labeled themselves as "solidly middle class," while another couple in the same state making $140,000 a year described themselves as "nowhere near what you consider middle class."[21]

Reputational Measures

Rather than having subjects estimate their own social standing, reputational measures of social class ask individuals to rank the social position of other individuals in the community with whom they are familiar. When employing these measures, researchers request key informants within a group (a coworker, manager, neighbor, member of the clergy, colleague) to provide preliminary judgments of other members' social class. Trained researchers, however, are responsible for making the definitive assignments of community members into the various social class positions.[32]

reputational measures
ways of determining social class based on individuals' ranking of others in a society

Although many social scientists regard reputational measures as the most accurate and thoroughly validated approach to investigate social class structures, reputational approaches hold lesser value to marketers and researchers of consumer behavior, who are interested in identifying specific class attributes that have a bearing on consumption patterns.

Objective Measures

Unlike subjective and reputational techniques of social class measurement, which rely on self- or peer-evaluations, respectively, studies that use objective measures apply relevant demographic and socioeconomic criteria in order to assess individuals' social class membership. Specific variables employed when using the objective method include amount or

objective measures
a method that applies relevant demographic and socioeconomic criteria to determine social class membership

source of income, location or type of residence, occupation, education, and possessions. These variables, as well as other factors, can be used separately or in combination to evaluate an individual's social standing.

Some investigations of social class rely on just one socioeconomic gauge in order to estimate an individual's social class membership. Such studies are said to employ single-variable indexes. Among the single-variable indexes used to measure social class, occupation is probably the most widely accepted sole indicator of social standing. To a great extent, occupation reflects level of education, determines income, and influences the type of people with whom someone associates, as well as the products and services bought to perform the occupational role. Other commonly accepted singular yardsticks of social class include an individual's level of formal education and amount or source of income. Education is likely to influence a person's beliefs, values, activities, and opinions. Income determines one's ability to purchase goods and services.[22]

Other sociologists have used possessions and property as indexes of social class.[23] Chapin's Social Status Scale offered a rating scheme for evaluating a family's social class that hinged on the presence of certain furniture items and accessories in the living room (types of floor covering, drapes, fireplace, etc.) and the condition of the room.[24] The quality of the neighborhood where a person lives and the dollar value of his or her residence, although seldom used as sole gauges of an individual's social standing, are useful to verify social class membership that has been assigned on the basis of a single variable such as occupation or income.

Because social class is a truly multidimensional phenomenon and synthesizes many different aspects of people's lifestyle, consumer researchers typically prefer to systematically combine and differentially weigh several socioeconomic measures into an overall index of social class. Such gauges, known as composite-variable indexes, better reflect the complexity of social class than do single-variable indexes. When composite-variable indexes are used, an individual's overall score is computed as a weighted average.

Evaluation criteria such as income source, occupational status, educational level, housing type, and dwelling areas can be rated on a multipoint scale from most to least prestigious or from excellent to poor.[25] For example, when rating income source on a 7-point scale, inherited wealth would be assigned a rating of 1, whereas public relief would receive a rating of 7. Other criteria such as occupation and education level can also be evaluated on multipoint scales.

single-variable indexes
objective measures of social class that employ one socioeconomic factor

composite-variable indexes
Objective measures of social class that combine several socioeconomic factors

Would the Consumer in China Pay $5 for a Big Mac?

The changing class structure in many developing countries due to rising incomes and escalating standards of living have attracted the attention of many U.S.-based businesses that aim to expand their operations abroad. The problem that faces most of them, however, is how to assess the purchasing power in a foreign country and how to determine which class represents a feasible group to pursue. Fortunately, two methods of measuring foreign consumers' income and purchasing power have been developed by economists to help marketers in their pursuits. These methods are the Socioeconomic Strata (SES) system and *Purchasing Power Parity* (PPP) analysis. The logic behind either method is simple: Household income in developing countries does not always equate with the comparatively high household income in the United States, thus restricting the ability of consumers in these countries to pay the same prices for similar goods and services. The fact that standards of living vary significantly from one country to another creates a pricing dilemma for American companies selling globally.

In one application of the SES system, Strategy Research Corporation classified Latino American households based on measures such as the number of durables in the household, employment of domestic servants, and the householder's education level. Based on the SES, the company was able to divide Latino American households into five social classes ranging from the elite at the top, to those society members who are struggling for necessities at the bottom. Similarly, the SES system was employed in a recent study to ascertain value perceived by consumers in Argentina, Brazil, Chile, Colombia, Costa Rica, and Mexico as these individuals considered baskets of retail offerings.

PPP analysis, on the other hand, differs from measures such as household income or GNP per capita. It is based on the cost of a standard *market basket* of products bought in each country expressed in U.S. dollars. For example, one application of the PPP using the fast-food industry as the basis for evaluating Purchasing Power Parity among different countries is called the "Big Mac Index." Using the price of McDonald's Big Mac as the basis for evaluating the food basket reveals that the U.S. price of $5.00 for the sandwich can command a mere $2.00 in China due to lower incomes, but may be sold at $7.50 in Norway where incomes are high. This method, thus, allows marketers to compare the relative price of a product in a particular country to what it would cost in the United States. In this manner, the price for the same product in each country can be estimated in view of the level of purchasing power in that nation. The World Bank now classifies all countries by the PPP system in its annual *World Bank Atlas.*[28]

Finding an easy measure for consumer demand and purchasing power in foreign countries is a familiar problem that most U.S. marketers have to face. To learn more about Purchasing Power Parity (PPP), visit http://www.investopedia.com/updates/purchasing-power-parity-ppp/ *and* http://data.worldbank.org/indicator/PA.NUS.PPP *and learn how PPP is calculated. In your opinion, is overvaluation or undervaluation of currencies with respect to their ability to acquire products a factor that affects the rank of individuals or households on the social class scale? Explain.*

Researchers would also assign each of the socioeconomic factors chosen to measure individuals' social class its own relative weight. For example, subjects' "income source" may be given a higher weight than their "dwelling area." Multiplying each socioeconomic criterion rating by its respective weighting and then summing, produces an individual's overall score. This composite score, in turn, is used to designate the individual's class standing.[26] Interestingly, Zaltman, LeMasters, and Heffring note that it is extremely difficult to define social class by cataloging its components. Although members of a social class and similarities in their attitudes may be influenced by their education levels, occupations, and financial wealth, "social class is not a combination of these factors but a fusion of effects resulting from these and other factors. This fusion becomes a unique entity with its own character that does not resemble any of its contributory factors."[27]

ISSUES RELEVANT TO THE SOCIAL CLASS STRUCTURE IN THE UNITED STATES

Now that we have addressed some of the procedures used by researchers to measure social class, let us shift our attention to some of the issues relevant to the topic. These issues include the changing class stature of women, social class versus income, status crystallization, the over- and underprivileged, and finally the issue of social mobility. We discuss each of these topics in the sections that follow.

The Changing Class Stature of Women

As women's economic clout grows in our society, it is changing the roles of males and females. More women now are participants in the labor force compared with the past four decades. Today, they constitute 47 percent of the total labor force and are projected to compose 51 percent of the total by the year 2018. For example, in 2015, of the 123 million women age sixteen years and above, 72 million (58.6 percent) were participants in the labor force; and among mothers with children under the age of three, 61 percent were in the labor force, as well as 71.1 percent of mothers with children under eighteen years of age.

Concerning the types of occupations that women occupy, they now hold 51 percent of managerial, professional, and technical positions, according to data provided by the U.S. Census Bureau. In some professions, women dominate the workforce. For instance in 2015, 75 percent of all those employed in the education and health services industry were women. Also, the employment rate of women equals that of males in the fields of training, library, arts/design, entertainment, sports, and media.

In terms of educational accomplishment, women today make up almost 60 percent of U.S. college students, and outnumber males in all levels of degrees earned including master's degrees, but parallel the rate for males in earning doctorates. The U.S. Department of Education predicts this achievement trend among women will continue. It represents a steady flow of annual female postsecondary degree recipients—a factor that will have significant ramifications for the composition of the future workforce in the United States.

With regard to the relative pay scale for women, the U.S. Bureau of Labor Statistics indicates that single childless women ages twenty-two to thirty in the majority of U.S. cities now have a higher median income than their male peers. Furthermore in 2015, in families where the both the wife and husband had earnings, the percentage of wives outearning their husbands was over one in three, at 38.1 percent of households (compared with 29 percent in 2012).

As women continue to make up a higher percentage of the workforce, they have increasingly achieved senior executive positions. For example in 2016, the Capitalist Reports listed twenty women who currently hold CEO positions at S&P 500 companies.

Today, women's educational and professional accomplishments have altered the traditional view of social class in our society.

Regarding family matters, data from the Council on Women and Girls indicate that women are marrying later, tend to have fewer children than in the past, and are giving birth to their first child at an older age. In addition, while more adult women live in married-couple families than in any other living arrangement, an ever-growing number of women raise children without a spouse. Concerning longevity, women tend to live longer than men, thus continue to outnumber men in

© Stephen Coburn/Shutterstock.com

the older-age categories. Furthermore, women continue to spend a greater share of their time engaged in household activities or caring for other family members. They also undertake more unpaid volunteer work than men. [29]

Social Class Versus Income

Although it is not uncommon for people to casually equate money with social class, social scientists still ponder the precise nature of the relation-

CONSUMER BEHAVIOR IN PRACTICE

For Richer, for Smarter . . . 'Til Death Do Us Part

America's matrimonial trends clearly indicate that the majority of marriages are between individuals who belong to the same social class. Clearly, individuals feel more comfortable when they are around people who are much like themselves. This phenomenon has been confirmed by looking at how closely a couple's "social ranks" match. Social ranking has been used by sociologists to reflect the extent of a couple's educational attainment—a measure that is less likely to change over time compared with the couple's income.

This trend toward educational homogeneity, or the tendency for men and women with similar educational achievement to marry each other, has had an obvious negative effect on the U.S. marriage rates, and has placed educated women in an adverse position in the matrimonial market. The increased educational attainment of women and their mass entry into the workforce since the 1970s had given them an edge over many eligible males. Today, for example, the number of women who receive a bachelor's or master's degree each year far surpasses the number of men who do so.[30] Since this trend is expected to continue into the future, it simply would indicate that more educated women are and would likely continue to

be available in the nuptial market. And herein lies the problem. Educated women are less likely to be attracted to males who lack comparable educational credentials. Less-educated men are less desirable to women because they do not fit the profile of what a woman looks for in a mate. An attractive companion has to be someone who shares similar interests, values, and views of the world as well as a partner who can make a similar economic contribution to the family.

From a male's point of view, on the other hand, less-educated men tend to feel somewhat threatened by the higher educational accomplishment of their female companion.[31]

Since many single Americans tend to look for marriage partners within their own social class, they often face the problem of infrequent opportunities to socially meet others. Marketers have seized this opportunity by providing dating/mating services to facilitate the task of meeting others online. Many dating websites have now proliferated the Internet, with some boasting membership of millions. Visit the website of one such service at www.e-Harmony.com, *a site that employs twenty-nine personality dimensions of participants to bring about successful matches. In your opinion, to what extent are such services successful in matching similar individuals? Will such services help to enhance or reduce the homogeneity trend in intraclass marriages prevalent in our society today?*

ship between income and other aspects of social class. The fact that some lower-class families earn lofty incomes while some higher-class families remain underprivileged has already been established. Coleman concluded that "class and income are not very well correlated."[32]

A number of authors have addressed the issue of whether social class or income better predicts consumption patterns. Both concepts appear to hold merit, and one is not a substitute for the other.[33] According to Stone, for example, buying decisions are less affected by income than by consumers' reference groups, social class, and cultural influences. Stone noted that the *ability* to buy needs to be distinguished from the *proneness* to buy.[34]

Similarly, Schaninger suggested that social class appears to be a better predictor than income for consumer purchases that require low-to-moderate dollar expenditures, have symbolic value, reflect an underlying lifestyle, or mirror homemaker roles (various food items and beverages, domestic or imported wines, some cosmetic and makeup items).[35] Social class also appears to be more relevant than income for predicting the method and place of purchase for highly visible, symbolic, and more costly items such as living room furniture. Income, on the other hand, appears to be a better predictor than social class in the case of products or activities that require major expenditures and reflect ability to pay. Examples include high-tech electronics, as well as major kitchen and laundry appliances, which are not perceived to be class-linked status symbols. Combined social class and income data, however, appear necessary in order to predict purchases of moderate-to-expensive, highly visible products such as homes, automobiles, electronics, and clothing that serve as symbols of status within a class.

Status Crystallization versus Incongruity

When we attempt to gauge an individual's social class membership, that person's score on one class indicator may or may not concur with his or her standing on other class indicators. Whenever multiple objective criteria are applied to ascertain an individual's social class, researchers often find some degree of inconsistency among the indicators they employ.[36] Consider the case of a truck driver who never finished high school and who lives in a modest home in the older section of town but who earns a very high income. Such an individual would exemplify low-status crystallization, a case known as status incongruity.

Thus, status crystallization refers to the extent to which different indicators of an individual's social stature (income, occupation, education, residence, ethnicity) tend to coincide with one another. As consumer researchers, we are often interested in the exceptions to the phenomenon of status crystallization—incongruities between a consumer's social class standing and his or her consumption-related patterns.

The concepts of status crystallization and incongruity help consumer researchers appraise the impact of inconsistencies on consumption patterns. For instance, in the case of the truck driver mentioned earlier who earns a high income but lives in a modest home, the excess discretionary income may be spent on luxury items such as expensive high-tech electronics, a speedboat, or a fancy automobile or motorcycle.

The Over- and Underprivileged

Popular notions that all members of a given social class have approximately equal income or that individuals' or households' class standing is the consequence of their income are serious fallacies. In fact, significant earning differentials can be observed within every social class. For example, in a recent Pew Research Center's Report on the middle class, four in ten Americans with incomes below $20,000 self-defined themselves as middle class, as did a third of those with incomes above $150,000.[37] Therefore, in addition to categorizing individuals and families by their class standing, we can further pigeonhole members of each class as:

1. fairly average wage earners,
2. those who make considerably more money than the average for their class, and
3. those who make notably less than the average for their class.[38]

Marketers recognize that the purchasing, spending, and consumption patterns of these three subgroups differ according to their relative incomes.[39]

Average individuals and families are those who fall into the middle-income range for their assigned social class. Such households are likely able to afford the residence location, type of home, furniture, appliances, automobiles, clothing, and food, as well as other possessions and services that their class peers might expect. If we were to consider average individuals within present middle class, we would readily observe that their households have been increasingly squeezed by sagging incomes. Declining family income and rising prices have affected their expenditures on various products and services such as food, clothing, housing, medical care, and education. Even though most members of this category have working spouses, reports indicate that even with dual incomes, average middle-class families in recent years tend to spend 32 percent less on clothing, 18 percent less on food, and 52 percent less on appliances compared with their expenditures before the Great Recession.

Those whose income level exceeds the median for their class are said to be the overprivileged. In these households, a good portion of earnings remains as discretionary income after basic necessities have been cared for. In other words, extra money is available to pursue some of the nicer things that life offers. For example, when the iPhone was introduced, it surprised management at Apple to learn that adoption spread over all social classes, and not just the upper social class. The innovators were found to be the overprivileged—those with elevated incomes—in every social class. A similar pattern exists for other product categories, such as luxury automobiles, more expensive home electronics, appliances, and recreational equipment. The market for such items is not restricted to the upper social classes but rather extends to the overprivileged within each class. However, because these households continue to share the values and symbols of other members of their own class, ownership of such niceties does not mean that they are viewed as members of the next higher social class.

overprivileged
households whose incomes exceed the median for their social class

The underprivileged are those individuals and families whose incomes are under the median for their social class. Because the earnings of underprivileged households fall well below the average for their class, these less-affluent households must economize and skimp just to afford the products and services that other members of their class deem proper and appropriate. Similarly, if we were to consider an underprivileged family within the present middle class, we would readily observe that it is financially difficult for such a household to make ends meet.

underprivileged
households whose incomes are below the median for their social class

Social Mobility

More than any other country in the world, the United States exhibits an *open class system*. In other words, individuals are not frozen into a fixed position along a social continuum by nature of their birth. Rather, it is possible to rise from rock bottom to top positions in industry and government. Because people are influenced by their socialization as children as well as by their present or aspired-to class standing, those who study the impact of social class on consumer behavior should take into account both individuals' past and present socioeconomic statuses.[40]

A study by Shimp and Yokum revealed a clear pattern of upward mobility (movement toward higher class membership) in U.S. society.[41] Nearly two-thirds of the households examined in this study included a spouse who had achieved higher social stature than his or her parents. In the meantime, social status remained the same for 25 percent of respondents and fell for a mere 8 percent. Most social mobility tends to be intergenerational (it occurs between generations) and is limited to the immediately adjacent social classes. In other words, children in a family may acquire slightly higher social standing than their parents. The parents, in turn, may have gained slightly higher standing than the grandparents.

Many people aspire to higher classes than they currently occupy. Higher strata serve as reference groups for those who have lesser standing but are on the move. Education, occupation, achievement, talent, and sometimes marriage are among the forces that propel upward mobility. Consider, for example, the cases of the late Steve Jobs, his successor Tim Cook, Bill Gates, and Mark Zuckerberg, who progressed from mere computer enthusiasts to heads of three of the largest companies in the world. Think about Ray Kroc, who leaped from being a modest salesman to the highest echelons of McDonald's; and Walt Disney, who advanced from an animation novice to the pinnacle of the world's largest entertainment empire.

The dynamic nature of an open class system is usually viewed in terms of upward social mobility. Wanting it all is a hallmark of the middle class, and many members of this group buy products with the symbols and allure of elevated status. Occasional splurging and treating oneself to the best are ways that consumers set themselves apart from their peers and bolster their self-image. Consequently, ads for top-of-the line products are often designed to be sensual, provocative, and elegant.[42]

Unfortunately, open class systems also mean that families or individuals can tumble on the social ladder, and some downward mobility has been observed in recent years. Due to a bleak job market, many members of Generation Y have been finding it difficult to secure entry-level employment that relates to their college degree or vocational training.[43] Many of those who have college degrees are now holding jobs that are unrelated to their training or which did not require a college diploma. Some of these young people in the United States are thus in danger of dropping out of the middle class.[44]

THE IMPACT OF SOCIAL CLASS ON CONSUMER BEHAVIOR

Characteristics that distinguish the various social classes also influence their behavior as consumers. Understanding the psychological differences between classes as well as the differences in their lifestyles can help marketers design effective strategies targeted to specific socioeconomic groups. This concluding section cites a number of generalizations regarding tendencies of the various classes and suggests likely influences on consumption. Although idiosyncrasies can be observed in the situations faced by specific individuals and households within a class, these general inclinations have important implications for marketers in terms of segmentation, targeting, and positioning.

While some product categories, such as purely functional staples like detergents and paper products, are classless, many of the more expensive and fashionable possessions that people own, like home furnishings and apparel, *are* expressions of class. Purchasing patterns are therefore likely to vary across social strata.

One indicator of class membership is income, which largely determines the types, quantity, and quality of products and services that consumers in a particular class can afford. For example, relative to its size, the upper class consumes a disproportionate share of services compared with the middle and lower classes.

Other gauges of social class, such as education and occupation, also appear to affect shoppers in terms of what they contemplate when evaluating and selecting products as well as how they gauge the social acceptability of merchandise. Clothing, for example, has always been a peculiarly resonant class symbol.[45] Members of various classes differ in what they regard to be in good taste or fashionable. Lower-middle-class consumers seem to like apparel items that offer an external point of identification. In this sense, they constitute prime targets for licensed goods, such as T-shirts and caps that bear the names of famous celebrities and athletes, admired organizations, and valued company trademarks. Upper-class consumers, on the other hand, prefer clothing that has a more subtle look and is free of supporting associations.

No retail store can equally appeal to all shoppers. Retailers like Nordstrom successfully target consumers in the upper and upper-middle classes.

Social class also influences shoppers' retail store choices. It is unlikely that any given store could simultaneously cater to all classes. For example, a study that dealt with shopping behavior and store avoidance of different social classes revealed that Kmart was seen as appealing to lower- and lower-middle-class customers, whereas Nordstrom was seen as appealing mainly to upper- and upper-middle-class consumers.[46] The relationship between social class and willingness to buy store brands is well established. Higher social class individuals tend to prefer national brands compared with middle classes, which tend to experiment with store brands.

Saving, investing, spending, and credit card usage patterns also seem to relate to social class. Higher-status consumers tend to be future oriented and confident in their financial discernment. They are willing to invest in insurance, stocks, and real estate. Lower-class consumers, on the other hand, tend to be interested in immediate gratification. Use of credit cards also differs according to social class. Whereas upper-status consumers use credit cards as an expedient substitute for cash, underclass consumers view credit as an indispensable means of fulfilling urgent needs that otherwise they could not afford to satisfy at the moment.

Social class additionally influences the recreational activities that people engage in during their leisure time. Upper-class consumers attend the theater, opera, and concerts; play polo and squash; and go to college football games. Playing golf, tennis, and racquetball are middle- to upper-class activities. Lower-class pastimes include watching TV, playing bingo, fishing, baseball, bowling, pool and billiards, and frequenting taverns, professional wrestling matches, and monster truck events.

Moreover, social class is assumed to have a bearing on consumers' media habits. Recognizing media-exposure and lifestyle differences between social classes can help advertisers allocate the advertising budget between various forms of traditional and electronic media, as well as select appropriate ad appeals. In ad messages, the appeal to class aspirations can be either subtle, as in ads from Ralph Lauren, or blatant, as in ads from Abercrombie & Fitch.

Psychological disparities between the classes regarding perceptions of the world may account for many of the dissimilarities in their consumption behaviors. Lower-status individuals, for instance, tend to have a rural identification, focus on the immediate past, and exhibit limited horizons. Members of the middle class, in contrast, tend to have an urban identification, focus on the future, have a broader view of the world, describe their experiences from diverse perspectives, and see themselves tied to global happenings.

We have observed that the social class structure in the United States is markedly different compared with that found in older societies. The unique values and beliefs held by members of our society regarding what determines an individual's standing in the class hierarchy largely explains our social class structure. These values and beliefs are integral parts of culture—aspects that determine how consumers in a society tend to think, feel, and act. The important influence of culture and its effect on consumer behavior are topics covered in the next chapter.

SUMMARY

Social classes are permanent status categories within a social system. Each class is an aggregate of people with similar socioeconomic positions, values, and behavioral patterns. Between the various social classes, sharp economic, social, and psychological disparities can be observed. Marketers' interest in social class stems from the fact that it provides a basis for segmenting and targeting markets.

Certain factors such as egalitarianism, the size of the middle class, opportunities for social mobility, and confusion of income with class membership obscure the recognition of divergent U.S. social classes. Unlike more rigid societies, countries like the United States exhibit a series of *status continua*. The class structure of the United States is evolving. A growing gap separates the affluent from everyone else. Both the higher and lower earnings groups are expanding.

Social class can be measured by employing subjective, reputational, or objective methods. Studies that follow an objective approach can use single-variable or composite-variable indexes to measure social class. Other relevant social class issues discussed include the changing class stature of women and status crystallization—the extent to which different indicators of an individual's social stature concur. In addition, every class has average, overprivileged, and underprivileged members. Significant differences in earnings and consumption patterns characterize these subgroups.

The United States exhibits an open class system, in which both upward and downward social mobility are possible. Most social mobility is intergenerational and limited to the immediately adjacent classes. Education, occupation, achievement, talent, and marriage can precipitate upward mobility. In recent years, some downward mobility has been observed.

Social class has a bearing on shopping and consumption patterns such as product and service choices; retail shopping and store selection; saving, investing, spending, and credit; as well as recreation and leisure activities.

Walmart Chases the Affluent

This case is about a meeting held by a top management group at Walmart's Corporate Headquarters to address merchandising and other policies for a new store that the firm was planning to open in Evergreen, Colorado. Evergreen is a town of upper-middle-class residents, consisting mainly of doctors, engineers, and other professionals whose income was double the national average. This move reflected a new Walmart strategy of locating stores in upscale, ritzy suburbs—a striking departure from the company's traditional philosophy of operating folksy, down-home stores designed with the working class in mind. As the committee members debated over store layout, as well as its merchandising strategy, a disturbing issue arose. Since the operating costs of such a store were expected to be exceptionally high, its profit margin would subsequently suffer drastically in view of Walmart's low-price strategy followed nationally.

Notes

1   Geraldine Trembath, "Uppercrust Brittania," *Hemispheres* (April 1996), pp. 66–71.
2   J. H. Myers and Jonathan Guttman, "Life Style: The Essence of Social Class," in William Wells (Ed.), *Lifestyle and Psychographics* (Chicago: American Marketing Association, 1974), pp. 235–256.
3   James E. Fisher, "Social Class and Consumer Behavior: The Relevance of Class and Status," in Melanie Wallendorf and Paul Anderson (Eds.), *Advances in Consumer Research 14* (Provo, UT: Association for Consumer Research, 1987), pp. 492–496.
4   T. Schjelderup-Ebbe, "Social Behavior of Birds," in C. Murchison (Ed.), *A Handbook of Social Psychology* (Worcester, MA: Clark University Press, 1935).
5   Al Ries and Jack Trout, *Positioning: The Battle for Your Mind* (New York: McGraw-Hill, 1981), p. 53.
6   Daniel W. Rossides, *Social Stratification* (Upper Saddle River, NJ: Prentice Hall, 1990).
7   Max Weber, in H. H. Gard and C. Wright Mills (Eds.), *From Max Weber: Essays in Sociology* (New York: Oxford University Press, 1946).
8   Fisher, "Social Class and Consumer Behavior: The Relevance of Class and Status."

9   Rebecca Piirto Heath, "The New Working Class," *American Demographics* (January 1998), pp. 51–55.

10 "Hilton Hotels & Resorts Named Best Hotel Chain by Executive Travel Readers," *Reuters* (July 9, 2008), www.reuters.com/article/pressRelease/i/US91869+09-Jul-2008+BW20080709.

11 Fisher, "Social Class and Consumer Behavior: The Relevance of Class and Status."

12 Philip A. Klein, "Institutionalists, Radical Economists, and Class," *Journal of Economic Issues* 16, no. 2 (June 1992), pp. 535–545.

13 William Thompson and Joseph Hickey, *Society in Focus* (Boston, MA: Pearson, 2005); Dennis Gilbert, *The American Class Structure: In an Age of Growing Inequality* (Belmont, CA: Wadsworth, 2002).

14 Pew Research Center, "The American Middle Class Is Losing Ground" (December 9, 2015), http://www.pewsocialtrends.org/2015/12/09/the-american-middle-class-is-losing-ground/; "Class Structure in the US: Models of US Social Classes," Boundless.com, https://www.boundless.com/sociology/textbooks/boundless-sociology-textbook/stratification-inequality-and-social-class-in-the-u-s-9/the-class-strcuture-in-the-usa; U.S. Census Bureau, "Income and Poverty in the United States: 2014."

15 The Annual World Wealth Report 2015, "North America High Net Worth Investment Individuals"; Robert Frank, "Record Number of Millionaires Living in the US," *CNBC* (March 7, 2016), http://www.cnbc.com/2016/03/07/record-number-of-millionaires-living-in-the-us.html; Robert Frank, "More Millionaires Than Ever Are Living in the US," *CNMC* (March 10, 2015), http://www.cnbc.com/2015/03/09/more-millionaires-than-ever-are-living-in-the-us.html.

16 Gillian B. White, "America's Poverty Problem Hasn't Changed," *The Atlantic* (September 16, 2015), http://www.theatlantic.com/business/archive/2015/09/americas-poverty-problem/405700/; Juliette Cubanski, Jiselle Casillas, and Anthony Damico, "Poverty Among Seniors: An Updated Analysis of National and State Level Poverty Rates Under the Official and Supplemental Poverty Measures," KFF.org (June 10, 2015), and http://kff.org/medicare/issue-brief/poverty-among-seniors-an-updated-analysis-of-national-and-state-level-poverty-rates-under-the-official-and-supplemental-poverty-measures.

17 Joaquim Moreira Salles, "The Wealth Gap Between Rich and Poor Is the Widest Ever Recorded," *Think Progress*, (December 18, 2014), http://thinkprogress.org/economy/2014/12/18/3605137/us-wealth-gap-at-its-widest-in-decades/; Dr. Andrew Chamberlain, "CEO to Worker Pay Ratios: Average CEO Earns 204 Times Median Worker Pay," A Glassdoor Economic Research Blog (August 25, 2015), https://www.glassdoor.com/research/ceo-pay-ratio/; "Chief Executive Officer (CEO) Salary (United States), http://www.payscale.com/research/US/job=Chief_Excecutive_Officer_(CEO)/salary; Nathaniel Popper, "C.E.O. Pay Is Rising Despite the Din," *The New York Times* (April 8, 2012), http://www.nytimes.com/2012/06/17/business/executive-pay-still-climbing-despite-a-shareholder-din.html?pagewanted=all;

Charles Riley, "Government Freezes GM CEO's Pay," *CNN Money* (April 6, 2012), http://money.cnn.com/2012/04/06/news/economy/treasury-gm-pay/index.htm; Bob Ettenhoff, "GuideStar Releases Free Report Defining Rules Governing Nonprofit Executive Compensation," *GuideStar* (September 22, 2011), http://www.globenewswire.com/newsroom/news.html?d=233083 and http://www.guidestar.org/rxa/news/news-releases/2011/free-guidestar-report-on-nonprofit-executive-compensation-rules.aspx; Craig A. Adoor et al., "Impacts of the Dodd-Frank Wall Street Reform and Consumer Protection Act on Executive Compensation in Corporate Governance," Husch Blackwell LLC (August 5, 2010), http://www.huschblackwell.com/impacts-of-the-dodd-frank-act-on-executive-compensation-and-corporate-governance/.

18 Renee O'Farrell, "Rise of the Dollar Stores: Three Undervalued Picks," Examiner.com (May 14, 2012), http://www.examiner.com/article/rise-of-the-dollar-stores-3-undervalued-picks-1.

19 Dan Schiller, "Marketing on the Net," *Le Monde Diplomatique* (November 1997), http://mondediplo.com/1997/11/internet.

20 Ibid.

21 Roshawan Watson, "The Impossible Question: Just Who Is the Middle Class?" *Watson Inc.* (February 10, 2011), http://www.roshawnwatson.com/impossible-question-just-who-is-middle/.

22 Rebecca Gardyn, "The Mating Game," *American Demographics* (July–August 2002), p. 34.

23 Janeen Arnold Costa and Russell W. Belk, "Nouveaux Riches as Quintessential Americans: Case Studies of Consumption in an Extended Family," *Advances in Nonprofit Marketing* 3 (Greenwich, CT: JAI Press, 1990), pp. 83–140.

24 F. Stuart Chapin, *Contemporary American Institutions* (New York: Harper, 1935), pp. 373–397.

25 Warner, Meeker, Eells, *Social Class in America: A Manual of Procedure for the Measurement of Social Status*; A. B. Hollingshead and F. C. Redlich, *Social Class and Mental Illness* (New York: John Wiley, 1958), p. 394; *Methodology and Scores of Socioeconomic Status*, Working Paper No. 15 (Washington, DC: U. S. Bureau of the Census, 1963); Coleman, "The Continuing Significance of Social Class to Marketing."

26 Ibid.

27 Sak Onkvisit and John J. Shaw, *International Marketing: Analysis and Strategy*, 2nd ed. (New York: Macmillan, 1993), p. 341.

28 B. A. Hamilton, "Creating Value in Retailing for Emerging Consumers: Breaking the Myths About Emerging Consumers," *The Coca-Cola Retailing Research Council Latin America* (May 1, 2003); Guillermo D'Andrea et al., "Breaking the Myth on Emerging Consumers in Retailing," *International Journal of Retail and Distribution Management* 34, no. 9 (2006), pp. 674–687.

29 U.S. Dept. of Labor Women's Bureau, "Data and Statistics: Women in the Labor Force," http://www.dol.gov/wb/stats/stats_data.htm; Anna Sutherland, "Why Do More Women Than Men Go to College?" *National Review* (October 14, 2015), http://www.nationalreview.com/article/425506/

gender-gap-college-fatherless-households; Mona Chalabi, "38 Percent of Women Earn More Than Their Husbands," *538.com* (February 8, 2015), http://538.com/datalab/38-percent-of-women-earn-more-than-their-husbands/; Ali Meyer, "Wives Earn More Than Husbands in 1 in 3 Families in US," *CNS New.com* (November 18, 2014), cnsnews.com; "Women in America: Indicators of Social and Economic Well-being," *Council on Women and Girls*, http://www.whitehouse.gov/administration/eop/cwg/data-on-women.

30 Liza Mundy, "Women, Money, and Power," *Time* (March 26, 2012), pp. 26–34.

31 Rebecca Gardyn, "The Mating Game," *American Demographics* (July–August 2002), p. 34.

32 Coleman, "The Continuing Significance of Social Class to Marketing," p. 273.

33 Charles M. Schaninger, "Social Class Versus Income Revisited: An Empirical Investigation," *Journal of Marketing Research* 18 (May 1985), pp. 192–208; Louis V. Dominquez and Albert L. Page, "Stratification in Consumer Behavior Research: A Re-examination," *Journal of the Academy of Marketing Science* 9 (Summer 1981), pp. 250–271.

34 Bob Stone, *Successful Direct Marketing Methods*, 2nd ed. (Chicago: Crain Books, 1979), p. 98.

35 Schaninger, "Social Class Versus Income Revisited: An Empirical Investigation."

36 Yoram Wind, "Incongruency of Socioeconomic Variables and Buying Behavior," in Philip R. McDonald (Ed.), *Proceedings of the Educators' Conference Series No. 30* (Chicago: American Marketing Association, 1969), pp. 362–367.

37 "Inside the Middle Class: Bad Times Hit the Good Life," *Pew Research Center* (April 9, 2008), http://pewsocialfriends.org/pubs/706/middle-class-poll.

38 Coleman, "The Continuing Significance of Social Class to Marketing."

39 Elizabeth Warren, "The New Economics of Middle Class: Why Making Ends Meet Has Gotten Harder," *Harvard Law School* (May 10, 2007); Elizabeth Warren, "A 2007 Filmed Presentation," www.youtube.com/watch?v=akVL7QY0S8A.

40 George P. Moschis and Gilbert A. Churchill, "Consumer Socialization: A Theoretical and Empirical Analysis," *Journal of Marketing Research* 15 (November 1978), pp. 599–609; Shimp and Yokum, "Extensions of the Basic Social Class Model Employed in Consumer Research."

41 Shimp and Yokum, "Extensions of the Basic Social Class Model Employed in Consumer Research."

42 Jaclyn Fierman, "The High-Living Middle Class," *Fortune* 115 (April 13, 1987), p. 27.

43 Lawrence Mischel and Elise Gould, "Inhospitable Job Market to Greet College Graduates," *Economic Policy Institute* (May 14, 2008), www.epi.org/content.cfm/webfeatures_snapshots_20080514.

44 Katherine S. Newman, "No Room for the Young," *New York Times* (May 16, 1993), p. E17.

45 Labich, "Class in America."

46 John P. Dickson and Douglas L. MacLachlan, "Social Distance and Shopping Behavior," *Journal of the Academy of Marketing Science*, 18, no. 2 (Spring 1990), pp. 153–161.

CHAPTER 14

CULTURE AND SUBCULTURES

LEARNING OBJECTIVES

- To grasp the meaning of culture and the way it is learned by the members of a society.
- To become cognizant of the five dimensions of culture proposed by Hofstede.
- To examine ten sociocultural dimensions proposed by Harris and Moran.
- To probe the concept of subcultures and recognize its importance in segmenting markets.
- To identify three major ethnic subcultures in the United States and examine their characteristics and purchasing patterns.
- To become cognizant of consumption subcultures.
- To explore marketing implications of culture and subcultures.

KEY TERMS

culture	direct questioning	term orientation
socialization	content analysis	values
enculturation	key informants	means—end chains
acculturation	power distance	norms
cultural lag	uncertainty avoidance	subcultures
ethnocentrism	individualism	rituals
ethnography	masculinity	

Historically, the American way of life has encroached on Europe for generations. Restaurants such as McDonald's and Pizza Hut, brands such as Nike and Disney, and American-made motion pictures, TV soaps, and news shows have found their way to major cities as well as many living rooms throughout Europe.

Although many Europeans were originally impressed and even fascinated by American novelties, stores, and shows, the appeal of these things seems to have waned, and sentiments in recent years seem to have taken the opposite direction. Many Europeans have started to fear that the American way of life is about to overtake their culture and rob them of their own rich heritage. Seeing that they are inundated with American expressions, products, and ideas, they are fearful that they may wake up one day and find themselves conforming to the American way of life.

Major differences exist between the mentalities of Europeans and Americans. The American mindset is sometimes described as a *Swatch-watch* mentality, accustomed to produce a product that is functional, appears attractively styled, sells for an affordable price, and has a relatively short product life. For a veteran German craftsman, whose exactitude and expertise are the culmination of many years of formal training and apprenticeship, the American outlook is viewed as lamentable.

Many differences in lifestyle also exist. In some European countries such as Germany, France, Norway, and Sweden, workers continue to receive high wages and extensive employee benefit packages. For example, in Germany, they are entitled to at least six weeks of vacation every year. Long lunch breaks and midday shop closings remain customary in Italy, Spain, and parts of France. In Germany, shops throughout the country close at 8:00 P.M. on weekdays and 4:00 P.M. on Saturdays. Stores are never open on Sundays. Such hours and high wages are customary in Europe and are perceived as entitlements.

Countries are taking a number of steps in an effort to preserve their cultural integrity and protect it from the American cultural invasion. A few years ago, Canada called together nineteen other governments to devise ways to ensure their cultural independence from the United States. Mexico is considering legislation requiring that a major percentage of its media programming remains in the hands of its citizens. In the arena of films, TV, and news, the governments in Britain, France, and Germany have designed programs to stabilize and promote homegrown films. There is also an obvious trend away from buying American TV services. In addition, many products—replicas of their American counterparts—have been developed in Europe as a defense against the flood of U.S. goods.[1]

An obvious trend in recent years is the growing negative sentiments on the part of consumers in many foreign countries toward U.S. products, stores, and programs. Learn about two cultures, the United Kingdom and Canada, by visiting http://www.odci.gov/cia/publications/factbook/docs/faqs.html. Simply click your mouse on each of the two nations in the menu provided. What cultural forces underlie resentment toward American products abroad? In your opinion, what strategies should U.S. marketers adopt to ease these feelings?

In this chapter, we deal with the issues of culture and subcultures. We broaden the scope of analysis and consider the marketing implications of cultural similarities and differences that prevail in world markets. We further investigate consumer behavior in a cultural setting and address issues such as values and modes of thinking and behaving. We also deal with similarities and dissimilarities in African, Hispanic, and Asian-American subcultures and investigate the impact of these characteristics on consumption behavior.

THE MEANING OF CULTURE

There are over 200 definitions of *culture* proposed by writers in the field. Although they are beneficial in profiling a culture, most of these definitions are broadly based and lack the specificity needed by marketers. Unlike sociologists and anthropologists, marketers are mainly interested in discovering those elements of culture that influence the patterns of consumer behavior for a particular product or service within a specific society. For example, devout Muslims do not partake of alcoholic beverages. Pork is not consumed by adherents of the Jewish and Islamic faiths, and beef is not eaten in the Hindu tradition. Western cultures tend to emphasize youth, whereas traditional Eastern societies hold persons of advanced age in high esteem. Such knowledge can be translated into culturally sensitive marketing strategies. For example, canned-meat processors can sell nonpork products and breweries can sell nonalcoholic beer in the Middle East.

For the purposes of this book, culture may be defined as a society's distinctive and learned mode of living, interacting, and responding to environmental stimuli. This mode is shared and transmitted between members. As people live with one another in a society, interaction between them

culture
a society's distinctive and learned mode of living, interacting, and responding to environmental stimuli

requires them to adjust to the social environment. Modes of conduct, standards of performance, and systems of dealing with interpersonal and environmental relations are established to ensure harmony and growth. Within this process, certain values and behaviors emerge as helpful and desirable whereas others appear to be ineffective or even harmful. The first are shared and rewarded, and the latter are discouraged or even punished. Thus, it can be said that culture functions to establish, enforce, and transmit group norms and values.

HOW IS CULTURE LEARNED?

socialization
the process by which we acquire knowledge to function productively in society

Standards of acceptable behavior are shared and passed along from one generation to the next in a continuation of the cultural heritage. The process by which individuals learn the norms and values of a culture is referred to as socialization. More specifically, socialization refers to the process by which individuals acquire the knowledge, skills, morals, and ethics necessary to function as productive members of a society. Cultural learning occurs in a variety of ways, including living in the family environment, formal schooling, observing and imitating the behavior of others who serve as role models, and simply interacting with other people within the society, either personally or online. Within the United States, the sharing of cultural norms and values is facilitated by such factors as a common language, schools, and places of worship, as well as the Internet and other types of mass media and advertising.

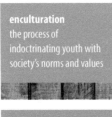

enculturation
the process of indoctrinating youth with society's norms and values

acculturation
the process of learning the norms, values, and behaviors of a different culture

From early childhood, we begin to absorb the norms, values, and behaviors deemed appropriate by our culture. The process of indoctrinating youth with the norms and values of a society is often referred to as enculturation. On the other hand, some individuals, for one reason or another, leave the society in which they were born and raised and take up residence in another culture. Such persons need to assimilate the norms, values, and behaviors of an unfamiliar culture. The term acculturation is often applied to the process of learning the norms, values, and behaviors of a culture different from that in which individuals were brought up.

Culture includes both material and abstract elements. Tangible aspects of a culture include its tools, technologies, architecture, currency, and works of art. Intangible aspects include religion, knowledge, traditions, ideals, and language. Culture provides the language in which people communicate with others and in which they ponder their most private thoughts.

GLOBAL OPPORTUNITY

When the Gift Box Is More Valuable Than Its Contents

Among the cultural values that people learn are those that deal with appropriate behavioral patterns. The universal practice of gift giving presents an interesting case. A recent study compared how Americans and the Japanese give gifts. The study revealed that most gift purchases in Japan take place in department or specialty stores that have an upscale market image, carry well-known brand names, and are fashionable places from which to buy. For Americans, being practical and more value oriented prompts many to include other outlets on the list such as discount stores, and food and drugstores.

Gift packaging and wrapping were also found to be of extreme importance by the Japanese compared with their American counterparts. Gift packaging and wrapping are so important in Japan that the package, in many cases, is more significant than the actual gift inside. Aware of this fact, Japanese product manufacturers often concentrate more effort on package design than on product contents.

Regarding the occasions on which gifts are given, over half of the gifts given by U.S. families are given during religious holidays such as Christmas and Easter. Other occasions for gift giving include family celebrations such as birthdays and anniversaries. In Japan, only 17 percent of the gifts are given during religious holidays. However, 32 percent of the gifts given during *Ochugen* and *Osebo* seasons in early summer and at yearend, are primarily for reciprocal giving between employers and employees. This is a direct result of the social- or work-group orientation of much Japanese gift giving.

Another issue in the study dealt with the value of the gift, which is an indication of the amount of respect or admiration one has for the receiver of the gift. Almost every Japanese person is brought up to be highly conscious of doing favors, which literally signifies one's honor to another. Conversely, in the United States, businesspeople fear that such a gift, particularly to superiors, may be misinterpreted and considered a form of a bribe or a means of flattery. Such concerns prevent many businesspeople from offering gifts or, at least, are factors in reducing their frequency or value.[2]

Cultural traditions influence what consumers consider appropriate as a gift, how much to pay for it, and where to buy it. Learn more about how Japanese traditions are being transmitted from one generation to the next by visiting http://www. japancorner.com/customs_traditions.asp. *In your opinion, what factors influence the formation of cultural traditions? How should marketers address the fact that foreign traditions often differ from our own? Explain using specific examples.*

Humans cannot think without language. Languages tend to vary across cultures, with many—but not all—being exclusive to a specific culture. Greek, for example, is spoken primarily in the Hellenic culture. English, on the other hand, is spoken in the U.S., Canadian, British, Irish, South African, New Zealand, and Australian cultures, among others.

Interestingly, the tangible and intangible components of a culture do not necessarily evolve at the same pace. Whereas mechanical and technical traits of a culture can mature quite rapidly, ideological traits of a culture tend to change more slowly. In recent years, breakthroughs in the fields of medicine and information systems, for example, have occurred so rapidly that we cannot possibly keep abreast of, take advantage of, or accept all the advances. In some cases, issues of morality and ethics have not had an opportunity to catch up and address what is right and wrong. A consequence of this unevenness in the pace of change can be friction among the components of a society, sometimes referred to as cultural lag. Cultural lag is the delay between the time that technological innovations are made available and the time the public accepts and makes use of them or rejects them and limits their use.

cultural lag
the time delay between the introduction of innovations and their acceptance

CULTURAL SENSITIVITY VERSUS ETHNOCENTRISM

In today's diverse culture, we must be able to understand, accept, and respect the views and actions of others, even though these views and actions may markedly differ from our own. Ethnocentrism refers to the tendency to make cross-cultural evaluations on the basis of prereflective beliefs and values that are rooted in one's own culture. Culture determines the way people think, feel, and act. As such, it becomes the lens through which individuals judge the world. Cultural programming can act as a sort of blinder to other people's ways of thinking, feeling, or acting. In other words, one's own views tend to become the *only* natural way to function in the world. The rest of the world is viewed through this cultural lens.[3] Ethnocentrism, per se, is not morally wrong. Its dangers become apparent, however, when individuals make cross-cultural judgments on the basis of such myopic beliefs. In doing so, one in effect declares the superiority of his or her own group above all others. Herein lie the perils of misunderstanding those who hold different views or perspectives. These different beliefs, attitudes, and behavior of people from other cultures can thus be perceived as wrong or somehow inappropriate.[4]

ethnocentrism
the tendency to make cross-cultural evaluations based on one's own beliefs and values

A recent case that reflects ethnocentrism is demonstrated by the feeling among the Japanese regarding the superiority of their domestically grown rice. The Japanese had always believed that their rice was unparalleled by that grown elsewhere. To the Japanese, domestic rice is sacred and represents the soul of the nation. A few years ago, when adverse weather conditions in Japan were predicted to cause a 10 percent shortage in the rice crop, panic ensued. In anticipation of the expected shortages, politicians suggested as a solution that domestic rice be blended with imported rice. As a consequence of this proposal, it was feared that there would be riots, hoarding of domestic rice, and even thefts. The emperor was enlisted to ease the predicted crisis; the Imperial Household Agency announced that he had consented "to eat foreign rice mixed with Japanese rice" and had survived. Fortunately for the Japanese, the "Great Rice Crisis" did not materialize. The rice crop was adequate to meet the demand.[5]

HOW TO ASSESS CULTURE

Culture can be studied in a number of different ways. Attempts to assess culture have employed such techniques as ethnography, direct questioning, content analysis, and consulting with key informants. Ethnography is the study of culture by observation. Anthropologists have been known to live in a foreign culture for lengths of time and unobtrusively scrutinize it from within.[6] Marketers sometimes observe shopping behavior or product-usage patterns abroad in order to determine the likelihood that their products will sell in these cultures. When attempting to sell cereal in Russia, Kellogg's observed what Russians customarily ate for breakfast. The firm discovered that cereal was seldom on the menu. Therefore, Kellogg's advertising had to help Russians form a new association and teach them a new dietary habit.

ethnography
the study of culture by unobtrusive observation

Direct questioning, a second method of studying culture, entails constructing and administering questionnaires that relate to the likelihood of product purchase and use. For example, in the Middle East, Nivea circulated a questionnaire to determine whether or not people sunbathed, how often they did so, and what people used to protect their skin from the rays of the sun. The company found a negative correlation between desire for beauty and tanning. In other words, appearance-conscious consumers tended to spend less time in the sun.

direct questioning
the study of culture through research questionnaires

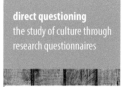

content analysis
the study of culture by reviewing its media or literature

key informants
individuals who are knowledgeable about a culture of interest

power distance
the degree to which society's members accept unequal power distribution

Content analysis, a third method of studying culture, entails attempting to assess cultural practices and values by reviewing the media or literature coming out of a society and searching for recurrent themes. Finally, marketers could consult with key informants who are familiar with the culture of interest. Key informants are knowledgeable persons, such as expatriates, who have lived in a foreign country for an extended period of time. Other examples of key informants include members of the diplomatic or commercial corps, as well as consulate and embassy personnel.

HOFSTEDE'S CULTURAL DIMENSIONS

From the perspective of consumer behavior, in order for us to analyze cultures in a meaningful manner, we must identify a number of sociocultural dimensions. Geert Hofstede, a Dutch researcher, has identified five cultural dimensions that help explain how and why people from various cultures behave as they do.[7] These dimensions are power distance, uncertainty avoidance, individualism, masculinity, and term orientation.

Power Distance

Power distance is the degree to which less-powerful members of a society accept the fact that power is not distributed equally. Societies in which people obey authority without question are labeled *high power distance* cultures. In *low power distance* cultures, on the other hand, people are seen as equals. Members of such societies place a great deal of value on independence and individuality. Hofstede found that many Latin American and Asian countries were typified by high power distance, whereas countries like the United States, Canada, and many European nations exhibited moderate to low power distance.

The effect of this dimension on consumer behavior can be observed in many areas, particularly in the areas of decision making and promotional strategies. In high power distance cultures, family decision making tends to be autocratic or paternalistic. Family members are inclined to obey the recommendations of the authority figure in the household. In promotions, the use of referents and authority figures in advertising can prove to be a highly successful strategy. Consumers in high power distance cultures value conformity and tend to behave as they are told. Conversely, in low power distance cultures, decisions are made after consulting with others.

Conviction of merits rather than blind obedience is the main motivation underlying behavior.

Uncertainty Avoidance

Uncertainty avoidance is the extent to which people feel threatened by ambiguous situations and have created institutions and beliefs for minimizing or averting uncertainty. People in societies characterized by *high uncertainty avoidance* attempt to reduce risk and attain security by developing systems and methods for dealing with ambiguity. They place significant trust in experts and their knowledge. Examples include Germany, Japan, and Spain. In such countries, many beliefs are formulated and rules or regulations are passed to ensure that people know what they are to do. High anxiety, stress, and concern with security characterize people who live in these societies. Conversely, in *low uncertainty avoidance* societies, such as Denmark, people have less of a need for structuring their activities and are willing to assume greater risk. They accept the uncertainty associated with the unknown and the notion that life must continue despite ambiguity and risk.

Uncertainty avoidance has applicability to consumer behavior and marketing in the areas of diffusion and adoption as well as branding, labeling, and channel strategy. The extent to which a culture is willing to try or accept new products and novel ideas is a function of the degree of uncertainty avoidance prevalent in that particular culture. Consumers in high uncertainty avoidance cultures are reluctant to accept innovations. The tendency of these consumers to prefer established brands, shop at well-known outlets, and seek information-laden product labels reflects their lower tolerance for accepting risk. Consumers in low uncertainty avoidance cultures, on the other hand, tend to perceive little or no risk in the purchase of new products and are much more likely to make innovative purchases than consumers who perceive a great deal of risk. The ad in Figure 14.1 from the LIFE Foundation emphasizes uncertainty avoidance by stressing the fact that this type of insurance is for the protection of the family members left behind after a loved one passes on.

Individualism

Individualism is the tendency of people to look after themselves and their immediate family only.[8] This dimension is the antithesis of *collectivism*, which is the tendency of people to belong to groups that look after each

uncertainty avoidance
the degree to which people feel threatened by ambiguity and uncertainty

individualism
a tendency of people to look after themselves and their immediate family only

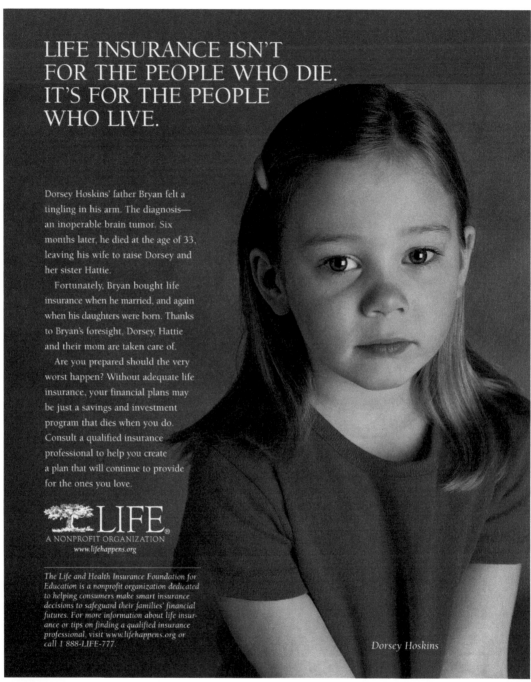

FIGURE 14.1

This ad from the LIFE Foundation emotionally depicts the foresight of a father who preserved the financial status of his family by purchasing life insurance before passing.

Helping Barbara Sullivan
live her American Dream

Before she had a third grade class, she had her own little "homeroom" of two girls and a boy. And somehow she's managed to treat them all with the same love and care.

For over 50 years, we've put our retirement and pension products to work to help make sure the American Dream has been safe and secure for the men and women who work so hard to make all our lives better. And the families they come home to.

401(k)
403(b)
457
ANNUITIES
TDA
RETIREMENT PLANS
LIFE INSURANCE

But we're not about to stop now. We've done our homework, and come up with programs that offer a serious choice of products. All without front-end charges, withdrawal fees or transfer charges,* from a local salaried consultant you get to know by name and who has a personal and professional interest in the financial well being of those we serve. For more information call us at **1-800-468-3785** or visit our web site at *www.mutualofamerica.com*

People like Barbara teach us lessons about hard work every day. Which is why it's so important that our programs score high marks.

MUTUAL OF AMERICA
the spirit of America

FIGURE 14.2

This ad from Mutual of America employs an other-directed approach. It informs the public that the firm's retirement and pension products have helped people like Barbara Sullivan, a devoted classroom teacher, to live her American dream by helping others.

other in exchange for loyalty. People in countries characterized by high individualism, such as the United States, Canada, Denmark, and France, tend to be self-sufficient and place strong emphasis on individual initiative. In such cultures, autonomy is given a high value. Consumers in highly individualistic societies tend to be inner directed and make individual decisions without reliance on or need for group support or approval. In contrast, countries with low individualism, such as Japan and Korea, tend to be other directed and place great importance on group decision making, affiliation, and approval of others.

From a consumer behavior perspective, consumers living in countries characterized by high individualism tend to rely on their own inner values or standards in evaluating new-product or service offerings and are likely to be innovative consumers. Consumers in societies with low individualism, on the other hand, tend to look to others for direction concerning what is acceptable. Consequently, they are less likely to be innovative consumers.

This cultural dimension may also have a bearing on the type of promotional messages that marketers employ in each culture type. Individualistic (inner-directed) consumers tend to prefer ads that emphasize product attributes and personal benefits. These consumers, in turn, apply their own values to evaluate the product. Collectivistic (other-directed) consumers tend to prefer ads that feature a social environment or stress social acceptance so as to appeal to their need for approval. The ad depicted in Figure 14.2 contains an other-directed appeal from Mutual of America. The ad stresses the company's continued effort to help individuals fulfill their American dream.

Masculinity

masculinity
the degree to which dominant values are success, money, and things

Masculinity (a descriptor that has nothing to do with gender) was described by Hofstede as the degree to which the dominant values in society are success, money, and things.[9] Hofstede measured this cultural dimension on a continuum ranging from masculinity to femininity. *Femininity*, in this view, is a situation in which the dominant values in society are caring for others and the quality of life. Countries such as the United States and other Western societies with a moderate-to-high masculinity index place great importance on earnings and recognition. People in such societies place high value on material possessions, achievement, and challenge. Achievement, in this view, is defined in terms of wealth and recognition. By contrast, in low-masculinity cultures (high-femininity cultures), such as Norway, achievement is defined in terms of human contacts and concern about the environment. People in such societies tend to place importance on cooperation, maintaining a friendly atmosphere, and employment security. The Pioneer and Peace Corps ads depicted in Figures 14.3 and 14.4 illustrate high-masculinity and low-masculinity themes, respectively. The first ad from Pioneer emphasizes power and control through innovations in sound and vision. The second ad from the Peace Corps emphasizes caring for others around the world.

From a consumer behavior perspective, the masculinity–femininity dimension represents a viable segmentation variable, because achievement in countries with high masculinity scores is expressed through material possessions. In such societies, possessions reflect a person's achievements. Possessions are social symbols and serve as a means of communication between people in a society. Prestigious products and brands find lucrative markets in such societies. In countries with low-masculinity scores, on the other hand, concern for the environment would tend to create demand for products and services that are ecologically friendly.

Term Orientation

A country's term orientation is another dimension added later by Hofstede to the original four dimensions cited earlier.[10] According to Hofstede, in contrast to short-term-oriented cultures, long-term-oriented cultures are characterized by patience, perseverance, respect for one's elders and

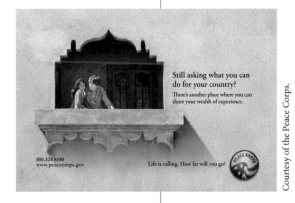

Courtesy of the Peace Corps.

FIGURE 14.3 AND 14.4

The dominant values of masculinity and femininity that characterize different cultures are exemplified here by contrasting themes in two ads from Pioneer and the Peace Corps.

ancestors, along with a sense of obedience and duty toward the larger good. Examples of long-term-oriented cultures are found in Asia, including China, Singapore, Taiwan, and Japan.

The effect of this dimension on consumer behavior may be observed in the strong influence that elderly members of the family or other significant groups possess over other individual members. In addition, a long-term orientation would direct people toward seeking more permanent solutions to their problems, rather than making temporary quick fixes. A long-term perspective is also demonstrated in the belief that one's culture is venerable and worth giving one's life for.

CONSUMER BEHAVIOR IN A CULTURAL SETTING

Like Hofstede, many researchers have examined cultural dimensions that reflect similarities and differences among cultures. In one such work, Harris and Moran identified a number of sociocultural dimensions that they selected on the basis of their relevance to products and services being marketed in various societies.[11] They suggested that the elements of culture can be divided into ten distinctive categories. These categories consist of communication and language, beliefs and attitudes, values and norms, sense of self and space, relationships, time and time consciousness, mental process and learning, rewards and recognitions, dress and appearance, and food and eating habits. Exhibit 14.1 depicts the interrelationship between these variables and consumer behavior within a cultural context. This section surveys the effect of each of these ten cultural dimensions on consumer behavior. In practice, however, each dimension cannot be treated as separate or mutually exclusive. Rather, these dimensions are highly interdependent and interrelated.

Communication and Language

Language as part of culture is the primary means of communication and the medium used to convey meaning, thoughts, and feelings. It embodies the culture's philosophy and heritage. Language is not only restricted to spoken and written words but also includes symbolic communication through spatial proximity, gestures, facial expressions, and body movements.

From a marketing perspective, at least two aspects of language must be investigated in any culture to gain a better understanding of that society. The

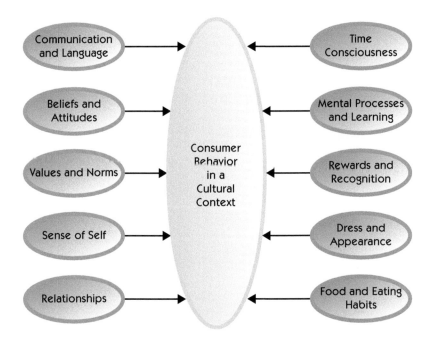

EXHIBIT 14.1

The Sociocultural Dimensions of Consumer Behavior

first deals with language as a *communication tool*. In this regard, marketers examine the relevance of explicit and implicit elements of language (the spoken word and silent components of communication). The second aspect deals with the *heterogeneity* of languages in a culture, or the number of languages and dialects spoken within the borders of a particular country. The traditional Pepsi can design depicted in Figure 14.5 communicates essentially the same image of Pepsi cross culturally, regardless of language differences.

Beliefs and Attitudes

Culture has a significant influence on beliefs and attitudes. For example, in Western cultures, the prevailing outlook is youth oriented.[12] Youth is admired, and considerable efforts and funds are allotted to looking and feeling younger. Many people join health clubs, subscribe to physical fitness programs, and frequent beauty salons. Some even undergo plastic surgery. In traditional societies, in contrast, old age carries great respect. Young people often seek advice and opinions from the elderly. In addition, beliefs, particularly religious beliefs, influence a culture's outlook on life and its meaning. Religions assert what is right and wrong, good and bad, and often are central to a culture because they influence the economic system, political structure, and social relationships between people.

FIGURE 14.5

"Fortunately, nothing's lost in the translation" is the tag line of this Pepsi ad. It communicates the thought that the brand is perceived uniformly throughout the world.

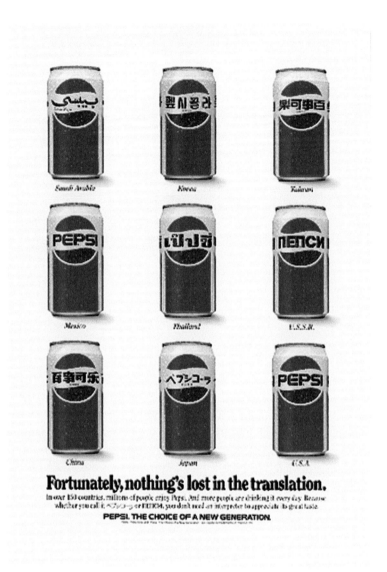

Values and Norms

Values are enduring beliefs that involve ideals, such as what a person should or ought to do, goals that are worth pursuing, and ways to pursue these goals. Culture may be analyzed and categorized on the basis of its norms and value systems. For example, through analysis of a culture's values, it is possible to draw conclusions about how these elements affect behavior and modes of consumption. Values may influence whether con-

values
ideals concerning what is right or wrong and goals worth pursuing

CONSUMER BEHAVIOR IN PRACTICE

An Aquarium with Six Black Fish Can Change Your Luck

Based on beliefs acquired from their homeland, many Asian Americans—especially those of Chinese ancestry—subscribe to *feng shui*, an ancient custom with roots deep in nature worship, Taoism, and yin and yang. *Feng shui* literally means "wind and water." Believers in this tradition profess that invisible power forces, called *chî* (chee) run through the world. A person's dwelling or place of business should attract a favorable *chî* and deflect an unfavorable one. If buildings, furniture, roads, and other human-made objects are placed in harmony with nature, it is believed that good fortune will prevail. If not, it is held that bad omens and great harm would befall the place and person(s) occupying it. It has been claimed, for example, that animals, such as dragons and tigers, reside beneath the surface of the earth. Consequently, humans must not cut into a dragon's flesh (exposing red earth), nor should they build under a tiger's mouth. Simply stated, buildings must fit the land's contours.

In order to ensure that buildings, offices, and furniture are arranged in harmony with nature, many Asian businesses operating in the United States retain the services of an expert **feng shui** practitioner, who examines the facilities and takes readings from a compass-like instrument covered with small Chinese characters. A geomancer may, for example, propose installing aquariums complete with black fish. Although these fish are fed, they are not pampered in fancy tanks. Rather, they are meant to die and be replaced. In doing so, the fish are presumed to absorb bad luck. Other likely recommendations include placing mirrors pointing out of offices to deflect bad luck, using wind chimes, plants, crystals, and weather vanes, among other things, in order to deflect unfavorable *chî*.

Many well-known American corporations operating in Asia, including Chase Manhattan and Citibank, use *feng shui* to help them achieve harmonious relationships with nature. These companies have found that this practice, which was originally used to ease the fears of local employees, really does work. After a Chase Manhattan bank manager, who had occupied a supposedly unlucky office in Hong Kong, was killed in an airplane crash, the bank moved its regional headquarters to a new building. Chase officials admit that the staff's concern about *feng shui* was one of the reasons for relocating, but these same officials also note that bank business seems to boom as a result of using this craft.[13]

Superstitions are part of the folklore of any culture, small or large. Businesses must be cognizant of and sensitive to these traditions when dealing with microcultures. To learn more about feng shui, visit http://www.fengshuiweb.co.uk/advice/business.htm. Think of some American superstitions. How might these superstitions affect the way a company designs its products, services, or brands? How might these same superstitions affect consumers' preferences for brands, institutions, and stores?

sumers regard a product or service as desirable or undesirable. For example, unlike Western cultures, people in Eastern cultures avoid sunbathing because dark skin is associated with the working social class. Therefore, to determine the acceptability or appeal of their products in various cultures, marketers often solicit the help of a technique known as means–end chains.[14] This analytical technique is simply a depiction of the postulated linkages between a product's *attributes, consequences* of that product's

means–end chains
depictions of linkages between product attributes, use consequences, and consumer values

use, and consumer *values* as they exist in a particular culture. Means–end chains are based on the premise that consumers do not buy physical products—they buy *benefits* that these products yield. Yet, obviously the benefits that consumers seek are culturally determined.

From its value system, a culture sets norms of behavior for the society. Norms are shared guidelines to accepted and expected behavior and provide standards against which people evaluate the appropriateness of their behavior.[15] Norms address matters and issues that range from work ethic to manner of dress, and as such, influence consumption patterns. In the United States, for example, material possessions and manifestation of wealth are encouraged. An overt display of success is acceptable. In other cultures, such as Japan and Germany, thrift is emphasized. In the United Kingdom, a conspicuous display of wealth is considered to be in bad taste.

norms
a society's shared guidelines regarding appropriate behavior

Sense of Self

Self-identity and self-worth are influenced by culture. Being modest and humble or being aggressive or macho are reflections of what a culture values and rewards. In the United States, traits such as aggressiveness, sense of independence, and assertiveness are expected and encouraged. In many Western societies, people gauge their accomplishments in terms of the status symbols they acquire. In Eastern societies, the opposite is true. For example, in Japan, child rearing emphasizes modesty and self-effacement. If aggressiveness is one of the desirable traits for U.S. salespersons, the Japanese would tend to be judged as poor salespeople.

Relationships

Personal and organizational relationships are subject to cultural influences. Culture, for example, determines the roles of managers and subordinates as well as how they relate to each other. In some traditional cultures, managers and subordinates are separated by various boundaries ranging from protocol to separate office facilities. In others, equality characterizes the operation.

The family unit is another common expression of cultural relationships. The family unit in Western industrialized countries consists of parents and children. In traditional societies, on the other hand, the family unit is extended to include others such as grandparents, uncles, aunts, and cousins—all living under the same roof. In such societies, business is kept within the family and passed from one generation to the next. Centers of authority and responsibility within the family also vary dramatically. In the Middle East, for example, the authority figure in the family is the male. Children play an insignificant role in the decision-making process. Whereas female roles in Western societies are equivalent to those of males, in other societies women's roles are sometimes restricted to managing the household.

Time Consciousness

Sense of time differs by culture. In the United States, Germany, and the United Kingdom, people are punctual. Promptness is the norm, and tardiness leads to embarrassing or even costly consequences. In Latin America and much of Africa and the Middle East, the clock is not so rigidly adhered to. A person can arrive at a meeting half an hour late and be considered early. Tardiness is acceptable and expected. Concerning social functions, it is not considered polite to arrive at a party on time. In much of the Middle East, Africa, and Latin America, hosts are likely to be annoyed if a guest arrives precisely on time. In Japan, arrival at a meeting is governed by rank—junior people are expected to arrive early and wait. Those with seniority arrive last.

Mental Processes and Learning

The way people think and the ease or difficulty with which learning occurs is another aspect that differentiates people from various cultures. In some cultures, such as the British, myopic thinking modes are the pattern. Data, material objects, and other stimuli or activities are viewed in terms of a particular goal or result.[16] Therefore, attention is directed to details and procedures rather than general principles or abstract concepts. In this case, an activity's detail takes priority over what the activity as a whole is all about. In other societies, such as the United States, people place practical considerations ahead of details or procedures. Many Middle Easterners may act on emotions; in contrast, Americans are taught to act on logic. In still other societies, such as the French, general principles are placed ahead of practical considerations. These modes of mental activity precede behavior, and as such affect consumer behavior.

Rewards and Recognition

The methods of rewarding individuals for exceptional performance or accomplishments differ widely within cultural contexts. Monetary rewards, recognition, medals, honors, expense accounts, and impressive titles are used differently in various cultures. Although the process of motivation is universal, the methods used to attain goals are quite different. In the United States, for example, recognition, security, and monetary awards are important reinforcement systems. In China, however, group affiliation is an important need and reinforcer. A desirable reward in this case may involve having a picture of an employee hung on the wall as "employee of the month." In Canada, a study of what motivates workers revealed that relationships at work rank first, followed by security, then recognition, and pay in fourth place.[17]

Dress and Appearance

The clothes and body adornments people use in different cultures vary according to climate and tradition. The traditional Japanese still wear the kimono, Arabs the abaya, Polynesians the sarong, Indians the sari, and Middle Easterners the jalabia. Although these articles of clothing may be designed first to protect against the elements, like white robes that reflect the Mideast sun's rays and allow for body ventilation, they may also be styled to maintain a sense of modesty and equality. Modesty is attained by covering most of the body, and equality through a look-alike appearance that eliminates distinctions between rich and poor.

Customs and traditions determine acceptable modes of dress, appearance, and hair length. Americans prefer loose-fitting suits, whereas

The sari is traditional garb for many Indian women. In addition to its attractiveness and colorfulness, the sari is styled to maintain a sense of modesty, because it covers most of a woman's body.

© v.s.anandhakrishna/Shutterstock.com

Europeans prefer tight-fitting attire. Many Latin American men prefer to grow a beard and mustache and have long hair, styles that are acceptable in their business circles. Many U.S. corporations, on the other hand, require their male employees to have a clean-shaven face and short haircuts.

Food and Eating Habits

Another way of observing culture is to note what people eat or refuse to eat, how food is prepared, when meals are served, and how quickly people eat. In Islamic countries, for example, pork is not eaten and liquor is not served. In most of Latin America, as well as in Africa and the Middle East, the main meal is served in the early afternoon, followed by a nap. Beer is the preferred drink in Germany, wine in France, and aquavit in Norway. Whereas most Americans are meateaters, in some cultures, such as India, many people consume little or no meat. Foods that are common in one culture may sound repulsive to members of another. Among the Chinese, dog and cat are delicacies. Hummus, felafel, and tabouli are staples in most Middle-Eastern households, but are less popular among many U.S. consumers who have been raised on hamburgers and hot dogs. In terms of how quickly people eat, individuals in the United States—especially those with active or stressful lifestyles—tend to eat quickly or even on the run. On the other hand, Italians and some South Americans make a ceremony out of dining and may leisurely spend a couple of hours or more at the dinner table.

So far we have seen that each culture tends to have its own customs and traditions. We have also recognized that cultural values determine how people in a particular society think, feel, and act. Today, sensitivity to these cultural dimensions is not a matter of choice for marketers—it is a practical necessity. Success in business hinges on the understanding that consumer behavior occurs within a cultural context and that the route to success lies within the confines of such sensitivity to cultural traditions.

Now let us move on to another culture-related issue—the view that culture is seldom homogeneous. Rather, a culture often consists of a number of subcultures or subgroups of individuals within the culture whose beliefs, experiences, traditions, and modes of behavior set them somewhat apart from those of the main culture. These unique patterns of various subcultures are a topic of interest to marketers in their pursuit of better ways to serve their customers.

subcultures
smaller, more homogeneous subsets of people within a larger culture

SUBCULTURES

Within countries such as the United States and Canada, nations characterized by plurality and multiculturalism, researchers use a variety of criteria to delineate subcultures. Among these criteria, subcultures have been identified on such bases as demographic, geographic, and lifestyle variables. Although such classifications may be somewhat useful for purposes of sociological research and market segmentation, they are less actionable for purposes of designing culturally sensitive marketing strategies. For this very reason, we limit our coverage of subcultures to two forms: the first is an overview of those subcultures that can be identified on the basis of ethnicity; and the second is subcultures that are identifiable through observed consumption choices of products or services that consumers make, such as consumption subcultures, brand communities, and tribes.

Ethnicity, one of the most popular bases for delineating subcultures, embraces such factors as the race, nationality, and religion to which individuals belong. Ethnicity also takes into account how strongly or weakly individuals feel connected to their heritage.[18] The amount of influence that consumers' ancestry exerts on them depends largely on the strength of their association and affiliation with the subculture. Some consumers strive to preserve the language and traditions of their native homeland. Others opt for rapid assimilation into the mainstream of their new society. In addition, differences can be observed between first-, second-, and third-generation members of the various ethnic subcultures.

To the extent that the members of an ethnic group share common beliefs and perceptions that differ from those of other ethnic groups or society as a whole, these individuals constitute a distinct ethnic subculture or market segment.[19] It must be pointed out, however, that ethnic groups (Black Americans, Hispanics, Asians) which exist within the marketplace are, of course, very diverse in composition and may need to be segmented further. We will begin with an overview of ethnic subcultures.

ETHNIC SUBCULTURES

The following sections briefly profile three major subcultures in U.S. society, namely Black, Hispanic, and Asian American consumers.

Black (African-American) Consumers

According to the U.S. Census Bureau in 2016, the number of Blacks in the nation, including those of more than one race, was around 45.7 million, or about 14.7 percent of the population. Projections reveal that by the year 2060, there will be 74.5 million Black American individuals in the United States, comprising 17.9 percent of the total U.S. population. One myth concerning Black Americans is that most are low income. However, while the median household income of Blacks was $35,481 in 2014, their income outpaced that of non-Hispanic whites at every annual household income level above $60,000. The largest increase for African-American households occurred in the number earning $200,000, with an increase of 138 percent, compared to the total population. Financially, Black Americans constitute a major force in the marketplace, with a buying power of nearly $1.2 trillion annually, projected to reach $1.4 trillion by 2020.

States with the largest Black populations in 2015 were New York with 3.3 million, Florida with 3.2 million, Texas with 3.2 million, Georgia with 3.1 million, California with 2.7 million, and North Carolina with 2.2 million.

With regard to education, there has been substantial educational growth among Blacks, with high school graduation rates exceeding 70 percent, outpacing the growth rate for all students nationwide. Furthermore, the percent of Black students enrolled in college recently soared to over 70 percent, exceeding that of whites and Hispanics.

Concerning employment, Black Americans made up 12 percent of the U.S. labor force. However, the unemployment rate for Blacks in 2015 was 9.2 percent, more than double that of whites, which was 4.4 percent in the same year.

Black Americans are younger than the general population. Their median age is thirty-one years, which is more than twelve years younger than the median age for whites, which is forty-three years. More than half of all Black Americans are between the ages of eighteen and thirty-four years. As these young individuals form families, buy homes, and build careers, their spending power is virtually certain to grow.

Although Black-American households spend less than average on many items, from food away from home to charitable contributions, millions of middle-class and upper-class Blacks have discretionary income to spend on other commodities. They are inclined to spend more on basic food ingredients and beverages, and tend to value the food preparation process.

African Americans are younger than the general population. As they form families, buy homes, and build careers, their spending power will grow.

© Andresr/Shutterstock.com

Other popular purchase categories include fragrances, personal health and beauty products, as well as household care and cleaning products.

In terms of reaching Black American consumers, technology today has fueled the highest level of media segmentation in history. New media alternatives have divided consumers into very specific segments, precipitating cultural differences—particularly among the Black digitally savvy millennials, in which 78 percent used the Internet in 2016.

Astute marketers have already acknowledged the importance as well as the diversity of the Black-American market. The belief that blacks are a demographic monolith or demonstrate a single mindset is a myth. Segmentation of the Black-American market usually reflects socioeconomic standing (income, education, occupation). Armed with this understanding, many companies have already targeted and positioned their products and services to the Black-American market. For example, numerous magazines, such as *Ebony, O* (the Oprah magazine), *Essence, Upscale, Sister, About Time, American Legacy*, and *Hope Today*, predominantly cover topics ranging from fashions to politics and social issues. Online magazines that address Black fashions and issues have emerged. Mass marketers like Kmart, Walmart, and Target have often courted the Black clothing market. Similarly, banks and brokerage firms have targeted Black investors.

Hispanic-American (Latino) Consumers

About half of all immigrants to the United States today—legal and illegal—come from Spanish-speaking countries. In 2014, Hispanics and their U.S.-born children accounted for 55.4 million individuals, representing around 17.4 percent of the population. Hispanics are projected to represent 19 percent of the population by 2020, and are estimated to increase to 119 million individuals in 2060, an increase of 115 percent. At that time, they will represent 29 percent of the U.S. population.

A recent report published by the Pew Hispanic Center found that Mexican-originated U.S. Hispanics represented the largest share of the total, at 64 percent. The second largest group is Puerto Rican Hispanics accounting for 9.5 percent. Other groups include Cubans (3.7 percent), Salvadorans (3.7 percent), Dominicans (3.3 percent), and Guatemalans (2.4 percent), as well as Colombians, Hondurans, and Peruvians. These figures show that Hispanics have rapidly surpassed Black Americans as the largest ethnic minority in the United States. In fact, the Hispanic population continues to grow at a rate faster than the black population, the Asian population, and the white population.

U.S. Hispanics are younger than Americans in general, with a median age of twenty-nine compared with forty-three for the nation as a whole. This youth orientation is due to the high birth rate that characterizes the Hispanic market. This youthful trend will have many ramifications both for the labor force and marketers.

On average, the Hispanic population falls at the lower end of the socio-economic scale. A 2015 report by the Pew Hispanic Center revealed that while the U.S. census indicates a median income of $40,963 for Hispanics in general, wide differences exist among the subgroups in this population.

From an educational perspective, in the year 2015, 14 percent of U.S. Hispanics age twenty-five and older were college graduates; and 64 percent of Hispanics age twenty-five years and older held a high school diploma.

In terms of spending patterns, expenditures on grocery items are high due to the fact that Hispanics tend to eat at home more often than non-Hispanic whites. Hispanics place high value on food and in-home meal preparation, as well as high priority on getting together to enjoy meals with the whole family.

© Rob Marmion/Shutterstock.com

From a marketing point of view, Hispanics in 2015 accounted for as much as $1.5 trillion in annual buying power, and this figure is projected to top $1.7 trillion in 2017, and $2 trillion by 2020. With this huge combined buying power of the aggregate Hispanic population, many U.S. companies are aggressively pursuing this market. Multinational companies known for personal care brands are now marketing their brands in Spanish both off- and online, including social media.

American Hispanics can be divided into three distinct acculturation segments. The first group is the *unacculturated* segment, which accounts for approximately 40 percent of this market. Members of this subgroup retain close ties to the culture of their country of origin and prefer to communicate in the Spanish language. The second subgroup, which constitutes around 32 percent of the total, is the *bicultural* segment, and consists of bilinguals who desire to retain much of their original culture while adopting many elements of U.S. society as well. The third subgroup is the *accultured* segment, accounting for 28 percent of Hispanics, whose members have moved beyond their roots and have adopted U.S. cultural and family values. Members of this segment prefer to communicate in English, and many no longer speak the Spanish language. This segmentation pattern has major implications for marketers, particularly in the areas of employment, store preferences (e.g., unacculturated members often prefer small *bodegas*), and promotional media types as well as languages used to reach the Hispanic community.[20]

ETHICAL DILEMMA

In Search of a Country

Throughout the history of the United States, immigration has been a major source of economic growth, vitality, demographic diversity, and innovation. According to recent Pew Research Center data, 63 percent of Americans believe that immigration is good for the country.

With the present challenge the United States is facing in addressing immigration from Latin America, this problem pales in comparison with what the European Union is encountering as it deals with millions of migrants seeking admission. For Americans who live on the western side of the Atlantic in a country largely settled and built by immigrants, this global issue raises fears and resentment in the hearts of many. For example, in the 2016 presidential campaign, a certain candidate brought the issue of immigration to the forefront with controversial views on illegal individuals arriving from Mexico. Such notions included negative depictions of them. This same candidate then proposed taking drastic measures to foil such attempts at infiltration.

These suggested actions to curtail the influx of immigrants coming into the country across its southern border happened to coincide with American public opinion and popular prejudices. This had particularly been the case as Americans continued to encounter the unaccompanied minors who had been trickling into the United States in steadily increasing numbers. Originally, it was Mexican children who made up the bulk of such

immigrants; however, a wave of individuals from Guatemala, Honduras, and El Salvador has also been arriving. This surge was caused by many factors, among which were recent U.S. policies toward unaccompanied children, rising crime and gang activity in Central American countries, as well as operations of smuggling networks, including drug cartels.

Many Americans believe that the main focus of the U.S. government in dealing with the issue of illegal immigration should be on developing a plan to integrate immigrants who are currently in the United States illegally, rather than to develop a plan for halting the flow of immigrants into the United States. In this case, those individuals who are already here would be placed on a path that would allow them to become U.S. citizens if they were to meet specific requirements, including paying taxes, passing a criminal background check, and learning English.[21]

Many U.S. citizens have mixed feelings on the issue of illegal immigrants. Learn more about the perception of Americans regarding immigration and how they prioritize this issue among the many serious problems that the United States faces today. Visit www.gallup.com/opinion/polling-matters/184262/american-public-opinion-immigration.aspxespv=2#9=Halimah+Abdullah%2c+5+things+you+need+to+know+about+the+immigration+crisis%2ccnn. What are the social, political, economic, and ethical ramifications associated with the issue of illegal immigration? Where do you stand on this matter? Defend your position.

Asian-American Consumers

In 2016, there were 18.2 million Asian-American consumers (Asian alone or in combination with one or more other races), constituting about 5.4 percent of the U.S. population, and projected to reach 20.9 million individuals by 2020. The Census Bureau labels Asians as a fast-growing racial group, estimated to increase in size by an astounding 128 percent by the year 2060. At that time, they will represent 9.3 percent of the total U.S. population. Like other subcultures, Asian Americans exhibit a strong ethnic identity and vast diversity. They are considerably more diverse than the Black- or Hispanic-American markets.

The term *Asian* is used to refer to many ethnic groups. The Census Bureau's category "Asian and Pacific Islander" covers more than seventeen countries. The Chinese comprise the single largest group (approximately 24 percent), followed by Filipinos (about 18 percent), Asian Indians (about 16.5 percent), Vietnamese (about 11 percent), Korean (about 11 percent), and Japanese (about 8 percent). Other subgroups include Laotions, Cambodians, Thais, Pakistanis, Hawaiians, Samoans, Guamanians, Fiji Islanders, among others. Within this group, however, generations—delineated by when they immigrated to the United States—distinguish between this large group's various members.

Well over half of Asian Americans live in three states: California (especially the Los Angeles and San Francisco areas), New York, and Hawaii. It has been estimated that four of ten Asian Americans live in California. They also account for 25 percent of immigrants in Los Angeles and New York. Clusters of Asian Americans are also found in Philadelphia and Washington, D.C., as well as a number of other large urban centers, such as Oakland, San Jose, San Diego, Orange County, and Chicago.

The median age of Asian Americans is roughly thirty-seven years, compared with forty-three years for the general population. Asian Americans are industrious and strongly driven to achieve a middle-class lifestyle. The most highly educated and affluent subculture, this group exhibits strong family ties and places a high value on education. In 2015, about 75 percent of Asian Americans age twenty-five and older held a bachelor degree or higher, which is well above the national average. In addition, 85 percent of Asian Americans age twenty-five and older had at least a high school diploma. Their median income was over $72,472, with certain segments such as Asian Indians earning over $90,000. In addition, 53 percent of Asian-American households had at least two wage earners, which is a higher proportion than other racial groups. Asian Americans and Pacific Islanders tend to hold executive, professional, and technical positions, and many run their own businesses. Nielsen Reports reveal that Asian Americans' purchasing power in 2015 amounted to $770 billion and is forecast to reach $1 trillion by the year 2018. Asians value well-known, premium-quality brands and are both able and willing to pay for them. They consider quality more important than price when selecting retail outlets to shop; 54 percent shop as a leisure activity compared to 50 percent of the general population. Asian Americans are highly status conscious. They are a good market for electronics/technically oriented products and services, automobiles, housing, as well as food.

The current revolution in electronic media has significantly facilitated the task of reaching the electronically savvy Asian-American market. For example, a 2015 report from Pew Research Center suggested that the Asian-American community outpaces other demographics in terms of adoption of digital media channels. While 85 percent of Americans are regular Internet users, within the Asian-American community, the percentage is higher at 97 percent. Thus, companies relying on social media marketing can more effectively target Asian Americans than most other demographics.[22]

MARKETING IMPLICATIONS OF CULTURE AND SUB-CULTURES

Marketers stand to profit from studying culture and subcultures. In reference to culture, this chapter has already demonstrated that the beliefs, values, norms, and traditions held by consumers within a culture influence the products/services they buy and use. When cultural values are deemed relevant to product consumption, marketers appeal to prevalent values and surround their brands with symbols of these values. For example, when advertising yogurt in Japan, Yoplait emphasized the product's pure, all-natural ingredients to capitalize on the Japanese love of nature.

Marketers also benefit from understanding subcultures. Delving into the psyche of members of a subculture to find out what is important to them and playing to their interest is simply good marketing practice. In this context, cultural *relevance* becomes a necessity. Cultural relevance requires understanding of a group's values, customs, and aspirations to permit presenting products and promotions in light of these unique characteristics. For example, a depiction of a family reunion in an ad for a smartphone service plan directed to the Hispanic-American subculture would be considered highly apropos and effective. This appropriateness is due to the tendency of Hispanic Americans to care for their families and value familial relationships. Cultural relevance also means avoiding symbols, icons, holidays, and heroes that are often meaningless to members of the subculture. For example, using highly paid supermodels and movie stars to advertise Cover Girl cosmetics is a plausible appeal when advertising to white America. For Hispanic and Asian Americans, a supermodel is simply just another pretty face.[23]

Interestingly, subcultures often exhibit different rituals than the major culture. Rituals are sets of symbolic behaviors that occur in a fixed sequence and tend to be repeated periodically.[24] Rituals can be private or public and often reflect widely held cultural or religious values. For example, private rituals include bowing one's head for grace before meals or burning incense and making food offerings to the spirits of one's God. Public rituals, on the other hand, include such things as giving some Asian-American employees gifts during *Ochugen* and *Osebo* Japanese holiday seasons or fasting during the month of Ramadan for practicing Muslims. Ritual situations are important to marketers because specific products are bought and consumed within the context of these occasions.

In this chapter, we have seen that people's traditions, norms, and values comprise the cultural component of their external environment. Culture is simply people—how they live, what they think, and what they hold in esteem. Cultural norms and values affect consumer decision making, because they establish limits regarding what a society deems desirable or at least acceptable.

We have also observed that within diverse cultures, subcultures may exist that have their own distinguishing tastes and consumption patterns. Members of subcultures are frequently prime targets for products or promotions designed specifically with them in mind. In our society, the existence and rapid growth of such subcultures is anticipated to hold ramifications in many areas, including the composition of the labor force, social services and taxation, and the demand for culturally sensitive products and services.

As we have learned from this chapter and the previous ones, the study of consumer behavior integrates many fields of knowledge. It focuses on the behavioral, social, and cultural aspects involved in the process of satisfying human needs and wants. We also know that consumption-related activities extend across geographic boundaries, making the investigation of consumer behavior a necessary undertaking anywhere in the world. Equipped with this consumer knowledge, we as marketers hope to be able to use this information to serve our customers and society better.

rituals
sets of symbolic behaviors that occur in a fixed sequence and tend to be repeated periodically

SUMMARY

Culture can be defined as a society's distinctive and learned mode of living, interacting, and responding to environmental stimuli. This response pattern is shared and transmitted between the members of a society. The process by which we learn the skills, norms, and values necessary to function as productive members of a society is referred to as socialization. Cultural learning occurs via living in a family environment, formal schooling, observing and imitating others, and simply by interacting with them. Within the United States, the sharing of cultural norms and values is facilitated by a common language, schools, places of worship, and the mass media.

Culture includes both tangible and intangible elements. Whereas mechanical traits of a culture evolve rapidly, its ideological traits change more slowly. This unevenness in the pace of change can create cultural lag or friction among the components of society.

Ethnocentrism refers to the tendency to make cross-cultural evaluations on the basis of pre-reflective beliefs and values that are rooted in our own culture. To avoid this kind of bias, marketers and researchers of consumer behavior learn about different cultures via such techniques as ethnography, direct questioning, content analysis, and using key informants.

Five cultural dimensions help explain how and why people from various cultures behave as they do. These dimensions are power distance, uncertainty avoidance, individualism, masculinity, and term orientation. A set of ten sociocultural dimensions offers a basis for comparing similarities and differences between cultures. These dimensions are communication and language, beliefs and attitudes, values and norms, sense of self and space, relationships, time and time consciousness, mental processes and learning, rewards and recognitions, dress and appearance, and food and eating habits.

Subcultures are smaller, more homogeneous subsets of people that exist within a larger, more diverse society. Within nations characterized by plurality and multiculturalism, researchers use a variety of criteria such as demographic, geographic, and lifestyle variables to delineate subcultures. Ethnicity, one popular basis for delineating subcultures, embraces such factors as the race, nationality, and religion that individuals belong to as well how strongly these individuals feel connected to their heritage. Three subcultures of particular importance to marketers today are Black-,

Hispanic-, and Asian-American consumers. Of course, these groups are very diverse in composition and may need to be segmented further.

Marketers stand to benefit from studying culture and subcultures because the beliefs, values, and attitudes held by people within a culture as well as the rituals they engage in can affect the products and services they buy and use. Such understanding is essential to develop sensitive and relevant marketing strategies.

CASE SYNOPSIS

Enabling the Disabled

This case cites an incident of a wheelchair-bound traveler who was denied boarding assistance from the staff of an airline. This incident of discrimination against the disabled, as well as others like it, has resulted in global efforts to enact legislation aimed at eradicating such forms of questionable behavior and securing equal rights and opportunities for persons with disabilities. In the United States alone, many such laws have been passed by federal and local governments covering domains such as work and the workplace, education, housing, transportation, communications, and public accommodations, among others.

Notes

1   Hedy Weiss, "The New Europe: What Europeans Think of Us—Fear and Fascination," *Chicago Sun-Times* (December 1, 1997), pp. 6–7; Hedy Weiss, "The New Europe: Nationalism—New Dangers, Old Dreams," *Chicago Sun-Times* (December 3, 1997), pp. 6–7; Hedy Weiss, "The New Europe: Prospects for a United Europe—Paying the Price of Unity," *Chicago Sun-Times* (December 4, 1997), pp. 6–7; Jeffrey E. Garten "'Cultural Imperialism' Is No Joke," *Business Week* (November 30, 1998), p. 26.
2   Nessim Hanna and Tanuja Srivastava, "Cultural Aspects of Gift Giving: A Comparative Analysis of the Significance of Gift Giving in the U.S. and Japan," in Samsinar Sidin and Ajay K. Manrai (Eds.), *Proceedings of the Eighth Biennial World Marketing Congress* VIII (Kuala Lampur, Malaysia: Academy of Marketing Science, 1997), pp. 269–273.
3   Barbara Applebaum, "Moral Paralysis and the Ethnocentric Fallacy," *Journal of Moral Education* 25, no. 2 (June 1996), pp. 185–200.

4   D. M. Gollnick and P. C. Chin, *Multicultural Education in a Pluralistic Society* (Columbus, OH: Merrill Publishing, 1986).

5   B. R. Schlender, "What Rice Means to the Japanese," *Fortune* (November 1, 1993), pp. 150–156; "Going Against the Grain in Japan," *The Economist* (April 23, 1994), p. 34.

6   Alison S. Wellner, "The New Science of Focus Groups," *American Demographics* (March 2003), pp. 29–33.

7   Geert Hofstede, *Culture's Consequences: International Differences in World Related Values* (Beverly Hills, CA: Sage, 1980).

8   Ibid.

9   Ibid.

10 Geert Hofstede, *Cultures and Organizations* (London: McGraw-Hill, 1991).

11 Philip R. Harris and Robert T. Moran, *Managing Cultural Differences* (Houston, TX: Gulf, 1985), pp. 58–61.

12 David Aviel, "Cultural Barriers to International Transactions," *Journal of General Management* 15, no. 4 (Summer 1990), pp. 5–20.

13 Olivia Wu, "Believers in Harmony with Old Chinese Practice," *Chicago Sun-Times* (February 14, 1996), p. 22; E. S. Browning, "When Fung Shui Speaks, Business Listens," *International Wildlife* 14 (September–October 1984), pp. 36–37; Patricia Corrigan, "Living in Harmony with Feng Shui," *Chicago Sun-Times* (November 10, 1996), p. 12CW.

14 T. Hofstede et al., "An Investigation into the Association Pattern Technique as a Quantitative Approach to Measuring Means–End Chains," *International Journal of Research in Marketing* 15, no. 1 (February 1998), pp. 37–50; Jonathan Gutman, "Means–End Chains as Goal Hierarchies" *Psychology & Marketing* 14, no. 6 (September 1997), pp. 545–560.

15 A. Birenbaum and E. Sagarin, *Norms and Human Behavior* (New York: Praeger, 1976).

16 Endel-Jakob Kolde, *Environment of International Business*, 2nd ed. (Boston: Kent, 1985), p. 423.

17 G. E. Popp, H. J. Davis, and T. T. Herbert, "An International Study of Intrinsic Motivation Composition," *Management International Review* 26, no. 3 (1986), p. 31.

18 Rohit Deshpandi, Wayne D. Hoyer, and Naveen Donthu, "The Intensity of Ethnic Affliation: A Study of the Sociology of Hispanic Consumptic," *Journal of Consumer Research* 13 (September 1986), pp. 214–219.

19 Elizabeth C. Hirschman, "An Examination of Ethnicity and Consumption Using Free Response Data," in *Proceedings of the Educators' Conference* (Chicago: American Marketing Association, 1982), pp. 84–88.

20 Jens Manuel Krogstad, "Hispanic Population Reaches Record 55 Million, But Growth Has Cooled," *Pew Research Center* (June 25, 2015), http://www.pewresearch.org/fact-tank/2015/06/25/u-s-hispanic-population-growth-surge-cools/; "Buying Power of Hispanic Consumers in the United States from 1990 to 2017 (in U.S. Dollars)," *Statista,* http://www.statista.com/statistics/251438/hispanics-buying-power-in-the-us/; Jens Manuel Krogstad,

"With Fewer New Arrivals, Census Lowers Hispanic Population Projections," *Pew Research Center* (December 16, 2014), http://www.pewresearch.org/fact-tank/2014/12/16/with-fewer-new-arrivals-census-lowers-hispanic-population-projections-2/; Sandra L. Colby and Jennifer M. Ortman, "Projections of the Size and Composition of the U.S. Population: 2014 to 2060," Current Population Reports, P25-1143 (Washington, DC: U.S. Census Bureau, 2014).

21 Halimah Abdullah, "5 Things You Need to Know About the Immigration Crisis," *CNN* (July 7, 2014), https://www.google.com/?ion=1&cspv=2#q=halimah+abdullah%2C+5+things+you+need+-to+know+about+the+immigration+crisis%22cnn; Frank Newport, "American Public Opinion and Immigration," *Gallup* (July, 2015), www.gallup.com/opinion/polling-matters/184262/american-public-opinion-immigration.aspxespv=2#9=Halimah+Abdullah%2c+5+things+you+need+to+-know+about+the+immigration+crisis%2ccnn; David Horsey, "Europe's Migrant Crisis Dwarfs U.S. Problems on the Mexican Border," *Los Angeles Times* (September 3, 2015), www.latimes.com/opinion/topoftheticket/la-na-tt-europe-migrant-crisis-20150902-story.html.

22 Michael Nam, "Report: Asian American Buying Power to Hit $1 Trillion by 2018," *DiversityInc.* (2015), www.diversityinc.com^News; "The Rise of Asian Americans," *Pew Research Center: Social & Demographic Trends* (2015-2016), www.pewsocialtrends.org^asianamericans; "FFF: Asian/Pacific American Heritage Month: May 2015 Release Number: CB15-FF.07," *U.S. Census News Room* (April 29, 2015); Jennifer Lee, "The Truth About Asian-Americans' Success," *CNN* (August 4, 2015), cnn.com^Lee-immigration-ethnic-capital; Colby and Ortman, "Projections of the Size and Composition of the U.S. Population: 2014 to 2060."

23 Shelly Reese, "Cultural Shock: When It Comes to Marketing to Ethnic Populations, What You Don't Know Can Hurt You," *Marketing Tools* 5 (May 1, 1998), p. 44.

24 B. Gainer, "Ritual and Relationships," *Journal of Business Research* (March 1995), pp. 253–260; C. Otnes and L. M. Scott, "Something Old, Something New," *Journal of Advertising* (Spring 1996), pp. 35–50.

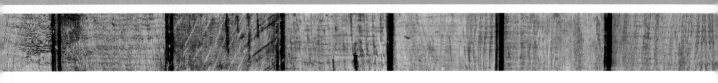

GLOSSARY

absolute (lower) threshold the lowest intensity level at which an individual can detect a stimulus

acculturation the process of learning the norms, values, and behaviors of a different culture

acquired needs drives that are conditioned by relationships with others in the environment

adaptation an indifference to a stimulus to which an individual has become overly accustomed

adoption the decision-making stages an individual goes through before accepting a product

affective component an individual's positive or negative reaction to an attitude object

agents of change entities that actively strive to reshape consumers' beliefs and behaviors

AIO inventories questionnaires designed to reveal consumers' activities, interests, and opinions

anticipatory aspirational reference groups groups a person has reasonable expectations of joining in the future

approach–approach conflict a situation in which a person faces a choice among two desirable alternatives

approach–avoidance conflict a situation in which a person must surrender resources to gain a desirable outcome

arousal a tension state resulting mainly from unfilled needs

aspirational reference groups groups in which a person seeks membership but lacks the qualifications to join

association tests tests based on the immediacy of subject's responses to stimulus words or phrases

attention the allocation of an individual's mental capacity to a stimulus or task

attitude change a shift in the valence of an attitude from negative to positive or vice versa

attitude object anything about which consumers can form an attitude

attitude toward the object an individual's overall appraisal (like or dislike) of an attitude object

attitude toward the behavior one's overall appraisal of an act based on its consequences and one's evaluation of these outcomes

attitudes learned predispositions to respond in a consistent manner to a given object

attribution efforts to ascertain the causes of events in our lives

availability-valence hypothesis a view that vivid information tends to be stored in memory with more links to other concepts

avoidance–avoidance conflict a situation in which a person faces a choice between two undesirable alternatives

behavior shaping the process of breaking down a complex behavior into a series of simple stages and reinforcing the learner at each step

behavioral (conative) component a person's action tendency or intentions with respect to an attitude object

behavioral segmentation a partitioning of the market based on attitudes toward or reaction to a product

bonding the connecting of a consumer and a product through an emotional tie

boomerang children grown children—now adults—who continue to live in or return to their parents' home

Boomers I cohort individuals age sixty-two through seventy (in 2016)

Boomers II cohort individuals age fifty-one through sixty-one (in 2016)

bottom-up processing physical characteristics of the stimulus drive perception

brand advocates consumers who speak on behalf of a company without monetary compensation

brand communities groups that are formed on the basis of a strong attachment to a firm or its products

brand equity the added value a brand name brings to a product beyond its functional worth

brand loyalty a consumer's consistent purchase of a specific brand within a product category; an attachment to brands that have proven satisfactory in the past

brand parity a situation where many consumers come to believe that no significant differences exist among brands

brand-specific goals particular alternatives in a product category from which consumers can choose

brand tribes networks of people gathering homogeneously around consumption activities or brands

central route to persuasion a view that under high involvement, consumers diligently process information provided in messages

centrality the extent of how closely an attitude reflects a person's core values and beliefs

chunk an organized grouping of data inputs

classical conditioning a view that learning involves linking a conditioned stimulus and an unconditioned stimulus

classical identification the case where one accepts influence in order to establish or maintain one's self-image within a group

closure the tendency to perceive complete structures even though some parts are missing

coercive power influence based on a group's ability to administer punishments

cognitive component what a person thinks he or she knows about an attitude object

cognitive consistency a view that we strive to maintain congruity between beliefs, emotions, and behavior

cognitive dissonance theory a view that inconsistency between a person's beliefs and behavior causes psychological tension

cognitive learning a view that humans are goal-oriented problem solvers and processors of information

cohort an aggregate of people who have undergone similar experiences and share common memories

compatibility the perceived property of a new product as being consistent with consumers' beliefs, values, experiences, and habits

compensatory decision rule a selection procedure where a high score on one attribute of a brand can make up for a low score on another

compliance the act of going along with a group to obtain approval

compliance-aggressiveness-detachment (CAD) scale a paradigm that classifies people based on how compliant, aggressive, and detached they are

composite-variable indexes objective measures of social class that combine several socioeconomic factors

concentration strategy a marketing effort that focuses on a single market segment

confirmation a stage where an adopter experiences postpurchase doubt and seeks reassurance for the decision made

congruity the relatedness of sequentially presented informational cues

conspicuous consumption the acquisition and exhibition of extravagant luxuries to portray one's ability to afford them

constructive processing   a tendency of consumers to tailor their cognitive effort to suit the task at hand

consumer behavior   the study of how consumers select, purchase, use, and dispose of goods and services to satisfy personal needs and wants

consumer satisfaction   the mental state of feeling adequately rewarded in a buying situation

consumption subcultures   distinguishable subgroups of society that share a strong commitment to a product, brand, or activity

content analysis   the study of culture by reviewing its media or literature

context   the setting in which a stimulus occurs affects how it is perceived

contiguity   the spatial or temporal nearness of objects

contingency   the notion that the conditioned stimulus should precede the unconditioned stimulus

continuous innovations   new products that require minimal, if any, adjustments in consumption routines

continuous reinforcement   a reinforcement schedule that rewards a desired behavior every time it occurs

cultural lag   the time delay between the introduction of innovations and their acceptance

culture   a society's distinctive and learned mode of living, interacting, and responding to environmental stimuli

customization strategy   a personalized marketing effort to suit individual customer's needs

decision   a stage where a prospect makes a choice to either adopt or reject an innovation

decision rules   alternative analytical procedures consumers use to process information and arrive at a selection

demographic segmentation   a partitioning of the market based on factors such as age, gender, income, occupation, education, and ethnicity

desires   passions that involve longing, yearning, and fervently wishing for something

determinant attributes   those features on which alternatives are believed to differ

differential threshold or just noticeable difference (JND)   the smallest increment in the intensity of a stimulus that a person can detect

diffusion   the spread of a new product or idea within the marketplace

direct questioning   the study of culture through research questionnaires

direction   an end toward which behavior is prompted

disclaimant reference groups groups to which a person previously belonged, but whose values one later rejects

discontinuance a consumer's decision to cease using a previously adopted product

discontinuous innovations unique products that significantly alter established consumption routines

divisibility the perceived property that a new product can be sampled in small quantities

dynamically continuous innovations new products that do not strikingly alter consumers' established usage patterns

early adopters the second tier of consumers (after the innovators) to adopt an innovation

early majority the third tier of consumers to adopt an innovation

ecological design the planning of physical space and other facets of the environment to modify human behavior

e-commerce buying and selling of products or services over electronic systems

egalitarianism a principle which advocates that all people are equal

ego a personality component that balances the id's hedonistic impulses and the superego's constraints

ego-defensive function the notion that some attitudes serve to protect an individual's ego or disguise a person's inadequacies

elaboration-likelihood model (ELM) a view that consumers' level of involvement determines the appropriate route to persuasion

emergent groups groups that spontaneously come into being

emotional motives those aroused by stressing sentiments, fantasies, and feelings

emotions feeling states such as joy or sorrow

enacted role the overt behavior displayed by an individual in a particular situation

encoding the process of employing symbols such as words or images to store a perceived idea

enculturation the process of indoctrinating youth with society's norms and values

ethnocentrism the tendency to make cross-cultural evaluations based on one's own beliefs and values

ethnography the study of culture by unobtrusive observation

evaluative criteria product characteristics consumers use to judge the merits of competing options

evoked set those few brands that come to mind when one thinks of a product category

expert power   influence based on a person's regard for an agent's knowledge or skill

exposure   the act of deliberately or accidentally coming into contact with environmental stimuli

expressive performance   social or psychological aspects of product performance that consumers regard as ends in themselves

extended problem solving   an elevated level of expended effort used in making risky and significant decisions

extended self   the self defined in terms of an individual's possessions

external search   the process of seeking information from exogenous sources

extrinsic motivation   behavior undertaken in order to acquire rewards

family   two or more persons, related either through birth, marriage, or adoption, living under one roof

family lifecycle   the sequence of stages that families tend to pass through

figure and ground   objects are perceived in relation to their background

fixation   a halt in personality progress at a particular developmental stage

focus groups   sessions where eight to twelve people—led by a moderator—freely discuss a topic

formal groups   highly organized groups with an explicit structure and specified goals and procedures

framing   a view that a given decision can be structured from either a gain or a loss perspective

frequency of purchase   the rate at which consumers purchase a product after the initial purchase

general sensation-seeking scale (GSSS)   a scale designed to measure individual differences in sensation-seeking tendencies

Generation X cohort   individuals age thirty-nine through fifty-one (in 2016)

Generation Y cohort (Millennials)   individuals age twenty-two through thirty-eight (in 2016)

Generation Z cohort   individuals age birth to early twenties (in 2016)

generational marketing   the cataloging of generations in terms of external events that occurred during their members' formative years

generic goals   nonspecific categories of products and services that can satisfy customer needs

geodemographic segmentation   a partitioning of the market by considering data on neighborhoods, zip codes, or census tracts

geographic segmentation   a partitioning of the market based on climate, location, surroundings, and terrain

Gestalt a view that people perceive cohesive wholes and formulate total impressions

goal the sought-after objective of motivated behavior

goals pursuits where an individual thinks impediments stand in the way of attaining a desired objective

Google effect information available online is less likely to be remembered than web-scarce information

group people who share beliefs, have role relationships, and experience interdependent behavior

grouping the tendency to perceive data chunks rather than separate units

hemispheric specialization of the brain a view that the left and right hemispheres of the brain process, organize, and encode information differently

heuristics simple rules of thumb consumers use as shortcuts to reduce shopping effort

high involvement a case in which consumers attach elevated relevance to a purchase

high-involvement learning a case where individuals are motivated to process information to be learned

high sensation seekers (HSS) persons with stronger-than-average need to seek novel, surprising, and more intense activities

homeostasis a self-regulating mechanism of the body that maintains harmony of all bodily systems

hypodermic needle model a view that the media have an immediate, direct, forceful impact on a mass audience

id a personality component that demands pleasure and immediate gratification

image a person's view of what a company, product, brand, or store is

image barrier a condition where a product or brand is unknown by the public or suffers from an unfavorable image

imagery the way consumers visualize sensory information in working memory

implementation a stage where a person acts on his or her decision to adopt

impulse purchases spontaneous and unplanned purchases made in response to environmental cues

individual factors the qualities of people that influence their interpretation of an impulse

individualism a tendency of people to look after themselves and their immediate family only

inertia a pattern of repeatedly buying a particular brand merely because it is familiar

influencer a person with above-average reach or impact via word of mouth in a relevant marketplace

informal groups groups in which structure, goals, and procedures are less explicit

information-processing approach an effort to provide facts to help consumers reach a logical conclusion

information retrieval the process of sifting through memory to activate previously stored information

innovators the first 2.5 percent of the market to adopt a new product

instincts genetically transmitted physical and behavioral characteristics of a species that enable it to survive in the environment

instrumental performance consumers' view of the utilitarian performance of the physical product as a means to an end

intensity the extent of how strongly an individual feels one way or the other about an attitude object

intention one's subjective resolution to behave in a certain way toward an attitude object

intermittent reinforcement a reinforcement schedule that rewards a desired behavior only occasionally

internal search the process of retrieving relevant information from memory

internalization an influence that occurs when individuals accept group norms and values as their own

intrinsic motivation behavior undertaken for the inherent pleasure of the activity itself

involvement the degree of personal relevance that a purchase holds for the consumer

key informants individuals who are knowledgeable about a culture of interest

knowledge a state of being exposed to and aware of an innovation's existence

knowledge function the notion that some attitudes provide people with a simple, predictable, and organized view of the environment

knowledge structures formations of related bits of information

laggards the fifth and last tier of consumers to adopt an innovation

late majority the fourth tier of consumers to adopt an innovation

learning process by which changes occur in the content or organization of a person's long-term memory

learning curve (experience effect) the notion that tasks become easier as the number of repetitions increases

left hemisphere the area of the brain that specializes in analytical thinking, verbalization, and algebraic calculations

legitimate power influence that occurs as a result of individuals' feelings of obligation

leveling a process in which details are omitted in order to simplify the memory structure

limited problem solving a reduced level of expended effort used in making less-risky decisions

long-term memory (LTM) the information warehouse in which data are organized and extendedly stored

low involvement a case in which consumers attach minimal personal relevance to a purchase

low-involvement learning a case where individuals are less motivated to attend to and process material to be learned

low sensation seekers (LSS) persons who prefer less-thrilling activities

m-commerce business transactions conducted via a portable or hand-held electronic device

market maven person who actively transmits marketplace information

market profile a portrait of the various market segments and competitors' positions in them relative to a specific product

market segmentation the act of dissecting the marketplace into sub-markets that require different marketing mixes

market targeting the process of reviewing market segments and deciding which one(s) to pursue

marketing concept an operating philosophy in which the consumer is the focus of all company activities

masculinity the degree to which dominant values are success, money, and things

mass communication relies on the mass media to disseminate information to a target audience

mass customization combining technology and customer information to tailor products and services to the specific needs of each customer

mass-market strategy a philosophy that presumes consumers are uniform and that broad-appeal products and marketing programs suffice

massed (concentrated) practice lengthy learning sessions scheduled over a brief time period

means–end chains depictions of linkages between product attributes, use consequences, and consumer values

membership reference groups groups to which a person currently belongs or qualifies for membership

misinformation effect a case where false assertions taint a person's recall of what actually occurred

mnemonic devices auditory or visual aids that promote retention of material by identifying it with easily remembered symbols

mood an individual's current frame of mind

moral anxiety the fear of feeling shame and guilt

motivation a state in which our energy is mobilized and directed in a selective fashion toward desirable goals

motivation research the study of the *why* aspects of consumer behavior

motivational conflict situations in which multiple needs simultaneously act on an individual

motive a state of tension that pushes an individual to act

multiattribute model a view that attitude objects have a number of desirable or undesirable features that differ in importance to the same individual

multisegment strategy a view that the market consists of multiple segments, and each requires its own marketing mix

multistep model a view that mass-media messages reach both opinion leaders and followers who then share that information with others

needs internal forces that prompt behavior toward goal-oriented solutions

negative reference groups groups with which individuals wish to avoid association or identification

negative reinforcement an inducement to repeat a behavior in order to remove an adverse situation

neo-Freudian theory a view that social variables rather than biological instincts and sexual drives underlie personality formation

neo-Pavlovian conditioning a view that reshapes traditional classical conditioning into a fully cognitive theory

neurotic anxiety the fear of the negative consequences of instinctual gratification

noncompensatory decision rule a selection procedure where a high score on one attribute of a brand cannot offset a low score on another

nonproductive reach the effort wasted on contracting consumers who are unlikely prospects

nonprogrammed decision a case in which a novel or infrequently encountered situation requires a customized solution

norms shared guidelines to accepted and expected behavior; a society's shared guidelines regarding appropriate behavior

objective measures a method that applies relevant demographic and socioeconomic criteria to determine social class membership

observability the perceived property that an innovation is visible and communicable to potential adopters

operant (instrumental) conditioning a view that learning is driven by the positive or negative consequences of behavior

opinion leaders knowledgeable, influential persons who casually provide advice

opinion leadership an agent's ability to informally incline the beliefs, attitudes, or behaviors of others

optimal stimulation level (OSL) a measurement of people's tendency to seek or avoid thrilling, challenging activities

overprivileged households whose incomes exceed the median for their social class

perceived role an individual's perceived obligations

perception the process of selecting, organizing, and interpreting sensations into a meaningful whole

perceptual categorization the tendency to group somewhat similar objects together

perceptual defense a tendency to block threatening or contradictory stimuli from extensive conscious processing

perceptual inferences beliefs based on prior experience that a person assigns to products or stores

perceptual map *n*-dimensional depiction that provides a visual profile of a number of brands for comparison purposes

perceptual overloading the inability to perceive all the stimuli that compete for an individual's attention at a given moment

perceptual vigilance an individual's ability to disregard much of the stimulation one receives through the senses

peripheral route to persuasion a view that under low involvement, consumers are less likely to process information provided in messages

personal communication involves two or more persons interacting directly with each other

personal influence any change in beliefs, attitudes, or behavior due to interpersonal communication

personality the sum total of an individual's inner psychological attributes

personality tests questionnaires designed to measure personality traits

personalization making a product personal to the consumer; a term related to customization

persuasion a stage where a prospect formulates a favorable or unfavorable attitude toward an innovation

physiological needs basic bodily requirements essential to maintain life

planned groups groups formed by persons or organizations for some specific purpose

positioning establishing a differentiating image for a product or service in relation to that of the competition

positive reinforcement an inducement to repeat a behavior to receive a pleasant consequence

possible self the self a person would like to or could become

postpurchase dissonance a state of doubting the wisdom of one's choice after making a purchase

power distance the degree to which society's members accept unequal power distribution

prescribed role the set of expectations held by others as to what modes of behavior should be displayed by an individual in a situation

primary groups small, intimate groups that meet regularly and communicate face-to-face

proactive interference a case where prior learning interferes with recall of recently learned material

product placement display of branded merchandise in movie scenes or TV shows

programmed decisions cases where consumers follow habitual routines to deal with frequently encountered situations

projective techniques the psychological techniques that reveal the real reasons behind consumption behaviors

prospect theory a view of how decision makers, under risk conditions, value different options and assess their outcomes

prototype matching the tendency to compare brands in a product category to the category's leading brand

proximity the tendency to assume relatedness due to spatial or temporal nearness

psychographic segmentation a partitioning of the market based on lifestyle and personality characteristics

psychographics a segmentation approach that classifies consumers based on their lifestyle

rate of adoption the relative speed with which consumers adopt an innovation

rational motives those aroused through appeals to reason and logic

reactance a situation in which one resists pressure to conform and behaves independently

reality (objective) anxiety the fear of tangible danger in the real world

reciprocal identification the case where a person accepts influence due to playing a complementary role with another individual

reference groups groups that provide a perspective for evaluating or patterning one's own behavior

referent power influence based on a person's desire to identify with an admired group

reinforcement schedule the pattern in which reinforcements are given

relative advantage the perceived property of a new product as better than its dated substitutes

repetition the frequency of pairing a conditioned stimulus with an unconditioned stimulus

repositioning modifying a brand, redirecting it, or stressing different features to boost sales

reputational measures ways of determining social class based on individuals' ranking of others in a society

retroactive interference a case where recent learning interferes with recall of previously learned material

reward power influence based on a group's ability to dispense rewards

right hemisphere the area of the brain that specializes in interpreting and recognizing visual patterns

risk barrier a condition where uncertainty lingers about adopting an innovation

rituals sets of symbolic behaviors that occur in a fixed sequence and tend to be repeated periodically

role-related product cluster the set of goods necessary for a person to play a given role competently

roles patterns of behavior performed by individuals within a given social context

salient attributes important aspects of a product that affect the choices consumers make

sandwich generation parents who simultaneously support both their kids and their elderly parents

schema a structure for understanding and interpreting new information

script the knowledge about procedures to follow in recurring situations

secondary groups groups in which regular, face-to-face contact is lacking

selective attention a tendency of individuals to heed information that interests them and to avoid information that is irrelevant

selective exposure a tendency of people to ignore media and ads that address topics that are unimportant to them

selective interpretation the act of combining relevant knowledge structures with expectations and intentions to derive meaning from a stimulus

selective sensitization a tendency to perceive more readily information that is consistent with one's needs and beliefs

self-concept the overall image that a person holds of him or herself

self-product congruence a tendency to select products that match some aspects of the self

sensation the responses of a person's sensory receptors to environmental stimuli and transmission of this data to the brain via the nervous system

sensory memory a storage system in which incoming data undergo preliminary processing

servicescape model for illustrating consumer perception patterns in specific consumption settings

sharpening a process of changing stimuli from ambiguous forms to more conventional ones

shopping pals other persons who accompany a consumer on a shopping trip

short-term memory (STM) a storage system in which an individual briefly holds a limited amount of information

simplicity the perceived property that an innovation is easy to understand, assemble, and operate

single-variable indexes objective measures of social class that employ one socioeconomic factor

situational self-image the physical and mental state a person is experiencing at a specific moment in time

situational variables environmental circumstances that constitute the context within which transactions occur

social class a societal rank assigned to large groups of people

social mobility movement upward and downward in the socioeconomic hierarchy

social networks online groups that serve to build relationships among individuals across political, economic, and geographic borders

socialization the process by which we acquire knowledge to function productively in society

spaced (distributed) practice brief learning sessions intermingled with rest periods scheduled over a lengthy time period

S-shaped diffusion curve a pattern of market acceptance for an innovation that begins with a slow start, followed by more rapid acceptance, and then a slowdown

status the relative position a person occupies along a group's social continuum

status crystallization the coincidence of the different indicators of an individual's social stature

stimulus discrimination the tendency to distinguish between, and respond differently to, similar—but nonidentical—stimuli

stimulus factors the physical characteristics of an object that produce physiological impulses in an individual

stimulus generalization the tendency to assign commonality to similar stimuli

stratification a system of classifying members of a population based on economic and social characteristics

subcultures smaller, more homogeneous subsets of people within a larger culture

subjective experience the notion that humans synthesize beliefs and experiences to gain insight into new situations

subjective measures ways of determining social class membership based on individuals' classification of themselves

subjective norms one's beliefs about what significant others think and inclinations to comply with their views

superego the social, moral, and ethical component of personality

surrogate consumer an agent who a consumer retains to guide, direct, or transact marketplace activities

surrogate indicators the cues that consumers rely on to place products into categories

symbolic aspirational reference groups groups in which one's chances of gaining membership are remote at best

symbolic innovations cases where a product conveys new social or psychological meanings

synesthesia fusing together of the human senses

teaser campaigns promotions that drop bits of information while withholding the particulars

terminal (upper) threshold the point beyond which further increases in the intensity of a stimulus produce no greater sensation

testimonials ads that depict a celebrity, expert, or ordinary consumer who endorses a brand

theory of reasoned action (TORA) a view that attitude toward the behavior, intentions, and subjective norms determine behavior

top-down processing an individual's experiences, goals, and expectations drive perception

tradition barrier a condition where cultural norms and values hamper product adoption

traditional model of attitudes a view that attitudes consist of three components: cognitive, affective, and behavioral

trait theory a view that classifies people according to their predominant response patterns

traits relatively permanent and consistent response patterns that characterize individuals

trialability the perceived property that a new product can be experienced before purchase

trickle-across model a view that influence flows horizontally among peers

trickle-down model a view that influence flows from celebrities and elite influentials to emulating recipients (the general public)

trickle-up model a view that influence flows upward from usual recipient emulators to the general public, as well as to celebrities and elite influentials

two-step model a view that it is opinion leaders who receive messages first from the mass media and then pass them on to others

uncertainty avoidance the degree to which people feel threatened by ambiguity and uncertainty

underprivileged households whose incomes are below the median for their social class

undifferentiated strategy a view that the market is a single large domain and that one marketing mix suffices

usage barrier a condition where an innovation is not part of a prospect's routines

utilitarian function the notion that some attitudes serve as a means to an end—gaining rewards or avoiding punishments

valence an attraction or repulsion felt toward an attitude object

VALS™ a segmentation approach that classifies consumers according to primary motivations and resources/innovation

value barrier a perceived lack of product performance relative to its price compared to that of substitute brands

value-expressive function the notion that some attitudes help consumers communicate the core values they revere to other people

values ideals concerning what is right or wrong and goals worth pursuing

vicarious learning behavior change due to observing others and the consequences of their actions

word of mouth (WOM) sharing of an opinion about a product, service or company between an independent source and a receiver

Zaltman Metaphor Elicitation Technique (ZMET) a test where respondents provide images that represent their feelings about a topic

INDEX

Behavior, 128
    attitudes determining, 182–85
    buyer, 6
    consequences of, 136
    consumer, 5–9, 330–32
    in cultural setting, 552
    impact of social class on, 531–33
    overt, 186
    product-relevant, 41
    reference group influence on, 418–19
    shaping, 139
    sociocultural dimensions of, 553
Behavioral component, 186–87
Behavioral segmentation, 57–60
    benefits, 58
    brand and store loyalty, 57
    marketing tactic sensitivity, 59–60
    usage rate, 57–58
Beliefs, 553
Bell, Alexander Graham, 373
Berners-Lee, Tim, 17
Bicultural segment, of Hispanic Americans, 564
Black Americans. *See* African Americans
Blackwell, Roger D., 5
Bonding, 250, 254
Boomerang children, 449–50
Boomers I cohort, 454
Boomers II cohort, 454
Bottom-up processing, 96–97
Brain hemispheres, learning and, 148–50
Brand
    advocates, 472
    attributes, 204
    communities, 397–98
    decision making and, 315
    equity, 116
    heuristic, 320
    image and, 111
    parity, 155
    reputation, 188
    as surrogate indicator, 107

switching, 155
    tribes, 398
Brand loyalty, 57, 126
    decision making and, 311
    development of, 154–55
    habit and, 152–55
    women and, 247
Brand-specific goals, 232
Business-to-business buying, 6
"Buy American" movement, 404–5
Buyer behavior, 6
    consumer behavior *versus,* 6
Buyers, 436
Buying decisions, 9–10
    impulsive, 11

C

Cartoons, 244
Cause marketing, 132
Center for Disease Control and Prevention (CDC), 4
Centrality, 177–78
Central route to persuasion, 206
Change
    agents of, 14, 371, 474
    attitude, 200–5
Children
    advertising to, 444
    boomerang, 449–50
    influence on family decision making, 441–44
    Internet and, 432
Children's Advertising Review Unit (CARU), 444
Children's Online Privacy Protection Act of 1998, 444
China
    fast food in, 328
    Hollywood actors and, 31–32
Chunk, 95
Clan hierarchies, 510
Classical conditioning, 131–36, 195
    formation of associations and, 131–34
    learning principles under, 134–36

importance of, 392–93
meaning of, 392–93
online communities and social networks,
    396–97
planned *versus* emergent, 395
primary *versus* secondary, 393
reference, 407–9
roles, 399–400
social, 393
social power and, 402–7
status, 400–2

H

Habit, 136
    brand loyalty and, 152–55
Hacktivists, social networking and, 21
Halo effect, 109
Haves *versus* have-nots, 513
Hemispheres, brain, 148–50
    left, 149
    right, 149
    specialization of, 148
Hemispheric specialization of the brain, 148
Herbal supplements, 377
    obesity and, 500
Heterogeneity, 553
Heuristics, 320
Hidden-camera commercials, 496
High involvement, 308
    learning, 130, 204
High self-monitors, 294
High sensation seekers (HSS), 237
High-urgency motivation, 224
Hispanic Americans, 562–64
    accultured segment of, 564
    bicultural segment of, 564
    consumers, 563–64
    marketing to, 49
    unaccultured segment of, 564
Hofstede, Geert, 546
Homeostasis, 236

Honeymooner stage, 446
Howard, John A., 5
Hybrid cars, 315
Hypodermic needle model, 478–79
Hypothetical value function, 322

I

Id, 271
Ideals-motivated consumers, 286
Identification, 415–16
    classical, 415
    of influencers, 485–86
    reciprocal, 415
Image
    barrier, 382
    brand equity, 116
    change, 114
    definition, 111
    management, 114
    perception and, 111–16
    promotion and, 113–14
    risk perception and, 116–17
    Western, 153
Imagery, 113–14
Implementation stage, in adoption process, 376
Impulse purchases, 310
Impulsive decision making, 11
Income, social class *versus*, 511
Incongruity, status crystallization *versus*, 527–28
Indexes
    composite-variable, 522
    single-variable, 522
India, pharmaceutical companies in, 476
Indirect influence, 443
Individual factors, 95–97
Individualism, 547, 550
Inference
    correlational, 110
    evaluation-based, 109
    perceptual, 108–11

CONSUMER BEHAVIOR *AN APPLIED APPROACH*

Postpurchase dissonance, 201
Power
      coercive, 403
      expert, 406–7
      legitimate, 405
      of personal influence, 474–75
      reference, 406
      reward, 402–3
      social, 402–7
      of word of mouth, 474–75
Power distance, 546–47
Practice
      massed, 139
      schedules, 139
      spaced, 139
Preferred-customer cards, 154
Preparers, 436
Pre-purchase deliberation, 11
Prescribed role, 435
Price
      affordability, 188
      expected, 108
      quality and, 108
      as surrogate indicator, 107–8
Primary groups, 393
Primary motivation, 286
PRIZM, 50–54
      census and, 50
      cluster assignments, 52
Proactive interference, 162
      dynamics of, 163
Problem recognition, 312–13
Problem solving
      extended, 310
      limited, 310
      stages in, 312
Product
      acquisitions, 313
      generic, 106
      image, 111
      involvement, 317
      new, 349
      obsolescence, 313
      placement, 497
      positioning, 70
      trial-size, 361
Product-relevant behavior, 41
Programmed decisions, 310–11
Projective techniques, 244
      cartoons, 244
      thematic apperception test, 244
Promotion
      applications of emotion, 253–56
      imagery and, 113–14
Prospect theory, 321
Prototype matching, 108
Proximity, 105
Psychographics, 41, 284–86
      VALS system, 286–89
Psychographic segmentation, 56–57
Psychological risk, 117
Psychology, 8
      Gestalt, 104–6
      social, 8
Punishment, 139
Purchase, 324–26
      frequency of, 368
Purchasing-behavior patterns, 155
      conversion, 155
      experimentation, 155
      reversion, 155
      vacillation, 155
Purchasing patterns, 531

Q

Q-sorting, 292
Quality, price and, 108
Questioning, direct, 545

R

Race, demographic segmentation by, 49
Rationality, of consumers, 307–8
Rational motives, 227–28

RATTER, 332

Reactance, 415

Readers, in groups, 399

Recall, likelihood of, 162–63

Recency, 195

Reciprocal identification, 415

Recognition, in cultures, 557–58

Recognized authority, 440

Reference group influence, 413–17

    compliance, 413–15

    on consumer behavior and marketing
      strategy, 418–19

    identification, 415–16

    internalization, 417

Reference groups, 407–17

    aspirational, 410

    definition, 407–8

    degrees of influence, 413–17

    disclaimant, 411

    dissociative, 411–13

    membership, 409–10

    negative, 411

    types of, 409–13

Referent power, 406

Reinforcement, 137

    continuous, 138

    intermittent, 138

    negative, 138

    positive, 137

    schedules, 138

Relationship marketing, 154

Relationships, 556–57

Relative advantage, 358–59

Repetition, 134

Repositioning, 71–72

Reputational measures, 521

Research, motivation, 243–47

Research and development (R&D), 351

Resources, 286

Response, 146

    conditioned, 135

    evaluative, 146

Retention, 156–59

Retroactive interference, 162

    dynamics of, 163

Reversion, 155

Reward power, 402–3

Rewards, 136, 152, 557–58

Right hemisphere, 149

Risk

    barrier, 381

    financial, 117

    functional, 117

    perception, 116–17, 318

    psychological, 117

    social, 117

Rituals, 568

Roadblocking, 93

Role-related product cluster, 399

Roles, 399

    of consumption, family, 434–36

    enacted, 435

    group, 399–400

    perceived, 435

    prescribed, 435

    traditional, 439

    of working mothers, 437

S

Safety, 19–23

Sales potential, 54

Salient attributes, 321

Sandwich generation, 450

Schema, 110

Scripts, 110

Search

    activity, 313–14

    external, 315–18

    internal, 314–15

    types of, 313–18

Search engine optimization method (SEO), 475

Search marketing, 316

Value-expressive function, 180–81
Value function, 322
    hypothetical, 322
Values, 554–56
Vanity sizing, 4
Variables
    moderating, 183
    situational, 101
Vicarious learning, 151
    advertisers and, 151
Video games, effect on children, 235
Virtual information, influence of, 15
Virtual reality (VR) technology, 361
Visibility, 70
Vision, 84–85

W

Web-enabled customer contact centers, 335
Wine industry, adoption and, 380
Women
    changing class stature of, 524–26

    live alone, 452–53
    multiple roles of working mothers, 437
    roles of, 430
Word of mouth (WOM) communication, 11, 470, 472, 482, 488, 493
    combating negative, 496–98
    power of, 474–75
    strategic applications of, 493
    vividness and impact of, 475–77
Workbench. *See* Short-term memory (STM)
Working class, 515–16
World Wide Web, 17

Y

YouTube, 25

Z

Zaltman Metaphor Elicitation Technique (ZMET), 247